PLEADINGS: PRINCIPLES AND PRACTICE

AUSTRALIA AND NEW ZEALAND
The Law Book Company Ltd.
Sydney : Melbourne : Perth

CANADA AND U.S.A.
The Carswell Company Ltd.
Agincourt, Ontario

INDIA
N.M. Tripathi Private Ltd.
Bombay
and
Eastern Law House Private Ltd.
Calcutta and Delhi
M.P.P. House
Bangalore

ISRAEL
Steimatzky's Agency Ltd.
Jerusalem : Tel-Aviv : Haifa

PAKISTAN
Pakistan Law House
Karachi

LITIGATION LIBRARY

PLEADINGS:

PRINCIPLES AND PRACTICE

by

Sir Jack Jacob, Q.C., LL.D., Dr. Juris
Fellow of University College London; Honorary Bencher of Gray's Inn;
(General Editor, The Supreme Court Practice)

and

Iain S. Goldrein, M.A. (Cantab.)
Barrister, Northern Circuit

WITH A FOREWORD BY
The Right Hon. The Lord Goff of Chieveley

LONDON
SWEET & MAXWELL
1990

Published in 1990 by
Sweet & Maxwell Limited of
183 Marsh Wall, London E14
Computerset by Promenade Graphics Limited, Cheltenham
Printed and bound by Butler and Tanner Limited, Frome, Somerset

British Library Cataloguing in Publication Data

Jacob, Sir, Jack I. H. *1908–*
Pleadings: Principles and Practice—(Litigation library).
1. Great Britain. High Court of Justice. Queen's Bench
Divison. Pleadings
I. Title II. Goldrein, Iain S. (Iain Saville) *1952–* III.
Series
344.20727

ISBN 0–421–40760–3

FOREWORD

I feel greatly honoured to have been invited to contribute a Foreword to this admirable book on "Pleadings: Principles and Practice" by Sir Jack Jacob and Mr. Iain Goldrein. As the authors explain in their Preface, the book finds its origin in the classic work of Bullen and Leake, now Bullen and Leake and Jacob. The authors have, very understandably, thought it right to separate the Principles and Practice of Pleadings from the Precedents we know so well, and to develop the Principles and Practice into a separate and substantial work. I have no doubt that this new work will be much read by students and practitioners, and will be of the greatest benefit to them.

All of us who have practised at the Bar have learned to appreciate both the importance of pleadings, and how difficult it is to draw a really good pleading. The mastery of the art of pleadings is, in the end, the fruit of experience; but, speaking for myself, I learned much from my pupil master, and much too from pleadings drawn by other skilled lawyers more experienced than myself. To draw a competent pleading in a difficult case requires a mastery both of the relevant facts, and of the applicable law; indeed, the very act of drawing the pleading may have the effect of elucidating the case for the pleader, since it requires a precise and accurate analysis of the case. But in the end, the function of pleadings is to define the issues in the case, for the benefit both of the parties and of the court, and for the better administration of justice; and well drawn pleadings should lead to the saving of costs, since they enable the parties to identify accurately the evidence they need to call, and to present economical arguments directed only to the matters at issue between them. Here we have a book which expounds, for the benefit of students and practitioners, the principles upon which good pleadings are based, and the science which underlies the art.

A novel feature of this book is the group of Appendices relating to other systems of law. This development, which I applaud, is one which will interest many readers. Those English lawyers who hear civil appeals from Scotland as well as from other parts of the United Kingdom have been startled by the strictness of the Scots system of pleadings, which would have earned the admiration of Baron Parke; but we have also learned to admire the discipline which underlies the system, directed as it is towards a very precise elucidation of the issues. At the other end of the scale is a system, which can (I believe) be broadly called the civil law system, in which the facts, the law and the evidence are together the subject of a statement of case which transcends the function of pleadings as known in the United Kingdom. In between these two extremes lies our own system of pleading, which seeks to combine the discipline of the

v

FOREWORD

Scots with a narrative form which should render pleadings not merely functional but also elegant, economical, informative and readable. The art of the English pleader lies in achieving all these desirable results.

I happily commend this book. I am confident that its many readers will derive much profit from it.

May 1990   The Right Hon. The Lord Goff of Chieveley

To Rose, my life-long companion
and mainstay
—Jack

and

To Margaret, for her abiding support
—Iain.

PREFACE

"The Principles of pleadings must be strictly observed"

per May LJ in *Lipkin Gorman* v *Karpnale Ltd* [1989] 1 W.L.R. 1340, 1352

"A perusal of the RSC Order 18 from end to end, with all the notes and quotations, constitutes a fascinating experience for a practitioner, in the nature of a trip through territory unknown to him and in a climate which he has not experienced in his daily life. No set of rules could have been more carefully devised; no judicial comment could be more cogently expressed; practice all too regrettably often reveals little relationship to the Rules; the judicial comments pass unregarded."

Report of the (Winn) Committee on Personal Injuries Litigation, 1968 Cmnd 3691 Para 237 p 71.

This book is virtually a new work. It is largely based on *The System of Pleadings*, which had formed Part I of the twelfth edition of Bullen and Leake and Jacob on *Precedents of Pleading*. True to its title, that edition was predominantly devoted to the comprehensive collection of precedents under the simple divide between Statements of Claim, Defences and Subsequent Pleadings, but, compared with the earlier edition, a greatly increased number of separate subjects dealt with in alphabetical order, each subject having its own explanatory notes. It is therefore, perhaps, not greatly surprising that the narrative exposition of the principles and practice of pleadings embodied in *The System of Pleadings* should have been somewhat overshadowed and much neglected. It became increasingly necessary to rescue the *System of Pleadings* from the obscurity into which it had fallen and to bring it out into the light in its own right.

The opportunity to do just that opened up when it was decided that it was feasible and desirable to produce a new edition of the *Precedents of Pleading*. In order to avoid the fate that overcame the *System of Pleadings*, it became more and more clear that it would be necessary to produce a new work, separate and apart from the *Precedents of Pleadings*, which would state the guiding principles and practice governing the subject of pleadings. To this end, the *System of Pleadings* was, as it were, taken down, thoroughly worked over, dusted, polished, cleaned and clarified, brought up to date and re-presented anew in this work in a way designed to make pleadings a live and vibrant subject.

The need for a separate work on the *Principles and Practice of Plead-*

ings, as a companion volume to the *Precedents of Pleading* is dictated by the crucial importance of pleadings in our machinery of Civil Justice.

Pleadings have in the past played, and they still continue to play, a predominant role in the practice and procedure of the Supreme Court, and in this respect they have provided a model for the conduct of civil litigation in the County Courts and other courts and tribunals and indeed however the proceedings are begun whether by writ or otherwise. Pleadings have been described as a science, and also as an art, but above all, they are a craft, in the sense that the drafting of pleadings calls for the exercise of skill and expertise, based on a complete understanding of the principles of pleadings. In our system of the judicial process, pleadings are neither formal nor formless, but they are based on realism, grounded on the world of fact, and designed to distill, with some exactness, the real matters in dispute between the parties. For this reason, the pleader must, so far as is possible, be in complete command of all the relevant facts and the applicable law, especially relating to the law of pleadings, and as a master of his craft, he must produce the appropriate pleading for the particular purpose for which it is required.

The admonition of Lord Justice May, that the principles of pleadings must be strictly observed carries with it the imperative message that a pleading which does not pass this test will be defective and rejected unless and until it can be put right to conform with those principles. Hence the need to grasp and master the basic rules and principles of pleadings. Moreover, the *cri de coeur* of the Winn Committee on Personal Injuries Litigation that practitioners have failed (and by all accounts are still continuing to fail) to conform to these rules and principles must of course be seriously heeded and should be reversed so that practitioners should follow the principles and apply the practice relating to pleadings.

In this respect, the pleader should remember, before signing his pleading, that he owes a duty, in the broad sense of that term, to his clients both lay and professional, to his fellow practitioners, to the Court and above all, be it said, to himself to produce a proper pleading for the matter in hand, worthy of the highest craftsmanship of his craft. It would be the height of folly to approach the stage of pleading in a cavalier fashion, on the basis for example, that "you can always amend", or "it will be alright at the trial" or "it is clear enough anyway". Many a good case may be, and some are, delayed or even defeated by a bad pleading, and equally, many a bad case may be, and some are, assisted or even won by a good pleading. Whatever the nature or the value of the case may be, the drafting of the pleadings should be regarded with its due sense of responsibility and the obligation to present the case of the party, whether a plaintiff or defendant, in the best possible fashion.

The title of this book emphasises the close connection and interaction between the principles and the practice of pleadings. These are not two separate parts or even aspects of the system of pleadings, but on the contrary, they dovetail to form together the integral subject of pleadings, describing the rules and principles and how they function in everyday practice. The book, accordingly, seeks to provide a complete, comprehensive and systematic exposition of the law and practice relating to pleadings at the present day. It contains the fundamentals for the full understanding and knowledge of the subject of pleadings which are essential to its mastery. It should enable anyone involved in the pleading process, and particularly the practitioner who is or may be called upon to plead or to advise on pleadings on behalf of any of the parties and whether in the High Court or County Court, to discharge his task with greater assurance and to better effect. That, at any rate, has been the objective we had set ourselves when preparing this work, and we can only hope that it has been fulfilled.

A special, somewhat unusual, and perhaps even a unique feature of the work is that it includes four Appendices, each dealing with the system of pleadings prevailing in a different jurisdiction, namely in Scotland, in West Germany, in the Federal Courts of the USA, and in the European Court of Justice. We decided to do this because we tend to believe that it would perhaps help to enable us to understand and appreciate our own system better by making a brief excursion into other jurisdictions to see how they conduct their affairs in the comparable area of pleadings.

Thus, for example, it would seem that in Scotland, there is a highly developed and disciplined system of pleadings, based on allegations of fact, but supported by the applicable or relevant law, whereas in West Germany there is hardly a recognisable system of pleadings since all the facts, the evidence and the law relied on have to be stated by the parties; on the other hand, in the Federal Courts of the USA, the system of pleadings is based not on allegations of fact but in stating a claim showing entitlement to relief supported by extensive, sometimes regarded as extravagant, discovery processes, while in the European Court, within well-defined limits of jurisdiction, the parties are required not only to allege the facts, but also the evidence relied on as to prove those facts, and the legal arguments supporting the claims or defences, as the case may be.

All these jurisdictions aim to achieve the same objective as we do, namely, to produce a just result, but we all go about this process in a different way. We claim for ourselves, however, that our system of pleadings constitutes a major contribution to the jurisprudence of civil procedure, especially in the comparative context. We hope very much that these appendices will be found interesting as well as useful.

PREFACE

We wish to express our great gratitude to the contributors:
Alastair Mennie, JH Scots Bar for Appendix A "Pleading practice in Scotland"; to Dr Volker Triebel, Rechtsanwalt, OLG, Barrister (Inner Temple) for Appendix B "Pleadings in West Germany"; to Michael V. Cerisi Attorney, Minnesota, for Appendix C "The Courts and Pleadings of the United States of America"; and to Philippa Watson Phd, Barrister, London and Brussels for Appendix D "The European Court of Justice".

This law is up to date to May 1, 1990

May 1990

Jack Jacob
Iain Goldrein

CONTENTS

CONTENTS

CONTENTS

CONTENTS

Table of Cases

TABLE OF CASES

TABLE OF CASES

TABLE OF CASES

TABLE OF CASES

TABLE OF CASES

xlvi

l

Table of Statutes

TABLE OF STATUTES

Table of Statutory Instruments

Nature and Functions of Pleadings

Agenda for Pre-Trial and Trial[1]

Pleadings—what they are   Pleadings are the written statements of the parties served by each party in turn upon the other which must set out in summary form the material[2] facts on which each party relies in support of his claim or defence, as the case may be.

Pleadings—what they include

   (a) Documents within the definition:
      (i) the statement of claim;
     (ii) defence[3];
    (iii) reply;
     (iv) counterclaim;
      (v) defence to counterclaim[4];
     (vi) pleadings subsequent thereto;
    (vii) a statement of claim indorsed on a writ of summons[5]; and
    (viii) particulars of pleadings.
   (b) Documents outside the definition:
      (i) a general indorsement on a writ[6];

---

[1] The phrase, an "agenda for trial" in the context of pleadings is taken from the judgment of Morris L.J. in the Court of Appeal decision of *Southport Corporation* v. *Esso Petroleum Company Ltd.* [1954] 2 Q.B. 182; [1954] 3 W.L.R. 200; [1954] 2 All E.R. 561. See also, p. 9, n. 54.

[2] See R.S.C., Ord. 18, r.7(1). The word "material" conceals the hidden question "What must pleadings *not* contain?"; and the answer is: "Allegations which are irrelevant, evidence and propositions of law."

[3] A letter is not a "defence"; see *Marshall* v. *Jones* (1888) 52 J.P. 423.

[4] See the former Supreme Court of Judicature (Consolidation) Act 1925, s.225.

[5] *Anlaby* v. *Praetorius* (1888) 20 Q.B.D. 764.

[6] *Murray* v. *Stephenson* (1887) 19 Q.B.D. 60.

    (ii) a petition;
    (iii) summons or preliminary act[7];
    (iv) an originating summons[8]; and
    (v) any affidavit or notice of appeal.[9]

Framing the issues Properly drafted, the pleadings should disclose clearly and precisely the real issues which are in dispute between the parties, as opposed to a recitation of the evidence which each party intends to adduce at trial. They are not mere narratives or provisional documents. The parties are bound by what they say in their pleadings which have the potential of forming part of the record, and, moreover, the court itself is also bound by what the parties have stated in their pleadings as to the facts relied on by them.

Issues—how many? As the parties are at liberty to join in one pleading various claims or various defences, the pleadings in an action may raise several issues either of fact or of law, or may raise issues both of fact and of law or of mixed fact and law.

Pleadings—their dual object in summary Pleadings serve a two-fold purpose:

(a) *First* To inform each party what is the case of the opposite party which he will have to meet before and at the trial; and

(b) *Secondly* Concurrently to apprise the court what are the issues. The identity of the issues is crucial, not only for the purposes of trial, but also for the purposes of all the pre-trial interlocutory proceedings.

The object of pleadings—in detail

(a) *First* To define with clarity and precision the issues or questions which are in dispute between the parties and fall to be determined by the court. In *Thorp* v. *Holdsworth*, Jessel M.R. said[10]:

> "The whole object of pleadings is to bring the parties to an issue, and the meaning of the rules of [Ord. 18] was to prevent the issue

---

[7] See R.S.C., Ord. 1, r. 4(1), but contrast the *inclusion* of petition and summons in section 225 of the Supreme Court of Judicature (Consolidation) Act 1925.

[8] *Lewis* v. *Packer* [1960] 1 W.L.R. 452.

[9] *Re Beldam's Patent* [1911] 1 Ch. 60 at 63. However, an affidavit in defence under Ord. 14 may be ordered "to stand as his defence": Queen's Bench Masters' Practice Form No. PF18, *Supreme Court Practice 1991*, Vol. 2, para. 218. See also p. 714, para. 214.

[10] (1876) 3 Ch.D. 637 at 639.

being enlarged, which would prevent either party from knowing when the cause came on for trial, what the real point to be discussed and decided was. In fact, the whole meaning of the system is to narrow the parties to definite issues, and thereby to diminish expense and delay, especially as regards the amount of testimony required on either side at the hearing."

(b) *Secondly*   To require each party to give fair and proper notice to his opponent of the case he has to meet to enable him to frame and prepare his own case for trial. In *Palmer* v. *Guadagni*, Swinfen Eady J. said[11]:

" . . . The pleadings must contain fair and proper notice of the issues intended to be raised. This is essential to prevent the other party being taken by surprise."

Again in *Esso Petroleum Co. Ltd.* v. *Southport Corporation*, Lord Normand said[12]:

"The function of pleadings is to give fair notice of the case which has to be met so that the opposing party may direct his evidence to the issue disclosed by them."

(c) *Thirdly*   To inform the court what are the precise matters in issue between the parties which alone the court may determine, since they set the limits of the action which may not be extended without due amendment properly made. In *The Why Not*, Phillimore J. said[13]:

"[The pleadings] are not to be considered as constituting a game of skill between the advocates. They ought to be so framed as not only to assist the party in the statement of his case but also the court in its investigation of the truth between the litigants."

In similar vein, in *Blay* v. *Pollard and Morris* Scrutton L.J. said[14]:

"Cases must be decided on the issues on the record; and if it is desired to raise other issues they must be placed on the record by amendment. In the present case the issue on which the judge decided

[11] [1906] 2 Ch. 494 at 497. See also R.S.C., Ord. 18, r. 8(1)(*b*).
[12] [1956] A.C. 218 at 238.
[13] (1868) L.R. 2 Al. & E. 265 at 266.
[14] [1930] 1 K.B. 628 at 634. See also *Esso Petroleum Co. Ltd.* v. *Southport Corporation* [1956] A.C. 218; *Qualcast (Wolverhampton) Ltd.* v. *Haynes* [1959] A.C. 743, *per*, Lord Somerville of Harrow at 758: "The point on which the plaintiff succeeded was not pleaded . . . The point not having been pleaded, it would be wrong to draw inferences adverse to the defendants which might well have been answered in evidence if the point had been pleaded"; *Waghorn* v. *George Wimpey & Co. Ltd.* [1969] 1 W.L.R. 1764; *Rawding* v. *London Brick Co.* (1971) 10 K.I.R. 207.

was raised by himself without amending the pleadings, and in my opinion he was not entitled to take such a course."

(d) *Fourthly*   To provide a brief summary of the case of each party, which is readily available for reference, and from which the nature of the claim and defence may be easily apprehended, and to constitute a permanent record of the issues and questions raised in the action and decided therein so as to prevent future litigation upon matters already adjudicated upon between the litigants or those privy to them.[15]

Analysis of pleading technique   The machinery by which the system of pleadings operates is founded upon the interaction of three basic principles, namely:

(a) each party must plead the material facts upon which he relies for his claim or defence[16];

(b) the material facts stated in the preceding pleading are deemed to be admitted if not expressly traversed,[17] or denied by implied joinder of issue[18]; and

(c) any fresh matter must be specifically pleaded which makes the claim or defence in the preceding pleading not maintainable or which might take the opposite party by surprise or which raises issues of fact not arising out of the preceding pleading.[19]

The machinery works by requiring the parties to serve their respective pleadings on each other within the times specified for each pleading or any extended time.[20]

Summary   At the close of pleadings, there should be revealed precisely the issues of fact and law between the parties. Documents relevant to such issues should be disclosed on discovery and further relevant information explored by way of interrogatories. Fudging the issues at the pleading stage drives a coach-and-four through effective and efficient discovery and the incisiveness of the precision required for interrogatories;

---

[15] See *Duchess of Kingston's Case* (1776) 2 Smith's *Leading Cases* (13th ed.) 644; *Outram v. Morewood* (1803) 3 East 346; *Hoystead v. Commissioner of Taxation* [1926] A.C. 155 (P.C.).

[16] See R.S.C., Ord. 18, r. 7(1).

[17] *i.e.* denied or not admitted.

[18] See R.S.C., Ord. 18, r. 13(1); the mere joinder of issue, express or implied, on a statement of claim or counterclaim is forbidden; see R.S.C., Ord. 18, r. 14(3). Thus, if no defence is served in answer to the statement of claim or no defence to counterclaim is served in answer to the counterclaim, there are no issues between the parties. The allegations of fact made in the statement of claim or counterclaim are deemed to be admitted and the plaintiff or defendant may enter, as the case may be, judgment in default of pleading under R.S.C., Ord. 19. See also, as to "unless" orders and default judgments.

[19] See R.S.C., Ord. 18, r. 8(1).

[20] See p. 42, *infra.*

it impairs an analytical advice on evidence as well as the preparation for trial and it undermines the effective presentation of the case at the trial.

Present Code of Pleading

Ord. 18 The revision of the Rules of the Supreme Court 1965, which was completed in two stages,[21] provided the opportunity to codify and consolidate the law regulating the practice and procedure of the Supreme Court.[22] In the course of that revision, the rules of pleading have been greatly simplified and clarified, and yet they have preserved substantially intact the system of pleadings prevailing since the Judicature Acts 1873–1875. They have, as it were, been decanted into one Order, R.S.C., Ord. 18, in which there are gathered together the rules of pleading which were before 1964 contained in several orders.[23] This Order, as it has since been amended from time to time, may properly be regarded as constituting at least the nucleus of a complete Code of Pleading.[24] It sets out all the main rules of pleading in a clear, systematic and comprehensive

---

[21] First, the partial revision in 1962, see Rules of the Supreme Court (Revision) 1962 (S.I. 1962 No. 2145), made on September 28, 1962, which came into operation on January 1, 1964, and next the entire revision, completed in 1965, see Rules of the Supreme Court (Revision) 1965 (S.I. 1965 No. 1776), made on September 30, 1965, which came into operation on October 1, 1966.

[22] See Jacob, "The Rules of the Supreme Court (Revision) 1965" (1966) *The Legal Executive*, p. 168. "The revised R.S.C. 1965," it was said, *ibid.*, "cut out a great deal of dead wood. They renew much old material. They restate earlier provisions and add several new provisions in clear and more direct language. Above all, their outstanding achievement is their simple, logical arrangement, providing the framework of a code of procedure . . . [They] have been rewritten by way of revision, and not reform. Therefore, although many changes of detail have been introduced, the structure has been retained. In fact, the Rules make comparatively few substantial changes and they do not fundamentally alter the methods of procedure in the Supreme Court."

[23] *i.e.* the pre-1964 Ord. 19 (Pleadings), Ord. 20 (Statement of Claim), Ord. 23 (Reply), Ord. 24 (Matters Arising Pending the Action) and Ord. 25 (Proceedings in Lieu of Demurrer).

[24] *Cf. Bruce* v. *Odhams Press Ltd.* [1936] 1 K.B. 697, *per* Scott L.J. at 712, where he referred to the former Rules as constituting "a complete Code of Pleading"; and see *per* Greer L.J. at 704. Other parts of the "Code" would no doubt include R.S.C., Ord. 19 (Default of Pleadings), Ord. 20 (Amendment), Ord. 72, r. 7 (pleadings in commercial actions), Ord. 76, rr. 7–10 (pleadings in probate actions), Ord. 80, r. 8 (pleadings of persons under disability), Ord. 82, rr. 3 and 7 (pleadings in defamation actions), and of course the Orders relating to causes of action, counterclaims and parties (Ord. 15), third party proceedings (Ord. 16) and interpleader (Ord. 17). In this context, also see the Report of the (Winn) Committee on Personal Injuries Litigation, Cmnd. 3691 (1968), para. 237, which, *inter alia*, reported: "A perusal of the R.S.C. Order 18 from end to end, with all notes and quotations, constituted a fascinating experience for a practitioner, in the nature of a trip through territory unknown to him in a climate which he has not experienced in his daily life. No set of rules could have been more carefully devised: no judicial comment could be more cogently expressed; practice all too regrettably often reveals little relationship to the Rules; the judicial comments pass unregarded."

way. It has swept away the last vestiges of pleading the general issue, by revoking the former plea of "not guilty by statute"[25] and the pre-1964 "plea in possession,"[26] and at the same time a number of obsolete and unnecessary provisions have also been revoked and not replaced.[27]

Changes effected by Ord. 18   The forms of pleadings which had been formerly prescribed[28] (which were themselves unsatisfactory and even insufficient),[29] have been wholly abrogated.

(a) Since 1964 there are no prescribed forms of pleadings.

---

[25] See the pre-1964 Ord. 19, r. 12, and Ord. 21, r. 19.

[26] See the pre-1964 Ord. 21, r. 21.

[27] Some of the former Rules which have been revoked and not replaced still substantially embody the current practice, and for this reason, it may be convenient to set out the more important of these.

The references are to the pre-1964 R.S.C.:

Ord. 19, r. 19. "When a party in any pleading denies an allegation of fact in the previous pleading of the opposite party, he must not do so evasively, but answer the point of substance. Thus, if it be alleged that he received a certain sum of money, it shall not be sufficient to deny that he received that particular amount, but he must deny that he received that sum or any part thereof, or else set out how much he received. And if an allegation is made with divers circumstances, it shall not be sufficient to deny it along with those circumstances."

Ord. 19, r. 20. "When a contract, promise or agreement is alleged in any pleading, a bare denial of the same by the opposite party shall be construed only as a denial in fact of the express contract, promise or agreement alleged, or of the matters of fact from which the same may be implied by law, and not as a denial of the legality or sufficiency in law of such contract, promise or agreement, whether with reference to the Statute of Frauds or otherwise."

Ord. 19, r. 26. "No technical objection shall be raised to any pleading on the ground of any alleged want of form."

Ord. 20, r. 7. "Where the plaintiff seeks relief in respect of several distinct claims or causes of complaint founded upon separate and distinct grounds, they shall be stated, as far as may be, separately and distinctly. And the same rule shall apply where the defendant relies upon several distinct grounds of defence, set-off or counterclaim founded upon separate and distinct facts."

Ord. 21, r. 2. "In actions upon bills of exchange, promissory notes, or cheques, a defence in denial must deny some matter of fact, *e.g.* the drawing, making, endorsing, accepting, presenting or notice of dishonour of the bill or note."

Ord. 21, r. 3. "In actions for a debt or liquidated demand in money 'a defence in denial' must deny such matters of fact, from which the liability of the defendant is alleged to arise, as are disputed, *e.g.* in actions for goods bargained and sold or sold and delivered, the defence must deny the order or contract, the delivery, or the amount claimed; in an action for money had and received, it must deny the receipt of the money or the existence of those facts which are alleged to make such receipt by the defendant a receipt to the use of the plaintiff."

[28] See the pre–1964 Ord. 19, r. 5, and Appendix C (Statements of Claim), Appendix D (Forms of Defence), Appendix E (Forms of Reply). The Common Law Procedure Act 1852 was the first to provide "Examples of Pleadings" which were to be adopted (see s.91 and Sched. B), and this was all the more necessary then, because of the need to assist the profession to deal with the numerous changes which it introduced into the system of pleadings (see ss.49–90).

[29] See *Wethered v. Cox* [1888] W.N. 165.

(b) The period prescribed by the Rules for the service of all pleadings has been made uniform, except, of course, when some other period is fixed by consent or under an order.[30]

(c) Pleadings may be served during the month of August if the parties consent as well as under an order.[31]

(d) A statement of claim may be served between the service of the writ and the acknowledgement of service by the defendant,[32] and service of the defence is regulated by rule.[33]

(e) There is a general power to order trial without pleadings or further pleadings where the issues between the parties are otherwise clearly defined.[34]

(f) The Rules substantially equate a counterclaim with a statement of claim.

(g) The Rules draw a sharp distinction:
  (i) between the reply which is an answer to the defence[35] and the defence to counterclaim which is an answer to the counterclaim[36]; and
  (ii) between a set-off which operates as a defence and a counterclaim which operates as a cross-action.[37]

(h) A pleading subsequent to a reply or defence to counterclaim may not be served without the leave of the court.[38]

(i) The moment when the pleadings are deemed to be closed is carefully defined.[39]

(j) The operation of an implied joinder of issue on the pleading last served at the close of pleadings is fully spelt out.[40]

(k) The entitlement of a party to plead any matter which has arisen since the issue of the writ is expressed in wider terms.[41]

---

[30] See p. 37 *et seq. infra.*

[31] See R.S.C., Ord. 18, r. 5.

[32] See *ibid.* r. 1. This may save time where the plaintiff intends to proceed for summary judgment under Ord. 14, when he has not indorsed his statement of claim on the writ; see R.S.C., Ord. 14, r. 1(1).

[33] See R.S.C., Ord. 18, r. 2. The court may order the affidavit of the defendant to stand as his defence; see Queen's Bench Masters Pratice Form No. PF14, *Supreme Court Practice 1991*, Vol. 2, para. 212.

[34] See R.S.C., Ord. 18, r. 21, and see p. 18, *infra.*

[35] See R.S.C., Ord. 18, r. 18. The defendant can enter a judgment on his counterclaim if the defendant defaults in the service of his defence to counterclaim, as if the counterclaim were a statement of claim; see R.S.C., Ord. 19, r. 8.

[36] See R.S.C., Ord. 18, r. 3.

[37] See *ibid.* rr. 17 and 18.

[38] *Ibid.*, r. 4.

[39] *Ibid.*, r. 20.

[40] *Ibid.*, r. 14(3). See p. 43 *et seq. infra.* However, there can be no joinder of issue, implied or express, on a statement of claim, or counterclaim.

[41] See R.S.C., Ord. 18, r. 9. It extends to "any pleading" and not only as formerly to a defence or reply, and to any matter which may have arisen, not only as formerly before, but also after, the time for service of the defence or reply.

(l) Particulars of pleadings may be required or ordered of any allegation of any condition of mind,[42] including knowledge,[43] or of any notice.[44]

(m) Particulars of pleadings may be ordered in the form of a statement of the nature of the case relied on.[45]

(n) A criminal conviction and a finding of paternity or adultery which is intended to be relied on as evidence in civil proceedings, must be specifically pleaded,[46] and so must any defence thereto.[47]

(o) The summary powers of the court to strike out pleadings are collected in one rule and have been extended to "abuse of the process of the court,"[48–49] which itself is derived from the inherent jurisdiction of the court.

(p) The Rules have revived and re-introduced the more expressive term "traverse" so as to emphasise its function of requiring the defendant to go over the same ground of the allegations which he intends to deny or not admit or as has been said[50] "to make the defendant take matter by matter and traverse each of them separately"; and as a matter of terminology the Rules have also substituted the term "the service" in place of "the delivery" of pleadings.

The Function of Pleadings

The machinery of the adversarial system   The function of pleadings has been described as a reflection of the rôle of the court[51] and as an aspect of the adversary system of civil proceedings[52]:

"As the parties are adversaries, it is left to each of them to formulate his case in his own way, subject to the basic rules of pleadings. . . . For the sake of certainty and finality, each party is bound by his own

---

[42] R.S.C., Ord. 18, r. 12(1).

[43] *Ibid.*, r. 12(4)(*a*).

[44] *Ibid.*, r. 12(4)(*b*).

[45] *Ibid.*, r. 12(3).

[46] *Ibid.*, r. 7A(1) and (2).

[47] R.S.C., Ord. 18, r. 7A(3).

[48–49] *Ibid.*

[50] *Per* Thesiger L.J. in *Byrd* v. *Nunn* (1877) 7 Ch.D. 284 at 287.

[51] The court acts as a kind of umpire to decide the matters in controversy between the parties; see, Holdsworth, *A History of English Law* (4th ed., 1926), Vol. IX, pp. 280–281. See also *Fallon* v. *Calvert* [1960] 2 Q.B. 201, *per* Pearce L.J. at 204: "In a civil suit the function of a court in this country . . . is not inquisitorial."

[52] See Jacob, "The Present Importance of Pleadings" (1960) *Current Legal Problems*, pp. 171, 174. "The judges sit in Court, not in order that they may discover the truth, but in order that they may answer the question, "How's that?" The English judge will, if he can, play the umpire rather than the inquisitor." See Pollock and Maitland (2nd ed., 1968), *The History of English Law*, Vol. II, p. 671; Holdsworth, *A History of English Law, supra*, Vol. 1, pp. 299–302 and Vol. IX, pp. 280–281, 318. Jacob, *The Fabric of English Civil Justice*, pp. 5–19.

pleading and cannot be allowed to raise a different or fresh case without due amendment properly made. Each party thus knows the case he has to meet and cannot be taken by surprise at the trial. The court itself is as much bound by the pleadings of the parties as they are themselves. It is no part of the duty or function of the court to enter upon any inquiry into the case before it other than to adjudicate upon the specific matters in dispute which the parties themselves have raised by their pleadings. Indeed, the court would be acting contrary to its own character and nature if it were to pronounce upon any claim or defence not made by the parties. To do so would be to enter the realms of speculation. . . . Moreover, in such event, the parties themselves, or at any rate one of them, might well feel aggrieved; for a decision given on a claim or defence not made, or raised, by or against a party is equivalent to not hearing him at all and may thus be a denial of justice.[53] The court does not provide its own terms of reference or conduct its own inquiry into the merits of the case but accepts and acts upon the terms of reference which the parties have chosen and specified in their pleadings. In the adversary system of litigation, therefore, it is the parties themselves who set the agenda for the trial by their pleadings[54] and neither party can complain if the agenda is strictly adhered to. In such an agenda, there is no room for an item called 'Any other business' in the sense that points other than those specified in the pleadings may be raised without notice."[55]

The rôle of the court   Subject to many exceptions, the court plays an inactive, passive and non-interventionist rôle in the machinery of civil justice which operates throughout the whole range of civil proceedings. It has no power or duty to determine what are the issues or questions in dispute between the parties save as may appear from the pleadings or other statements of the parties.

The need to avoid tunnel-vision[56]

"One last word of caution. I think we should be careful not to be mesmerised by our present system of pleadings and feel, as did the lawyers and judges before 1875 and certainly before 1830, that the system does not need radical change as this might inflict damage on the law. The rule that all material facts must be pleaded presupposes

---

[53] See *Esso Petroleum Co. Ltd.* v. *Southport Corporation* [1956] A.C. 218; [1955] 3 All E.R. 864; *per*, Lord Radcliffe at 241.

[54] See *Esso Petroleum Co. Ltd.* v. *Southport Corporation* [1954] 2 Q.B. 182; [1954] 2 All E.R. 56; *per*, Morris L.J. at 207.

[55] See Jacob, *loc. cit.* at n. 52.

[56] Jacob, *The Fabric of English Civil Justice* (Hamlyn Lectures), (1987), p. 91.

that each party already knows what they are, but in truth, as is often the case, at the time of the pleading the party may not know all the material facts and may only suspect what they are. This doubt raises the question whether we should, as the Federal courts and most of the State Courts in the United States have done, move from the system of 'fact-pleading' to the system of 'notice-pleading.'[57] Under such a system a party is entitled to state broadly the nature of the claim made or the defence raised without being required to plead facts or particulars. The system of pleading facts produces precise issues or questions for judicial decision, while the system of 'notice-pleading' puts forward the claim itself made or the defence raised for decision; one is bounded by facts already known or alleged, the other looks beyond to facts to be discovered to support the claim or defence made or raised. Notice-pleading therefore inevitably requires a wide and extensive basis for discovery processes in order to ascertain what are the facts relating to the claim or defence made or raised. Nevertheless, it may be claimed that such a system of pleading would get closer to the attainment of justice, in the sense of enabling the judicial determination, as well as any pre-trial settlement, to be made on the true merits of the case rather than on the narrower factual matrix constructed by the pleadings of the parties."[58]

Cardinal Importance of Pleadings

Clarity and precision It is well to emphasise the cardinal importance of pleadings in the system of civil litigation. This is particularly so in the High Court but applies equally in the county court.[59] A party is not well served if his pleading is drafted in a hurried, shoddy, slipshod, unthinking manner, on the basis that whatever is stated in the pleading will do and may be developed by particulars or discovery or evidence at the trial or may be amended in due course.[60] Conversely, a party is well served

---

[57] See Appendix C.

[58] See Appendix C. It may be wise to raise a word of caution as to notice-pleading; since it greatly increases the range of discovery, it carries with it the attendant risk of increased costs and delay.

[59] See *Beresforde* v. *Chesterfield Borough Council*; [1989] E.G. 176, (C.A.). The inelegance of pleading style was raised by the Court of Appeal in relation to a county court action.

[60] It is of great importance that all fundamental issues should be properly pleaded. To take a point at the trial which has not been properly pleaded is not a satisfactory springboard for success; *per* Russell L.J. in *Eley* v. *King and Chasemore*; [1989] 22 E.G. 109 (C.A.). Similarly in *James* v. *Eastleigh Borough Council* [1989] 3 W.L.R. 123 at 130, Sir Nicholas Browne-Wilkinson V.-C. said: "The plaintiff has failed to plead the case in the only way it could succeed and justice does not require him to be given leave to amend at this

whose pleading states his case with clarity and precision, with full particulars and details, with understanding of the law, an insight into the substantive rights of the parties, and intelligent anticipation of how the case of the party will need to be prepared and presented to the court. The one kind of pleading lays bare the weakness of the party's case; and the other kind clothes it with strength and substance. The drafting of a pleading is the equivalent of laying the foundation on which to build the claim or defence of a party, and as the foundation is laid, whether badly or well and truly, so will the claim or defence be weak and fall or be well sustained and upheld. Pleadings should therefore be drafted with all due care and circumspection, and they require the exercise of much skill and not a little art, to fulfil their whole function.

The pleadings underpin the whole litigation   The influence and importance of pleadings is pervasive throughout all the stages of an action, and thus pleadings play a central, if not predominating, part in civil litigation. As has been said[61]:

> "Pleadings do not only define the issues between the parties for the final decision of the court at the trial; they manifest and exert their importance throughout the whole process of the litigation. They contain the particulars or the allegations of which further and better particulars may be requested or ordered, which help still further to narrow the issues or reveal more clearly what case each party is making. They limit the ambit and range of the discovery of documents and the interrogatories that may be ordered. They show on their face whether a reasonable cause of action or defence is disclosed. They provide a guide for the proper mode of trial and particularly for the trial of preliminary issues of law or of fact. They demonstrate upon which party the burden of proof lies, and who has the right to open the case. They act as a measure for comparing the evidence of a party with the case which he has pleaded. They determine the range of admissible evidence which the parties should be prepared to adduce at the trial. They delimit the relief which the court can award. They provide the basis for the defence of *res judicata* in subsequent proceedings by reference to the record in the earlier proceedings."

Setting the bounds of the controversy   The very nature and character of pleadings demonstrates their significant and overwhelming importance,

---

late stage." In contrast the skilful use of pleading enabled the plaintiff to invoke R.S.C., Ord. 14 in *Newton Chemical Ltd.* v. *Arsenis* [1989] 1 W.L.R. 1297 (C.A.), by scrupulously avoiding express allegations of fraud or deceit.

[61] Jacob, "The Present Importance of Pleadings" (1960) *Current Legal Problems*, pp. 175–176.

for the attention of the parties as well as the court is naturally focused on and riveted to the pleadings as being the nucleus around which the whole case revolves throughout all its stages. The respective cases of the parties can only be considered in the light of and on the basis of the pleadings, which act as fetters upon them, binding and circumscribing them closely and strictly to their own cases as pleaded, subject only to the power of amendment to free them from such fetters so as to put forward the real questions in controversy between the parties. Each party may thus be assumed to have put forward the best case he has in the best way he can in his pleading, and in this sense the pleadings manifest the true substantive merits of the case.[62] Thus pleadings continue to play an essential part in civil actions, and their primary purpose is to define the issues and thereby to inform the parties in advance of the case they have to meet. It is thus bad law and bad practice to shrug off a criticism as a "mere pleading point"[63]; and indeed, the principles of pleading must be strictly observed.

The pleadings uphold the right to a fair trial   The system of pleadings is thus primarily designed to bring the parties to an issue or issues on which alone the court can adjudicate between them, but it is also designed to fulfil some of the fundamental principles of natural justice, such as: that each party should have fair and due notice of what case he has to meet; that each party should have a reasonable opportunity of answering the claim or defence of his opponent; and that each party should have a reasonable opportunity of preparing his case on the basis of the issues disclosed in the pleadings. On this basis the fundamental right of each party to a fair trial is well founded.

The Machinery of Pleadings in Action

A technique for resolving issues of fact   The system of pleadings is targeted at cases where there is or is likely to be a dispute as to questions of fact or of mixed law and fact between the parties to the proceedings. This is emphasised by the requirement that certain categories of actions must be begun by writ.[64] These categories have as their common denominator

---

[62] Jacob, *ibid.* at n. 61, pp. 176–177.

[63] *Farrell* v. *Secretary of State for Defence* [1980] 1 W.L.R. 172 at 180; [1980] 1 All E.R. 166 at 173, *per* Lord Edmund-Davies (action by widow alleging negligence, assault and battery by soldiers in Northern Ireland).

[64] See R.S.C., Ord. 5, r. 2, which provides that the following proceedings must be begun by writ, namely, proceedings: (a) in which a claim is made by the plaintiff for any relief or remedy for any tort, other than trespass to land; (b) in which a claim made by the plaintiff is based on an allegation of fraud; (c) in which a claim is made by the plaintiff for damages for breach of duty (whether the duty exists by virtue of a contract or of a provision made by or under an Act or independently of any contract or any such provision) where the damages claimed consist of or include damages in respect of the death of any person or in respect of personal injuries to any person or in respect of damages to any property; or (d) in which a claim is made by the plaintiff in respect of the infringement of

a likelihood that they will embrace factual disputes between the parties. Conversely, the category of proceedings which are to be commenced by originating summons[65] include any proceedings in which there are unlikely to be any substantial disputes of fact,[66] although even in such case the court has power to order the proceedings to continue as if begun by writ, and to give directions for the service of pleadings.[67] The courts have strongly deplored the absence of pleadings in cases where difficult issues of law and of fact are involved. This is because, without pleadings, the issues cannot be clearly defined.[68]

Claim The plaintiff must serve the statement of claim on the defendant. Whether it is indorsed on the writ or not, it must contain in summary form *only* the material facts on which he relies for his claim[69] together with the relief or remedy which he claims.[70]

Defence—in summary The defendant in answer to the statement of claim must serve his defence on the plaintiff.[71] He may take all or any of the following courses:

(a) he may expressly make admissions;
(b) he may expressly traverse, *i.e.* deny, or refuse to admit, any of the material facts stated by the plaintiff;

a patent. A parallel can also be drawn with proceedings by way of judicial review under R.S.C., Ord. 53. Notice of application for leave to apply for judicial review has to be made in the Prescribed Forms, Form 86A (*Supreme Court Practice 1991*, Vol. 2, para. 84) which provides that the grounds on which relief is sought have to be stated and such grounds must be supported "by an affidavit which verifies the facts relied on." In other words, there is a basic similarity or affinity with the system of pleadings, in that the facts relied on have to be stated as being sufficient to support the grant of relief. The issue or question in proceedings begun by originating summons or originating notice of motion is, as in the case of pleadings, inextricably dependent on the factual situation, so that at bottom the issue or question has to emerge from the facts relied on by the parties. Similar, albeit less formal, machinery is employed in proceedings before tribunals and arbitrations.

[65] See R.S.C., Ord. 5, r. 4(2)(*a*), which includes proceedings in which the sole or principal question at issue is, or is likely to be, one of the construction of an Act or of any instrument made under an Act, or of any deed, will, contract, or other document, or some other question of law. Proceedings by originating summons or originating motion must be supported by affidavit evidence.

[66] See R.S.C., Ord. 5, r. 4(2)(*b*).

[67] See R.S.C., Ord. 28, r. 8; see also *Re Deadman decd.*, *Smith* v. *Garland* [1971] 1 W.L.R. 426, distinguishing *Re 462 Green Lane, Ilford, Gooding* v. *Borland* [1971] 1 W.L.R. 138.

[68] See *General Electric Co. (of U.S.A.)* v. *General Electric Co. Ltd.* [1972] 1 W.L.R. 729 (H.L.), *per* Lord Diplock at 735; *per* Wynn-Parry J. in *Re Camkin's Questions* [1957] 1 W.L.R. 255.

[69] See R.S.C., Ord. 18, r. 7(1).

[70] *Ibid.*, r. 15(1).

[71] Otherwise, he will be in default of defence; see p. 232, *infra.*

- (c) he may deny or admit the facts alleged but avoid their effect by asserting fresh facts which afford an answer to them ("confession and avoidance");
- (d) he may plead collateral matter to destroy or defeat any claim made against him;
- (e) he may raise a question of law as to any claim made by the plaintiff; and
- (f) he may raise a cross-claim against the plaintiff by way of set-off or counterclaim. If he confines his cross-claim to a set-off against the plaintiff's claim, it will operate as a defence. If he also pleads his cross-claim as a counterclaim, he must add his counterclaim to the defence. Any counterclaim operates for pleading purposes as if it were a statement of claim thus rendering the defendant a plaintiff to the counterclaim. Accordingly, the defendant must plead all the material facts upon which he relies for his counterclaim, together with the relief or remedy which he claims.

If the defendant intends to raise any fresh facts or matters in answer to the claim, he must explicitly and clearly inform the plaintiff of the nature of his defence together with the material facts upon which he relies.[71a]

Reply   The plaintiff, in answer to the defence may, though he need not, serve a reply. If no reply is served, all the material facts alleged in the defence will be deemed to be denied by virtue of the implied joinder of issue.[72] But if the plaintiff does serve a reply, he may expressly join issue upon the defence, in which case he must plead any special defences:

- (a) which he alleges make the defence not maintainable; or
- (b) which might take the defendant by surprise; or
- (c) which raise issues of fact not arising out of the defence.[73]

Defence to counterclaim   Just as the counterclaim is the equivalent of a statement of claim, so the defence to counterclaim is the equivalent of a defence.[74] Thus the plaintiff must expressly traverse such material facts pleaded in the counterclaim, otherwise they will stand admitted. Similarly, he must take the same positive assertive position in his defence to counterclaim as the defendant is required to take in his defence.[75]

Only facts in issue have to be proved   Any fact in the statement of claim which is admitted in the defence, because it is expressly admitted or because it is impliedly admitted by the omission of the defendant to tra-

[71a] See R.S.C., Ord. 18, r. 8.
[72] See R.S.C., Ord. 18, r. 14(1).
[73] *Ibid.*, r. 8(1).
[74] See R.S.C., Ord. 19, r. 8.
[75] See p. 13, *supra*.

verse it expressly, ceases to be in controversy between the parties. Thus, no evidence will be required or admitted to prove such fact. Pleadings are required to be served between the parties only in actions begun by writ of summons, and not by any other mode.[76]

Pleadings in Particular Proceedings

The significance of the rules Pleadings in actions in the High Court of Justice are mainly regulated by the Rules of the Supreme Court 1965 as amended. They have the force and effect of a statute and ordinarily apply to all actions begun by writ in the Queen's Bench Division, including the Admiralty Court and the Commercial Court, in the Chancery Division and on the hearing of appeals in such actions before the Court of Appeal.

Practice and procedure—variations The theme is struck by the application of the Rules to proceedings in the Queen's Bench Division, but there are some variations in the practice and procedure relating to pleadings in other divisions of the High Court.

Chancery actions Although the material facts relied on for the claim or defence must be stated in a summary form,[77] it is often necessary and fairly common practice to state them in rather more detail than is usual in an ordinary common law action.[78] A Chancery pleading is ordinarily less laconic and more informative than a pleading in a common law action.

Admiralty actions The pleadings should set out the facts in the fullest detail. Where the court orders the preliminary acts to be opened, it may additionally order the action to be tried without pleadings,[79] and it may make a like order when ordering the trial of an Admiralty action as a short cause.[80] The right of any shipowner or other person to rely by way of defence on any provisions of the Merchant Shipping Acts 1894–1965, which limit the amount of his liability in connection with a ship or other property, is expressly saved.[81]

Commercial actions The pleadings must be in the form of points of claim or points of defence or of counterclaim, defence to counterclaim or reply, and they must be as brief as possible.[82] In practice however, they

---

[76] As to the continuation of proceedings begun by originating summons as if begun by writ, see R.S.C., Ord. 28, r. 8.

[77] See R.S.C., Ord. 18, r. 7(1).

[78] See *Heap* v. *Marris* (1877) 2 Q.B.D. 630; *Mayor &c., of the City of London* v. *Horner* (1914) 111 L.T. 512 (C.A.).

[79] R.S.C., Ord. 75, r. 18(3).

[80] *Ibid.*, r. 31.

[81] R.S.C., Ord. 18, r. 22.

[82] R.S.C., Ord. 72, r. 7(1). See *Practice Direction (Commercial List)* [1962] 1 W.L.R. 1216.

15

are usually not much distinguishable from pleadings in other common law actions. Moreover, in commercial actions no particulars shall be applied for or ordered except such particulars as are necessary to enable the party applying to be informed of the case he has to meet, or as are for some other reason necessary to secure the just, expeditious and economical disposal of any question at issue in the action.[83] It has been said that since its foundation the Commercial Court has strongly set its face against unduly long and complex pleadings. From the outset it was recognised that most commercial disputes did not involve issues which were so complicated that they could only be identified by means of obtuse or intricately worded pleadings.[84]

Official Referees' business[85] It is common practice for pleadings or particulars of pleadings to be ordered to be served in the form of a "Scott Schedule", a document divided into separate columns setting out the full description of each item in dispute between the parties, the contention of each party against each item as to liability or amount or both, with a final column for the use of the court.[86] In this way the parties are required in the Scott Schedule to give full particulars of their respective cases in respect of each item in issue, even though a party may thereby have to state not only that he denies that the charge for any particular claim is reasonable but also what he contends is a reasonable and proper charge for such item.[87]

Third party proceedings Pleadings are not served between the defendant and the third party except pursuant to an order of the court made under the summons for third party directions.[88]

Interpleader proceedings[89] In these, or any other kind of proceeding[90] in which it may become apparent that there are or might be difficult or complex issues of fact or of mixed fact and law, the court may order the parties, (one of whom will be directed to be plaintiff on the issue and the other to be defendant on the issue) to serve pleadings on each other in order to define the issues between them.

[83] R.S.C., Ord. 72, r. 7(2); see, however, *Astrovlanis Compania Naviera S.A.* v. *Linard* [1972] 2 Q.B. 611; [1972] 2 All E.R. 1301, (C.A.); *Palamisto General Enterprises S.A.* v. *Ocean Marine Insurance Ltd.* [1972] 2 Q.B. 625; [1972] 2 All E.R. 1112, (C.A.).

[84] See Colman, *Practice and Procedure of Commercial Court* (2nd Ed., 1986), in particular pp. 41–47 inclusive.

[85] See R.S.C., Ord. 36.

[86] See Chitty and Jacob, *Queen's Bench Forms* (21st ed., 1987), Forms 1477–1488.

[87] This is so, notwithstanding *James* v. *Radnor County Council* (1890) 6 T.L.R. 240.

[88] See R.S.C., Ord. 16, r. 4. The same position applies in claims and issues between co-defendants (Ord. 16, r. 8), and in claims by third and subsequent parties (Ord. 16, r. 9).

[89] See R.S.C., Ord. 17.

[90] *e.g.* proceedings under R.S.C., Ord. 49, r. 5.

Probate actions

(a) The plaintiff must, unless the court gives leave to the contrary or unless a statement of claim is indorsed on the writ, serve his statement of claim on every defendant who acknowledges service in the action. Such service must be prior to the expiration of six weeks after acknowledgement of service by that defendant or of eight days after the filing by that defendant of an affidavit of testamentary scripts,[91] whichever is later.

(b) If the defendant alleges that he has any claim or is entitled to any relief or remedy in respect of any matter relating to the grant of probate of the will, or letters of administration of the estate, of the deceased person which is the subject of the action, he must add to his defence a counterclaim in respect of that matter[92]; and if the plaintiff fails to serve a statement of claim, the defendant may nevertheless, with the leave of the court, serve a counterclaim and the action shall then proceed as if the counterclaim were the statement of claim.[93]

(c) If the plaintiff disputes the interest of a defendant, he must allege in his statement of claim that he denies the interest of that defendant.[94] Further, the party who disputes the interest by virtue of which another party claims to be entitled to a grant of letters of administration must show in his own pleading that if the allegations made therein are proved he himself would be entitled to an interest in the estate.[95]

(d) Any party who pleads that at the time when a will, the subject of the action, was alleged to have been executed the testator did not know and approve of its contents must specify the nature of the case on which he intends to rely. That defence must be pleaded as a condition precedent to support any allegation which would be relevant in support of any other ground or defence such as, that the will was not duly executed, or that at the time of its execution the testator was not of sound mind, memory and understanding, or that its execution was obtained by undue influence or fraud.[96]

(e) If any party defaults in the service of his pleading on any other party, such other party may apply to the court for an order for the trial of the action, and the court may order the action to be tried on affidavit evidence.[97]

[91] R.S.C., Ord. 76, r. 7.
[92] *Ibid.*, r. 8(1).
[93] *Ibid.*, r. 8(2).
[94] *Ibid.*, r. 9(1).
[95] *Ibid.*, r. 9(2).
[96] *Ibid.*, r. 9(3).
[97] *Ibid.*, r. 10.

Dispensing with Pleadings

Principle   The court has power, on the application of the plaintiff or the defendant who has given notice of intention to defend, to order that the action shall be tried without pleadings or further pleadings.[98]

Practice   The power extends to actions begun by writ other than one' which includes a claim by the plaintiff for libel, slander, malicious prosecution or false imprisonment or a claim based on an allegation of fraud.[99]

When?   By its nature, this power is exceptional, since it is a departure from the normal practice that the issues or questions in controversy between the parties should be defined by their pleadings. The instances in which the court would be likely to exercise the power to dispense with pleadings or further pleadings are likely to be very few.[1] However, the policy underlying the power is that, in certain cases, the issues between the parties have already been or can be stated with clarity and precision and that, as the object of pleadings is or can be thus achieved, the pleadings can properly be dispensed with.[2]

How?   The court can direct the parties to prepare a statement of the issues in dispute, or in default of agreement by them, it may settle the statement itself.[3] The court must then, or if it refuses to dispense with

---

[98] R.S.C., Ord. 18, r. 21(1). This power should not be confused with the parallel power to order the trial of a preliminary point of law or preliminary issues, under R.S.C., Ord. 33, rr. 3 and 4(3), nor should it be confused with the trial of proceedings begun by originating summons where the sole or principal question at issue is one of construction or in which there is unlikely to be a substantial dispute of fact, under R.S.C., Ord. 5, r. 4.

[99] R.S.C., Ord. 18, r. 21(4).

[1] See, *e.g. Union of India* v. *Compania Naviera Aeolus S.A.* [1962] 1 Q.B. 1 at 6 (claim for declaration indorsed on the writ); *Jones Construction Co.* v. *Alliance Assurance Co.* [1960] 1 Lloyd's Rep. 264 (claim for declaration plus points of claim in Commercial Court); *Asfar & Co.* v. *Blundell* [1896] 1 Q.B. 123; *Rayner* v. *Rederiaktiebolaget Condor* [1895] 2 Q.B. 289; *Central Argentine Ry.* v. *Marwood* [1915] A.C. 981 (mutual admissions or agreed statement of facts); *Hill* v. *Scott* [1895] 2 Q.B. 371 (C.A.); and *Buchanan & Co.* v. *London and Provincial Marine Insurance Co.* (1895) 65 L.J. Q.B. 92 (letters stating the points to be decided).

[2] See the Final Report of the (Evershed) Committee on *Supreme Court Practice and Procedure*, Cmd. 8878 (1953), pp. 32 *et seq.* On the basis of the recommendation there made, R.S.C., Ord. 14B was introduced in 1955 providing for a rather elaborate and cumbersome procedure for dispensing with pleadings, but this procedure was not much used especially after the decision in *Commissioner of Customs and Excise* v. *Anco Plant and Machinery Co. Ltd.* [1956] 1 W.L.R. 1048 (see Jacob, "*The Present Importance of Pleadings*" (1960) *Current Legal Problems*, p. 180), and accordingly Ord. 14B was revoked by the Rules of the Supreme Court (Revision) 1962 (S.I. 1962 No. 2145) and replaced by R.S.C., Ord. 18, r. 21, which provides a much more simplified procedure, though even this is used rather infrequently.

[3] R.S.C., Ord. 18, r. 21(2).

pleadings it may, give directions for the further conudct of the action as if on a summons for directions.[4]

Historical Perspective

Why pleadings?   The system of pleadings is the English mechanism for enabling and, indeed, requiring the parties to state the real issue or issues between them for determination by the court. In the earliest days of the common law it was the appropriate mode of trial which determined how the real matters in controversy should be presented to the decision making process. In medieval times there were two such processes. Questions of law were determined by the court, *i.e.* the judges, and questions of fact were determined by the verdict of the jury. Even questions of law, however, have to be based on the factual situation, which may afford an explanation as to how the whole system of pleadings came to be based on allegations of fact.

The significance of pleadings   The system of pleadings has played a predominant rôle in the machinery of English civil justice from the earliest days of the common law to the present time. Its history affords an outstanding illustration of the capacity of the fabric of English civil justice to absorb fundamental changes while remaining substantially the same as before, which is the secret of its historical continuity from the old order to the new.

The common law/Chancery dichotomy   Before the Judicature Acts 1873–1875, two independent systems of pleading prevailed side by side under two equally independent systems of judicature: the common law system in the superior courts of common law, and the equity system in the Court of Chancery. The two systems of pleading had different historical roots, operated in the context of different systems of procedure, fulfilled quite different functions and served wholly different machinery for the bringing of a claim before the court. The rules of pleading, which prescribed the manner in which the parties were to state their respective cases, aimed at different objectives. As Sir William Holdsworth has put it[5]:

> "Under the common law procedure a plaintiff must choose some one of the forms of action, and the procedural rules which he must obey were determined largely by his choice. Under the equity procedure, on the other hand, the procedure was generally by bill and answer, and uniform for all sorts of cases. We have seen that the common law rules of pleading aimed at the production of an issue by the

---

[4] *Ibid.*, r. 21(3).
[5] Holdsworth, *A History of English Law*, Vol. IX, p. 336.

mutual allegations of the parties. In equity, on the other hand, the rules of pleading aimed, not at the production of an issue, but at getting all the facts before the court in so complete a fashion that the court could do complete justice to the parties . . . But the systems of pleading prevailing in the two jurisdictions, though fundamentally divergent, were never completely distinct . . . Although the Chancellors set their faces against the importation into the Chancery of the technical formalities of the common law system of pleading, and though in equity pleading never had the same fatal effect as mistakes in common law, some of the ideas and technical terms of the common law were received. Equity knew such pleas as demurrers, replications, and rejoinders; and it sometimes adopted common law rules as to the manner in which these pleas should be drawn. And so, when the fusion of jurisdiction came with the Judicature Acts, it was possible to create a more uniform system of pleading than of procedure.''

Common law procedure—the historical backdrop   The orality of pleading was the characteristic of the medieval system. The parties were opposed to each other in verbal altercation at the bar of the court, which made for great freedom in the statement of the case. They knew of no system of written pleading. The debate between the opposing counsel, carried on subject to the advice or the rulings of the judge, allowed the parties considerable latitude in pleading to the issue.[6] In the present context, *Waldon* v. *Marshall*[6a] affords a characteristic example of medieval oral pleading where the plaintiff succeeded in an action against a veterinary surgeon who had undertaken to cure his horse but had negligently killed it:

> "William Walden brought a writ against one J. Marshall, and alleged by his writ *quod praedictus Johannes manucepit equum pradiciti Willelmi de infirmitate (curare), et postea praedictus Johannes ita negligenter curam suam fecit quod equum suum interiit.* Kirton: We challenge the writ, because it makes mention of *contra pacem*, and in his count he has counted of his cure *ita negligenter* so that the horse died, so that he should not have said 'against the peace.'
>
> And the judges were of opinion that the writ was ill framed. And then the writ was read, and he had not said *contra pacem* in the writ, and the writ was held to be good.
>
> Kirton: Because he has counted that he had undertaken to cure his horse of his malady, for which he should have had an action of covenant, judgment of the writ.

[6] *Ibid.*, p. 635.
[6a] Y.B. Mich. 43 Ed.3, f.33, pl.38 in the year 1370.

Belknap: That we cannot have without a Deed; and this action is brought because you did your cure *ita negligenter* that the horse died, wherefore it is right to maintain this special writ according to the case; for we can have no other writ.

Kirton: You could have a writ of trespass, that he killed your horse, generalment.

Belknap: A general writ we could not have had, because the horse was not killed by force, but died by default of his cure . . .

And then the writ was adjudged good . . . "

The formalism of the old common law   At common law, the predominating feature of the system of pleading was the requirement that the plaintiff must choose the form of action in which to bring his claim.[7] The primary objective of pleadings was to distill an issue by the mutual allegations of the parties.[8] Originally, all pleading was oral, though when the plea was uttered, it would be recorded in the roll of the court. When the parties stood opposite to each other, the plaintiff had to state his case by his own mouth or that of his pleader called the *narrator* or *advocatus*. It was a formal statement "bristling with sacramental words, an omission of which would be fatal."[9] The plaintiff had to offer to prove its truth. The defendant had to preface his defence by a flat denial of all the plaintiff had said by defending "the charge word for word with painful accuracy"[10] but after that he could urge any other pleas or "exceptions" he liked, though in such case he had likewise to offer to prove his case. In

[7] Pollock and Maitland, *History of English Law* (2nd ed., 1968), Vol. 2, pp. 558–573. "Today we can say much of actions in general and we can say little of any procedure that is peculiar to actions of particular kinds. On the other hand, in the middle ages one could say next to nothing about actions in general while one could discourse at great length about the mode in which an action of this or that sort was to be pursued and defended." See also Maitland, *Forms of Action* 1909, reprinted 1971, at pp. 1 and 2: "English law knows a certain number of forms of action, each with its own uncouth name, the Writ of right, an assize of *novel disseisin* or of *mort d'ancestor*, a writ of entry *sur disseisin* in the *per and cui*, a writ of *besaiel*, of *quare impedit*, an action of covenant, debt, detinue, replevin, trespass, assumpsit, ejectment, case. This choice is not merely a number of queer technical names, it is a choice between methods of procedure adapted to cases of different kinds . . . When it comes to pleadings each form of action has some rules of its own . . . The differences between the settled forms of actions have been of very great practical importance—"a form of action" has implied a particular original process, a particular mesne process, a particular final process, a particular mode of pleading, of trial, of judgment. [The litigant] may find that, plausible as his case may seem, it just will not fit any one of the receptacles provided by the Courts and he may take to himself the lesson that where there is no remedy there is no wrong."

[8] For the history of the development of the common law system of pleadings, see Holdsworth, *A History of English Law*, Vol. III, pp. 627 *et seq.*, (3rd ed., 1922), Vol. IX, pp. 336 *et seq.*, and for the history of the development of the system of equity pleading, see pp. 376 *et seq.*

[9] See Pollock and Maitland, *supra*, p. 605.

[10] See *ibid.*, p. 607. By the end of the thirteenth century, he was allowed to employ a more general form of negation.

21

due course a regular, rigid sequence of pleadings was developed which continued in substantially the same mould until the reforms of the Judicature Acts 1873–1875.[11] The parties had ultimately to reach an issue, which could be either an issue of law by way of demurrer or an issue of fact which had to be single and certain.[12] The issue when reached was formally tendered and accepted, and was decided by the court or the jury according as it was an issue of law or of fact.[13]

The flaws in common law procedure   For the medieval lawyer pleading was oral. Only at about the beginning of the sixteenth century was this system superseded by the system of written pleadings, which, when complete, were entered on the record.[14] As time went on, the system of pleading tended to grow more elaborate, more rigid and technical and numerous defects and abuses had become engrafted onto the system which went far to destroy its utility,[15] and to make the whole system extremely difficult and abstruse.[16] Nevertheless, the rules of pleading, archaic though they were, continued to possess great practical importance, for the disregard of them might mean the failure of the action, and a skilful use of them might enable a just claim to be delayed, if not

---

[11] The first pleading was the declaration (or count or *narratio*) in which the plaintiff stated his case. The defendant made answer by a demurrer, which raised an issue of law or a plea, and of these there were many kinds, which had to be raised in a precise order, so that to raise a plea lower in the series operated to waive or renounce a plea higher in the series. The order of pleas was: (1) to the jurisdiction of the court; (2) to the disability of the plaintiff or defendant; (3) a plea in abatement to the court; or (4) to the writ, contending it to be irregular; and (5) a plea in bar, which was an answer on the merits to the action. The answer could itself take the form of a traverse (or denial) or a confession and avoidance, which pleaded other facts to destroy the legal effect of the facts admitted. To the traverse, the plaintiff could demur or join issue upon it, and to a confession and avoidance the plaintiff could plead a replication by way of traverse, or confession and avoidance. To the replication the defendant could in like manner plead a rejoinder, to which the plaintiff could plead a surrejoinder, to which the defendant could plead a rebutter, and to which lastly the plaintiff could plead a surrebutter.

[12] See Co.Litt. 126a: "Issue, *Exitus*, a single, certain and material point issuing out of the allegations or pleas of the plaintiff and defendant, consisting regularly upon an affirmative and negative to be tried by twelve men."

[13] See Holdsworth, *supra*, Vol. III, p. 630.

[14] *Ibid.*, pp. 639 *et seq.* The primary function of the pleadings however remained the same, namely to produce a precise, clear and certain issue of law or fact for determination by the court.

[15] Among these defects and abuses may be mentioned, the device of a demurrer to the evidence, the device of the doctrine of colour, the device of a protestation, the device of a special traverse, the device of the multiplication of counts, *i.e.* stating the same facts in different forms in different counts, and the recourse to sham pleas.

[16] See the First Report of the Common Law Procedure Commission (1851): "The rules which govern the form and application of the special traverse are so technical and artificial as to perplex the practitioner. . . . The rules as to when an inducement may or may not be traversed, and how the pleading may be answered by the opposite party, are extremely difficult and abstruse."

defeated.[17] Special pleading had thus become a distinct branch of the law; and equally, a class of special pleaders became a distinct order in the legal profession.

The earlier nineteenth century reforms   Attempts were made from time to time to remedy the defects of the system of pleading,[18] but without much success. Indeed the Hilary Rules 1834,[19] which greatly extended the area of special pleading, proved to be a disastrous mistake.[20] This was because they created a multitude of new pleading questions, exposing the parties to a variety of new points, and thus inadvertently resulted in increasing the expense and delay of litigation. However, the Common Law Procedure Acts 1852[21] and 1854[22] greatly improved the system of pleading. They achieved this result by minimising the importance of forms of action, abolishing all fictitious averments, and demurrers for want of form, limiting the sphere of special pleading, allowing a party to plead and demur at the same time to the same matter and introducing equitable defences.

Chancery procedure—the theory   In the Court of Chancery, pleadings were conducted by written statements of the parties which were entered on the rolls by the registrars. The first pleading of the plaintiff was the bill in equity which contained nine parts and which the defendant was obliged to answer.[23] The bill became a complex, prolix, repetitive docu-

---

[17] Holdsworth, *supra*, Vol. IX, p. 307. It would be out of place to deal with the complex problems relating to parties both at common law and in equity before the Judicature Acts 1873–1875. One or two illustrations of the then prevailing technicalities may be enough. At common law, for example, the misjoinder of a party or the non-joinder of necessary and proper parties could prove fatal by a plea in abatement or demurrer for want of parties. For the constitution of an action and ejectment for the recovery of land, it became necessary to invent two fictitious characters, the renowned John Doe and Richard Roe. In equity, too, artificial procedural devices were also employed. Thus, for example, whereas all the parties who might be affected by the decree were required to be before the court, yet since what happened to one co-plaintiff, such as death or marriage, could disentitle all the ohers to any relief, the artificial practice was developed of having a single plaintiff, preferably an infant, and the others made defendants, who should have been co-plaintiffs, and if any one of them died or married, the action would have to be reconstituted either by amendment or more generally by a bill of revivor.

[18] *Ibid.* pp. 315 *et seq.*

[19] See 10 Bing. 453–475. These Rules were made by the judges under the Common Law Procedure Act 1833, s.1.

[20] See Holdsworth, *supra*, Vol. IX, p. 325; and see Holdsworth, *"The New Rules of Pleading of the Hilary Term, 1834"* [1923] 1 Camb.L.J. 261.

[21] See ss.49–90.

[22] See ss.83–86 (equitable defences).

[23] See Holdsworth, *supra*, Vol. IX, pp. 379 *et seq.* The first part is the address; the second part is the names of the plaintiffs; the third part is the stating part; the fourth part is the charge of confederacy; the fifth part is the charging part; the sixth part is the allegation that all this is contrary to equity and can only be remedied by a court of equity; the seventh part is the relief sought; and the ninth part is the prayer of process.

23

ment which repeated the case of the plaintiff three times,[24] and inevitably the answer became elaborate and intricate. The parties were allowed to plead further to their respective bills and answers, but in due time the place of further pleadings was taken by the practice of amending the bill (which was liberally allowed and which led to the filing of what were called "fishing bills"), and also by the machinery of the exceptions to and amendments of the answer. Ultimately the parties joined issue and proceeded to the examination of witnesses.

Chancery procedure—nineteenth century reforms The result was that the equity system of pleading was quite as artificial and technical as the common law system and it was infinitely more dilatory and expensive. The Chancery Practice Amendment Act 1852 introduced many reforms into the system of equity pleadings, requiring the bill to state the material facts, matters and circumstances relied on, but not to contain interrogatories. It also abolished the practice of excepting the bills and answers for impertinence.

Consequence of nineteenth century reforms to Chancery procedure
The reforms made in the systems of common law and equity pleadings still left the two systems very distinct from each other. This position continued until the Judicature Acts 1873–1875 and the Rules of Court made thereunder swept away both the old systems and replaced them by the uniform modern system of pleading which has basically prevailed ever since.[25] The modern system of pleadings seeks to combine the best features of the two former systems of pleading: the brevity and the simplified forms of the common law, with the equity principles of stating facts and not the legal conclusion which the pleader puts upon the facts.[26]

---

[24] See Lord Bowen, "Progress in the Administration of Justice during the Victorian Period," in *Select Essays in Anglo-American Legal History*, Vol. 1, p. 524: "A bill in a Chancery suit was a marvellous document which stated the plaintiff's case at full length and three times over. There was first the part in which the story was circumstantially set forth. Then came the part which 'charged' its truth against the defendant or, in other words, which set it forth over again in an aggrieved form. Lastly came the interrogating part which converted the original allegations into a chain of subtly framed inquiries addressed to the defendant, minutely dovetailed and circuitously arranged so as to surround a slippery conscience and to stop up every earth." (This should not of course be confused with the fact that the bill in Chancery finished up with having nine parts.)

[25] It is worth remembering that many of the fundamental principles of the modern system of pleading are the same as those of the older systems, such as the rules that parties must plead material facts, that they must not plead evidence, that a traverse must not be too wide or too narow, that a negative pregnant is evasive, that there must be no departure in pleading, that an objection in point of law may be taken though not by way of demurrer, see Holdsworth, *supra*, Vol. IX, p. 329.

[26] Holdsworth, *supra*, Vol. IX, p. 407. See First Report of the Judicature Commissioners (1859): "Common law pleadings are apt to be mixed averments of law and fact, varied and multiplied in form, and leading to a great number of useless issues while the facts

Equitable claims and defences   One of the primary objectives of the Judicature Acts 1873–1875 was to ensure that law and equity should be concurrently administered in the High Court of Justice and in the Court of Appeal.[27] As Sir George Jessel M.R. said in *Salt* v. *Cooper*[28]:

" . . . the main object of the [Judicature] Act was to assimilate the transaction of Equity business and Common Law business by different Courts of Judicature. It has been sometimes inaccurately called 'the fusion of Law and Equity'; but it was not any fusion, or anything of the kind; it was the vesting in one tribunal the administration of Law and Equity in every cause, action, or dispute which should come before that tribunal."

Accordingly, the rules and doctrines by which equity had modified and supplemented the system of common law are recognised in every Division of the High Court of Justice, and effect must be given to this in all cases in which they are properly applicable. The court must therefore give effect to all equitable claims and defences in what would formerly have been mere common law actions.[29] Although the Judicature Acts

which lie behind them are seldom clearly discoverable. Equity pleadings, on the other hand, commonly take the form of a prolix narrative of the facts relied on by the party with copies or extracts of deeds, correspondence, and other documents, and other particulars of evidence, set forth at needless length. The best system would be one, which combined the comparative brevity of the simpler forms of common law pleading with the principle of stating, intelligibly and not technically, the substance of the facts relied upon as constituting the plaintiff's or the defendant's case, as distinguished from his evidence."

[27] Since incorporated in the Supreme Court of Judicature (Consolidation) Act 1925, s.36.

[28] (1880) 16 Ch.D. 544 at 549.

[29] Supreme Court Act 1981, s.49(1) and (2). Subs. (1) deals with the precedence of the rules of equity; subs. (2) deals with the avoidance of multiplicity of proceedings. Section 49 lies at the heart of the administration of civil justice in England and Wales, since it embodies, in a concentrated form, the fundamental objectives of the Judicature Acts 1873–1875, namely: (a) to bring about the concurrent jurisdiction of law and equity in all civil causes and matters in all civil courts on the basis that in any matter where there is a conflict or variance between the rules of equity and the rules of the common law, the rules of equity shall prevail; and, simultaneously, (b) to secure that the court will be empowered to determine finally all matters in dispute between the parties and to avoid all multiplicity of proceedings.

These objectives were formulated in the celebrated section 25(10) and the seven subsections of section 24 of the Judicature Act 1873, replaced respectively by section 44 and sections 36–43 of the Judicature Act 1925. By a great economy of language all these provisions are replaced by this single section of the Act. This somewhat surprising achievement has been accomplished because, hidden within the provisions of the section, but fundamental to its construction, understanding and operation are words which have the effect of bringing back into operation the very provisions of the Judicature Act 1925, which this section has replaced and by that route reviving the very provisions of the Judicature Act 1873 which the provisions of the Judicature Act 1925 had replaced. In this context, the words in section 49(1) "shall continue" have a crucial importance and significance. They constitute a statutory direction to every court exercising jurisdiction in England and Wales in any civil cause or matter to carry on in the future to administer law and equity precisely as they did before the Act. This means of course, that the cases decided and the law and practice prevailing under these former provisions will themselves continue to have the same authority, value, influence and power as they did before

1873–1875 put an end to the two-fold system of courts and thereby avoided multiplicity of proceedings, they touched upon procedure rather than principle. Thus generally, they did not alter the rights of the parties or enable remedies to be given where they previously would not have been given. They merely amended or improved the procedure for giving effect to those rights.[30]

the Act. Again, in this context the words in section 49(2) "as hitherto" also have the same importance and significance, because those words also constitute statutory direction to every court to give the same effect in the future as it did before the Act to the matters specified in the subsection, and to exercise its jurisdiction in the way stated in the subsection which is the same way as stated in section 43 of the Judicature Act 1925 and section 24(7) of the Judicature Act 1873. Thus, the earlier case law and practice and procedure under the former provisions have been preserved under this Act. Indeed, it should also be remembered in interpreting this section that the Act of 1981 is a consolidation statute with amendments and that the whole thrust of the Act is to preserve the former procedure and practice of the Supreme Court as enacted in the Judicature Act 1925, replacing the comparable provisions of the Judicature Act 1873. Moreover, the use of substantially the same language in this section of the 1981 Act, as was used in the former provisions of the Judicature Act 1925, and the Judicature Act 1873 dealing with the same subject matter gives rise to the presumption that the same meaning will be attached to the words in the 1981 Act as was given under the former statutes (see *Lennon* v. *Gibson & Howes Ltd.* [1919] A.C. 709 (P.C.). See *Supreme Court Practice 1991*, Vol. 2, para. 5187.

[30] *North London Ry.* v. *Great Northern Ry.* (1883) 11 Q.B.D. 30 at 36; *Stumore* v. *Campbell* [1892] 1 Q.B. 314 at 316; *British South Africa* Co. v. *Companhia de Mozambique* [1893] A.C. 602 at 628.

CHAPTER 2

Formal Requirements of Pleadings

Introduction

Since 1964 there have been no forms of pleadings prescribed by the rules of court.[1] There are however, several formal requirements with which pleadings must conform.[2] They constitute the framework in which the parties must construct their pleadings and so enable them to state with greater clarity and precision the substantive content of their respective cases. They impart to the whole range of pleadings a consistency and uniformity which enhance their effect and their significance. Pleadings which comply with the formal requirements become immediately recognisable as such and cannot be mistaken for or confused with any other documents produced in the litigation process.

Non-compliance   Any non-compliance with these formal requirements does not render the pleading a nullity, but is an irregularity which may be amended or waived.[3] These requirements, however, should be observed with great care,[4] so that the pleading should be drawn in such manner as not to prejudice, embarrass or delay the fair trial of the action.[5]

---

[1] The Common Law Procedure Act 1852, s.91, first introduced forms of pleadings which could be adopted as "sufficient" but were to be used with such modifications as were necessary to meet the facts of the case. They were intended to afford "examples of pleading" which the profession were to follow. Under the Judicature Acts 1873–1875, forms of pleadings were prescribed for all pleadings (see the pre-1964 R.S.C., Ord. 19, r. 5, and Appendices C, D and E); they provided the profession with the minimum guidance but were unsatisfactory and indeed insufficient (see *The Isis* (1883) 8 P.D. 227; *Wethered* v. *Cox* [1888] W.N. 165). In course of time, they fell into desuetude, and they were finally abrogated by the Rules of the Supreme Court, (Revision) 1962 (S.I. 1962 No. 2145) as from January 1, 1964.

[2] See R.S.C., Ord. 18. rr. 6 and 15(3), and see *infra*.

[3] R.S.C., Ord. 2, r. 1. See *Smalley* v. *Robey & Co. Ltd.* [1962] 1 Q.B. 577; [1962] 2 W.L.R. 245; [1962] 1 All E.R. 133 (C.A.) (omission of name of division of High Court to which action assigned and name of district registry); *Brady* v. *Barrow Steel Works Ltd.* [1965] 2 Q.B. 182; [1965] 2 W.L.R. 244; [1965] 2 All E.R. 639, (wrong index letter in title and omission of asigned division and name of district registry). The provision of the pre-1964 R.S.C., Ord. 19 r. 26, that "no technical objection shall be raised to any pleading on the ground of any alleged want of form," still governs the present practice.

[4] See *Marshall* v. *Jones* (1888) 52 J.P. 423.

[5] See R.S.C. Ord. 18, r. 19(1)(c). and see p. 223, *infra*.

FORMAL REQUIREMENTS OF PLEADINGS

Heading and Title

Heading of pleading Every pleading must bear on its face:

(a) the year in which the writ in the action was issued[6];

(b) the letter and number of the action, which appear in the right-hand corner of the pleading, *e.g.* "1990 W. No. 8739"[7];

(c) the Division of the High Court to which the action is assigned[8];

(d) the name of the Judge, if any, to whom it is assigned[9];

(e) if the action is proceeding in a district registry, the name of the district registry must be added[10];

(f) the description of the pleading, *e.g.* "statement of claim" or "defence," and so forth[11];

(g) the date upon which the pleading was served[12] and by whom[13];

(h) in the case of a statement of claim the date upon which the writ in the action was issued and specifically the relief or remedy claimed[14];

(i) if the action is begun or is transferred to proceed as "Official Referees' Business" the words "Official Referees' Business" must be added in the top left-hand corner of the pleading. After it has been allocated, there should also be added the name of the Official Referee to whom it has been allocated[15];

(j) if the action is begun in, or transferred to, the Commercial Court, these words must be added in the top left-hand corner of the pleading: "Commercial Court"[16];

(k) these requirements should appear on the right-hand or left-hand corner of the pleading, as may be appropriate in the circumstances, as appears from the following specimen:

---

[6] R.S.C., Ord. 18, r. 6(1)(*a*).

[7] The *year* is that in which the action is commenced; the *letter* is the initial letter of the surname of the plaintiff, or the first plaintiff if there be more than one, or in case of a limited company, corporation or firm, the first letter of the name of that party; and the *number* shows how many writs have already been issued during the current year to plaintiffs whose surnames or names commenced with that letter. The year, letter and number provide the way in which the action is distinguished in the Cause Book or the Cause Index Card.

[8] R.S.C., Ord. 18, r. 6(1)(*c*).

[9] R.S.C., Ord. 18, r. 6(1)(*c*).

[10] See R.S.C., Ord. 6, rr. 1, 7(2) and App. A. Form No. 2. See also *Smalley* v. *Robey & Co. Ltd.* [1962] 1 Q.B. 577; [1962] 2 W.L.R. 245; [1962] 1 All E.R. 133, C.A.

[11] See R.S.C., Ord. 18, r. 6(1)(*d*).

[12] *Ibid.* r. 6(1)(*e*).

[13] See R.S.C., Ord. 18, r. 6(4).

[14] *Ibid.* r. 15(1) and (3).

[15] See R.S.C., Ord. 36, rr. 2(1), 3 and 5(3).

[16] See R.S.C., Ord. 72, r.4(1).

IN THE HIGH COURT OF JUSTICE   1990 B. No. 1234

QUEEN'S BENCH DIVISION

[DISTRICT REGISTRY.]

[COMMERCIAL COURT.]

[Official Referees' Business. Before His Honour Judge Q.C. O.R.]

Writ issued the _____ day of _____ , 1990

Between

A B .... Plaintiff

and

C D .... Defendant

STATEMENT OF CLAIM

1.

2.

3.

4. [*Separate paragraphs for each allegation.*]

5.

6.

7.

And the Plaintiff claims:

(1)

(2) [*Separate paragraphs for each head of relief or remedy claimed.*]

(Signed) _____

Served the _____ day of _____ , 19 __ , by Messrs. XY & Co. of _____ [agents for YZ & Co. of _____]. Solicitors for the Plaintiff [*or* by the Plaintiff acting in person].

Title   Every pleading must bear on its face the title of the action.[17] This consists of the names of each plaintiff and of each defendant. In this

---

[17] R.S.C., Ord. 18 r. 6(1)(*b*).

respect, save for a few rare exceptions,[18] the statement of claim or other pleading must correspond exactly with the writ of summons.[19] Thus:

(a) the forenames and the surname of every plaintiff and of every defendant should be stated in full and correctly on the writ of summons and every pleading.[20] In any case where doubt might otherwise arise as to the sex or, when relevant, the description of a party, the appropriate description must be added in the title of the writ, provided that it is known or can readily be ascertained.[21] In the case of a female party, it is not necessary for her description to be stated in the writ, whether before or after her name; but nevertheless, where it would make it more convenient for the purpose of identity, service, execution or otherwise, a female party may describe herself or be described as "Miss" or "Mrs" as the case may be the term; or by adding after her name "wife of *AB*" or "married woman" or "spinster" or "widow" as the case may be; the term *feme sole* should only be used to describe a divorced woman[22];

(b) in the case of a limited liability company, the full name of the company should be accurately stated. A company may be classed either as "a public company" or as "a private company." The name of a public company must end with the words "Public Limited Company" which are generally abbreviated as "plc".[23] The name of a private company must end with the word "Limited" which is generally abbreviated as "Ltd."[24] If appropriate, the title should alternatively record "a company Limited by Guarantee." Where a limited company changes its name *pendente lite*, it must file at the appropriate court office a written notice of

---

[18] See p. 32, *infra*.

[19] The importance of the title of an action lies in the fact that all the orders made in the action and the judgment and all enforcement proceedings based thereon must correspond in all particulars with the title as it appears in the writ.

[20] See R.S.C., Ord. 6, r. 1, and App. A, Form No. 1. The description or occupation of the parties need not appear in the title; but personal titles including titles by courtesy, and names of dignity should be stated, see *Chitty & Jacob's Queen' Bench Forms* (21st ed. 1987), Form 1307. The description of a female party need not appear in the title. If the plaintiff does not know the Christian or forename of the defendant, he may sue him by his surname only.

[21] Queen's Bench Masters' Practice Directions No. 17(1), (Description of parties), *Supreme Court Practice 1991*, Vol. 2, para. 731.

[22] *Ross* v. *Collins* [1964] 1 W.L.R. 425: [1964] 1 All E.R. 561, *per* Russell L.J.

[23] Companies Act 1985, s.27(3). The Welsh equivalent is "ccc," *ibid*. If a limited company is in liquidation this fact should not appear in the title, but the indorsement of the writ should add after the name and address of the solicitors. "The plaintiffs are a limited company in liquidation. Their liquidator is XY of (state address of liquidator). The address of the plaintiff is the same (or as the case may be)." If a receiver has been appointed, the fact should also not appear in the title (see *Gough's Garages Ltd.* v. *Pugsley* [1930] 1 K.B. 615).

[24] *Ibid*. ss. 25 and 27.

the change of name and serve a copy on all other parties and thereafter the new name must be substituted for the former name which must be mentioned in brackets. However, this requirement does not apply where the name of the company is simply re-registered with the words "Public Limited Company" or its Welsh equivalent[25];

(c) in the case of a corporation, the full corporate name should be used, and statutory corporations must receive their full statutory title;

(d) in the case of a firm, the firm name should be stated in full, adding "trading as a firm"[26];

(e) if either party is an infant, this fact should appear in the title, with the addition that he sues or is sued by his next friend or guardian *ad litem* as the case may be[27];

(f) if either party is a mental patient, it is undesirable to state this fact in the title, but it is necessary to state that he sues or is sued by his next friend or guardian *ad litem* as the case may be[28];

(g) if a party sues or is sued in a representative or other special capacity, *e.g.* as an executor or administrator of the estate of a deceased person or as the trustee of a bankrupt, this fact should also be stated in the title[29];

(h) if a party sues or is sued in a dual capacity, as may sometimes be the case, the fact that he sues or is sued in both capacities should be stated in the title.

(3) Problems of description and misdescription

(a) *Misnomer*   A name wrongly spelt, in a manner *idem sonans*, is not a material misnomer.[30] Thus a misspelling of the name, if it does not alter the sound, would not be a variance such as, *e.g.* "M'Nicoll" and "M'Nicholl." If there be a misnomer on the writ, the defendant, if he gives

---

[25] Queen's Bench Masters' Practice Directions, No. 17(3) (*Change of name—limited company*), *Supreme Court Practice 1991*, Vol. 2, Part 3A, para. 731.

[26] See R.S.C., Ord. 81, r. 1. An individual carrying on business in a firm's name must *sue* in his own name and not in the name of the firm, but he may be *sued* either in the firm's name or in his own name, see R.S.C., Ord. 81, r. 9, and *Mason* v. *Mogridge* (1892) 8 T.L.R. 805. If such a defendant's trade name is one that might be mistaken for the name of an individual, the words "a trade name" should be added in brackets after the name of the defendant in the title.

[27] See R.S.C., Ord. 80, r. 2 and notes thereto.

[28] *Ibid.*

[29] See R.S.C., Ord. 6, r. 3(1). If a limited liability company is in liquidation this fact should not appear in the title, but the indorsement of the writ should add after the name and address of the solicitors, "The plaintiffs are a limited company in liquidation. Their liquidator is XY of [*state address of liquidator*]. The address of the plaintiff is the same [*or as the case may be*]." If a receiver has been appointed, the fact should also not appear in the title (see *Gough's Garages Ltd.* v. *Pugsley* [1930] 1 K.B. 615).

[30] *R.* v. *Shakespeare* (1808) 10 East 83; *Ahitbol* v. *Benedetto* (1810) 3 Taunt. 225.

notice of intention to defend can take no advantage of it. But the misnomer should be corrected by the plaintiff in the statement of claim, if any is served, by inserting the right names, with a statement that the party misnamed had sued or been sued by the name on the writ. Where there is an inaccuracy in the statement of the name of the defendant on the writ, it may be corrected by the defendant in his acknowledgement of service and in such case the plaintiff should adopt the correction in his statement of claim. However, where a person executes a deed by a wrong name, he may be sued by the name in which he executed it.[31] Where either party has been described in the writ by a wrong name, either the title of the writ should be amended or the heading of the statement of claim should be as follows:

Between   *A B* (by whom the writ of
summons was issued
herein under the
name of *E B*)

.... Plaintiff

and

C D... Defendant

or

Between

A B .... Plaintiff

and

C D sued as *F D* .... Defendant
[*or* against
whom the writ of
summons was issued
herein under the
name of *F D*]

(b) *Wrong service*   What of the situation where a person is served with a writ issued against another person? The person is not bound "to give notice of intention to defend" but if he does not do so, proceedings cannot properly be taken against him in default of giving such notice. Nevertheless, his best course would be to give notice of intention to defend and then, before serving a defence, apply to have the service of the writ set

---

[31] See *Mountain (Alexander) & Co.* v. *Rumere* [1948] 2 K.B. 436; [1948] 2 All E.R. 482 (C.A.); cited in *Establissement Baudelot* v. *Graham* [1953] 2 Q.B. 271, at 278.

aside under R.S.C., Ord. 12, r. 8. The acknowledgement of the service of the writ or even giving notice of intention to defend will not constitute a waiver of any irregularity in the service by reason of R.S.C. Ord. 12, r. 7 which to this extent has reversed the case of *Harris* v. *Taylor*.[32]

(c) *Abbreviation*   If on the face of a negotiable or other written instrument the name of any party is not set out in full, but an initial letter, or some other contraction of any Christian name or forename is used, his name may be set out on the writ in the same manner.[33]

Multiple parties

(a) *Using prescribed form*   Where the parties to an action are numerous, whether as plaintiffs or defendants, so that it is not practicable to include all their names and addresses on the prescribed (or adapted) form of Writ of Summons, the issuing party may prepare and annex a schedule setting out in full detail the parties in question. On the face of the writ, however, there must be a clear reference to the schedule, as for example "*AB* and the other plaintiffs" or "*CD* and the other defendants, set out in the schedule annexed hereto," and the schedule must be securely annexed to the writ.[33a]

(b) *Using typescript*   As an alternative method to using such a schedule, the plaintiff, or his solicitor, may prepare the form of writ in typescript, with the names and addresses of the parties appearing in their proper places. So long as an embossing machine is available for this purpose, the court officer will emboss a replica of the Royal Arms upon the writ, since no writ may be issued unless it bears the replica of the Royal Arms.[33b]

(c) *Describing the plaintiffs*   Where there are multiple plaintiffs or defendants, the better practice, which is simple, helpful and clear, is to list the names of all the plaintiffs or all the defendants in the title, each on a separate line, with the appropriate numeral in brackets before or after the name of each. When all the names of all the plaintiffs have been set out, and not before, there should appear the single word "plaintiffs." Then, and only then, there should be inserted an "and" separating all the plaintiffs from all the defendants, and after that all the defendants should be similarly listed, each on a separate line, with the appropriate numeral in brackets for the name of each.

---

[32] [1915] 2 K.B. 580.

[33] See *Lynne's Case Mayor* 10 Co.Rep. 122b; *Williams* v. *Bryant* (1839) 5 M. & W. 447.

[33a] Queen's Bench Masters' Practice Direction No. 12(5), (Numerous Parties), *Supreme Court Practice 1991*, Vol. 2, para. 731.

[33b] See R.S.C., Ord. 1, r. 9(2).

(d) *Directing the writ to each defendant* The writ will then be directed to each defendant and accordingly, the name and address of each defendant must be stated in the writ.

(e) *Names and addresses of plaintiffs* Equally, the name and residence of each plaintiff at whose instance the writ was issued must be stated at the end of the writ.

Description of pleading

Beneath its heading and title, every pleading must bear on its face its own description, *i.e.* by the words "statement of claim" or "defence" or "reply," as the case may be.[34] If the defendant raises a counterclaim against the plaintiff, he must add his counterclaim to his defence,[35] and the description of the pleading will then be "defence and counterclaim," though the body of the pleading should be divided into two sections, the first described as "defence"and the second described as "counterclaim." In such case, the plaintiff must in his reply add his defence to the counterclaim,[36] and the description of the pleading will then be "reply and defence to counterclaim." Similarly, the body of the pleading should be divided into two sections, the first described as "reply" and the second described as "defence to counterclaim."[37]

Paragraphs, Figures and Signatures

Paragraphs of pleading Every pleading must, if necessary, be divided into paragraphs numbered consecutively, and each allegation should so far as convenient be contained in a separate paragraph.[38] This requirement is designed to ensure, so far as possible, that the allegations in every pleading are stated with clarity, and precision, and that long narratives are avoided. It is the hallmark of a good pleading that each allegation is stated in a separate paragraph. It is equally desirable that each head of the relief or remedy claimed should be stated in separate paragraphs of the prayer of the statement of claim.

Figures in pleading In every pleading, dates, sums and other numbers must be expressed in figures and not in words.[39] This requirement is designed to simplify the ready assimilation of dates, sums and other numbers in pleadings.

[34] R.S.C., Ord. 18, r. 6(1)(*d*).
[35] R.S.C., Ord. 15, r. 2(1).
[36] R.S.C., Ord. 18, r. 3(3).
[37] See *Chitty & Jacob's Queen's Bench Forms* (21st ed, 1987), Forms Nos. 242 and 243.
[38] R.S.C., Ord. 18, r. 6(2).
[39] *Ibid.* r. 6(3), and see *Love* v. *Pharaoh* [1954] 1 W.L.R. 190; [1954] 1 All E.R. 120n; (figures in affidavits). It is an undesirable practice to follow the figures by their equivalent in words, whether in brackets or not, as if for the sake of emphasis or accuracy.

Signature of pleading   Every pleading must be signed by counsel, if it has been settled by him. If not, it must be signed by the solicitor for the party or by the party himself if he is acting in person.[40] The signature should appear at the end of the pleading.[41] Counsel's signature is a matter

> "to which the Court was in the habit of paying—as it ought to pay and as it always will be warranted in paying hereafter, as it has done heretofore—the greatest possible respect . . . [It] was to that extent a voucher that the case was not a mere fiction."[42]

The signature of counsel reflects his responsibility for the formulation of the case of a party, which requires the exercise of great care, skill and art to present with clarity, precision and effectiveness.[43]

Date and Indorsement of Service of Pleadings

Date   Every pleading must bear on its face the date on which it is served.[44] If it is amended after service by leave or otherwise, it must, unless the court otherwise directs, be re-served and the date and authority of such amendment and of such re-service must also be shown on its face.

Indorsement   The writ must be indorsed with the name or firm and business address of the solicitor by whom it is served and if the solicitor is the agent of another, with the name or firm and business address of his

---

[40] R.S.C., Ord. 18, r. 6(5). Also note C.C.R., Ord. 50, r. 6 which requires every pleading or other document settled by counsel to be signed by him. Apparently there is no requirement for a solicitor who settles any pleading or document to sign it, which may be a lacuna in the rules and the better practice is for the solicitor to add his signature.

[41] The signature of a legal executive or clerk in the employ of a solicitor in the name of the solicitor is sufficient (see *R.* v. *Kent Justices* (1873) L.R. 8 Q.B. 305; *France* v. *Dutton* [1891] 2 Q.B. 208; *London County Council* v. *Agricultural Food Products* [1955] 2 Q.B. 218; [1955] 2 W.L.R. 925; [1955] 2 All E.R. 229), and it should ordinarily be an actual signature, not a lithographed one (see *R.* v. *Cowper* (1890) 24 Q.B.D. 533), though possibly the use of a rubber stamp may be sufficient though this is an undesirable practice (*Goodman* v. *Eban (J.) Ltd.* [1954] 1 Q.B. 550; [1954] 2 W.L.R. 581; [1954] 1 All E.R. 763). The signature must be printed, typed or written on the copy pleading which is served. If the copy pleading served is unsigned, it is an irregularity which may be amended or corrected by the court under R.S.C., Ord. 2, r. 2, or if it is serious enough, then R.S.C., Ord. 12, r. 8, see *Fick and Fick Ltd.* v. *Assimakis* [1958] 1 W.L.R. 1006 (C.A.); [1958] 3 All E.R. 182, C.A.

[42] *Great Australian Gold Mining Co.* v. *Martin* (1877) 5 Ch.D. 1, *per* James L.J. at 10.

[43] A special responsibility devolves on counsel who settles a pleading containing allegations of fraudulent conduct on the part of the opposite party or allegations setting up justification as a ground of defence to a claim for damages for libel or slander, since such allegations should not be pleaded unless there is "clear and sufficient evidence to support" them (see *Associated Leisure Ltd.* v. *Associated Newspapers Ltd.* [1970] 2 Q.B. 450, *per* Lord Denning M.R. at 456).

[44] R.S.C., Ord. 18, r. 6(1)(*e*).

principal.[45] If the litigant is acting in person, the writ must be indorsed with his name and address.[46]

Paper to be Used for Pleadings

Every pleading, as a document prepared by a party for use in the Supreme Court, must be printed, written clearly and legibly or typewritten otherwise than by means of a carbon and may be produced partly by one of those means and partly by another or others of them.[47] The paper used must be of durable quality, of A4 ISO size with at least $1\frac{1}{2}$ inch wide margin on the left side of the face of the paper and on the right side of the reverse.[48]

---

[45] *Ibid.* r. 6(4)(*b*).
[46] *Ibid.* r. 6(4)(*a*).
[47] R.S.C., Ord. 66, r. 2(1). A document is deemed to be printed if produced by type lithography or stencil duplicating (Ord. 66, r. 2(2)).
[48] R.S.C., Ord. 66, r. 1(1).

CHAPTER 3

Service and Close of Pleadings

Service of Pleadings Between Parties

It is the responsibility of each party to prepare, produce and serve his pleading upon the opposite party. This is a fundamental feature of the adversary system of civil proceedings under which the parties have the primary responsibility, subject to the rules and orders of the court, for preparing and conducting their respective cases at all stages of the proceedings before trial. Pleadings in the High Court[1] are thus documents *inter partes* and not documents of the court. They are served by each party upon the other and not upon the court, nor are copies sent to or filed with the court.[2]

Sequence of Service of Pleadings

Sequence   The pleadings in an action are required to be served in an orderly sequence by each party upon the other in turn. This is an essential part of the machinery of the system to enable each party to give the other due notice of his case, to enable each party to answer or otherwise deal with the case of the opposite party and thus to arrive at the issues or questions between them.

Sequential service—the practice   The sequence in which the pleadings are required to be served, unless the court orders otherwise:

---

[1] The text of this chapter deals with the practice of the High Court relating to the service of pleadings. However, if or when the boundaries of the jurisdiction of the county court is extended, the function of pleadings in that jurisdiction will greatly increase and assume an importance approximating to their rôle in the High Court. Some of the present salient provisions of the County Court Rules are: the particulars of claim must be filed with the court (C.C.R., Ord. 6, r. 1). Any admission, defence or counterclaim must be delivered to the court office (C.C.R., Ord. 9, r. 2). Service of these "pleadings" may be either by the bailiff or other officer of the court or by a party or his solicitor (C.C.R., Ord. 7).

[2] A copy of the statement of claim indorsed on the writ of summons is filed at the office at which the writ is issued (see R.S.C., Ord. 6, r. 7(5)), but this is so by virtue of its being the writ and not of its being a pleading. Moreover, for the purposes of setting an action down for trial, the pleadings have to be lodged with the proper officer of the court (R.S.C., Ord. 34, r. 3(1)(*b*)), when they will then constitute the "record" of the action, but they are not required to be filed.

(a) *First* The plaintiff must serve his statement of claim upon the defendant or upon each defendant if there is more than one.[3]

(b) *Secondly* A defendant who gives notice of intention to defend must serve his defence upon the plaintiff[4] and if he intends to make a counterclaim, he must add the counterclaim to his defence.[5]

(c) *Thirdly* The plaintiff on whom a defendant serves a defence must serve his reply on the defendant if so required,[6] and if the defendant serves a counterclaim the plaintiff must, if he intends to defend it, serve on the defendant his defence to counterclaim.[7] Where the plaintiff serves both a reply and a defence to counterclaim, he must include them in the same document.[8-9]

Time for Service of Pleadings Without Order

Without order—when? Save in cases where the leave or order of the court is required, the pleadings in an action are required to be served by the parties on each other without the leave or order of the court.[10]

---

[3] R.S.C., Ord. 18, r. 1.
[4] *Ibid.* r. 2(1).
[5] R.S.C., Ord. 15, r. 2(1).
[6] R.S.C., Ord. 18, r. 3(1).
[7] *Ibid.* r. 3(2).
[8-9] *Ibid.* r. 3(3).
[10] Until 1893, pleadings were delivered as a matter of course between the parties without the leave or order of the court, unless the parties agreed to dispense with them, which was very rare. In 1893, presumably following the recommendation of the Coleridge Committee on Procedure, which had reported in 1880 (see 25 S.J. 911), the plaintiff was given power to declare on his writ that he intended to proceed to trial without pleadings, and in such cases there were no pleadings unless, on the application of the defendant, the Master ordered otherwise. This practice, intended to discourage parties from serving pleadings, was also virtually ignored, with the result that in 1897, the rules of court were amended to provide that, save in specified cases, as where the writ was specially indorsed or a statement of claim was filed in default of appearance, pleadings could only be delivered by the parties pursuant to the leave or order of the Master either on the summons for directions under the pre-1964 R.S.C., Ord. 30, or under Ord. 14, and it thereafter became irregular for either party, save in such specified cases, to deliver any pleading without such leave or order. In practice, however, the court granted leave to the parties to serve their respective pleadings on each other almost as a matter of course, and the rules requiring leave became otiose but remained in force until 1933, when the rules were amended by Rules of the Supreme Court (No. 1) 1933, requiring pleadings to be delivered between the parties without leave of the court, unless the court otherwise ordered. This practice has been adopted by the Rules of the Supreme Court (Revision) 1962 (S.I. 1962 No. 2145) followed by the revised Rules of the Supreme Court 1965 (S.I. 1965 No. 1776) which as amended from time to time are currently in force, under which pleadings up to the stage of a reply are required to be served by rule without the leave or order of the court. In *Clough* v. *Clough* [1968] 1 W.L.R. 525); [1968] 1 All E.R. 1179 (C.A.) the action was dismissed for want of prosecution for default in the service of the statement of claim.

Timing   They must be served within the time prescribed by the rules for each pleading respectively, unless such time has been duly extended.[11] While an application for an interlocutory injunction is a good reason for the court to extend the time for service of the statement of claim, it is not a good reason why the time prescribed by the rule for the service of that pleading should be disregarded.[12]

The purpose of the time-table   The time-table for the service of pleadings is intended to provide for the orderly progress and due expedition of an action, and should accordingly be adhered to. Failure to comply with the prescribed time will expose the party to the sanctions resulting from default of pleading.[13] These sanctions are provided by way of a disciplinary measure in order to goad the parties to serve their respective pleadings within the time allowed to them by the rules or by an order of the court.

The terms of the time-table   Unless the court gives leave to the contrary, the times prescribed for the service of pleadings without an order are:

(a) *Statement of claim*   If it is indorsed on the writ of summons, the indorsement itself constitutes the statement of claim and it is of course served on the date when the writ is served.[14] If the statement of claim is not indorsed on the writ:

(i) it may accompany the writ, and thus be served on the same date as the writ; or

(ii) if not served before, it must be served within 14 days after the defendant has given notice of intention to defend.[15]

(b) *Defence*   In relation to the service of the defence, it is the defendant who gives notice of his intention to defend who must serve his defence before the expiration of 14 days after the time limited for acknowledging service of the writ.[16] If, however, the plaintiff has first served on that defendant a summons for summary judgment under Order 14, the time for service of the defence is automatically extended until the hearing of that summons. If an order is made on the summons giving leave to

---

[11] See p. 42 *infra*.

[12] *Hytrac Conveyors Ltd.* v. *Conveyors International Ltd.* [1983] 1 W.L.R. 44; [1982] 3 All E.R. 415; (C.A.), in which the action was dismissed for default of the due service of the statement of claim.

[13] See p. 42 *infra*.

[14] See R.S.C., Ord. 18, r. 1, and see *Anlaby* v. *Praetorius* (1888) 20 Q.B.D. 764 (C.A.); *Cassidy & Co.* v. *M'Aloon* (1893) 32 L.R.Ir. 368.

[15] R.S.C., Ord. 18, r. 1. As to the service of a statement of claim on a defendant who is in default of giving notice of intention to defend see R.S.C., Ord. 13, r. 6.

[16] R.S.C., Ord. 18, r. 2(1).

defend, the defence must be served within 14 days after the making of such order or within such other period as may be specified therein.[17]

(c) *Reply* If one is called for, it must be served within 14 days after the service of the defence.[18] If the defendant has served a counterclaim on the plaintiff, his reply (if any) and defence to counterclaim must be served within 14 days after the service on him of the counterclaim to which it relates.[19]

Service of Pleadings Pursuant to Order

Pleadings pursuant to order—when? In some instances, pleadings cannot be duly served without the leave or order of the court.

Long vacation Pleadings may not be served during the month of August except with the leave of the court or with the consent of all parties to the action.[20] Thus the time for service of a pleading runs throughout all the vacations except only during the month of August.[21]

Order 14 If an order is made on a summons for summary judgment under Ord. 14 giving the defendant leave to defend, it will have effect as if it required him to serve his defence within 14 days after the making of the order or within such other period as may be specified therein.[22] In practice, an order is made requiring the defendant to serve his defence within a specified period.

---

[17] *Ibid.* r. 2(2).

[18] *Ibid.* r. 3(1) and (4).

[19] *Ibid.* r. 3(2) and (4).

[20] *Ibid.* r. 5. The service of a pleading during the long vacation without leave of the court or consent of the parties is an irregularity which may be waived under R.S.C., Ord. 2, r. 2 (see *MacFoy* v. *United Africa Co. Ltd.* [1962] A.C. 152; [1961] 3 W.L.R. 1405; [1961] 3 All E.R. 1169.). It should be observed that the rule applies only to the month of August so that the time for the service of pleadings runs during the month of September and all the other vacations in the same manner as during the sittings of the court. See also R.S.C., Ord. 3. The word "pleading" does not include an affidavit nor a notice of appeal, *e.g.* a petition of appeal from the comptroller of patents. *Re Beldam's Patent* [1911] 1 Ch. 60 at 63: and see as to particulars of objection to a petition for extension of a patent. *In the matter of Stearn's Patents* [1911] 28 R.P.C. 663); nor does the rule refer to anything but an amending, serving or filing (*Re Beldam's Patent, supra*); nor does it apply to matrimonial causes (Matrimonial Causes Rules 1977, r. 25). In *Re C.P.C. (U.K.) Ltd. and Re Patents Act 1949* (unrep.) Buckley L.J. confirmed that service of a notice of appeal is not the service of a pleading within the meaning of this rule, and r. 3, and Ord. 64, r. 1(1)(*d*).

[21] As to the definition of "vacation" see R.S.C., Ord. 1, r. 4 (means "the interval between the end of any of the sittings mentioned in Order 64, rule 1, and the beginning of the next sittings.)"

[22] R.S.C., Ord. 14, r. 6, and Ord. 18, r. 2(2).

Third party and subsequent proceedings   In third party and subsequent proceedings,[23] and in proceedings between co-defendants,[24] pleadings may not be served between the parties except pursuant to an order of the court.

Trial of issues   Pleadings may be ordered to be served by the court when giving directions for the trial of issues in interpleader[25] or garnishee[26] proceedings, or when the court orders the separate trial of separate issues.[27]

Pleadings subsequent to reply   No pleading subsequent to a reply or a defence to counterclaim may be served without the leave of the court.[28] Such leave will not be granted as of course but only where its requirement is clearly established.[29] For example, where the plaintiff:

- (a) raises a counterclaim to the defendant's counterclaim, and the defendant desires to serve a defence to that counterclaim[30]; or
- (b) where the defendant raises a counterclaim for damages for libel and slander and he intends to plead express malice on the part of the plaintiff[31]:
  - (i) where the plaintiff pleads fair comment on a matter of public interest, or
  - (ii) the plaintiff pleads qualified privilege to the defendant's counterclaim for damages for libel or slander; or
- (c) where otherwise the defendant intends to raise matters which must be specifically pleaded.[32]

The court thus has control over the service of pleadings subsequent to the reply, so as to prevent the proliferation of pleadings. Such proliferation may readily have the effect of causing confusion, rather than clarification of the issue(s).

A pleading subsequent to the reply or defence to counterclaim must be served within the time specified by the leave or order of the court for its

---

[23] See R.S.C., Ord. 16, rr. 4 and 9, and see Queen's Bench Masters' Practice Forms. PF, 20 and 21, *Supreme Court Practice 1991*, Vol. 2, paras. 220, 221.
[24] See R.S.C., Ord. 16, r. 8.
[25] See R.S.C., Ord. 17, r. 5(1).
[26] R.S.C., Ord. 49, r. 6.
[27] See R.S.C., Ord. 33, r. 3 and r. 4(2).
[28] R.S.C., Ord. 18, r. 4.
[29] See *Harry* v. *Davey* (1875–76) 2 Ch.D. 721; *Norris* v. *Beazley* (1877) 35 L.T. 845. The pleading should normally be prepared and produced to the court at the time of the application for leave, so that the court can see by its terms whether there is a real need for it. Such leave cannot be obtained *ex parte*; *Monck* v. *Smythe* [1895] 1 Ir.R. 200.
[30] R.S.C., Ord. 15, r. 2(2) and see *Faulk (Lewis) Ltd.* v. *Jacobwitz* (1944) 171 L.T. 36.
[31] See R.S.C., Ord. 82, r. 3(3).
[32] See p. 112, *infra*.

service. The pleading subsequent to the reply of the plaintiff is called a rejoinder.[33]

Extension of Time for Service of Pleadings

By consent The time within which any pleading is required to be served, whether by rule or order or direction of the court, may be extended by consent given in writing[34] without any order of the court being made for that purpose.[35]

By order If, however, such consent is not forthcoming, the court has power to extend the time for the service of pleadings.[36] It may do so even though the application for such extension is not made until after the expiration of the period when the pleading should have been served.[37] It is the duty of the party who desires such extension to make application therefor by a "time" summons, which is made returnable, unless otherwise ordered, two days from the date of its issue.[38]

Final "unless" or conditional orders Any extension of time granted may be marked "final," which indicates that no further extension will be granted save in exceptional or changed circumstances. Where the court makes an "unless" or conditional order that a party is required to do an act within a specified time, but the order to do that act is not complied with within the time specified, the court nevertheless retains the power to extend the time within which such act should be complied with.[39] On the other hand, it must be emphasised that although the court has jurisdiction to extend the time where an "unless" order has been made and not

---

[33] Pleadings subsequent to a rejoinder are extremely rare, if they exist, but if leave is granted for their service, they will presumably retain their former names, *i.e.* surrejoinder to be served by the plaintiff, rebutter to be served by the defendant, and surrebutter to be served by the plaintiff.

[34] In practice, the consent is often given in an oral informal way, *e.g.* on the telephone, and such consent is equally effective and respected.

[35] R.S.C., Ord. 3, r. 5(3).

[36] *Ibid.* r. 5(1).

[37] *Ibid.* r. 5(2).

[38] The costs of any application to extend time are borne by the party applying unless the court otherwise orders (R.S.C., Ord. 62, r. 6(6)). See also Queen's Bench Masters' Practice Directions No. 23(8), *Supreme Court Practice 1991*, Vol. 2, Part 3A, para. 733. The summons must be served at least one day before the return date. The issue or services of such a summons does not of itself operate to extend any period of time or to stay proceedings.

[39] *Samuels* v. *Linzi Dresses Ltd.* [1981] Q.B. 115; [1980] 2 W.L.R. 836; [1980] 1 All E.R. 803 (C.A.). This decision of the Court of Appeal not only did not follow the cases of *Whistler* v. *Hancock* (1878) 3 Q.B.D. 83; *Wallis* v. *Hepburn* (1878) 3 Q.B.D. 84 (Ex.D); *King* v. *Davenport* (1879) 4 Q.B.D. 402, D.C. and *Script Phonograph Co. Ltd.* v. *Gregg* (1890) 59 L.J. Ch. 406, but it may be said that it has overruled those cases, since they do not any longer express the present state of the law. (See *Bacal Contracting Ltd.* v. *Modern Engineering (Bristol) Ltd.* [1980] 2 All E.R. 655, where these cases were in fact treated as having been overruled.

complied with, the power to do so should be exercised cautiously and the court will not automatically extend the time of a party who has failed to comply with the order of the court except on stringent terms either as to payment of costs or bringing money into court or the like. Orders as to time are made to be complied with and are not lightly to be ignored.[40] The making of a consent order requiring a party to comply with the terms of the order within a specified time, failing which his claim would be struck out, does not preclude the parties returning to the court to ask for an extension of time.[41] An "unless" order in the form of an order that "unless the defendants within [10] days" comply with an earlier order as to discovery "the plaintiff should have leave to sign judgment," is bad and a judgment entered in pursuance of such an order will be set aside, since such an order does not comply with the requirements of R.S.C., Ord. 42., r. 2(1), that a judgment or order which requires a person to do an act must itself specify the time after service of the judgment or order, or some other time, within which the act is to be done.[42] An "unless" order which is bad for failure to specify a commencement date for the time in which the act required by the order is to be done is irregular rather than void, and the irregularity is capable of being cured under R.S.C., Ord. 2, r. 1. But the court will not exercise its discretion to cure the irregularity where the circumstances do not justify the making of the original order.[43]

Abridgement   The court also has power to abridge the time for the service of pleadings prescribed by the rules.[44]

Close of Pleadings

Rationale   In order to ensure that pleadings should not run on indefinitely but rather be brought to a definite conclusion, the rules fix the precise date on which pleadings are deemed to be closed.[45] The close of pleadings is of vital significance, not only as part of the system of pleadings, but also as determining the date by reference to which further steps in the action are required to be taken.

Threefold significance   The importance of the close of pleadings is thus threefold:

[40] *Samuels* v. *Linzi Dresses Ltd.* [1981] Q.B. 115; [1980] 2 W.L.R. 836; [1980] 1 All E.R. 803, (C.A.).
[41] *Greater London Council* v. *Rush and Tomkins* (1984) 81 L.S.Gaz. 2624 (C.A.).
[42] *Van Houten* v. *Foodsafe Ltd.* (1980) 124 S.J. 277 (C.A.); *Hitachi Sales (U.K.)* v. *Mitsui Osk Lines* [1986] 2 Lloyd's Rep. 574 (C.A.).
[43] *Hollis* v. *Jones (R.B.)* (*a firm*), The Times, October 6, 1984 (C.A.).
[44] R.S.C., Ord. 3, r. 5(1).
[45] R.S.C., Ord. 18, r. 20, replacing the pre-1964 Ord. 27, r. 13, which however did not fix the date for the close of pleadings.

(a) at the close of pleadings there is an implied joinder of issue on the pleading last served[46];

(b) the close of pleadings determines the date by reference to which the parties are required to make automatic mutual discovery by exchanging lists of documents without an order of the court[47]; and

(c) the close of pleadings determines the date by reference to which the summons for directions must be issued[48] (or automatic directions in actions for personal injury take effect).

Deemed to be closed—when?   The pleadings are deemed to be closed in the following circumstances:

(a) if no reply or defence to counterclaim is served at the expiration of 14 days after service of the defence[49];

(b) if a reply is served, at the expiration of 14 days after the service of the reply[50];

(c) if no reply but only a defence to counterclaim is served, at the expiration of 14 days after the service of the defence to counterclaim.[51]

Outstanding request for particulars—does not bar closure   The date on which pleadings are deemed to be closed is in no way dependent upon the fact that a request or an order for further and better particulars has been made but has not been complied with by that time.[52]

Amendment—does not bar closure   Moreover, pleadings are deemed to be closed, notwithstanding that one or other party may desire or apply to amend his pleadings or that pleadings are in fact subsequently amended.

---

[46] R.S.C., Ord. 18, r. 14(2)(a).

[47] R.S.C., Ord. 24, r. 2(1). Lists of documents are required to be exchanged within 14 days after the pleadings in the action are deemed to be closed (ibid.). There are a number of exceptions to this rule under which a party is not required to make discovery of documents except under an order of the court: See Ord. 24, r. 2(2) (defendant to an action arising out of vehicle accidents on land); Ord. 77, r. 12(1) (the Crown as a party to an action).

[48] R.S.C., Ord. 25, r. 1(1). The summons for directions must be issued within one month after the pleadings in the action are deemed to be closed (ibid.) irrespective of whether the parties have exchanged lists of documents without an order.

[49] R.S.C., Ord. 18, r. 20(1)(b).

[50] Ibid. r. 20(1)(a).

[51] Ibid. r. 20(1)(a). If, of course, the time for the service of the reply or the defence to counterclaim or both is extended by the written consent of the parties or by order of the court, the pleadings will not be deemed to be closed until the expiry of such further extended time.

[52] R.S.C., Ord. 18, r. 20(2). This rule expressly disposes of a widespread misconception that an outstanding request or order for further and better particulars of pleadings in some way prevents their being or being treated as "closed."

44

Principal Rules of Pleading

Principal Rules of Pleading

System of fact pleading The principal rules of pleading, with particular reference to R.S.C., Ord. 18, r. 7(1), enshrine the overriding principle that the system of pleadings is a system of fact pleading. This appears all the clearer and more emphatically when the terms of the rule are analysed and it is broken down into its constituent elements. Such analysis throws into relief the basic principles of the system of pleadings.

Source material The principal rules of pleading are encapsulated in R.S.C., Ord. 18, r. 7(1) which provides as follows:

" . . . every pleading must contain, and contain only, a statement in a summary form of the material facts on which the party pleading relies for his claim or defence, as the case may be, but not the evidence by which those facts are to be proved, and the statement must be as brief as the nature of the case admits."[1]

What Ord. 18, r. 7 achieves This rule is of fundamental importance to the whole system of pleading:

(a) it lays down the guiding principles governing the entire system;

---

[1] R.S.C., Ord. 18, r. 7(1), repeats verbatim the substantive terms of Ord. 19, r. 4 in the 1875 Rules of Court, about which Brett L.J. remarked in *Philipps* v. *Philipps* (1878) 4 Q.B.D. 127 at 132, "I know that great pains were taken to draw rule 4." The rule was first made in 1875 (see the Rules of Court set out in the First Schedule to the Supreme Court of Judicature Act 1875). The words "and contain only" were added by way of emphasis by the Rules of the Supreme Court 1883. The rule is subject to the further provisions of r. 7 which deal with what are and what are not material facts to be pleaded: (a) as to pleading the effect of a document or purport of a conversation (r. 7(2), and see p. 59, *infra*): (b) as to pleading presumptions of law (r. 7(3), and see p. 68, *infra*): and (c) as to pleading conditions precedent (r. 7(4), and see (condition precedent) p. 57, *infra*). The rule is further subject to r. 7A (pleading criminal convictions, etc., see p. 58, *infra*) r. 10 (pleading a departure, see p. 161, *infra*) r. 11 (pleading a point of law, see (point of law) p. 65 *infra*) and r. 12 (particulars of pleading, see p. 165, *infra*)

    (b) it effected, in its original form,[1a] a radical change from the former system by requiring material facts only to be pleaded. "Pleadings are now to be merely concise statements of facts which the party pleading deems material to his case."[2]

Constituent elements   R.S.C., Ord. 18, r. 7(1) is particularly succinct and needs to be analysed to reveal that it contains several strands, each of which is a principal rule of pleading in itself:

    (a) every pleading must state material facts only;
    (b) every pleading must state all material facts;
    (c) every pleading must state the material facts, but not the evidence to prove those facts;
    (d) every pleading must state the material facts, and not law; and
    (e) every pleading must state the material facts in a summary form.

Pleading Material Facts Only

The significance of "only"   Every pleading must state *only* those facts which are material. This rule is itself based upon the underlying principle of the Judicature Acts 1873–1875, namely, the function of the court is, so far as possible, to determine all matters in controversy between the parties and to avoid multiplicity of proceedings concerning such matters.[3] In the great majority of cases, the matters in controversy between the parties are matters of fact, and the function of the system of pleading is to ascertain what are the facts that are in controversy between them. Even when the matters in controversy between the parties are a question of law, still the facts have to be ascertained, whether by determination, admission or agreement. In all cases, therefore, it is the factual situation which lies at the basis of every claim or defence. For this reason, the rule insists that material facts only should be pleaded.

"Fact" and "Material"—an analysis   The pleader must plead "facts," and such facts must be "material." The requirement that the pleader must state "facts" means, not only that he must not plead law,[4] but also that he must not plead arguments, reasons, theories or conclusions. The facts pleaded should be pleaded with precision[5] and "certainty" and must not be left to be inferred from vague or ambiguous expressions or

---

[1a] See *ibid.*
[2] *Per* Brett J. in *Lord Hammer* v. *Flight* (1876) 24 W.R. at 347.
[3] See now Supreme Court Act 1981, s.49.
[4] See p. 51, *infra.*
[5] See, *per* Kay J. in *Re Parton, Townsend* v. *Parton* (1882) 30 W.R. 287: "Although pleadings must now be concise, they must also be precise."

from statements of circumstances consistent with a different conclusion. If material details are omitted, particulars of the facts relied on may be requested or ordered.

What facts are material?   The facts must be "material," *i.e.* relevant to the claim or defence, as the case may be. Accordingly, facts that are irrelevant or immaterial to the claim or defence may be struck out.[6] On the other hand, allegations may be material though not necessary to establish a cause of action or ground of defence.[7] Any fact which the party is entitled to prove at the trial is relevant and therefore material to be pleaded,[8] even though it may relate only to the quantum of damages or the type of relief claimed. Thus, the plaintiff is allowed to plead matters which merely tend to increase the amount of damages recoverable, especially where such matters are matters of aggravation,[9] and the defendant may plead matters in mitigation of damages.[10] The principle was thus stated by Lord Selborne L.C.[11]:

> "The rule provides that, 'Every pleading shall contain as concisely as may be a statement of the material facts on which the party pleading relies.' If those words, 'material facts,' are to be confined to matters which are material to the cause of action, that is to say, facts which must be proved in order to establish the existence of the cause of action, then no doubt the facts in this paragraph[12] were not properly pleaded. But in my opinion those words are not so confined, and must be taken to include any facts which the party pleading is entitled to prove at the trial. . . .
> . . . [There] is no chance of the defendant being taken by surprise at the trial by having charges sprung upon him of which he had no notice."

"Material"—examples   The question whether any fact is or is not material to be pleaded depends mainly on the special circumstances of the particular case. Thus, according to the particular circumstances of a

---

[6] *Davy v. Garrett* (1878) 7 Ch.D. 473; *Rassam v. Budge* [1893] 1 Q.B. 571; *Murray v. Epson Local Board* (I.) [1897] 1 Ch. 35.
[7] *Gaston v. United Newspapers* (1915) 32 T.L.R. 143.
[8] See *Millington v. Loring* (1880) 6 Q.B.D. 190, *per* Brett L.J. at 196.
[9] *Millington v. Loring, supra*; *Whitney v. Moignard* (1890) 24 Q.B.D. 630.
[10] *Plato Films Ltd. v. Speide* [1961] A.C. 1090 (H.L.); [1961] 2 W.L.R. 470; [1961] 1 All E.R. 876, overruling *Wood v. Durham* (1888) 21 Q.B.D. 501; *Goody v. Odhams Press Ltd.* [1967] 1 Q.B. 333; [1966] 3 W.L.R. 460; [1966] 3 All E.R. 369; (C.A.).
[11] *Millington v. Loring, supra*, at 194–195.
[12] *I.e.* that in reliance on the promise of marriage the plaintiff permitted sexual intercourse "whereby the defendant infected her with venereal disease."

case, it may be material to plead knowledge, or notice, or intention, or other condition of mind, or in a few cases motive, and in some cases it may be necessary to give details of time, place, or pedigree,[13] though as a rule the precise wording of a document or conversation is not material.[14]

Pleading "All" Material Facts[15]

Each party must plead all the material facts on which he relies for his claim or defence, as the case may be. In other words, he must plead all the facts which he must prove to establish a legally complete or viable cause of action or ground of defence, and no averment must be omitted which is essential to success. All those facts must be pleaded which must, not may, amount to a cause of action.[16] In *Philipps* v. *Philipps*, Cotton L.J. said[17]:

> "The statement of claim, of necessity, must set out all the facts material to prevent the defendant being taken by surprise, because it is the first pleading, and that which ought to be referred to for the purpose of seeing whether there is a cause of action. . . .
> . . . In my opinion it is absolutely essential that the pleading, not to be embarrassing to the defendants, should state those facts which will put the defendants on their guard and tell them what they have to meet when the case comes on for trial."

Moreover, a party will not be entitled to give any evidence at the trial of any relevant facts which he has not pleaded.

> "If parties were held strictly to their pleadings under the present system they ought not to be allowed to prove at the trial . . . any fact which is not stated in the pleadings. Therefore, again, in their pleadings they ought to state every fact upon which they must rely to make out their right or claim."[18]

Thus, where the evidence at the trial establishes different facts from those pleaded by the plaintiff, the action will be dismissed.[19] If the plaintiff's

---

[13] *Palmer* v. *Palmer* [1892] 1 Q.B. 319.
[14] R.S.C., Ord. 18. r. 7(2) and *Darbyshire* v. *Leigh* [1896] 1 Q.B. 554.
[15] R.S.C., Ord. 18, r. 12.
[16] See *West Rand Central Gold Mining Co. Ltd.* v. *R.* [1905] 2 K.B. 391 at 399, *per* Lord Alverstone C.J.; and see *Ayers* v. *Hanson* [1912] W.N. 193.
[17] (1878) 4 Q.B.D. 127 at 138, 139.
[18] *Per* Brett L.J. in *Philipps* v. *Philipps* (1878) 4 Q.B.D. 127 at 133.
[19] *Waghorn* v. *George Wimpey & Co. Ltd.* [1969] 1 W.L.R. 1764; [1970] 1 All E.R. 474; and see *Rawding* v. *London Brick Co.* (1971) 4 K.I.R. 207; *Lloyde* v. *West Midlands Gas Board* [1971] 1 W.L.R. 749; [1971] 2 All E.R. 1240, (C.A.) (new trial ordered).

cause of action or his title to sue depends on a statute, he must plead all facts necessary to bring him within that statute.[20]

Pleading Material Facts, not Evidence

Fact/evidence dichotomy   Every pleading must contain only a statement of the material facts on which the party pleading relies and not the evidence by which they are to be proved.[21] The function of evidence is to prove or disprove the facts in issue as between the parties and not to identify what those issues are. Thus, evidence has generally no place in the system of pleadings. A paragraph, therefore, which amounts to pleading evidence, ought to be struck out:

> "It is an elementary rule in pleading, that, when a state of facts is relied on, it is enough to allege it simply, without setting out the subordinate facts which are the means of producing it, or the evidence sustaining the allegation."[22]

All facts which tend to prove the fact in issue will be relevant at the trial, but they are not "material facts" for pleading purposes. In *Philipps* v. *Philipps*, Brett L.J. said[23]:

> "I will not say that it is easy to express in words what are the facts which must be stated and what matters need not be stated. I know that great pains were taken to draw rule 4 [now r. 7(1)], and it is difficult to state the matter more clearly than in that rule. The distinction is there pointed out that every pleading shall contain a statement of the material facts on which the party pleading relies, but not the evidence by which they (that is, those material facts) are to be proved. The distinction is taken in the very rule itself, between the facts on which the party relies and the evidence to prove those facts. Erle C.J., expressed it in this way. He said that there were facts that might be called the *allegata probanda*, the facts which ought to be proved, and they were different from the evidence which was adduced to prove those facts. And it was upon that expression of opinion of Erle C.J., that rule 4 [now r. 7(1)] was drawn. The facts which ought to be stated are the material facts on which the party pleading relies."

---

[20] *Seear* v. *Lawson* (1880) 16 Ch.D. 121; *Read* v. *Brown* (1889) 22 Q.B.D. 128; *Davis* v. *James* (1884) 26 Ch.D. 778.
[21] See *per* Farwell L.J. in *North-Western Salt Co. Ltd.* v. *Electrolytic Alkali Co. Ltd.* [1913] 3 K.B. 422 at 425.
[22] *Per* Lord Denman C.J. in *Williams* v. *Wilcox* (1838) 8 Ad. & E. 314 at 331; and see *Stewart* v. *Gladstone* (1879) 10 Ch.D. 626 at 664.
[23] (1878) 4 Q.B.D. 127 at 132–133.

Evidence, as opposed to "material" facts—examples

(a) A pleading should not allege admissions made by the opposite party, since this is a matter of evidence.[24]

(b) Again a statement of account which is relied on by way of evidence or admission, and not as a stated or settled account, should not be alleged in the pleading.[25]

(c) " . . . in . . . a scuttling case, it is sufficient to state the . . . procuring and conniving as a fact. The rest is evidence."[26]

Exclusion of evidence—the rationale   The reasons for excluding matters of evidence from being pleaded are:

(a) pleadings would otherwise become long and obtuse, with each party stating his own account or version of the facts;

(b) the pleadings would have the effect of confusing instead of clarifying the issues or questions between the parties.

Exception to exclusion of evidence   An important exception to the rule that a pleading must exclude any allegation of evidence is provided by the rule that if a party intends to adduce evidence that a person has been convicted of a criminal offence by or before a court in the United Kingdom or a court martial, he must plead the conviction relied on, together unto its date, the court that made it, and the issue to which the conviction is relevant.[26a]

The abiding risk of "surprise"   The effect of excluding matters of evidence from pleadings is that, although the pleadings should operate to eliminate the element of surprise as to the material facts in dispute between the parties, yet there may still be "surprise" at the trial as to the oral evidence which each party may adduce to support his case. The observation of Cotton L.J.[27] about the old system of pleading at common law that it " . . . was to conceal as much as possible what was going to be proved at the trial . . . " applies with equal force under the present system

---

[24] *Davy* v. *Garrett* (1878) 7 Ch.D. 473 (C.A.); *Williamson* v. *London and North Western Ry.* (1879) 12 Ch.D. 787 at 793; *Lumb* v. *Beaumont* (1884) 49 L.T 772; *Spedding* v. *Fitzpatrick* (1888) 38 Ch.D. 410 at 414; *Briton Medical and General Life Association Co. Ltd.* v. *Britannia Fire Association and Whinney* (1888) 59 L.T. 889.

[25] See *Kleinberger* v. *Norris* (1937) 183 L.T.J. 107 (C.A.).

[26] *Astrovlanis Compania Naviera S.A.* v. *Linard* [1972] 2 Q.B. 611: [1972] 2 All E.R. 647, *per* Lord Denning M.R. (in a dissenting judgment).

[26a] See R.S.C., Ord. 18, r. 7A(1). The rule extends also to a conviction by Court Martial, and to findings of adultery or paternity.

[27] *Spedding* v. *Fitzpatrick* (1888) 38 Ch.D. 410 at 414.

of pleading as to the oral evidence by which the material facts pleaded are to be proved at the trial.[28]

In this context, however, it should be remembered that under the power of the Court to direct the parties to serve on the other party the written statements of the oral evidence which that party intends to adduce at the trial. The element of "surprise" about the oral evidence at the trial should be greatly diminished.[29] Indeed this power is expressly conferred where the court thinks fit to exercise it for the purpose of disposing fairly and expeditiously of the cause or matter and saving costs, and this purpose should effectively reduce or even eliminate "surprise" as to the oral evidence at the trial.

Pleading Material Facts, not Law

Legal consequences of pleaded facts   A necessary corollary of the first principle of pleading that material facts only are to be stated is that matters of law or mere inferences of law should not be stated as facts or pleaded at all.[30] Thus if the material facts are alleged it is not necessary to plead the legal result. If for convenience this is pleaded, the party is not bound by, or limited to, the legal result he has alleged. He may rely on any legal consequence which may properly flow from the material facts pleaded.[31] In *Karsales (Harrow) Ltd.* v. *Wallis*, Denning L.J. said[32]:

> "I have always understood in modern times that it is sufficient for a pleader to plead the material facts. He need not plead the legal consequences which flow from them. Even although he has stated the legal consequences inaccurately or incompletely, that does not shut him out from arguing points of law which arise on the facts pleaded."[33]

---

[28] See Jacob, "The English System of Civil Proceedings" (1963–64) 1 C.M.L.Rev. 299: "The English pleading is, therefore, a rather laconic document, somewhat reserved and uncommunicative, setting forth merely the bare outline of the case, which is left to be developed in full flood at the trial."

[29] R.S.C., Ord. 38, r. 2A and see *Supreme Court Practice 1991*, Vol. I, para. 38/2A/1. Also see *Comfort Hotels Ltd.* v. *Wembley Stadium Ltd.* [1988] 1 W.L.R. 872; [1988] 3 All E.R. 53. Exchange of witness statements can now be ordered in all proceedings in the High Court: Rules of the Supreme Court (Amendment No. 2) 1988 (S.I 1988 No. 1340). Such exchange is now the norm in the Chancery Division; see *Practice Direction (Chancery 1/89)* [1989] 1 All E.R. 764.

[30] *Per* Farwell L.J. in *North-Western Salt Co. Ltd.* v. *Electrolytic Alkali Co. Ltd.* [1913] 3 K.B. 422 at 425; *Middlesex County Council* v. *Nathan* [1937] 2 K.B. 272. For the distinction between pleading law and raising a point of law, see p. 65, *infra*.

[31] *Re Vandervell's Trusts (No. 2)*; *White* v. *Vandervell Trustees Ltd.* [1974] Ch. 269 (C.A.); [1974] 3 W.L.R. 256; [1974] 3 All E.R. 205.

[32] [1956] 1 W.L.R. 936 at 941: [1956] 2 All E.R. 866.

[33] See also *Lever Bros. Ltd.* v. *Bell* [1931] 1 K.B. 557, *per* Scrutton L.J. at 582: " . . . the practice of the Courts has been to consider and deal with the legal result of pleaded facts, though the particular legal result alleged is not stated in the pleadings. . . . "

Avoiding the pleading of law—examples

(a) If a party alleges that he is *entitled* to a particular **right** or goods or property, or that the opposite party is under a *liability* or a *duty* to act in a specified way or that a *legal relationship* exists between two or more persons, such allegations are conclusions of law or of mixed fact and law. The plaintiff must set out in his pleading the facts which, in his opinion, give him that right or title or which impose on the defendant that liability or duty.[34]

(b) Similarly, the defendant must allege the facts upon which he relies as a defence,[35] and he must deal explicitly with the facts alleged by the plaintiff.[36]

(c) An apparent exception exists in the case of foreign law, which must be adequately pleaded, since it is a matter of fact.[37]

Pleading Material Facts in Summary Form

The material facts must be stated in a summary form and the pleadings should be as brief as the nature of the case will admit.[38] The material facts should accordingly be stated:

(a) briefly;

(b) succinctly;

(c) in strict chronological order.

Thus, so far as possible:

(a) unnecessary allegations or details should not be pleaded, *e.g.* citations from public statutes, or propositions of law, or the precise words of documents or conversations, unless they are material[39];

(b) a party should not plead to:

    (i) any matter of law set out in his opponent's pleading or to any matter of fact which is not alleged against him[40]; nor

    (ii) to any particulars of pleadings; nor

    (iii) to the prayer of the statement of claim or counterclaim; nor

---

[34] See, *per* Willes J. in *Gautret* v. *Egerton* (1876) L.R. 2 C.P. 371, cited with approval by Lord Alverstone C.J. in *West Rand Central Gold Mining Co.* v. *R.* [1905] 2 K.B. 391; and see *Selangor United Rubber Estates Ltd.* v. *Cradock* [1965] Ch. 896; [1965] 2 W.L.R. 67; [1964] 3 All E.R. 709.

[35] R.S.C., Ord. 18, rr. 7(1) and 8.

[36] *Ibid.* r. 13.

[37] See *Ascherberg, Hopwood & Crew Ltd.* v. *Casa Musicale Sonzogno di Petro Ostali S.N.C.* [1971] 1 W.L.R. 1128; [1971] 3 All E.R. 38; [1971] 1 W.L.R. 173 (C.A.). Another rare exception is the need to plead a private Act of Parliament if passed before 1850, or since that date if the Act itself so provides (see Interpretation Act 1978, s.3).

[38] R.S.C., Ord. 18, r. 7(1).

[39] *Ibid.* r. 7(2).

[40] See *Rassam* v. *Budge* [1893] 1 Q.B. 571.

(iv) to the claim for damages.[41] For the sake of clarity, however, it is common practice to deal with these matters in the pleadings.

The court has an inherent jurisdiction to deal with prolix documents,[42] but no pleading is prolix which merely states the material facts, however numerous.

Alternatives to "Fact" Pleading

U.S.A. The replacement in the American Federal System and most State jurisdictions of Fact-Pleading by Notice-Pleading under which the initial complaint is merely a short and plain statement of the claim showing that the plaintiff is entitled to relief, has affected the rules as to discovery in those jurisdictions. The process of fishing discovery has been fully legitimated. It is permissible for a party to employ the discovery processes, both oral and documentary, to ascertain and discover facts which until then were unknown and which will establish or support the claim.[43]

European mainland Similarly in the continental systems, the whole of the evidence of the parties and their witnesses would have been obtained before the final day of reckoning or judgment, including all the oral, documentary and tangible evidence which the court, in its search for the truth, would have gathered.

Canada In Canada, at the pre-trial stage, the parties are entitled to examine each other, and with the leave of the court, any other witness, under their system of what is called "Examination for Discovery,"[44] which has the effect of revealing the whole of the cases of the parties, thus enabling them to effect a greater volume of settlements and to do so on a fairer basis by knowing what the material evidence would likely to have been at the trial.

The inter-action with discovery In the American Federal and many state systems, the processes of discovery are employed, in some instances perhaps extravagantly, to ascertain the entirety of the evidence which will be available to be adduced at the trial by each of the parties, and

[41] See R.S.C., Ord. 18, r. 13(4).
[42] See *Hill* v. *Hart-Davis* (1884) 26 Ch.D. 470.
[43] See *Hickman* v. *Taylor* 329 U.S. 495 (1947); 67 S.Ct. 385. "The deposition-discovery rules are to be accorded a broad and liberal treatment. No longer can the time-honoured cry of "fishing expedition" serve to preclude a party from inquiring into the facts underlying his opponent's case. Mutual knowledge of all the relevant facts gathered by both parties is essential to proper litigation. To that end, either party may compel the other to disgorge whatever facts he has in his possession," *per* Justice Murphy delivering the opinion of the U.S. Supreme Court.
[44] See, *e.g.* Ontario Rules of Civil Procedure, Rule 31, as amended (Reg. 786/1984).

which will be known and may be used by both the parties at the pre-trial stage.

In England, too, the trend has also markedly been towards the more open system of pre-trial disclosures of evidence, including the relevant oral evidence of the parties, their witnesses and experts who adduced at the trial. So far as documentary evidence is concerned, the rules and the practice of the court enable the parties to obtain or impel the fullest disclosure of all relevant documents, subject to the right of any party to withhold disclosure or a recognised ground of privilege.[45] So far as the oral expert evidence is concerned, it may not be adduced at the trial, unless the parties agree, or the court has given leave and directed that the substance of the evidence be disclosed in the form of a written report, at the pre-trial stage, to the opposite party,[46] and moreover, the court may direct the expert to meet "without prejudice" and prepare a statement indicating those parts of the evidence on which they are, and those on which they are not, in agreement.[47] Discovery of evidence may be obtained by interrogatories served in the first instance without leave by one party or the other or may be ordered by the court,[48] and the answers may be used at the trial.[49] And lastly, the court may direct the parties to exchange the witnesses' statements of the real evidence to be adduced at the trial.[50]

All those methods of obtaining or procuring the pre-trial evidence of facts and expert opinions do not in any way lessen or diminish the importance of pleadings as being the central core on or around which the whole of the proceedings must be conducted and ultimately determined if necessary. On the contrary, the methods of pre-trial discovery are themselves constrained and bound by the issues or questions arising from the pleading of the parties. The scope and extent of the pre-trial discovery processes are measured and dictated by the pleadings of the parties, and they do not spill over or beyond what is to be found in those pleadings, just as they will not be allowed to do so in respect of the real evidence of the trial itself.

---

[45] See R.S.C., Ord. 24, Ord. 25, r. 8.
[46] See R.S.C., Ord. 38, rr. 36–44, and Ord. 25, r. 8.
[47] See R.S.C., Ord. 38, r. 38.
[48] See R.S.C., Ord. 26, rr. 1–4.
[49] See R.S.C., Ord. 26, r. 7.
[50] See R.S.C., Ord. 38, r. 2A.

CHAPTER 5

Subsidiary Rules Of Pleadings

Introduction

Subsidiary—as opposed to primary—rules of pleading   In addition to the principal rules of pleading, there are a number of rules or principles which operate as ancillary to the principal rules. They assist the system of pleading to fulfil its functions with greater clarity, precision and effectiveness. The main subsidiary rules or principles which operate in this way are explained below. These are, however, by no means exhaustive. Thus there are special provisions regarding defences, which require particular grounds of defence to be specifically pleaded.[1] or which deal with specific defences, such as tender[2] or set-off,[3] and there are general provisions regarding particulars of pleading[4] and the mode of pleading a counterclaim.[5] The subsidiary rules and principles dealt with below may affect all pleadings, and are accordingly so grouped together and dealt with in alphabetical order.

Layout of chapter   The list of topics is in alphabetical order since there is no way of comparing the importance of one subsidiary rule as against another. The list sets out some of the more striking subsidiary rules which are of great importance in practice.

Alternative and Inconsistent Allegations

Meaning   Either party may in a proper case include in his pleading alternative and inconsistent allegations of material facts, as long as he

---

[1] See pp. 112 and 130, *infra.*
[2] See p. 135, *infra.*
[3] See p. 139, *infra.*
[4] See p. 165, *infra.*
[5] See p. 148, *infra.*

does so separately and distinctly. He may also claim relief thereunder in the alternative and he may rely upon several different rights alternatively, although they may be inconsistent.[6] However, in an action for rectification the plaintiffs were held not to be allowed to allege two claims in the alternative based on inconsistent assertions of the parties' common continuing intention since such allegations demonstrated at the outset that there was no certain intention which would found such a claim.[7]

Pleading technique Whenever alternative cases are alleged, the facts relating to such cases should be stated separately, so as to show on what specific facts each alternative head of relief is claimed.[8] So a defendant may:

- (a) "raise by his statement of defence without leave, as many distinct and separate, and therefore inconsistent, defences as he may think proper . . . "[9];
- (b) rely upon several distinct grounds of defence, set-off or counter-claim, founded upon separate and distinct facts.

A defence is not embarrassing, merely because it contains inconsistent grounds of defence, provided they are not fictitious.[10]

On the other hand, different plaintiffs cannot claim inconsistent alternative relief,[11] and a party must not in a subsequent pleading make any allegation of fact, or raise any new ground or claim inconsistent with a previous pleading of his.[12]

Condition of Mind

A material fact Where a party pleading alleges any condition of the mind of any person, be it any disorder, mental disability, or malice, fraudulent intention or other condition of mind, he must expressly allege such condition of mind as a fact and he must state the particulars of the

---

[6] See *Philipps* v. *Philipps* (1878) 4 Q.B.D. 137 at 134.

[7] *Pearce C.H. & Sons Ltd.* v.*Stonechester Ltd. The Times*, November 17, 1983 (C.A.).

[8] *Davy* v. *Garrett* (1878) 7 Ch.D. 473 at 489; *Watson* v. *Hawkins* (1876) 24 W.R. 884.

[9] See *per* Thesiger L.J. in *Berdan* v. *Greenwood* (1878) 3 Ex. D. 251 at 255; *Hawkesley* v. *Bradshaw* (1880) 5 Q.B.D. 302; *Coote* v. *Ford* [1899] 2 Ch. 93.

[10] *Re Morgan; Owen* v. *Morgan* (1887) 35 Ch.D. 492. In this case, where there was a claim against the executor of the husband in respect of sums of money and stock alleged to have been received by the husband as trustee, for the separate use of the wife, the defence pleaded: (a) that the sums had not been received; (b) if received, not as trustee; (c) if received, payment; (d) alternatively, gift by the wife to the husband; (e) alternatively, accord and satisfaction; (f) alternatively, set-off; (g) the Statute of Limitation; and (h) laches and delay.

[11] *Smith* v. *Richardson* (1878) 4 C.P.D. 112.

[12] R.S.C. Ord. 18, 10(1); and see p. 165 *infra*, "No Departure Permitted."

facts on which he relies.[13] "Knowledge" is a special condition of the mind and is dealt with separately.[14]

Necessary particulars Particulars of the facts relied on to support such condition of mind must be pleaded or they will be ordered. If an allegation is made that a person, including a party, had or did not have a particular intention, particulars will be ordered of any overt acts and any other facts relied on to support the allegation.[15]

Conditions Precedent

Meaning A condition precedent is a condition agreed between the parties or imposed by statute, the fulfilment of which is necessary before a party becomes entitled to sue.
Thus:

(a) it is not of the essence of the cause of action, but it has been made essential to it;
(b) it is not a substantive or constituent element of a cause of action, but it has been superimposed upon it as an additional formality which must be fulfilled so as to give rise to the entitlement to sue.

The fulfilment of a condition precedent necessary for the case of a party is to be implied in his pleading.[16] Thus:

(a) a general averment of the due performance of all conditions precedent need not be alleged[17]
(b) it is unnecessary for a party to state in his pleading that a thing has been done or an event has occurred, being a thing or event the doing or occurrence of which constitutes such a condition precedent.[18]

Conditions precedent—the shifting burden of proof If the defendant intends to rely upon the non-fulfilment of a condition precedent, he must expressly allege what was the condition precedent and the material facts relied on to show that it has not been duly performed or fulfilled or that

---

[13] See R.S.C., Ord. 18, r. 12(1)(*b*).
[14] See p. 62, *infra*. Keeping to the alphabetical order of these subsidiary rules as to pleadings.
[15] *Feeney* v. *Rix* [1968] Ch. 693; [1968] 3 W.L.R. 376; [1968] 3 All E.R. 22 (C.A.).
[16] R.S.C., Ord. 18, r. 7(4).
[17] *Gates* v. *Jacobs W.A. & R.J.* [1920] 1 Ch. 567 (due performance of the statutory conditions for service of notice under s.146 of the Law of Property Act 1925 is implied and need not be expressly pleaded). For the pre-1875 requirement to plead such a general averment, see *per* Lord Goddard C.J. in *Bond Air Services Ltd.* v. *Hill* [1955] 2 Q.B. 417 at 427.
[18] R.S.C., Ord. 18, r. 7(4). Thus an allegation that the plaintiff was ready and willing to perform the contract may be implied (*Jefferson* v. *Paskell* [1916] 1 K.B. 57 at 74).

the event has not occurred.[19] But if the defendant properly pleads non-performance or non-fulfilment of a condition precedent, the burden of proving its due fulfilment or performance then shifts to the plaintiff.[20]

Distinguishing between conditions precedent and material facts   A material fact which is of the essence of a cause of action, and is not a mere condition precedent, must still be pleaded. Thus, *e.g.*:

(a) the requirement that notice of dishonour of a bill of exchange was duly given (except to an acceptor), or was waived, or excused is an essential constituent in an action on the bill. And such fact must be pleaded with all necessary particulars.[21]

(b) in an action by the assignee of a debt or legal chose in action, it is an essential requirement that the assignment was in writing and that notice in writing thereof was duly given to the debtor and such facts must accordingly be pleaded, otherwise the plaintiff would have no title to sue.[22]

Criminal Convictions

Exception to the rule against pleading evidence   The Civil Evidence Act 1968, s.11(1), made criminal convictions by or before any court in the United Kingdom, or by a court-martial there or elsewhere, admissible in evidence in civil proceedings whether the person was convicted upon a plea of guilty or otherwise and whether or not he is a party to the civil proceedings.[23] This provision requires a criminal conviction to be pleaded, even though it constitutes a matter of evidence. Its object is to give the opposite party fair notice that such criminal conviction is intended to be relied on.

Plaintiff pleading technique   If a party wishes to rely on this provision to adduce evidence of such criminal conviction, he must include in his pleading a statement of his intention to do so with particulars of the con-

---

[19] *Abbs* v. *Matheson & Co.* (1898) 104 L.T.J. 268; *Bond Air Services Ltd.* v. *Hill* [1955] 2 Q.B. 417; [1955] 2 W.L.R. 1194; [1955] 2 All E.R. 476: and see *Whiting* v. *East London Waterworks* [1884] W.N. 10.

[20] *Bank of New South Wales* v. *Laing* [1954] A.C. 135; [1954] 2 W.L.R. 25; [1954] 1 All E.R. 213.

[21] *Fruhauf* v. *Grosvenor & Co.* (1892) 61 L.J. Q.B. 717; *May* v. *Chidley* [1894] 1 Q.B. 451; *Roberts* v. *Plant* [1895] 1 Q.B. 597.

[22] *Seear* v. *Lawson* (1880) 16 Ch.D. 121; *Read* v. *Brown* (1888) 22 Q.B.D. 128.

[23] This provision abolished the rule in *Hollington* v. *Hewthorn F. & Co. Ltd.* [1943] K.B. 587 (C.A.). Of course, the conviction must still be a subsisting one, *ibid.* A paragraph in a pleading referring to a foreign conviction will however be struck out following *Hollington* v. *F. Hewthorn & Co. Ltd.* (*ibid.*) because the Civil Evidence Act 1968 has no application to foreign convictions; *Union Carbide Corporation* v. *Natarin Ltd.* [1987] F.S.R. 538 (C.A.).

viction and the date thereof, the court or court-martial which made the conviction and the issue in the proceedings to which the conviction relates.[24]

Pleading convictions—the shifting burden of proof   The effect of pleading and proving a criminal conviction is to shift the *legal* burden of proof to the convicted party to allege and disprove the offence, though he may discharge such burden on the balance of probabilities.[25]

Defendant pleading technique   Where a pleading contains a statement of the intention of a party to rely on section 11 of the Civil Evidence Act 1968, the opposite party must either expressly or impliedly admit the criminal conviction relied on, or, if he desires to contest such conviction, he must do so expressly in one of three ways, *i.e.* (a) deny the conviction; or (b) allege that it was erroneous, and if so give particulars of the facts and matters relied on; or (c) deny that it is relevant to any issue in the proceedings.[26]

Convictions and defamation claims   Although there is no express provision requiring a criminal conviction in a defamation action to be pleaded in reliance on section 13 of the Civil Evidence Act 1968 (which makes a conviction in such action conclusive evidence of the commission of the offence), nevertheless it is still desirable that a criminal conviction relied on in such an action should be pleaded.[27]

Effect of Document or Purport of Conversation

General rule   Where any document or conversation is referred to in any pleading, the precise words of the document or conversation should not be stated, but only the effect of the document or the purport of the conversation should be briefly stated.

---

[24] R.S.C., Ord. 18, r. 7A(1). Similar requirements are provided for pleading findings of adultery in matrimonial proceedings and adjudications of paternity in affiliation proceedings in reliance on s.12 of the Civil Evidence Act 1968; see R.S.C., Ord. 18, r. 7A(2), but not in the County Court.

[25] *Stupple* v. *Royal Insurance Co. Ltd.* [1971] 1 Q.B. 50; [1970] 3 W.L.R. 217: [1970] 3 All E.R. 230, (C.A.); *Taylor* v. *Taylor* [1970] 1 W.L.R. 1148; [1970] 2 All E.R. 609 (C.A.). *Wauchope* v. *Mordecai* [1970] 1 W.L.R. 317; [1970] 1 All E.R. 417 (C.A.) A similar effect operates when pleading and proving a finding of adultery in matrimonial proceedings; see *Sutton* v. *Sutton* [1970] 1 W.L.R. 183; [1969] 3 All E.R. 1348.

[26] R.S.C., Ord. 18, r. 7A(3). Similar provisions apply to contesting findings of adultery and adjudications of paternity, *ibid.*

[27] See *Levene* v. *Roxhan* [1970] 1 W.L.R. 1322; [1970] 3 All E.R. 683, (C.A.).

Exception But if the precise words of a document or conversation are themselves material, they must be set out in full in the pleading[28] but only insofar as it is necessary to show what the alleged effect is.[29] Thus:

(a) it is not ordinarily necessary to set out verbatim the entire terms of a written contract, but only to state briefly the effect thereof and to specify the particular terms in respect of which any breach is alleged;

(b) it is not ordinarily necessary to set out the precise words used by the parties when making an oral contract or taking part in any conversation relied on.

However:

(a) in an action of libel or slander, the plaintiff must set out verbatim in his statement of claim the very words on which he relies to found his claim;[30]

(b) it may be necessary to set out the precise words of a clause in a will, which the court will have to interpret.[31]

Documents—legal effect—pleading

(a) Where the legal effect of the document is stated, the pleader takes upon himself to give the true meaning of the instrument, whatever its terms may be.

(b) Where the document is set out verbatim, he leaves the construction of it to the court, except that the meaning is often necessarily assumed in alleging the breach.[32]

Generally therefore, the best course is to state the legal effect of the documents relied on, especially where they are lengthy or numerous. However, where their meaning is doubtful, and it is desired to raise in the easiest and most direct form the question of their sufficiency to support the action, it may be advisable to set them out verbatim. But a pleading which sets out verbatim immaterial documents, or documents which are only material as containing matters of evidence, may be struck out.[33]

---

[28] R.S.C., Ord. 18, r. 7(2); and see *per* Lord Mansfield in *Bristow* v. *Wright* (1781) 2 Doug. K.B. 665.

[29] See *Philipps* v. *Philipps* (1878) 4 Q.B.D. 127 (C.A.); *Davis* v. *James* (1884) 26 Ch.D. 778; *Riddell* v. *Earl of Strathmore* (1887) 3 T.L.R. 329.

[30] *Harris* v. *Warre* (1879) 4 C.P.D. 125; *Collins* v. *Jones* [1955] 1 Q.B. 564; [1955] 2 W.L.R. 813; [1955] 2 All E.R. 145, but the jury may be invited to say whether words to the "like effect" were used; see *per* Bankes L.J. in *Tournier* v. *National Provincial and Union Bank of England Ltd.* [1924] 1 K.B. 461.

[31] *Darbyshire* v. *Leigh* [1896] 1 Q.B. 554.

[32] If documents are referred to in a pleading, they become part of the pleading, and it is open to the court to look at them without the necessity for an affidavit exhibiting them (*Day* v. *Hill (Park Lane)* [1949] 1 K.B. 632: [1949] 1 All E.R. 219, C.A.).

[33] See R.S.C., Ord. 18, r. 19.

Pleading from documents—how? In stating what the pleader contends is the legal effect of an instrument (having due regard to conciseness), he should follow the terms and order of the document itself and not attempt to reform it or to use supposed equivalent expressions; but he should omit all portions of the document not material to the case. Where a contract or other document is stated *verbatim*, the pleading must in some way show its application to the facts stated, as by identifying the parties, and so forth, and it may sometimes be necessary to add an express allegation for this purpose. Where it is necessary to state the pleadings in a previous action, their effect should be concisely stated so far as material; it is not necessary to set them in full.[34]

Challenging a pleading founded on a document Where the plaintiff has set out in his claim the legal effect of a document on which he relies, and the defendant, while admitting the document itself, wishes to dispute the construction thus put upon it, he may in his defence deny the construction put upon it by the plaintiff and state its effect according to his own construction.

Judicial Notice

Examples of matters which need not be pleaded It is unnecessary to plead matters of which the court takes judicial notice. Such matters are for example:

  (a) the law of the realm and the general law of nations:
  (b) all public Acts of Parliament, and all private Acts passed since 1850, unless the contrary is expressly provided by any such statute[35];
  (c) the law and custom of Parliament, including the privileges and procedure of each branch of the legislature;
  (d) the prerogatives of the Crown;
  (e) the maritime and ecclesiastical laws;
  (f) the articles of war in the land, marine and air services;
  (g) royal proclamations;
  (h) the custom of merchants where such custom has been settled by judicial determinations;
  (i) the customs of the City of London, which have been certified by the Recorder;
  (j) the rules and course of procedure of the superior courts; and the limits of their jurisdiction;
  (k) the power of the ecclesiastical courts, and the limits of their jurisdiction;

---

[34] *Houstoun* v. *Sligo* (1885) 29 Ch.D. 448.
[35] See Interpretation Act 1978, s.3.

    (l) the division of England into counties, provinces, and dioceses;
   (m) the commencement and ending of legal terms and sittings;
   (n) coincidence of the years of the reign of any sovereign of this country with the years of our Lord;
   (o) the coincidence of the days of the week with days of the month;
   (p) the order of the months;
   (q) the meaning of ordinary English words and terms of art;
   (r) the names and quantities of legal weights and measures;
   (s) the relative values of the coin of the realm.

Examples of matters which should be pleaded   But judicial notice is not taken of the following;

    (a) foreign or Commonwealth law;
    (b) Scottish law;
    (c) particular local customs or usages;
    (d) customs of foreign countries or courts of justice;
    (e) of the existence of a war between foreign countries;
    (f) of the situation of any particular place.

Any of these matters when relied upon must be alleged like other facts. Even in the case of a matter of which the court takes judicial notice, it is necessary to allege any facts which are required to connect that matter with the facts on which the right of action or defence rests.[36]

Knowledge

Materiality   The element of "knowledge" is a special condition of mind for the purpose of pleading. Where it is material that a person had or had not knowledge of some fact, matter or thing, the pleader must expressly allege such knowledge or absence of knowledge as a fact.[37]

Particulars   Particulars of knowledge volunteered should be pleaded or the court may order them to be given.[38] Such particulars should consist

---

[36] A more complete enumeration of the matters of which the court does and does not take notice (including those above specified) may be found in Roscoe, *Evidence in Civil Actions* (20th ed.), pp. 82, *et seq.*

[37] As to when it is material to allege and prove that a party had knowledge of a fact, see *Griffiths* v. *London and St. Katharine Docks Co.* (1884) Q.B.D. 259; *Imperial Loan Co. Ltd.* v. *Stone* [1892] 1 Q.B. 599; *Osborn* v. *Chocqueel* [1896] 2 Q.B. 109; *Baker* v. *Snell* [1908] 2 K.B. 825; *Broughton* v. *Snook* [1938] Ch. 505.

[38] R.S.C., Ord. 18. r. 12(4)(*a*). This rule reversed the pre-1964 R.S.C., Ord. 19, r. 22, and negatived *Burgess* v. *Beethoven Electric Equipment Ltd.* [1943] 1 K.B. 96, (C.A.)

of any specific facts, documents or overt acts relied on to show knowledge, on the part of the person concerned, of some fact, matter or thing.

"Ought to know"   Particulars of the facts and circumstances relied on will be ordered of an allegation that a party "ought to know" or "ought to have known" some fact, matter or thing.[39]

"Grounds for belief", etc.   Similarly, if a party puts forward a positive allegation that he had grounds for belief, or reasonable and probable cause for doing what he did, he may be ordered to give particulars of the facts and matters he relies on,[40] but otherwise such particulars are not ordinarily ordered to be given.[41]

Matters Whenever Arising

General rule   Ordinarily, the material facts to be pleaded are those which existed at the date of the issue of the writ, since the rights of the parties are in the ordinary way crystallised at that date. But occasionally the rights of the parties may be affected by events or circumstances which happen or take place after the issue of the writ. Accordingly, either party may in any pleading plead any matter which has arisen at any time therein before or since the issue of the writ.[42] The generality of this provision extends to:

(a) any pleading (and not only to a defence or reply); and
(b) to matters whenever arising and not only to matters which have arisen before the time for the service of the defence or reply has expired.[43]

Limits to the general rule   The generality of this provision is expressly limited in two respects[44]:

---

[39] *Fox v. Wood H. (Harrow) Ltd.* [1963] 2 Q.B. 601; [1962] 3 W.L.R. 1513; [1962] 3 All E.R. 1100.

[40] See *Alman* v. *Oppert* [1901] 2 K.B. 576 (C.A.); and see *per* Lord Denning M.R. in *Stapeley* v. *Annetts* [1970] 1 W.L.R. 70; [1969] 3 All E.R. 1541.

[41] *Cave v. Torre* (1886) 54 L.T. 515; *Roberts v. Owen* (1890) 6 T.L.R. 172; *Stapeley* v. *Annetts, supra.*

[42] R.S.C., Ord. 18, r. 10.

[43] These limitations were contained in the pre–1964 R.S.C., Ord. 24, rr. 1 and 2. The pre–1964 practice of a "confession of defence" contained in the former Ord. 24, r. 3 under which the plaintiff could deliver such a "confession" as to matters that have arisen after the commencement of the action and sign judgment for costs, has been abolished.

[44] See R.S.C., Ord. 18, r. 9.

   (a) a party may not in any pleading raise any allegation of fact or any
     new ground of claim inconsistent with his previous pleading[45];
     and
   (b) the plaintiff may not in his statement of claim raise any allegations
     or make any claim in respect of a cause of action which is not
     mentioned in his writ.[46]

Moreover, this provision as to pleading material facts whenever arising is also subject to the general powers of amendment of pleadings.[47]
Thus in a proper case a party may by amendment raise matters arising
before or since the issue of the writ. If a party desires to plead any matter
arising after the issue of the writ, he must make a specific averment to
that effect.[48] So far as the statement of claim is concerned, in addition to
the limitation above mentioned,[49] the plaintiff cannot plead matters
which have arisen since the issue of the writ which have the effect of
adding a cause of action accruing since that date.[50]

Pleading subsequent to the claim

(a) *Defence*   The defendant may plead any matter of defence which has
arisen since the issue of his writ, such as a release or bankruptcy of the
plaintiff,[51] but performance after action brought may not amount to a
defence.[52]

(b) *Counterclaim*   It may be founded on matters which have arisen since
the issue of the writ,[53] though in such a case it must be pleaded as so arising.[54]

---

[45] *Ibid.* r. 10.
[46] *Ibid.* r. 15(2).
[47] See R.S.C., Ord. 20.
[48] *Champion* v. *Formby* (1878) 7 Ch.D. 373. The matters relied on should be preceded by a
clear statement that they arose after the issue of the writ; see *Ellis* v. *Munson* (1876) 35
L.T. 585 (C.A.).
[49] See n. 63, *supra.*
[50] See *Eshelby* v. *Federated European Ltd.* [1932] 1 K.B. 254 (D.C.); (C.A.) (claim for
instalments falling due after issue of writ).
[51] See *Foster* v. *Gamgee* (1876) 1 Q.B.D. 666; *Champion* v. *Formby, supra*; *Re May* (1885)
28 Ch.D. 516; *Barker* v. *Johnson* (1889) 60 L.T. 64. In the case of the bankruptcy of the
plaintiff, the defendant may apply to stay the action instead of pleading the bankruptcy
in bar *Warder* v. *Saunders* (1882) 10 Q.B.D. 114; and see Insolvency Act 1986, ss.7 and
9). A receiving order arising since issue of writ may not be pleaded by the defendant (see
Re Berry [1896] 1 Ch. 939).
[52] See *Callander* v. *Hawkins* (1887) 2 C.P.D. 592.
[53] *Beddall* v. *Maitland* (1881) 17 Ch.D. 174 at 180.
[54] *Wood* v. *Goodwin* [1884] W.N. 17. As to the plaintiff raising a counterclaim arising out
of matters since the service of the defendant's counterclaim, see *Toke* v. *Andrews* (1882)
8 Q.B.D. 428; *Renton Gibbs & Co. Ltd.* v. *Neville & Co.* [1900] 2 Q.B. 181.

(c) *Reply*   The plaintiff may plead matters amounting to an estoppel arising after the issue of the writ.[55]

Notice

Pleading technique   Where it is material that a person had notice of some fact, matter or thing, the pleader must expressly allege such notice as a fact, and particulars of such notice may be ordered.[56]

"Notice" as distinct from "knowledge"   "Notice" and "knowledge" are not synonymous, and an allegation that a party had notice is not an allegation of a condition of mind.[57] Although the rule[57a] deals with both knowledge and notice, they are clearly made separate by the particulars which have to be given of each such allegation. It is these particulars that differentiate the one topic from the other.

Example   Where it was alleged that bankers did not receive a cheque and the proceeds thereof "as purchasers for value without notice," particulars were ordered showing how and when such notice was given and the circumstances from which it was to be inferred.[58]

Point of Law

Raising, not pleading—the distinction   While it is a principal rule of pleading that a party must plead material facts only and not law,[59] yet every party is permitted by his pleading to raise a point of law.[60] The dis-

---

[55] *Morrison Rose & Partners* v. *Hillman* [1961] 2 Q.B. 266; [1961] 3 W.L.R. 301; [1961] 2 All E.R. 891 (C.A.).

[56] R.S.C., Ord. 18, r. 12(4)(*b*); reversing the pre-1964 Ord. 19, r. 28.

[57] *Cresta Holdings Ltd.* v. *Karlin* [1959] 1 W.L.R. 1055; [1959] 3 All E.R. 656 (C.A.).

[57a] R.S.C., Ord. 18, r. 12(4).

[58] See *Cresta Holdings Ltd.* v. *Karlin, ibid.*

[59] See p. 51, *supra.*

[60] R.S.C., Ord. 18, r. 11. This rule replaced the pre-1964 Ord. 25, r. 2, which was made by the Rules of the Supreme Court 1883, which also by Ord. 25, r. 1, abolished demurrers. Under the pre–1883 system of pleading, a demurrer was the formal mode in pleading for disputing the sufficiency in law of the pleading of the other side. The effect of a demurrer was that the party demurring thereby confessed on the record that, for the purposes of the demurrer, all the matters of fact pleaded were to be taken as true (see *Hancocke* v. *Prowd* 1 Wms. Saund. 336 at 337, n. 3), but denied that they were sufficient in their legal effect to constitute the right or defence which was maintained by the other side, and thus an issue of law was raised which was decided by the court after argument. Before the Common Law Procedure Act 1852, the party demurring could not also plead a traverse or a confession and avoidance, though he could raise a *special demurrer* by expressly stating his grounds of objection, *e.g.* on the ground of duplicity, repugnancy, want of particularity, argumentativeness, etc.; or otherwise raise a *general demurrer*. Under the Common Law Procedure Act 1852, ss.50–52, there was only one kind of demurrer (see s.89 for its form), and it became possible both to demur and to plead to the facts (see, *e.g. Williams* v. *Great Western Ry.* (1874) L.R. 9 Ex. 157). This rule implements the recommendations of the (Evershed) Report of the Committee on Supreme Court Practice and

tinction between pleading law which is not permitted, and raising a point of law which is permitted, is that by pleading law a party would in effect be pleading conclusions of law, which could obscure the facts of the case. On the other hand, by raising a point of law a party would help to define or identify or isolate an issue or question of law on the facts as pleaded. It is a constitutional principle of great importance that questions of construction of all legislation, primary and secondary, are questions of law to be determined authoritatively by courts of law. Moreover, no court of law and no tribunal has any discretion, in order to meet what it thinks is the justice of a particular case, to vary the meaning of the words of primary or secondary legislation from case to case. This is the function of Parliament or the body responsible for the secondary legislation.[61]

Raising a point of law—how An objection in point of law may be pleaded together with any number of traverses and special pleas. Each objection should, however:

    (a) be stated in a separate paragraph following those which deal with the facts;

    (b) raise a point of substance, not a merely technical objection to some defect of form; and

    (c) state succinctly the grounds for the objection.[62]

Any point of law which necessitates legal argument, as, *e.g.* the validity of a custom,[63] or a question of jurisdiction,[64] or *lex fori*[65] or whether a statement was absolutely privileged,[66] may be raised under this rule, but not the question whether words complained of are defamatory.[67] A point of law which requires serious and prolonged argument should ordinarily be raised in the pleading and dealt with, if appropriate, as a preliminary issue rather than by summons to strike out the opponent's pleading under R.S.C., Ord. 18, r.19.[68] Where, however, the court is satisfied, even after substantial argument, that the pleading does not

---

Procedure that the pleadings of a party "should plead points of law of what may be called a special character, e.g. reliance on some particular statute or rules or regulations or such as go to the validity of the cause of action" (see Cmnd. 8878 (1962), para. 120).

[61] *Energy Conversion Devices Inc's Appliction* [1983] R.P.C. 231, *per* Lord Diplock.

[62] *Anderson* v. *Midland Ry.* [1902] 1 Ch. 369 at 370.

[63] *British, etc., Shipping Co.* v. *Lockett* [1911] 1 K.B. 264.

[64] *Chatenay* v. *Brazilian Telegraph Co.* [1891] 1 Q.B. 79.

[65] *Hansen* v. *Dixon* (1907) 96 L.T. 32.

[66] *Isaacs* v. *Cooke* [1925] 2 K.B. 391.

[67] *Morris* v. *Saunders Universal Products* [1954] 1 W.L.R. 67, (C.A.) (whether words complained of were defamatory).

[68] See *Addis* v. *Crocker* [1961] 1 Q.B. 11; [1960] 3 W.L.R. 339; [1960] 2 All E.R. 629; and see *Dadswell* v. *Jacobs* (1887) 34 Ch.D. 278 at 284; *Hubbuck and Sons Ltd.* v. *Wilkinson, Heywood & Clark Ltd.* [1899] 1 Q.B. 86 at 91; *Worthington* v. *Belton* (1902) 18 T.L.R. 438.

disclose a reasonable cause of action or ground of defence, it will order the pleading to be struck out.[69]

Litigation strategy To raise a substantial point of law on the facts as pleaded is a convenient course, especially where it may dispose of the whole action,[70] since it may enable the point to be tried as a preliminary issue.[71] Where the point of law is going to be decisive of the litigation it should be raised under this rule.[72] Thus, the court may:

(a) allow a preliminary point of law to be tried on the facts as pleaded in a great variety of cases[73];

(b) may allow such a point to be argued without pleadings[74];

(c) allow the pleading to be amended to raise the point for trial as a preliminary issue.[75]

Alternatively, the preliminary point of law may be kept open for argument before the House of Lords.[76]

Tactics

(a) An objection in point of law must be taken clearly and explicitly, and the point itself should be precisely defined.[77]

(b) Where all the allegations in the statement of claim are admitted but an objection in point of law is raised in the defence, no evidence will be admitted at the trial since there is no issue of fact on the pleadings.[78]

(c) If a party does not raise a point of law in his pleading, he may nevertheless at the trial raise any point of law open to him.[79]

(d) The parties are not entitled by their pleadings to raise abstract or hypothetical questions of law or to raise questions of law on

---

[69] See *Williams & Humbert Ltd.* v. *W. & H. Trade Marks (Jersey) Ltd.* [1986] A.C. 368; [1986] 2 W.L.R. 24; [1986] 1 All E.R. 129 (H.L.); *McKay* v. *Essex Area Health Authority* [1982] Q.B. 1166; [1982] 2 W.L.R. 890; [1982] 2 All E.R. 771 (C.A.).

[70] See *Independent Automatic Sales Ltd.* v. *Knowles & Foster* [1962] 1 W.L.R. 974; and see *The Mayor, Aldermen and Citizens of Manchester* v. *Williams* [1891] 1 Q.B. 94.

[71] See R.S.C., Ord. 33, rr. 3 and 4 (2).

[72] *Everett* v. *Ribbands* [1952] 2 Q.B. 198 at 206; applied in *Carl Zeiss Stiftung* v. *Smith Herbert & Co.* [1969] 1 Ch. 93 and see *Waters* v. *Sunday Pictorial Newspapers* [1961] 1 W.L.R. 967 at 974.

[73] See *Supreme Court Practice 1991*, Vol. I, para. 18/11/3, (Cases).

[74] See *Ramage* v. *Womack* [1900] 1 Q.B. 116; *Roberts* v. *Charing Cross, Euston and Hampstead Ry.* (1903) 87 L.T. 732.

[75] *Lever* v. *Land Securities Co. Ltd.* (1894) 70 L.T. 323.

[76] See *Cummings* v. *London Bullion Co.* [1952] 1 K.B. 327; [1952] 1 All E.R. 383 (C.A.).

[77] See *National Real Estate and Finance Co.* v. *Hassan* [1939] 2 K.B. 61: "care should be taken that a real point of law is being raised and that there should be a clear definition of what the point of law raised is," *ibid.* 77.

[78] *Pioneer Plastic Containers Ltd.* v. *Commissioners of Customs and Excise* [1967] Ch. 597; [1967] 2 W.L.R. 1085; [1967] 1 All E.R. 1053.

[79] *Independent Automatic Sales Ltd.* v. *Knowles and Foster* [1962] 1 W.L.R. 974: [1962] 3 All E.R. 27; and see *per* Lindley J. in *Stokes* v. *Grant* (1878) 4 C.P.D. 25 at 28.

hypothetical sets of facts, even if they are agreed between the parties,[80] and especially if the hypothesis is false or fictitious.[81]

Presumptions

The principle   A party need not allege any fact if:

(a) it is presumed by law to be true; or
(b) the burden of disproving it lies on the other party, unless the other party has specifically denied it in his pleading.[82]

Examples   Thus:

(a) the plaintiff suing on a dishonoured bill of exchange need not allege that it was given for good consideration[83]:
(b) the plaintiff suing on a contract for the sale of land need not allege compliance with section 40 of the Law of Property Act 1925.[84]

But material facts must be pleaded   The material facts which are alleged to give rise to such presumption or onus should themselves be pleaded. Thus, the fact that the defendant was the owner of a motor vehicle is "material" because if proved, it is prima facie evidence that the driver was his servant or agent.[85] And it is for the defendant to plead and prove facts to rebut such inference.[86] The plaintiff, however, need not expressly

---

[80] *Sumner* v. *William Henderson & Sons* [1963] 1 W.L.R. 823 (C.A.); and see *Stephenson, Blake & Co.* v. *Grant, Legros & Co.* (1917) 86 L.J. Ch. 439. See also *Avon County Council* v. *Howlett* [1983] 1 W.L.R. 605 (C.A.); applying *Adams* v. *Naylor* [1946] A.C. 543 at 555, (*per* Lord Uthwatt; hypothetical state of facts without substance or reality). Appellate Court will decline to hear "academic appeals" or those in which the issues are dead or the parties no longer have any interest in the result or there is no dispute or further dispute between the parties to be resolved (*Ainsbury* v. *Millington* [1987] 1 W.L.R. 379; [1987] 1 All E.R. 929 H.L. *Glasgow Navigation Co.* v. *Iron Ore Company* [1910] A.C. 293; *Sun Life Assurance Company of Canada* v. *Jervis* [1944] A.C. 111 (H.L.). On the question of the attitude of the appellate courts to "academic" appeals, see also *National Coal Board* v. *Ridgway* [1987] 3 All E.R. 582 (C.A.); and *Star Cinemas (London) Ltd.* v. *Barnett. The Times*, December 9, 1987 (C.A.).
[81] *Royster* v. *Cavey* [1947] K.B. 204; [1946] 2 All E.R. 642 (C.A.); *Whall* v. *Bulman* [1953] 2 Q.B. 198 at 202, *per* Denning L.J. On the other hand, in what is sometimes called a "friendly" action, the parties may raise a genuine and live point of law precisely for the purpose of resolving a doubtful issue or question, as for example, where there are conflicting decisions in the lower courts. (See *Thorne* v. *Motor Trade Association* [1937] A.C. 797).
[82] R.S.C., Ord. 18, r. 7(3).
[83] See Bills of Exchange Act 1882, s.30.
[84] See *Catling* v. *King* (1887) 5 Ch.D. 660 (C.A.). If, of course, the contract was in writing, this fact should be pleaded in the statement of claim as a material fact.
[85] *Barnard* v. *Sully* (1931) 47 T.L.R. 557.
[86] See *Rambarran* v. *Gurrucharran* [1970] 1 W.L.R. 556; [1970] 1 All E.R. 749 (P.C.); *Hewitt* v. *Bonvin* [1940] 1 K.B. 188.

plead the doctrine of *res ipsa loquitur*[87] although, of course, he must allege the material facts on which the doctrine may be invoked.

Presumption of continuity　This presumption may be mentioned as being especially important to the pleader, namely that there is a presumption of the continuance of the existing state of things, in the absence of any statement to the contrary, *i.e.* if a particular state of things is once alleged in the pleadings as existing, it is, in general, presumed that the state of things has continued, unless the pleadings contain something to negative it.

---

[87] *Bennett* v. *Chemical Construction (G.B.) Ltd.* [1971] 1 W.L.R. 1571; [1971] 3 All E.R. 822 (C.A.). The doctrine is in essence no more than a common sense approach, not limited by technical rules, to the assessment of the effect of evidence in certain circumstances (see *per* Megaw L.J. in *Lloyde* v. *West Midlands Gas Board (I.)* [1971] 1 W.L.R. 749 at 755): [1971] 2 All E.R. 1240 at 1287.

CHAPTER 6

Statement of Claim

Function of the Statement of Claim

Function The statement of claim is the first pleading in actions begun by writ. Since its central purpose is to formulate a cause of action against the defendant, it must show a viable legal and enforceable claim against the defendant. It should also state such material facts as to enable the defendant to know the case he has to meet.[1] In contrast, the general indorsement of the writ is a concise statement of the nature of the claim made or the relief or remedy required in the action.[2]

Pleading requirements The statement of claim must state in summary form the material facts on which the plaintiff relies for his claim[3] and it must also state specifically the relief or remedy which he claims.[4] This does not mean that the plaintiff is required to frame his claim in any formal legal shape, or that he is confined to any specified legal forms or to any specific relief or remedy.[5] It is not enough, however, for the statement of claim merely to state the material facts and to claim specific relief or remedy; there must be an inner connection, a legal nexus, between the facts relied on and the relief or remedy claimed. The material facts relied

---

[1] See p. 6, *supra.*
[2] See R.S.C., Ord. 6, r. 2(1)(*a*).
[3] See R.S.C., Ord. 18, r. 7(1), and see p. 52, *supra.*
[4] R.S.C., Ord. 18, r. 15(1).
[5] See p. 92, *infra.* "[The] practice of the Courts has been to consider and deal with the legal result of pleaded facts, though the particular legal result alleged is not stated in the pleadings" (*Lever Bros. Ltd.* v. *Bell* [1931] 1 K.B. 557, *per* Scrutton L.J. at 582, 583).

on must disclose a reasonable cause of action against the defendant. The statement of claim is otherwise liable to be struck out.[6] Thus when dismissing an action for default in serving the statement of claim Whitford J. observed[7]:

> "It is not right, in my judgment, that the plaintiffs should start an action apparently not in a position even to know what form of statement of claim they should make until possibly after an Anton Piller order has been secured and the evidence upon an application for an interlocutory injunction has been taken through to the end."[8]

Pleading Technique

Consistency of description The pleader should always refer to the same person, document or thing by the same name throughout his pleading.

Identifying the parties The plaintiff and defendant should not be mentioned by name; they should always be called "the plaintiff" and "the defendant," or, if more than one, 'the male plaintiff," "the female plaintiff," "the defendant Smith," "the defendant Robinson," "the defendant company," or, if both defendants bear the same surname, "the defendant Henry Marbles," "the defendant John Marbles."

Identifying non-parties The name of any other person, not a party to the suit, should be given in full, if known, the first time he is mentioned. Afterwards he can be referred to by his surname only, as "the said Johnson."

Use of paragraphs Unless the case is short and simple, when the claim may be stated shortly in one paragraph,[9] the statement of claim should state the material facts relied on fully, clearly and precisely. It should ordinarily be divided into paragraphs numbered consecutively. Each allegation should so far as convenient be contained in a separate paragraph.[10]

---

[6] See R.S.C., Ord. 18, r. 19(1)(a), and see p. 217, *infra*.

[7] *Hytrac Conveyors Ltd.* v. *Conveyors International Ltd.* [1983] 1 W.L.R. 44; [1982] 3 All E.R. 415. This was an *Anton Piller* case in which an order was obtained by the plaintiff before the issue of the writ against 11 defendants. The writ was issued on the following day against the defendants, but the statement of claim had not been served 12 weeks after the issue of the writ. Whitford J. went on to say: "It is . . . particularly important where questions of infringement of copyright are concerned and where questions of confidence are concerned that in the clearest possible terms the exact ambit of the plaintiff's claim in these regards should be made known." The Court of Appeal expressly agreed with this approach.

[8] [1983] 1 W.L.R. 44; [1982] 3 All E.R. 415, (C.A.).

[9] See *Chitty and Jacobs' Queen's Bench Forms* (21st ed., 1987). Forms 14–30 (these forms are for the endorsement of the statement of claim on the writ).

[10] R.S.C., Ord. 18, r. 6(2).

Distinguishing each head of claim and relief   Where the plaintiff seeks relief in respect of several distinct claims or causes of complaint founded upon separate and distinct grounds, such grounds should be stated separately and distinctly.[11] So far as possible, the facts or group of facts relied on should be stated in chronological order.

Pleading claims in the alternative   Where claims are made in the alternative the facts on which each alternative claim is founded should be separately and distinctly stated.[12]

Representative parties   Where a plaintiff sues or a defendant is sued both in a representative capacity and also in his own right, this should be clearly stated and facts must be separately and distinctly alleged to justify the claim in each capacity.

Particulars   All necessary particulars must be inserted in the body of the claim unless they exceed three folios, *i.e.* 216 words, in which case that fact must be stated and reference made to particulars already served or to be served with the statement of claim. Further, every pleading must contain the necessary particulars of any claim, defence or other matter pleaded including, without prejudice to the generality of the foregoing,

(a) particulars of any misrepresentation, fraud, breach of trust, wilful default or undue influence on which the party pleading relies,

(b) where a party pleading alleges any condition of the mind of any person, whether any disorder or disability of mind or any malice, fraudulent intention or other condition of mind except knowledge, particulars of the facts on which the party relies, and

(c) where a claim for damages is made against a party pleading, particulars of any facts on which the party relies in mitigation of, or otherwise in relation to, the amount of damages.[13]

---

[11] The practice provided by the pre-1964 R.S.C., Ord. 20, r. 7 remains though the rule has itself disappeared.

[12] See *Davy* v. *Garrett* (1878) 7 Ch.D. 473 at 489.

[13] R.S.C., Ord. 18, r. 12 as amended by The Rules of the Supreme Court (Amendment No. 4) 1989 SI 1989 No. 2427 (L. 20). It may be helpful to state in summary the effect of these Rules namely,

(a) to reduce from 12 to 4 months the time for which a writ or an originating summons is valid for service (except an originating summons under Order 97, rule 6 where, as now, the summons is valid for 2 months) and to amend the rules on extending validity (*Rules 2 to 7*);

(b) to require a party against whom a claim for damages is made to plead any facts on which he relies in mitigation of the amount of damages (*Rules 8 to 11*):

(c) to require the provision of a medical report and of a detailed statement of special damages with the statement of claim in an action claiming damages for personal injuries (*Rules 12 to 16*);

(d) to require the Court to consider whether a split trial should be ordered on the summons for directions and to enable the Court in an acton for personal injuries to

Form of Statement of Claim

Structure   The statement of claim is not required to be pleaded in any particular form or to be cast in any particular mould or pattern. For the sake both of clarity and precision, it is however, the practice for the statement of claim to be divided into three related parts, namely:

    (a) matters of inducement;
    (b) substantive content or body of the pleading;
    (c) prayer for relief.

To follow this form or pattern greatly assists in formulating a clear and effective statement of claim.

Matters of inducement   It is customary to commence a statement of claim with some introductory averments, such as:

    (a) who the parties are;
    (b) what business they carry on;
    (c) how they are related or connected in reference to the subject matter of the claim; and
    (d) other surrounding circumstances leading up to the dispute.

These are called "matters of inducement" or "preliminary averments"; they are useful because they explain or clarify what follows, though they are not essential to the cause of action.[14-15] They should be stated as concisely as possible.

> make of its own motion an order providing for the issue of liability to be tried before any issue as to damages;
>
> (e) to enable interrogatories to be administered (on not more than two occasions) without a court order;
>
> (f) to require a defendant to specify in an offer to submit to a provisional award the type of disease for which an application for an award of further damages may subsequently be made;
>
> (g) to strengthen the power of the Court to penalise in costs a party who unjustifiably fails to make admissions of facts of documents;
>
> (h) to extend to proceedings begun by originating summons the power of the Court to order affidavits or particulars of any claim to stand as informal pleadings and to enable the Court to require points of claim to be provided;
>
> (i) to enable a party to an action for libel or slander, who has not accepted a payment into court but is contemplating doing so, to apply to the judge for a statement to be made clearing his name;
>
> (j) to extend to actions for malicious prosecution and false imprisonment the procedure for actions for libel or slander whereby a party who is either contemplating accepting a payment into court or has already done so, to apply to the judge for a statement to be made clearing his name;
>
> (k) to require a party seeking summary possession of land to indicate whether or not residential premises are situated on the land;
>
> (l) to amend the form of acknowledgement of sevice.
>
> [14-15] It should be remembered that sometimes "matters of inducement" may be very material to the cause of action or claim, *e.g.* in actions of defamation, where the allegation that the plaintiff carries on a particular trade, business or profession may provide the basis for

Substantive Content of Statement of Claim

Essential requirements   The statement claim of claim must disclose a cause of action in every plaintiff and a legal liability in every defendant.

Contract   If the action be brought on a contract, the statement of claim must set out:

(a) the terms of the contract;
(b) its date and parties and how made;
(c) the consideration for it if it is not under seal;
(d) the breach of it;
(e) the consequent loss and damage;
(f) all special damage must be set out in full detail.

Tort   If in tort the statement of claim must set out:

(a) the facts giving the right of the plaintiff which the defendant has violated or infringed, unless that right be one which every person possesses; and
(b) then should follow details of the defendant's tortious act and the loss and damage which has in consequence been occasioned to the plaintiff.

Recovery of land   The claim must state:

(a) that the plaintiff has a right to the immediate possession of the land; and
(b) that the defendant is wrongfully in possession.

All these matters must be stated concisely and yet with sufficient detail to enable the defendant to know precisely what case he has to meet.

Significance of the Concept: "A Cause of Action"

Definition   A cause of action has been defined as being:

> "every fact which it would be necessary for the plaintiff to prove, if traversed, in order to support his right to the judgment of the Court. It does not comprise every piece of evidence which is necessary to prove each fact, but every fact which is necessary to be proved."[16]

his cause of action; or in actions for breach of contracts for the sale of goods, where allegations that the seller sells goods in the course of a business may provide the basis for claiming damages for breach of warranty as to the merchantable quality or fitness of the goods for the purpose supplied (see Sale of Goods Act 1979, s.14(2), (3)). *Read* v. *Brown* (1888) 22 Q.B.D. 128, *per* Lord Esher M.R. at 131; and see *Cooke* v. *Gill* (1873) L.R. 8 C.P. 107, *per* Brett J. at 108; *Hernaman* v. *Smith* (1855) 10 Ex. 659, *per* Parke B. at 666.

[16] *Per* Lord Esher M.R. in *Coburn* v. *College* [1897] 1 Q.B. 702, 707 (C.A.), approved and applied in *Central Electricity Board* v. *Halifax Corporation* [1963] A.C. 785; [1962] 3 All E.R. 715.

75

This definition has been held to mean that:

> "if the plaintiff alleges the facts which, if not traversed, would prima facie enable him to recover, then he makes out a cause of action."[16a]

A more general and trenchant statement of the meaning is:

> "simply a factual situation the existence of which entitles one person to obtain from the court a remedy against another person."[17]

What facts are "necessary to be proved?"   Thus a cause of action is constituted by the "bundle" or aggregate of facts which the law will recognise as giving the plaintiff a substantive right to make the claim against the defendant for the relief or remedy which he is seeking.[18] The factual situation on which the plaintiff relies to support his claim must be capable of being recognised by the law as giving rise to a substantive right capable of being claimed or enforced against the defendant, and in this respect there is a close connection between the procedural law relating to the pleading of the statement of claim and the substantive law relating to what is recognised as a legally viable cause of action. But where a plaintiff requires any aid from an illegal transaction to establish his cause of action, the court will not give him any aid but will dismiss the action.[19]

The law/fact interface   It is necessary for the statement of claim to fulfil its function, that the elements or components, which together constitute the substantive right which is being claimed or enforced, must be alleged as the material facts in the pleading. What these "elements or components" are will depend upon the particular substantive right which is being raised in the pleading. The pleader who is settling a statement of claim has, as it were, to look over his shoulder and examine the substantive law in order to ascertain and allege the material facts which constitute the elements or components of the particular substantive right which he intends to raise and to form the basis of the claim for the relief or remedy against the defendant.

[16a] Per Lord Reid in *Central Electricity Board* v. *Halifax Corporation supra.*

[17] *Letang* v. *Cooper* [1965] 1 Q.B. 232, *per* Diplock L.J. at 242.

[18] See *Trower & Sons Ltd.* v. *Ripstein* [1944] A.C. 254, *per* Lord Wright at 263.

[19] *Bedford Insurance Co. Ltd.* v. *Instituto de Resseguros do Brazil* [1985] Q.B. 966. But if the plaintiff is in the position of an innocent party and did not know that effecting or carrying out a contract of re-insurance would involve the defendants in contravening the Insurance Companies Act 1974, he is entitled to enforce the contract; *Stewart* v. *Oriental Fire and Marine Insurance Co. Ltd.* [1985] Q.B. 988.

[19a] See *Securities and Investments Board* v. *Pantell* [1989] 3 W.L.R. 698 (right of action conferred on S.I.B. for the benefit of investors by section 6 of the Financial Services Act 1986); *Virgo Steamship Co. S.A.* v. *Skaarup Shipping Corp, The Kapeton Georgis* [1988] 1 Lloyd's Rep. 352. And see *Garden Neptune Shipping* v. *Occidental Worldwide Investments Corp.* [1989] 1 Lloyd's Rep. 305.

A cause of action—not forms of action A cause or right of action may be created or conferred by statute and in such event, the facts relied on must be pleaded to show that the claim comes within the ambit of the relevant statutory provisions.[19a] The phrase cause of action is not identical with the subject-matter of a complaint nor is it akin to "forms of action" which have been abolished,[20] such as the actions of assumpsit, debt, covenant, trespass, case, trover or conversion, detinue (except in some points of view) and replevin. The pleader does not have to cast his claim to suit the particular "form of action" by which to obtain the relief or remedy which he is seeking, but rather to state material facts on which he relies to obtain relief or remedy against the defendant.

An objective perspective Since the Judicature Acts 1873–1875, which did not affect causes of action, the dominating feature of the English system of civil justice as regards claims made in courts is that they have to be expressed so as to disclose a reasonable cause of action. As a matter of pleading, this requirement means that the plaintiff must state all the material facts on which he relies which in the aggregate and read as an integral whole would show that he had a legal right or claim entitling him to relief or remedy from the court against another person. This requirement presupposes that at the time of making his claim the plaintiff knows full well what are the entire facts on which he can rely to make such a claim. No doubt in many, perhaps even in a majority of cases, those facts are within his knowledge at the time; but equally, there is little doubt that in many, and certainly a significant number of cases, the plaintiff does not or may not know what those facts are at that time. He can only find out or discover those facts at a later time either from the defendant or from other source or from both such sources. This requirement therefore that he must at the very commencement of the proceedings state the facts

---

[20] See Maitland, *Forms of Action at Common Law* (1936) and Sutton, *Personal Actions at Common Law*. The historical and terminological connections between "forms of action" and "causes of action" were explained by Diplock L.J. in *Letang* v. *Cooper* [1965] 1 Q.B. 232 at 243 as follows: "The Judicature Act, 1873, abolished forms of action. It did not affect causes of action; so it was convenient for lawyers and legislators to continue to use, to describe the various categories of factual situations which entitled one person to obtain from the court a remedy against another, the names of the various "forms of action" by which formerly the remedy appropriate to the particular category of factual situation was obtained. But it is essential to realise that when, since 1873, the name of a form of action is used to identify a cause of action, it is used as a convenient and succinct description of a particular category of factual situation which entitles one person to obtain from the court a remedy against another person. To forget this will indeed encourage the old forms of action to rule us from their graves." It is, however, often necessary to appreciate the distinctions between the old forms of action in order to understand some of the earlier decisions of the courts and properly to construe statutes passed before the Judicature Acts.

on which he relies to show a reasonable cause of action may operate to defeat justice.[21]

Joinder of Causes of Action[22]

Rationale The joinder in one action of several causes by the same plaintiff against the same defendant is permitted in specified circumstances without the leave of the court. But otherwise such joinder is permitted only with the leave of the court.[23] One of the overriding objectives of the Judicature Acts 1873–1875 was to ensure that, so far as possible, all matters in controversy between the parties should be completely and finally determined, and all multiplicity of proceedings concerning any of these matters should be avoided.[24]

Without leave In the following circumstances, the plaintiff is entitled as of right and without the leave of the court to claim in one action any relief against the same defendant in respect of more than one cause of action:

   (a) if the plaintiff claims, and the defendant is alleged to be liable, in the same capacity in respect of all the causes of action[25]; or
   (b) if the plaintiff claims, or the defendant is alleged to be liable, in the capacity of executor or administrator of an estate in respect of one or more of the causes of action and in his personal capacity but with reference to the same estate in respect of all the others.[26]

---

[21] For this reason, the concept and practice relating to "cause of action" may be considered too high a price to pay in the administration of civil justice; the plaintiff is required to jump too high a hurdle to reach out to justice. If this is right, it should be sufficient to require the plaintiff to set forth a short and plain statement showing that he is entitled to relief and a demand for judgment for such relief. This proposal is, as everyone knows, drawn directly from the American Federal Rules of Civil Procedure which have entirely eliminated the expression "cause of action." If adopted in England, it would of course greatly alter the present system based on causes of action and the pleading of material facts, and it would have to be accompanied by a greatly enlarged process of discovery. It would not be surprising if this proposal raised some criticism and perhaps loud lamentations about the fate and the future of English civil justice. But the question that cannot be stilled is whether, if a person does in truth and in fact have a lawful claim against another, should not the procedural rules be so structured as to entitle him to obtain the appropriate relief or remedy from the courts? See Jacob, *The Fabric of English Civil Justice* (Hamlyn Lectures) (1987), p. 85.

[22] Also see "Joinder of Parties" in Chapter 14, p. 243. The two subjects of Joinder of Parties and Joinder of Causes of Action are complementary and are dealt with in one Order of the R.S.C., namely, Ord. 15, r. 1 deals with joinder of causes of action and Ord. 15, r. 4 deals with joinder of parties.

[23] See R.S.C., Ord. 15, r. 1.

[24] See now s.49(2) of the Supreme Court Act 1981 which is derived from the Supreme Court of Judicature (Consolidation) Act 1925, s.43. Section 49(2) is explained in paras. 5187 *et seq.* of the *Supreme Court Practice 1991*, Vol. 2.

[25] See R.S.C., Ord. 15, r. 1(a).

[26] *Ibid.*, r. 1(b).

Accordingly, if the following two conditions set out below are satisfied any number of different causes of action, whether legal or equitable, whether of contract or of tort, may be included in the same proceeding—subject only to the power of the court subsequently to exclude any cause of action which cannot conveniently be tried with the others.[27]

(a) Where there is only one plaintiff and one defendant, or where all the plaintiffs and all the defendants are interested in every cause of action.

(b) Where two or more persons have been properly joined as plaintiffs, the question—"what causes of action can be joined with claims in respect of which they were joined as plaintiffs?"—depends upon the rule permitting joinder of causes of action.[28]

Causes of action and relief: not to be confused   The same cause of action may entitle the plaintiff to relief of various kinds; therefore no leave is necessary to join a claim for a receiver,[29] or an account, or an injunction, or for a declaration which merely tends to establish the plaintiff's right to possession, as all these are simply machinery to enforce the plaintiff's one cause of action.[30]

The defendant's riposte—severance

(a) *Principle*   If causes of action are improperly joined, the defendant should apply to have them struck out or to have the proceedings set aside or amended.[31] Strictly he should not plead the objection in his defence.[32]

(b) *Practice*   The proper course is to apply by summons at the earliest practicable time to have the misjoinder rectified as being an irregularity.[33] The same person cannot be both a plaintiff and a defendant in the same action.[34]

Claims by personal representatives   Personal claims by or against an executor or administrator which do not have any reference to the estate cannot be joined in the same action without leave.[35] If such joinder will not cause inconvenience it may be allowed.[36] Thus, joinder of causes of

---

[27] *Ibid.*, r. 5(1).
[28] *Harris* v. *Ashworth* [1962] 1 W.L.R. 193; [1962] 1 All E.R. 438.
[29] See *Gwatkin* v. *Bird* (1882) 52 L.J. Q.B. 263.
[30] *Gledhill* v. *Hunter* (1880) 14 Ch.D. 492; *Allen* v. *Kennet* (1876) 24 W.R. 845; *Read* v. *Wotton* [1893] 2 Ch. 171, dissented from in *Wheeler* v. *Keeble (1914) Ltd.* [1920] 1 Ch. 57.
[31] *Hunt* v. *Worsfold* [1896] 2 Ch. 224.
[32] *Wilmott* v. *Freehold House, etc. Co.* (1885) 51 L.T. 552; *Re Derbon* (1888) 58 L.T. 519.
[33] See R.S.C., Ord. 2, r. 2.
[34] *Ellis* v. *Kerr* [1910] 1 Ch. 529 at 537. Nor can he be applicant and respondent to the same summons (*ibid.*); and see *Re Phillips* [1931] W.N. 271.
[35] See R.S.C., Ord. 15, r. 1(b), and see *Whitworth* v. *Darbishire* (1893) 41 W.R. 317.
[36] See R.S.C., Ord. 15, r. 1(c), reversing *Tredegar* v. *Roberts* [1914] 1 K.B. 283.

action would ordinarily be allowed where a widow claims in her capacity as administratrix of the estate of her deceased husband and in her personal capacity for personal injuries arising out of the same accident. The name of a person who is a party in more than one capacity must be inserted in the record, showing that he sues or is sued both personally and in his representative capacity.[37]

Leave

(a) *When required*   In circumstances other than those specified, the court has power to give leave for several causes of action to be joined in the same action,[38] in whatever capacity the claims are made by or against a party.

(b) *How obtained*   Such leave should be obtained on an application made *ex parte* before the writ is issued; although it can be given by the Master after issue of the writ in which the causes of action have been improperly joined. In such case the application should be made on summons. Such a joinder is an irregularity only, and an objection to the writ on that ground will be treated as waived if the defendant, without raising it, takes any step in the action which would be neither necessary nor useful if he intended to rely on that objection.[39]

(c) *When joinder disallowed*   Where it appears to the court that the joinder of two or more causes of action in the same action may embarrass or delay the trial or is otherwise inconvenient, the court may order separate trials of such causes of action or make such other order as may be expedient.[40] The power to do so is discretionary in the light of the circumstances of each particular case.[41] In particular the court will consider whether the plaintiff has needlessly enlarged the area of dispute.[42]

How the court exercises its discretion   The court had very wide powers to protect a defendant against being prejudiced by the joinder of parties or of causes of action which cannot conveniently be tried together. The claims of several plaintiffs may arise out of the same series of transactions, and there may be questions of fact or law common to them all, yet the common factor may be completely put into the background by the issues peculiar to the separate plaintiffs. Moreover, at the date of the issue of the writ a common question of law or fact may arise, which may

[37] See *Hardie & Lane Ltd.* v. *Chiltern* [1928] 1 K.B. 663, *per* Sargant L.J.
[38] R.S.C., Ord. 15, r. 1(c).
[39] *Lloyd* v. *Great Western Dairies Co.* [1907] 2 K.B. 727. And see further as to steps which have been held to waive objections, *Fry* v. *Moore* (1889) 23 Q.B.D. 395 (C.A.); *Moore* v. *Gamgee* (1890) 25 Q.B.D. 244; *The Assunta* [1902] P. 150.
[40] R.S.C., Ord. 15, r. 5(1).
[41] See *Thomas* v. *Moore* [1918] 1 K.B. 555.
[42] See *per* Collins M.R. in *Saccharin Corporation* v. *Wild* [1903] 1 Ch. 410 at 442.

disappear as soon as the defence is served, *e.g.* several persons injured in a motor coach accident join in one action, where at the time of the issue of the writ liability had not been admitted; if the defendants serve a defence admitting liability the continued joinder of the several plaintiffs would probably be found inconvenient and embarrassing.[43]

Court's options[44]   The powers of the court under this rule may be exercised in diverse ways, *e.g.*

(a) order separate trials;
(b) confine the action to some of the causes of action, and exclude the others;
(c) order the plaintiff or plaintiffs to elect which cause of action shall be proceeded with[45] or which plaintiff should proceed and which be struck out or stayed[46];
(d) prevent a defendant from being embarrassed or put to expense by being required to attend proceedings in which he has no interest;
(e) make such other order as may be expedient.[47]

Actions of Contract

In all cases   In actions founded on contract, the pleader should always state with full particulars the material facts relating to the contract, namely, the parties to the contract, its date and how it was made, whether orally or in writing or under seal or how otherwise and, where necessary the consideration.

Oral contracts   If the contract was made orally, particulars should be given of the date when, and the persons between whom the contract was made, and if there is any special significance about it, the place where it was made.

Contracts in writing   If a written contract is contained in several documents, these should all be identified. It is not necessary, as a rule, to set them out verbatim; it is sufficient for the plaintiff to state what he alleges to be their effect.[48]

---

[43] See *Supreme Court Practice 1991*, Vol. 1, para. 15/5/1.
[44] *i.e.* court's options when application comes before order under R.S.C., Ord. 15, r. 1. And see *Supreme Court Practice 1991*, Vol. 1, para. 15/5/1.
[45] *Universities of Oxford and Cambridge* v. *Gill* [1899] 1 Ch. 55.
[46] *Sandes* v. *Wildsmith* [1893] 1 Q.B. 771.
[47] Under R.S.C., Ord. 33, r. 4(2) the court may order that different questions whether of fact or law be tried at different places or by different modes of trial and that one or more questions may be tried before the others.
[48] See R.S.C., Ord. 18, r. 7(2).

THE STATEMENT OF CLAIM

Partly oral and partly in writing   If the contract was made partly orally and partly in writing, this fact should be alleged. The necessary particulars relating to the oral part and the identity of the documents relating to the written part should be given. If the contractual relationship is to be implied or inferred from a series of letters or conversations or otherwise from a number of circumstances or the conduct of the parties, the contract should be alleged as a fact, but full particulars should be given of the facts and matters relied on as giving rise to the contract alléged.[49]

Consideration   Unless the contract is under seal, the consideration for it must be set out. Where the consideration for the covenant or promise is in the alternative, it should be stated according to the fact.[50]

Agency   Where the contract is made by either party through an agent, it is proper though perhaps not strictly necessary[51] to state the fact and name the agent.

Express terms   Next, the pleader should state clearly whether the claim made arises *under* the terms of the contract, and if so he should set out the terms relied on and state how the claim arises thereunder, or whether the claim made is for damages for *breach of contract*. If the claim is for breach, he should state the relevant terms of the contract and allege with full particulars the precise breach or breaches of contract relied on, and the nature and extent of the loss and damage alleged to have been occasioned thereby.[52]

Implied terms   It is usual to state all the covenants or promises before alleging any of the breaches, though this is a matter of discretion. If any terms of the contract are alleged to be implied, particulars should be given of the facts and matters relied on as giving rise to the alleged implied terms.

Executed contracts—the simple claim in debt   Where the consideration is executed and a debt or liquidated amount has therefore accrued due and is payable at the date of writ, a very short and simple mode of statement, similar to the old *indebitatus* counts, is sufficient.[53] Such forms are not applicable where an entire contract remains still open and in part unperformed.

---

[49] See *Brogden* v. *Metropolitan Railways* (1877) 2 App.Cas. 666; *Hussey* v. *Horne-Payne* (1879) 4 App.Cas. 311.
[50] See *Penny* v. *Porter* (1801) 2 East 2; *Bullen and Leake* (3rd ed.), p. 60.
[51] *Higgins* v. *Senior* (1841) 8 M. & W. 834 at 844.
[52] See *Turquand* v. *Fearon* (1879) 4 Q.B.D. 280.
[53] See thereon *Bank of New South Wales* v. *Laing* [1954] A.C. 135; [1954] 2 W.L.R. 25; [1954] 1 All E.R. 213.

But not all terms have to be pleaded Where there are several covenants in the same deed, or several promises in the same instrument or forming parts of one oral contract, it is sufficient to state those covenants or promises only of which breaches are to be afterwards alleged. This is, of course, provided that the parts omitted do not materially qualify or alter the nature of the covenants or promises alleged to have been broken.[54]

Two contracts Where the action is brought on two or more distinct deeds or contracts, each deed or contract, and the breach or breaches of it, should be separately stated and the claim under each should be clearly identified.[55]

Variation alleged Where an agreement between the parties has been altered or modified by a subsequent agreement, the plaintiff may either:

(a) state the agreements in their order according to the fact[56]; or
(b) he may state the contract as it stands modified or altered, without noticing the original terms.[57]

Pleading the breach

(a) *Generally* It must be carefully drafted and all necessary particulars given. It should be stated in the words of the contract either negatively or affirmatively according to whether the contract is negative or affirmative. As a rule the words "and" and "all" in the contract must be changed into "or" and "any" in the breach.

(b) *Contracts containing more than one promise* Identify precisely how the defendant has fallen short of the contractual promise. If the contract is to do more things than one, or to do one or other of two things, the plaintiff must either state expressly that the defendant has done none of them, or else set out precisely what and how much he has done or not done.[58] Where the effect only of the contract is stated, the breach should be alleged in words co-extensive therewith. In either case particulars of the breach should be given, and these will narrow the generality of the preceding allegation.[59]

(c) *Exceptions and provisos* If the covenant or agreement as alleged in the statement of claim contains any exception or proviso it will be necess-

---

[54] *Cotterill* v. *Cuff* (1812) 4 Taunt. 285; *Tempest* v. *Rawling* (1810) 13 East 18.
[55] See R.S.C., Ord. 18, r. 6(2) and see *Watson* v. *Hawkins* (1876) 24 W.R. 884.
[56] See the averment in *Carr* v. *Wallachian Petroleum Co.* (1866) L.R. 1 C.P. 636 at 637.
[57] *Boone* v. *Mitchell* (1822) 1 B. & C. 18.
[58] *Legh* v. *Lillie* (1860) 6 H. & N. 165.
[59] *Harris* v. *Mantle* (1789) 3 Term Rep. 307; *Carpenter* v. *Parker* (1857) 3 C.B.(N.S.) 206 at 243; *Byrd* v. *Nunn* (1877) 5 Ch.D. 781; *affirmed* (1878) 7 Ch.D. 284, followed in *Collette* v. *Goode* (1878) 7 Ch.D. 842; but see the remarks on this case in *Edevain* v. *Cohen* (1889) 41 Ch.D. 563 at 566; *ibid.*, 43 Ch.D. 187 (C.A.). And see *Mona Oil Equipment* v. *Rhodesia Railways* [1949] 2 All E.R. 1014, *per* Devlin J. at 1017.

ary to qualify the breach accordingly as, *e.g.* where there is a covenant to repair premises, except damage by fire, it must appear that the defendant failed to repair other damage than damage by fire; and where the covenant is to repair a fence, except on the west side thereof, the breach should show that the want of repair was in parts of the fence other than on the west side.[60] In relation to such a covenant the breach must be alleged in such a manner as to show that the case does not fall within the proviso or exception. But if the exception occurs in some distinct and separate part of the deed or document, no reference need be made to it; it will be for the defendant to set it up, if he relies on it.

It should be noted that a judgment for a claim in debt arising upon a contract does not create an estoppel to preclude a claim for damages for breach of contract since such a claim raises a different cause of action.[61]

Repudiation   Repudiation is a statement or conduct by a contracting party evincing an intention no longer to be bound by the terms and provisions of the contract. The claims for damages for breach of contract and for repudiation of contract are not necessarily co-extensive. Pleading "repudiation of contract" must be carefully drafted and all necessary particulars given.

Actions of Tort

Introduction   Unlike claims in contract where (subject to implied terms and statutory modification) the parties create and regulate the relationship they have agreed between themselves, in actions in tort the right which is alleged to have been violated is not one peculiar to the plaintiff, but is common to everyone. In such cases it is unnecessary to plead the existence of the right for it is implied by law.

Rights which do not have to be pleaded   These rights include the right to security of life and limb, liberty and reputation.

In such cases the pleading should merely state the violation of the right, as, for instance, that the defendant assaulted and beat the plaintiff, or that the defendant imprisoned the plaintiff, or that the defendant wrote or published or spoke of the plaintiff certain defamatory words. Similarly, in ordinary actions for damages to rights of property, it is as a rule sufficient merely to state that the property was the plaintiff's.

Pleading the factual basis for the right   Where the right which the defendant has infringed is one special to the plaintiff, such as an easement

---

[60] Com. Dig. Pleader (C), 47.
[61] *Lawlor* v. *Gray* [1984] 3 All E.R. 345.

or a trade mark, the facts which gave the plaintiff that right must be stated in the statement of claim. Thus, in an action for infringing a patent, the plaintiff should allege the existence of the patent and his property therein.[62] So, where a plaintiff claims a right of way, he must define the course of the path, state its *termini*, and show how the right vested in him, whether by prescription or grant, or the pleading may be struck out or amended as embarrassing.[63] The pleader is not, however, bound to name the parties to or to give the dates of any alleged lost grants, for these exist only by presumption of law.[64]

Breach arising from relationship between the parties   Where the pleader alleges that a breach of duty arises from any given relationship between the parties he should state with full particulars the precise relation from which the duty is alleged to arise.[65] This is the basis of the employer's duty of care.[66] By virtue of the contract of employment, the employer brings the employee into the ambit of Lord Atkin's neighbour *dictum*— one so closely and directly affected by the employer's act. That relationship must be pleaded to establish the existence of the duty of care.

When the mode of doing the act is the gist of the action   In some actions sounding in tort the act complained of is not actionable in itself, but is made so by the way in which it is done. Here it must be shown in the pleading that the act was committed in a certain manner—"negligently," "maliciously," "without reasonable or probable cause," or with knowledge of a certain fact; such matters constitute a necessary part of the statement of the wrongful act. Examples are claims for driving negligently, for malicious prosecution and for keeping an animal of a non-dangerous species under section 2(2) of the Animals Act 1971.

State of mind   A pleading which alleges a condition of the mind as a fact must be supported by particulars of the facts relied on.[67] Hence, in order to establish that the defendant ought reasonably to have contemplated the result which in fact happened and that the damage claimed is therefore not too remote, it is often necessary to set out in the claim facts which show that the defendant knew or ought to have known that such damage would probably result from his act, and further, that such facts

[62] Infringement of rights to intellectual property are of course conceptually identical to claims for trespass to real property.
[63] *Harris* v. *Jenkins* (1883) 22 Ch.D. 481.
[64] *Palmer* v. *Guadagni* [1906] 2 Ch. 494, referred to in *Wade and English* v. *Dixon and Cardus* [1937] 3 All E.R. 900.
[65] *Selangor United Rubber Estates Ltd.* v. *Cradock* [1965] Ch. 896; [1965] 2 W.L.R. 67; [1964] 3 All E.R. 709 (fiduciary relationship between customer and bank).
[66] See *Matthews* v. *Kuwait Bechtel Corpn.* [1959] 2 Q.B. 57.
[67] R.S.C., Ord. 18, r. 12, r. 1(b), negativing *Burgess* v. *Beethoven Electric Equipment Ltd.* [1943] K.B. 96 at 100 *and see note §13 supra.*

were known to the defendant at the time when he entered into the contract or committed the tort.[68] But where, on the facts alleged, the act complained of gives no right of action, mere general allegations, such as that the act was done "wrongfully," "unlawfully," or "improperly," are redundant epithets which add nothing to the plaintiff's case.[69]

Breach of statutory duty A claim for damages for breach of statutory duty is a specific common law right, which is not to be confused, in essence, with a claim for negligence. The same damage may be caused by conduct, which might equally be characterised as ordinary negligence at common law, or as a breach of statutory duty, or it may be due to either cause. The correct pleading should allege each cause of action separately.[70] An allegation that a party has been guilty of bad faith or lack of good faith is the equivalent of an allegation of dishonesty (though not necessarily of a financial nature) and proper particulars of such an allegation must be pleaded, otherwise the allegation will be struck out.[71] Similarly in order to claim that a person is liable as a constructive trustee, it is necessary to plead clearly and unequivocally that he had known that the breach of trust in respect of which it was sought to make him liable was dishonest or fraudulent. It is not enough merely to plead that the defendant was aware or ought to have been aware of the facts necessary to show a dishonest breach of the trust.[72]

Allegation of Damage

Damage—not necessarily a pre-requisite In many actions it is unnecessary to allege that the plaintiff has suffered any actual loss or damage, *e.g.*:

(a) on proof of a contract and the breach of it by the defendant, the plaintiff is entitled to judgment for a nominal amount although he may have suffered no pecuniary loss[73];

---

[68] See *Overseas Tankships (U.K.) Ltd.* v. *Miller Steamship Co. Pty. (The Wagon Mound) (No. 2)* [1967] 1 A.C. 617; [1966] 3 W.L.R. 498; [1966] 2 All E.R. 709 and *Karavias* v. *Callinicos* [1917] W.N. 323; *Victoria Laundry* v. *Newman* [1949] 2 K.B. 528.

[69] See *Day* v. *Brownrigg* (1879) 10 Ch.D. 294 at 302, and see *Gautret* v. *Egerton* (1867) L.R. 2 C.P. 371; *Boots* v. *Grundy* (1900) 82 L.T. 769 at 771. It is necessary to allege what must, not what may, be a cause of action (*West Rand Central Mining Co.* v. *R.* [1905] 2 K.B. 391 at 400); see also *Bradford (Mayor)* v. *Pickles* [1895] A.C. 587 at 594.

[70] See *London Passenger Transport Board* v. *Upson* [1949] A.C. 155, *per* Lord Wright at 167–169: [1949] 1 All E.R. 60.

[71] *Cannock Chase District Council* v. *Kelly* [1978] 1 W.L.R. 1; [1978] 1 All E.R. 152; (C.A.).

[72] *Belmont Finance Corporation Ltd.* v. *Williams Furniture Ltd.* [1979] Ch. 250; [1978] 3 W.L.R. 712; [1979] 1 All E.R. 118.

[73] *Perestrello e Companhia Limitada* v. *United Paint Co. Ltd.* [1969] 1 W.L.R. 570; [1969] 3 All E.R. 479, (C.A.) See also *Domsalla* v. *Barr (Trading as A.B. Construction* [1969] 1 W.L.R. 630; [1969] 3 All E.R. 487 (C.A.). The mere allegation that the plaintiff has suffered "damage" or the prayer that the plaintiff claims "damages" is not enough to entitle him to recover more than general or nominal damages as the case may be.

(b) in actions for trespass to land, or for defamatory words actionable *per se*, no actual damage need be alleged. In such cases it is sufficient to state generally "whereby the plaintiff has suffered damage."[74]

Damage—a pre-requisite where special loss is claimed   Whenever the plaintiff has suffered any "special damage," this must be alleged in the statement of claim with all necessary particulars. The plaintiff will not be allowed at the trial to give evidence of any special damage which is not claimed explicitly in his statement of claim or particulars.[75]

General and special loss—the distinction   General damage is such as the law will presume to be the natural and probable consequence of the defendant's act. It arises by inference of law and may be averred generally. Special damage, on the other hand, is such a loss as the law will not presume to be the consequence of the defendant's act, but such as depends in part, at least, on the special circumstances of the particular case. It must therefore be always explicitly claimed on the pleading, as otherwise the defendant would have no notice that such items of damage would be claimed from him at the trial.[76]

Examples of Pleading Practice in Relation to Loss and Damage

Particulars   Where the plaintiff claims that he has suffered damage, *e.g.* injury, of a kind which is not the necessary and immediate consequence of the wrongful act complained of, it is his duty to plead full particulars to show the nature and extent of the damages claimed, *i.e.* the amount which he claims to be recoverable, irrespective of whether they are general or special damages. This operates fairly to inform the defendant

---

[74] *Marzetti* v. *Williams* (1830) 1 B. & Ad. 415.

[75] *Hayward* v. *Pullinger & Partners Ltd.* [1950] 1 All E.R. 581, and see in *Anglo-Cyprian Trade Agencies Ltd.* v. *Paphos Wine Industries Ltd.* [1951] 1 All E.R. 873, *per* Devlin J. at 875, and *Longdon-Griffiths* v. *Smith* [1951] K.B. 295, *per* Slade J. See *Fleming* v. *Bank of New Zealand* (1900) A.C. 577 at 587. See *Ilkiw* v. *Samuels* [1963] 1 W.L.R. 991, *per* Diplock L.J. Special damage in the sense of a monetary loss which the plaintiff has sustained up to the date of trial must be pleaded and particularised, otherwise it cannot be recovered, for the plaintiff will not be allowed to give any evidence of it at the trial.

[76] If sufficient details are not given, the plaintiff will be ordered to give particulars of the special damage with dates and items. If the plaintiff alleges that certain customers have ceased to deal with him, he must give their names, or the allegation will be struck out; particulars of alleged loss of business also will be ordered (*Watson* v. *North Metropolitan Tramways Co.* (1886) 3 T.L.R. 273). If ambiguous expressions are used in the statement of claim which may or may not amount to an allegation of special damage, the master will order "particulars of special damage, if any, claimed"; and if the plaintiff does not then give particulars, it will be taken that he does not claim any special damage. No particulars are ever ordered of general damage (*London and Northern Bank Ltd.* v. *Newnes* (1900) 16 T.L.R. 433).

of the case he has to meet and to assist him in computing, if he so desires, a payment into court.[77]

Future loss   The plaintiff must plead any special circumstances which he alleges will lead to his sustaining in the future losses which would not in the ordinary way be expected to flow from the wrongful act complained of.[78] If the plaintiff is able to base his claim for damages upon a precise or perhaps estimated calculation, he must plead particulars of the facts which make such a calculation possible.[79]

Liabilities already incurred   Any expense which the plaintiff has reasonably incurred in consequence of the defendant's tort or breach of contract should be stated as special damage. It is not necessary that the plaintiff should have actually paid the amounts, if he is clearly liable to pay them.[80]

Nexus between conduct complained of and damage.   No damages can be recovered for a loss actually sustained, unless it be either the direct consequence of the defendant's act or such a consequence as a reasonable man would have contemplated. It must be proved by evidence at the trial that the loss alleged as special damage was in fact incurred, and that it was the direct result of the defendant's conduct, as neither fact will be presumed in the plaintiff's favour. All other damage is held to be "remote."[81] A mere speculation of loss is not sufficient, though damages may be recovered for a prospective loss which is reasonably certain to occur.[82]

Loss of custom   A general loss of business or custom may, however, in some cases, be alleged and proved without having recourse to particular instances.[83]

General and special loss—several, not joint   Where both general and special damage exist, the plaintiff can recover for both. Where both are

---

[77] *Perestrello e Companhia Limitada* v. *United Paint Co. Ltd.* [1969] 1 W.L.R. 570 (loss of profits for breach of contract).

[78] *Domsalla* v. *Barr* (*Trading as A.B. Construction*) [1969] 1 W.L.R. 630; [1969] 3 All E.R. 487 (C.A.). (A lost chance of promotion should be specifically pleaded.)

[79] *Perestrello e Companhia Limitada* v. *United Paint Co. Ltd., supra.*

[80] *Richardson* v. *Chasen* (1847) 10 Q.B. 756; *Josling* v. *Irvine* (1861) 30 L.J. Ex. 78; *Spark* v. *Heslop* (1859) 28 L.J.Q.B. 197. Where special damage is an essential part of the cause of action it must have accrued before writ. See *Ward* v. *Lewis* [1955] 1 W.L.R. 9; [1955] 1 All E.R. 55 (slander only on proof of special damages).

[81] See notes to *Hadley* v. *Baxendale* and *Vicars* v. *Wilcocks* in *Smith's Leading Cases* (13th ed.), Vol. 11, pp. 501–575.

[82] *Phillips* v. *London and South Western Ry.* (1880) 5 Q.B.D. 78.

[83] *Ratcliffe* v. *Evans* [1892] 2 Q.B. 524; but see *Weinberger* v. *Inglis* [1918] 1 Ch. 133 at 138.

alleged and the plaintiff fails to prove the special damage, he can still recover his general damage, unless special damage is essential to his cause of action.[84]

Age—personal injury claims In personal injury actions the plaintiff's age is a material fact on the issue of damages and should be pleaded.[85]

Actions for personal injuries In such actions in which the damages claimed consist of or include a claim for (a) loss of earnings; (b) loss of future earnings; (c) medical and other expenses relating to or including the cost of care, attention, accommodation or appliances; or (d) loss of pension rights, particulars must be prepared by the party making such claim, where appropriate in the form of a schedule, and must be served upon all the parties against whom such claim is made. Such service must be effected in London not later than seven days after the case appears in the Warned List, and outside London not later than the lodging of the certificate of readiness. Every party upon whom such particulars have been served must by way of answer, indicate in writing whether and to what extent each item claimed is agreed, and, if not agreed, the reason why not and any counter-proposal. Such answer must be made, in London not later than seven days after such particulars have been served, and outside London not later than 14 days after the lodging of the certificate of readiness. Where there is a fixed date of trial, the plaintiff's particulars must be served not less than 28 days before the date and the answer not later than 14 days thereafter.[85a]

Aggravated damages In order to ascertain the nature and extent of the injury done to the plaintiff, it is often material to consider the circumstances under which the wrongful act was committed.[86] Such matters of aggravation should therefore be pleaded in the statement of claim.[87]

---

[84] *Ratcliffe* v. *Evans, supra.*

[85] *Practice Direction (Personal Injuries: Pleading)* [1974] 1 W.L.R. 1427.

[85a] Practice Note (Personal Injury Action: Special Damages) [1984] 1 W.L.R. 1147, issued by the Lord Chief Justice. Also see n. 13 on page 73.

[86] In certain torts, particularly those of defamation, false imprisonment, malicious prosecution and wrongful eviction of a lessee, the measure of damages may be affected by the conduct, character, and circumstances of both plaintiff and defendant. These factors are said to go in aggravation or mitigation of the damage. Thus the damage is most commonly aggravated, and the damages correspondingly increased, by the defendant's bad motives or wilfulness, see McGregor, *Damages* (15th ed. 1988), para. 1664 *et seq.*

[87] See *Rookes* v. *Barnard* [1964] A.C. 1129, *per* Lord Devlin at 1221: "[The court] can take into account the motives and conduct of the defendant where they aggravate the injury done to the plaintiff. There may be malevolence or spite or the manner of committing the wrong may be such as to injure the plaintiff's proper feelings of dignity and pride." See also *Millington* v. *Loring* (1880) 6 Q.B.D. 190; *Whitney* v. *Moignard* (1890) 24 Q.B.D. 630; and *Newman* v. *Smith* (1705) 2 Salk. 642, cited in *Dix* v. *Brookes* (1717) 1 Str. 61.

Thus, in an action of trespass for entering the plaintiff's house, the defendant may allege that the defendant did so under a false charge that the plaintiff had stolen goods therein.[88]

Exemplary damages   A claim for exemplary damages must be specifically pleaded together with the facts relied on.[89] The object of the rule is to give the defendant fair warning of what is going to be claimed together with the relevant facts relied on, and thus to prevent surprise at trial, to avoid the need for any adjournment of trial on this ground, and, at the same time to extend the ambit of the discovery before trial. A claim for exemplary damages is an exceptional form of award and if may be awarded only three categories as laid down by the House of Lords namely,[90] where there has been oppressive arbitary or unconstitutional action of servants of the government,[91] the cases in which the defendants conduct has been calculated by him to make a profit for himself which may well exceed the compensation payable to the plaintiff,[92] and a case in which exemplary damages are expressly allowed by statutes. In the Chancery Division, where the practice is normally to try liability before quantum, the court may at trial, having found a case for exemplary damages, leave the question of quantum to the subsequent inquiry but

---

[88] *Bracegirdle* v. *Orford* (1813) 2 M. & S. 77; and see *Merest* v. *Harvey* (1814) 5 Taunt. 442; *Bell* v. *Midland Ry.* (1861) 10 C.B.(N.S.) 287 at 307, 308. *Nichols Advanced Vehicles Systems Inc.* v. *Rees* (1979) R.P.C. 127.

[89] R.S.C., Ord. 18, r. 8(3) has two parts to it. First, it requires that the claim for exemplary damages must itself be specifically pleaded, and this must be done in the body of the statement of claim, and not merely in the prayer, and it must be made in addition to any other claim for damages. Secondly, it requires the facts on which the party relies to support his claim for exemplary damages to be pleaded. This is an expression of the cardinal rule that "every pleading must contain, and contain only, a statement in a summary form of the material facts on which the party pleading relies for his claim or defence" (Ord. 18, r. 7(1)). A claim for exemplary damages is an exceptional form of award, and it is awardable only in three categories of cases as laid down by the House of Lords in the speech of Lord Devlin in *Rookes* v. *Barnard* [1964] A.C. 1129 at 1226–1227, and approved by the House of Lords in *Broome* v. *Cassell & Co. Ltd.* [1972] A.C. 1027, namely: (1) cases where there has been oppressive, arbitrary or unconstitutional action by servants of the Government; (2) cases in which the defendant's conduct has been calculated by him to make a profit for himself which may well exceed the compensation payable to the plaintiff; and (3) cases in which exemplary damages are expressly allowed by statute; see, *e.g.* the Reserve and Auxiliary Forces (Protection of Civil Interests) Act 1951, s.13(2) and possibly the Copyright Act 1956, s.17(3). Note that aggravated or exemplary damages may be awarded for the use of unjustifiable force in an assault by a police constable: *Flavius* v. *Commissioner of Metropolitan Police* (1982) 132 New L.J. 532. Or for unlawful arrest, *Holden* v. *Chief Constable of Lancashire* [1986] Q.B. 380; [1986] 3 All E.R. 836.

[90] *Rookes* v. *Barnard* [1964] A.C. 1129, *per* Lord Devlin 1226–1227, affirmed by the House of Lords in *Broome* v. *Cassell & Co. Ltd.* [1972] A.C. 1027.

[91] See *Holden* v. *Chief Constable of Lancashire* [1987] 3 Q.B. 380; [1986] 3 All E.R. 836, C.A. (wrongful arrest by a police officer).

[92] *Catnic Components Ltd* v. *Hill & Smith Ltd.* [1983] F.S.R. 562.

with an indication that such damages should be given[93]; or it may be left to the inquiry altogether.[94]

Nevertheless, it is still necessary to plead a claim for exemplary damages so as to enable the trial judge to form a view of the flagrancy of the defendant's acts, and he should give a direction or indication that such damages should be awarded on the inquiry as to quantum. Exemplary damages may be awarded in the county court even when not specifically pleaded, since the county court rules do not require a claim for exemplary damages to be specifically pleaded.[95]

Even if they could be awarded in an action of deceit, the plaintiff is not entitled to exemplary damages where the defendant had already spent a considerable time in gaol for the fraud perpetrated on the plaintiff, for that would offend the principle that a man is not to be punished twice for the same offence; but a moderate award of aggravated damages may be made in such an action for injured feelings and mental suffering.[96]

Continuing torts As a general rule damages can only be claimed up to the date of writ. But damages under any continuing cause of action, such as a nuisance or a breach of a covenant to repair, may be claimed down to the time of their assessment.[97]

Anticipatory damages These are not recoverable.[98]

Mesne profits May be claimed from the date of the defendant's entry on the premises until possession be given up to the plaintiff.[99]

Tax In assessing damages for personal injuries or wrongful dismissal regard must be had to the liability of the plaintiff for tax,[1] and particulars which are material to the question of liability for tax should be

---

[93] As in *Nichols Advanced Vehicle Systems Inc.* v. *Rees* [1979] R.P.C. 127.

[94] *The Lady Anne Tennant* v. *Associated Newspapers Group Ltd.* [1979] F.S.R. 298; *Sillitoe* v. *McGraw-Hill Book Co.* [1983] F.S.R. 545; *Catnic Components Ltd.* v. *Hill & Smith Ltd.* [1983] F.S.R. 512.

[95] *Drane* v. *Evangelou* [1978] 1 W.L.R. 455 (C.A.) (unlawful eviction of a tenant by harassment—award of £1,000 exemplary damages).

[96] *Archer* v. *Brown* [1985] Q.B. 401; [1984] 3 W.L.R. 350; [1984] 2 All E.R. 267.

[97] R.S.C., Ord. 37, r. 6.

[98] *West Leigh Colliery Co.* v. *Tunnicliffe* [1908] A.C. 27; *Kennard* v. *Cory* [1922] 1 Ch. 265 at 274.

[99] *Southport Tramways Co.* v. *Gandy* [1897] 2 Q.B. 66; and see *Canas Property Co. Ltd.* v. *K.L. Television Services Ltd.* [1970] 2 Q.B. 433; [1970] 2 W.L.R. 1133; [1970] 2 All E.R. 795.

[1] *British Transport Commission* v. *Gourley* [1956] A.C. 185; [1955] 3 All E.R. 796; *Parsons* v. *B.N.M. Laboratories Ltd.* [1964] 1 Q.B. 95; [1963] 2 All E.R. 658 (C.A.); *Tantalus* v. *Telemachus* [1957] P. 47 and *cf. Island Tug and Barge* v. *Owners of S.S. Makedonia* [1958] 1 Q.B. 365; [1958] 1 All E.R. 236.

given.[2] Such a claim must be made in the body of the statement of claim and not merely in the prayer, and it must be made in addition to any other claim for damages. The facts relied on to support such a claim must be alleged with full particulars.

Prayer for Relief or Remedy

Introduction   At its conclusion, the statement of claim must specify the relief or remedy which the plaintiff claims.[3] This is called "the prayer" and is traditionally introduced with the words: "And the plaintiff claims [*as may be*]." Thereafter there should be set out separately and distinctly in numbered (or lettered) paragraphs each head of relief or remedy which is claimed.

Absence of prayer   If the plaintiff omits to ask for any relief or remedy claimed in the writ, he will be deemed to have abandoned that claim.[4]

Costs   Costs need not be specifically claimed,[5] nor is it strictly necessary to ask for "general or other relief," since the court will grant the plaintiff the remedies to which he appears to be entitled,[6] provided it is not "inconsistent with that relief which is expressly asked for."[7]

Pleading the prayer in the alternative   The plaintiff may claim his relief or remedy in the alternative. Moreover, there is nothing to prevent the plaintiff from setting up two or more inconsistent sets of material facts and claiming relief or remedy thereunder in the alternative, *e.g.* a claim for money had and received or alternatively damages for breach of contract,[8] since he is entitled to rely upon several different rights alternatively, although they may be inconsistent.[9]

Alternative claims and judgment in default   The plaintiff may obtain judgment in default of defence in the alternative which he selects, provided that his allegations entitle him to such relief or remedy.[10]

---

[2] *Phipps* v. *Orthodox Unit Trusts Ltd.* [1958] 1 Q.B. 314; [1957] 3 All E.R. 305.
[3] R.S.C., Ord. 18, r. 15(1).
[4] *Ibid.*; and see *Lewis & Lewis* v. *Durnford* (1907) 24 T.L.R. 64.
[5] It should be remembered that, subject to the rules of court, costs are in the discretion of the Court, see Supreme Court Act 1981, s.51(1) and R.S.C., Ord. 62, r. 3–11.
[6] See *Hulton* v. *Hulton* [1916] 2 K.B. 642, affirmed [1917] 1 K.B. 813; *Harrison-Broadley* v. *Smith* [1964] 1 W.L.R. 456; [1964] 1 All E.R. 867 (C.A.).
[7] *Cargill* v. *Bower* (1878) 10 Ch.D. 502 at 508.
[8] See *Bagot* v. *Easton* (1877) 7 Ch.D. 1.
[9] *Philipps* v. *Philipps* (1878) 4 Q.B.D. 127 at 134; *Re Morgan, Owen* v. *Morgan* (1887) 35 Ch.D. 492. The material facts should however be stated separately, so as to show distinctly on what facts each head of relief or remedy is claimed (*Davy* v. *Garrett* (1877) 7 Ch.D. 473 at 489; *Watson* v. *Hawkins* (1876) 24 W.R. 884).
[10] *Farrant* v. *Olver* [1922] W.N. 47; *Glover* v. *Broome* [1926] W.N. 46.

Multiple defendants   Recovery of judgment against one party on a contract is no bar to action by the same plaintiff against another party with regard to the same subject-matter if the contract be not the same.[11] Where different causes of action in respect of the same subject-matter are joined some words should be added in the judgment making it clear that the plaintiff cannot have double satisfaction.[12]

If there be different claims for debt, damages or other relief or remedy by different plaintiffs or against different defendants, the pleading must clearly show by and against whom each separate claim is made, as, for instance:

> The plaintiffs, *A B* and *C D*, claim, etc.;
> The plaintiff, *C D*, in the alternative claims, etc.; *or*
> The plaintiff claims against the defendant, *G H*, etc.;
> In the alternative, the plaintiff claims against the defendant, *I K*, etc.

Claims and Judgments in Foreign Currency

Jurisdiction   The English court has power to give judgment for a sum of money expressed in a foreign currency.[13] This power may be exercised even where the foreign currency is payable under a contract the proper law of which is English law.[14] The court has further power to award damages for breach of contract in foreign currency[15] and to award damages for tort in a foreign currency.[16] In both these cases the court has power to award damages in the currency that best expresses the plaintiff's loss.[17] It does not matter whether the foreign currency is that of a Member State of the European Community[18] or the currency of any

---

[11] *Isaacs* v. *Salbstein* [1916] 2 K.B. 139 (C.A.).

[12] *Morris (B. O.) Ltd.* v. *Perrott and Bolton* [1945] 1 All E.R. 567.

[13] *Miliangos* v. *George Frank (Textiles) Ltd.* [1976] A.C. 443; [1975] 3 All E.R. 801; (H.L.); overruling *Re Scandinavian Bank Group plc* [1988] Ch. 87; [1987] 2 All E.R. 70; *Re Lines Bros. Ltd.* [1983] Ch. 1; *Re United Railways of Havana and Regla Warehouses Ltd.* [1961] A.C. 1007; [1960] 2 All E.R. 332; pursuant to the *Practice Statement (Judicial Precedent)* [1966] 1 W.L.R. 1234; and affirming the decision of C.A. [1975] Q.B. 487.

[14] *Barclays Bank International Ltd.* v. *Levin Brothers (Bradford) Ltd.* [1977] Q.B. 270 (dishonoured bills of exchange accepted payable in England but expressed in foreign currency).

[15] *Kraut (Jean) A.G.* v. *Albany Fabrics Ltd.* [1977] Q.B. 182; [1976] 3 W.L.R. 872; [1977] 1 All E.R. 116.

[16] *Eleftherotria (Owners of the M.V.)* v. *Despina R (Owners of the M.V.)* [1979] A.C. 685 (H.L.); affirming [1978] Q.B. 396; overruling *Di Ferdinando* v. *Simon, Smits & Co.* [1920] 3 K.B. 409 (C.A.).

[17] *Services Europe Atlantique Sud (SEAS)* v. *Stockholms Rederiaktiebolag Svea, The Folias(I.)* [1979] A.C. 685; [1979] 1 All E.R. 421 (H.L.); affirming [1979] Q.B. 491 (C.A.); reversing [1978] Q.B. 396.

[18] *Schorsch Meier GmbH* v. *Hennin* [1975] Q.B. 416; [1975] 1 All E.R. 152 (C.A.).

other state.[19] The judgment will be for payment of the amount of the foreign currency or its sterling equivalent[20] converted for the purposes of the enforcement of the judgment at the time of payment, *i.e.* the date on which enforcement process is taken or authorised in terms of sterling.[21]

Charterparties and demurrage   Where a charterparty provides that demurrage is to be calculated in U.S. dollars and does not provide for it to be paid in sterling the reasonable inference is that the money of payment as well as the money of account, is U.S. dollars, even though the freight is payable in sterling and the contract is to be governed by English law. The rate of exchange for demurrage is that prevailing at the date of the payment of the demurrage and not at the date of the bill of lading, and therefore the owners are entitled to the difference between the amount of sterling actually paid at the date of the bill of lading and the sum required to be paid at the rate of exchange ruling at the date of payment and to have the balance awarded in U.S. dollars.[22]

Company liquidation   In the case of liquidation of a company, the practice of converting a foreign currency judgment into sterling as at the date of its enforcement does not apply. Instead the foreign currency debt must be proved according to its sterling equivalent since that was in accordance with the general rule for the valuation of liabilities on a winding up value at the date of the commencement of the winding up.[23] But in a wholly solvent liquidation, the liquidator should make good a shortfall in the full contractual foreign currency debt before he pays anything to the shareholders.[24]

Which foreign currency?   Where there is more than one eligible[25] foreign currency in which the judgment may be given, then in the absence of an agreed currency of account and payment, the judgment would be expressed in the currency in which the plaintiff's loss was felt or which most expressed his loss.[26]

Tort—personal injuries   In an action by a foreign national for damages for personal injuries suffered during a visit to England, the damages for

[19] *Miliangos* v. *George Frank (Textiles) Ltd.* [1976] A.C. 443; [1975] 3 All E.R. 801, (H.L.).
[20] *Ibid.*
[21] *Ibid.*
[22] *Veflings (George) Rederi A/S* v. *President of India* [1979] 1 W.L.R. 59; [1979] 1 All E.R. 380 (C.A.).
[23] *Re Lines Bros. Ltd. (In Liquidation)* [1983] Ch. 1 (C.A.).
[24] *Ibid.*, *per* Brightman L.J.
[25] The applicable principles are those stated by Lord Wilberforce in *Services Europe Atlantique Sud (SEAS)* v. *Stockholms Rederiaktiebolag Svea, The Folias* [1979] A.C. 685; [1978] 3 W.L.R. 804; [1979] 1 All E.R. 421.
[26] *Société Française Bunge S.A.* v. *Belcan N.V.; The Federal Huron* [1985] 3 All E.R. 378.

out of pocket expenses will be assessed in the currency of his country, since his loss is most closely linked with that currency. But damages for pain, suffering and loss of amenity will be assessed in sterling.[27]

Time for entering judgment   If the court does express its judgment for the payment of money in a foreign currency, the judgment will be entered in that currency or its sterling equivalent at the time of payment. The prescribed forms of judgment should be appropriately amended for this purpose.[28]

Election and judicial discretion   It is not clear whether the plaintiff has the right to elect that the judgment should be expressed in sterling or in a foreign currency. It would seem that the court retains a residual discretion and that it will exercise this discretion having regard to all the circumstances including the position of the parties and the fluctuations in the rates of exchange between the currency of the contract and sterling during the period between the date when the cause of action, whether in contract or tort, arose and the date of judgment. There may well be cases in which although the plaintiff may elect that the judgment should be expressed in sterling, yet the defendant may wish, or it might otherwise be just, that the judgment should be expressed in the foreign currency of the contract and *vice versa*.

Different Kinds of Relief or Remedy: The Principles

Introduction   The same cause of action may entitle the plaintiff to relief or remedies of different kinds, which may be claimed separately, collectively or in the alternative. The plaintiff in an action may also ask for many different kinds of equitable relief or remedy such as an injunction, a declaration of right or title, an account, specific performance of a contract, or the appointment of a receiver.

Supreme Court Act 1981

(a) Section 49 of the Supreme Court Act 1981 gives to the High Court and the Court of Appeal power to "grant, either absolutely or on such terms and conditions as the court thinks just, all such remedies whatsoever as any of the parties thereto may appear to be entitled to in respect of any legal or equitable claim properly brought forward by them in the cause or matter, so that, as far as possible, all matters in controversy between the parties may be completely and finally determined, and all multiplicity of legal proceedings concerning any of those matters avoided."

---

[27] *Hoffmann* v. *Sofaer* [1982] 1 W.L.R. 1350.
[28] *Practice Direction (Judgment: Foreign Currency)* [1976] 1 W.L.R. 83.

(b) By section 61, however, certain matters are assigned to the Chancery Division, and a plaintiff therefore should not bring an action in the Queen's Bench Division in respect of any of these matters. But this section does not prevent anyone, who has been made a defendant in an action in the Queen's Bench Division, from seeking any equitable relief by way of counterclaim.

Examples of Different Kinds of Relief or Remedy

Account   An account may be claimed in the Queen's Bench Division in cases devoid of complexity[29]; though as a general rule it is assigned to the Chancery Division.[30] In the Queen's Bench Division it may be taken either by a master, or a district registrar,[31] or by an official referee,[32] who is not bound to take the account in the strict way usually adopted before a master in Chancery Chambers, but may adopt any other method that in his opinion will best advance the ends of justice.[33] The court may at any stage of the proceedings in any cause or matter direct any necessary accounts to be taken.[34]

Damages   The plaintiff in settling a statement of claim for debt or damages is not restricted to the figures (if any) given on the writ. If he names a figure, he should claim the largest amount which he is likely to recover; for, in the absence of amendment, he cannot recover more than the amount claimed.[35] An amendment, however, in this respect may be allowed at any time before judgment is entered and perfected.[36] Where the plaintiff's claim is for a debt or liquidated demand and can be ascertained exactly, it is better to claim only the precise amount. Where, however, the damages are unliquidated, it is not necessary or usual to insert any specific figure as the precise amount of damages claimed.[37] In an action for damages for personal injuries, it is good practice to plead specifically a claim for loss of future earning capacity in order to give fair notice to the defendant.[38]

---

[29] See R.S.C., Ord. 43, r. 1; and see *York* v. *Stowers* [1883] W.N. 174. However, if it is complicated or difficult it may be commenced as "Official Referees' Business" see R.S.C., Ord. 33, r. 2.

[30] See Supreme Court Act 1981, s.61 and Sched. 1, para. 1(*f*).

[31] *Re Bowen* (1882) 20 Ch.D. 538.

[32] See R.S.C., Ord. 36, rr. 1 and 9, and see *Rochefoucauld* v. *Boustead* [1897] 1 Ch. 196. Under R.S.C., Ord. 36, r. 10, an account may be taken before a special referee with the consent of the parties.

[33] *Re Taylor, Turpin* v. *Pain* (1880) 44 Ch.D. 128.

[34] See R.S.C., Ord. 43, r. 2.

[35] *Wyatt* v. *Rosherville Gardens Co.* (1886) 2 T.L.R. 282.

[36] As to entering and perfecting a judgment see *Supreme Court Practice 1991*, Vol. 1, para. 42/1/4.

[37] See *London and Northern Bank Ltd.* v. *George Newnes Ltd.* (1900) 16 T.L.R. 433 at 434; *Thompson* v. *Goold* [1910] A.C. 409 (H.L.).

[38] *Chan Wai Tong* v. *Li Ping Sum* [1985] A.C. 446 (P.C.), *per* Lord Fraser.

Declaration of right   The court has power to make binding declarations of right without ordering either of the parties to pay any money or to restore any land or goods or to do any other specific act and whether or not any consequential relief is or could be claimed.[39] This power is limited only by the discretion of the courts.[40] The court may make a declaration, even where it refuses to grant an injunction or to give any other relief.[41] While it is undesirable that judges should make declarations as to the true construction of documents on motions for judgment in default of defence,[42] in an exceptional case, it may well be the only relief possible.[43] But a declaration will not be made against a party who has never asserted a right or formulated a specific claim.[44] Where, however, sufficient reason is shown, parties to a mercantile contract are entitled to ask the court for a declaration whether they are bound by the contract or not.[45]

Injunction[46]   An injunction is an order or judgment of the court by which a party to an action is required to do or refrain from doing a particular act, *e.g.* not to build a wall to such a height that it will become a nuisance to the plaintiff by diminishing the access of light to his ancient windows. In some cases the plaintiff can obtain a mandatory injunction, namely an order requiring the defendant to do a certain act, *e.g.* to pull down so much of the wall which he has erected as is a nuisance to the plaintiff. The court has power, if it thinks fit, to award damages in lieu of an injunction.[47] An injunction should be claimed whenever there is any reason to apprehend any repetition of the defendant's unlawful act. In

---

[39] R.S.C., Ord. 15, r. 16, and see *Ellis* v. *Duke of Bedford* [1899] 1 Ch. 494 at 515; *Honour* v. *Equitable Life Society* [1900] 1 Ch. 852. Such a declaration can be made without ordering either of the parties to pay any money or to restore land or goods or to do any other specific act and whether or not any consequential relief is or could be claimed.

[40] *Russian Commercial and Industrial Bank* v. *British Bank for Foreign Trade* [1921] 2 A.C. 438, and see *Guaranty Trust Co. of New York* v. *Hannay & Co.* [1915] 2 K.B. 536 (where the validity of the rule was upheld); *Hanson* v. *Radcliffe Urban Council* [1922] 2 Ch. 490 at 507; *Gibson* v. *Union of Shop, Distributive and Allied Workers* [1968] 1 W.L.R. 1187; [1968] 2 All E.R. 252.

[41] *Llandudno U.D.C.* v. *Woods* [1899] 2 Ch. 705; *West* v. *Gwynne* [1911] 2 Ch. 1.

[42] *New Brunswick Ry.* v. *British and French Trust Corporation* [1939] A.C. 1.

[43] *Guardian Assurance Co.* v. *Sutherland* [1939] 2 All E.R. 246; and see *Jenkins* v. *Price* [1907] 2 Ch. 229; *West* v. *Gwynne* [1911] 2 Ch. 1.

[44] *Re Clay* [1919] 1 Ch. 66 (C.A.); *Nixon* v. *Att.-Gen.* [1930] 1 Ch. 566; *Re Barnato, Joel* v. *Sanges* [1949] Ch. 258; *Mellstrom* v. *Garner* [1970] 1 W.L.R. 603; [1970] 2 All E.R. 9 (C.A.) (no breach and no threat or intention to commit a breach of agreement); *Midland Bank plc.* v. *Laker Airways Ltd.* [1986] Q.B. 689; [1986] 1 All E.R. 526 (declaration refused for no liability under English law where no threat to take proceedings in English courts).

[45] *Société Maritime* v. *Venus Shipping Co.* (1900) 9 Com.Cas. 289 (a chargee of land may apply to the court for a declaration that he is entitled to the charge); *West Ham Corpn.* v. *Sharp* [1907] 1 K.B. 445, cited in *Poole Corpn.* v. *Moody* [1945] 1 K.B. 350.

[46] The jurisdiction flows from s.37(1) of the Supreme Court Act 1981.

[47] Supreme Court Act 1981, s.50. See *Leeds Industrial Co-operative Society* v. *Slack* [1924] A.C. 851 and *Kennaway* v. *Thompson* [1981] Q.B. 88; [1980] 3 W.L.R. 361; [1980] 3 All E.R. 329 (C.A.).

such case it must be averred in the body of the pleading that the defendant intends to repeat the unlawful act, unless such an intention is already apparent[48] from the nature of the case of the facts pleaded.[49-50]

Receiver[51]   A receiver is a person who is appointed by the court to protect and preserve, in the interests of both parties, property which is the subject-matter of litigation, until the case is decided. It is his duty to collect and receive, pending the proceedings, the rents, issues and profits of land or personal estate which it does not seem reasonable to the court that either party should collect or receive. He may also be authorised to employ the money in his hands in executing necessary repairs or making any other improvements which the condition of the property urgently requires. He is an officer of the court, not the agent of or trustee for the parties,[52] and is answerable to the court for misconduct or neglect. Any interference with him in the discharge of his duties is a contempt of the court which appointed him.

A plaintiff is, in a proper case, entitled to a receiver, even though he has not asked for one on his writ or statement of claim.[53] The court has jurisdiction to appoint a receiver in all cases in which it appears to be just or convenient to make such an order. If the defendant may be in possession of the property,[54] the court will give the receiver possession of the property so far as is necessary for the preservation of the plaintiff's rights.[55]

Specific performance   Claims for the specific performance of a contract for the sale or leasing of land are specially assigned to the Chancery Division and will not therefore be entertained by the Queen's Bench Division.[56] On the other hand, actions for the specific performance of

---

[48] Injunctions may be final (with which this text deals) or interlocutory. Interlocutory injunctions may be awarded by reference to the criteria set out in *American Cyanamid* v. *Ethicon Ltd.* [1975] A.C. 396; [1975] 1 All E.R. 504 or the exceptions thereto; or they may be of the "Mareva" and/or "Anton Piller" categories. Further discussion as to these interlocutory remedies are set out in Goldrein & Wilkinson, *Commercial Litigation: Preemptive Remedies* (1987).

[49-50] *Stannard* v. *Vestry of St. Giles* (1882) 20 Ch.D. 190 at 195. For claims for an injunction, see Bullen & Leake and Jacob's *Precedents of Pleadings*.

[51] A receiver may be appointed in all cases in which it appears to be just and convenient to do so; see s.37(1) of the Supreme Court Act 1981. Applications for the appointment of a receiver are regulated by R.S.C., Ord. 30.

[52] *Boehm* v. *Goodall* [1911] 1 Ch. 155; *Viola* v. *Anglo-American Cold Storage Co.* [1912] 2 Ch. 305.

[53] *cf. Salt* v. *Cooper* (1881) 16 Ch.D. 544.

[54] *Gwatkin* v. *Bird* (1882) 52 L.J. Q.B. 263; *Foxwell* v. *Van Grutten* [1897] 1 Ch. 64. Also see *Derby & Co. Ltd.* v. *Weldon (No. 3 and No. 4)*, *The Times*, December 26, 1988.

[55] *Charrington & Co.* v. *Camp* [1902] 1 Ch. 386.

[56] Supreme Court Act 1981, s.61(1) and Sched. 1(*a*). Strictly speaking the leasing of land is not assigned to the Chancery Division by the Statute, but is treated as such by virtue of R.S.C., Ord. 86 which deals with summary judgment for specific performance.

contracts not relating to land can be and often are brought in the Queen's Bench Division, *e.g.* a contract for the sale of shares. In particular, in any action brought in the Queen's Bench Division for the breach of a contract to deliver specific or ascertained goods, the court may, if it thinks fit, on the application of the plaintiff, by its judgment direct that the contract shall be performed specifically, without giving the defendant the option of retaining the goods on payment of damages.[57]

Provisional damages   A claim for provisional damages must be specifically pleaded together with the facts relied on.[58] It is a condition precedent to the making of an award for provisional damages that such a claim has been pleaded.[59] The facts relied on should include those set out in section 32A of the Supreme Court Act 1981, so as to satisfy the court that the action is one to which that section applies.[60] These facts are that there is a chance that at some time in the future the plaintiff will develop some serious disease or suffer some serious deterioration in his physical or mental condition. The prayer in the statement of claim should include "an order for the award of provisional damages under section 32A of the Supreme Court Act 1981."

Interest

Pleading—condition precedent to recovery   Any claim for interest under section 35A of the Supreme Court Act 1981[61] or otherwise must be specifically pleaded.[62] If the plaintiff does not plead his claim for interest, no interest will be awarded by the court, whether on the debt or damages unless and until the pleading is duly amended.[63]

Rationale   The requirement of the rules that any claim for interest must be specifically pleaded reflects the fundamental principle that the plead-

---

[57] Sale of Goods Act 1979, s.52; R.S.C., Ord. 14, r. 9; *Jones & Sons Ltd.* v. *Tankerville (Earl)* [1909] 2 Ch. 440.
[58] R.S.C., Ord. 18, r. 8(3). Note that the County Court does not have power to award provisional damages.
[59] R.S.C., Ord. 37, r. 8(1)(*a*).
[60] Ibid., r. 8(1)(*b*).
[61] For interest in the county court see the County Courts Act 1984, s.69.
[62] R.S.C., Ord. 18, r. 8(4). This rule applies to a pleading, whether indorsed on the writ or not; but it does not apply to a general indorsement claiming a debt or damages. See *Butler (Edward) Vintners Ltd.* v. *Grange Seymour International Ltd., The Times,* June 9, 1988 (C.A.). The general indorsement is required to state the nature of the claim made and the relief or remedy required in the action; see Ord. 6, r. 2(1)(*a*). In virtue of this provision, the general practice is for the plaintiff to include in the general indorsement a claim to entitlement of interest whether under s.35A of the Supreme Court Act 1981 or otherwise. By this practice the plaintiff gives the defendant fair notice of the nature and extent of his claim and at the same time formulates the plaintiff's claim to interest from the very commencement of the action.
[63] *Ward* v. *Chief Constable of Avon and Somerset* (1985) 129 S.J. 606, C.A.

ing should give fair notice to the opposite party of the nature and extent of the claim which is being made against him, and to the relevant facts relied upon so as to enable that party to meet such claim and to prevent surprise at the trial. Thus, if the defendant has due notice of the plaintiff's intention specifically expressed in his pleading to seek an award of interest he will know the nature and extent of the plaintiff's claim and he can better calculate what sum (if any) he should pay into court in satisfaction of the claim, or what sum he can fairly offer to settle the claim or even whether in all the circumstances he should allow the plaintiff to enter judgment in default of pleading.[64]

Pleading interest and the payment-in   If no interest has been pleaded, the defendant need not include an element of interest in any payment into court that he may make in satisfaction of the claim.[65] It should be stressed that this position will apply even in actions for personal injuries or death, since although in such actions the court is under a statutory duty to award interest on the amount for which judgment is given[66] yet such duty is subject to the rules of court which provide that a claim for interest must be specifically pleaded.[67]

The rule appears to require the claim for interest to be pleaded in the body of the pleading, even if it is claimed under section 35A of the Supreme Court Act 1981, although it has been held that it is sufficient if the claim for interest, at any rate under section 35A of the Supreme Court Act 1981 is made only in the prayer and not also in the body of the pleading.[68] It must of course also be repeated in the prayer.[69]

Pleading the grounds for the claim to interest   If interest is being claimed under another statutory provision, the pleading should specifically identify that statute or provision, together with the rate at which and the period for which the interest is being claimed.[70] If the claim for interest is under a contract, express or implied or under mercantile usage,

---

[64] See R.S.C., Ord. 18, r. 15(1).
[65] See R.S.C., Ord. 22, r. 1(8).
[66] Supreme Court Act 1981, s.35A(i) and (ii).
[67] See *Supreme Court Practice 1991*, Vol. 1, para. 18/8/10.
[68] See *Supreme Court Practice 1991*, Vol. 1, para. 18/8/10.
[69] *McDonald's Hamburgers* v. *Burgerking (U.K.) Ltd.* [1987] F.S.R. 112. In this context it may be worth remarking that the prayer in the statement of claim is ordinarily treated and regarded as being an adjunct or supplement to that pleading in the sense that it is a summary of the relief or remedy claimed on the basis of the material facts relied on in support of the claim. This explains why a separate rule is provided precisely to require that the relief or remedy must be specifically stated in the statement of claim; see R.S.C., Ord. 18, r. 15(1). On the other hand, the claim to the entitlement of interest whether under statute or otherwise, is a material fact which like other material facts is required to be pleaded and this explains why a separate rule is provided that the claim for interest must be specifically pleaded (see R.S.C., Ord. 18, r. 8(4)).
[70] *Ibid.*

the contractual term relied upon or otherwise the relevant facts and matters relied upon for entitlement to interest must be sufficiently pleaded, as should the rate at which and the period for which interest is being claimed. Moreover, if the plaintiff claims to have incurred a special loss by way of additional interest charges resulting from the defendant's breach of contract which was reasonably foreseeable, he must plead the facts and matters relied upon to recover such interest and charges.[71]

If the plaintiff claims to be entitled to interest under the equitable jurisdiction of the court to award interest as ancillary relief in respect of equitable remedies such as specific performance or the taking of an account, the facts and matters relied upon must be specifically pleaded. Under this jurisdiction, interest may be ordered to be paid where money has been obtained and retained by fraud or where money has been withheld or misapplied by an executor, trustee or anyone else in a fiduciary position and in such case the court has an inherent power to order the payment of interest at whatever rate is equitable in the circumstances. If in such case the plaintiff seeks an award of compound interest, he should specifically so state in his pleading which should contain all the material facts relied upon and should include such a claim in his prayer.

If the plaintiff claims to be entitled to interest on the judgment debt which he may obtain at a higher rate than that payable for the time being on judgment debts he must specifically plead the contractual term relied upon to support such claim. In such case, the judgment itself should expressly specify the higher rate which will accrue on the judgment debt until payment, otherwise the judgment debt will only carry interest at the rate current at the time of judgment is entered under the Judgments Act 1838, s.17.

Recovery of Land

Historical background It was a rule of the common law that anyone who was out of possession must recover the land by the strength of his own title, and not by reason of any defect in the title of the person in possession.[72] This rule still remains the law; and to it may be traced most, if not all, the special features of the procedure in an action for the recovery of land. Every presumption is still made in favour of the person in possession. Even when it was clear that the person in possession had no right to be there, still the claimant in ejectment could not turn him out unless he could show in himself a title which was—prima facie, at all events— good against all the world. If some third person had a better title than the

---

[71] *Ibid.* See also *Supreme Court Practice 1991*, Vol. 1, para. 6/2/9.

[72] *Martin* v. *Strachan* (1744) 5 Term Rep. 107n. at 110n. Lee C.J. laid down the rule that the plaintiff must recover by "strength of his own title, and not by the weakness of the defendant's title"; and see *Lyell* v. *Kennedy* (1882) 20 Ch.D. 484 at 488, 490.

claimant, the action failed even though such third person had not placed the defendant in possession.

Practice points

    (a) The land of which the plaintiff seeks to recover possession must be in England or Wales, although a court of equity can entertain questions as to specific performance of contracts and other equitable matters affecting land abroad.[73] It cannot place a plaintiff in possession of such land.[74]

    (b) The general rule is that an English court will not adjudicate on questions relating to the title to, or the right to the possession of, immovable property out of the jurisdiction of that court. The exceptions to this rule depend on the existence between the parties to the suit in England of some personal obligation arising out of contract or implied contract, fiduciary relation, or fraud, or other conduct which in the view of an English court of equity would be unconscionable, and do not depend for their existence on the law of the *locus* of the immovable property.[75]

Being out of possession—a pre-requisite The plaintiff in an action for the recovery of land is always a person who is out of possession but claims to have a right to the immediate possession of the land. Where there is no suggestion that the defendant received possession from the plaintiff, or has paid him rent, then as a general rule the onus lies on the plaintiff of strictly proving his title, and he must state his title in full detail in his pleading, deducing it step by step through the various mesne assignments.[76]

Exceptions to the general rule To this rule there are two exceptions:

(a) *Prior possession* Prior possession, however short, is a sufficient prima facie title against a wrongdoer. Thus, if the plaintiff was recently in possession, and has been ejected by the defendant wrongfully and not by process of law, it is enough for him to plead these facts.[77]

(b) *Estoppel* Where the defendant is estopped from denying the plaintiff's title, as, for instance, where the relation of landlord and tenant existed between them. A tenant is estopped from denying that his land-

---

[73] *Penn* v. *Baltimore* (1750) 1 Ves.Sen. 444.

[74] *British South Africa Co.* v. *Companhia de Mocambique* [1893] A.C. 602, discussed and distinguished in *The Tolten* [1946] P. 135.

[75] *Deschamps* v. *Miller* [1908] 1 Ch. 856; see also *Sydney Municipal Council* v. *Bull* [1909] 1 K.B. 7.

[76] *Philipps* v. *Philipps* (1878) 4 Q.B.D. 127; followed in *Davis* v. *James* (1884) 26 Ch.D. 778.

[77] *Asher* v. *Whitlock* (1865) L.R. 1 Q.B. 1.

lord who put him in possession of the land then had title so to do, or that his landlord from whom he has accepted a lease then had title to grant that lease, or that his landlord to whom he paid rent then had title to receive that rent. Hence, where a landlord seeks to recover the possession of the demised premises from his late tenant, it is only necessary for him to show in the statement of claim the creation of the relationship of land-lord and tenant, its determination before action, and the defendant's con-tinued possession of the premises. He should state the date of any lease or written agreement under which the premises were held, the date of any assignment of the reversion and the date of the determination of the defendant's tenancy. But it is not necessary for him to trace his own title except from the date of the lease.

Pleading points

(a) *Joinder*   If he desires to recover the whole of the premises mentioned on his writ, he should as a general rule join as a defendant every person who is in possession of any part of them. He will be prima facie entitled to a verdict on proof that the land is his; for the ownership of land involves a right to the possession of it, unless the owner has voluntarily parted with possession to some third person.

(b) *Right of entry*   In any case the statement of claim must show that there was a right of entry in the plaintiff at the date of the writ; or if mesne profits be claimed from an earlier date, at that earlier date.

A defendant's riposte   The defendant must plead specifically every ground of defence on which he relies, and a plea that he is in possession of the land by himself or his tenant is not sufficient.[78] If the defendant asserts that he is in possession of the land by the permission of the plain-tiff, he thereby admits that the plaintiff had the right so to place him in possession. In other words, he admits the plaintiff's title at that date, though he may contend that it has since determined, as, for instance, if the lessor himself had only a leasehold interest.[79]

Summary proceedings for possession of land   Where a person claims possession of land which he alleges is occupied solely by a person or per-sons (not being a tenant or tenants holding over after termination of the tenancy) who entered into or remained in occupation without his licence or consent or that of any predecessor in title of his, the proceedings may

---

[78] R.S.C., Ord. 18, r. 8(2).
[79] *Barwick* v. *Thompson* (1798) 7 T.R. 488; *Cuthbertson* v. *Irving* (1859–1860) 4 H. & N. 742; 6 H. & N. 135; *Delaney* v. *Fox* (1857) 2 C.B.(N.S.) 768. Where the defendant did not receive possession from the plaintiff, the latter will also have to prove his derivative title from the party by whom the defendant was originally admitted into possession.

be brought by originating summons.[80] The purpose of these provisions is not to provide a new remedy but rather a new procedure for the recovery of possession of land which is in wrongful occupation by trespassers. The machinery is designed to overcome the apparent short-comings of the procedural law as it was, namely:

(a) by providing the procedure for claiming possession of land where not every wrongful occupier could properly be identified (these provisions overcome the question whether an order for possession of land could be made and enforced in *ex parte* proceedings in which no person was named as defendant);

(b) by shortening the steps of the time taken for obtaining a final order for possession of land, these provisions overcome the question as to whether such an order can be made on an interlocutory application or by way of a final judgment or order.

Mesne Profits

Definition

(a) *Trespass* If a person who has no title enters into possession of land, the rents or profits which he receives or makes or which he might have received or made therefrom during his occupation are called mesne profits. He must pay these over to the true owner as compensation for the trespass which he has committed.

(b) *Holding over* As soon as a tenant's interest in the premises that were demised to him is legally determined, his remaining in occupation without the consent of his landlord will be wrongful, and is in law a trespass for which damages in respect of mesne profits may be recovered.

Contrast with rent "Rent" is the money which is payable by a tenant to his landlord for the use and occupation of land under a contract express or implied. A claim for rent is therefore liquidated. In contrast, the amount to which the plaintiff is entitled for mesne profits must be assessed by the court. It is not necessarily commensurate with the rent reserved in the expired lease, as the value of the premises may have either increased or fallen during the tenancy. Rent must be claimed up to the date at which the defendant ceased to be a tenant; mesne profits from the date at which he first became a trespasser. If, as is usually the case, the defendant became a trespasser before the date of the writ, the statement of claim must show that a right of entry accrued to the plaintiff at that earlier date. Mesne profits may be claimed up to the time when possession is given up to the plaintiff.[81]

[80] R.S.C., Ord. 113, r. 1.
[81] *Southport Tramways Co.* v. *Gandy* [1897] 2 Q.B. 66.

Pleading practice—the interaction between rent and mesne profit
Where the defendant's interest is determined by a forfeiture, it is the service of the writ and not its mere issue, which constitutes the notional re-entry and unequivocal determination of the tenancy by the landlord. In such action, therefore, the date from which mesne profits are recoverable is the date of the service of the writ, and not the date of its issue. Accordingly, the proper practice in such case is to claim rent up to the date of the service of the writ, and mesne profits from that date up to the date of delivery of possession.[82]

Trap for the unwary Care must be taken not to claim rent for any period after the date of the forfeiture; otherwise the forfeiture may be waived[83] unless a prior action has been brought for the recovery of the land on such forfeiture and the writ has been served in such action.[84]

The special case of the assignee or under-tenant Cases sometimes occur in which a tenant has assigned his term or underlet the demised premises, and the assignee or under-tenant refuses or neglects to give up possession to the landlord on the determination of the tenancy. In such cases it is the duty of the tenant to deliver up complete possession of the premises to his landlord; it is therefore no defence for him to plead that the premises are occupied by his assignee or under-tenant, who refuses to give them up; and the tenant is liable both for mesne profits whilst his assignee or under-tenant holds over, and for the costs of ejecting him.[85] It is the correct course in such a case to claim the costs expressly in the statement of claim. The assignee or under-tenant should be made a defendant to the action as well as the tenant, so as to secure recovery of possession.

Judgment for possession does not bar a subsequent claim for mesne profits A plaintiff is not bound to claim mesne profits in the action by which he seeks to recover possession of land. If the plaintiff sues first for possession alone and recovers judgment, and issues execution thereon, such judgment and execution are no bar to a subsequent action for mesne profits. The judgment in the former action will assist the plaintiff in the second action, for, if pleaded:

---

[82] *Canas Property Co. Ltd.* v. *K.L. Television Services Ltd.* [1970] 2 Q.B. 433 (C.A.); overruling in part *Elliott* v. *Boynton* [1924] 1 Ch. 236 (C.A.)

[83] *Dendy* v. *Nicholl* (1858) 4 C.B.(N.S.) 376; see also *Keith Prowse & Co.* v. *Telephone Co.* [1894] 2 Ch. 147; *Elliott* v. *Boynton* [1924] 1 Ch. 236; referred to in *Oak Property Co.* v. *Chapman* [1947] K.B. 886 at 898; and see Smith's *Leading Cases*, (13th ed.), Vol. 1, pp. 38 *et seq.*

[84] *Grimwood* v. *Moss* (1872) L.R. 7 C.P. 360; *Serjeant* v. *Nash* [1903] 2 K.B. 304.

[85] *Harding* v. *Crethorn* (1793) 1 Esp. 57; *Chitty* v. *Tancred* (1840) 7 M. & W. 127 at 130; *Henderson* v. *Squire* (1869) L.R. 4 Q.B. 170 at 174.

(a) it will be conclusive evidence of the plaintiff's title at the date of the writ in such original action as against the same defendant and persons claiming under him[86]; and

(b) prima facie evidence of the defendant's possession at the same date.[87]

Interim payment The court has jurisdiction to grant an interim payment if satisfied that the plaintiff's action includes a claim for possession of land and, if the action proceeded to trial, the defendant would be held liable to pay to the plaintiff a sum of money in respect of the defendant's use and occupation of the land during the pending of the action, even if a final judgment or order were given or made in favour of the defendant.

Altering, Modifying or Extending the Claim Indorsed on the Writ

The statement of claim can only amplify the writ—not extend it Where the statement of claim is not indorsed on the writ, but is a separate document, whether served with the writ or later, it must, in general, confine itself to the causes of action mentioned in the general indorsement[88] on the writ. Subject to such limitation, the plaintiff is permitted in his statement of claim to alter, modify or extend any claim made by him in the indorsement of the writ without amending the indorsement.[89] Thus if the facts necessary to establish the claim in the writ would suffice to establish some other, perhaps narrower, cause of action, because they are the same as, or include or form part of the facts giving rise to the cause of action mentioned in the writ, the plaintiff is entitled to add in the statement of claim a new cause of action different from the one mentioned in the writ without amending the writ.[90] But this does not entitle the plaintiff completely to change the cause of action indorsed on the writ,[91] or to introduce an entirely new and additional cause of action,[92] or to introduce a claim which the court has no jurisdiction to entertain.[93]

Curing defects in the writ A defect in the writ may be cured by a proper statement of claim which may operate in the same way as the obtaining

---

[86] *Wilkinson* v. *Kirby* (1854) 15 C.B. 430; *Harris* v. *Mulkern* (1876) 1 Ex.D. 31 at 36.

[87] *Pearse* v. *Coaker* (1869) L.R. 4 Ex. 92; applied in *Elliott* v. *Boynton* [1924] 1 Ch. 236.

[88] R.S.C., Ord. 6, r. 2(1)(a). (The indorsement should consist only of a concise statement of the nature of the claim made or the relief or remedy required in the action.)

[89] R.S.C., Ord. 18, r. 15(2); and see *Large* v. *Large* [1877] W.N. 198; *Johnson* v. *Palmer* (1879) 4 C.P.D. 258.

[90] See *Brickfield Properties Ltd.* v. *Newton* [1971] 1 W.L.R. 862; [1971] 1 W.L.R. 862; [1971] 3 All E.R. 328 (C.A.).

[91] *Cave* v. *Crew* (1893) 62 L.J. Ch. 530; *Ker* v. *Williams* (1886) 30 S.J. 238.

[92] *United Telephone Co.* v. *Tasker* (1888) 59 L.T. 852.

[93] *Waterhouse* v. *Reid* [1938] 1 K.B. 743 (C.A.) (a claim for which leave to serve out of the jurisdiction would not have been granted under R.S.C., Ord. 11, r. 1).

of leave to amend,[94] though the omission from the statement of claim of any cause of action mentioned or relief claimed in the writ will operate as an election by the plaintiff to abandon it.[95] However, the plaintiff is not entitled to alter the parties to the action, without amendment of the writ, or to make any other amendment except in the claim.

No Function of Statement of Claim to Anticipate Defence

Cross one's bridges only when one comes to them   The statement of claim should not anticipate a defence that may never be made,[96] for that would be "like leaping before one comes to the stile."[97] "It is no part of the statement of claim to anticipate the defence and to state what the plaintiff would have to say in answer to it."[98] This practice follows from the principle that the statement of claim should state the material facts relied on at the date when it is served.

Examples of anticipation—to be avoided

(a) In an action for a specific performance of an agreement to purchase land, the plaintiff should not in his statement of claim allege waiver by the defendant of any alleged default or breach of agreement or other ground which would disentitle the defendant to determine the agreement.[99]

(b) The plaintiff should not in his statement of claim allege any matter of fact as to which the burden of proof lies on the defendant.[1]

(c) Pleading that a condition precedent has been performed, since it is for the defendant to aver that it has not.[2]

Example of anticipation—to be adopted   It is sometimes convenient and desirable to allege facts which are clearly material and affect the substratum of the claim made. Thus:

---

[94] *Hill* v. *Luton Corporation* [1951] 2 K.B. 387, and see *Grounsell* v. *Cuthell and Linley* [1952] 2 Q.B. 673.

[95] *Cargill* v. *Bower* (1878) 10 Ch.D. 502 at 508; *Lewis & Lewis* v. *Durnford* (1907) 24 T.L.R. 64; *Harries* v. *Ashford* [1950] 1 All E.R. 427.

[96] See *Hall* v. *Eve* (1876) 4 Ch.D. 341, *per* Bramwell J. at 348.

[97] *Sir Ralph Bovy's Case* (1672) 1 Vent. 193, *per* Hale C.J. (claim on a bond need not allege defendant was of full age when he executed it).

[98] *Hall* v. *Eve* (1876) 4 Ch.D. 341, *per* James L.J. at 345, who added "That would be a return to the old inconvenient system of pleading in Chancery, which ought certainly not to be encouraged, when the Plaintiff used to allege in his bill imaginary defences of the Defendant and make charges in reply to them."

[99] *Hall* v. *Eve, supra.*

[1] R.S.C., Ord. 18, r. 7(3); and see *Victors* v. *Davies* (1844) 12 M. & W. 758 (claim for money lent need not allege *request* for loan).

[2] R.S.C., Ord. 18, r. 7(4); see *Hotham (Sir Richard)* v. *East India Co.* (1787) 1 Term Rep. 638.

(a) the facts relating to an acknowledgment sufficient to take the case out of the Limitation Acts may and should ordinarily be pleaded in the statement of claim[3]; and

(b) so should facts showing lack of actual or constructive knowledge of material facts of a decisive character within the relevant period to entitle the plaintiff to the benefit of the leave obtained for the purposes of the Limitation Act 1980.

Do not amend the claim through the medium of the reply   If the plaintiff intends to meet any answer raised by the defendant by raising a new or fresh cause of action or ground of claim, he must do so by amending the statement of claim, and not by doing so in the reply, for that would be a "departure."

Withdrawal of Claim

Can the plaintiff withdraw his claim

(a) *Without leave*   The plaintiff is entitled to withdraw any particular claim made by him in the action begun by writ without leave as against all or any of the defendants, provided he does so by serving notice of such withdrawal on the defendant concerned not later than 14 days after service of the defence on him, or if there are two or more defendants, of the defence last served.[4-5] The notice of withdrawal must be in writing and must be clear and unequivocal and it must specify the particular claim which is being withdrawn, but no particular form of notice is necessary.[6]

(b) *With leave*   Where, however, such notice of withdrawal has not been served or has not been effectively served within the specified time, the leave of the court is required for the withdrawal by the plaintiff of any particular claim made by him in the action. The court may order such claim to be struck out as against all or any of the parties against whom it is made on such terms as to costs, the bringing of a subsequent action or otherwise as it thinks just.[7]

Withdrawal—does not generate an issue estoppel   Subject to any such terms imposed by the court, the fact that a party has withdrawn a particular claim made by him in the action will not be a defence to a subsequent action for the same, or substantially the same, cause of action.[8]

---

[3] *Busch* v. *Stevens* [1963] 1 Q.B. 1.
[4-5] R.S.C., Ord. 21, r. 2(1).
[6] See *The Pomerania* (1879) 4 P.D. 195; *M'Ilwraith* v. *Green* (1884) 14 Q.B.D. 766 (C.A.); *Spencer* v. *Watts* (1889) 23 Q.B.D. 350 (C.A.).
[7] R.S.C., Ord. 21, r. 3(1). The application for such leave is made by summons or by notice under the summons for direction, R.S.C., Ord. 21, r. 3(2).
[8] R.S.C., Ord. 21, r. 4.

Co-plaintiff—one withdraws   A co-plaintiff suing in respect of a separate cause of action may withdraw without leave, for his withdrawal will not affect the right of his co-plaintiffs to continue the action.[9] But one of two or more co-plaintiffs cannot withdraw without the consent of the others, if he is a necessary party to the claim by them.[10]

---

[9] *King* v. *Sunday Pictorial Newspapers Ltd.* (1924) 41 T.L.R. 229. Equally, where two plaintiffs claim in the alternative either can discontinue or withdraw without leave; *ibid.*
[10] See *Re Matthews, Oates* v. *Mooney* [1905] 2 Ch. 460.

CHAPTER 7

The Defence

Function of the Defence

Introduction   The function of the defence is to state the grounds and the material facts on which the defendant relies for his defence.[1] Great care is necessary in drafting a defence, and none the less so because the defendant may amend his defence once without leave before the close of pleadings.[2]

Object   The primary object of the defence is:

(a) to inform the plaintiff precisely how much of the statement of claim the defendant admits and how much he denies; and

(b) what grounds and facts the defendant relies on to defeat the claim of the plaintiff.

Pleading requirements   In his defence, the defendant must deal specifically with every material allegation contained in the statement of claim traversing it or admitting it, or admitting it with some stated qualification. He may object if he wishes, that the statement of claim or some specified part of it is bad in law. He must state in a summary form the material facts on which he relies for his defence, but not the evidence by which he will seek to prove those facts at the trial.[3] He may plead any set-off or counterclaim which he desires to set up.

Examples of pleading techniques   In answer to the statement of claim, the defendant in his defence may take any one, or some, or all the following courses:

[1] See R.S.C., Ord. 18, r. 7(1).
[2] See R.S.C., Ord. 20, r. 3(1), see p. 189, *infra.*
[3] *Ibid.*

(a) he may deny or refuse to admit the facts, or some of them, stated by the plaintiff;
(b) he may confess or admit them, and avoid their effect by asserting fresh facts which afford an answer to them;
(c) he may admit the facts stated by the plaintiff, and may raise a question of law as to their legal effect;
(d) he may state facts giving rise to a set-off; or
(e) he may plead a counterclaim.

Matters which must be specifically pleaded If the defendant intends to rely upon them, the following matters must be expressly pleaded:

(a) any matter which he alleges makes the claim of the plaintiff not maintainable, as, *e.g.* performance, release, any relevant statute of limitation, fraud, or any fact showing illegality[4];
(b) any matter which, if not specifically pleaded, might take the plaintiff by surprise[5]; or
(c) any matter which raises issues of fact not arising out of the statement of claim.[6]

Further Ord. where the statement of claim contains a claim for damages, the defendant must plead the particulars of any facts on which the party relies in mitigation of, or otherwise in relation to the amount of damages."

Pleading in the alternative Where the defendant relies on several distinct grounds of defence, set-off, or counterclaim, founded upon separate and distinct facts, they must be stated, as far as may be, separately and distinctly.[7] Any number of defences may be pleaded together—in the alternative or otherwise—although they are obviously inconsistent. A defendant may raise by his defence, without leave, as many distinct and separate, and therefore inconsistent, defences as he may think proper.

The overriding discretion of the court The ambit of the defendant's right to plead is circumscribed by the overriding power of the court to strike out or amend any defence or any part thereof which does not disclose a reasonable defence,[8] or is scandalous, frivolous or vexatious, or

---

[4] See R.S.C., Ord. 18, r. 8(1)(*a*).
[5] *Ibid.* r. 8(1)(*b*).
[6] *Ibid.* r. 8(1)(*c*).
[7] See the pre–1964 R.S.C., Ord. 20, r. 7, see note 12, p. 73, *supra.*
[8] See *Waters* v. *Sunday Pictorial Newspapers* [1961] 1 W.L.R. 967; [1961] 2 All E.R. 758; and see *Kemsley* v. *Foot* [1952] A.C. 345; [1952] 1 All E.R. 501; *Initial Services Ltd.* v.*Putterill* [1968] 1 Q.B. 396; [1967] 3 W.L.R. 1032; [1967] 3 All E.R. 145.

may tend to prejudice or embarrass or delay the fair trial of the action, or is otherwise an abuse of the process of the court.[9]

Defences which are not embarrassing A defence is not embarrassing merely because it contains:

(a) inconsistent averments,[10] provided such averments are not fictitious[11]; or
(b) prolix statements or a statement which the other party traverses as untrue.

Defences which are embarrassing It is embarrassing if a plea leaves the plaintiff in doubt as to what a defendant has admitted and what he has denied.[12]

Drafting the defence—considerations for the pleader Before drafting a defence, counsel for the defendant should:

(a) carefully consider the statement of claim and the way in which the action is framed against the defendant. It ought to be noted that the defence of want of jurisdiction should be specifically pleaded. But the court may allow an objection to the jurisdiction to be raised at the trial, though not previously raised by the pleadings, and will treat the pleadings as amended accordingly.[13] On the other hand, the defendant should not wait to plead this defence, but should, after giving notice of intention to defend and within the time limited for serving his defence, apply by summons or motion to stay or dismiss the action[14];
(b) if he thinks that no reasonable cause of action is shown at all, or that the only cause of action shown is frivolous, or vexatious, or otherwise an abuse of the process of the court, he may think it right to apply to strike out the statement of claim.[15] Such an application should be made promptly, as a rule before the defence is served;
(c) he should consider whether before service of the defence the claim is properly pleaded and whether any portion of it is scandalous or

---

[9] See R.S.C., Ord. 18, r. 19; and see p. 223 *infra*.
[10] *Child* v. *Stenning* (1877) 5 Ch.D. 695.
[11] *Re Morgan* (1887) 35 Ch.D. 492 at 496.
[12] *Fleming* v. *Dollar* (1888) 23 Q.B.D. 388.
[13] *Crosfield* v. *Manchester Ship Canal Co.* [1904] 2 Ch. 123 at 142 (C.A.).
[14] *Rothmans of Pall Mall (Overseas) Ltd.* v. *Saudi Arabian Airlines Corp.* [1981] Q.B. 368; [1980] 3 All E.R. 359 (C.A.).
[15] See R.S.C., Ord. 18, r. 19, and see p. 211 *et seq. infra*.

embarrassing, and if so he may think it right to apply to strike out such portion[16];

(d) he should further consider whether before service of the defence any further and better particulars of the statement of claim are necessary or desirable in order to enable him to plead, or for some other special reason, in which case he may consider it right to apply for such particulars before the defence,[17] or he may consider that he is entitled to such particulars but only after he has served his defence[18];

(e) he should also consider whether the action:

   (i) is fit for transfer to the Commercial Court[19]; or

  (ii) should be referred for trial as official referees' business[20]; or

 (iii) should be stayed under the Arbitration Act 1950, s.4, or Arbitration Act 1979, s.1, in which case application for such stay should be made before the service of the defence, or taking any other step in the action[21]; or

  (iv) should be transferred to the county court[22];

(f) the defendant's counsel must also consider whether the proper parties have been placed on the record. If he considers that the proper parties are not before the court, his remedy is to apply to add or strike out or substitute a plaintiff or defendant.[23] The court

---

[16] *Ibid.*

[17] See R.S.C., Ord. 18, r. 12(5).

[18] *Imasa Ltd.* v. *Technic Inc.* [1981] F.S.R. 554.

[19] See R.S.C., Ord. 72.

[20] See R.S.C., Ord. 36, r. 1.

[21] As to what is a "step in the action" within the meaning of this section, see *County Theatres, etc. Ltd.* v. *Knowles* [1902] 1 K.B. 480, followed in *Ochs* v. *Ochs* [1909] 2 Ch. 121; *Parker Gaines* v. *Turpin* [1918] 1 K.B. 358 (summonses for mutual discovery). Serving an affidavit in opposition to a summons under R.S.C., Ord. 14 and attending the first hearing consitutes a "step" in the action (see *Turner & Goudy* v. *McConnell* [1985] 1 W.L.R. 898; [1985] 2 All E.R. 34; *Rumput (Panama) S.A.* v. *Islamic Republic of Iran Shipping Lines, The Leage* [1984] 2 Lloyd's Rep. 259). On the other hand, opposing the summons under Ord. 14 but raising the matter of the arbitration clause and at the same time taking out a summons to stay the action does not amount to taking a "step." See *Supreme Court Practice,* Vol. 2, para. 5718. *Pitchers Ltd.* v. *Plaza (Queensbury) Ltd.* [1940] 1 All E.R. 151 (C.A.). As a general proposition, correspondence or negotiations between parties or their solicitors do not constitute a "step in the action" but an application to the court or the service of a pleading, including a request for particulars, does. The phrase "taking a step in the action" contemplates some positive procedural act on the part of the defendant rather than merely parrying a blow by the plaintiff (*Roussell-Oclof* v. *G.D. Searle & Co. Ltd.* [1978] 1 Lloyd's Rep. 225 (defending application for interlocutory injunction is a step)).

[22] See County Courts Act 1984, s.40 (actions in contract or tort): s.50 (actions for recovery of land): s.54 (equity proceedings).

[23] See R.S.C., Ord. 15, r. 6, and see *Kendall* v. *Hamilton* (1879) 4 App.Cas. 504; *Pilley* v. *Robinson* (1888) 20 Q.B.D. 155; *Performing Right Society* v. *London Theatre* [1924] A.C. 1.

will make an order to add a defendant more readily than to add a plaintiff.[24] Moreover, a fresh plaintiff cannot be added without his consent in writing.[25] However, the law regarding the joinder of defendants has been changed by virtue of the Civil Liability (Contribution) Act 1978, by virtue of which take the reference to the abrogation of para. (3) of r. 4 of Ord. 15, to the note, a defendant cannot apply to have a person added as a defendant on the ground that he is jointly liable with himself on the contract sued upon[26];

(g) if causes of action which cannot be conveniently tried together are joined in the same action, the court will order them to be tried separately,[27] or on the application of the defendant the court may give directions, confining the action to such of the causes of action as can conveniently be disposed of together, and excluding other claims[28];

(h) the defendant's counsel must further consider whether it is a proper case for bringing third party proceedings against a third party, in which case he will be entitled to do so without leave before the service of the defence[29];

(i) consideration must be given to the expiry of the relevant period of limitation, which defence must always be raised by an express plea[29a].

Pleading style

(a) *Each material fact should be pleaded to*   Counsel for the defendant should commence his pleading by dealing with the material facts alleged in the statement of claim in the order in which they are alleged, either

---

[24] *Wilson, Sons & Co.* v. *Balcarres, etc., Co.* [1983] 1. Q.B. 422; *Roberts* v. *Holland* [1893] 1 Q.B. 665.

[25] R.S.C., Ord. 15, r. 6(2).

[26] The result is that where the liability of two or more persons is several, or several as well as joint, the plaintiff may choose which of them he wishes to sue and he need not join, nor can he be compelled to join, the other persons also liable to him even if their liability is under a joint contract only. If the defendant desires to obtain a contribution or indemnity from the other joint co-contractor, he may make his claim to obtain a contribution under the 1978 Act or at common law, but this is no longer of any concern to the plaintiff. The defendant is no longer entitled to apply that all the persons jointly liable should be joined by the plaintiff as defendants in the action, and that unless and until he did so, the action should be stayed. The former practice regulating this procedure has ceased to apply (see the cases cited in *Supreme Court Practice 1979*, para. 15/4/10A).

[27] See R.S.C., Ord. 15, r. 5: *Bagot* v. *Easton* (1878) 7 Ch.D. 1; as to form of order limiting number of causes of action to be sued on, see *Saccharin Corpn.* v. *White* (1903) 88 L.T. 850.

[28] See R.S.C., Ord. 15, r. 5.

[29] See R.S.C., Ord. 16, r. 1.

[29a] See R.S.C., Ord. 18, r. 8(1).

admitting or traversing each of them. If he should omit to deny any material allegation of fact in the statement of claim or to state expressly that he does not admit it, *he will be deemed to admit it.*[30] This rule is of crucial importance in the machinery of pleadings, since it compels every allegation of fact in the statement of claim to be dealt with "matter by matter", and thus to ensure that the parties are brought clearly and precisely to defined issues.

(b) *Law need not be pleaded to*   He need not, however, traverse any allegation of law. Strictly, matters of law should not appear in a pleading. If the plaintiff in his statement of claim asserts a right in himself without showing on what facts his claim of right is founded, or asserts that the defendant is indebted to him or owes him a duty without alleging the facts out of which such indebtedness or duty arises, his pleading is bad and may be struck out. If, however, the plaintiff asserts certain facts and then states the inference of law which he draws from them, they will stand admitted unless the defendant expressly denies them. But he need not, though in practice he usually does, deny that they create the alleged right or duty. That is a question of law, which he should raise by an objection in point of law, on the argument of which he will be taken to have admitted such of the facts as are not specifically denied.

Defences can arise post writ   The defendant is entitled to plead any matter of defence which may have arisen subsequently to the commencement of the action upon a specific averment to that effect.[31]

Form of the Defence

Preamble   The defence must bear on its face the description that it is the "defence"[32] and the heading to a defence must be the same as that on the statement of claim to which it is pleaded with the exception of the words "writ issued on——19—." If only the initials of the first names of any parties appear on the statement of claim, the defendant may fill them in by setting out the full names; he may also correct any mis-spellings, *e.g.* Johnston for Johnson. At the end of the pleading must appear the signature of counsel or other person who drafted the pleading as in a statement of claim,[33] and also the words "Served on——19—by Messrs.——."

---

[30] See R.S.C., Ord. 18, r. 13(1).
[31] See R.S.C., Ord. 18, r. 9 and see *Champion* v. *Formby* (1878) 7 Ch.D. 373; *Barker* v. *Johnson* (1889) 60 L.T. 64.
[32] See R.S.C., Ord. 18, r. 6(1)(*d*).
[33] *Ibid.* r. 6(5).

Format   The defence is not required to follow any particular form, but:

(a) it must, if necessary, be divided into paragraphs numbered consecutively[34];

(b) each allegation must, so far as convenient, be contained in a separate paragraph[34];

(c) each distinct ground of defence should, therefore, be stated in a separate paragraph; and such paragraphs may be introduced by a few words of explanation;

(d) a paragraph which is applicable only to a part of a claim, or to one of several distinct grounds of claim, should be prefaced by words which show distinctly that it is pleaded only to that part of the plaintiff's claim or to that ground of claim to which it is germane. Thus:

    (i) "In the alternative the defendant says that. . . . ";

    (ii) "If, the defendant did [*so and so*], which he denies, he says that. . . . ";

    (iii) "If, contrary to what the defendant contends, the plaintiff did [*so and so*], the defendant says that. . . . ";

    (iv) "And in further answer to paragraph 3 of the Statement of Claim [*or* as to the alleged breach of the covenant to repair], the defendant says that. . . . ";

    (v) "As to £—, part of the money claimed by the plaintiff in this action, the defendant says that. . . . ";

(e) it is desirable both from the point of view of convenience and clarity to observe some kind of order in the framing of a defence, such as gathering together:

    (i) admissions and denials;

    (ii) objections in point of law;

    (iii) special defences;

    (iv) set-off;

    (v) counterclaim.

But the different grounds of claim alleged by the plaintiff should, where practicable, be dealt with *seriatim* in the order in which they are alleged.

Pleading to distinct grounds of claim   In dealing with each distinct ground of claim it is usually convenient to state the defences relied upon in the following order:

(a) Denials or refusals to admit, and any affirmative statements inserted for the purpose of explaining such denials or refusals to

---

[34] *Ibid.* r. 6(2).

admit, should precede any matter alleged by way of confession and avoidance.

(b) Of defences by way of confession and avoidance, those alleging a justification or excuse should generally be placed before those alleging a satisfaction or discharge.

(c) Ordinary defences, such as jurisdiction, leave and licence, payment or release, are frequently placed before more special and complicated ones. However, the general practice is to plead the expiry of any relevant limitation period at the end rather than the beginning of the defence.

(d) Where a particular plea affords an answer to two or more grounds of claim it may be pleaded with some words of introduction showing precisely to which grounds of claim it is intended to apply.

(e) A set-off or counterclaim is always reserved to the end.

(f) Where the defendant pleads an objection in point of law, as well as a defence upon the facts, such objection should if practicable be raised at the beginning.[35]

More than one defendant   Where there are two or more defendants, they may at their discretion either join in one defence or serve separate defences.[36] If separate defences are served in an action in which the plaintiff has but one and the same cause of action against all the defendants then, as a rule, the defence of one defendant is available to the other defendants.[37] Where they join in the same defence, they should traverse for both and also for each of them, thus:

> "the defendants deny that they were, or that either of them was, guilty of the alleged, or any, negligence as alleged or at all."

Where they sever in their defence, each must serve a separate pleading; these will be headed respectively, "Defence of the defendant *C.D.*" and "Defence of the defendant *E.F.* "

Admissions—Express or Implied by Non-Traverse

Admissions may be express or implied   An admission in the defence[38]

---

[35] Presumably such a defence would assume that the facts pleaded by the plaintiff are not being challenged and on that footing, the court may be asked under R.S.C., Ord. 33, r. 3 to order the trial of a preliminary issue as the point of law raised.

[36] For exceptions to this rule, see *Earle* v. *Kingscote* [1900] 1 Ch. 203; *Cole* v. *De Trafford and Wife* [1917] 1 K.B. 911; *Liverpool Adelphi Loan Association* v. *Fairhurst* (1854) 9 Ex. 422. As to joint tortfeasors who sever in their defence, see *Greelands Ltd.* v. *Wilmshurst* [1913] 3 K.B. 507.

[37] *Pirie* v. *Richardson* [1927] 1 K.B. 448.

[38] An admission made in a pleading, which is to be encouraged, should be distinguished from pleading an admission which is not permitted as it is contrary to the basic rule

may be made expressly, or may arise by implication from the non-traverse of a material fact in the statement of claim.[39]

What should be admitted   The defendant ought properly to admit in his defence material facts as to which there is really no controversy, and conversely he ought not to deny plain and acknowledged facts which it is neither in his interest nor in his power to disprove.[40]

How to admit   An express admission in the pleading ought to be clear, bold and unambiguous, and should specify precisely what it is that is being admitted. Furthermore, it is an undesirable practice to make what is substantially an affirmative allegation under the guise of an "admission."

Implied admissions   An implied admission arises in the defence where the defendant does not traverse any allegation of fact made by the plaintiff in his statement of claim. This is the effect of the general rule that any allegation of fact made by a party in his pleading, save as to damages, is deemed to be admitted unless it is traversed by the party in his pleading, or a joinder of issue operates as a denial of it.[41] The effect of a traverse, if properly pleaded, is that the party who makes the allegation has to prove it; the effect of an allegation which is admitted or treated as admitted is that the party who makes it need not prove it. Thus, if the facts pleaded in the statement of claim are admitted, there is no issue between the parties on that part of the case which is concerned with those matters of fact and, therefore, no evidence is admissible in reference to those facts.[42] An implied admission has the same value and effect as if it were an express

---

precluding the pleading of the evidence, see R.S.C., Ord. 18, r. 7(1). An admission by a party may be made "by his pleading or otherwise in writing, that he admits the truth of the whole or any part of the case of any other party" (R.S.C., Ord. 27, r. 1). Moreover, either party may serve on the other, not later than 21 days after the action is set down for trial or any extended time, a notice requiring him to admit, for the purpose of that cause or matter only, such facts or such part of his case as may be specified in the notice (see R.S.C., Ord. 27, r. 2(1)), and unless the facts specified in such notice are admitted within seven days or any extended time, the costs of proving such facts must be paid by the opposite party unless the court otherwise orders (see R.S.C., Ord. 62, r. 6(7)). Further, "[at] the hearing of the summons for directions, the Court shall endeavour to secure that the parties make all admissions . . . which ought reasonably to be made by them . . . " (R.S.C., Ord. 25, r. 4).

[39] See R.S.C., Ord. 18, r. 13(1).
[40] See *Lee Conservancy Board* v. *Button* (1879) 12 Ch.D. 383, *per* Malins V.-C., affirmed (1881) 6 A.C. 685.
[41] R.S.C., Ord. 18 r. 13(1). The rule applies equally to a counterclaim, see R.S.C., Ord. 18 r. 13(3).
[42] *Pioneer Plastic Containers Ltd.* v. *Commissioners of Customs and Exercise* [1967] Ch. 597; [1967] 2 W.L.R. 1085 [1967] 1 All E.R. 1053.

admission,[43] but of course the plaintiff must show that the matters in question are clearly pleaded in order to fix the defendant with an admission.[44]

Circumstances where an implied admission does not arise   An implied admission by non-traverse will, however, not arise, where:

(a) there is a denial by joinder of issue[45]; or
(b) there is an omission to plead to the claim for damages[46]; or
(c) there is an omission to plead to particulars[47]; or
(d) the defence of an infant or a patient is concerned.[48]

Advantages of making admissions

(a) *Costs*   It is not always advisable to traverse every disputed allegation in the statement of claim, since to do so may render the defendant liable to costs, which he might have avoided by admitting facts which the plaintiff will be required to prove and which he is in no position reasonably to controvert or challenge.[49]

(b) *The right to begin*   By making proper and sufficient admissions, the defendant may be able to obtain the right to begin at the trial, and thereby also the right to reply, since if the proof of any issue at the trial lies upon the plaintiff, he has the right to begin, which also generally involves the right to reply.[50]

Tactical denials   On the other hand, it is sometimes important to traverse an allegation in the statement of claim, in order to compel the plaintiff to call a particular witness whom the defendant may wish to cross-examine so as to prove some fact which is essential to his case, as for the purpose of cross-examining the witness on other matters material to the case.[51]

---

[43] See *Byrd* v. *Nunn* (1877) 5 Ch.D. 781, affirmed 7 Ch.D. 284, (C.A.); *Green* v. *Sevin* (1879) 13 Ch.D. 589; *Collette* v. *Goode* (1878) 7 Ch.D. 842 (specific denial held to qualify general denial); *Symonds* v. *Jenkins* (1876) 34 L.T. 277 (title not denied).
[44] *Ash* v. *Hutchinson & Co. (Publishers)* [1936] Ch. 489 at 503.
[45] R.S.C., Ord. 18, r. 14. Any allegation as to the amount of damages must be separately traversed.
[46] *Ibid.* r. 13(4).
[47] See *Chapple* v. *Electrical Trades Union* [1961] 1 W.L.R. 1290.
[48] See R.S.C., Ord. 80, r. 8.
[49] *Cf.* R.S.C., Ord. 62, r. 6(7).
[50] See *Grunther Industrial Developments* v. *Federated Employers Insurance Association* [1973] 1 Lloyd's Rep. 394 (C.A.); *Seldon* v. *Davidson* [1968] 1 W.L.R. 1083; [1968] 2 All E.R. 755; *Mercer* v. *Whall* (1845) 5 Q.B. 447; and, as to the order of speeches, see R.S.C., Ord. 35, r. 7.
[51] See *Pinson* v. *Lloyds and National Provincial Foreign Bank Ltd.* [1941] 2 K.B. 72, *per* Stable J. at 82.

Withdrawing an admission   In a proper case, a party who has made any admission unwarily or under a bona fide mistake or prematurely will be allowed to amend or withdraw it on such terms as may be just.[52]

Admissions—no particulars   Particulars will not be ordered of an admission, express or implied, made in a pleading.[53]

Judgment on admissions   Where sufficient admissions are made by the defendant, by his defence or otherwise, the plaintiff may apply for such judgment or order as from those admissions he may be entitled to, without waiting for the trial; and the court may give such judgment or make such order on such application as it thinks just.[54]

Traverse by Denial or Non-Admission

Traverse—what is it   A traverse in the defence is a denial of an allegation of fact made in the statement of claim.

What does a traverse do

(a) It negates such an allegation.
(b) It operates to contradict what is alleged and to put it in issue.
(c) It casts upon the plaintiff the burden of proving the allegations denied.[55]

In principle, there is no reason why the defendant should not put the plaintiff to the proof of his whole case. Indeed it is a legitimate and well-recognised method of pleading, which on occasion may serve a useful purpose.[55a]

Traverse—how?   A traverse must be made by a denial or by a statement of non-admission; and it may be made either expressly or by necessary implication.[56]

Every allegation of fact made in the statement of claim, except as to damages, which the defendant does not intend to admit must be specifi-

---

[52] *Hollis v. Burton* [1892] 3 Ch. 226. *Cf.* R.S.C., Ord. 27, r. 2(2).
[53] *Fox v. H. Wood (Harrow) Ltd.* [1963] 2 Q.B. 601 (C.A.).
[54] See R.S.C., Ord. 27, r. 3, see *Guinness plc v. Saunders* [1990] 2 W.L.R. 324; [1990] 1 All E.R. 652 (H.L.); (C.A.). The jurisdiction of the court under this rule is discretionary, see *Lancashire Welders Ltd. v. Harland & Wolff Ltd.* [1950] 2 All E.R. 1096; *Showell v. Bowron* (1883) 52 L.J.Q.B. 284; *Mersey Steamship Co. v. Shuttleworth & Co.* (1883) 11 Q.B.D. 531. Such application may be made even after the action is set down for trial (see *Rutter v. Tregent* (1879) 12 Ch.D. 758; *Brown v. Pearson* (1882) 21 Ch.D. 716; *Smith v. Davies* (1884) 28 Ch.D. 650), but the plaintiff may be penalised in costs for his delay (see *Tottenham v. Foley* [1909] 2 Ir.R. 500 (C.A.)).
[55] See Bullen and Leake, *Precedents of Pleading* (3rd ed.,) p. 436.
[55a] See "Tactical Denials" on p. 120.
[56] R.S.C., Ord. 18, r. 13(2).

cally traversed by him in his defence. A general denial of such allegations or a general statement of non-admission of them is not a sufficient traverse of them.[57]

Bad pleading   The rule requiring the traverse to be specific applies equally whether by his traverse the defendant "denies" or "does not admit." The refusal to admit must be stated as specifically as a denial, so that the plaintiff will thereby know precisely what is admitted and what is put in issue.[58] Thus, a statement in the defence that "the defendant puts the plaintiff to proof of the several allegations" in the statement of claim is not a proper or sufficient traverse,[59] nor is it a proper or sufficient traverse for the defendant to plead that he "does not admit the correctness of the statements set forth in paragraphs 1, 2, 3 and 6 of the statement of claim and requests further proof thereof."[60]

Denying and not admitting—interactions   There is no difference in effect between *denying* and *not admitting* an allegation.[61] The distinction usually observed is that a party denies any matter which, if it had occurred, would have been within his own knowledge, while he refuses to admit matters which are not within his own knowledge. Sometimes the distinction is simply a matter of emphasis, a denial being more emphatic than a non-admission. In short, a traverse must not be ambiguous or equivocal or evasive.[62] The defendant may, of course, admit one portion of a statement made by the plaintiff and at the same time deny another portion of it, provided he makes it perfectly clear how much he admits and how much he denies. Thus, he may say:

> "The defendant admits that he made to the plaintiff the representation set out in paragraph 3 of the statement of claim, but denies that he did so falsely or fraudulently or with any intention to mislead the plaintiff as alleged or at all."

Traverse must be Specific, not General

Each material fact must be traversed   As the effect of the traverse in the defence is to contradict an allegation of fact[63] in the statement of claim, it

---

[57] R.S.C., Ord. 18. r. 13(3). The rule applies equally to the counterclaim as to the defence to counterclaim, *ibid.*

[58] *Thorpe v. Holdsworth* (1876) 3 Ch.D. 637 at 640; *Hall v. London and North Western Ry.* (1877) 35 L.T. 848 at 849; *Smith v. Gamlen* [1881] W.N. 110.

[59] *Harris v. Gamble* (1878) 7 Ch.D. 877.

[60] *Rutter v. Tregent* (1879) 12 Ch.D. 758.

[61] See *Hall v. London and North Western Ry.* (1877) 35 L.T. 848, *per* Grove J.; and *Warner v. Sampson* [1959] 1 Q.B. 297, *per* Hodson L.J. at 319.

[62] See p. 126 *infra.*

[63] See *Supreme Court Practice 1991.*

must not be vague or general or evasive. Rather it must be specific and must deal with each allegation of fact and, as regards each, must answer the point of substance.[64]

Examples

(a) *Debt*　In an action for a debt or liquidated demand, a mere denial of the debt is inadmissible.[65] It does not operate as a traverse, which should deal specifically with the facts relied on as giving rise to the debt such as a claim for the price of goods sold or work done or services rendered or a loan or as the case may be.

(b) *Bill of exchange*　In an action on a bill of exchange, promissory note or cheque, a defence must deny some matter of fact, such as the drawing, making, endorsing, accepting, presenting or notice of dishonour.[66]

(c) *Sale of goods*　In an action for goods bargained and sold or sold and delivered, a defence in denial must deny the order or contract, the delivery or the amount claimed.

(d) *Money had and received*　In an action for money had and received, a defence in denial must deny the receipt of the money or the existence of those facts which are alleged to make such receipt by the defendant a receipt to the use of the plaintiff.[67]

(e) *Copyright*　If the plaintiff alleges that the defendant has infringed his copyright, the defendant must deny each act of infringement alleged, and also, if he wishes, the validity of the plaintiff's copyright.

It is, however, only necessary to deal in this way with the main allegations which are the foundation of the action, *e.g.* those which assert that the parties entered into a certain contract, or that the defendant committed a certain tort. In such cases, if the terms of the contract are set out in the claim, the defendant must deny specifically each term which he disputes.

Matters of inducement　There are, in most statements of claim, certain introductory averments which are known as "matters of inducement," *i.e.* matters which are explanatory only of the facts and not essential to the cause of action. All these matters may be answered by the defendant by a general denial, such as, "save as hereinbefore expressly admitted the defendant denies each and every allegation contained in the statement of

---

[64] See *Thorp* v. *Holdsworth* (1876) 3 Ch.D. 637 at 639, 640; *Tildesley* v. *Harper* (1878) 7 Ch.D. 403; *British and Colonial Land Association* v. *Foster & Robins* (1888) 4 T.L.R. 574.

[65] See the pre-1964 R.S.C., Ord. 21, r. 1.

[66] See the pre-1964 R.S.C., Ord. 21, r. 2.

[67] See the former R.S.C., Ord. 21, r. 2.

claim as though each such allegation was herein set out and specifically traversed." This will have the same effect as if he had separately set out each of such allegations and then sepecifically denied it. It is often useful to use this comprehensive form of traverse in dealing with a lengthy statement of claim.[68]

Matters of law   The requirement that every traverse must be specific, applies only to allegation of fact and, therefore, matters of law should not be traversed.

Deny only what in fact is claimed   The defendant should not traverse any matter which the plaintiff has not actually alleged against him, although he might or ought to have done so.[69]

Cross bridges only when one comes to them   Do not anticipate any matter the plaintiff might raise in his reply.

Damages, etc.   Although the defendant is not strictly required to traverse the claim for damages or their amount,[70] or matters alleged as particulars, or the prayer or claim for relief, it is nevertheless common practice for the defendant to deal specifically with these allegations and to traverse them by denial or non-admission. If, however, the defendant intends himself to raise specific questions or issues in relation to damages, such as, *e.g.* that they are too remote and are not recoverable or that they were not caused or contributed to by the wrongful acts complained of, he must specifically raise such issues as to remoteness or causation in his defence.

Every material fact must be dealt with   Because the traverse is generally expressed in the negative, it is especially necessary to be careful that *every* material allegation of fact is specifically dealt with. Thus, in traversing a statement it is generally necessary to change the word "and," whenever it occurs, into "or" and the word "all" into "any." Thus, if the plaintiff asserts:

> "The defendant broke and entered the said shop and seized, took and carried away all the furniture, stock-in-trade, and other effects which were therein.";

the correct traverse will be:

> "The defendant denies that he broke or entered the said shop or seized, took or carried away any of the furniture, stock-in-trade, or

[68] See *Adkins v. North Metropolitan Tramways Co.* (1893) 63 L.J.Q.B. 361; *Lancaster (John) Radiators Ltd.* v. *General Motor Radiator Co.* [1946] 2 All E.R. 685, (C.A.); and see p. 126 *infra*.
[69] *Rassam* v. *Budge* [1893] 1 Q.B. 571.
[70] See R.S.C., Ord. 18, r. 13(4).

other effects which were therein, as alleged in (paragraph—) of the statement of claim or at all."

Compound averments   Sometimes two traverses are necessary completely to deny one allegation in the statement of claim. This is so whenever it is desired to traverse a compound allegation, consisting of several distinct facts. Thus, if the plaintiff has averred that:

"The defendant broke and entered the plaintiff's close called Blackacre.";

the defendant, if he wishes to deny at the trial not merely the alleged trespasses, but also the ownership of the close, must expressly traverse both, and each in a separate paragraph, thus:

"1. The defendant denies that the close called Blackacre is or was the plaintiff's close as alleged or at all;
2. The defendant denies that he broke or entered the said close as alleged or at all."

In fact, each several allegation contained in a statement of claim which is denied by the defendant should be categorically denied in the defence.

A bill of lading example   If the statement of claim alleges that "a bill of lading of goods shipped by the plaintiff was signed by *A B* as the defendant's agent," it would not be correct simply to state in the defence that the defendant denies or does not admit the paragraph in question. The proper mode of denying such a paragraph is to single out the particular part of it which the defendant desires to deny *e.g.* that *A B* was the defendant's agent, and to deny that only. Alternatively, if it is desired to deny the whole, then the defence should break up the compound allegation and deny each part of it separately. Thus, the defendant might plead two or more of the following allegations:

(a) No goods were shipped by the plaintiff.
(b) No bill of lading was given for any goods shipped by the plaintiff.
(c) No bill of lading for any goods shipped by the plaintiff was signed by *A B* as the defendant's agent.
(d) *A B* was not the defendant's agent to sign any such bill.
(e) No bill of lading for any goods shipped by the plaintiff was signed by any agent of the defendant.

Historical background to the sweeping up traverse   Although a general denial or a general statement of non-admission of allegations of fact is not a sufficient traverse of them[71] and although the practice until 1893

---

[71] See R.S.C., Ord. 18, r. 13(3).

required the defendant to traverse specifically every allegation of fact made in the statement of claim,[72] yet since 1893[73] it has become common practice for the defendant to plead a general denial or general statement of non-admission, provided, however, he is specific when he does so, as for example:

> "each of the allegations contained in paragraph [6] of the statement of claim is denied"; or
> "each of the allegations contained in paragraph [6] of the statement of claim is denied other than [*some allegation*] which is specifically admitted."[74]

The principle is that it is not necessary for the pleader to copy out each allegation of fact which he denies or refuses to admit, so long as he makes clear which allegation of fact he is traversing.[75] Indeed, nowadays, almost every defence contains a sweeping general denial, as for example:

> "Save as is hereinbefore expressly admitted, the defendant denies each and every allegation contained in the statement of claim as though the same were herein set out and traversed seriatim."[76]

This practice should not generally be adopted in dealing with essential allegations, which should be traversed specifically.[77] It is nevertheless a convenient practice in dealing with a long or complicated statement of claim, especially with allegations which are more or less immaterial, or to ensure that there will be no implied admission arising from the non-traverse of a material allegation.[78]

Traverse must not be Evasive

The principle Where the defendant traverses any allegation of fact in the statement of claim, whether by denial or refusal to admit, he must not

---

[72] See *Thorp* v. *Holdsworth* (1876) 3 Ch.D. 637; *Byrd* v. *Nunn* (1878) 7 Ch.D. 284 at 287; *Jones* v. *Quinn* (1878) 40 L.T. 135; *Green* v. *Sevin* (1879) 13 Ch.D. 589 at 594, 595.
[73] See *Adkins* v. *North Metropolitan Tramways Co.* (1893) 63 L.J.Q.B. 361.
[74] *Ibid*; and see also *Harris* v. *Gamble* (1878) 7 Ch.D. 877; *Smith* v. *Gamlen* [1881] W.N. 110; *Rutter* v. *Tregent* (1879) 12 Ch.D. 758; *British and Colonial Land Association* v. *Foster and Robins* (1888) 4 T.L.R. 574; *Burdett and Harris* v. *Humphage* (1892) 92 L.T.J. 294. An extreme instance of the use of the general denial is the case of *Lancaster (John) Radiators Ltd.* v. *General Motor Radiator Co. Ltd.* [1946] 2 All E.R. 685 (C.A.).
[75] See *Grocott* v. *Lovatt* [1916] W.N. 317: general denial held sufficient though irregular.
[76] See *Warner* v. *Sampson* [1959] 1 Q.B. 297, Lord Denning M.R. at 310–311.
[77] See *Wallersteiner* v. *Moir* [1974] 1 W.L.R. 991, Lord Denning M.R. at 1002.
[78] See R.S.C., Ord. 18 r. 13(1), and see p. 118 *supra*.

do so evasively but must answer the point of substance.[79] This is a basic rule of pleading, since a traverse which is evasive,[80] or ambiguous, or equivocal or does not answer the point of substance will not amount to a specific traverse of the allegation. Thus, if it be alleged that the defendant received a certain sum of money, it will not be sufficient to deny that he received *that* particular sum. He must deny that he received that sum or any part thereof or else set out how much he received.[81] As a further example, if the allegation is made with divers circumstances it will not be sufficient to deny it along with those circumstances.[82] In such case, the allegation of each circumstance should be traversed specifically.

Avoid the incomplete admission The defendant must deal specifically with every allegation of fact made by the plaintiff. He must clearly admit or deny it. Any half-admission or half-denial is evasive. Thus, where it is alleged that an agreement or terms of arrangement were arrived at, a defence in these words "The terms of the arrangement were never definitely agreed upon as alleged" is evasive.[83] As Jessel M.R. said[84]:

> "[The defendant] is bound to deny that any agreements or any terms of arrangement were ever come to, if that is what he means; if he does not mean that, he should say that there were no terms of arrangement come to, except the following terms, and then state what the terms were; . . . "

The defence therefore, must not contain evasive denials or denials which are ambiguous or do not show clearly what are the specific facts that are denied and thus placed in issue between the parties.

Dealing with the real point of substance The phrase "answering the point of substance" in this connection means the real gist and significance of the allegation traversed as distinct from comparatively immaterial details. A traverse is usually framed in terms of the allegation denied. But there is danger in following those terms too closely, as to do so might often render it doubtful how much the defendant intended to admit and how much he wishes to deny. The defendant must make the purport and effect of his denial clear and distinct,[85] Thus,

---

[79] R.S.C., Ord. 18, r. 13(1); and see *Byrd* v. *Nunn* (1877) 5 Ch.D. 781, affirmed 7 Ch.D. 284 (authority of agent not specifically put in issue); *Collette* v. *Goode* (1878) 7 Ch.D. 842 (specific denials qualify general denial); *Tildesley* v. *Harper* (1878) 7 Ch.D. 403, affirmed 10 Ch.D. 93.

[80] See the pre-1964 R.S.C., Ord. 19, r. 19.

[81] See pre-1964 R.S.C., Ord. 19, r. 19.

[82] *Ibid.*; and see *Lane* v. *Alexander* (1608) Yel. 122.

[83] *Thorp* v. *Holdsworth* (1876) 3 Ch.D. 637.

[84] *Ibid.* at 641.

[85] *Thorp* v. *Holdsworth* (1876) 3 Ch.D. 637.

THE DEFENCE

(a) If the plaintiff asserts that—"the defendant on——19—, offered Edward Smith, the plaintiff's manager, a bribe of £—," it is evasive for the defendant to plead merely: "the defendant denies that he on——19—, offered Edward Smith, the plaintiff's manager, a bribe of £—,".[86]

This would be consistent with his having offered Smith a bribe of £— on some other day or a bribe of a different amount on the day specified. The substance of the allegation is that a bribe was offered, and this must be denied in a certain manner which leaves no room for doubt. The proper traverse would be: "The defendant denies that he offered the alleged or any bribe to Edward Smith or any other servant or agent of the plaintiff as alleged or at all.".

(b) If the statement of claim contains an allegation that the defendant did a certain act in a certain manner, e.g. that he wrongfully entered certain premises or unlawfully removed certain goods, a literal traverse of this allegation—such as, "The defendant never wrongfully entered the said premises," or "the defendant denies that he unlawfully removed the said goods"—would be ambiguous. It is not clear whether the defendant intends to deny the fact of entry or removal, or whether he means to assert that he had a right to act as he did. Such a traverse will be construed as denying the bare act only, and not its wrongful character under the particular circumstances.[87] The defect may often be cured by adding the phase "or at all," if the defendant desires to raise both points, e.g. "the defendant never entered the said premises wrongfully, or at all." But it is better as a rule to raise each defence in a separate paragraph or clause, alleging in the first that "the defendant never entered the said premises," and in the second setting out the facts which justify the entry, if any.

(c) A literal traverse of the allegation, so frequent in a statement of claim for defamation, that "the defendant falsely and maliciously wrote (or spoke) certain words" is open to the same objection. It purports to be merely a denial of the fact of publication, but it insinuates two additional defences, justification and privilege, both of which pleas must be specially pleaded.[88]

Traverse material facts—not particulars A plaintiff, when alleging a material fact, should add details of time and place and amount or other surrounding circumstances. But it is not proper for the defendant, when

[86] See *Tildesley* v. *Harper* (1878) 7 Ch.D. 403.
[87] See *Myn* v. *Cole* (1606) Cro.Jac. 87.
[88] *Belt* v. *Lawes* (1882) 51 L.J.Q.B. 359; *Penrhyn* v. *Licensed Victuallers' Mirror* (1890) 7 T.L.R. 1; *Fleming* v. *Dollar* (1889) 23 Q.B.D. 388.

denying that material fact, to traverse at the same time those details and circumstances; for by so doing he will obscure the issue and render it impossible for the plaintiff certainly to know what it is that the defendant really means to dispute. Thus, if the statement of claim alleges that the plaintiff and the defendant entered into a certain agreement on such a date and at such a place, it would be improper for the defendant simply to aver in his defence, "The defendant never agreed as alleged." He should add some words, such as "or at all," to show that he is not merely denying that the agreement was entered into on that day or at that place. So, if the allegation was:

> "The plaintiff handed £137 to the defendant at his office, No. 286 Fleet Street, E.C., in the presence of A B,"

the correct traverse would be simply:

> "The plaintiff denies that he handed to the defendant £137 or any other sum as alleged or at all."

Denial of Negative Allegation

The negative pregnant problem   The defendant should take special care when he traverses a negative allegation made in a statement of claim. Such a traverse necessarily involves a double negative. Although in ordinary parlance a double negative must involve an affirmative proposition, for the purposes of pleading, the denial of a negative allegation does not necessarily involve the making of a positive or affirmative proposition.[89] Whether it does so or not depends upon whether it is a *mere* traverse or a traverse which, though negative in form, is pregnant with an affirmative.

A denial to a negative does not necessarily generate a negative pregnant   In the first place, therefore, the denial of a negative allegation may operate as a bare traverse and no more, whereby the defendant simply puts the plaintiff to the proof of the negative alleged.[90] In such case, if it is not possible to read into the mere denial of a negative allegation any affirmative allegation beyond that which is necessarily implied from such a traverse, particulars will not be ordered.[91] In such a case, however, once the plaintiff establishes a prima facie case, the defendant will be pre-

---

[89] See *Pinson* v. *Lloyds and National Provincial Foreign Bank Ltd.* [1941] 2 K.B. 72, *per* Stable J. at 84.
[90] *Ibid.*; *Weinburger* v. *Inglis* [1918] 1 Ch. 133; *La Radiotechnique* v. *Weinbaum* [1928] Ch. 1.
[91] *Ibid.*; and see *Dukes' Court Estates Ltd.* v. *Associated British Eningeering Ltd.* [1948] Ch. 458; *Chapple* v. *Electrical Trades Union* [1961] 1 W.L.R. 1290.

cluded from setting up an affirmative case in answer, for that would be to set up a case which he has not pleaded.[92]

Particularising the negative pregnant   On the other hand, the denial of a negative allegation may contain either the double negative or affirmative allegation and nonetheless so because the affirmative case is concealed albeit imperfectly, in a negative shell. If, therefore, it is clear to the court either from the nature of the case or from the admission of counsel or otherwise, that it is intended to set up an affirmative case, particulars of such an affirmative case must be given or will be ordered, for otherwise there will be doubt as to what are the issues to be determined between the parties.[93]

Denial of a negative allegation—may be embarrassing   Where the denial of a negative allegation leaves the matter in doubt as to what its true nature is, the pleading will be defective as embarrassing and evasive and it will be either ordered to be struck out, or amended, or particulars may be ordered of any affirmative case relied on.

Special Grounds of Defence

Introduction   The defendant must in his defence specifically plead any matter, *e.g.* performance, release, any relevant statute of limitation, fraud, or any fact showing illegality:

(a) which he alleges makes any claim of the plaintiff not maintainable; or
(b) which, if not specifically pleaded, might take the plaintiff by surprise; or
(c) which raises issues of fact not arising out of the statement of claim.[94]

In addition the defendant in an action for the recovery of land must plead specifically every ground of defence on which he relies, and a plea that he is in possession of the land by himself or his tenant is not sufficient.[95]

---

[92] *Ibid.* Hence particulars were refused of mere denials of negative allegations: *Howard* v. *Borneman* [1972] 1 W.L.R. 863.

[93] *Machulich* v. *Machulich* [1920] P. 439 (denial of acting without reasonable cause); *Pinson* v. *Lloyds and National Provincial Foreign Bank Ltd. supra* (denial of acting without authority); *I.R.C.* v. *Jackson* [1960] 1 W.L.R. 873 (denial of failure to comply with notice without reasonable excuse).

[94] R.S.C., Ord. 18, r. 8(1). As to release, see p. 132 *infra*.

[95] R.S.C., Ord. 18, r. 8(2). This rule abolishes an obsolete survival of the pre-1964 system of pleading the general issue, under which (see the former R.S.C., Ord. 21, r. 21) a plea that the defendant was in possession of the land by himself or his tenant put in issue the whole of the plaintiff's case.

These requirements operate to compel the defendant who intends to raise a special ground of defence or to raise an affirmative case to destroy any claim of the plaintiff, to plead specifically the matter he relies on for such purpose. Contributory negligence must be specifically pleaded by way of defence to a plaintiff's claim for negligence, and in the absence of such a plea, the trial judge is not entitled to find that the plaintiff's negligence had contributed to the accident.[96] Such defences must not be insinuated under an apparent traverse. Charges of dishonesty, cruelty, bad workmanship or other misconduct, etc., must always be specifically pleaded, as it would be manifestly unfair that the defendant should be allowed to give evidence of any such matters without previous notice to the plaintiff. All equitable defences must be specifically pleaded and with due particularity. Similarly, a failure to plead negligence against a specified person precludes the court from finding that person guilty of negligence.[97]

Purpose of the rule   Accordingly the defendant has the duty to state any special defence or any new fact on which he will rely at the trial,[98] as otherwise the plaintiff may legitimately complain that he has been taken by surprise. These fresh facts must be pleaded in a summary form, and yet with sufficient particularity to enable the plaintiff to know what is the case which he will have to meet; though of course the evidence by which they are to be proved need not be stated.

Whether the action be founded on contract or on tort, all new facts or special defences must be expressly pleaded. Thus, when a contract, promise, or agreement is alleged in the statement of claim, a bare denial by the defendant will be constructed only as a denial in fact of the express contract, promise, or agreement alleged or of the matters of fact from which the same may be implied by law, and not as a denial of the legality or sufficiency in law of such contract, promise, or agreement.[99] It is, therefore, often not enough for the defendant to deny an allegation in the statement of claim; he must go further and dispute its validity in law or set up some affirmative case of his own in answer to it.

Special defence and traverse—interactions   A special defence differs in its essence from a traverse. The office of a traverse is to contradict, not to

---

[96] *Fookes* v. *Slaytor* [1978] 1 W.L.R. 1293 (C.A.). See also *Supreme Court Practice*, Vol. 1, para. 18/12/8.
[97] *Farrell* v. *Secretary of State for Defence* [1980] 1 W.L.R. 72 (H.L.).
[98] See *Re Robinson's Settlement, Gant* v. *Hobbs* [1912] 1 Ch. 717, *per* Buckley L.J. at 728. The court nevertheless has power to give effect to defences which are not pleaded, *ibid.*; and see *Pirie* v. *Richardson* [1927] 1 K.B. 448 at 453.
[99] See the pre-1964 R.S.C., Ord. 20, r. 19; see p. 132 *infra*.

excuse or justify, the act complained of. Its object is to compel the plaintiff to prove the truth of the allegation traversed, not to dispute its sufficiency in point of law. All matters justifying or excusing the act complained of must be specially and separately pleaded.[1] In other words, a traverse denies; a special defence, as a rule, "confesses and avoids." For example:

(a) It is one thing for a defendant to deny that he entered into the contract alleged in the statement of claim; it is another thing for him to admit that he did so contract and then plead new matters to show that the contract was void from its inception or that it has been subsequently rescinded or performed.

(b) Again, where the plaintiff complains of acts done by the defendant which are prima facie tortious, it is one thing for the defendant to deny that he ever did such acts, and quite another thing for him to admit that he did the acts and then assert that he was justified in doing them by reason of certain facts not hitherto mentioned.

(c) If he simply denies that he ever entered into a contract he will not be permitted to set up at the trial that he was induced to enter into it by fraud or that it was made for an illegal consideration, or that it was a wager within the Gaming Act 1845,[2] or that the plaintiff's right of action, if any, is barred by the Limitation Act 1980 or the expiry of any other limitation period.

(d) If the plaintiff complains that the defendant has trespassed upon his freehold farm, and the defendant merely denies that the plaintiff is the owner in fee simple of that farm, he cannot at the trial set up that he holds an unexpired lease of the farm and therefore was entitled to enter thereon.[3]

(e) A mere denial of an allegation that the defendant assaulted or beat the plaintiff will not enable the defendant to maintain at the trial that he did so in self-defence.

(f) Nor will the bare averment that the defendant never spoke or published libellous words "falsely, maliciously, or at all" entitle him to contend that the words were true or that they were spoken on a privileged occasion.

---

[1] *Att.-Gen.* v. *Mayor of Sheffield* (1912) 106 L.T. 367.

[2] The defence that a contract is a wager within the Gaming Acts 1845–1892, must be specifically pleaded; and the facts which are relied on to bring the transaction within either of those Acts must be stated: *Colborne* v. *Stockdale* (1710) 1 Strange 493; *Grizewood* v. *Blane* (1852) 11 C.B. 526; *Harmer* v. *Rowe* (1827) 6 M. & S. 146; *Willis* v. *Lovick* [1901] 2 K.B. 195; and see *Ladup Ltd.* v. *Shaikh* [1983] Q.B. 225; [1982] 3 W.L.R. 172 (illegality under Gaming Act 1968, s.16(1)).

[3] See *Doe* v. *Wright* (1839) 10 Ad. & E. 763; *Ryan* v. *Clark* (1849) 14 Q.B.D. 65; *Delaney* v. *T. P. Smith Ltd.* [1946] K.B. 393.

(g) Particulars of a defence that the plaintiff is abusing a dominant position within the EEC contrary to Article 86 of the Treaty of Rome must be given. A mere general denial is embarrassing because the defendant does not know what case he has to meet, or what matters are relevant to discovery.[4]

(h) The circumstances in which the defence of "Act of State" is available are very ill-defined, and it is still in the process of being worked out in the cases. It is for the courts to determine in any particular case, if it comes up, whether as a matter of policy (*i.e.* the policy of the law) the defence of Act of State should be available.[5]

Pleading techniques for special defences Any number of defences may be pleaded together, although obviously inconsistent with each other, providing they are not embarrassing; but each special defence must be stated clearly and distinctly and in a separate paragraph.

Moreover, each defence by way of justification or excuse must cover the whole ground of the claim to which it is pleaded, unless it be intended to apply to a part only of such claim, in which case it should be limited by prefix "As to so much of the statement of claim as alleges, etc.," or, "As to paragraph 4 of the statement of claim."

Special defences can be pleaded with traverses Both traverses and special defences can be pleaded to the same statement of claim, but the special defence must not be mixed up with the traverse or embodied into a plea denying the facts alleged.[6] Consequently, the defendant must be careful not merely to traverse where he ought to plead a special defence.

Confession and Avoidance

Meaning The term "confession and avoidance" is the description of a plea in the defence which, while expressly or impliedly admitting or confessing or assuming the truth of the material facts alleged in the statement of claim, seeks at the same time to avoid or destroy the legal consequences of those facts. The plea is invoked by alleging fresh or additional facts to establish some legal justification or excuse, or some other ground for avoiding or escaping legal liability.[7] The defendant, as it were, "con-

[4] *Application des Gaz S.A. v. Falks Veritas Ltd.* [1975] F.S.R. 363.
[5] *Buttes Gas & Oil Co. v. Hammer (Nos. 2 & 3)* [1982] A.C. 888; [1981] 3 All E.R. 616.
[6] *Belt v. Lawes* (1882) 51 L.J.Q.B. 359; *Penrhyn v. Licensed Victuallers' Mirror* (1890) 7 T.L.R. 1.
[7] See *Frankum v. Lord Falmouth* (1835) 2 Ad. & E. 452; *Lush v.Russell* (1850) 5 Ex. 203.

fesses" the truth of what is alleged against him but proceeds immediately to "avoid" the effect of such allegations.

Examples

(a) The defence that the written contract sued on was subsequently altered in a material way is a plea of confession and avoidance, since he admits the contract but seeks to avoid it.[8]

(b) The defence that the defendant has a lien on the goods claimed by the plaintiff is a plea of confession and avoidance, since he admits the entitlement of the plaintiff to their possession but justifies their detention.

(c) When the defendant seeks to justify or excuse the acts complained of, as when raising the plea of self-defence to an action for assault.

(d) The plea of licence to an action for trespass.

(e) The plea of justification or publication on a privileged occasion in an action of defamation.

Material facts and burden of proof The defendant must plead all the material facts relied on as constituting an "avoidance" of what he otherwise confesses or admits to. The burden of proof is upon him to prove those facts. The plea of confession and avoidance should be stated clearly and distinctly and in a separate paragraph. It may justify or excuse or avoid liability to the whole of the claim to which it is pleaded, but if it is intended to apply to a part only of such claim, it must be clearly limited by an appropriate prefix or description of such parts as, "as to paragraph 8 of the statement of claim, the defendant says . . . ," or as may be.

Pleading techniques A plea of confession and avoidance may be, and often is, raised as an alternative to a traverse of the allegations made in the statement of claim. This is the safe course, as the defendant gets the best of both worlds, since he denies those allegations, but alternatively confesses and avoids them. If, however, the plea of confession and avoidance is the sole plea to such allegations, the defendant will be bound by his confession, and will be precluded thereby from denying the facts as alleged in the statement of claim.[9]

The defendant should not confess and avoid where a mere traverse is sufficient. For he will then introduce additional matter which he may have to prove, instead of putting the plaintiff to proof of his allegations. It is not always wise for the defendant to set up an affirmative case, especially if there is a ground for anticpating that the plaintiff may fail to establish a prima facie case.

---

[8] See *Hemming* v.*Trenery* (1839) 9 Ad. E. 926; *Crediton (Bishop)* v. *Exeter (Bishop)* [1905] 2 Ch. 455.

[9] *Hewitt* v. *Macquire* (1851) 7 Exch. 80.

Defence of Tender

Pleading techniques   If the defendant intends to rely on a defence of tender before action:

(a) he must specifically allege in the defence that he made such tender before action; and

(b) he must also plead in his defence that he has paid into court the amount of such tender; and

(c) he must pay such amount into court and give notice of such payment in to the plaintiff, (for his tender will not be available as a defence unless and until such payment into court has been made).[10]

The defence of tender is excepted from the general rule that any payment into court must not be pleaded or disclosed to the trial judge until all questions of liability and damages have been decided.[11]

Tender before action—when applicable   The defence of tender before action brought is a good defence only to an action to recover a debt or liquidated claim.[12] It cannot be pleaded as a defence to a claim for unliquidated damages.[13] If the defence of tender succeeds or if it is admitted and the plaintiff accepts the money paid into court, it is the defendant who has succeeded in the action, as the action ought not to have been brought.[14] But if the defence is defective or the tender was in respect of an unliquidated claim, the plea would be bad and the plaintiff would be entitled to the full amount claimed with costs.[15]

Denials of Damages

Exceptions to the general rule   Any allegation that a party has suffered damage and is deemed to be traversed unless specifically admitted.[16] This provision renders unnecessary any specific denial of damage alleged to have been suffered, whether the damage alleged is general or

---

[10] R.S.C., Ord. 18, r. 16. The amount paid into court may exceed the amount tendered and it need not include any element of interest unless it is in respect of a debt bearing contractual or statutory interest. See *Laing (John) Construction Ltd.* v. *Dastur* [1987] 1 W.L.R. 686 (C.A.), applied in *Smith* v. *Springer* [1987] 1 W.L.R. 1720; [1987] 3 All E.R. 252; (C.A.).

[11] See R.S.C., Ord. 22, r. 7.

[12] *The Mona* [1894] P. 265; and see *Griffiths* v. *Ystradyfodwg School Board* (1890) 24 Q.B.D. 307.

[13] *Davys* v. *Richardson* (1888) 21 Q.B.D. 202 at 205 (C.A.) *Laing (John) Construction Ltd.* v. *Dastur* [1987] 1 W.L.R. 686; [1987] 3 All E.R. 247.

[14] *Griffiths* v. *Ystradyfodwg School Board, supra.*

[15] *Read's Trustee in Bankruptcy* v. *Smith* [1951] Ch. 439.

[16] R.S.C., Ord. 18, r. 13(4).

special and whether the damage alleged is or is not part of the cause of the action.[17]

When special damage is essential to cause of action   Where, however, special damage is an essential ingredient of the cause of action, it is generally advisable, if not necessary, to deal specifically with such damage in the defence by raising an objection in point of law; for example that "the claim of the plaintiff is not maintainable without proof of special damage and none is alleged," or "that the special damage alleged is not sufficient in point of law to sustain the action."[18]

What in fact happens, in practice   In practice, the defence almost invariably contains a traverse, by denial or non-admission, of the damage, injury or loss alleged to have been suffered or sustained by the plaintiff.

Positive averments as to a loss—to be pleaded in defence   If the defendant intends to raise at the trial any question as to the causation or remoteness of the damage alleged, he must give fair warning of his intention to do so and such allegation should be specifically raised in the defence. For the same reason, if the defendant intends to set up a positive case to show that the plaintiff failed to take reasonable steps to mitigate his loss or damage, such an allegation should be specifically raised in the defence with supporting particulars.

Defamation actions   In a defamation action, the defendant may plead matters relied on in mitigation of damages only, but such plea must be limited to the general reputation of the plaintiff supported by particulars of the respects or the relevant sector of his life in which his reputation was bad. It may not extend to specific facts, which accordingly must not be pleaded[19] nor may the defendant plead in mitigation of damages only any fact which would tend to justify the acts complained of in the statement of claim, or otherwise support a defence to the action which has not been pleaded.[20] If the defendant does not rely on justification, he must serve on the plaintiff at least seven days before the trial particulars of the matters as to which he intends to give evidence in chief with a view to

---

[17] See R.S.C., Ord. 18, r. 12(1)(c), and see also *Wilby* v. *Elston* (1849) 8 C.B. 142; *Wood* v. *Earl of Durham* (1888) 21 Q.B.D. 501 at 506, 508; *Goldrei, Foucard & Son* v. *Sinclair and Russian Chamber of Commerce in London* [1918] 1 K.B. 180 (C.A.).

[18] An alternative course for the defendant is to apply to strike out the action as not disclosing a reasonable cause of action; see, *e.g. Ward* v. *Lewis* [1955] 1 W.L.R. 9 (action for slander dismissed for want of plea of special damage).

[19] *Plato Films Ltd.* v. *Spiedel* [1961] A.C. 1090, applying *Scott* v.*Sampson* (1882) 8 Q.B.D. 491, and overruling *Wood* v. *Earl of Durham* (1888) 21 Q.B.D. 501; and see *Waters* v. *Sunday Pictorial Newspapers Ltd.* [1961] 1 W.L.R. 967; [1961] 2 All E.R. 758 (C.A.).

[20] *Ibid.*; and see *Associated Newspapers Ltd.* v. *Dingle* [1964] A.C. 371; [1962] 3 W.L.R. 229; [1962] 2 All E.R. 737; *Watt* v. *Watt* [1905] A.C. 115.

mitigation of damages. These particulars must include circumstances in which the defamatory matter was published or as to the character of the plaintiff, otherwise he will not be allowed to give such evidence at the trial without the leave of the judge.[21]

[21] R.S.C., Ord. 82, r. 7.

CHAPTER 8

Set-Off and Counterclaim

Introduction

In addition to the matters which are strictly answers to the plaintiff's claim, the defendant may have a cross-claim against the plaintiff which entitles him to refuse to pay the amount demanded from him. This may be either a set-off or a counterclaim.[1] It should, however, be noted that although every set-off can be pleaded as a counterclaim, if the defendant so desires it, not every counterclaim can be pleaded as a set-off. But both alike must be specially pleaded.

The set-off/counterclaim distinction   The essential distinction between a set-off and a counterclaim is that:

(a) a set-off is in the nature of a defence, whereas a counterclaim is in the nature of a cross-action.[2] If the plaintiff obtains judgment or the action is stayed, discontinued or dismissed, the set-off also comes to an end,[3] whereas in such events a counterclaim may still be proceeded with[4];

(b) under a set-off, the defendant can recover nothing against the plaintiff, for he can only use the set-off as a defence or answer to the plaintiff's claim equal to the amount of the set-off. As it is only a defence, the plaintiff cannot obtain security for costs in respect of a set-off raised by a foreign defendant[5] or an impecunious

---

[1] The subjects of set-off and counterclaim were dealt with together in the pre-1964 R.S.C., Ord. 19, r. 3, but for the sake of both clarity and accuracy they are now distinguished one from the other and treated separately, set-off under R.S.C., Ord. 18, r. 17, and counterclaim under R.S.C., Ord. 15, rr. 2, 3 and 5(2).

[2] See *Stoke* v. *Taylor* (1880) 5 Q.B.D. 569; *Gathercole* v. *Smith* (1881) 7 Q.B.D. 626. (C.A.); *Hanak* v. *Green* [1958] 2 Q.B. 9; [1958] 2 All E.R. 141; (C.A.).

[3] *Gathercole* v. *Smith, supra.*

[4] R.S.C., Ord. 15, r. 2(3).

[5] See R.S.C. Ord. 23, r. 1; *N.V. Beleggings Compagnie "Uranus"* v. *Bank of England* [1948] 1 All E.R. 465 (C.A.); *affirming* [1948] 1 All E.R. 304.

limited company[6] as he may in the case of a separate and independent counterclaim[7];

(c) the set-off is treated as a defence for the purposes of the judgment, execution, costs and taxation, since judgment is given for the plaintiff in the action only for the amount, if any, of the excess of his claim over the amount found due to the defendant on the set-off[8];

(d) a set-off may be raised only in respect of to a claim by the plaintiff to a sum of money, whether such sum a be claim for debt or damages.

A set-off is thus a claim by the defendant to a sum of money, whether of an ascertained amount or not, which is relied on as a defence to the whole or part of the claim made by the plaintiff.[9]

Set-off—when arising? The defence of set-off may be raised in one of three sets of circumstances, namely:

(a) a set-off of mutual debts;

(b) in certain cases a setting up of matters of complaint which, if established, reduce or even extinguish the claim; and

(c) reliance upon equitable set-off and reliance as a matter of defence upon matters of equity.[10]

Historical Background

Common law At common law, a defendant who had any cross-demand or cross-claim against the plaintiff could not raise it as a defence in the plaintiff's action, but had to bring a cross-action. This inflexible position was to some extent remedied by the statutes of set-off[11] which first conferred the right to plead a set-off. Under these statutes, however, the

---

[6] See Companies Act 1985, s. 726(1) and *Accidental and Marine Insurance Co.* v. *Mercati* (1866) L.R. 3 Eq. 200.

[7] See *New Fenix Compagnie Anonyme d'Assurances de Madrid* v. *General Accident Fire and Life Assurance Corporation* [1911] 2 K.B. 619; *Strong* v. *Carlyle Press* (No. 2) [1893] W.N. 51.

[8] See *Stooke* v. *Taylor, supra; Neale* v. *Clarke* (1879) 4 Ex. D. 286.

[9] See R.S.C., Ord. 18, r. 17.

[10] *Hanak* v. *Green* [1958] 2 Q.B. 9, *per* Morris L.J. at 23.

[11] *i.e.* the Insolvent Debtors Relief Act 1729, s.13, and the Debtors Relief Amendment Act 1735, s.4. These statutes were repealed by the Civil Procedure Acts Repeal Act 1879, and the Statute Law Revision and Civil Procedure Act 1883, subject to a saving clause, s.4(1) of the Act of 1879, and were replaced by s.39(1)(a) of the Supreme Court of Judicature (Consolidation) Act 1925 (which re-enacted s.24(3) of the Supreme Court of Judicature Act 1873), and R.S.C., Ord. 18, r. 17.

claims on both sides had to be liquidated debts or money demands which could be ascertained with certainty at the time of pleading, so that the set-off of the defendant would operate as a defence to reduce or extinguish the money claim of the plaintiff.[12]

Exceptions to the general rule   At common law, a convenient practice developed[13] and the rule became established in contracts for the sale of goods and for work and labour, that:

> "it is competent for the defendant . . . not to set off, by a proceeding in the nature of a cross action, the amount of the damages which he has sustained by breach of the contract, but simply to defend himself by shewing how much less the subject-matter of the action was worth, by reason of the breach of contract."[14]

The intervention of the equity jurisdiction   In addition to the statutes of set-off, and the common law remedy of setting up a breach of warranty in diminution or extinction of the price of goods or work and labour, the courts of equity allowed what was called an "equitable set-off," *i.e.* where the defendant had some equitable ground for being protected against the claim.[15] Since the Judicature Acts 1873–75, equitable defences may be relied upon in actions at law[16] and accordingly an equitable set-off may be raised in any court. On the other hand, the Judicature Acts have conferred no new rights of set-off.[17] Accordingly, not every cross-claim may be presented as a set-off, even if in amount it equals or overlaps the claim. Nor does the mere fact that the cross-claim is in some way related to the transaction which gave rise to the claim serve to invest the cross-claim with the quality of set-off.[18]

---

[12] See *Stooke* v. *Taylor* (1880) 5 Q.B.D. 569, *per* Cockburn C.J. at 576; and see *Pellas* v. *Neptune Marine Insurance Co.* (1879) 5 C.P.D. 34; *Sovereign Life Assurance Co.* v. *Dodd* [1892] 2 Q.B. 573 at 577, 578.

[13] See *King* v. *Boston* (1789) 7 East 481n.

[14] *Mondel* v. *Steel* (1841) 8 M. & W. 858, *per* Parke B. at 871; applied in *Gilbert-Ash (Northern) Ltd.* v. *Modern Engineering (Bristol) Ltd.* [1974] A.C. 689 (H.L.). See also *Davis* v. *Hedges* (1871) L.R. 6 Q.B. 687; *Bow, McLachlan & Co.* v. *Ship "Camosun"* [1909] A.C. 597 at 610. The rule has been embodied in statutory form in s.53 of the Sale of Goods Act 1979, under which the buyer may "set up against the seller the breach of warranty in diminution or extinction of the price."

[15] See *Rawson* v. *Samuel* (1841) Cr. & Phil. 161, *per* Lord Cottenham L.C. at 178; *Morgan & Son Ltd.* v. *S. Martin Johnson & Co. Ltd.* [1949] 1 K.B. 107; [1948] 2 All E.R. 196; (C.A.); *Hanak* v. *Green* [1958] 2 Q.B. 9; [1958] 2 All E.R. 141; (C.A.).

[16] See now Supreme Court Act 1981, s.49(2).

[17] *Stumore* v. *Cambell & Co.* [1892] 1 Q.B. 314, *per* Lord Esher M.R. at 316, and *per* Lopes L.J. at 318; and see *Baker* v. *Adam* (1910) 102 L.T. 248 at 251.

[18] *Hanak* v. *Green, supra, per* Morris L.J. at 23.

Nature of a Set-off

Crystallisation   A set-off must have accrued at the commencement of the action.[19]

A shield—not a sword[20]   The plea of set-off can only be used by way of defence to the plaintiff's action. Claims cannot therefore be the subject of set-off, unless they exist between the same parties and in the same right.[21]

Examples

(a) Against a claim made by the plaintiff as executor or trustee, the defendant cannot set off a debt to him personally.[22]

(b) Conversely, to a claim against the defendant as executor, a debt due to him personally cannot be set off.[23]

(c) A set-off may be raised by the defendant against the claim made against him, if as a result his wrongful act or conduct a particular benefit has accrued to the plaintiff which would otherwise not have accrued. Such benefit must, however, be related to a particular head of damages claimed. Therefore, where as the result of the defendant's negligence, sub-tenants of the plaintiff were given notice to quit part of the premises, which they duly vacated, a benefit accrued to the plaintiff *i.e.* to re-let or occupy the vacated premises, which would not otherwise have accrued to them. The defendant was accordingly entitled to set off the value or amount of such accrued benefit against the plaintiff's claim for damages.[24]

(d) A tenant who counterclaims for damages for defects appearing in premises which cause them to become partially unfit for use may set off such counterclaim against the landlord's claim for unpaid rent.[25]

(e) To a claim against an executor personally, a debt due to him as executor cannot be set off.[26]

---

[19] *Richards* v. *James* (1848) 2 Ex. 471; *Smith* v. *Betty* [1903] 2 K.B. 317.

[20] *Stooke* v. *Taylor* (1880) 5 Q.B.D. 569, *per* Cockburn C.J. at 576.

[21] *David* v. *Rees* [1904] 2 K.B. 435; *Lister* v. *Hooson* [1908] 1 K.B. 174; *Lord* (*Trustee of* v. *Great Eastern Ry.* [1908] 1 K.B. 195.

[22] *Rees* v. *Watts* (1855) 11 Ex. 410; *Newell* v. *National Provincial Bank of England* (1876) 1 C.P.D. 496; *Stumore* v. *Campbell* [1892] 1 Q.B. 314 (C.A.) (claim for money held in trust, set-off of debt not allowed); *Re Gregson* (1887) 36 Ch.D. 223 at 227; *Re Gedney, Smith* v. *Grummitt* [1908] 1 Ch. 804.

[23] *Re Dickinson, Bute* v. *Walker* [1888] W.N. 94; *Phillips* v. *Howell* [1901] 2 Ch. 773.

[24] *Nadreph Ltd.* v. *Willmett & Co.* [1978] 1 W.L.R. 1537; [1978] 1 All E.R. 746.

[25] *British Anzani (Felixstowe)* v. *International Marine Management (U.K.)* [1980] Q.B. 637; [1979] 3 W.L.R. 451; negativing *Hart* v. *Rogers* [1916] 1 K.B. 646.

[26] *Nelson* v. *Roberts* [1893] 69 L.T. 352.

(f) Against a claim by the plaintiff, a debt due from his agent personally cannot be set off (unless the plaintiff authorised or allowed
the agent to contract as principal).[27]

(g) To a claim to a several debt, a claim to a joint debt cannot be set
off.[28]

On the other hand, the defendant can set off a debt originally due from
the plaintiff to a third party which the latter has assigned to the defendant.[29]

Charter-parties In relation to the charter-parties, a change has come
about in modern times between hire payable under a time charter-party
and freight payable under a voyage charter-party. "Freight" is payable
for carrying a quantity of cargo from one place to another, and "hire" is
payable for the right to use a vessel for a specified period of time, irrespective of whether the charterer uses it for carrying cargo or lays it up out
of use. Accordingly the rule that "freight" must be paid in full without
deductions for short delivery or cargo damage cannot be applied automatically to time charter "hire."[30] Thus in the case of a time charter-party
the charterer is entitled to deduct from the hire the amounts of his valid
claims. *i.e.* sums quantified by reasonable assessment made in good faith,
even though such sums are not agreed or established, which arise under a
clause in the charter-party which gives rise to such deductions or which
constitute an equitable set-off. Such a cross-claim arises out of the same
transaction or is closely connected with it, or is one which goes directly to
impeach the plaintiff's demands, *i.e.* so closely connected with such
demands that it would be manifestly unjust to allow the plaintiffs to
enforce payment without taking into account the cross-claim.[31]

Nature of a Cross-Claim

Ambit

(a) A cross-claim may be raised by way of set-off even when the claim

---

[27] *George* v. *Clagett* (1797) 7 T.R. 359; and see *Richardson* v. *Stormont Todd & Co. Ltd.*
[1900] 1 Q.B. 701. (C.A.).
[28] *Re Pennington & Owen Ltd.* [1925] Ch. 825, (C.A.).
[29] *Bennett* v. *White* [1910] 2 K.B. 643 (C.A.).
[30] *Aries Tanker Corporation* v. *Total Transport Ltd., The Aries* [1977] 1 W.L.R. 185;
[1977] 1 All E.R. 398; (H.L.).
[31] *Federal Commerce and Navigation Co.* v. *Molena Alpha Inc.* [1978] Q.B. 927; [1978] 3
All E.R. 1066 (C.A.) (though this point was left open in the House of Lords in the same
case); [1979] A.C. 757 disapproving *Seven Seas Transportation Ltd.* v. *Atlantic Shipping
Co. Ltd.* [1975] 2 Lloyd's Rep. 188, and approving *Compania Sud Americana de
Vapores* v. *Shipmari B.V., The Teno* [1977] 2 Lloyd's Rep. 289.

or cross-claim or both are for unliquidated amounts or one is for debt and the other for damages.[32]

(b) A claim founded on tort may be opposed to one founded on contract and vice versa.[33] Where, however, the cross-claim is for damages, it must arise out of the same transaction as the claim.[34]

(c) For the purposes of summary judgment under Order 14, in an action on a dishonoured bill of exchange or cheque, no set-off will be allowed for damages for breach of contract, save in exceptional circumstances.[35] If, however, the action does go to trial, there is no reason why a claim for damages for breach of warranty may not be raised as a set-off by way of defence, as it certainly can be raised by way of counterclaim.

The Crown   A set-off or counterclaim may be raised in an action by or against the Crown, save that:

(a) no set-off or counterclaim can be raised against the Crown in proceedings by the Crown for the recovery of taxes, duties or penalties, nor can a claim for repayment of taxes, duties or penalties be pleaded by way of set-off or counterclaim[36];

(b) leave of the court must be obtained to raise a set-off or counterclaim in proceedings by or against the Crown in the following two cases:

(i) where the Crown sues or is sued in the name of a government department to which the set-off or counterclaim does not relate; and

(ii) where the Crown sues or is sued in the name of the Attorney-General.[37]

Pleading a Set-off

Where claim exceeds set-off   Where a claim by a defendant to a sum of money, whether of an ascertained amount or not, is relied on as a defence

---

[32] See R.S.C., Ord. 18, r. 17; *Newfoundland Government* v. *Newfoundland Ry.* (1888) 13 App. Cas. 199 at 213; *Bankes* v. *Jarvis* [1903] 1 K.B. 549; *Lawrence* v. *Hayes* [1927] 2 K.B. 111; *Harris (Oscar) Son & Co.* v. *Vallarman & Co.* [1940] 1 All E.R. 185; *cf. Hart* v. *Rogers* [1916] 1 K.B. 646 at 651; *McCreagh* v. *Judd* [1923] W.N. 174.

[33] *Stooke* v. *Taylor, supra* at 576; and see *Morgan & Son Ltd.* v. *Martin Johnson & Co. Ltd.* [1949] 1 K.B. 107 (C.A.).

[34] *Morgan & Son Ltd.* v. *Martin Johnson & Co. Ltd., supra; Hanak* v. *Green, supra*; and see *McCreagh* v. *Judd* [1923] W.N. 174; *Bankes* v. *Jarvis* [1903] 1 K.B. 549, *per* Channell J.

[35] *James Lamont & Co. Ltd.* v. *Hyland Ltd.* [1950] 1 K.B. 585: [1950] 1 All E.R. 341 (C.A.); *Brown Shipley & Co. Ltd. Alicia Hosiery* [1966] 1 Lloyd's Rep. 668 (C.A.); *Saga of Bond Street Ltd.* v. *Avalon Promotions Ltd.* [1972] 2 Q.B. 325; [1972] 2 All E.R. 545; (C.A.).

[36] R.S.C., Ord. 77, r. 6(1).

[37] R.S.C., Ord. 77, r. 6(2).

to the whole or part of a claim made by the plaintiff, it may be included in the defence and set off against the plaintiff's claim, whether or not it is also added as a counterclaim.[38] Where, however, the claim is not such as to be the subject of a set-off, the defendant can only avail himself of it by pleading it as a counterclaim. The question as to what is a set-off is to be determined as a matter of law and is not in any way governed by the language used by the parties in their pleadings.[39]

Where set-off exceeds claim If the amount of such cross-demand exceeds the amount of the plaintiff's liquidated claim, the defendant may plead in his defence a set-off of part of the debt due from the plaintiff, and may counterclaim for the residue of it, so as to recover judgment against the plaintiff for the excess. Hence, it is usual to find in such a defence, the following paragraph by way of introduction of the counter-claim:

> "Further and without prejudice to the foregoing, the defendant will seek to set off so much of his counterclaim herein as will extinguish or diminish the amount of the plaintiff's claim in diminution or extinction of the plaintiff's claim ."

Set-off is pleaded generally One defence of set-off may be pleaded generally to the whole claim to which the defence is applicable, without specifying how much is intended to apply to each ground of claim.[40] The defence of set-off is taken distributively. Thus, if issue is joined upon a defence of payment, and the defendant fails to prove such payment to the full amount alleged, he is nevertheless entitled to avail himself of the partial payment proved as a defence *pro tanto*. The plaintiff in such case will be entitled to judgment on that issue for the residue of his demand not covered by the defence pleaded.

Set-off and interest Interest may be claimed in a defence of set-off whether under section 35A of the Supreme Court Act 1981 or otherwise and, of course, such a claim must be specifically pleaded.[40a] Where interest is merely claimable as damages, it is not the subject of a defence of set-off, though it may be the ground of a counterclaim.

The pleading of a set-off should be particularised A defence of set-off should state with some particularity the debt or other matter sought to be set off. The requisite degree of particularity is not readily to be defined and must depend upon the circumstances. The facts should, however, be

---

[38] R.S.C., Ord. 18, r. 17. There is no need for a separate heading of "set off" to be made in the defence.

[39] *Hanak* v. *Green* [1958] 2 Q.B. 9, *per* Morris L.J. at 26, citing *Sharpe* v. *Haggith* (1912) 106 L.T. 13.

[40] *Noel* v. *Davis* (1838) 4 M. & W. 136.

[40a] See R.S.C., Ord. 18, r. 8(4).

145

stated in such a manner as will put the opposite party on his guard and prevent surprise.[41]

Pleaded set-off—plaintiff's options   If an admitted set-off is equal in amount to the claim, and is pleaded by way of defence only, the plaintiff may discontinue the action.[42] If it be pleaded as a counterclaim, the plaintiff may in his reply admit it, and state his willingness to have it set off against his claim. If the admitted set-off is larger in amount than the claim, and there is a counterclaim for the excess, the plaintiff may discontinue the action and pay money into court on the counterclaim.[43]

When issue is joined without a reply   Where a set-off is pleaded by way of defence and not by way of counterclaim and the plaintiff merely wishes to deny the material facts alleged in such defence, as, for example, the contract or consideration on which the set-off is alleged to have been founded, no reply is necessary to traverse specifically such facts one by one.[44]

When a reply is needed to a pleaded set-off   But if the plaintiff relies on any grounds of reply to a defence of set-off such as, if not specifically raised, would be likely to take the defendant by surprise, or would raise issues of fact not arising out of the previous pleadings, as for instance, fraud, the expiry of the relevant period of limitation, release, payment, performance, facts showing illegality either by statute or common law or Statute of Frauds, he should serve a reply.[45] So, too, if the plaintiff relies on the non-fulfilment of conditions precedent to the case of the defendant he should state such non-fulfilment in his reply.[46]

Nature of Counterclaim

Introduction   A counterclaim is substantially a cross-action, and not merely a defence to the plaintiff's claim. It is a cross-claim which the defendant may raise in the very action brought against him by the plaintiff, instead of himself bringing a separate, independent action against the plaintiff.

Historical perspective   At common law, such a cross-claim could not be raised, since the law did not allow the action of the plaintiff against the

---

[41] *Weinberger* v. *Inglis* [1918] 1 Ch. 133 at 138; *Pinson* v. *Lloyds, etc., Bank* [1941] 2 K.B. 72.

[42] See R.S.C., Ord. 21, r. 2.

[43] See R.S.C., Ord. 22, r. 6.

[44] See R.S.C., Ord. 18, r. 14(1). See also *Williamson* v. *London & North Western Ry.* (1879) 12 Ch.D. 787.

[45] See R.S.C., Ord, 18, r. 8(1) (payment made and accepted before action is complete discharge of a debt); *Beaumont* v. *Greathead* (1846) 2 C.B. 494 at 499 (*secus* after action commenced); *Société des Hotels Le Touquet* v. *Cummings* [1922] 1 K.B. 451.

[46] See R.S.C., Ord. 18, r. 7(4).

defendant to be met by an independent claim of the defendant against the plaintiff. The defendant had to bring a separate cross-action.[47] The right to maintain a counterclaim was first introduced by the Judicature Act 1873,[48] and the procedure by counterclaim has been greatly extended in its operation and application by the rules. Thus, as far as is practicable, the counterclaim is assimilated to the position of a statement of claim indorsed on a writ of summons.[49]

Counterclaim—an independent action A counterclaim is a separate and independent action which is tried together with the original action.[50] As Bowen L.J. said in *Amon v. Bobbett*[51]:

[47] See *Stooke v. Taylor* (1880) 5 Q.B.D. 569, *per* Cockburn C.J. at 576.

[48] s.24(3) re-enacted as s.39 of the Judicature Act 1925 and now encapsulated in Supreme Court Act 1981, s.49, under which every judge of the High Court and of the Court of Appeal has power to grant to any defendant in respect of any estate, right or title, legal or equitable, claimed or asserted by him, all such relief against the plaintiff as such defendant shall have properly claimed by his pleading to the same extent as if the defendant had brought an action against the plaintiff for the purpose.

[49] In R.S.C., Ord. 15, r. 3(2) so far as practicable the counterclaim is assimilated to the position of a statement of claim indorsed on a writ of summons. Under these Rules the position of a counterclaim is as follows:
(1) Defendant may counterclaim against plaintiff.
(2) Defendant may counterclaim against added party along with plaintiff or for relief relating to or connected with the original subject-matter of the action, (r. 3(1)) and with leave serve it out of the jurisdiction (see r.3(5)).
(3) Defendant may apply for summary judgment on counterclaim (see Ord. 14, r. 5) even against a co-defendant, see R.S.C. Ord. 15, r. 3(5A) which negatived the decision in *C. E. Heath plc v. Ceram Holding Co.*; [1988] 1 W.L.R. 1219 C.A.
(4) Plaintiff may counterclaim to counterclaim by defendant (para. (2) and see *Renton Gibbs & Co. v. Neville* [1900] 2 Q.B. 181).
(5) Third party procedure applies to a counterclaim (Ord. 16, r. 11, and see *The Normar* [1968] P. 362 (defendant counterclaiming against counterclaim of third party)).
(6) Rules of pleading apply to counterclaim and defence to counterclaim as though they are respectively a statement of claim and a defence (see Ord. 18, r. 18).
(7) Defendant counterclaiming against added party may enter, or apply by summons or motion for, judgment in default of acknowledgment of service against such party under Ord. 15, r. 3(5).
(8) Defendant counterclaiming against plaintiff may enter, or apply by summons or motion for, judgment in default of defence to counterclaim under Ord. 19, r. 8.
(9) Counterclaim may be amended without leave (see Ord. 20. r. 3).
(10) Counterclaim may be discontinued or withdrawn without leave (see Ord. 21, r. 2(b)).
(11) Rules of payment into court apply to a counterclaim, so that, (i) the defendant must state whether his payment in has taken his counterclaim into account (see Ord. 22, r. 2), and (ii) payment into court may be made to satisfy a counterclaim.
(12) Counterclaim may be made in an action begun by originating summons (see Ord. 28 r. 7).

[50] A counterclaim, however, is not an "action" within the definition in s.151(1) of the Supreme Court Act 1981 (see *Kinnaird v. Field (No. 2)* [1905] 2 Ch. 306; *McGowan v. Middleton* (1883) 11 Q.B.D. 464 at 468), nor is the defendant a "plaintiff" within the definition there given (see *ibid.*; *Lewin v. Trimming* (1888) 21 Q.B.B. 230 at 235).

[51] (1889) 22 Q.B.D. 543 at 548; and see *Stumore v. Campbell & Co.* [1892] 1 Q.B. 314, *per* Lord Esher M.R. at 317 (for all purposes except those of execution a claim and a counterclaim are two independent actions).

147

"A counterclaim is . . . to be treated, for all purposes for which justice requires it to be so treated, as an independent action."

Thus, it is so treated for the purpose of being continued if judgment is given in the plaintiff's action, or if the plaintiff's action is stayed, discontinued, or dismissed,[52] or for the purpose of security for costs,[53] or for the purpose of a stay under section 4 of the Arbitration Act 1950,[54] or section 1 of the Arbitration Act 1979, or for the purpose of the Limitation Act 1980.[55]

Principles as to pleading a counterclaim   The rules of pleading apply to a counterclaim and to a defence to counterclaim as though they are respectively a statement of claim and a defence.[56] Similarly, the rules relating to the joinder of causes of action apply to a counterclaim as if it were a separate action and as if the person making the counterlcaim were the plaintiff, and the person against whom it is made a defendant.[57] A mere statement of intention to make a counterclaim is not enough,[58] nor is the service or filing of a "notice of counterclaim" without there being any previous pleadings[59]: but a statement in an affidavit in the proceedings of the intention to counterclaim is sufficient.[60] Accordingly, if the defendant in any action alleges that he has any claim or is entitled to any relief or remedy against a plaintiff in the action in respect of any matter, whenever and however arising, he may, subject to the power of ordering separate trials of claim and counterclaim[61] instead of bringing a separate

[52] R.S.C., Ord. 15, r. 2(3); and see *McGowan* v. *Middleton, supra.* If the defendant applies to dismiss the plaintiff's action for want of prosecution, he will ordinarily be required to submit to an order dismissing his counterclaim at the same time, at any rate where the counterclaim arises out of the same events as were to be investigated in the action (*Zimmer Orthopaedic Ltd.* v. *Zimmer Manufacturing Co. Ltd.* [1968] 1 W.L.R. 1349; [1968] 3 All E.R. 449. (C.A.)). In this context it should be noted that the fact that an action has been stayed by order of the court pending the giving by the plaintiff of security for the defendant's costs does not excuse delay if the plaintiff could, at any time during the relevant period, have caused the stay to be lifted by giving the security or by making an appropriate application to the court (*Thomas Storey Engineers Ltd.* v. *Waites Dove Bitumastic Ltd. The Times,* January 21, 1989, (C.A.)).
[53] See R.S.C., Ord. 23, r. 1; and see *Sykes* v. *Sacerdoti* (1885) 15 Q.B.D. 423; *Lake* v. *Haseltine* (1885) 55 L.J.Q.B. 205; otherwise if the counterclaim is in substance a defence to the action, see *Neck* v. *Taylor* [1893] 1 Q.B. 560. The court has no jurisdiction to order a foreign plaintiff to give security for *damages* under a counterclaim (*The James Westoll* [1905] P. 47).
[54] *Spartali & Co.* v. *Van Hoorn* [1884] W.N. 32; *Chappell* v. *North* [1891] 2 Q.B. 252.
[55] See *Lowe* v. *Bentley* (1928) 44 T.L.R. 388. For the purposes of s.28 of the Act, a claim by way of set-off or counterclaim is deemed to be a separate action and to have been commenced on the same date as the action in which it is pleaded.
[56] R.S.C., Ord. 18, r. 18.
[57] R.S.C., Ord. 15, r. 2(2).
[58] *The Saxicava* [1924] P. 131; and see *The Salybia* [1910] P. 25.
[59] *The Gniezno* [1967] 3 W.L.R. 705.
[60] *Bildt* v. *Foy* (1892) 9 T.L.R. 34; *affirmed ibid.* at 83; *Whiteley's Case* [1900] 1 Ch. 365.
[61] R.S.C., Ord. 15, r. 5(2), and see p. 155 *infra.*

action, make a counterclaim in respect of that matter. Where he does so, he must add the counterclaim to his defence.[62]

Examples

(a) A claim founded on tort may be opposed to one founded on contract or vice versa.[63]

(b) The counterclaim need not be an action of the same nature as the original action or even analogous thereto.[64]

(c) An equitable counterclaim may be raised in an action-at-law, and a legal counterclaim in an action in the Chancery Division.[65]

(d) The counterclaim need not arise against the plaintiff in the same capacity in which he sues,[66] nor in the case of a counterclaim against the plaintiff only, need it be connected with the plaintiff's claim[67]: though in the case of a counterclaim against the plaintiff along with an added party, this is necessary.[68]

(e) To a joint claim by two plaintiffs, a counterclaim may be made against them jointly or a separate counterclaim may be made against each of them,[69] or the defendant may counterclaim against one plaintiff and deny all liability to the other.

In summary, therefore, if the defendant has a valid cause of action of any description against a plaintiff, there is no necessity for him to bring a separate cross-action, since he can make a counterclaim in the same action against the plaintiff.

Conditions precedent to a successful counterclaim   The claim set up by the counterclaim must be one in respect of which the defendant could maintain a separate action,[70] and it must be of such a nature that the court would have jurisdiction to entertain it as a separate action.[71] A

---

[62] R.S.C., Ord. 15, r. 2(1). *Beddall* v. *Maitland* (1881) 17 Ch.D. 174 at 187; and see *Ellis* v. *Munson* (1876) 35 L.T. 585, (C.A.) (counterclaim arising after action brought must be pleaded as so arising). *Mostyn* v. *West Mostyn Coal and Iron Co.* (1876) 1 C.P.D. 145 (irrelevant that counterclaim exceeds claim).

[63] *Stooke* v. *Taylor* (1880) 5 Q.B.D. 569, *per* Cockburn C.J. at 576.

[64] *Beddall* v. *Maitland* (1881) 17 Ch.D. 174, *per* Fry J. at 181.

[65] *Fleming* v. *Loe* [1902] 2 Ch. 359 (C.A.).

[66] *Re Richardson, Richardson* v. *Nicholson* [1933] W.N. 90 (C.A.) (counterclaim against plaintiff as executor who had sued in his personal capacity), not following *Macdonald* v. *Carington* (1878) 4 C.P.D. 28.

[67] *Gray* v. *Webb* (1882) 21 Ch.D. 802; *Quin* v. *Hession* (1878) 40 L.T. 70.

[68] R.S.C., Ord. 15, r. 3.

[69] *Manchester Sheffield and Lincolnshire Ry. and London and North Western Ry.* v. *Brooks* (1877) 2 Ex.D. 243. See also, *Hall* v. *Fairweather* (1901) 18 T.L.R. 58 (judgment on counterclaim against one of two plaintiffs); *Eyre* v. *Moreing* [1884] W.N. 58 (counterclaim against two partners against separate claim by one of them).

[70] *Pellas* v. *Neptune Marine Insurance Co.* (1879) 5 C.P.D. 34 (C.A.); *Newell* v. *National Provincial Bank of England* (1876) 1 C.P.D. 496.

[71] *Bow, Maclachlan & Co.* v. *The Camosun* [1909] A.C. 597; *Williams Brothers* v. *E.T. Agius Ltd.* [1914] A.C. 510 at 522.

defendant, therefore, cannot maintain a counterclaim in respect of a matter for which he could not as plaintiff sue the person against whom the counterclaim is set up,[72] e.g. a counterclaim against a foreign sovereign, unless it is really in the nature of a defence and is immediately connected with the claim.[73]

Counterclaims—when/how tried? Subject to the power to order the separate trials of claim and counterclaim,[74] the issues of fact raised by the claim and counterclaim should as a rule be tried together, as that was the defendant's object in pleading the counterclaim.[75] If both claim and counterclaim succeed, there may be two judgments, one in favour of the plaintiff on his claim and the other for the defendant on his counterclaim,[76] though execution will issue only for the balance. Nevertheless, where a defendant establishes a counterclaim against the claim of the plaintiff and there is a balance in favour of one of the parties, the court may give judgment for the balance, while retaining its discretion with respect to costs.[77]

Counterclaim exceeds claim—practice Ordinarily a counterclaim may exceed the amount of the plaintiff's claim. If successful, the defendant may be entitled to judgment for the balance.[78] In two cases however, the amount of the defendant's cross-claim, even if pleaded as a counterclaim, cannot exceed the amount of the plaintiff's claim; namely:

(a) where the defendant claims as assignee the amount of a debt owing by the plaintiff which has been assigned to him[79]; and

(b) where the defendant raises a counterclaim against a sovereign plaintiff.[80]

Counterclaiming to a counterclaim The plaintiff on whom a counterclaim is served may himself serve a counterclaim to that counterclaim on the defendant even though the cause of action on which it is founded

---

[72] *Turner v. Hednesford Gas Co.* (1878) 3 Ex. D. 145 (C.A.); *Factories Insurance Co. Ltd. v. Anglo-Scottish General Commercial Insurance Co. Ltd.* (1913) 29 T.L.R. 312 (C.A.).

[73] *South African Republic v. La Compagnie Franco-Belge* [1897] 2 Ch. 487; *Union of Soviet Republics v. Belaiew* (1925) 42 T.L.R. 21.

[74] R.S.C., Ord. 15, r. 5(2); and see p. 158, *infra.*

[75] *Piercy v. Young* (1880) 15 Ch.D. 475.

[76] The position is different, of course, in the case of a set-off, where there can be only one judgment; see *Provincial Bill Posting Co. v. Low Moor Iron Co.* [1909] 2 K.B. 344; *Sharpe v. Haggith* (1912) 106 L.T. 13.

[77] R.S.C., Ord. 15, r. 2(4), and see *Hanak v. Green* [1958] 2 Q.B. 9 (C.A).

[78] R.S.C., Ord. 15, r. 2(4).

[79] *Young v. Kitchin* (1878) 3 Ex.D. 127; *Government of Newfoundland v. Newfoundland Ry.* (1887) 13 App. Cas. 199.

[80] *High Commissioner for India v. Ghosh* (1960) 1 Q.B. 134; and see *Duke of Brunswick v. King of Hanover* (1844) 6 Beav. 1 at 38.

arose after the issue of the writ,[81] or he may bring in a third party in respect of the claim raised by the counterclaim,[82] and the defendant claiming against a third party may counterclaim against the counterclaim made by a third party.[83]

Pleading a Counterclaim—Practice

Essentials   The principles of pleading which govern a counterclaim are substantially the same as those which would apply to a statement of claim in a cross-action brought by the defendant against the plaintiff:

(a) It should have the word "counterclaim" prefixed to it as a heading, so as to distinguish it from what is pleaded merely as a matter of defence to the plaintiff's claim. However, the absence of such heading would not invalidate a counterclaim which was otherwise properly pleaded.[84]

(b) It must also contain a statement in a summary form of the material facts relied on, but not the evidence by which they are to be proved.[85] Such statement must, when necessary, be divided into paragraphs numbered consecutively.[86]

Paragraph numbering   Where the defendant pleads both a defence and a counterclaim, the paragraphs of the counterclaim are usually numbered as though they were a continuation of the paragraphs of the defence.

Joinder   Several different causes of action may be joined in the same counterclaim. For the purpose of determining what claims may or may not be so joined, regard must be had to the same provisions with respect to the joinder of different causes of action in a statement of claim.[87] If the defendant relies upon several distinct grounds of counterclaim founded upon separate and distinct facts, such grounds of counterclaim must be stated, as far as may be, separately and distinctly. The facts pleaded as supporting a counterclaim must, of course, be such as would be sufficient to support an action brought by the defendant for the same cause of complaint; otherwise the counterclaim will be open to an objection that it does not disclose a reasonable cause of action.[88]

---

[81] See *Toke* v. *Andrews* (1882) 8 Q.B.D. 428; *Renton Gibbs & Co. Ltd.* v. *Neville & Co.* [1900] 2 Q.B. 181 (C.A.); *Lewis Faulk Ltd.* v. *Jacobwitz* [1944] Ch. 64.
[82] See R.S.C., Ord. 16, r. 1; *Lewis Faulk Ltd.* v. *Jacobwitz* [1944] Ch. 64.
[83] See *The Normar* [1968] P. 362; [1968] 2 W.L.R. 704; [1968] 1 All E.R. 753.
[84] *Lees* v. *Patterson* (1878) 7 Ch.D. 866.
[85] R.S.C., Ord. 18, r. 7(1).
[86] *Ibid.* r. 6(2).
[87] See R.S.C., Ord. 15, r. 2(2).
[88] See R.S.C., Ord. 18, r. 19.

SET-OFF AND COUNTERCLAIM

Grounds of defence as counterclaim—when? The defendant is not allowed to rely for his counterclaim upon matters which have been stated simply as grounds of defence to the plaintiff's claim, and are not specifically referred to in the counterclaim unless he has repeated them or incorporated them by reference in his counterclaim, as he is at liberty to do.[89]

Particulars Particulars of the matters relied upon as supporting the counterclaim must be given in all cases where they are required to be given, and, if sufficient particulars are not given, an order may be made for further and better particulars.[90]

The prayer A counterclaim, like a statement of claim, must state specifically the claim made and the relief or remedy sought by the defendant,[91] though where the defendant has specifically stated the particular remedy or relief claimed it is unnecessary for him to add a claim for general or other relief, which may always be given as if it had been asked.

What if defence is exclusively the counterclaim Where the defendant pleads no other defence than a counterclaim, the allegations of fact contained in the statement of claim except allegations as to claim for damages will be taken to be admitted by him.[92] The court has, however, a discretion whether to make an order for judgment on such admissions in respect of a pecuniary claim where there is a substantial counterclaim for debt or damages to an equal or greater amount.[93]

Time limits The time allowed for serving on the plaintiff a counterclaim or a defence containing a counterclaim is the same as that for serving a defence.

Counterclaim can be in respect of "post-writ" facts A counterclaim may, subject to the court's power of disallowance or exclusion, be pleaded in respect of matters arising after action brought.[94] In such a case the counterclaim must show, either by express statement or by the dates therein mentioned, or otherwise, that the matters relied upon arose after

---

[89] See *Birmingham Estates Co.* v. *Smith* (1880) 13 Ch.D. 506; *Benbow* v. *Low* (1880) 13 Ch.D. 553.

[90] R.S.C., Ord. 18, r. 12(3).

[91] *Ibid.* r. 18(*a*).

[92] *Ibid* r. 13(3).

[93] See R.S.C., Ord. 27, r. 3; and see *Showell* v. *Bowron* (1883) 52 L.J.Q.B. 284; *Mersey Steamship Co.* v. *Shuttleworth* (1883) 11 Q.B.D. 468; affirmed at 531.

[94] Supreme Court Act 1981, s.49, continuing as hitherto the provisions of s.39 and 43 of the Judicature Act 1925. *Beddall* v. *Maitlaind* (1881) 17 Ch.D. 174; *Toke* v. *Andrews* (1882) 8 Q.B.D. 428; *Wood* v. *Goodwin* [1884] W.N. 17.

action brought, otherwise it will be deemed to have been pleaded in respect of matters arising before action.[95]

Counterclaim against Plaintiff and Added Party

Introduction The defendant may in special circumstances make his counterclaim against the plaintiff and some other person, whether already a party to the action (*e.g.* a co-defendant) or not.

Joinder of additional party Where the defendant alleges that such other person is liable to him along with the plaintiff in respect of the subject-matter of the counterclaim, or claims against such other person any relief relating to or connected with the original subject-matter of the action, he may join such other person as a party against whom the counterclaim is made.[96]

Pre-condition to counterclaiming against a new party The defendant can make a counterclaim against an additional party only if the plaintiff is also a defendant to the counterclaim,[97] and such a counterclaim must be in respect of or relate to or be connected with the subject-matter of the plaintiff's claim,[98] although it need not be an action of the same nature as the original action.[99] The defendant's counterclaim against the plaintiff and the additional party may be made against them jointly or in the alternative,[1] and may also be made against the plaintiff in the alternative only.[2]

Pleading practice Where the defendant makes a counterclaim against the plaintiff and an additional party, the title of the action must show that this had been done,[3] as follows:

---

[95] *Ellis* v. *Munson* (1876) 35 L.T. 585; and see R.S.C., Ord. 18, r. 9.

[96] R.S.C., Ord. 15, r. 3(1); and see Supreme Court Act 1981, s.49 as n. 94 above. This procedure is alternative and additional to the third party procedure under R.S.C., Ord. 16.

[97] *Harris* v. *Gamble* (1877) 6 Ch.D. 748; and see *Furness* v. *Booth* (1876) 4 Ch.D. 586.

[98] R.S.C., Ord. 15. r. 3(1); and see *Padwick* v. *Scott* (1876) 2 Ch.D. 736; *Barber* v. *Blaiberg* (1882) 19 Ch.D. 473; *S. F. Edge Ltd.* v. *Weigel* (1907) 97 L.T. 447. This requirement is not necessary where the plaintiff is the sole defendant to a counterclaim, see p. 147, note 50 *supra*.

[99] *Re Richardson, Richardson* v. *Nicholson* [1933] W.N. 90; disapproving *Macdonald* v. *Carington* (1878) 4 C.P.D. 28; and see *McEwan* v. *Crombie* (1884) 25 Ch.D. 175 at 177.

[1] *Smith* v. *Buskell* [1919] 2 K.B. 362; and see *Child* v. *Stenning* (1878) 7 Ch.D. 413; *Dear* v. *Sworder* (1876) 4 Ch.D. 476.

[2] R.S.C., Ord. 15 r. 3(1) thus has the effect of negativing *Times Cold Storage Co.* v. *Lowther* [1911] 2 K.B. 100, decided under the former Ord. 21, r. 11.

[3] R.S.C., Ord. 15. r. 3(2).

SET-OFF AND COUNTERCLAIM

Title of Counterclaim against Plaintiff and Co-defendant

IN THE HIGH COURT OF JUSTICE   19__ B. No. __
QUEEN'S BENCH DIVISION

BETWEEN   A B .... Plaintiff

                                and

                                C D .... First Defendant
                                and XY   Second Defendant
                                                                (by original action)

                                And between the said C D .... Plaintiff

                                and

                                the said A B .... First Defendant
                                and the said XY .... Second Defendant
                                                                (by counterclaim)

Although in the "further title" which is required to be added, the counterclaiming defendant is described as plaintiff by counterclaim, and the plaintiff and the person joined along with him are described as defendants by counterclaim, this method of description should *not* be followed in the body of the pleading, as it might produce confusion, and it is better that in the body of the counterclaim the defendant in the action should continue to be described as the "defendant," or the "defendant C D," as the case may be, and the plaintiff in the action as "the plaintiff."

Service on additional party   A copy of the counterclaim must be served on the person not already a party to the action, together with a prescribed form of acknowledgment of service, who will become a party to it as from the time of service with the same rights in respect of his defence to the counterclaim and otherwise as if he had been duly served in the ordinary way by the party making the counterclaim.[4] For practical purposes, such a counterclaim is the equivalent of a writ and the proceedings arising from it as an action. Thus the party making the counterclaim is in the position of a plaintiff and the party against whom it is made in the

---

[4] R.S.C., Ord. 15, r. 3(2). A copy of the counterclaim required to be served on a person not already a party to the action must be indorsed with a form of acknowledgment of service in Form No. 14 in R.S.C., Appendix A (*Supreme Court Practice 1991*, Vol. 2, para. 9) with such modification as the circumstances may require (R.S.C., Ord. 15, r. 5). The copy of the counterclaim required to be served on a person who is not already a party to the action must be indorsed with the notice in Form 17 in R.S.C., Appendix A (*Supreme Court Practice 1991*, Vol. 2, para. 12) addressed to that person (Ord. 15, r. 3 (6)).

position of a defendant in the action.[5] If, however, the added party to the counterclaim is already a party to the action, the defendant must serve the counterclaim upon him within the time specified for the service of his defence on the plaintiff.[6]

Rights of additional party   An additional party properly brought in by counterclaim may himself counterclaim against the defendant who brought him in, and he may also employ the third party procedure as against the plaintiff whose co-defendant to the counterclaim he has thus become.[7]

Separate Trials

Splitting claim from counterclaim   Where it appears to the court, on the application of a person against whom a counterclaim is made that the subject-matter of the counterclaim ought for any reason to be disposed of by a separate action, the court may order the counterclaim to be struck out or may order it to be tried separately or make such other order as may be expedient.[8] The court thus has ample powers to protect the plaintiff or any added party against whom a counterclaim is made where it appears that the joinder of the counterclaim may embarrass or delay the trial of the action or is otherwise inconvenient.[9] The fact that the defendant cannot otherwise bring an independent action against the plaintiff is not a sufficient ground for refusing to strike out a counterclaim.[10]

Consolidation, etc.   Where the defendant in one action brings an independent action against the plaintiff, the court has power to order the two actions to be consolidated, or that they be tried at the same time, or one immediately after the other, or may order either of them to be stayed until after the determination of the other.[11]

---

[5] R.S.C., Ord. 15, r. 3(5).

[6] *Ibid.* r. 3(3).

[7] This is the effect of R.S.C., Ord. 15, r. 3(2) reversing *Street and Edmunds* v. *Gower* (1877) 2 Q.B.D. 498 and *Alcoy and Gandia Railway and Harbour Co.* v. *Greenhill* [1896] 1 Ch. 19.

[8] R.S.C., Ord. 15, r. 5(2).

[9] *Cf.* R.S.C., Ord. 15, r. 5(1). See *Gray* v. *Webb* (1882) 21 Ch.D. 802 (exclusion of counterclaim on the ground that it would unduly delay the action); *Fendall* v. *O'Connell* (1885) 52 L.T. 538 (exclusion of counterclaim as being embarrassing); *McLay* v. *Sharp* [1877] W.N. 216, and *Padwick* v. *Scott* (1876) 2 Ch.D. 736 (exclusion of counterclaim by defendant against plaintiff and co-defendant); but see *Dear* v. *Sworder* (1876) 4 Ch.D. 476; *The Normar* [1968] P. 362; [1968] 2 W.L.R. 704; [1968] 1 All E.R. 753 (exclusion of part of counterclaim by one defendant against another on the ground of inconvenience to plaintiff).

[10] *South African Republic* v. *La Compagnie Franco-Belge* [1897] 2 Ch. 487.

[11] See R.S.C., Ord. 4, r. 10.

Costs of Claim, Set-off and Counterclaim

The significance of the set-off/counterclaim distinction   As regards the question of costs, the distinction between a set-off and a counterclaim is of great importance.

Judgment for the defendant   Where the defendant establishes a set-off to an amount equal or greater than the amount of the plaintiff's claim, he thereby defeats the action, and is entitled, subject to the discretion of the court, to the general costs of the action as well as the costs of his set-off.[12] Even in the case of an equitable set-off, if the plaintiff's claim is extinguished, the proper order is to enter judgment for the defendant with costs on the claim and for the balance of the amount of the counterclaim with costs.[13]

Judgment for plaintiff and defendant   Where, however, the plaintiff succeeds on his claim and the defendant merely succeeds in establishing a cross-claim which can only be relied on by way of counterclaim, the plaintiff's claim, even if it is overtopped by the proved amount of the counterclaim, has not been defeated. Thus, subject to the discretion of the court, the plaintiff having succeeded in establishing his claim, is entitled to the general costs of the action save insofar as they were increased by the counterclaim. In contrast, the defendant is merely entitled to the costs of and incidental to his counterclaim.[14] Thus, subject to judicial discretion, where the plaintiff succeeds on his claim and the defendant on his counterclaim, each party is entitled to the costs which he had to incur to recover the sum on the claim and counterclaim respectively, such costs being set off against each other.[15] If both parties fail, the same principle is applied.[16]

Principle   The principle is that if the defendant establishes a set-off, the plaintiff only "recovers" the amount, if any, by which his proved claim exceeds the amount of the set-off.[17] In contrast, if the defendant estab-

---

[12] See *Baines* v. *Bromley* (1881) 6 Q.B.D. 691 at 694; *Bowker* v. *Kesteven* (1882) 47 L.T. 545; *Lund* v. *Campbell* (1885) 14 Q.B.D. 821; *Provincial Bill Posting Co.* v. *Low Moor Iron Co.* [1909] 2 K.B. 344.

[13] *Childs* v. *Gibson*; *Childs* v. *Blacker* [1954] 1 W.L.R. 809; [1954] 2 All E.R. 243; *Hanak* v. *Green* [1958] 2 Q.B. 9; [1958] 2 W.L.R. 755; [1958] 2 All E.R. 141; (C.A.).

[14] *Medway Oil and Storage Co.* v. *Continental Contractors* [1929] A.C. 88, where the cases are reviewed; and see *Sharpe* v. *Haggith* (1912) 106 L.T. 13; *Chell Engineering Ltd.* v. *Unit Tool and Engineering Co. Ltd.* [1950] 1 All E.R. 378, C.A.; *Lowther* v. *Lewin* (1965) 109 S.J. 33.

[15] *Chell Engineering Ltd.* v. *Unit Tool and Engineering Co. Ltd.*, *supra*. For the principles of taxation on such an order, see *Atlas Metal Co.* v. *Miller* [1898] 2 Q.B. 500; *Medway Oil and Storage Co.* v. *Continental Contractors*, *supra*.

[16] *James* v. *Jackson* [1910] 2 Ch. 92.

[17] *Ashcroft* v. *Foulkes* (1856) 18 C.B. 261; *Stooke* v. *Taylor* (1880) 5 Q.B.D. 569.

lishes a cross-claim which is not capable of being pleaded as a defence by way of set-off and can only be relied upon by way of counterclaim, the plaintiff is deemed to "recover" the whole amount of his proved claim.[18] Such order does not always give a "just result" and it is desirable that the court consider making a special order as to costs.[19]

Special orders as to costs Where exactly the same sum was recovered on both claim and counterclaim, no order was made except that the plaintiff should pay the costs of both.[20] So, again, where the defendant admits the claim but succeeds on the counterclaim, which was the substantive issue between the parties, the successful defendant may be awarded the whole costs,[21] or the order may be that the plaintiff do have the costs up to the date of admission and the defendant do have the costs on the counterclaim which was the only matter litigated,[22] or the plaintiff may be awarded half these costs.[23]

Scale of costs Where the defendant succeeds on his counterclaim, he is entitled to costs on the High Court scale, since sections 19 to 20 of the County Courts Act 1984 do not apply to a counterclaim.[24]

---

[18] *Stooke* v. *Taylor, supra; Baines* v. *Bromley* (1881) 6 Q.B.D. 691 at 694.
[19] See *Chell Engineering Ltd.,* v. *Unit Tool and Engineering Co. Ltd. supra, per* Denning L.J. at 383; and see *Hanak* v. *Green* [1958] 2 Q.B. 9; [1958] 2 All E.R. 141; (C.A.).
[20] *Sprange* v. *Lee* [1908] 1 Ch. 424.
[21] *Childs* v. *Blacker* [1954] 1 W.L.R. 809; [1954] 2 All E.R. 243 (C.A.).
[22] *N.V. Amsterdamsche, etc.* v. *H. & H. Trading Agencies Ltd.* [1940] 1 All E.R. 587 (C.A.).
[23] *Procter and Lavender* v. *G. T. Crouch* (1966) 110 S.J. 273.
[24] *Blake* v. *Appleyard* (1878) 3 Ex.D. 195; *Chatfield* v. *Sedgwick* (1879) 4 C.P.D. 459; *Amon* v. *Bobbett* (1889) 22 Q.B.D. 543.

CHAPTER 9

Reply and Subsequent Pleadings

Function of Reply

Leave   A reply may be served by the plaintiff in answer to the defence of the defendant without leave.[1]

When   It is necessary for the plaintiff to serve a reply in the following cases:

(a) if the defendant has pleaded a counterclaim which the plaintiff desires to contest: for he must, in his reply and defence to counterclaim, deal specifically with every allegation of fact contained in the counterclaim of which he does not admit the truth, except the claim for damages.[2]

(b) if he desires to admit, so as to save unnecessary costs, some of the facts alleged in the defence, while denying others, or if he desires to admit the facts, or some of the facts, alleged in the defence, and to meet them by asserting new and additional facts:

(c) if he desires to plead an objection in point of law:

(d) if he desires to plead in answer to the defence that it misstates the cause of action.

No reply—joinder   In many cases it is unnecessary to serve a reply. If no reply is served to a defence which is unaccompanied by a counterclaim, there is an implied joinder of issue on that defence,[3] which means that the material allegations of fact in the defence are deemed to be denied.[4]

Joinder of issue—effect   A joinder of issue operates as a denial of all material allegations in the defence: if pleaded to the whole defence, and if

---

[1] R.S.C., Ord. 18, r. 3(1). As to the time for the service of a reply, see R.S.C., Ord. 18, r. 3(4).

[2] R.S.C., Ord. 18, rr. 18 and 13(3). There can be no joinder of issue, implied or express, on a counterclaim; see R.S.C., Ord. 18, r. 14(3).

[3] R.S.C., Ord. 18, r. 14(4). The amount of the damages is not deemed to be traversed and therefore must be specifically traversed.

[4] *Ibid*. r. 14(1).

pleaded only to a part of the defence, to a denial of all such allegations in that part.[5] The reply should answer the whole of the matters to which it is pleaded.

Pleading Technique

Multiple and inconsistent averments   The plaintiff in reply may rely either on legal or on equitable grounds of reply or on both and may plead alternative or inconsistent grounds of reply if he thinks fit.

Reply should plead if possible to the particular grounds of the defence   Where any particular ground of reply applies only to a part of the grounds of defence alleged by the defendant, the paragraph stating that ground of reply should be so expressed as to show distinctly that it is pleaded only to that part.

Pleading points

(a) In replying to a defence the plaintiff may make use of a comprehensive form of tranverse called "a joinder of issue," which runs as follows: "The plaintiff joins issue with the defendant upon his defence." The effect of this sentence is to deny every material allegation of fact in the defence.[6]

(b) The plaintiff may, however, if he wishes, as a matter of course, admit certain allegations in the defence, and join issue on the rest, thus: "The plaintiff joins issue with the defendant on paragraphs 3 and 4 of the defence."

(c) If a reply be served which does not traverse an allegation in the defence, that allegation will be deemed to be admitted.[7]

The reply—a vehicle for positive averments   Frequently the plaintiff must do something more than merely traverse the defence. For a joinder of issue merely contradicts the facts alleged by the defendant: and the plaintiff may often need to set up some affirmative case of his own in answer to those facts. Indeed the proper function of the reply is precisely to raise, in answer to the defence, any matters which must be specifically pleaded, which make the defence not maintainable or which otherwise might take the defendant by surprise or which raise issues of fact not arising out of the defence.[8]

---

[5] *Ibid.* r. 14(4).
[6] *Ibid.* r. 14(2) (*b*) and (4).
[7] *Ibid.* r. 13(1).
[8] *Ibid.* r. 8(1) (*a*), (*b*) and (*c*).

160

Example of positive averment—the pleading technique of confession and avoidance   The reply is the proper place for meeting the defence by using the technique of confession and avoidance.[9] Thus, *e.g.*:

(a) in order to defeat the defence of the Limitation Act, the plaintiff must specifically plead in his reply any fact upon which he relies to take the case out of the statute[10]; or

(b) in order to defeat the defence of the absence of a note or memorandum in writing to satisfy the Law of Property Act 1925, s.40, the plaintiff must specifically plead in his reply part performance relied on[11]; or

(c) in order to defeat a defence justifying the determination of an agreement, the plaintiff must specifically plead in his reply any waiver relied on or any facts relied on to disentitle the defendant to determine the agreement[12]; or

(d) in actions for libel or slander, if the plaintiff intends to set up express malice in answer to the defence setting up publication on a privileged occasion, or as being fair comment on a matter of public interest, he must serve a reply setting out the facts on which he relies.[13]

The Rule against Departure

No departure from causes of action set out in original claim   The plaintiff must not set up in his reply a new cause of action which is not raised either on the writ or in the statement of claim. This is because the plaintiff must not in his reply make any allegation of fact, or raise any new ground of claim inconsistent with his statement of claim.[14] Inconsistent for this purpose does not mean "mutually exclusive" but merely new or different.[15]

"Departure"—meaning   In other words, the reply must not contradict or "depart" from the statement of claim, or it will be ground for an application to strike out the reply in which the defect occurs. For example:

(a) if a plaintiff claims rent on his writ, he cannot claim the same sum in his reply as damages for unlawfully "holding over"[16]; or

[9] See in *Hall* v. *Eve* (1876) 4 Ch. D. 341, *per* James L.J. at 345.
[10] See *Chandler* v. *Vilett* (1670) 2 Wms. Saund. 120 (plaintiff an infant); *Skeet* v. *Lindsay* (1877) 2 Ex. D. 314 (acknowledgement in writing); but see *Busch* v. *Stevens* [1963] 1 Q.B. 1; *Betjemann* v. *Betjemann* [1895] 2 Ch. 474 (concealed fraud).
[11] *Ungley* v. *Ungley* (1877) 5 Ch. D. 887.
[12] *Hall* v. *Eve* (1876) 4 Ch. D. 341.
[13] R.S.C., Ord. 82, r. 3(3).
[14] R.S.C., Ord. 18, r. 10(1).
[15] See *Herbert* v. *Vaughan* [1972] 1 W.L.R. 1128; [1972] 3 All E.R. 122.
[16] *Duckworth* v. *McClelland* (1865) 2 L.R. Ir. 527.

(b) if the statement of claim alleges merely a negligent breach of trust, the reply must not assert that such breach of trust was fraudulent[17]; or

(c) if the statement of claim alleges undue influence exercised on the deceased by the defendant, the reply must not allege that in the alternative it was exercised by the deceased's husband.[18]

Such inconsistent claims should be pleaded, if at all, alternatively in the statement of claim: and the plaintiff may amend or apply to amend his statement of claim in order to plead such allegations or claims in the alternative.[19]

The "new assignment"   Although the plaintiff is not allowed to make a "departure" in his reply, he may "new assign." A new assignment was a pleading in the nature of a special reply, which explained the declaration in a manner as to point out the real or supposed mistake of the defendant, and to show that the defence pleaded was either wholly inapplicable to the causes of action relied upon by the plaintiff, or was applicable only to a part of them. Such a reply is very seldom necessary under the present system of pleading owing to the greater particularity now required in a statement of claim, but it is still sometimes used.[20] As a rule, however, if there be any mistake or possible ambiguity as to the precise nature or extent of the acts complained of or of the right which the defendant relies on as justifying those acts, the pleadings already served should be amended or further particulars ordered.

Defence to Counterclaim

As if the counterclaim were the statement of claim   For the purposes of pleading, a counterclaim is assimilated with a statement of claim, and the defence to counterclaim with a defence. Accordingly, a counterclaim served by the defendant on the plaintiff,[21] or on the plaintiff and an added party,[22] operates as if the counterclaim were a statement of claim and the defendant making it a plaintiff.[23]

Pleading to a counterclaim   If the plaintiff on whom a defendant serves a counterclaim intends to defend it, he must serve on that defendant a

---

[17] *Kingston* v. *Corker* (1892) 29 L.R. Ir. 364.

[18] *Herbert* v. *Vaughan, supra.*

[19] R.S.C., Ord. 18, r. 10(2).

[20] See *Breslauer* v. *Barwick* (1876) 24 W.R. 901; *Collett* v. *Dickinson* (1878) 26 W.R. 403; *Renton Gibbs* v. *Neville* [1900] 2 Q.B. 181.

[21] See R.S.C., Ord. 15, r. 2.

[22] *Ibid.* r. 3.

[23] See R.S.C., Ord. 15 r. 2(2) and Ord. 18, r. 18.

defence to counterclaim.[24] If he serves both a reply and a defence to counterclaim, he must include them in the same document.[25]

Pleading a reply and defence to counterclaim   It must be made perfectly clear how much of the pleading which is called the Reply and Defence to Counterclaim applies to the defence and how much to the counterclaim. For this purpose, the pleading is formally divided into two parts: the first part, which deals with the defence, is headed the "Reply"; and the second part, which deals with the counterclaim, is headed the "Defence to Counterclaim." Thus, it would generally commence with a joinder of issue on the whole or some part of defence; then may follow special pleas to the defence. Lastly comes the defence to the counterclaim, which is subject to substantially the same rules of pleading as a defence to a statement of claim.

Counterclaim—joinder of issue   Since there can be no joinder of issue, implied or express, on a counterclaim,[26] the plaintiff or the added party must specifically traverse every allegation of fact in the counterclaim which he does not intend to admit; for otherwise he will be deemed to admit such allegation.[27] Accordingly, every ground of defence relied on must be specifically pleaded in the defence to counterclaim as it is in a defence,[28] including every defence relied on to an action for the recovery of land,[29] the defence of tender,[30] and the defence of set-off.[31]

Defence to counterclaim—service   The defence to counterclaim must be served by the plaintiff before the expiration of 14 days after the service on him of the counterclaim to which it relates.[32] An added party on whom a counterclaim is served must himself, if he intends to defend it, serve his defence to counterclaim as if it were a defence to a statement of claim.[33]

Judgment in default   If the plaintiff or the added party makes default in the service of his defence to counterclaim, the defendant is entitled to

---

[24] R.S.C., Ord. 18, r. 3(2).
[25] *Ibid.* r. 3(3).
[26] *Ibid.* r. 14(3).
[27] *Ibid.* r. 13(1).
[28] *Ibid.* r. 8(1).
[29] *Ibid.* r. 18(*b*).
[30] *Ibid.*
[31] *Ibid.*
[32] *Ibid.* r. 3(4).
[33] R.S.C., Ord. 15, r. 3(2). He must do so before the expiration of 14 days after the expiration of the time entered for his appearance to the counterclaim. See R.S.C., Ord. 15, r. 3(5).

proceed to enter judgment in default of defence as if the counterclaim were a statement of claim.[34]

Joinder of Issue

When At the close of pleadings[35] there is an implied joinder of issue on the pleading last served.[36] Thus:

(a) there is a joinder of issue on the reply, if there is one; or
(b) on the defence, or the defence to counterclaim, if there is no reply.

Meaning of "joinder" The effect of this rule[37] is to ensure that the parties are ultimately, but definitely, brought to an issue, and that at the close of pleadings[38] the issues between the parties are clearly and precisely defined. Thus:

(a) if no defence is served in answer to the statement of claim or no defence to counterclaim is served in answer to the counterclaim, there are no issues between the parties. The allegations of fact made in the statement of claim or counterclaim are deemed to be admitted[39] and the plaintiff or defendant, as the case may be, may enter, or apply for, judgment in default of pleading[40]; or
(b) if no reply is served in answer to a defence, the allegations of fact in the defence are deemed to be denied.

Subsequent Pleadings

No pleading subsequent to a reply or a defence to counterclaim may be served except with the leave of the court.[41] Such leave to serve a rejoinder or subsequent pleading will not be granted unless it is really required, so as to raise matters which must be specifically pleaded.[42] The practice is that the draft subsequent pleading proposed to be served should be produced to the court on the hearing of the application for leave to serve it.

---

[34] R.S.C., Ord. 19, r. 8 and see p. 238, *infra*.
[35] See p. 43, *supra*.
[36] R.S.C., Ord. 18, r. 14(2)(a).
[37] *Ibid.* r. 14.
[38] As to when pleadings are deemed to be closed see R.S.C., Ord. 18, r. 20.
[39] *Supreme Court Practice 1991*, Vol. 1, para. 19/2/2.
[40] R.S.C., Ord. 19, rr. 2–8.
[41] R.S.C., Ord. 18, r. 4. The pleadings subsequent to a reply, if leave to serve is granted, retain their old names: rejoinder (by defendant), surrejoinder (by plaintiff), rebutter (by defendant) and surrebutter (by plaintiff).
[42] See p. 46 *et seq.*, *supra*; and see *Harry* v. *Davey* [1876] 2 Ch. D. 721; *Norris* v. *Beazley* (1877) 35 L.T. 845. Such leave cannot be obtained *ex parte* (*Monck* v. *Smythe* [1895] 1 Ir. R. 200), but only on summons, when the proposed pleading should be produced at the hearing.

CHAPTER 10

Particulars of Pleadings

Necessary Particulars of Pleadings

Introduction   The practice as to particulars demands in every pleading such a sufficiency of detail as will elucidate the issues to be tried and prevent "surprise" at the trial. No hard-and-fast line can be laid down as to the degree of particularity which is required of the pleader and which an opponent may demand of him when formulating his claim or defence. It is, however, essential that each party should give to his opponent a fair outline of the case which will be raised against him at the hearing, and for this purpose he must set out in the body of his pleading all particulars which are necessary to enable his opponent properly to prepare his case for any interlocutory proceeding and for trial.

Definition   Every pleading must contain the necessary particulars of any claim, defence or other matter pleaded.[1] For this purpose particulars may be described as the details of the case set up[2] and they form part of the pleadings[3] by which a party is bound as much as he is by his pleading.[4]

Particulars of what?   Particulars are required only of material facts and not of evidence.[5] They must be distinguished from the mode by which the case of a party is to be proved.[6] Nevertheless, where the essential details

---

[1] R.S.C., Ord. 18. r. 12(1).
[2] See *The Rory* (1882) 7 P.D. 117 at 121.
[3] See *United Telephone Co.* v. *Smith* (1889) 61 L.T. 617; and see *Arnold and Butler* v. *Bottomley* [1908] 2 K.B. 151, *per* Vaughan Williams L.J. at 155.
[4] *Yorkshire Provident Life Assurance Co.* v. *Gilbert* [1895] 2 Q.B. 148 (C.A.); *Symonds* v. *City Bank* (1886) 34 W.R. 364; *Woolley* v. *Broad* [1892] 2 Q.B. 317.
[5] See *Benbow* v. *Low* (1880) 16 Ch.D. 93 at 95; *Cave* v. *Torre* (1886) 54 L.T. 515; *Briton Medical and General Life Association Ltd.* v. *The Britannia Fire Association and Whinney* (1888) 59 L.T. 889.
[6] See *Duke and Sons* v. *Wisden & Co.* (1897) 77 L.T. 67, *per* Lindley L.J. at 68.

or elements of any claim, defence or other matter pleaded are necessary, they must be contained in every pleading, which otherwise will fail to comply with the overriding requirement that all material facts relied on must be pleaded.[7]

How much particularity   The precise degree of particularity required in any particular case cannot of course be predicated, but as much certainty and particularity must be insisted on as is reasonable having regard to the circumstances and the nature of the facts alleged.[8] As Cotton L.J. stated in *Philipps* v. *Philipps*[9]:

> "What particulars are to be stated must depend on the facts of each case. But in my opinion it is absolutely essential that the pleading, not to be embarrassing to the defendants, should state those facts which will put the defendants on their guard and tell them what they have to meet when the case comes on for trial."

Particulars of a pleading should therefore indicate to the opposite party the nature of the evidence required by him.[10]

Rule requirements   In the following cases, because of the seriousness, gravity or importance of the allegation relied on, there is an express requirement that the necessary particulars relied on to support such allegation must be contained in the pleading:

(a) misrepresentation, fraud, breach of trust, wilful default, or undue influence on which the party pleading relies[11];

(b) particulars of the facts on which the party relies must be contained in the pleading where he alleges any condition of the mind of any person, whether any disorder or disability of mind or any malice, fraudulent intention or other condition of mind except knowledge[12]; although;

---

[7] See R.S.C., Ord. 18, r. 7(1).

[8] See *Ratcliffe* v. *Evans* [1892] 2 Q.B. 524, *per* Bowen L.J. at 533, who added: "To insist upon less would be to relax old and intelligible principles. To insist upon more would be the vainest pedantry."

[9] (1878) 4 Q.B.D. 127 at 139; and see *Weinberger* v. *Inglis* [1918] 1 Ch. 133. "[P]articulars should be limited to what is really reasonably necessary to enable the party seeking them to know what case he has to meet," *per* Jenkins L.J. in *Phipps* v. *Orthodox Unit Trusts Ltd.* [1958] 1 Q.B. 314 at 321 (C.A.). In this case particulars of the plaintiff's tax liability were ordered where he was claiming damages for wrongful dismissal.

[10] See *Elkington* v. *London Association for the Protection of Trade* (1911) 27 T.L.R. 329; and see *per* Lord Radcliffe in *Esso Petroleum Co.* v. *Southport Corporation* [1956] A.C. 218 at 241.

[11] R.S.C., Ord. 18, r. 12(1)(*a*).

[12] *Ibid.* r. 12(1)(*b*).

(c) Where a claim for damages is made against a party pleading particulars of any facts relied on in mitigation of, or otherwise in relation to, the amount of damages[13];

(d) In an action for personal injuries, the plaintiff must serve with his statement of claim[14];

   (1) a medical report, *i.e.* a report substantiating all the personal inquiries alleged in the statement of claim which the plaintiff proposes to adduce in evidence as part of his case at the trial[15] and

   (2) a statement of the special damages claimed, *i.e.* a statement giving full particulars of the special damages claimed for expenses and losses, already incurred and an estimate of any future expenses and losses including loss of earnings and of pension rights.[16]

(e) in an action under the Fatal Accidents Act 1976 as amended, the plaintiff must set out in or serve with his statement of claim particulars of the person or persons for whom and on whose behalf the action is brought and the nature of the claim in support of which damages are sought to be recovered.[17]

(f) In an action for defamation, there is an express requirement that particulars must be given of certain allegations, namely,

   (i) particulars of what is sometimes called a legal or true innuendo, *i.e.* that the words or matters complained of were used in a defamatory sense other than their ordinary meaning[18];

   (ii) particulars of the "rolled-up" plea, *i.e.* particulars stating which of the words complained of are alleged to be statements of fact, and of the facts and matters relied on in support of the allegation that the words are true[19];

   (iii) particulars of an allegation that the defendant was actuated by express malice to defeat the defence of fair comment on a matter of public interest or publication on a privileged

[13] *Ibid.* r. 12(1)(*c*). The *amount* of damages will no longer be deemed to be traversed; see R.S.C., Ord. 18, r. 13(4); and particulars must be given of any ground, including a plea in mitigation on which it is open to the defendant to contest the amount of damages.

[14] The Court may order a later specified date within which such service may be made or make such other order as it thinks fit, including dispensing with such service or staying the proceedings: R.S.C., Ord. 18, r. 12(1B).

[15] *Ibid.* r. 12(1A)(*a*) and (1C).

[16] *Ibid.* r. 12(1A)(*b*) and (1C).

[17] Fatal Accidents Act 1976, s.2(4); and see R.S.C. Ord. 80, r. 11(2). For other instances in which necessary particulars are required to be served by express provisions, see R.S.C., Ord. 76, r. 9(3) (nature of the case relied on to support certain defences in a probate action); Ord. 77, r. 3 (particulars in proceedings against the Crown).

[18] R.S.C., Ord. 82, r. 3(1); and see *Lewis* v. *Daily Telegraph* [1964] A.C. 234: [1963] 2 All E.R. 151 especially *per* Lord Reid.

[19] R.S.C., Ord. 82, r. 3(2).

occasion, *i.e.* particulars of the facts and matters from which such malice is to be inferred[20]; and

NOTE—Ord. 82, r. 7, has been revoked by R.S.C. (amendment No. 4) 1989]

Functions of Particulars

"Opening up" the other side's case The function of particulars is to carry into operation the overriding principle that the litigation between the parties, and particularly the trial, should be conducted fairly, openly and without surprises and incidentally to save costs.[21] In earlier times, by way of contrast, as Cotton L.J. has said,[22] "[t]he old system of pleading at common law was to conceal as much as possible what was going to be proved at the trial."

Analysis of the purpose of particulars

(a) To inform the other side of the nature of the case they have to meet as distinguished from the mode in which that case is to be proved.[23]

(b) To prevent the other side being taken by surprise. As Cotton L.J. stated[24].

"The object of particulars is to enable the party asking for them to know what case he has to meet at the trial, and so to save unnecessary expense, and avoid allowing parties to be taken by surprise."

(c) To enable the other side to know what evidence they ought to be prepared with and to prepare for trial.[25] As Lord Radcliffe said[26]:

"It seems to me that it is the purpose of such particulars that they should help to define the issues and to indicate to the party who asks for them how much of the range of his possible evidence will be relevant and how much irrelevant to those issues. Proper use of them shortens the hearing and reduces costs. But

---

[20] *Ibid.* r. 3(3).

[21] See *Supreme Court Practice 1991*, Vol. 1, para. 18/12/2, cited with approval by Edmund Davies L.J. in *Astrovlanis Compania Naviera S.A.* v. *Linard* [1972] 2 Q.B. 611 at 620.

[22] In *Spedding* v. *Fitzpatrick* (1888) 38 Ch.D. 410 at 414.

[23] *Duke and Sons* v. *Wisden & Co.* (1897) 77 L.T. 67, *per* Lindley L.J. at 68; and see *Young & Co.* v. *Scottish Union Co.* (1908) 24 T.L.R. 73, *per* Buckley L.J. at 74; *Aga Khan* v. *Times Publishing Co.* [1924] 1 K.B. 675 at 679.

[24] In *Spedding* v. *Fitzpatrick* (1888) 38 Ch.D. 410 at 413: and see also *Newport Dry Dock Co.* v. *Paynter* (1886) 34 Ch.D. 88, *per* Cotton L.J. at 93; *Thomson* v. *Birkley* (1882) 31 W.R. 230; *Hennessey* v. *Wright* (1888) 57 L.J.Q.B. 594; *The Rory* (1882) 7 P.D. 117; *Weinberger* v. *Inglis* [1918] 1 Ch 133, *per* Astbury J. at 138.

[25] See *Thorp* v. *Holdsworth* [1876] 3 Ch.D. 637, *per* Jessel M.R. at 639; *Spedding* v. *Fitzpatrick* (1889) 38 Ch.D. 410, *per* Cotton L.J. at 413; *Elkington* v. *London Association for the Protection of Trade* (1911) 27 T.L.R. 329 at 320.

[26] In *Esso Petroleum Co. Ltd.* v. *Southport Corporation* [1956] A.C. 218 at 241.

if an appellate court is to treat reliance upon them as pedantry or mere formalism, I do not see what part they have to play in our trial system."

(d) To limit the generality of the pleadings[27] or of the claim or the evidence.[28]

(e) To limit and define the issues to be tried and as to which discovery is required.[29]

(f) To tie the hands of the party so that he cannot without leave go into any matter not fairly included therein,[30] and conversely if a party should omit to request or apply for an order for particulars which ought to have been given, the opposing party will be entitled to give evidence at the trial of any fact which supports any material allegation in his pleading.[31]

Analysis of what is *not* the function of particulars   Particulars are not a substitute for:

(a) necessary averments in the pleading;

(b) to state the material facts omitted in order, by filling the gaps, to make good an inherently bad pleading[32]; nor should a request for particular be used

(c) to obtain information which can only be obtained by interrogatories[33] and the court will not sanction any attempt to administer interrogatories in the guise of seeking particulars.[34]

Request and Orders for Particulars

First—a request   This is appropriate and perhaps necessary where the opposite party:

(a) pleads material facts too broadly, generally or vaguely; or

(b) does not condescend to particulars; or

---

[27] *Saunders* v. *Jones* (1877) 7 Ch.D. 435, *per* Thesiger L.J.
[28] *Millbank* v. *Milbank* [1900] 1 Ch. 376 at 385.
[29] *Yorkshire Provident Life Assurance Co.* v. *Gilbert* [1895] 2 Q.B. 148; and see *Milbank* v. *Milbank supra, per* Vaughan Williams L.J. at 385. See also *Thomson* v. *Birkley* (1883) 31 W.R. 230, *per* Watkin Williams J.: "[Particulars] limit inquiry at the trial to matters set out in the particulars. They tend to narrow issues and ought to be encouraged."
[30] *Philipps* v. *Philipps* (1878) 4 Q.B.D. 127, *per* Brett L.J. at 133; and see *Woolley* v. *Broad* [1892] 2 Q.B. 317.
[31] *Dean and Chapter of Chester* v. *Smelting Corporation Ltd.* (1902) 85 L.T. 67; *Hewson* v. *Cleeve* [1904] 2 Ir.R. 536.
[32] *Bruce* v. *Odhams Press Ltd.* [1936] 1 K.B. 697, *per* Scott L.J. at 712, and again in *Pinson* v. *Lloyds and National Provincial Bank* [1941] 2 K.B. 72 at 75.
[33] *Young & Co.* v. *Scottish Union Co.* (1907) 24 T.L.R. 73 at 74.
[34] *Lister & Co.* v. *Thompson* (1891) 7 L.T.R. 107.

(c) if the particulars given are insufficient or inadequate or he omits to plead necessary particulars, the opposite party may attack the pleading by making a written request for the required particulars.

The importance of making such an application is that otherwise a party will be taken to waive such particulars and he cannot at the trial exclude specific evidence in support of a general allegation.[35] The application should first be made by letter, otherwise the court may refuse to order particulars to be served.[36]

Only then—by order If the request is not complied with or refused, or if a party considers that the particulars supplied do not give him the information to which he is entitled, he may then apply to the court for an order for further and better particulars.[37] The court may order a party, on such terms as it thinks just, to serve on any other party particulars of any claim, defence or other matter stated in his pleading or in any affidavit of his ordered to stand as a pleading, or a statement of the nature of the case on which he relies.[38]

Modern practice—a tendency to particularise more fully The tendency of modern practice is to incline to particularise and to respond to a valid request for further and better particulars of pleading, more fully.[39]

Greater particularity—advantages and disadvantages

(a) *Advantages* Giving the necessary particulars of pleading not only helps in preparing a case and in stating it with certainty and confidence but also manifests the strength of the party's case. In contrast, the withholding of particulars may suggest a possible weakness in the case and a desire to spring surprise as to the oral evidence at the trial.

(b) *Disadvantages* Particulars of pleadings beyond those that are really necessary may fetter the hands of a party too closely,[40] or lay on him an increased burden of proof,[41] or may disclose more of his case at that stage than may be wise. Hence, the situation can arise where one party will seek to compel the opposite party to reveal, by particulars, more

[35] *Dean and Chapter of Chester* v. *Smelting Corporation Ltd.* (1902) 85 L.T. 67; *Hewson* v. *Cleeve* [1904] 2 Ir.R. 536; and see p. 169, *supra*.
[36] R.S.C., Ord. 18, r. 12(6). As a rule where a party omits without excuse to apply for particulars by letter, he will have to pay the costs of obtaining the order for such particulars to be served.
[37] See R.S.C., Ord. 18. r. 12(3).
[38] *Ibid.*; and see *James* v. *Smith* [1891] 1 Ch. 384.
[39] This is perhaps reflected in the rule itself: R.S.C., Ord. 18, r. 12(3).
[40] See *James* v. *Smith* [1891] 1 Ch. 384.
[41] See *West* v. *Baxendale* (1850) 9 C.B. 141.

fully the case which he has pleaded and to tie him down to narrower issues, whereas the opposite party will seek to keep the issues as wide and general as possible and then to withhold as much of his case as he can.

Procedure

Making the application—when? The application should be made within a reasonable time after the necessity for it has arisen. It should not be delayed. Ordinarily the application is made on, and *not* before, the summons for directions or by notice under such summons.[42] It is generally unnecessary to support such application by any affidavit.[43]

The significance of "delay" Although the court has power to order particulars of pleadings at any time,[44] yet, the court may refuse to order such particulars which a party would otherwise be entitled to where there has been inexcusable delay in making the application, or the application is made at a late stage. This is because there might be a substantial risk of the trial being delayed or of other prejudice being occasioned to the opposite party.[45] Thus, an application for particulars was refused, *inter alia*, because it was made just 12 days before the trial.[45–46]

Applying for particulars in the alternative The application for particulars may be made alternative to an application to strike out or to compel the amendment of a defective or embarrassing pleading.[47] In some cases, the particulars ordered may really amount to an amendment of the pleading.[48]

When particulars will not be ordered The court will not make an order for particulars:

(a) if it is satisfied that the other party cannot give them;
(b) if it would be oppressive or unreasonable to make such an order; or

---

[42] Unless, of course, the particulars are necessary or desirable to enable the defendant to serve his defence; see R.S.C., Ord. 18, r. 12(5). In actions for personal injuries in which automatic directions take effect under R.S.C., Ord. 25, r. 8, such an application should ordinarily be made after close of pleadings.

[43] See *Sachs* v. *Spielman* (1887) 37 Ch.D. 295 at 304, 305; *Roberts* v. *Owen* (1890) 6 T.L.R. 172; *Blackie* v. *Osmaston* (1884) 28 Ch.D.119.

[44] See *Thomson* v. *Birkley* (1882) 47 L.T. 700.

[45–46] *Astrovlanis Compania Naviera S.A.* v. *Linard* [1972] 2 Q.B. 611; [1972] 2 All E.R. 647 and see *Gouraud* v. *Fitzgerald* (1888) 37 W.R. 265.

[47] See *Seligmann* v. *Young* [1884] W.N. 93.

[48] See *Milbank* v. *Milbank* [1900] 1 Ch. 376, *per* Vaughan Williams L.J. at 385; and see *Bruce* v. *Odhams Press Ltd.* [1936] 1 K.R. 697, *per* Scott L.J. at 712–714.

(c) if what sought to be particularised is a mere admission[49] or a mere traverse[50];

(d) particulars will not as a rule be ordered of any immaterial allegation.[51] Particulars will also as a rule not be ordered of allegations as to which the burden of proof lies on the applicant.[52] However, particulars may be ordered of an allegation which it was not necessary for the pleader to have inserted[53];

(e) no particulars are ever ordered of general damage.[54]

When is it "oppressive or unreasonable?" Particulars will not be ordered where the information is not in the possession of either party or could only be obtained with great difficulty or expense or laborious research or exhaustive inquiry. However, in such cases the court may order a party to give the best particulars he can, with liberty to supplement them within a specified time after the discovery of documents.[55]

What if the party applying for particulars knows the true facts The mere fact that the applicant may or even must know the true facts of the case is not itself an objection to an order for particulars being made, because he is entitled to know the nature of the case being made against him and to tie down the other side by his particulars.[56]

"Fishing" applications for particulars will be dismissed The rule relating to particulars is a rule of pleading only.[57] If the only object of the application is to obtain particulars of the evidence of the other party or some other clue to such evidence, or to obtain the names of witnesses, it will be dismissed.[58] But if particulars of material facts are clearly necessary to enable the applicant properly to prepare for trial, the information

[49] Fox v. H. Wood (Harrow) Ltd. [1963] 2 Q.B. 601 (C.A.).
[50] Weinberger v. Inglis [1918] 1 Ch. 133; Perlak Petroleum Maatschappij v. Deen [1924] 1 K.B. 111 at 114.
[51] Cave v. Torre (1886) 54 L.T. 515 at 518; Gibbons v. Norman (1886) 2 T.L.R. 676; General Stock Exchange v. Bethell (1886) 2 T.L.R. 683.
[52] Cheeseman v. Bowaters United Kingdom Paper Mills Ltd. [1971] 1 W.L.R. 1773; [1971] 3 All E.R. 513; (C.A.).
[53] See Gaston v. United Newspapers Ltd. (1915) 32 T.L.R. 143 (C.A.).
[54] James v. Radnor County Council (1890) 6 T.L.R. 240; Roberts v. Owen (1890) 6 T.L.R. 172, but see Orient Steam Navigation Co. v. Ocean Marine Insurance Co. (1886) 34 W.R. 442. In proceedings before the Official Referee, such particulars are ordinarily ordered in the form of a Scott Schedule, see Chitty and Jacob, Queen's Bench Forms (21st ed., 1987), paras. 1478 et seq.
[55] See Marshall v. The Inter-Oceanic Steam Yachting Co. (1885) 1 T.L.R. 394; Higgins v. Weekes (1889) 5 T.L.R. 238; Williams v. Ramsdale (1887) 36 W.R. 125; Harbord v. Monk (1878) 38 L.T. 411.
[56] Harbord v. Monk, supra; Keogh v. Incorporated Dental Hospital of Ireland [1910] 2 Ir.R. 166.
[57] See Leitch v. Abbott (1886) 31 Ch.D. 374, per Bowen L.J. at 378.
[58] Temperton v. Russell (1893) 9 T.L.R. 318 at 321; Briton Medical, etc. Association v. Britannia Fire Association (1888) 59 L.T. 889.

must be given, even though it discloses some portion of the evidence on which the other party proposes to rely at the trial.[59] This is so even where the plaintiff is privileged from producing documents which would disclose such evidence.[60]

Particularising the "negative pregnant" If a traverse, though negative, is "pregnant" with an affirmative allegation,[61] particulars of such affirmative allegation will be ordered.[62] If however, the traverse is a mere denial, even though of a negative allegation, and it is not possible to read into it an affirmative allegation, particulars will be refused.[63]

The order for particulars The order for particulars should specify with clarity and precision:

(a) what particulars are required to be served; and
(b) the paragraph in the pleading and the particular allegation in relation to which the particulars are being ordered, so that the particulars given will relate to the specific allegation to which it relates.

An order so drafted enables all parties to see exactly which part of which pleading is made the subject of the order for particulars. Moreover, it will help show what particulars are in fact being given in response to the order and thus enable these particulars to be placed immediately after the pleadings to which they relate at the time of the setting down of the action pursuant to R.S.C., Ord. 34, r. 3(2).

Further, the order will ordinarily limit the time when the particulars are to be served, and if necessary, the time for pleading after they are served. The order may provide the form in which the particulars are to be given, as, for example, by marking a position on a plan.[64] The order may also impose terms in the event of a party failing to serve the particulars ordered. It is not the practice to impose such terms when the order is first made. However, in the event of a failure to comply with the order the court may go on to provide:

---

[59] *Zierenberg* v. *Labouchere* [1893] 2 Q.B. 183 at 187, 188; *Bishop* v. *Bishop* [1901] P. 325; *Wootton* v. *Sievier* [1913] 3 K.B. 499 (C.A.); and *cf. Eade* v. *Jacobs* (1878) 3 Ex.D. 335; *Marriott* v. *Chamberlain* (1886) 17 Q.B.D. 154; *Spiers and Pond Ltd.* v. *John Bull Ltd. and Odhams Press Ltd.* (1916) 114 L.T. 641 (cases as to interrogatories).

[60] *Milbank* v. *Milbank* [1900] 1 Ch. 376; and see *Sachs* v. *Speilman* (1887) 37 Ch.D. 295.

[61] See *Machulich* v. *Machulich* [1920] P. 439; *La Radiotechnique* v. *Weinbaum* [1928] Ch. 1.

[62] *Pinson* v. *Lloyds and National Provincial Bank* [1941] 2 K.B. 72 (C.A.); *Inland Revenue Commissioners* v. *Jackson* [1960] 1 W.L.R. 873; [1960] 3 All E.R. 31; and see p. 129, *supra.*

[63] *Duke's Court Estates Ltd.* v. *Associated British Engineering Ltd.* [1948] Ch. 458; [1948] 2 All E.R. 137; *Chapple* v. *Electrical Trades Union* [1961] 1 W.L.R. 1290. But see *Regina Fur Co. Ltd.* v. *Bossom* [1958] 2 Lloyd's Rep. 425 at 428.

[64] See *Tarbox* v. *St. Pancras Borough Council* [1952] 1 All E.R. 1306 (C.A.).

(a) that if proper particulars are not served within a specified time, the action shall stand dismissed or the defence struck out[65]; or
(b) that the allegation of which particulars are ordered should be struck out from the pleading; or
(c) that the party be precluded from giving evidence in support of such allegation.[66]

In summary, the dividing line between particulars and evidence may sometimes be difficult to draw.[67]

"Particulars" do not stop the pleading clock An order for particulars does not operate as a stay of proceedings or give any extension of time for pleading. If necessary, therefore, the order should specify the time for pleading after the particulars ordered are served; and moreover, pleadings are deemed to be closed notwithstanding that any request or order for particulars has been made but has not been complied with.[68]

Applying for Particulars before Defence

Usually—no A request for particulars of the statement of claim can be used as an instrument for delay. To prevent such potential abuse, an order for particulars will not be made before the service of the defence, unless the order is necessary or desirable to enable the defendant to plead, or for some other special reason.[69]

When Particulars before defence are necessary or desirable where otherwise:

(a) the defendant would be prejudiced or embarrassed in his pleading[70]; or
(b) to enable the defendant to decide how to plead.[71]

Thus, where the defendant genuinely desires to consider making a payment into court, particulars of special damage will ordinarily be ordered before defence, as, for example, in actions for wrongful dismissal.[72] On

[65] See *Davey* v. *Bentinck* [1893] 1 Q.B 185 (C.A.).
[66] See *Young* v. *Geiger* (1848) 6 C.B. 541; *Ibbetti* v. *Leaver* (1847) 16 M. & W. 770.
[67] See R.S.C., Ord. 18. r. 20(2); and see p. 165, *supra*, note five.
[68] It may be that the right course is to end such issues as to particulars by introducing the more open system of pre-trial disclosure of admissible evidence relied on by both parties.
[69] R.S.C., Ord. 18, r. 12(5). This rule was added in 1919 (R.S.C. March 1919) as the pre-1964 Ord. 19, r. 7B.
[70] See *Selangor United Rubber Estates Ltd.* v. *Cradock* [1965] Ch. 896; [1964] 3 All E.R. 709; (particulars of the relation under which the duty between the parties is alleged to arise).
[71] *Bruce* v. *Odhams Press Ltd.* [1936] 1 K.B. 697 (C.A.).
[72] See *Monk* v. *Redwing Aircraft Ltd.* [1942] 1 K.B. 182 (C.A.); *Phipps* v. *Orthodox Unit Trusts Ltd.* [1958] 1 Q.B. 314; [1957] 3 All E.R. 305; (C.A.).

the other hand, although the defendant may be entitled to the particulars requested, they will not be ordered before the defence if they are not necessary or desirable at that stage. Thus, where the defendant intends to contest the issue of whether he is an accounting party, particulars of the sums alleged to have been paid to him will not be ordered before the defence.[73]

Particulars before Discovery or Discovery before Particulars

General rule Particulars of pleadings will usually be ordered before the discovery of documents or the administration of interrogatories. That is because the party pleading presumably knows the material facts on which he relies to support his claim or defence.[74] Thus where the defendant pleads justification in an action of defamation, the court will generally order him to serve particulars before discovery, and will not allow him to avoid giving particulars of justification until after discovery.[75] Moreover, particulars may be ordered to be served before discovery or interrogatories with liberty to supplement them by serving further particulars after discovery or interrogatories.

Exceptions to the general rule Where the circumstances are such that the party pleading does not know the facts necessary to enable him to give the particulars requested, but his opponent knows or ought to know them, the party applying for particulars may be ordered to give discovery or answer interrogatories before the party pleading is required to serve particulars.[76] As Bowen L.J. said in *Millar* v. *Harper*[77]:

> "It is good practice and good sense that where the Defendant knows the facts and the Plaintiffs do not, the Defendant should give discovery before the Plaintiff delivers particulars."

[73] *Sharer* v. *Wallace* [1950] 2 All E.R. 463.
[74] Thus in *Cyril Leonard & Co.* v. *Simo Securities Trust* [1972] 1 W.L.R. 80; [1971] 3 All E.R. 1318 (C.A.), in an action for wrongful dismissal, the defendants were ordered to serve the best particulars they could give before discovery of the alleged failures to exercise due care, skill and diligence to justify the dismissal.
[75] *Arnold and Butler* v. *Bottomley* [1908] 2 K.B. 151; *Zierenberg* v. *Labouchere* [1893] 2 Q.B. 183 (C.A.): *Goldschmidt* v. *Constable & Co.* [1937] 4 All E.R. 293 (C.A.); see, however, *Russell* v. *Stubbs* [1913] 2 K.B. 200n. (discovery before particulars of person to whom libel published).
[76] See *Philipps* v. *Philipps* (1878) 4 Q.B.D. 127, *per* Bramwell B. at 130, 131, and observations thereon *Philipps* v. *Philipps* (1879) 5 Q.B.D. 60 (C.A.); and see *Sachs* v. *Speilman* (1887) 37 Ch.D. 295; *Edelston* v. *Russell* (1888) 57 L.T. 927; *Maxim Nordenfelt Guns and Ammunition Co.* v. *Nordenfelt No. 2)* [1893] 3 Ch. 122 (C.A.); *Waynes Merthyr Co.* v. *Radford & Co.* [1896] 1 Ch. 29; *Stirling-Winthrop Group Ltd.* v. *Farbenfabriken Bayer A.G.* [1969] R.P.C. 274.
[77] (1888) 38 Ch.D. 110 at 112 (discovery of chattels in inventory before particulars of chattels claimed).

Again where a party has good grounds for his claim but can plead it only in a general way, he will be allowed discovery before being ordered to serve detailed particulars. As Bowen L.J. again said in *Leitch* v. *Abbot*[78]:

> "[T]he very fact that the pleader is unable to plead except in general terms, is in many cases the very reason why he should have discovery from the other party, so as to enable him to plead [the fraud] in detail."

No hard and fast rule can be laid down and each case will turn on its own facts.[79]

Discovery before statement of claim   Although the court has jurisdiction to order discovery of documents before the service of pleadings, *e.g.* a statement of claim, the discretion to do so should be exercised only in exceptional circumstances. Accordingly, it would decline to order the defendants to give discovery before the plaintiffs served their statement of claim, *e.g.* in a passing-off action in which the plaintiffs had alleged serious allegations of a deliberate intention to mislead the public through their packaging and advertising campaigns.[80]

Form and Service of Particulars

In the pleading itself   Particulars are ordinarily embodied in the pleading. They follow immediately after the paragraph containing the allegation of which they constitute the necessary particulars under the title "Particulars," describing what they are particulars of, *e.g.*"Particulars of Negligence" or particulars of Special Damage.

Separate—but accompanying pleadings   If the particulars are served separately they must be referred to in the pleading. as, *e.g.*:
   (a) "The particulars of the said breaches of covenants exceed three folios and are served separately herewith." They should also be intituled like a pleading, and headed "Particulars" with a state-

---

[78] (1886) 31 Ch.D. 374 at 379 (action against stockbroker alleging fraud); and see *Whyte* v. *Ahrens* (1884) 26 Ch.D. 717 (C.A.) (discovery before particulars in action alleging fraud and receipt of secret commissions by agents).

[79] *Waynes Merthyr Co.* v. *Radford* [1896] 1 Ch. 29; *Russell* v. *Stubbs Ltd.* [1913] 2 K.B. 200 (C.A.); and note *Barham* v. *Huntingfield* (*Lord*) [1913] 2 K.B. 193 (C.A.); *Ross* v. *Blakes' Motors Ltd.* [1951] 2 All E.R. 689 (C.A.). Where a fiduciary relation exists between the parties, discovery will generally be ordered before service of particulars. See *Zierenberg* v. *Labouchere* [1893] 2 Q.B. 183; and see *Waynes Merthyr Co.* v. *Radford & Co. supra,* but the practice is not restricted to such cases: *Ross* v. *Blakes Motors Ltd. supra.*

[80] *R.H.M. Foods Ltd.* v. *Bovril Ltd.* [1982] 1 W.L.R. 661; [1982] 1 All E.R. 673; (C.A.), distinguishing *A. J. Bekhor & Co. Ltd.* v. *Bilton* [1981] Q.B. 923; [1981] 2 All E.R. 565.

ment identifying the paragraph and the allegation of which they are the necessary particulars, as for example "Particulars of breaches of covenant under paragraph [6] of the statement of claim" or as the case may be and they should if necessary be signed and served as a pleading, stating the date of their service;

(b) Where it is necessary to give particulars of debt, expenses or damages, and those particulars exceed three folios,[81] they must be set out in a separate document referred to in the pleading and the pleading must state whether the document has already been served and, if so, when, or is to be served with the pleading, as for example, "the particulars of the special damages exceed three folios and are served separately herewith [or will be served after discovery]."

(c) In an action for personal injuries there must be served with the statement of claim a medical report and a statement of the special damages claimed.[82]

Particulars pursuant to request or order If the particulars are served pursuant to a request or under an order of the court, they become part of the pleading of which they are the necessary particulars.[83] Thus, they should be served, not in the form of a letter, but as a formal document in the same way as a pleading. It must bear the title of the action, a description of the pleading of which they are the necessary particulars, and a statement showing whether they are served pursuant to a request or an order of the court. The particulars should be set out under each paragraph of the request or order as follows[84]:

General Form of Particulars

IN THE HIGH COURT OF JUSTICE   19__. B. No. __
  QUEEN'S BENCH DIVISION

Between   *A B* .... Plaintiff

                                 and

                                 C D .... Defendant

---

[81] A folio is 72 words, every figure being counted as a word.

[82] R.S.C., Ord. 18, r. 12(1A).

[83] Any request or order for particulars and the particulars given constitute part of the requisite documents which must be lodged on setting down the action for trial, see R.S.C., Ord. 34, r. 3(1)(b) and *Supreme Court Practice 1991*, Vol. 1, para. 34/3/2.

[84] R.S.C., Ord. 18, r. 12(7).

PARTICULARS OF PLEADINGS

FURTHER AND BETTER PARTICULARS OF THE STATEMENT OF CLAIM [THE DEFENCE *OR AS MAY BE*] PURSUANT TO THE REQUEST [OR ORDER OF MASTER _____.] DATED _____.

[*Here state the request or order for the particulars in numbered or lettered paragraphs and sub-paragraphs, and the further and better particulars given after each item*] '

Served the _____ day of _____ 19__ by _____

Signed _____

Signature If the particulars are settled by counsel, they must be signed by him, and if not, by the party's solicitor or by the party acting in person.[85]

Amendment of Particulars

General rule A party who has served particulars of his pleading cannot amend or withdraw or add to them without the leave of the court.

Exceptions Particulars incorporated in the pleading may be amended once without leave before the pleadings are deemed to be closed.[86]

Leave Accordingly, leave to amend, withdraw or add to particulars must be obtained on the summons for directions or notice thereunder.[87]

Amendment—when allowed If the application is made a reasonable time before trial, it will generally be allowed on terms of the applicant paying the costs thrown away in any event.

Amendment—when refused

(a) If the other party to the action would be seriously prejudiced by such amendment or some injury would be caused which could not be compensated by costs.[88]

---

[85] See R.S.C., Ord. 18, r. 6(5).

[86] See R.S.C., Ord. 20, r. 3(1).

[87] See *Yorkshire Provident Assurance Co.* v. *Gilbert* [1895] 2 Q.B. 148, *per* Lindley L.J. at 152; *Spedding* v. *Fitzpatrick* (1888) 38 Ch.D. 410, *per* Lopes L.J. at 413; *Woolley* v. *Broad* [1892] 2 Q.B. 317 (C.A.); *Cropper* v. *Smith* (1884) 26 Ch.D. 700. In actions for personal injuries such leave may be obtained in a separate summons for the purpose required under R.S.C., Ord. 25, r. 8(3).

[88] *Clarapede* v. *Commercial Union Association* (1883) 32 W.R. 262 (C.A.).

178

(b) If it is sought thereby to introduce a new cause of action to the prejudice of the other party, *e.g.* to raise a charge of fraud for the first time.[89]

(c) Or to increase the amount claimed in the action after the defendant has made a payment into Court on the basis of the amount claimed.[90]

(d) Or at a late stage in the action, especially if the nature and extent of the amount claimed constitute a substantial change.[91]

Amendment at trial   At the trial leave to amend particulars may be refused[92]. The amendment of even a date will only, as a rule, be allowed upon terms.[93]

Voluntary Particulars

When   It sometimes happens that a party who, in compliance with a request or an order, has given all the particulars then within his knowledge, subsequently discovers new matter which he desires to add to the particulars already served so as to enable him to prove them at the trial.

How

(a) *The safer course* is to apply for leave to serve further particulars. Without such leave he has strictly no right to add anything to those already served and by which he is bound.[94]

(b) *Alternative*   If, however, further particulars are served without an order and are accepted by the opposite party, they will supersede or supplement the original particulars. The irregularity is waived by receiving the fresh particulars and continuing the proceedings in the action without making any objection.[95]

(c) *Tactics*   Serve the voluntary particulars under cover of a letter stating that if no objection is expressed within 21 days, the irregularity will be deemed to have been waived.

---

[89] *Cocksedge* v. *Metropolitan Coal Consumers' Association Ltd.* (1892) 65 L.T. 432; *Hendriks* v. *Montague* (1881) 17 Ch. D. 638 at 642.

[90] *Sanders* v. *Hamilton* (1907) 96 L.T. 679. The court may, however, so frame its order as to prevent prejudice to the defendant, by providing *e.g.*, that if the defendant should increase the amount of the payment into court, such increase should operate as if it was made at the date of the original payment into court.

[91] *Perestrello e Companhia Limitada* v. *United Paint Co. Ltd.* [1969] 1 W.L.R. 570; [1969] 3 All E.R. 479 (C.A.).

[92] *Moss* v. *Malings* (1886) 33 Ch.D. 603.

[93] *McCarthy* v. *Fitzgerald* [1909] 2 Ir.R. 445. The present practice is more flexible.

[94] *Yorkshire Provident Co.* v. *Gilbert* [1895] 2 Q.B. 148; *Emden* v. *Burns* (1894) 10 T.L.R. 400; and see the principle discussed in *Kent Coal Concessions* v. *Duguid* [1910] A.C. 452 (H.L.)(E.).

[95] *Fromant* v. *Ashley* (1853) 1 E. & B. 723.

If fair and proper particulars have been served without leave, an application to have them set aside could rarely be attended with any material advantage, as, on application under such circumstances, an order would probably be made that the fresh particulars should stand.

Particulars of Specific Matters Pleaded

Introduction The general rule that every pleading must contain the necessary particulars of any claim, defence or other matter pleaded applies to allegations of every kind contained in every pleading. It would therefore overburden this work to set out here in the form of a list or otherwise, the many and diversified allegations of which particulars may be required or ordered, and if so what those particulars should be.[96]

Examples of particulars required by rule Without prejudice to the generality of the rule requiring necessary particulars to be given of any claim, defence or other matter pleaded, it is expressly provided that necessary particulars must be given of the following allegations[97]; namely:

    (a) misrepresentations[98];

    (b) fraud[99];

    (c) breach of trust[1];

    (d) wilful default[2];

    (e) undue influence[3];

    (f) any condition of the mind of any person, whether any disorder or disability of mind or any malice[4];

---

[96] *Supreme Court Practice 1991*, Vol. 1, paras. 18/12/3 *et seq.*

[97] See R.S.C., Ord. 18, r. 12(1).

[98] Section on "Misrepresentation," p. 166, *infra.*

[99] See section on "Fraud," p. 166 *infra.*

[1] See *Re Anstice* (1885) 54 L.J.Ch. 1104; *Re Symons* (1882) 21 Ch.D. 757; *Smith* v. *Armitage* (1883) 24 Ch.D. 727; *Re Wrightson* [1908] 1 Ch. 789 at 799. Moreover, it is not enough to plead all the facts necessary to show a dishonest breach of trust on the part of the defendant or to plead that the defendant was aware or ought to have been aware of those facts, since it is necessary clearly and unequivocally to plead knowledge on the part of the defendant of the dishonesty of that breach of trust: *Belmont Finance Corporation Ltd.* v. *Williams Furniture Ltd.* [1979] Ch. 250; [1978] 3 W.L.R. 712; [1979] 1 All E.R. 118 (C.A.).

[2] *Ibid.*

[3] P. 166 *supra*, and see *Bruty* v. *Edmundson* [1917] 2 Ch. 285, at 292; *affirmed* [1918] 1 Ch. 112.

[4] In probate actions, particulars of the nature of the unsoundness, and of the character of the undue influence and the acts alleged in the exercise of it, with necessary dates, must be given (see R.S.C., Ord. 76, r. 9(3) but not of the names of the persons present (*Re Shrewsbury* [1922] P. 112). While a party cannot under cover of a plea of want of knowledge and approval affirmatively plead in substance an allegation of undue influence or fraud without specifically introducing it as an alternative plea, nevertheless a party may plead allegations, which if proved, might constitute evidence that could

(g) fraudulent intention or other condition of mind[5];

(h) the facts on which a party relies to support an allegation of knowledge[6];

(i) particulars of any notice alleged[7];

(j) particulars of any facts in which the party relies in mitigation of, or otherwise in relation to the amount of damages.[8]

(k) particulars are also expressly required to be given of certain allegations in defamation actions[9];

(l) in actions under the Fatal Accidents Act 1976.[10]

Particulars in other pleadings   Instances of some of the other more common kinds of claims, defences and other matters pleaded of which particulars may be required or ordered include the following[11]:

(a) account[12];

(b) account stated or settled[13];

(c) assignment[14];

(d) breach of statutory duty[15];

(e) concealed fraud[16];

---

immediately assist proof of the relevant alternative plea under R.S.C., Ord. 76, r. 9(3) (*Re Stott (dec'd.), Klouda* v. *Lloyds Bank Ltd.* [1980] 1 W.L.R. 246; [1980] 1 All E.R. 259).

[5] See *Feeny* v. *Rix* [1968] Ch. 693 (intention); *Alman* v. *Oppert* [1901] 2 K.B. 576 (belief).

[6] See R.S.C., Ord. 18, r. 12(4)(*a*); and see p. 85, *supra*.

[7] See R.S.C., Ord. 18, r. 12(4)(*b*); and see p. 65, *supra*.

[8] R.S.C., Ord. 18, r. 12(1)(*c*).

[9] See R.S.C., Ord. 82, r. 3. and see p. 167, *supra*.

[10] See Fatal Accidents Act 1976, ss.2(4) and 4; and see p. 167, *supra*. For other provisions expressly requiring particulars to be given see p. 166, *supra*.

[11] See the appropriate sections of the statement of claim and defence relating to each of these instances.

[12] No particulars necessary of claim for general account (see *Augustinus* v. *Nerinckx* (1880) 16 Ch.D. 13; *Sharer* v. *Wallace* [1950] 2 All E.R. 463; *Re Wells, Decd.* [1962] 1 W.L.R. 397) but particulars necessary of claims for specific or definite sums (see *Blackie* v. *Osmaston* (1884) 28 Ch.D. 119; *Carr* v. *Anderson* (1901) 18 T.L.R. 206; *Kemp* v. *Goldberg* (1887) 36 Ch.D. 505 at 507). In a patent action if an account of profits is ordered the names and addresses of purchasers of the infringing article must, if possible, be given: *Saccharin Corp* v. *Chemicals and Drugs Co.* [1900] 59 L.J. Ch. 820.

[13] In an action on stated accounts, the defendant is entitled to particulars of the "debts or claims in respect of which the said accounts are alleged to have been on both sides or on one side only, and stating the nature and amount of each such debt or claim," *Kleinberger* v. *Norris* (1937) 183 L.T.J. 107.

[14] Particulars necessary to show absolute assignment in writing and notice in writing of assignment to defendant (see s.25(6) of the Supreme Court of Judicature (Consolidation) Act 1925); and see *Seear* v. *Lawson* (1880) 16 Ch.D. 121; *Read* v. *Brown* (1888) 22 Q.B.D. 128; *Bradley* v. *Chamberlyn* [1893] 1 Q.B. 439 at 441.

[15] See p. 86.

[16] Full particulars necessary (see *Riddell* v. *Earl of Strathmore* (1887) 3 T.L.R. 329; *Betjemann* v. *Betjemann* [1895] 2 Ch. 474; *Bulli Coal Mining Co.* v. *Osborne* [1899] A.C. 351). The fraud alleged must be the fraud of the person setting up the Statute of Limitation or of some one through whom he claims: *Re McCallum* [1901] 1 Ch. 143. But

    (f) condition[17];

    (g) consideration[18];

    (h) conspiracy[19];

    (i) contract[20];

    (j) contributory negligence[21];

    (k) credits[22];

    (l) damages[23];

    (m) defamation[24];

    (n) false entries[25];

    (o) false imprisonment[26];

"fraud" in s.32 of the Limitation Act 1980, is not confined to "fraud in the ordinary sense," *i.e.* to give rise to an independent cause of action for deceit: *Beaman* v. *A.R.T.S. Ltd.* [1949] 1 K.B. 550 (C.A.). On the other hand "fraud," in this context, envisages unconscionable conduct in regard to the parties' relationship and the trustee's conduct will not be regarded as "unconscionable" when he did not know that he was acting in breach of trust, and in such a case there would be no "concealment" by him: *Bartlett* v. *Barclays Bank Trust Co. Ltd.* (*Nos. 1 and 2*) [1980] Ch. 515; [1980] 2 W.L.R. 430; [1980] 1 All E.R. 139.

[17] Particulars necessary of express condition (see *Abbs* v. *Matheson* (1898) 104 L.T.J. 268). Particulars of implied condition may also be ordered.

[18] Particulars of consideration to support agreement (see *Cooke* v. *Rickman* [1911] 2 K.B. 1125, *per* Bankes J. at 1130). If the consideration is for any agreement not under seal it is a material fact and must be pleaded except in the case of a negotiable instrument where it is presumed.

[19] In an action for conspiring to induce certain persons by threats to break their contracts with the plaintiffs, the defendant is entitled to particulars, stating the name of each such contractor, the kind of threat used in each case, and when and by which defendant each such threat was made, and whether verbally or in writing; if in writing, identifying the document; but he is not entitled to the names of the workmen in the employ of those contractors whom it is alleged the defendant threatened to "call out" (*Temperton* v. *Russell and Others* [1893] 1 Q.B. 715 at 319). So where the plaintiff alleged that certain directors had instigated the defendant to do something, Kay J. held that the plaintiff ought to state whether such instigation was verbal or in writing, and if verbal by whom it was made, and if in writing the date of such writing (*Briton Medical, etc., Association* v. *Britannia Fire Assn.* (1888) 59 L.T. 889).

[20] See section on "Contract," p. 81 *et seq. supra.*

[21] *Atkinson* v. *Stewart and Partners* [1954] N.I.L.R. 146: *Martin* v. *M'Taggart* [1906] 2 Ir.R. 120; *Toppin* v. *Belfast Corporation* [1909] 2 Ir.R. 181.

[22] Particulars of amount of credit allowed (*Godden* v. *Corsten* (1879) 5 C.P.D. 17; *Kemp* v. *Goldberg* (1887) 36 Ch.D. 505).

[23] See p. 167 *supra.*

[24] See p. 167 *supra.*

[25] See *Newport Dry Dock Co.* v. *Paynter* (1886) 34 Ch.D. 88; *Harbord* v. *Monk* (1878) 38 L.T. 411.

[26] Where the defendant justified the arrest of the plaintiff on the ground that the defendant had reasonable and probable cause for suspecting that a felony had been committed, and that the plaintiff had committed it, he was ordered to give particulars of the alleged felony and also of the reasonable and probable cause for suspicion, but not of the names of those who had given him information against the plaintiff (*Green* v. *Garbutt* (1912) 28 T.L.R. 575 (C.A.); and see *Stapeley* v. *Annets* [1970] 1 W.L.R. 20; [1969] 3 All E.R. 1541, (C.A.)). In a wartime case the plaintiff, having been detained by an order of the Home Secretary, brought an action for false imprisonment and pleaded the terms of the order under which he was detained. There was no suggestion of *mala fides.* The defendant, in his defence, admitted having made the order. The defendant was empowered to

(p) goods sold[27];
(q) lump sums claimed[28];
(r) money claims[29];
(s) negligence[30];
(t) passing-off actions[31];

act "if he has reasonable cause to believe any person to have been, or to be a member of . . . an organisation and that it is necessary to exercise control over him." The plaintiffs applied for particulars of the grounds upon which the defendant had "reasonable cause to believe." It was held that these particulars ought not to be ordered (*Liversidge* v. *Anderson* [1942] A.C. 206, Lord Atkin dissenting.

[27] Particulars necessary of value of goods, price of each claim, and date and amount of each delivery (*Parpaite Frères* v. *Dickinson* (1878) 38 L.T. 178).

[28] Where the claim is for a lump sum, particulars of items must be given (*Philipps* v. *Philipps* (1878) 4 Q.B.D. 127 at 131). Where a bill has been delivered before action, giving items of work and labour done, and subsequently a writ is issued claiming a lump sum for such work and labour, the defendant is entitled to particulars showing how that lump sum is arrived at by reference to the several items of the bill (*Hall* v. *Symons* (1892) 92 L.T.J. 337). Where the plaintiff gives credit for a lump sum, and sues for a balance, he must give particulars of the items of which such credit is composed (*Godden* v. *Corsten* (1879) 5 C.P.D. 17). If he claims a lump sum for money paid, he must give the items and state when and to whom each such payment was made (*Gunn* v. *Tucker* (1891) 7 T.L.R. 280). Where a railway company had charged different rates for carrying different consignments of goods over the same distances, it was ordered to give particulars as to each rate, "distinguishing the charges for conveyance from the terminal charge (if any) and from the dock charges (if any); and if any terminal charges or dock charges be included, specifying the nature and detail of the terminal charges or dock charges in respect of which they are made" (*L. & N.W.R.* v. *Lee* (1891) 7 T.L.R. 603, upheld in the Court of Appeal; but particulars of specific charges are premature, where raising the rate in respect of a whole class may be justified. *The Mansion House Association* v. *G.W.R.* [1895] 2 Q.B. 141). *Cf.* cases cited in *Supreme Court Practice* 1988, Vol. 1, para. 18/12/3 (Account).

[29] Particulars necessary of dates and items of claim; see *Gunn* v. *Tucker* (1891) 7 T.L.R. 280.

[30] Particulars must always be given in the pleading, showing in what respects the defendant was negligent. The statement of claim "ought to state the facts upon which the supposed duty is founded, and the duty to the plaintiff with the breach of which the defendant is charged" (*per* Willes J. in *Gautret* v. *Egerton* (1867) L.R. 2 C.P. 371, cited with approval by Lord Alverstone C.J. in *West Rand Central Gold Mining Co.* v. *R.* [1905] 2 K.B. 391 at 400; *The Kanawha* (1913) 108 L.T. 433). Then should follow an allegation of the precise breach of that duty, of which the plaintiff complains, and, lastly, particulars of the injury and damage sustained. An allegation of negligence on the ground that a party was driving when under the influence of drink must be expressly pleaded, otherwise cross-examination to suggest insobriety should not be allowed (*Bills* v. *Roe* [1968] 1 W.L.R. 925; [1968] 2 All E.R. 636, (C.A.)). Where the plaintiff relies upon "all the provisions of the Highway Code," particulars may be ordered of the particular provisions relied on (*Wells* v. *Weeks* (*Practice Note*) [1965] 1 W.L.R. 45; [1965] 1 All E.R. 77n.).

[31] If the plaintiff proposes to allege at the trial that the defendant purposely made his goods to resemble in appearance the goods of the plaintiff with the intention of misleading the public, this must be explicitly pleaded in the statement of claim (*Claudius, Ash, Sons & Co. Ltd.* v. *Invicta Manufacturing Co.* (1912) 29 R.P.C. 465 (H.L.)). See *Supreme Court Practice 1991*, Vol. 1, para. 18/12/23 (misrepresentation). If the defendant in such an action merely denies the allegations of the plaintiff, and makes no affirmative allegation, he will not be ordered to deliver particulars of his traverse—the onus being on the plaintiff (*La Radiotechnique* v. *Weinbaum* [1928] 1 Ch. 1).

(u) recovery of land;
(v) rights of way[32];
(w) secret process/trade secrets[33];
(x) wrongful dismissal.[34]

Special damage   The plaintiff will not be allowed at the trial to give evidence of any special damage which is not claimed explicitly, either in his pleading or particulars.[35] Special damage in the sense of a monetary loss which the plaintiff has sustained up to the date of trial must be pleaded and particularised; otherwise it cannot be recovered. If special damage be claimed in the statement of claim, but not with sufficient detail, particulars will be ordered with dates and items, *e.g.* if the plaintiff alleges that certain customers have ceased to deal with him, he must give their names, or the allegation will be struck out. Particulars of alleged loss of business will be ordered even after the defence has been served.[36] If ambiguous expressions are used in the statement of claim which may or may not

[32] Particulars necessary of *terminus a quo* and *terminus ad quem*, and of title: see *Harris* v. *Jenkins* (1882) 22 Ch.D. 481; *Pugh* v. *Savage* [1970] 2 Q.B. 373; [1970] 2 W.L.R. 634; [1970 2 All E.R. 353.

[33] Particulars may be ordered as to what features of the process are alleged to be secret. See *Printers & Finishers Ltd.* v. *Holloway* (Practice Note) [1965] 1 W.L.R. 1; [1964] 3 All E.R. 54n. An order for the inspection of the process by an expert is a substitute for such particulars, so that there is a duty to explain to him what elements are claimed to be secret, and why: *Printers & Finishers, supra.* Cases of alleged breach of confidence ought to be clearly and precisely pleaded, and particulars of the confidential information must be given. Moreover, some particularity of what is alleged to have been taken is required: *Speed Seal Products Ltd.* v. *Paddington* [1986] 1 All E.R. 91; [1984] F.S.R. 77. In an action for misuse of trade secrets, it will often be necessary, even before defence, for the plaintiff to specify precisely what it is he alleges are the trade secrets relied upon. For this purpose, the court may impose safeguards *e.g.* a condition that the particulars be not filed with the pleadings and that the defendants shall undertake not to make or permit use of them, save such use as may be necessary for the purposes of the proceedings: *John Zink Co. Ltd.* v. *Wilkinson* [1973] F.S.R.1. If the plaintiffs do their best to give particulars of the trade secrets relied upon, then they cannot be struck out for non-compliance with an order to serve such particulars, although the statement of claim may, in the circumstances, then prove to be vexatious and an abuse of the process of the court (*John Zink Co. Ltd.* v. *Lloyd's Bank Ltd.* [1975] R.P.C. 385. See also *Reinforced Plastics Applications (Swansea) Ltd.* v. *Swansea Plastics & Engineering Co. Ltd.* [1979] F.S.R. 182.

[34] Particulars should be given of the period of time claimed to constitute a reasonable notice and also of the special damage alleged, whether other employment or employments had been obtained since the alleged dismissal, and if so, when, with whom, date of commencement, salary and terms of payment, the nature of the employment and whether it is still continuing and if not when determined (*Monk* v. *Redwing Aircraft Co. Ltd.* [1941] 1 K.B. 182 (C.A.), and also particulars of the taxable income and allowances of the plaintiff (*Phipps* v. *Orthodox Unit Trusts Ltd.* [1958] 1 Q.B. 314 (C.A.)) at any rate where the damages claimed are or likely to be under £5,000; see *Parsons* v. *B.N.M. Laboratories* [1964] 1 Q.B. 95; [1963] 2 All E.R. 658 (C.A.); *Bold* v. *Brough, Nicholson & Hall* [1964] 1 W.L.R. 201; [1963] 3 All E.R. 849.

[35] *Hayward* v. *Pullinger & Partners Ltd.* [1950] 1 All E.R. 581; *Anglo-Cyprian Trade Agencies Ltd.* v. *Paphos Wine Industries Ltd.* [1951] 1 All E.R. 873.

[36] *C. Watson* v. *North Metropolitan Tramways Co.* (1887) 3 T.L.R. 273.

amount to an allegation of special damage, the Master will order "particulars of special damage, if any, claimed," and if the plaintiff does not then give particulars, it will be taken that he does not claim any special damage. It would seem, for example, that a claim for "damages for breach of contract" would entitle the plaintiff to nominal damages only unless he gives particulars of special damage. The expenditure of managerial time in remedying an actionable wrong done to a trading concern could properly form the subject-matter of special damage which could be claimed by the concern. If, however, the plaintiff fails to plead and prove such special damage, the court will not speculate on the quantum by awarding, as the damages under that head, a percentage of the plaintiff's total damages.[37] In the Chancery Division particulars of damage will in some cases be ordered when an inquiry into damages is directed.[38] An inquiry as to damages for use of confidential information in breach of confidence will not be confined to the particulars of breaches pleaded and proved but will extend to cover the same field as the terms of the injunction granted.[39] In personal injury actions, any benefits accrued, whether by way of unemployment benefit or from other sources, should be disclosed at the earliest possible moment on the pleading.[40]

In a personal injury action, the plaintiff must serve with the statement of claim on such later date as may be specified by order, a statement of the special damages claimed, that is, a statement giving full particulars of the special damages claimed for expenses and losses already incurred and an estimate of any future expenses or losses including loss of earnings and of pension rights.[41]

For clarity and convenience, this statement should be made in the form of a schedule, as for example:

(a) Loss of earnings already suffered
(b) Estimated loss of future earnings stating how the estimate is made up
(c) Expenses already incurred include medical and other expenses in relation to the cost of care, attention, accommodation or appliances
(d) Estimates of future expenses, stating how this is made up[41a]
(e) Pension rights.[42]

---

[37] *Tate and Lyle Food Distribution Ltd.* v. *Greater London Council* [1983] 2 A.C. 509; [1983] 2 W.L.R. 649; [1983] 1 All E.R. 1159.

[38] *Turnock* v. *Sartoris* (1889) 33 S.J. 58; but see *Maxim Nordenfeld, etc. Co.* v. *Nordenfelt* [1893] 3 Ch. 122.

[39] *National Broach and Machine Co. Ltd.* v. *Churchill Gear Machines* [1965] 1 W.L.R. 1199; [1965] 2 All E.R. 961 (C.A.).

[40] *Cheeseman* v. *Bowaters United Kingdom Paper Mills Ltd.* [1971] 1 W.L.R. 1773; [1971] 3 All E.R. 513 (C.A.).

[41] R.S.C., Ord. 18, r. 12(1A), (1B) and (1C).

[41a] See p. 89.

[42] See *Practice Note (Personal injury action special damages)* [1984] 1 W.L.R. 1127; [1984] 3 All E.R. 161.

Damages Particulars must be given of special, but not of general damage. Where the plaintiff claims that he has suffered damage, *i.e.* injury, of a kind which is not the necessary and immediate consequence of the wrongful act, it is his duty to plead full particulars to show the nature and extent of the damages. Thus, he must set out the amount which he claims to be recoverable, irrespective of whether they are general or special damages, so as fairly to inform the defendant of the case he has to meet and to assist him in computing a payment into court. The mere statement or prayer that he claims "damages" will not support a claim for such damages.[43] Equally, the plaintiff must plead any special circumstances which he alleges will lead to his sustaining in the future losses which would not in the ordinary way be expected to flow from the wrongful act, *e.g.* inability to set up in business on his own account.[44] *A fortiori*, if the plaintiff is able to base his claim for damages upon a precise calculation, he must plead particulars of the facts which make such a calculation possible[45]; and presumably, such particulars should also be pleaded where the plaintiff bases his claims, not on a precise, but on an estimated calculation of his damages. In an action for damages for personal injuries, a claim for loss of future earning capacity should be specifically pleaded in order to give fair notice to the defendant.[46] A claim for exemplary damages must be specifically pleaded together with the facts on which the party pleading relies.[47] Equally, a claim for aggravated damages should be specifically pleaded and the facts relied on to support such claim should also be pleaded.[48]

Pleading to Particulars

Historical perspective Before the Supreme Court Judicature Acts 1873–1875, it was not the practice for the plaintiff to set out in his declaration any details which were not a necessary part of the cause of action; such matters were stated, if at all, in a separate document, subsequently delivered, which was called "Particulars." And it was then a

---

[43] As to the proper way of pleading special damages, at any rate arising from breach of contract of sale, see *Anglo-Cyprian Trade Agencies Ltd.* v. *Paphos Wine Industries Ltd.* [1951] 1 All E.R. 873 at 875; as to the special damage in libel or slander, see *Supreme Court Practice 1991*, Vol. 1, para. 18/12/31 (Slander).

[44] *Domsalla* v. *Barr (Trading as A.B. Construction)* [1969] 1 W.L.R. 630; [1969] 3 All E.R. 487, (C.A.).

[45] *Perestrello e Companhia Limitada* v. *United Paint Co. Ltd.* [1969] 1 W.L.R. 570; [1969] 3 All E.R. 479.

[46] *Per* Lord Fraser in *Chan Wai Tong* v. *Li Ping Sum* [1985] A.C. 446 (P.C.).

[47] See R.S.C., Ord. 18, r. 8(3) and see *Supreme Court Practice 1991*, Vol. 1, para. 18/8/6 (Exemplary Damages).

[48] See R.S.C, Ord, 18, r. 15(1) requiring the specific statement of the relief or remedy claimed. *Rookes* v. *Barnard* [1964] A.C. 1129, *per* Lord Devlin.

clear rule that the defendant must not plead to anything stated in the particulars, but only to the matters alleged in the declaration.

History is the living of the past in the present The rules of pleading at present in force require a plaintiff to insert in a summary form all necessary facts in his statement of claim[49]; but it still remains the rule that the defendant need not plead to any matter which is only alleged under the head of "Particulars."

What if material facts are pleaded as particulars? It is unfortunately not unknown that a plaintiff inserts in his particulars allegations of fact which should have been set out in the body of the pleading. In such case, unless they are so serious as to necessitate the taking out of a summons to amend the statement of claim as being embarrassing, they should be pleaded to as though they had been stated in their proper place.

Exchange of Witnesses' Statements of Facts[50]

Introduction The High Court has power, for the purpose of disposing of an action fairly and expeditiously and of saving costs, to order the parties to disclose to each other the written statements of the oral evidence intended to be adduced at the trial. In effect, in appropriate cases, the parties may be ordered to exchange the "proofs" of their witnesses' evidence as to facts.

Distinguishing from pleadings This rule proceeds on the footing that the parties will exchange the proofs of their witnesses' "evidence." Thus whereas pleadings deal with the facts only and do not and should not include evidence, this rule is supplementary and complementary to that rule. The issues between the parties will continue to be determined by reference to their pleadings and the power of the court to order exchange of witnesses' statements will not operate to widen or narrow the ambit of the issues arising from their pleadings. Indeed, statements of the witnesses exchanged are not evidence in themselves and they do not become evidence at the trial until they are "put in," evidence at the trial and unless the other party agrees, the witness whose statement is being so put in is called to verify the truth of its contents.[51] The statements cannot be used at any stage of the pre-trial process but only at the trial.

---

[49] See R.S.C., Ord. 18, r. 7(1).

[50] R.S.C., Ord. 38, r. 2A. See *Supreme Court Practice 1991*, Vol. 1, para. 38/2A/1. See also *Comfort Hotels Ltd.* v. *Wembley Stadium Ltd.* [1988] 1 W.L.R. 872; [1988] 3 All E.R. 53; in which the validity of this rule was unsuccessfully challenged.

[51] *Fairfield Maybee Ltd.* v. *Shell (U.K.) Ltd.* [1939] 1 All E.R. 576.

An "opening up" technique   Exchange of witness statements is thus an added method of "opening up" the cases of the parties. It develops the principle of a more open system of pre-trial discovery. The requirement to disclose one's evidence is another method of "attacking" the way a case is being prepared and presented by the opposite party.

Amendment of Pleadings

General Principles of Amendment of Pleadings

Introduction: purposes of the power to amend   The wide and extensive powers of amendment vested in the courts are designed to prevent the failure of justice due to procedural errors, mistakes and defects and they are exercised to further and serve the aims of justice. The powers of amendment are intended to make more effective the function of the courts to determine the true substantive merits of the case, to have more regard to substance than to form, and thus to free the parties and the court from the technicalities or formalities of procedure and to correct errors and defects in the proceedings.[1]

Practice   The object of the amendment of pleadings is to enable the parties to alter their pleadings so as to ensure that the litigation between them is conducted, not on the false hypothesis of the facts already pleaded or the relief or remedy already claimed, but rather on the basis of the true state of the facts or the true relief or remedy which the parties really and finally intend to rely on or to claim.[2] For example:

(a) where fresh information has come to hand, as when interrogatories have been fully answered by the party's opponent; or

(b) where documents the existence of which unknown to him, have been disclosed and which will necessitate the re-shaping of his statement of claim or defence; or

---

[1] See *G. L. Baker Ltd.* v. *Medway Building & Supplies Ltd.* [1958] 1 W.L.R. 1216, *per* Jenkins L.J. at 1236, where he said that the proposed amendment raised what "was a vital point in the case and that unless it was adjudicated upon, the real matter in issue between the parties would not be decided, for the case would proceed on an assumed state of the facts which, more likely than not, was wholly at variance with and bore no relation to the true facts of the case."

[2] See *G. L. Baker Ltd.* v. *Medway Building and Supplies Ltd.*, *supra, per* Jenkins L.J.: "The case shown on the pleading was a case which had no relation to any remotely probable state of facts."

189

(c) where his opponent may have raised some well-founded objections to his pleading, in which case it will be advisable for him to amend at once before it is too late.

The leave of the court[3]   The court has wide and ample powers to allow the amendment of pleadings. Thus a party has generally little difficulty in obtaining leave to amend his own pleadings, provided his application is not left to a stage so late in the proceedings that to allow an amendment then would be unjust to his opponent.[4] "However negligent or carelessness may have been the first omission, and however late the proposed amendment, the amendment should be allowed if it can be made without injustice to the other side. There is no injustice if the other side can be compensated for by costs."[5] If on the other hand the amendment will put the other side into such a position that they must be injured, it ought not to be made.[6] In *Tildesley* v. *Harper*, which may be taken as a *locus classicus*, Bramwell L.J. said[7]:

"My practice has always been to give leave to amend unless I have been satisfied that the party applying was acting *mala fide*, or that, by his blunder, he had done some injury to his opponent which could not be compensated for by costs or otherwise."[8]

In *Cropper* v. *Smith*, the practice was expressed on the basis of a wider principle by Bowen L.J.[9]:

---

[3] At common law there was very little room for amendment of pleadings, but amendments of mistakes were allowed, as it was said, in furtherance of justice (see *Rex* v. *Mayor, etc. of Grampound* (1798) 7 Term Rep. 699) whilst the proceedings remained in paper, *i.e.* until judgment was signed and during the term in which it was signed. Such amendments were made by summons and order at a judge's chambers, and after the statute of 1820 (1 Geo. IV., c. 55), s.1, they were allowed to be made by judges on circuit.

[4] *Kirby* v. *Simpson* (1835) 3 Dowl. 791: and see *Steward* v. *North Metropolitan Tramways Co.* (1886) 16 Q.B.D. 556.

[5] *Per* Brett M.R. *Clarapede* v. *Commercial Union Association* (1883) 32 W.R. 262 at 263.

[6] See *Clarapede* v. *Commercial Union Association supra, per* Brett M.R.: and see *Indigo Co.* v. *Ogilvy* [1891] 2 Ch. 31, *per* Lindley L.J.: *The Alert* (1894) 72 L.T. 124, *per* Jeune P.: *Hunt* v. *Rice and Son Ltd.* [1937] 3 All E.R. 715 (C.A.).

[7] *Tildesly* v. *Harper* (1878) 10 Ch.D. 393 at 396. See also *per* Lord Bramwell in *Australian Steam Navigation Co.* v. *Smith and Sons* (1889) 14 App.Cas. 318 at 320.

[8] See also *Steward* v. *North Metropolitan Tramways Co.* (1886) 16 Q.B.D. 556; *Re Trufort* (1885) 53 L.T. 498 at 500; *G.L. Baker Ltd.* v. *Medway Building and Suppliers Ltd.* [1958] 1 W.L.R. 1216; [1958] 3 All E.R. 540, (C.A.); and see *Cropper* v. *Smith* (1884) 26 Ch.D. 700, *per* Bowen L.J. at 711: "I have found in my experience that there is one panacea which heals every sore in litigation, and that is costs. I have very seldom, if ever, been unfortunate enough to come across an instance, where a person has made a mistake in his pleadings which has put the other side to such a disadvantage as that it cannot be cured by the application of that healing medicine."

[9] (1884) 26 Ch.D. 700 at 710–711. In *Shoe Machinery Co.* v. *Cutlan* [1896] 1 Ch.D. 108 at 112. A. L. Smith L.J. expressed his "emphatic" agreement with these observations. See also *Roe* v. *Davies* (1876) 2 Ch.D. 729 (contrasting the "old" and the "new" practice).

"I think it is a well established principle that the object of Courts is to decide the rights of the parties, and not to punish them for mistakes they make in the conduct of their cases by deciding otherwise than in accordance with their rights. . . . I know of no kind of error or mistake which, if not fraudulent or intended to overreach, the Court ought not to correct, if it can be done without injustice to the other party. Courts do not exist for the sake of discipline, but for the sake of deciding matters in controversy, and I do not regard such amendment as a matter of favour or of grace . . . It seems to me that as soon as it appears that the way in which a party has framed his case will not lead to a decision of the real matter in controversy, it is as much a matter of right on his part to have it corrected, if it can be done without injustice, as anything else in the case is a matter of right."

An amendment ought therefore as a rule to be allowed if thereby the real substantial question in controversy can be raised between the parties and to avoid multiplicity of legal proceedings.[10]

The rule as to amendment—in context It should be stressed that the powers of amendment are wide and extensive and are comprehensive in the sense of applying to all the areas of the civil litigation process. Thus:

(a) these powers extend to amendment of the writ (R.S.C., Ord. 20, rr.1 and 5), amendment of pleadings (Ord. 20, r.5), parties (Ord. 15, rr. 6 and 7), striking out or adding or substituting parties and changes of parties, and amendments relating to non-compliance with the rules (Ord. 2). Non-compliance with the rules would not render the document or the proceedings a nullity, but will amount to an irregularity which the court will have power to correct;[10a]

(b) the powers to amend contained in the rules are curative in the sense that they save rather than destroy;

(c) the exercise of the powers of amendment is discretionary and confers what may be called an unfettered judicial discretion on the court to grant or refuse leave to amend having regard to all the circumstances of the case for the purposes of serving the ends of justice.

Amendment without Leave

When? A party may, without the leave of the court, amend any pleading of his own at any time before the pleadings are deemed to be closed.[11]

---

[10] See R.S.C., Ord. 20, r. 8(1); Supreme Court Act 1981, s.49(2) replacing the Supreme Court of Judicature (Consolidation) Act 1925; s.43; *Kurtz* v. *Spence* (1887) 36 Ch.D. 770; *The Alert* (1894) 72 L.T. 124.

[10a] See *Singh* v. *Atom brook Ltd.* [1989] 1 W.L.R. 810; [1989] 1 All E.R. 385, (C.A.)

[11] R.S.C., Ord. 20, r. 3. As to the close of pleadings, see p. 43, *supra*.

AMENDMENT OF PLEADINGS

When he does so, he must serve the amended pleading on the opposite party.[12] This right extends to the statement of claim, whether indorsed on the writ or not, the defence, counterclaim, defence to counterclaim and reply.[13] It can be exercised only once and only before the close of pleadings. The right to amend pleadings without leave may not be exercised during the month of August except in the case of the statement of claim indorsed on the writ.[14]

The right to amend—but not to add   The right conferred to amend pleadings without leave, is intended to save time and costs in straightforward cases. It does not give any wider or different right to amend. Amendments therefore should not be made without leave, which could not or might not have been allowed to be made if application for such leave had been sought, *e.g.*, to add a cause of action to the statement of claim which has occurred after the issue of the writ.[15] Accordingly, whenever an amendment of a pleading is made without leave, the opposite party may apply to the court to disallow the amendment.[16] If the court is satisfied that leave to make the amendment or any part of it would have been refused at the time the amendment was made, it will order the amendment or that part of it to be struck out on such terms as to costs or otherwise as it thinks just.[17]

The right to amend is reciprocal   Where an amended statement of claim is served on the defendant, he may, if he has already served his defence, amend his defence.[18] Where an amended defence is served on the plaintiff, he may, if he has already served a reply, amend his reply.[19] Where a party has pleaded to a pleading which is thereafter properly amended without leave and served on him and he does not amend his own plead-

[12] R.S.C., Ord. 20, r. 3(1).
[13] There would seem to be no good reason by this right should not extent to particulars or further particulars of pleadings, but see, however, *Yorkshire Provident Co.* v. *Gilbert and Rivington* [1895] 2 Q.B. 148; *Emden* v. Burns (1894) 10 T.L.R. 400.
[14] R.S.C., Ord. 18, r. 5.
[15] See *Eshelby* v. *Federated European Bank* [1932] 1 K.B. 254; affirmed *ibid.* 423 (C.A.); *Tottenham Local Board of Health* v. *Lea Conservancy Board* (1886) 2 T.L.R. 410.
[16] R.S.C., Ord. 20, r. 4(1).
[17] R.S.C., Ord. 20, r. 4(2) and (3); see *Bourne* v. *Coulter* (1884) 50 L.T. 321.
[18] R.S.C., Ord. 20, r. 3(2)(a). For this purpose, the defence includes a counterclaim (R.S.C., Ord. 20, r. 3(4)). The period for service of the defence or amended defence is either the normal period for the service of the defence or the period of 14 days after service of the amended defence, whichever expires later (R.S.C., Ord. 29, r. 3(2)(b)). Where an amended counterclaim is served by the defendant on a party, other than the plaintiff, against whom the counterclaim is made, the counterclaim is treated for this purpose as if it were a statement of claim, and as if the defendant were the plaintiff and the person against whom it is made were the defendant (R.S.C., Ord. 20, r. 3(5)).
[19] R.S.C., Ord. 20, r. 3(3)(a). For this purpose, the reply includes a defence to counterclaim (R.S.C., Ord. 20, r. 3(4)). The period for service of the reply or amended reply is 14 days after service of the reply or amended reply is 14 days after service of the amended defence (R.S.C., Ord. 20, r. 3(3)(b)).

ing, he will be taken to rely on it in answer to the amended pleading. There will thus be an implied joinder of issue[20] as if the amendment had been contained in the original pleading. If, however, he does amend his own pleading, he is not entitled to introduce any amendments that he chooses. He can only make such amendments as are consequential upon the amendments made by the opposite party.[21]

Amendment by Consent of Parties

Rule   Any pleading in any cause or matter may, by written agreement between the parties, be amended at any stage of the proceedings.[22]

A limited power   This rule does not have effect in relation to an amendment to a counterclaim which consists of the addition, omission or substitution of a party.[23]

Practice   Although the parties may agree in writing to amend pleadings, the pleadings should in fact be actually amended in accordance with the usual practice, *e.g.* a first amendment in red ink and so forth.[24] If the statement of claim indorsed on the writ is amended, an amended copy of the writ must be filed. The parties may agree the costs of the amendment, otherwise the party making the amendment will bear the costs, unless the court otherwise orders.[25]

Amendment with Leave—Time to Amend

The power   The court has power,[26] at any stage of the proceedings, to allow the plaintiff to amend his writ[27] or any party to amend his pleading

---

[20] *i.e.* under R.S.C., Ord. 18, r. 14(2).

[21] *Squire* v. *Squire* [1972] Ch. 391; [1972] 2 W.L.R. 363; [1972] 1 All E.R. 891, (C.A.).

[22] R.S.C., Ord. 20, r. 12(1).

[23] *Ibid.* r. 12(2) *Bradford & Bingley Building Society* v. *Borders* [1941] 2 All E.R. 205 (H.L.).

[24] See Queen's Bench Masters' Practice Directions No. 20 (Amendment), *Supreme Court Practice 1991*, Vol. 2, para. 732, and the amended pleading should carry the legend "Amended pursuant to R.S.C., Ord. 20, r. 12."

[25] See R.S.C., Ord. 62, r. 6(5).

[26] This power is additional to its power to add, substitute or strike out parties or to order the carrying on of proceedings owing to a change of parties under R.S.C., Ord. 15, rr. 67–8, and see p. 211, *infra*, and to its power to grant leave to amend after the expiry of the current period of limitation under R.S.C., Ord. 20, r. 5(2)–(5); see p. 202, *infra*.

[27] The plaintiff may, without leave, make any amendment to his writ *before* it is served on any party in the action (R.S.C., Ord. 20, r. 1(3)), and he may also, without leave, amend the writ once before the pleadings are closed, but such amendments must not consist of the addition, omission or substitution of a party or alteration of the capacity in which a party to the action sues or is sued or the addition or substitution of a new cause of action (see R.S.C., Ord. 20, r. 1(1) and (3)).

on such terms as to costs or otherwise as may be just and in such manner, if any, as it may direct.[28]

The power may be exercised "at any stage of the proceedings" Accordingly amendments may be allowed before or at the trial or after trial or even after judgment or on appeal.[29]

The discretion in theory The power is discretionary[30] ánd is to be exercised so as to do what justice may require in the particular case, as to costs or otherwise.[31] As a general rule, however late the amendment is sought to be made, it should be allowed if it is made in good faith and if it will not do the opposite party some injury or prejudice him in some way that cannot be compensated for by costs or otherwise.[32] However, different considerations will apply to different stages of the proceedings or to the different nature of the amendments sought.

Exercise of the discretion—practice

(a) *Before trial* Leave to amend is readily granted[33] on terms that the costs of and occasioned by the amendment, including the costs of the application, are to be paid in any event by the party amending.[34] The application for leave to amend, should, nevertheless, be made promptly, and if not made within a reasonable time, it may be refused.[35] Moreover, even before trial, the court will not readily give leave to amend where there is ground for believing that the application is not made in good faith, or where the amendment seeks to introduce for the first time allegations of fraud[36] or to raise the plea of justification in a defamation action.[37] So:

---

[28] R.S.C., Ord. 20, r. 5(1).

[29] See *The Duke of Buccleuch* [1892] P. 201; *G.L. Baker Ltd.* v. *Medway Building and Supplies Ltd.* [1958] 1 W.L.R. 1216; [1958] 3 All E.R. 540, (C.A.); and see *Copthall Stores Ltd.* v. *Willoughby's Consolidated Co.* [1916] 1 A.C. 167; *Ley-Hamilton* (1935) 153 L.T. 384 (H.L.).

[30] *Riding* v. *Hawkins* (1889) 14 P.D. 56.

[31] *Roe* v. *Davies* (1876) 2 Ch.D. 729 at 733.

[32] See *Clarapede* v. *Commercial Union Association* (1883) 32 W.R. 262; *Steward* v. *North Metropolitan Tramways Co.* (1886) 16 Q.B.D. 556.

[33] See *Clarapede* v. *Commercial Union Association, supra*; *Re Trufort, Trafford* v. *Blanc* (1885) 53 L.T. 498; *Att-Gen.* v. *Pontypridd Waterworks Co.* [1908] 1 Ch. 388; *Frazer & Haws Ltd.* v. *Burns* (1934) 49 Lloyd's Rep. 216 (C.A.).

[34] The costs are always in the discretion of the court and in some cases they will be reserved to abide the event or made costs in the cause or reserved to the trial judge (see *Roe* v. *Davies* (1876) 2 Ch.D. 729).

[35] See *Clark* v. *Wray* (1885) 31 Ch.D. 68; *Zacklynski* v. *Polushie* [1908] A.C. 65 at 69.

[36] The court will ask why this new case was not presented originally, and may require to be satisfied as to the truth of the proposed amendment. Although it has been stated that it is "the universal practice, except in the most exceptional circumstances, not to allow an amendment for the purpose of adding a plea of fraud where fraud had not been pleaded in the first instance" (*per* Lord Esher M.R. in *Bentley* v. *Black* (1893) 9 T.L.R. 580 at 580; *cf. Hendriks* v. *Montague* (1881) 17 Ch.D. 638 at 642); amendment is allowed at an early stage. Ther is, indeed, no rule of practice that allegations of fraud have to be

   (i) the plaintiff may add a new cause of action and the defendant a
      new ground of defence; or
  (ii) either party may re-frame or re-formulate his case so as to bring
      out the real question in controversy between them.

(b) *At the trial*   Leave to amend may be granted, when to do so will not
cause injustice to the other side, and on proper terms as to costs, and the
adjournment of the trial, if necessary.[38] As a rule, leave to amend at the
trial will not so readily be given. Nevertheless, even where the amendment is substantial so as to completely change the plaintiff's cause of
action or nature of claim, leave to amend may be given on proper
terms.[39] However, leave to amend will not so readily be given:

   (i) where the necessity for such amendment was obviously apparent
      long before the trial and was not then asked for[40]; or

---

pleaded at the outset, and amendments alleging fraud are no different from other amendments which are allowed on the general principle that the real matters in controversy
between the parties are before the court (*Atkinson* v. *Fitzwalter* [1987] 1 W.L.R. 201;
[1987] 1 All E.R. 483, (C.A.) citing with approval the *Supreme Court Practice 1991*,
Vol. 1, para. 20/5–8/22). In a libel action, an amendment to add a plea of justification
with proper particulars may be allowed even if it is itself alleged fraud (*ibid.*). In special
circumstances amendments alleging fraud may be allowed at the trial though an adjournment would usually be granted, see *Riding* v. *Hawkins* (1898) 14 P.D. 56. But such an
amendment should not be allowed by the Court of Appeal (*Bradford, etc., Building
Society* v. *Borders* [1941] 2 All E.R. 205 H.L.). See *Lawrence* v. *Lord Norreys* (1888) 39
Ch.D. 213. But where an allegation of fraud has failed, an amendment will not generally
be allowed to set up a claim independently of the charge of fraud (*Noad* v. *Murrow*
(1879) 40 L.T. 100; *Halsey* v. *Brotherhood* (1880) 43 L.T. 366 at 370). Equally, when
an allegation is based on fraud, an amendment should not be allowed to raise an issue of
mutual mistake, see *Bell* v. *Lever Brothers* [1932] A.C. 161; but see *Nocton* v. *Ashbur-
ton* [1941] A.C. 932.
[37] *Associated Leisure Ltd.* v. *Associated Newspapers Ltd.* [1970] 2 Q.B. 450; [1970] 3
W.L.R. 101, (C.A.). Where leave to amend is granted shortly before the date of trial, the
court may in its discretion adjourn the date of the trial so as to enable further preparation
of the case on the matters raised by the amendment (*ibid., per* Lord Denning M.R.).
[38] See for example *Budding* v. *Murdock* (1875) 1 Ch.D. 42 (claim amended): *King* v. *Corke*
(1875) 1 Ch.D. 57; *Dallinger* v. *St. Albyn* (1879) 41 L.T. 406 (claim amended): *Nobel's
Explosives Co.* v. *Jones, Scott & Co.* (1881) 17 Ch.D. 721 (claim amended); *De Bergue*
v. *De Bergue* [1880] W.N. 191 (defence amended); *Blenkhorn* v. *Penrose* (1880) 43 L.T.
668 at 670 (defence amended); *Laird* v. *Briggs* (1881) 19 Ch.D. 22 (C.A.); *Parkinson* v.
Noel [1923] 1 K.B. 117 at 120 (claim for mesne profits added at trial); *Schlesinger and
Joseph* v. *Mostyn* [1932] 1 K.B. 349 (claim for damages added); *Telsen Electric Co. Ltd.*
v. *Eastwick and Sons* [1936] 3 All E.R. 266 (defences added); *Mussen* v. *Van Diemen's
Land Co.* [1938] Ch. 253.
[39] *Budding* v. *Murdoch* (1875) 1 Ch.D. 42; *Northampton Coal, Iron and Waggon Co.* v.
Midland Waggon Co. (1878) 7 Ch.D. 500 (security for costs ordered as a term); *Hub-
bock* v. *Helms* (1887) 56 L.J. Ch. 536.
[40] *Hipgrave* v. *Case* (1885) 28 Ch.D. 356 at 361. The trial judge may require evidence that
the party applying to amend could not with reasonable diligence have discovered the new
facts sooner (*Moss* v. *Malings* (1886) 33 Ch.D. 603).

(ii) where the amendment would involve a complete change in the nature of the claim or the whole character of the action[41]; or

(iii) where the amendment involves setting up an entirely different claim from that which the defendant came to meet[42]; or

(iv) where the amendment raises an entirely new ground of defence or counterclaim[43]; or

(v) where an amendment introduces for the first time a charge of fraud.[44]

Application to amend at trial—practice points

(a) *Formulation*   The exact amendment should be formulated and stated in writing[45] and submitted at the earliest possible time to the opposite party and the court[46]; and an opportunity must always be allowed to the opposite party to consider it and to meet the new matter and if reasonably necessary the trial should be adjourned for this purpose.[47] In such case, the party amending will be ordered to pay, not only any costs of the amendment, but also the costs thrown away by the adjournment.[48]

(b) *When applied for?*   Where the amendment has become necessary by reason of a variance between the statement of claim and the evidence given at the trial, it should be asked for at the conclusion of the plaintiff's case.[49] The court is reluctant to give leave to amend at a late stage of the trial unless there is strong justification for doing so. Accordingly such leave will as a rule be refused after the close of evidence on both sides,[50]

[41] See *Newby* v. *Brotherhood* (1880) 15 Ch.D. 514; affirmed (1881) 19 Ch.D. 386 (C.A.); *Clarke* v. *Yorke* (1882) 52 L.J. Ch. 32; *Gibbons* v. *Westminster Bank Ltd.* [1939] 2 K.B. 882.

[42] See *Ellis* v. *Manchester Carriage Co.* (1876) 2 C.P.D. 13 at 16.

[43] *Tuck* v. *Southern Counties Deposit Bank* (1889) 42 Ch.D. 471 (C.A.); *James* v. *Smith* [1891] 1 Ch. 384; *Aronson* v. *Liverpool Corporation* (1913) 29 T.L.R. 325; *Berners* v. *Fleming* [1925] Ch. 264; *Hills and Grant Ltd.* v. *Hodson* [1934] Ch. 53.

[44] *Behn* v. *Bloom* (1911) 132 L.T.J. 87; and see p. 166, *supra*.

[45] See *per* Farwell L.J. in *Hymans* v. *Stuart King* [1908] 2 K.B. 696 at 724.

[46] See *Practice Note* [1947] W.N. 185.

[47] *Winchelsea* v. *Beckley* (1886) 2 T.L.R. 300; *J. Leavey & Co.* v. *Hirst* [1944] K.B. 24 (C.A.). Where the charges of fraud had been anticipated, an adjournment may not be necessary; see *Riding* v. *Hawkins* (1889) 14 P.D. 56; *Bourke* v. *Davis* (1888) 44 Ch.D. 110 at 12; *Smith* v. *Roberts* (1892) 9 T.L.R. 77 (C.A.).

[48] *Ascherberg, Hopwood and Crew Ltd.* v. *Casa Musicale Sonzogno di Pietro Ostali S.N.C.* [1971] 1 W.L.R. 1128; [1971] 3 All E.R. 38, (C.A.); and see *Jacobs* v. *Schmaltz* (1890) 62 L.T. 121 at 122; *King* v. *Corke* (1875) 1 Ch.D. 57; *Bowden's Patents Syndicate Ltd.* v. *Herbert Smith & Co.* [1904] 2 Ch. 86.

[49] *Rainy* v. *Bravo* (1872) L.R. 4 P.C. 287; and see *Nicholson* v. *Brown* [1897] W.N. 52; and see *The Ballylesson* [1968] 1 Lloyd's Rep. 69 (amendment allowed after hearing evidence from master of plaintiff's ship).

[50] *Edevain* v. *Cohen* (1889) 41 Ch.D. 563 and 43 Ch.D. 187 (C.A.); *James* v. *Smith* [1891] 1 Ch. 384 and 389; *Soar* v. *National Coal Board* [1965] 1 W.L.R. 886; [1965] 2 All E.R. 311, (C.A.). In *Loutfi* v. *C. Czarnikow Ltd.* [1952] 2 All E.R. 823 (leave to amend was given after the close of the case).

especially where it could result in a party being confronted with an entirely new case.[51]

(c) *Appeal on amendment during trial*   Where a substantial amendment is sought at the trial, which is likely to be crucial to one party or the other, and the trial is likely to be long or protracted, the judge may adjourn the trial to enable an appeal to be taken against his ruling giving or refusing leave to amend and will resume the trial after the hearing of the expedited appeal.[52]

(d) *The position after judgment*   Generally speaking, after judgment has been entered, an amendment of the pleadings will rarely be granted[53] except to correct accidental slips or omissions.[54]

On appeal

(a) *Court of Appeal*   It will not usually interfere with the discretion of the judge in allowing or refusing an amendment of pleadings.[55] That notwithstanding, it will allow an amendment in a proper case, which has been refused below[56], or disallow an amendment which has been allowed below[57], or vary the terms on which an amendment was allowed.[58] Moreover, the Court of Appeal has power itself to grant or refuse leave

---

[51] *Rawding* v. *London Brick Co.* (1971) 9 K.I.R. 194.

[52] It is highly undesirable that there should be appeals to the Court of Appeal in the course of trials of actions. It is altogether better than matters of an interlocutory nature should work themselves out in the course of the trial without interlocutory recourse to the Court of Appeal before the facts had been completely determined and the trial had been concluded. The Civil Division of the Court of Appeal may hear appeals in the course of the trial but only in exceptional circumstances. The reason is not just that it interrupts the trial, although that is usually, a sufficient reason, but that if it became the practice to give leave to appeal in the course of a trial, the Court of Appeal will soon be overwhelmed with appeals, many of which might prove academic: *McGarry (E) (Electrical)* v. *Burroughs Machines*, April 14, 1986, C.A.T. No. 346.

[53] See *The Dictator* [1892] P. 64; *The Duke of Buccleuch* [1892] P. 201.

[54] See R.S.C., Ord. 20, r. 11, and see *Att-Gen.* v. *Corporation of Birmingham* (1880) 15 Ch.D. 423; *Hurst* v. *Hurst* (1882) 15 Ch.D. 278 (C.A.); *Durham Brothers* v. *Robertson* [1898] 1 Q.B. 765 at 774; *Noad* v. *Murrow* (1879) 40 L.T. 100; *Clarke* v. *Yorke* (1882) L.J. Ch. 32. On the other hand, if the jury find a larger amount of damages than the plaintiff has claimed in the statement of claim, the trial judge may amend the pleading, so as to enable the plaintiff to recover the full amount awarded to him by the verdict, but unless the pleading is amended, the plaintiff cannot have judgment for more than has been claimed; see *Chattel* v. *Daily Mail Publishing Co. Ltd.* (1901) 8 T.L.R. 165 (C.A.).

[55] See *Byrd* v. *Nunn* (1877) 7 Ch.D. 284; *Australiam Steam Navigation Co.* v. *Smith* (1889) 14 App.Cas. 318.

[56] See *Laird* v. *Briggs* (1881) 19 Ch.D. 22; *Clarapede* v. *Commercial Union Association* (1883) 32 W.R. 262; *Kurtz* v. *Spence* (1887) 36 Ch.D. 770; *Hunt* v. *Rice & Son Ltd.* [1937] 3 All E.R. 715.

[57] See *Newby* v. *Sharpe* (1878) 8 Ch.D. 39.

[58] *Hollis* v. *Burton* [1892] 3 Ch. 226; *Farquhar North & Co.* v. *Lloyd Ltd.* (1901) 17 T.L.R. 568.

to amend pleadings,[59] and in a proper case will allow the pleadings to be amended[60] and to order a new trial on the issues raised by the amended pleadings.[61] However, a plaintiff who wishes to plead a case which he is bound to lose at first instance as a result of a prior decision of the court should nevertheless plead the case before trial or at the latest by amendment at the trial, for he will not be granted leave to amend at the appeal stage by the Court of Appeal.[62]

(b) *House of Lords*   It may also itself grant[63] or refuse[64] leave to amend. It will be slow to permit amendments where a party had ample opportunity of raising an alternative plea at the trial but had not thought fit to do so.

Amendments not Allowed

Introduction   The essential basis for asking for leave to amend is that the application is genuine and necessary. The circumstances in which amendments of pleadings may be sought are infinitely various and a decision granting or refusing leave in a particular case may be no ground for refusing or granting leave in another. Each case must be decided having regard to all the surrounding circumstances of the particular case, including any protective terms as to costs or otherwise to compensate for or mitigate the altered position of the opposite party. Nevertheless, the cases in which leave to amend has or has not been granted afford a guide for deciding whether or not to grant such leave in substantially the same or similar circumstances.

Absence of "good faith"   The first and paramount consideration is whether the application for leave to amend is made in good faith; *i.e.* for the purpose of raising "the real question in controversy between the parties."[65] Indeed the first question the court asks itself when dealing with an application for leave to amend is: "Is this genuine or, what lies behind the application?" The amendment must not be dishonest, nor intended to overreach the opposite party, or made for any other ulterior motive. The

[59] See R.S.C., Ord. 59, r. 10(1). As to the inherent power of the Court of Appeal to amend the record, see *Clack* v. *Wood* (1882) 9 Q.B.D. 276; *Thynne* v. *Thynne* [1955] P. 272; [1955] 3 W.L.R. 465; [1955] 3 All E.R. 129.
[60] See *G.L. Baker* v. *Medway Building and Supplies Ltd.* [1958] 1 W.L.R. 1216; [1958] 3 All E.R. 540, (C.A.); *Curran* v. *William Neill & Son (St. Helen's) Ltd.* [1961] 1 W.L.R. 1069; [1961] 3 All E.R. 108.
[61] *Ibid.* and see *Ellis* v. *Scott (No. 2)* [1965] 1 W.L.R. 276; [1965] 1 All E.R. 3, (C.A.).
[62] *Williams* v. *Home Office (No. 2)* [1982] 1 All E.R. 564. (C.A.).
[63] See *Fraser* v. *Balfour* (1918) 87 L.J.K.B. 1116; *Harnett* v. *Fisher* [1927] A.C. 573 at 577 and 583. See also, *Copthall Stores* v. *Willoughby's Consolidated Co.* [1916] 1 A.C. 167 (amendment allowed on appeal to Privy Council).
[64] *Ley-Hamilton* (1935) 153 L.T. 384 at 385.
[65] See R.S.C., Ord. 20, r. 8(1).

amendment must be based on facts which are substantially true and germane to the matters in controversy between the parties. If, therefore, the court is not satisfied as to the truth and substantiality of the proposed amendment, it will be refused.[66] Such an amendment will only be allowed, even at an early stage, if the circumstances justify it.[67] In special circumstances it may be allowed at the trial.[68] In any event, an amendment to introduce a charge of fraud for the first time should not be allowed by the Court of Appeal.[69]

Materially—an off-shoot of the paramount requirement of good faith The court will look at the materiality of any proposed amendment.[70] It will, as a rule, refuse leave to make immaterial and useless amendments[71] or merely technical or trivial amendments.[72] Thus:

(a) an amendment which if made would set up a claim or defence which is bad in law will not be allowed[73];

(b) nor will an amendment to add an unnecessary counterclaim be allowed[74];

(c) nor to add a claim to recover only nominal damages[75]; and

(d) where the plaintiff's claim as originally framed is unsupportable an amendment which would leave the claim equally unsupportable would not be allowed.[76]

These are only examples to provide a "guide." They are not exhaustive.

---

[66] See *Lawrence* v. *Lord Norreys* (1888) 39 Ch.D. 213, *per* Stirling J. at 221, and *per* Bowen L.J. at 235; and see also *Lawrence* v. *Lord Norreys* (1890) 15 App.Cas. 210. As to adding a charge of fraud see p. 166, *supra*.

[67] See *Lever* v. *Goodwin* (1887) 36 Ch.D. (C.A.); *Symonds* v. *City Bank* (1886) 34 W.R. 364, *Hendriks* v. *Montagu* (1881) 50 L.J.Ch. 257 at 260. The statement of Lord Esher M.R. in *Bently* v. *Black* (1893) 9 T.L.R. 580, that "[i]t had for a long time been universal practice, except in the most exceptional circumstances, not to allow amendments for the purpose of adding a plea of fraud where fraud had not been pleaded in the first instance" should be read subject to the requirement that the court is satisfied about the *bona fides* of the application and the charge of fraud."

[68] See *Riding* v. *Hawkins* (1889) 14 P.D. 56 (C.A.); and see *Behn* v. *Bloom* (1911) 132 L.T.J. 87 (amendment at trial refused).

[69] *Bradford Third Equitable Benefit Building Society* v. *Borders* [1941] 2 All E.R. 205 (H.L.).

[70] *Ibid.*.

[71] *Wood* v. *Earl of Durham* (1888) 21 Q.B.D. 501.

[72] *Sinclair* v. *James* [1894] 3 Ch. 554; *Durham Brothers* v. *Robertson* [1898] 1 Q.B. 765; *Bevan* v. *Barnett* (1897) 13 T.L.R. 130, and see *Litchfield* v. *Dreyfus* [1906] 1 K.B. 584.

[73] *Collette* v. *Goode* (1876) 7 Ch.D. 842; *Dillion* v. *Balfour* (1886) 20 lr. L.T. 600; and see *Edevain* v. *Cohen* (1889) 41 Ch.D. 563; 43 Ch.D. 187.

[74] *Central Queensland Meat Co.* v. *Gallop* (1892) 2 Q.B. T.L.R. 225; *Machado* v. *Fontes* [1897] 2 Q.B. 231, (C.A.).

[75] *Marshall* v. *Langley* [1889] W.N. 222; *Factories Insurance Co. Ltd.* v. *Anglo-Scottish General Commercial Insurance Co.* (1913) 29 T.L.R. 312 (C.A.).

[76] *McManus* v. *Fortescue* [1907] 2 K.B. 1 at 5.

Defamation—plea of justification   An application for leave to amend the defence in a defamation action to add a plea of justification will be closely inquired into. Justification, like fraud, should not be pleaded unless there is clear evidence to support it. It will be allowed if the court is satisfied that the defendant has shown due diligence in making his inquiries and investigations. It may be refused if the defendant has been guilty of delay or has not made proper inquiries earlier.[77-78]

Withdrawal of admission   Where an amendment seeks to withdraw an admission, the court will inquire into the circumstances in which the admission was made. It will grant such leave only:

(a) where the admission was made inadvertently[79]; or
(b) where new facts have come to light justifying its withdrawal.

Changing of character of action   Although the court will not refuse an amendment simply because it will introduce a new case or a new ground of defence,[80] leave will be refused where the amendment would change the action into one of a substantially different character. The party seeking amendment should proceed by way of fresh action.[81]

New cause of action   Leave to amend will also be refused where the cause of action sought to be introduced by the amendment arose after the date of the writ,[82] or where the amendment would re-introduce a claim that had been abandoned.[83]

Limitation   An amendment will not be allowed which will prejudice the rights of the opposite party as existing at the date of the proposed amendment.[84] Such an amendment would do the opposite party an injury which could not be compensated for by costs or otherwise.[85] (And an

---

[77-78] *Associated Leisure Ltd.* v. *Associated Newspapers Ltd.* [1970] 2 Q.B. 450; [1970] 3 W.L.R. 101, (C.A.) Also see *Atkinson* v. *Fitzwalter* [1987] 1 W.L.R. 201; [1987] 1 All E.R. 483.

[79] See *Clarke* v. *Yorke* (1882) 31 W.R. 62; *Hollis* v. *Burton* [1892] 3 Ch. 226 at 23.

[80] *Budding* v. *Murdock* (1875) 1 Ch.D. 42; *Hubuck* v. *Helms* (1887) 56 L.J.Ch. 536 at 539.

[81] See *Raleigh* v. *Goschen* [1898] 1 Ch. 73 at 81; *Edevain* v. *Cohen* (1889) 41 Ch.D. 563 at 567. See also *Halsey* v. *Brotherhood* (1880) 15 Ch.D. 514 and (1881) 19 Ch.D. 386 (leave refused and original action dismissed, without prejudice to second action based on proposed amendment).

[82] *Tottenham Local Board* v. *Lea Conservancy* (1886) 2 T.L.R. 410; *Eshelby* v. *Federated European Bank Ltd.* [1932] 1 K.B. 254; *ibid.* 429 (C.A.).

[83] *Creed* v. *Creed* [1913] 1 Ir.R. 48; *Ingall* v. *Moran* [1944] 1 K.B. 160 (C.A.); *Finnegan* v. *Cementation Co. Ltd.* [1953] 1 Q.B. 688 (C.A.).

[84] *Harries* v. *Ashford* [1950] 1 All E.R. 427. See, however, *Knox & Dyke Ltd.* v. *Holborn Borough Council, Law Journal Newspaper*, May 23, 1931, p. 355.

[85] See *Weldon* v. *Neal* (1887) 19 Q.B.D. 394, *per* Lord Esher M.R. at 395.

amendment which would put the opposite party in such a position that they must be injured ought not to be made.[86] On this principle, and subject to the powers of the court to allow amendments notwithstanding the expiry of the current period of limitation[87]:

(a) the plaintiff will not be allowed to reframe his case or his claim by an amendment of the writ or statement of claim if it would deprive the defendant of an accrued right to rely on the Limitation Acts.[88] But if the amendment sought does not constitute a new cause of action it will be allowed, even after the expiry of the relevant period of limitation[89] provided that:
   (i) it relies on the same or substantially the same facts as already pleaded; and
   (ii) constitutes no more than a different or additional approach to those facts;

(b) again, the addition or substitution of a party, whether as plaintiff or defendant, will not be allowed where to do so would be to prevent the defendant or added defendant from relying on the Limitation Acts[90];

(c) similarly, the defendant will not be allowed, by way of amendment, to raise a new ground of defence where to do so would prejudicially affect the position of other persons,[91] or prevent the plaintiff from suing a third person because the period of limitation against that person has already expired,[92] unless the defendant was:

---

[86] See *Tildesley* v. *Harper* (1878) 10 Ch.D. 393 at 397; *Clarapede* v. *Commercial Union Association* (1883) 32 W.R. 262 at 263.

[87] *Steward* v. *North Metropolitan Tramways Co.* (1886) 16 Q.B.D. 556 (C.A.).

[88] See *Weldon* v. *Neal* (1887) 19 Q.B.D. 394; *Lancaster* v. *Moss* (1899) 5 T.L.R. 476; *Laird* v. *Briggs* (1881) 19 Ch.D. 22 at 28 and 34.

[89] *Collins* v. *Herts. Country Council* [1947] K.B. 598; [1947] 1 All E.R. 633; *Doran* v. *J.W. Ellis & Co. Ltd.* [1962] 1 Q.B. 583; *Robinson* v. *Unicos Property Corporation Ltd.* [1962] 1 W.L.R. 520; [1962] 2 All E.R. 24, (C.A.); *The Katcher I (No. 1)* [1968] 1 Lloyd's Rep. 232; *Chatsworth Investment Ltd.* v. *Cussins (Contractors) Ltd.* [1969] 1 W.L.R. 1; [1969] 1 All E.R. 143; *Brickfield Properties Ltd.* v. *Newton* [1971] 1 W.L.R. 862; [1971] 3 All E.R. 328. See also *Marshall* v. *London Passenger Transport Board* [1936] 3 All E.R. 83; *Green* v. *Kursaal (Southend-on-Sea) Estates Ltd.* [1937] 1 All E.R. 732.

[90] *Mabro* v. *Eagle Star and British Dominion Insurance Co.* [1932] 1 K.B. 485 (C.A.) (adding plaintiff refused); *Lucy* v. *W.T. Henleys Telegraph Works Co. Ltd.* [1970] 1 Q.B. 393; [1969] 3 All E.R. 456, (C.A.) (adding defendant refused). See, however, *Att-Gen.* v. *Pontypridd Waterworks Co.* [1908] 1 Ch. 388 (plaintiff added on terms limiting cause of action to date of amendment), and *Ayscough* v. *Bullar* (1889) 41 Ch.d. 341 (C.A.) (adding plaintiff with title to sue).

[91] See *Forbes* v. *Samuel* [1913] 3 K.B. 706.

[92] *Steward* v. *North Metropolitan Tramways Co.* (1886) 16 Q.B.D. 556 (C.A.); *Hudson* v. *Ferneyhough* (1889) 61 L.T. 722.

(i) not at fault in failing to discover the negligence or breach of duty of that person earlier[93]; or

(ii) the amendment consists of allegations of contributory negligence against the plaintiff, even though they might form the basis of a claim for negligence against his employers which has been statute barred.[94]

But an amendment to alter the capacity in which a party sues may be allowed[95] if the new capacity is one which that party had at the commencement of the proceedings or has since acquired.[96] This will allow a party to amend the capacity in which he or she sues as executor or executrix after the grant of probate since this would relate back to the date of death.[97] The rule will also allow a party to amend the capacity in which he or she sues as administrator or administratrix after the grant of administration even though this may take place after the issue of the writ, thus negativing the earlier cases on the subject.[98]

Amendment after Expiry of Limitation Period

An exception to the general rule   The practice of the court that amendments should not be allowed which might have the effect of depriving a party of the defence of the Limitation Act 1980 has to some extent been modified afresh by the powers conferred on the court to grant such amendments after the expiry of any relevant period of limitation.[99]

Rationale for the exception   The object of these powers is to prevent certain defects in the writ or pleading from being fatal and to enable the court to cure the specified defects in an action begun after the relevant time limit has expired.[1]

---

[93] *Weait* v. *Jayanbee Joinery Ltd.* [1963] 1 Q.B. 239; [1962] 3 W.L.R. 323; [1962] 2 All E.R. 568, (C.A.).

[94] The exercise of the court's discretion must also embrace consideration of the prospects of disapplying any time bar under s.33 of the Limitation Act 1980.

[95] R.S.C., Ord. 20, r. 5(2).

[96] *Ibid.* rr. 5(2) and (4).

[97] See *Stebbings* v. *Holst & Co. Ltd.* [1953] 1 W.L.R. 608; [1953] 1 All E.R. 925; *Bowler* v. *John Mowlem & Co.* [1954] 1 W.L.R. 1445; [1954] 3 All E.R. 556. Also see Limitation Act 1980, s.35(7).

[98] See *Ingall* v. *Moran* [1944] K.B. 160 (C.A.); *Hilton* v. *Sutton Steam Laundry* [1946] K.B. 65 (C.A.); *Burns* v. *Campbell* [1952] 1 K.B. 15; *Finnegan* v. *Cementation & Co. Ltd.* [1953] 1 Q.B. 688 (C.A.).

[99] R.S.C., Ord. 20, r. 5(2)–(5). These rules have been twice unsuccessfully attacked as constituting a change of the substantive rights of the parties and are not matters of "practice and procedure," within s.87 of the Supreme Court Act 1981, and thus *ultra vires* the Rule Committee to make them; see *Rodriguez* v. *Parker* [1967] 1 Q.B. 116; [1966] 3 W.L.R. 546; [1966] 2 All E.R. 349, (C.A.); *Mitchell* v. *Harris Engineering Co. Ltd.* [1967] 2 Q.B. 703; [1967] 3 W.L.R. 447; [1967] 2 All E.R. 682.

[1] See *Rodriguez* v. *Parker, supra, per* Neil J. at 127. citing *Supreme Court Practice 1991*, Vol. 1, para. 20/5 1–18/7.

Extent of court's power   Where an application is made to the court for leave to amend the writ or any pleading after any relevant period of limitation current at the date of the issue of the writ has expired, the court may nevertheless grant such leave in specified circumstances,[2] relating to:

(a) correcting the name of a party[3];
(b) altering the capacity of a party[4]; and
(c) adding or substituting a new cause of action.[5]

Amendment as to name   An amendment to correct the name of a party will be allowed, after the expiry of any limitation period, notwithstanding that the effect of doing so will be to substitute a new party, provided that the court is satisfied that:

(a) the mistake sought to be corrected was a genuine mistake and was not misleading; or
(b) such as not to cause any reasonable doubt as to the identity of the person intending to sue or intended to be sued.[6]

It should be noted that section 35(2) of the Limitation Act 1980 is imperative in its terms that the court must not allow such a new claim to be made in the course of any action after the expiry of any time limit under the Act which would affect a new action brought to enforce that claim (except as provided by section 33 of the Act which provides a discretionary power to extend the time-limits in respect of actions for damages for personal injuries or death or as provided by rules of court). R.S.C. Ord. 20, rr. 5(1) and (2) do not allow a general relaxation against the governing principle that any amendment after the expiry of the limitation period will not be allowed.[7]

---

[2] R.S.C., Ord. 20, r. 5(2) and also see Limitation Act 1980, s.35 at R.S.C., Ord. 15, r. 6.
[3] R.S.C., Ord. 20, r. 5(3).
[4] *Ibid.* r. 5(4).
[5] *Ibid.* r. 5(5).
[6] R.S.C., Ord. 20, r. 5(3), and see Limitation Act 1980, s.35(6)(a) and see *Rodriguez v. Parker* [1967] 1 Q.B. 116; [1966] 3 W.L.R. 546; [1966] 2 All E.R. 349; *Mitchell v. Harris Engineering Co. Ltd.* [1967] 2 Q.B. 703 (C.A.); and see also *Davies v. Elsby Brothers Ltd.* [1961] 1 W.L.R. 170 (C.A.); (*quaere* whether this case would have been decided differently under the rule); *Whittam v. W.J. Daniel & Co. Ltd.* [1962] 1 Q.B. 271 (C.A.). The word "mistake" in this rule should not be narrowly construed as meaning "error without fault" (*Mitchell v. Harris Engineering Co. Ltd., supra, per* Russell L.J.) Also see *Teltscher Brothers Ltd. v. London & India Dock Investments Limited* [1989], 1 W.L.R. 770 (transposition of names of parties under a genuine mistake).
[7] *Braniff v. Holland & Harman and Cubitts (Southern)* [1969] 1 W.L.R. 1533; [1969] 3 All E.R. 959, (C.A.); *Brickfield Properties Ltd. v. Newton* [1971] 1 W.L.R. 862, Edmund Davies L.J. at 879, and *per* Cross L.J. at 881, thus negativing *per* Lord Denning in *Chatsworth Investment Ltd. v. Cussins (Contractors) Ltd.* [1969] 1 W.L.R. 1 at 5; and in *Sterman v. E. W. & W. J. Moore* [1970] 1 Q.B. 596 at 604. Salmon L.J. *ibid.* at 605; and *per* Sachs L.J. in *Brickfield Properties Ltd. v. Newton, supra,* at 874.

Amendment as to capacity An amendment of the capacity in which a party sues, whether as plaintiff or defendant by counterclaim, may be allowed after the expiry of a limitation period, if the capacity in which, if the amendment is made, the party will sue is one in which at the date of the issue of the writ or the making of the counterclaim, he might have sued.[8]

Amendment as to cause of action An amendment may be allowed, after the expiry of any limitation period, notwithstanding that the effect of the amendment would be to add or substitute a new cause of action, provided that the new cause of action arises out of the same facts or substantially the same facts as a cause of action in respect of which relief has already been claimed in the action by the party applying for leave to make the amendment.[9]

Limitation and amendment—a summary In relation to an action to which the Limitation Act 1939 applies (this will of course be progressively more rare), an amendment to add a defendant takes effect, not by way of relating back to the date of the original writ but on the date on which he is effectively joined as a party, *i.e.* the date of the service of the amended writ on him or such as serving his own defence.[10] On the other hand in actions to which the Limitation Act 1980 applies, the relation back theory of amendment is expressly provided for by statute. It is provided that any new claim made in the course of the action will be deemed to have been commenced on the same date as the original action.[11] For this purpose it is provided that "a new claim" means any claim by way of set-off or counteraction and any claim involving either: (i) the addition or substitution of a new cause of action; or (ii) the addition or substitution of a new party.[12] It should be stressed that where a defendant has acquired an entitlement to plead a time bar, that entitlement constitutes

---

[8] R.S.C., Ord. 20, r. 5(4), and see *Stebbings* v. *Holst & Co. Ltd.* [1953] 1 W.L.R. 608 *Bowler* v. *John Mowlem & Co.* [1954] 1 W.L.R. 1445; [1954] 3 All E.R. 556, (C.A.).

[9] R.S.C., Ord. 20 r. 5(5); see Limitation Act 1980, s.35(5)(*a*); and see *Chatsworth Investments Ltd.* v. *Cussins (Contractors) Ltd.* [1969] 1 W.L.R. 1 (amendment to add novation of contract allowed); *Brickfield Properties Ltd.* v. *Newton* [1971] 1 W.L.R. 862; [1971] 3 All E.R. 328; (amendment on same facts to allege negligence in *design* as well as *supervision* of building allowed). See also *Collins* v. *Hertfordshire County Council* [1947] K.B. 598; [1947] 1 All E.R. 633; *Doran* v. *J.W. Ellis & Co. Ltd.* [1962] 1 Q.B. 583; *Robinson* v. *Unicos Property Corporation Ltd.* [1962] 1 W.L.R. 520 (C.A.). The following cases would very likely have been decided differently under the rule: *Marshall* v. *London Passenger Transport Board* [1936] 3 All E.R. 83 ad *Batting* v. *London Passenger Transport Board* [1941] 1 All E.R. 228, but *quaere* whether the following cases still fall outside the scope of the rule: *Weldon* v. *Neal* (1887) 19 Q.B.D. 394 and *Lancaster* v. *Moss* (1889) 15 T.L.R. 476.

[10] *Ketteman* v. *Hansel Properties Ltd.* [1987] A.C. 189; [1987] 2 W.L.R. 312; [1988] 1 All E.R. 38; and see *Gawthrop* v. *Boulton* [1979] 1 W.L.R. 268; [1978] 3 All E.R. 615.

[11] See Limitation Act 1980, s.35(1).

[12] *Ibid.* s.35(2).

an accrued right of which he cannot be deprived by subsequent legislation providing for a longer limitation period, whether or not such legislation is to be classified as procedural, since such legislation will not be construed retrospectively unless such a construction is unavoidable on the language used.[13]

Effect of Amendment

Introduction An amendment of the writ or pleadings duly made, with or without leave, takes effect, not from the date when the amendment is made, but from the date of the original document which it amended. This rule applies to every successive amendment of whatever nature and at whatever stage the amendment is made. Thus, an amendment made to the writ dates back to the date of its original issue, and the action continues as though the amendment had been inserted from the beginning.[14] As to amending the writ, Collins M.R. said[15]:

> "The writ as amended becomes the origin of the action, and the claim thereon indorsed is substituted for the claim originally indorsed."

However, by virtue of its powers under R.S.C., Ord. 20, r. 5(1) to direct the terms on which the amendment is being allowed, the court may impose a term that the amendment of the writ shall take effect from a date specified in the order later than the date of the issue of the writ.[16]

Pleadings Similarly in the pleadings:

> "Once pleadings are amended, what stood before amendment is no longer material before the court and no longer defines the issues to be tried."[17]

This rule as to the effect of an amendment is the reason why a plaintiff may not amend his writ by adding a cause of action which has accrued to

---

[13] *Yew Bon Tew* v. *Kenderan Bas Maria* [1983] A.C. 553; [1982] 3 W.L.R. 1026; [1982] 3 All E.R. 833 (P.C.). In this context it should be noted that the Limitaton Act is procedural, in the sense that it bars the remedy but not the claim and thus a limitation defence has to be pleaded. See *Ronex Properties Ltd.* v. *John Laing Construction Ltd.* [1983] Q.B. 398; [1982] 3 W.L.R. 875; [1982] 3 All E.R. 961; expressly approving *Dismore* v. *Milton* [1938] 3 All E.R. 762.

[14] *Sneade* v. *Wotherton Barytes and Lead Mining Co. Ltd.* [1904] 1 K.B. 295.

[15] *Ibid.* at 297. This effect of the amendment of the writ explains why the plaintiff may not amend his writ by adding a cause of action which has accrued to him *after* the issue of the writ; see *Eshelby* v. *Federated European Bank* [1932] 1 K.B. 254, *affirmed, ibid.* at 423.

[16] *Liverpool Roman Catholic Archdiocesan Trustees Inc.* v. *Gibberd*; H.H. Judge Fox-Andrews Q.C., O.R.; February 5, 1986, unreported.

[17] *Warner* v. *Sampson* [1959] 1 Q.B. 297 at 321 (C.A.).

him since the issue of the writ.[18] Further, this rule lies at the root of the difficulties which arise when an amendment is sought which will or might prejudice the other party or deprive him of a defence which has already accrued to him.

Amendment as to remedy   Where, however, the amendment sought to be made relates to matters going to the remedy claimed rather than introducing a new cause of action, the court will grant leave to amend the original pleadings in order to allege facts arising subsequent to the date of the writ or counterclaim, *e.g.* the acceptance of the repudiation of contract and a claim for further loss arising out of such repudiation and a declaration relating to such repudiation and its acceptance.[19] However, by virtue of its powers under Ord. 20, r. 5(1) to direct the terms on which the amendment is being allowed, the court may impose a term that the amendment of the writ shall take effect from a date specified in the order later than the date of the issue of the writ.[20]

Costs   The fact that the pleading has been amended, will not, moreover, affect the incidence of subsequent costs, even though the action is decided on the point raised by the amendment.[21]

Practice on Amendment of Pleadings

Leave   In all cases except where amendment is allowed without leave[22] the party seeking or requiring the amendment of any pleading must apply to the court for leave or order to amend.[23]

Formulation   The proposed amendments should be specified[24] either by stating them, if short, in the body of the summons, notice or other appli-

---

[18] *Eshelby* v. *Federated European Bank Ltd.* [1932] 1 K.B. 254; affirmed at 423; see also *Halliard Property Co. Ltd.* v. *Jack Segal Ltd.* [1978] 1 W.L.R. 377; [1978] 1 All E.R. 1219.

[19] *Tilcon Ltd.* v. *Land and Real Estate Investment Ltd.* [1987] W.L.R. 46; [1987] 1 All E.R. 615.

[20] See *Liverpool Roman Catholicd Archdiocesan Trustees Inc.* v. *Gibberd*; H.H. Judge Fox-Andrews Q.C., O.R.; February 5,d 1986, unreported. Also see *Leicester Wholesale Fruit Market Ltd.* v. *Grundy* [1988] C.I.L.L. 42 (C.A.).

[21] *Nottage* v. *Jackson* (1883) 11 Q.B.D. 627 (C.A.).

[22] See R.S.C., Ord. 20, rr. 1 and 3, and see p. 191, *supra.*

[23] See R.S.C., Ord. 20, r. 5(1). Although the court has power "of its own motion" to require or order the amendment of any pleading (see R.S.C., Ord. 20, r. 8(1), and see also R.S.C., Ord. 15, r. 6(2)) this power is rarely, if ever, exercised. For an isolated instance of its exercise by Field J., see *Nottage* v. *Jackson supra*, at 638. See also *Liverpool Roman Catholic Archdiocesan Trustees Inc.* v. *Gibberd*; H.H. Judge Fox-Andrews Q.C., O.R.; February 5, 1986, unreported.

[24] See *Lawrence* v. *Lord Norreys* (1888) 39 Ch.D. 213; *Derrick* v. *Williams* [1939] 2 All E.R. 559.

cation,[25] or by referring to them therein.[26] In practice, leave to amend is given only when and to the extent that the proposed amendments have been properly and exactly formulated,[27] and in such case, the order giving leave to amend binds the party making the amendment and he cannot amend generally.

Service of application—on whom?   Where it is clearly realised from the start, that on an application for leave to amend to add a defendant there would be reasoned opposition to the making of the order, the more convenient course to follow is to serve the summons on the proposed party to be added. This enables the matter to be dealt with directly before the joinder takes place, rather than to obtain the order in the absence of the added defendant who would have to give notice of intention to defend and then apply[28] to be dismissed from the action.[29] This practice should not be confined to the Chancery Division but should be extended and applied to the Queen's Bench Division. The practice is useful, though it is not clear whether the person so served becomes a party to the action, *e.g.* for the purposes of costs, rights of appeal or otherwise, but his consent to be so treated may be enough for such purposes.

Affidavit—when?   An affidavit in support of the application for leave to amend is not ordinarily required, except in the case of an amendment of a writ issued for service out of the jurisdiction[30] and in cases where it is necessary to satisfy the court that the amendment is made in good faith.[31]

Date from which order takes effect   The order to amend, like any other order, takes effect from the day of its date, *i.e.* the day it is pronounced, given or made.[32]

Drawing up the order   If a party does not amend the document in accordance with the order giving leave to amend before the expiration of the period specified for that purpose in the order (or, if no period is so

---

[25] If the Court of Appeal is being asked for leave to amend, the proposed amendments should be set out in notice of appeal; see *G. L. Baker Ltd.* v. *Medway Building & Supplies Ltd.* [1957] 1 W.L.R. 1216, *per* Willmer L.J.

[26] If a statement of claims does not disclose a cause of action relied on, an opportunity to amend may be given even though the formulation of the amendent is not before the court: *CBS Songs Ltd.* v. *Amstrad* [1988] Ch. 61; [1988] 1 W.L.R. 364.

[27] See *Derrick* v. *Williams, supra; Hyams* v. *Stuart King* [1908] 2 K.B. 696, *per* Farwell J. at 724; *J. Leavey & Co.* v. *Hirst & Co.* [1944] K.B. 24, *per* Lord Greene M.R. at 27.

[28] The application is made under R.S.C., Ord. 12, r. 8.

[29] *Per* Walton J. in *Gawthrop* v. *Boulton* [1979] 1 W.L.R. 268; [1978] 3 All E.R. 615.

[30] *Holland* v. *Leslie* [1894] 2 Q.B. 346 at 348 and *ibid.* at 450.

[31] See p. 198, *supra.*

[32] R.S.C., Ord. 42, r. 3.

specified, of a period of 14 days after the order was made), the order shall cease to have effect, without prejudice, however, to the power of the court to extend the period.[33]

Extending time   On the application to extend the time, the opposite party is entitled to be heard. The practice is that the court would wish to be satisfied that the opposite party has consented to the order being drawn up out of time. If the court is not so satisfied, it will direct a summons to be issued. On the hearing of such summons, if the opposite party can show that there has been inordinate delay and that during the time between the making of the order and its drawing up the limitation period has expired, he may persuade the court to refuse to extend the time. In such a case the party seeking to amend will be in the same position as if leave to amend had been refused. The same position could arise for other reasons or circumstances than the expiry of the limitation period.

Exceptionally—leave may be general   Sometimes, though rarely, leave may be given to amend a pleading generally.[34] Even in such case, the party amending is not entitled to introduce in his pleading amendments which would not have been allowed if he had properly and exactly formulated his proposed amendments, and the court may strike out such amendment.[35]

Costs   Terms are generally imposed, such as the payment of all costs of and occasioned by the amendments.

Amendment by court of its own motion   R.S.C., Ord. r. 8 empowers the court to order an amendment to be made of its own motion.[36] The court, however, very rarely exercises this power. "In a civil suit the function of a court in this country . . . is not inquisitorial"[37]; its function is to act as a kind of umpire[38] and it plays not an active but only a passive role in relation to the raising of the issues for its consideration and determination. It is not the duty of the court to force upon the parties amendments for

---

[33] R.S.C., Ord. 20, r. 9, it should be noted that if the party who has obtained an order to amend makes amendments which are not authorised by the order, the proper course is for his opponents to apply to have the amendment disapplied with costs.

[34] Leave to amend generally is ordinarily given, however, when the pleading of a party is struck out and he is given the opportunity to reframe his case; see p. 219, *infra*.

[35] *Busch* v. *Stevens* [1963] Q.B. 1; [1962] 2 W.L.R. 511; [1962] 1 All E.R. 412.

[36] *C.f.* R.S.C., Ord. 25, r. 3.

[37] *Fallon* v. *Calvert* [1960] 1 All E.R. 281 at 282.

[38] See Pollock and Maitland. *The History of English Law*. Vol. 2, p. 671; Holdsworth, *History of English Law*. Vol. 9, pp. 280–282.

which they do not ask.[39] Nevertheless, the power contained in this rule is valuable and significant.[40] It enables the court, by persuasion if possible and by order if necessary, to raise the real point at issue between the parties, and to ensure that its proceedings are free from errors and defects.

Form Where the amendments allowed to be made with or without leave in a writ, pleading or other document are so numerous or of such nature or length that to make written alterations of the document so as to give effect to them would make it difficult or inconvenient to read, a fresh document, amended as authorised, must be prepared. Subject to this and any direction given by the court, the amendments so authorised should be effected by making in writing the necessary alterations of the documents.[41]

Indorsement The amended writ, pleading or other document must be indorsed with a statement that it has been amended, specifying:

(a) the date on which it was amended;
(b) the name of the judge, master or registrar by whom the order, if any, allowing the amendment was made;
(c) the date thereof; and
(d) if the amendment was made without leave, the rule in pursuance of which the amendment was made.[42]

Colour The amendments when made should make it clear what has been deleted and what has been added or altered, so that the court when reading the amended pleading should be able to see at once the exact nature and extent of the amendments made. For this reason, the amendments should be made in different coloured ink. The first amendment is red, the second or re-amendment is green, the third or re-re-amendment in violet and the fourth amendment is yellow.[43]

---

[39] Per Fry L.J. in *Cropper* v. *Smith* [1883] 26 Ch.D. 700 at 715.
[40] For an instance of its exercise by Field J., see *Nottage* v. *Jackson* (1883) 11 Q.B.D. 627 at 638; see also *Liverpool Roman Catholic Archdiocesan Trustees Inc.* v. *Gibberd* H.H. Judge Fox-Andrews Q.C., O.R.; February 5, 1986, unreported (order for amendment of writ and statement of claim to add a new cause of action to the deemed to have effect at a specified date after the issue of the writ).
[41] See R.S.C., Ord. 20, r. 10(1).
[42] *Ibid.* r. 10(2)
[43] See Queen's Bench Master's Practice Directions No. 20 (Amendment), *Supreme Court Practice 1991*, Vol. 2, para. 732. A party is nevertheless entitled to amend his pleading once without leave in any colour he chooses; see *Re Langton* [1960] 1 W.L.R. 246; [1960] 1 All E.R. 657, (C.A.).

AMENDMENT OF PLEADINGS

Amending the Record

Rationale Since cases must be decided on the issues on the record, it is essential that amendments made should be embodied in the record of the court.[44-45] As Lord Russell of Killowen said[46]:

> "Any departure from the cause of action alleged, or the relief claimed in the pleadings, should be preceded, or, at all events, accompanied, by the relevant amendments, so that the exact cause of action alleged and relief claimed shall form part of the court's record, and be capable of being referred to thereafter should necessity arise. Pleadings should not be 'deemed to be amended' or 'treated as amended.' They should be amended in fact."[47]

Amendment at trial—post-date the judgment Where an issue which is not raised on the pleading is nevertheless opened at the trial and all the evidence called so that the court is seized of all relevant material and the defendants do not assert that they were prejudiced by the defect in the pleading, the plaintiffs should be granted leave to amend their pleadings to raise that particular issue, even though the charge, being one of professional negligence, ought to have been pleaded in the first instance clearly and with particularity.[48] On the other hand, if the trial judge should extend some latitude in relation to the cross-examination, this will not *per se* broaden the pleaded issues, but it may give rise to a successful application for leave to amend if such cross-examination proves fruitful.[49] Where amendments are allowed at the trial, the record must be amended, and the Court of Appeal may refuse to hear an appeal until this has been done, and the party in default will be penalised in costs.[50] The pleadings should be amended *before* judgment is pronounced, otherwise the record will be incomplete, and the judgment will be post-dated to the date on which the amended pleadings are completed.[51]

[44-45] See *Blay* v. Pollard and Morris [1930] 1 K.B. 628, *per* Scrutton L.J.

[46] *London Passenger Transport Board* v. *Moscrop* [1942] A.C. 332 at 347.

[47] See *e.g. Smith* v. *Roberts* (1892) 9 T.L.R. 77 (C.A.); *Shickle* v. *Lawrence* (1886) 2 T.L.R. 776 at 777, where the cases continued as though the issues which were being fought had been fully raised on the pleadings.

[48] *Buckland* v. *Farmar & Moody* [1979] 1 W.L.R. 221; [1978] 3 All E.R. 929, (C.A.).

[49] See *per* Lord Edmund-Davies in *Farrell* v. *Secretary of State for Defence* [1980] 1 W.L.R. 180; [1980] 1 All E.R. 166.

[50] See *Practice Note* [1927] W.N. 288.

[51] *Luby* v. *Newcastle-under-Lyme Corporation* [1965] 1 Q.B. 214; [1964] 3 W.L.R. 500; [1964] 3 All E.R. 169, (C.A.).

CHAPTER 12

Striking out pleadings

Summary Powers to Strike Out Pleadings, Dismiss Actions and Enter Judgment

Introduction   The court is clothed with wide and ample powers which are both useful and necessary to:

- (a) enforce the rules of pleadings by striking out or amending pleadings; and concurrently
- (b) stay or dismiss proceedings which are:
  - (i) an abuse of its process, such as frivolous, vexatious or harassing proceedings: or
  - (ii) manifestly groundless or in which there is clearly no cause of action or ground of defence in law or in equity.

        Although the court will not permit a plaintiff "to be driven from the seat of judgment" except where his cause of action is incontestably bad,[1] yet a stay or even a dismissal of proceedings may "often be required by the very essence of justice to be done,"[2] so as to prevent parties from being harassed and put to expense by frivolous, vexatious or hopeless litigation.[3]

Such powers are derived from two complementary sources, namely:

---

[1] See *Dyson v. Att.-Gen.* [1911] 1 K.B. 410, *per* Fletcher-Moulton L.J. at 419.

[2] See *Metropolitan Bank* v. *Pooley* (1885) 10 App.Cas. 210, *per* Lord Blackburn at 221.

[3] *Supreme Court Practice 1991*, Vol. 1, para. 18/19/4, cited by Lawton L.J. in *Riches* v. *Director of Public Prosecutions* [1973] 1 W.L.R. 1019 at 1027.

STRIKING OUT PLEADINGS

(a) the express powers conferred on the court by R.S.C., Ord. 18. r. 19[4]; and

(b) the inherent jurisdiction of the court.[5]

A concurrent jurisdiction   The powers conferred by the rule are, generally speaking, additional to and not in substitution for the powers arising under the inherent jurisdiction. These two sources of powers are generally cumulative, and not mutually exclusive. Thus in any given case a party may invoke, and the court is able to proceed under, either or both heads of jurisdiction. As Lord Esher said in *Davey* v. *Bentinck*[6]:

> "As to the question whether an order dismissing the action as frivolous and vexatious is right, such an order might be supported on either of two grounds – that is, either directly under the Rules of Court, or under the inherent jurisdiction of the Court to prevent oppression."

Extent of the express jurisdiction under the Rule[7]   The court may at any stage of the proceedings order to be struck out or amended any pleading or the indorsement of any writ in the action, or anything in any pleading or in the indorsement, on the ground that:

(a) it discloses no reasonable cause of action or defence, as the case may be; or

(b) it is scandalous, frivolous or vexatious; or

(c) it may prejudice, embarrass or delay the fair trial of the action; or

(d) it is otherwise an abuse of the process of the court.

Effect of the rule   It empowers the court[8]:

(a) by summary process, *i.e.* without the benefit of pre-trial procedures of and without a trial in the normal way:

    (i) to stay or dismiss an action where the pleading discloses no reasonable cause of action; or

[4] This rule has conveniently amalgamated, simplified and extended the pre-1964 R.S.C., Ord. 19, r. 27 (which dealt with unnecessary or scandalous matter in pleadings), and R.S.C., Ord. 25, r. 4 (which dealt with pleadings not disclosing a reasonable cause of action or answer and actions shown by the pleadings to be frivolous or vexatious), which themselves were introduced by the Rules of Court scheduled to the Supreme Court of Judicature Act 1875. The pre-1964 Ord. 25, r. 1 abolished the demurrer. On the abolition of the demurrer see *per* Lindley M.R. in *Hubbuck* v. *Wilkinson, Heywood and Clark* [1899] 1 Q.B. 86 at 91.
[5] See Jacob, "The Inherent Jurisdiction of the Court" (1970) 23 *Current Legal Problems* pp. 23 *et seq.*; "The Reform of Civil Procedural Law" (1982) page 22.
[6] [1893] 1 Q.B. 185 at 187. See also *Willis* v. *Earl Beauchamp* (1886) 11 P.D. 59, *per* Bowen L.J. at 63 and *Metropolitan Bank* v. *Pooley* (1885) 10 App.Cas. 210 *per* Lord Blackburn at 220–221.
[7] R.S.C., Ord. 18, r. 19(1).
[8] R.S.C., Ord. 18, r. 19(3).

      (ii) to enter judgment against a party where his pleading discloses no reasonable cause of action or ground of defence[9]; or

      (iii) where the action or defence is shown to be frivolous or vexatious[10] or is otherwise an abuse of the process of the court;

    And:

  (b) to strike out any pleading[11] or indorsement or any matter contained therein, which does not conform to the overriding rule that the pleading must contain only material facts to support a party's claim or defence.[12] It must not therefore be, or contain any matter which is, scandalous, frivolous or vexatious or which may prejudice, embarrass or delay the fair trial of the action or is otherwise an abuse of the process of the court.[13]

The powers of the court under the rule and under its inherent jurisdiction constitute the sanction for compelling parties to comply with the rules of pleading and the practice of the court relating to pleadings.[14]

Invoking the summary powers of the court – the practice Two important considerations arise concerning the exercise of the powers of the court, whether under R.S.C., Ord. 18, r. 19 or under the inherent jurisdiction of the court, namely:

  (a) the powers may be exercised by "summary process"; and

  (b) the court has power to order or grant leave to amend any pleading or indorsement, so as to cure and save the pleading or proceedings.

"Summary Process" The exercise of the court's powers by "summary process" means that the court may exercise its jurisdiction without the benefit of pre-trial discovery or other pre-trial processes and without a trial, *i.e.* without hearing the evidence of witnesses examined and cross-examined orally and in open court.[15] Thus by summary process, the

---

[9] See *South Hetton Coal Co.* v.*Haswell & Co.* [1898] 1 Ch. 465; *Dominion Iron & Steel Co.* v. *Baron Invernairn* [1927] W.N. 277.

[10] *Lawrance* v. *Palmer* (1890) 15 App.Cas. 210; *Wyatt* v. *Palmer* [1899] 2 Q.B. 106; *Lea* v. *Thursby* (1904) 90 L.T. 265; *Emerson* v. *Grimsby Times & Telegraph Co.* (1926) 42 T.L.R. 238.

[11] So far as applicable, the rule applies to an originating summons and a petition as though it were a pleading; see R.S.C., Ord. 18, r. 19(3), and *Re Bartlett & Berry's Contract*(1897) 76 L.T. 751.

[12] See R.S.C., Ord. 18, r. 7(1); and see p. 46 *et seq.*, *supra.*

[13] See *Supreme Court Practice 1991*, Vol. 1, para. 18/19/1.

[14] Also see *ROFA Sport Management A.G.* v. *D.H.L. International (U.K.) Limited* [1989] 1 W.L.R. 902 (C.A.) where it was held that a stay of proceedings is not equivalent to a dismissal or discontinuance and that therefore an action which has been stayed even by consent remains in being.

[15] See R.S.C., Ord. 38, r. 1.

court adopts a method of procedure which is different from the normal plenary trial procedure.[16] The difference is:

    (a) no discovery or other pre-trial processes;
    (b) no oral evidence; and
    (c) no cross-examination.

The result is that where these powers are invoked, and the action is stayed or dismissed or judgment is entered against the defendant, the party affected may thereby be deprived of the pre-trial processes of discovery and so forth and a plenary trial.

How "Summary" is this "process"? Because the party would be deprived of pre-trial and trial processes the court will exercise its coercive powers to terminate proceedings only with the greatest care and circumspection and only in the clearest case.[17]

Amendment The court also has power to amend any pleading or indorsement or any matter therein.[18] This power is additional to the general powers of the court to allow amendments of pleading.[19] Its incorporation in R.S.C., Ord. 18, r. 19 emphasises that, in a suitable and proper case, the court may exercise both its coercive and its corrective powers at the same time. The object of this additional power is precisely to allow the court to enable a party to reform or restate his pleading or claim or defence without offending the rules of pleading and also without offending the other sub-paragraphs of the rule.[19a]

General Principles for Exercise of Summary Powers under Order 18, Rule 19

"Circumspection" – the touchstone Because the powers under R.S.C., Ord. 18, r. 19, are coercive in operation and are exercised by summary process[20] the court exercises these powers only with the greatest care and circumspection and only in the clearest cases. As Fletcher-Moulton L.J. said in *Dyson* v. *Att.-Gen.*[21]:

> "To my mind it is evident that our judicial system would never permit a plaintiff to be driven from the judgment seat in this way with-

---

[16] See *Jacob, op. cit.*, p. 29; and see *Metropolitan Bank* v. *Pooley* (1885) 10 App.Cas. 210, *per* Lord Blackburn at 220–221.
[17] See *infra*.
[18] See R.S.C., Ord. 18, r. 19(1).
[19] See R.S.C., Ord. 20, rr. 3, 5 and 8; and see p. 193, n. 26, *supra*.
[19a] *i.e.* R.S.C., Ord. 18, r. 19(a), (b), (c) and (d).
[20] See p. 215, *supra*.
[21] [1911] 1 K.B. 410 at 419.

out any Court having considered his right to be heard, excepting in cases where the cause of action was obviously and almost incontestably bad."

Similarly, Lindley M.R. observed in *Hubbuck & Sons Ltd.* v. *Wilkinson, Heywood & Clark*[22]:

"The . . . summary procedure [*i.e.* under rule 19] is only appropriate to cases which are plain and obvious, so that any master or judge can say at once that the statement of claim as it stands is insufficient, even if proved, to entitle the plaintiff to what he asks."

How the court exercises its discretion in practice The power to strike out any pleading or any part of a pleading under this rule is not mandatory, but permissive and confers a discretionary jurisdiction to be exercised having regard to the quality and all the circumstances relating to the offending pleading[23]; and a reasonable latitude must be given, for this rule was not intended to enable parties to bring forward special demurrers in a new shape.[24]

Thus, the summary procedure under this rule can only be adopted when it can be clearly seen that:

(a) a claim or answer is on the face of it "obviously unsustainable"[25];
(b) the case is clear beyond doubt[26]; or
(c) the case is unarguable.[27]

Framing the application An application invoking the powers of the rule may be made on all or any of the grounds mentioned in the rule. Such grounds must however be expressly specified in the summons. Furthermore, the application may be (and ordinarily is) made both under this

---

[22] [1899] 1 Q.B. 86 at 91; and see *Drummond-Jackson* v. *British Medical Association* [1970] 1 W.L.R. 688; [1970] 1 All E.R. 1094, (C.A.), *per* Lord Pearson.

[23] See *Carl Zeiss Stiftung* v. *Rayner and Keeler Ltd.* (No. 3) [1970] Ch. 506; [1969] 3 All E.R. 897; *Hampshire County Council* v. *Shonleigh Nominees* (I.) [1970] 1 W.L.R. 865; [1970] 2 All E.R. 144.

[24] *Tomkinson* v. *South Eastern Ry.* (No. 2) (1887) 57 L.T. 358; *Rock* v. *Purssell* (1887) 84 L.T.J. 45.

[25] See *Att.-Gen. of the Duchy of Lancaster* v. *London and North Western Ry.* [1892] 3 Ch. 274, *per* Lindley L.J. at 277.

[26] See *Kellaway* v. *Bury* (1892) 66 L.T. 602, *per* Lindley L.J. at 602; and see *Dominion Iron & Steel Co.* v. *Baron Invernairn* [1972] W.N. 277.

[27] See *Nagle* v. *Feilden* [1966] 2 Q.B. 633, *per* Salmon L.J. at 651; [1966] 1 All E.R. 689; *Republic of Peru* v. *Peruvian Guano Co.* (1887) 36 Ch.D. 489, *per* Chitty J. at 496, a pleading will not be struck out under this rule "unless it is demurrable and something worse than demurrable"; *Waters* v. *Sunday Pictorial Newspapers Ltd.* [1961] 1 W.L.R 967; [1961] 2 All E.R. 758 (C.A.).

rule *and* concurrently under the inherent jurisdiction of the court.[28] The application should specify precisely what order is being sought, *e.g* to strike out, or to stay or dismiss the action or to enter judgment and precisely what is being attacked and on what grounds, whether the whole pleading or indorsement or only parts thereof, and if so the alleged offending parts should be clearly specified.[29]

Evidence – when?

(a) Where the only ground on which the application is made is that the pleading discloses no reasonable cause of action or defence, no evidence is admissible.[30]

(b) In applications on any of the other grounds mentioned in the rule or where the inherent jurisdiction of the court is invoked, affidavit evidence may be, and ordinarily is, used. Where however the facts are in dispute it is not permissible to try the action on affidavits.[31] Where an application to strike out pleadings involves a prolonged and serious argument, the court should, as a rule, decline to proceed with the argument unless it not only harbours doubts about the soundness of the pleading but, in addition, is satisfied that striking out would obviate the necessity for a trial or substantially reduce the burden of preparing for a trial. Thus where the court is satisfied, even after substantial argument both at first instance and on appeal, that the defence does not disclose a reasonable ground of defence, it will order it to be struck out.[32] However, if the court is satisfied that a claim by the plaintiff does not disclose a reasonable cause of action, even though the court is so satisfied after a relatively long and elaborate hearing, the right course for the court is to strike out that claim, even if the defendant has still to

---

[28] See *Vinson v. Prior Fibres Consolidated Ltd.* [1906] W.N. 209; *Day* v. *William Hill (Park Lane) Ltd.* [1949] 1 K.B. 632; [1949] 1 All E.R. 219 (C.A.). It is desirable to state expressly that the application is made under "the inherent jurisdiction of the court."

[29] *Williamson* v. *London and North Western Ry.* (1879) 12 Ch.D. 787 at 790; *Carl Zeiss Stiftung* v. *Rayner and Keeler Ltd. (No. 3)* [1970] Ch. 506; [1969] 3 All E.R. 897.

[30] R.S.C., Ord. 18, r. 19(2); and see *Republic of Peru v. Peruvian Guano Co.* (1887) 36 Ch.D. 489; *Att.-Gen. of Duchy of Lancaster* v. *London and North Western Ry.* [1892] 3 Ch. 274; *Wenlock* v. *Maloney* [1965] 1 W.L.R. 1238; [1965] 2 All E.R. 871. But on an application to strike out an originating summons on the ground that it discloses no reasonable cause of action, the prohibition in para. (2) against adducing evidence on the application itself does not apply to an affidavit already put in as supporting the originating summons, and affidavits used before the Master without objection cannot be excluded before the judge *(Re Caines, Knapman v. Servian* [1978] W.L.R. 540; [1978] 2 All E.R. 1.

[31] See *Wenlock* v. *Moloney* [1965] 1 W.L.R. 1238; [1965] 2 All E.R. 871 (C.A.) (where the Master delivered a reserved judgment in 21 pages).

[32] *Williams & Humbert Ltd.* v. *W. & H. Trade Marks (Jersey) Ltd.* [1986] A.C. 368; [1986] 2 W.L.R. 24; [1986] 1 All E.R. 129; affirming [1985] 3 W.L.R. 501 (C.A.).

meet other viable claims by the plaintiff. This is because he is entitled under this rule to be relieved from having to meet a claim which discloses no reasonable cause of action.[33]

When? Notwithstanding that the application may be made "at any stage of the proceedings," it should always be made promptly and as a rule soon after the service of the offending pleading,[34] Exceptionally however it may be made after the pleadings are closed.[35] The court may refuse to hear such an application after the action is set down for trial.[36]

Pleadings Disclosing no Reasonable Cause of Action or Ground of Defence

Not akin to a demurrer The court may order the pleading to be struck out or amended, and the action may be ordered to be stayed or dismissed or judgment to be entered accordingly.[37] The use of the term "reasonable" in the phrase employed in this rule namely "reasonable cause of action or defence", suggests that the rule is more favourable to the pleading objected to than the old procedure by demurrer, and effect must be given to the word "reasonable."[38] It has been said that to a limited extent this procedure has taken the place of the old demurrer which was abolished in 1875,[39] but the predominant judicial view is that it does not do

---

[33] *McKay* v. *Essex Area Health Authority* [1982] Q.B. 1166; [1982] 2 W.L.R. 890; [1982] 2 All E.R. 771; (C.A.) (No. 2) [1988] Ch. 114; [1987] 3 All E.R. 909. The case of *Smith* v. *Croft* [1986] 1 W.L.R. 580; [1986] 2 All E.R. 551, appears to go further than ordinary cases on the problem in as much as the court decided to follow the procedure to strike out under Ord. 18, r. 19 rather than the procedure for determining the preliminary issue of law under Ord. 33, r. 3. It is to be contrasted for example, with what happened in the case of *Addis* v. *Crocker* [1961] 1 Q.B. 11; [1960] 3 W.L.R. 339; [1960] 2 All E.R. 629. That case related to the question of whether absolute privilege attached to the publication of the findings of the disciplinary committee of the Law Society. Devlin J. set aside the order striking out the action as disclosing no cause of action and intimated that the point should be decided as a preliminary issue of law under Ord. 33, r. 3 which in fact happened. That case might today be decided differently under the more robust approach in *Smith* v. *Croft, ibid.*

[34] See *Att.-Gen. of Duchy of Lancaster* v. *London and North Western Ry., supra.* (before defence served); *Wright* v. *Prescot Urban District Council* (1916) 115 L.T. 772 (after service of statement of claim).

[35] See *Tucker* v. *Collinson* (1886) 16 Q.B.D. 562, *per* Brett M.R.

[36] See *Cross* v. *Earl Howe* (1892) 62 L.J. Ch. 342; *Fletcher* v. *Bethom* (1893) 68 L.T. 438.

[37] R.S.C., Ord. 18, r. 19(1)(a). As to the meaning of "cause of action," see p. 75, *supra.*

[38] See *Republic of Peru* v. *Peruvian Guano Co.* (1887) 36 Ch.D. 489, *per* Chitty J. at 495, where he said "there is some difficulty in affixing a precise meaning to the term "reasonable cause of action" used [in this rule.] In point of law, and consequently in the view of a Court of justice, every cause of action is a reasonable cause."

[39] See *Burstall* v. *Beyfus* (1884) 26 Ch.D. 35, *per* Lord Selbourne; *Michael* v. *Spiers and Pond Ltd.* (1909) 25 T.L.R. 740 at 741: *Emerson* v. *Grimsby Times and Telegraph Co.* (1926) 42 T.L.R. 238, *per* Banks L.J.

so at all except in very clear cases.[40] A reasonable cause of action means a cause of action with some chance of success when only the allegations in the pleading are considered.[41] The pleading will not be looked at with the same strictness as it would have been under the old demurrer. The question is not whether it discloses a good cause of action or answer, but whether it discloses a reasonable one.[42]

What is "reasonable"?   As long as the statement of claim, including any particulars, discloses *some* cause of action or *some* question fit to be decided by the court, whether it be a question of law or of fact or of mixed fact and law, the action should be allowed to proceed. It is irrelevant that the case is weak or not likely to succeed at the trial.[43]

Cases where the rule is inapplicable   The rule does not apply where:

  (a) there is an arguable or a seriously arguable point[44]; or

  (b) there is a question of difficulty or an important point of law;[45] if a serious point of law arises on the pleadings, the court may order it to be tried as a preliminary issue, or[46];

  (c) the action involves a serious investigation of ancient law and questions of general importance[47]; or

---

[40] See *Evans v. Barclays Bank and Galloway* [1924] W.N. 97 (C.A.); *Parsons v. Burton* [1883] W.N. 215, *per* Field J.; *Dyson v. Att.-Gen.* [1911] 1 K.B. 410, *per* Cozens-Hardy M.R. at 414, and *per* Fletcher-Moulton L.J. at 419. The demurrer was abolished by the former R.S.C., Ord. 25, r. 1. A demurrer was the proceeding by which a party objected that his opponent's pleading disclosed no cause of action, or no defence or answer, as the case might be in point of law. The question then was, whether the cause of action, defence or answer was good in point of law, not whether it was *reasonable*.

[41] See *Drummond-Jackson v. British Medical Association* [1970] 1 W.L.R. 688; [1970] 1 All E.R. 1094, *per* Lord Justice Pearson.

[42] See *Dadswell v. Jacobs* (1887) 34 Ch.D. 278, *per* Cotton L.J. at 281; *Worthington & Co. v. Belton* (1902) 18 T.L.R. 439 (C.A.); and see *Kellaway v. Bury* (1892) 66 L.T. 599, *per* Lindley L.J. at 602: "[The pleading will not be looked at] through the glasses of an old special pleader."

[43] *Moore v. Lawson* (1915) 31 T.L.R. 418 (C.A.); *Boaler v. Holder* (1886) 54 L.T. 298; *Wenlock v. Moloney* [1965] 1 W.L.R. 1238; [1965] 2 All E.R. 871, (C.A.); *Drummond-Jackson v. British Medical Association* [1970] 1 W.L.R. 68; [1970] 1 All E.R. 1094, (C.A.); *Home Office v. Dorset Yacht Co. Ltd.* [1970] A.C. 1004; [1970] 2 All E.R. 294 (H.L.); *Roy v. Prior* [1971] A.C. 470; [1970] 2 All E.R. 729.

[44] *Evans v. Barclays Bank and Galloway* [1924] W.N. 97 (C.A.); *Roberts v. Charing Cross, Euston and Hampstead Ry.* (1903) 87 L.T. 732; *London Corporation v. Horner* (1914) 111 L.T. 512 (C.A.); *Nagle v. Fielden* [1966] 2 Q.B. 633; [1966] 2 W.L.R. 1027; [1966] 1 All E.R. 689; *Barton, Thompson & Co. v. Stapling Machines Co.* [1966] Ch. 499; [1966] 2 W.L.R. 1429; [1966] 2 All E.R. 222.

[45] *Att.-Gen of Duchy of Lancaster v. London and North Western Ry.* [1892] 3 Ch. 274 (C.A.).

[46] See *Addis v. Crocker* [1961] 1 Q.B. 11; [1960] 3 W.L.R. 339; [1960] 2 All E.R. 629, (C.A.).

[47] *Dyson v. Att.-Gen.* [1911] 1 K.B. 410, but see, however, *Sirros v. Moore & Others* [1975] Q.B. 118; [1974] 3 All E.R. 776 C.A., where a claim for false imprisonment against a judge was summarily struck out.

(d) the transaction is a complicated one giving rise to questions which ought to be tried[48]; or

(e) the statement of claim shows that the cause of action arises outside the statutory period of limitation,[49] unless the defendant clearly intends to raise the limitation defence and there is nothing before the Court to suggest that the plaintiff could escape from that defence in which event the action will be struck out on being frivolous vexatious and on abuse of the processes of the court[50]; or

(f) a claim will not be struck out because the defendant may have a defence under the Statute of Frauds 1677; or under section 40 of the Law of Property Act 1925[51] or under the Statute of Frauds Amendment Act 1828.[52]

Pleadings capable of being cured by amendment

(a) *Situation*   The statement of claim or defence as pleaded discloses no reasonable cause of action or defence because some material averment has been omitted or because the pleading is defectively stated or formulated.

(b) *Approach of the court*   While striking out the pleading, the court will not dismiss the action or enter judgment, but may give the party

[48] *Lea* v. *Thursby* (1904) 89 L.T. 744, *affirmed* 90 L.T. 265 (C.A.); and see *Wyatt* v. *Palmer* [1899] 2 Q.B. 106 at 110 (important questions to be discussed). Similarly, where an application to strike out pleadings involves a prolonged and serious argument, the court should, as a rule, decline to proceed with the argument unless it not only harbours doubts about the soundness of the pleading but, in addition, is satisfied that striking out would obviate the necessity for a trial or substantially reduce the burden of preparing for a trial, and therefore, where the court is satisfied, even after substantial argument both at first instance and on appeal, that the defence does not disclose a reasonable ground of defence, it will order it to be struck out (*Williams & Humbert Ltd.* v. *W. & H. Trade Marks (Jersey) Ltd.* [1986] A.C. 368; [1986] 2 W.L.R. 24; 1 All E.R. 129 (H.L.); affirming [1985] 3 W.L.R. 501 (C.A.). However, if the court is satisfied that a claim by the plaintiff does not disclose a reasonable cause of action, even though the court is so satisfied after a relatively long and elaborate hearing, the right course for the court is to strike out that claim, even if the defendant has still to meet other viable claims by the plaintiff, since he is entitled under this rule to be relieved from having to meet a claim which disclosed no reasonable cause of action (*McKay* v. *Essex Area Health Authority* [1982] Q.B. 1166; [1982] 2 W.L.R. 890; [1982] 2 All E.R. 771, (C.A.).

[49] *Ronex Properties* v. *John Laing Construction Ltd.* [1983] Q.B. 398; [1982] 3 W.L.R. 875; [1982] 3 All E.R. 96), (C.A.); approving and applying *Dismore* v. *Milton* [1938] 3 All E.R. 762 (C.A.); and see *Dawkins* v. *Penrhyn (Lord)* (1878) 4 App.Cas. 51; *Murray* v. *Secretary of State for India* [1931] W.N. 91. The position is the same where a new claim is added under s.35(1)(*b*) of the Limitation Act 1980 (*Kenneth* v. *Brown* [1988] 1 W.L.R. 582 (C.A.)).

[50] *Riches* v. *Director of Public Prosecutions* [1973] 1 W.L.R. 1019 (C.A.) as explained in *Ronex Properties Ltd.* v. *John Laing Constructor Ltd* (1983) Q.B. 398; [1973] 2 All E.R. 935.

[51] See *Fraser* v. *Pape* (1904) 91 L.T. 340 (C.A.).

[52] See *Worthington & Co.* v. *Belton* (1902) 18 T.L.R. 439 (C.A.).

leave to amend and if necessary to serve a fresh pleading to correct or cure the defects appearing in the original pleading.[53]

A statement of claim setting out   Two causes of action will not be struck out because one of them may be bad.[54]

Pleadings incapable of cure   If the court is satisfied that the pleading discloses no reasonable cause of action or defence, as the case may be, and that no amendment, however ingenious, will correct or cure the defect, the pleading will be struck out and the action dismissed or judgment entered accordingly.[55]

Examples of when amendment cannot cure:

(a) In an action on contract the statement of claim will be struck out and the action dismissed:
   (i) if it appears clearly that there is no contract between the plaintiff and the defendant[56]; or
   (ii) if there is no contract valid in law[57]; or
   (iii) if there is an illegal contract[58]; or
   (iv) if the action be brought to obtain relief which the court has no power to grant[59]; or
   (v) if the relief be asked on a ground which is no ground for such relief.[60]

(b) Where the statement of claim discloses on its face a perfectly good defence to the action, as, for example, in an action for defamation that the occasion of publication was absolutely privileged,[61] the action will be stayed or dismissed.

(c) Where it is clear that the action must fail, or the pleading discloses a case which the court is satisfield will not succeed, or that no

---

[53] If a statement of claim does not disclose a cause of action to be relied on, an opportunity to amend may be given even though the formulation of the amendment is not before the court: *CBS Songs Ltd.* v. *Amstrad*; [1988] A.C. 1013; [1988] 2 W.L.R. 1191; [1987] R.P.C. 417.

[54] *Grosvenor* v. *White* (1989) 61 L.T. 663.

[55] See *Republic of Peru* v. *Peruvian Guano Co.* (1887) 36 Ch.D. 489; *Goodson* v. *Grierson* [1908] 1 K.B. 761; *Woods* v. *Lyttleton* (1909) 25 T.L.R. 665 (C.A.).

[56] *South Hetton Coal Co.* v. *Haswell & Co.* [1898] 1 Ch. 465.

[57] *Humphrys* v. *Polak* [1901] 2 K.B. 385.

[58] *Shaw* v. *Shaw* [1965] 1 W.L.R. 537; [1965] 1 All E.R. 638.

[59] *Dreyfus* v. *Peruvian Guano Co.* (1889) 41 Ch.D. 151; *Wing* v. *Burn* (1928) 44 T.L.R. 258.

[60] *Johnston* v. *Johnston* (1884) 33 W.R. 239 (C.A.).

[61] *Lilley* v. *Roney* (1892) 61 L.J.Q.B. 727; *Hodson* v. *Pare* [1899] 1 Q.B. 455; *Law* v. *Llewellyn* [1906] 1 K.B. 487; *Bottomley* v. *Brougham* [1908] 1 K.B. 584; *Burr* v. *Smith and Others* [1909] 2 K.B. 306; *Beresford* v. *White* (1914) 30 T.L.R. 591 (C.A.), but see *Addis* v. *Crocker* [1961] 1 Q.B. 11; [1960] 3 W.L.R. 339; [1960] 2 All E.R. 629, (C.A.).

relief can be granted at the trial, the action will be stayed or dismissed.[62]

Scandalous Pleadings may be Ordered to be Struck Out or Amended[63]

Scandalous matters which are susceptible to striking out. Allegations in a pleading are scandalous if they state matters which are indecent or offensive or are made for the mere purpose of abusing or prejudicing the opposite party.[64] Moreover, any "unnecessary" or "immaterial" allegations will be struck out as being scandalous if they contain any imputation on the opposite party or make any charge of misconduct or bad faith against him or anyone else.[65] Again, if degrading charges are made which are irrelevant, or if, though the charge be relevant, unnecessary details are given, the pleading becomes scandalous.[66] One of two defendants may apply to strike out scandalous passages from the defence served on him by the other.[67]

Scandalous matters which are not susceptible to being struck out, etc. A pleading or allegation which is scandalous, as, *e.g.*, by making

[62] *Barrett* v. *Day* (1890) 43 Ch.D. 435; *In the Estate of Hall* [1914] P. 1; and see also *Vacher & Sons Ltd.* v. *London Society of Compositors* [1913] A.C. 107 (claim for defamation against trade union barred by s.4(1) of the Trades Disputes Act 1906 (now repealed)); *Rondel* v. *Worsley* [1969] 1 A.C. 191; [1967] 3 W.L.R. 1666; [1967] 3 All E.R. 993; (claim against barrister for negligence); *Blackburn* v. *Att.-Gen.* [1971] 1 W.L.R. 1037; [1971] 2 All E.R. 1380 (claim impugning prerogative powers of the Crown to enter into treaties); *Thorne* v. *University of London* [1966] 2 Q.B. 237 (claim against University for negligence of examiner); *Hubbuck & Sons* v. *Wilkinson, Heywood & Clark* [1899] 1 Q.B. 86 (C.A.) (claim in respect of statement made by defendant that his goods were superior to those of the plaintiff); *Appleson* v. *Littlewood (H.) Ltd.* [1939] 1 All E.R. 464 (C.A.) (claim against football pool based upon contract containing an honour clause); *Prince* v. *Gregory* [1959] 1 W.L.R. 177; [1959] 1 All E.R. 133 (C.A.); *Fowler* v. *Lanning* [1959] 1 Q.B. 426; [1959] 2 W.L.R. 241; [1959] 1 All E.R. 290.

[63] R.S.C., Ord. 18, r. 19(1)(*b*). As to scandalous matter in affidavits, see R.S.C., Ord. 41, r. 6. The court also has an inherent power to expunge scandalous matter in any record or proceeding; see *Re Miller* (1884) 54 L.J. Ch. 205 (bill of costs).

[64] *Christie* v. *Christie* (1873) L.R. 8 Ch.App. 499 (C.A.): *Cashin* v. *Cradock* (1876) 3 Ch.D. 376; *Coyle* v. *Cuming* (1879) 40 L.T. 455 (action for rectification of marriage settlement; allegation that husband committed assault on young girl struck out); and see also *Rubery* v. *Grant* (1872) 42 L.J. Ch. 19; *Lee* v. *Ashwin* (1885) 1 T.L.R. 291.

[65] *Lumb* v. *Beaumont* (1884) 49 L.T. 772; *Pearse* v. *Pearse* (1873) 29 L.T. 453 (allegations of adultery against wife in answer to action in respect of her private property struck out); *Brooking* v. *Maudslay* (1886) 55 L.T. 343 (charges of dishonest conduct not relied on); *Smith* v. *British Marine Mutual Insurance Association* [1883] W.N. 176 (in action on marine policy allegations of proceedings before an official inquiry made to discredit and prejudice plaintiffs struck out); *Murray* v. *Epsom Local Board* [1897] 1 Ch. 35 (imputation that one member of board opposing plaintiff for his own private interest struck out); *Markham* v. *Wernher, Beit & Co.* (1902) 18 T.L.R. 763 (H.L.).

[66] *Blake* v. *Albion Life Assurance Society* (1876) 45 L.J.Q.B. 663.

[67] *Bright* v. *Marner* [1878] W.N. 211 (costs).

charges of dishonesty, immorality or outrageous conduct, cannot be struck out, if it is necessary or relevant to any issue in the action.[68] As Lord Selborne in *Christie* v. *Christie*[69] said:

> "The sole question . . . is whether the matter alleged to be scandalous . . . would be admissible in evidence to shew the truth of any allegation in the [pleading] that is material with reference to the relief that is prayed."

Thus, however grave the imputations they involve, whether of immorality of otherwise, if they are material to the issue *i.e.* will affect the result of the action if proved to be true, they are not scandalous within the meaning of the rule.[70]

Evidence   When considering whether particular passages in a pleading are scandalous, regard must be had to the nature of the action, and whether they are in any way relevant to any of the issues of the action. For this purpose affidavit evidence may be admissible, but the court will not go into the question of their truth or falsehood.

Frivolous or Vexatious Pleadings and Actions

Introduction   Any pleading or indorsement of the writ which is frivolous or vexatious may be ordered to be struck out or amended, and the action may be ordered to be stayed or dismissed or judgment to be entered, as the case may be.[71]

Frivolous – meaning   A pleading or an action is frivolous when it is without substance or unarguable.

Thus, a proceeding may be said to be frivolous when:

    (a) a party is trifling with the court[72]; or

    (b) when to put it forward would be wasting the time of the court[73]; or

    (c) when it is not capable of reasoned argument; or

    (d) it is without foundation; or

    (e) where it cannot possibly succeed; or

---

[68] *Christie* v. *Christie* (1873) L.R. 8 Ch. 499 (C.A.); *Cracknall* v. *Janson* (1879) 11 Ch.D. 1 at 13; *Everett* v. *Prythergch* (1841) 12 Sim. 363; *Rubery* v. *Grant* (1872) L.R. 13 Eq. 443.

[69] (1873) L.R. 8 Ch. 499 at 503; and see *Cashin* v. *Cradock* (1876) 3 Ch.D. 376; *Whitney* v. *Moignard* (1890) 24 Q.B.D. 630.

[70] *Millington* v. *Loring* (1880) 6 Q.B.D. 190 (C.A.); and see *ibid., per* Brett L.J. at 196: "The mere fact that these matters state a scandalous fact does not make them scandalous within the meaning of [the] rule"; and see *Appleby* v. *Franklin* (1885) 17 Q.B.D. 93.

[71] R.S.C., Ord 18. r. 19 (1)(*b*).

[72] See, *e.g. Chaffners* v. *Goldsmid* [1894] 1 Q.B. 186 (action against M.P. for refusing to present a petition).

[73] *Dawkins* v. *Prince Edward of Saxe-Weimar* (1876) 1 Q.B.D. 499, *per* Mellor J.

(f) where the action is brought or the defence is raised only for annoyance; or

(g) to gain some fanciful advantage[74]; or

(h) when it can really lead to no possible good.[75]

Vexatious – meaning   A pleading or an action is vexatious when it lacks bona fides and is hopeless or oppressive and tends to cause the opposite party unnecessary anxiety, trouble and expense.[76] So, it is vexatious and wrong to make solicitors parties to an action merely in order to obtain discovery from them.[77]

The approach of the court   This jurisdiction to strike out a pleading or dismiss an action should not be exercised merely because the facts disclosed are improbable or it is difficult to believe that they could be proved.[78] It should be exercised judicially[79] in plain and obvious cases. As Lindley L.J. said[80]:

"It appears to me that the object of the rule is to stop cases which ought not to be launched—cases which are obviously frivolous or vexatious, or obviously unsustainable."

For this purpose, the court is entitled to go behind the pleadings, and to inquire summarily what are the true facts and circumstances of the case. It may admit affidavit evidence.[81]

Pleadings Tending to Prejudice, Embarrass or Delay Fair Trial

Introduction   Any pleading or indorsement of writ which may prejudice, embarrass or delay the fair trial of the action may be ordered to be struck out or amended.[82] The power is designed:

[74] See Jacob, *op. cit.*
[75] See *Willis* v. *Earl Beauchamp* (1886) 11 P.D. 59, *per* Bowen L.J. at 63 (action brought to revoke letters of administration after nearly 90 years struck out). Cotton L.J. at 65 described the action as "hopeless . . . and would lead to no good result."
[76] See Jacob, "The Inherent Jurisdiction of the Court" (1970) 23 *Current Legal Problems* 41.
[77] *Burstall* v. *Beyfus* (1884) 26 Ch.D. 35; and see *Dreyfus* v. *Peruvian Guano Co.* (1889) 41 Ch.D. 151 (claim for discovery in aid or proceedings in a foreign court dismissed); *Farnham* v. *Milward* [1895] 2 Ch. 730.
[78] See *Higgins* v. *Woodhall* (1889) 6 T.L.R. 1, *per* Lord Halsbury L.C.
[79] See *Lawrence* v. *Lord Norreys* (1888) 39 Ch.D. 213.
[80] *Att.-Gen. of Duchy of Lancaster* v. *London and North Western Ry.* [1892] 3 Ch. 274 at 277. See also *Young* v. *Holloway* [1895] P. 87, *per* Jeune J. at 90: the pleading must be "so clearly frivolous that to put it forward would be an abuse of the process of the court." See also *Lovell* v. *Williams* (1938) 62 Lloyd's Rep. 349; *Day* v. *William Hill (Park Lane) Ltd.* [1949] 1 K.B. 632; [1949] 1 All E.R. 219, (C.A.), (action involving gaming debts framed in the guise of an account stated struck out).
[81] See *Remmington* v. *Scoles* [1897] 2 Ch. 1.
[82] R.S.C., Ord. 18, r. 19(1)(*c*).

(a) to prevent pleadings from:
    (i) being evasive; or
    (ii) from concealing or obscuring the real questions in controversy between the parties; and
(b) to ensure, as far as the pleadings are concerned, a trial on fair terms between the parties in order to obtain a decision which is the legitimate object of the action.[83]

The touchstone – intelligibility   While parties must not be too ready to find themselves "prejudiced" or "embarrassed" by the pleadings of the opposite party, still each party may claim *ex debito justitiae* to have the opposite party's case "presented in an intelligible form, so that he may not be embarrassed in meeting it."[84] The principle has been thus stated by Bowen L.J. in *Knowles* v. *Roberts*[85]:

> "It seems to me that the rule that the Court is not to dictate to parties how they should frame their case, is one that ought always to be preserved sacred. But that rule is, of course, subject to this modification and limitation, that the parties must not offend against the rules of pleading which have been laid down by the law; and if a party introduces a pleading which is unnecessary, and it tends to prejudice, embarrass, and delay the trial of the action, it then becomes a pleading which is beyond his right."

Embarrassing – meaning   A pleading is embarrassing which:

(a) is ambiguous or unintelligible[86]; or
(b) states immaterial matter and so raises irrelevant issues which may involve expense, trouble and delay and thus will prejudice the fair trial of the action; or
(c) contains unnecessary or irrelevant allegations[87]; or
(d) involves a claim or defence[88] which a party is not entitled to make use of; or

---

[83] See *Berdan* v. *Greenwood* (1878) 3 Ex.D. 251, *per* Thesiger L.J. at 256, adding a liberal interpretation to the words 'fair trial of the action'."
[84] See *Davy* v. *Garrett* (1878) 7 Ch.D. 473, *per* James L.J. at 486.
[85] (1888) 38 Ch.D. 263 at 270.
[86] See *Davy* v. *Garrett, supra*; and see *Cashin* v. *Craddock* (1876) 3 Ch.D. 376; *Harbord* v. *Monk* (1878) 38 L.T. 411; *Lumb* v. *Beaumont* (1884) 49 L.T. 772.
[87] *Rassam* v. *Budge* [1893] 1 Q.B. 571 (defence justifying words other than those complained of); and see *Davy* v. *Garrett, supra*; *Blake* v. *Albion Society* (1876) 45 L.J.Q.B. 663 (claim alleging other transactions with other people of the same kind as the transaction sued on); *Brooking* v. *Maudslay* (1886) 55 L.T. 343; *Murray* v. *Epsom Local Board* [1897] 1 Ch. 35.
[88] See *Heugh* v. *Chamberlain* (1877) 25 W.R. 742, *per* Jessel M.R.; and see *Knowles* v. *Roberts* (1888) 38 Ch.D. 263 (claim not entitled to be raised); *Preston* v. *Lamont* (1876) 1 Ex.D. 367 (ground of defence not entitled to be raised); *Smith* v. *British Marine Insurance* [1883] W.N. 176 (defence not allowed to be raised).

(e) the defendant does not make clear how much of the statement of claim he admits and how much he denies[89]; or

(f) is a plea of justification leaving the plaintiff in doubt what the defendant has justified and what he has not[90]; or

(g) involves denials in a defence where they are vague or ambiguous[91] or are too general.[92]

Examples of pleading within the rule

(a) Failing sufficiently to state the plaintiff's title in an action for the recovery of land.[93]

(b) In an action on the covenants in a lease brought by an assignee of the lessor.[94]

(c) Failing sufficiently to define the way claimed in an action claiming a right of way.[95]

Examples of pleading outside the rule

(a) The mere fact that an allegation is unnecessary is no ground for striking it out.[96]

(b) Nor is a pleading embarrassing because it contains allegations which are inconsistent[97] or stated in the alternative[98] provided they are pleaded clearly and distinctly and in separate paragraphs.

(c) The mere fact that statements in a pleading may be difficult to deal with does not render them "prejudicial" or "embarrassing" if they are material facts and are otherwise properly pleaded.

(d) Mere prolixity, *i.e.* stating material facts at unnecessary length or with unnecessary detail, is not sufficient ground for striking out.[99]

---

[89] *British and Colonial Land Association* v. *Foster & Robins* (1888) 4 T.L.R. 574; *Stokes* v. *Grant* (1879) 4 C.P.D. 25.

[90] *Fleming* v. *Dollar* (1889) 23 Q.B.D. 388; and see *Davis* v. *Billing* (1891) 8 T.L.R. 58.

[91] *Byrd* v. *Nunn* (1877) 7 Ch.D. 284.

[92] *British and Colonial Land Association* v. *Foster & Robins, supra*; *Copley* v. *Jackson* [1884] W.N. 39. The case of *Thornhill* v. *Weeks* (No. 2) [1913] 2 Ch. 464 in which the court declined to strike out the defence of a district council which "neither claimed nor denied" the existence of a public right of way appears to be exceptional and must be treated as decided on its own particular circumstances.

[93] *Philipps* v. *Philipps* (1878) 4 Q.B.D. 127; *Sutcliffe* v. *James* (1879) 40 L.T. 875; *Palmer* v. *Palmer* [1892] 1 Q.B. 319.

[94] *Davis* v. *James* (1884) 26 Ch.D. 778.

[95] *Harris* v. *Jenkins* (1882) 22 Ch.D. 481. See also *Stokes* v. *Grant* (1879) 4 C.P.D. 25 (not sufficiently or explicitly stating objection in point of law); *Riddell* v. *Strathmore* (1887) 3 T.L.R. 329 (not sufficiently stating facts to support allegation of concealed fraud).

[96] See *Rock* v. *Purssell* (1887) 84 L.T.J. 45.

[97] *Child* v. *Stenning* (1877) 5 Ch.D. 695; *Re Smith* (1884) 9 P.D. 68; *Re Morgan* (1887) 35 Ch.D. 492.

[98] *Bagot* v. *Easton* (1877) 7 Ch.D. 1.

[99] *Davy* v. *Garrett* (1878) 7 Ch.D. 473 at 487, 488; *Heap* v. *Marris* (1877) 2 Q.B.D. 630; *Weymouth* v. *Rich* (1885) 1 T.L.R. 609.

    (e) A pleading is not embarrassing merely because it is probable that the allegations made may ultimately turn out to be untrue in fact.[1]

    (f) Nor because points of laws are stated or alleged which may then turn out to be bad.[2]

    (g) Nor because it states facts which the party who pleads them is entitled to prove.[3]

The approach of the court   The question whether a pleading is embarrassing or prejudicial is one for the court to decide in view of the particular facts and circumstances of the case.[4] The court is inclined to give "a reasonable limit" and will only strike out irrelevant or unnecessary matter where it clearly is so.[5] Accordingly, unless the pleading as it stands is really and seriously embarrassing, it is often wiser to leave it unamended or to apply for further and better particulars.[6]

Severance   Where the matter which is wrongly or improperly pleaded is severable from the rest of the pleading, the order to strike out will usually be limited to that part of the pleading.[7]

Abuse of Process

Introduction   Any pleading or indorsement of writ which is an abuse of the process of the court may be ordered to be struck out or amended and the action may be stayed or dismissed or judgment entered accordingly, as the case may be.[8] This express power conferred on the court is derived from and is parallel with the inherent jurisdiction of the court to prevent the abuse of its process.[9]

Meaning   The term "abuse of process" is often used interchangeably with the terms "frivolous" or "vexatious" either separately or more

---

[1] *Turquand* v. *Fearon* (1879) 4 Q.B.D. 280; *Re Morgan* (1887) 35 Ch.D. 492.

[2] *Tomkinson* v. *South Eastern Ry.* (1887) 3 T.L.R. 822.

[3] *Lawrence Scott and Electrometers Ltd.* v. *General Electric Co. Ltd.* (1938) 55 R.P.C. 233.

[4] See *Russell* v. *Stubbs* [1913] 2 K.B. 200n., *per* Lord Halsbury.

[5] See *Tomkinson* v. *South Eastern Ry.* (*No. 2*) (1887) 57 L.T. 358, and *London Corporation* v. *Horner* (1914) 111 L.T. 512, *per*, Pickford L.J. at 514 "their irrelevancy must be quite clear and apparent at the first glance."

[6] See *Kemsley* v. *Foot* [1952] A.C. 345; [1952] 1 All E.R. 501.

[7] See, for instance, *Blake* v. *Albion Life Ass. Co.* (1876) 45 L.J.Q.B. 663; *Knowles* v. *Roberts* (1888) 38 Ch.D. 263. But where the matter which is faulty or defective is so intermixed with the rest of the pleading as not to be severable from it without difficulty, the whole of the pleading containing it may be struck out, as in *Cashin* v. *Cradock* (1882) 3 Ch.D. 376 or *Williamson* v. *London and North Western Ry.* (1879) 12 Ch.D. 787.

[8] R.S.C., Ord. 18, r. 19(1)(*d*).

[9] See Jacob, "The Inherent Jurisdiction of the Court" (1970) 23 *Current Legal Problems* p. 40.

usually in conjunction.[10] An action is an abuse of the process of the court where it is "pretenceless" or "absolutely groundless,"[11] and the court has the power to stop it summarily and prevent the time of the public and the court from being wasted.[12]

Circumstances where the court will strike out   The term "abuse of the process of the court" is a term of great significance. It connotes that the process of the court must be carried out properly, honestly and in good faith; and it means that the court will not allow its function as a court of law to be misused but will in a proper case, prevent its machinery from being used as a means of vexation or oppression in the process of litigation.[13] It follows that where an abuse of process has taken place, the court will intervene to stay or even dismissal of proceedings, "although it should not be lightly done, yet it may often be required by the very essence of justice to be done."[14]

Inherent Jurisdiction of the Court

Introduction   Apart from all rules and orders, the court has an inherent jurisdiction to stay or dismiss every action which is an abuse of its process or is frivolous or vexatious and to strike out all pleadings which are shown to be frivolous or vexatious. This inherent jurisdiction is distinct from the powers of the court conferred by the rules but is a most important adjunct to those powers.

Origins   From the earliest times the court exercised the power under its inherent jurisdiction by summary process to terminate proceedings which were frivolous or vexatious or which were an abuse of process.[15] In *Metropolitan Bank* v. *Pooley* Lord Blackburn said[16]:

---

[10] *Castro* v. *Murray* (1875) L.R. 10 Ex. 213 (action against the clerk of the petty bag office in the Court of Chancery for refusal to seal a writ of error); and see *Dawkins* v. *Prince Edward of Saxe-Weimar* (1876) 1 Q.B.D. 499 (action against members of a military court of inquiry for damages for a conspiracy); *Metropolitan Bank* v. *Pooley* (1885) 10 A.C. 210; and see p. 212, *supra*.

[11] See *Castro* v. *Murray, supra, per* Bramwell B. at 218; and see *Dawkins* v. *Prince Edward of Saxe-Weimar, supra, per* Blackburn J. at 502.

[12] See *Dawkins* v. *Prince Edward of Saxe-Weimar, supra, per* Mellor J. at 503.

[13] *Ibid.* and see *Supreme Court Practice 1991*, vol. 1, para. 18/19/9. Also see Jacob "The Inherent Jurisdiction of the Court" (1970) Vol. 23, p. 51, *Current Legal Problems*; "*The Reform of Civil Procedural Law* (1982) p.221.

[14] See *Metropolitan Bank* v. *Pooley* (1885) 10 App.Cas. 210, *per* Lord Blackburn at 221.

[15] See, *Tidds' Practice* 9th ed., 1828, Vol. 1, pp. 515 *et seq.*; and see also Winfield, *Abuse of Legal Process*, pp. 228–243; *Veale* v. *Saunders* (1669 1 Wms. Saund. 575; *Johnson* v. *Stephens & Carter Ltd.* [1923] 2 K.B. 857 (C.A.).

[16] (1885) 10 App.Cas. 210 at 220–221.

"[F]rom early times (I rather think, though I have not looked at it enough to say, from the earliest times) the Court had inherently in its power the right to see that its process was not abused by a proceeding without reasonable grounds, so as to be vexatious and harassing – the Court had the right to protect itself against such an abuse; but that was not done upon demurrer, or upon the record, or upon the verdict of a jury or evidence taken in that way, but it was done by the Court informing its conscience upon affidavits, and by summary order to stay the action which was brought under such circumstances as to be an abuse of the process of the Court; and in a proper case they did stay the action."

Meaning   The term "inherent jurisdiction of the court" is obviously a term of wide significance and it has been defined as being:

"The reserve or fund of powers, a residual source of powers, which the court may draw upon as necessary whenever it is just and equitable to do so and in particular to ensure the observance of the due process of law, to prevent improper vexation or oppression, to do justice between the parties and to secure a fair trial between them."[17]

Application—how should it be framed?   Where an application is made to the inherent jurisdiction of the court, all the facts and circumstances can be gone into. Affidavits are admissible.[18] The jurisdiction may be exercised even when the facts are in dispute.[19]

The court's discretion – to be exercised with circumspection   Lord Herschell has said[20]:

"It is a jurisdiction which ought to be very sparingly exercised, and only in the very exceptional cases. I do not think its exercise would be justified merely because the story told in the pleadings was highly

---

[17] See Jacob, "The Inherent Jurisdiction of the Court" (1970) 23 *Current Legal Problems* Vol. 23, p. 51. This definition has been adopted and applied by the Court of Appeal of Manitoba in *Montreal Trust Co.* v. *Churchill Forest Industries (Manitoba) Ltd.* [1971] 21 *Dominion Law Reports* (3rd ed.) 75.

[18] *Willis* v. *Earl Howe* [1893] 2 Ch. 545 at 554; *Vinson* v. *The Prior Fibres Consolidated Ltd.* [1906] W.N. 209; *Norman* v. *Matthews* (1916) 85 L.J.K.B. 857, and [1906] W.N. 209 (C.A.); and see *Remmington* v. *Scoles* [1897] 2 Ch. 1; *Critchell* v. *London and South Western Ry.* [1907] 1 K.B. 860.

[19] *Lawrance* v. *Lord Norreys* (1890) 15 App.Cas. 210.

[20] *Ibid.*, at 219. He added that the story told in the affidavits left him with the impression "that [it] is a myth which has grown with the progress of the litigation and has no substantial foundation." See also *Goodson* v. *Grierson* [1908] 1 K.B. 761.

improbable, and one which it was difficult to believe could be proved."

Examples of dismissal

(a) The court has inherent jurisdiction to stay an action which must fail, as, for instance, an action brought in respect of an act of State.[21]

(b) An action brought by an infant suing by a next friend which clearly is brought in the interest of the next friend and not of the infant.[22]

(c) An action which the plaintiff cannot prove and which is without any solid basis.[23]

(d) If a party seeks to raise a new question which has already been substantially decided between the same parties by a court of competent jurisdiction in a former action, this fact may be brought before the court by affidavit, and the statement of claim, though good on the face of it, may be struck out, and the second action dismissed even though the matter is not technically *res judicata*.[24] But if there be any "matter of fact fit to be investigated," the court will refuse to stay it.[25]

Identifying the grounds of the application Frequently an application may be made both under the powers contained in the rules and under the inherent jurisdiction of the court to strike out a pleading or to dismiss or to stay an action or to enter judgment,[26] but in such case, the summons should clearly state the fact and indicate precisely what order is being sought.

---

[21] *Chatterton* v. *Secretary of State for India* [1895] 2 Q.B. 189; *Salaman* v. *Secretary of State for India* [1906] 1 K.B. 613.

[22] *Huxley* v. *Wootton* (1912) 29 T.L.R. 132.

[23] *Lawrance* v. *Lord Norreys* (1890) 15 App.Cas. 210; *Willis* v. *Earl Howe* [1893] 2 Ch. 545.

[24] *Reichel* v. *Magrath* (1889) 14 App.Cas. 665; *MacDougall* v. *Knight* (1890) 25 Q.B.D. 1; *Stephenson* v. *Garnett* [1898] 1 Q.B. 677; *Cooke* v. *Rickman* [1911] 2 K.B. 1125; *Greenhalgh* v. *Mallard* [1947] 2 All E.R. 255; and see *Conquer* v. *Boot* [1928] 2 K.B. 336; *Green* v. *Weatherill* [1929] 2 Ch. 213.

[25] *Blair* v. *Crawford* [1906] 1 Ir.R. 578 at 587; *Goodson* v. *Grierson* [1908] 1 K.B. 761; *Electrical Development Company of Ontario* v. *Att.-Gen of Ontario* [1919] A.C. 687.

[26] See *Coxon* v. *Gorst* [1891] 2 Ch. 74; *Day* v. *William Hill (Park Lane) Ltd.* [1949] 1 K.B. 632; [1949] 1 All E.R. 219.

CHAPTER 13

Default of Pleadings

Default of Pleadings

Introduction   The system of pleadings embodies appropriate sanctions for:

(a) default by the parties in serving their respective pleadings within the time-table prescribed by the rules or any duly extended period[1]; or

(b) default in complying with orders of the court for service of further and better particulars of pleadings.

Function   These sanctions are intended:

(a) to secure due compliance with the requirements of the rules or orders of the court; and

(b) alternatively, to dispose of proceedings without trial, where the parties do not prosecute or defend with due diligence.

Setting aside   In appropriate circumstances, these sanctions are tempered by the power of the court to set aside judgments entered in default of pleadings.[2]

Default in Service of Statement of Claim

How is the court's power invoked?   If the plaintiff defaults in the service of his statement of claim within the time prescribed by the rules[3] or any duly extended period[4] the defendant is not entitled immediately or as of right to sign judgment[5] nor to have the action dismissed. He must apply to the court for an order to dismiss the action for want of prosecution.

---

[1] See R.S.C., Ord. 3, r. 5.

[2] R.S.C., Ord. 19, r. 9; and see p. 239, *infra*.

[3] See R.S.C., Ord. 18, r. 1; and see p. 37 *et seq.*, *supra*.

[4] See p. 42, *supra*.

[5] The position is different in the case of a default of defence in relation to specified categories of claim; see p. 234, *infra*.

The court may by order dismiss the action or make such other order on such terms as it thinks fit.[6]

The power is discretionary   Since the power to dismiss is discretionary[7] the service of the statement of claim before the hearing of the summons to dismiss does not automatically cure the default or preclude the court from dismissing the action for want of prosecution.[8] The power may be exercised notwithstanding that the plaintiff has obtained an *Anton Piller* order against the defendants or some of them, since the principle is that those who make charges which warrant such an order being made must state at the very commencement of their action what they are and what facts they are based upon.[9]

"Unless" orders   If the order to dismiss is an "unless" order, *i.e.* conditional upon the service of the statement of claim, its terms should be precise and unambiguous as to the date and time of such service.[10]

Dismissal – a bar to fresh proceedings?   An order to dismiss an action for default in the service of the statement of claim does not operate as a bar to the commencement of a fresh action on the same facts[11] unless the order contains some express provision to that effect[12] though the court has an inherent jurisdiction to dismiss the second action as an abuse of the process of the court.[13] This is especially so if the first action has been dismissed for contumelious conduct on the part of the plaintiff or on the ground of abuse of process.[14]

Default of Defence

Introduction   Where the defendant has given notice of intention to defend, but defaults in the service of his defence within the time pre-

---

[6] R.S.C., Ord. 19, r. 1.
[7] See *Gilder* v. *Morrison* (1882) 30 W.R. 815; *Canadian Oil Works Corporation* v. *Hay* (1878) 38 L.T. 549; and see *Eaton* v. *Storer* (1882) 22 Ch.D. 91, *per* Jessel M.R. at 92; *Higginbottom* v. *Aynsley* (1876) 3 Ch.D. 288.
[8] *Clough* v. *Clough* [1968] 1 W.L.R. 525; [1968] 1 All E.R. 1179; negativing *Ernest Lyons Ltd.* v. *Sturges & Co.* [1918] 1 K.B. 326, decided under the pre-1964 R.S.C., Ord. 27, r. 1.
[9] *Hytrac Conveyors Ltd.* v. *Conveyors International Ltd.* [1983] 1 W.L.R. 44; [1982] 3 All E.R. 415.
[10] *Abalian* v. *Innous* [1936] 2 All E.R. 834; *Kaye* v. *Levinson* [1950] 1 All E.R. 594; [1950] 1 All E.R. 594; and see p. 00, *supra.*
[11] *Department of Health and Social Security* v. *Ereira* [1973] 3 All E.R. 421 (C.A.).
[12] *Pople* v. *Evans* [1969] 2 Ch. 255; [1968] 3 W.L.R. 97; [1968] 2 All E.R. 743; *Magnus* v. *National Bank of Scotland* (1888) 57 L.J. Ch. 902.
[13] *Stephenson* v. *Garnett* [1898] 1 Q.B. 677 (C.A.); *Spring Grove Securities Ltd.* v. *Deane* (1972) 116 S.J. 844 (C.A.); and see *Hart* v. *Hall & Pickles Ltd.* [1969] 1 Q.B. 405; [1968] 3 W.L.R. 744; [1968] 3 All E.R. 291.
[14] See *Janov* v. *Morris* [1981] 1 W.L.R. 1389; [1981] 3 All E.R. 780; approved in *Palmer* v. *Birks* (1986) 83 L.S.Gaz. 121.

scribed by the rule[15] or any duly extended time. Various courses are open to the plaintiff depending upon the nature of his case.[16–17]

Condition precedent to default procedure The plaintiff may not proceed on any such course until after the defendant is actually in default of defence.[18] In particular, if he enters judgment before the prescribed or extended time for the service of the defence has in fact expired, the judgment will be irregular and the defendant will be entitled to have it set aside as of right.[19]

Late service of defence If the defendant serves his defence after the expiration of the prescribed or extended time but before judgment has been entered, the plaintiff cannot disregard it. Such service (albeit late) will generally prevent him from entering judgment, even though it is not served until after the plaintiff has served his summons or motion for judgment in default of defence. However, in such circumstances the defendant may be ordered to pay the costs occasioned by the delay.[20]

When the plaintiff can apply for judgment as of right

(a) *Categories of action* Subject to the plaintiff establishing due default on the part of the defendant, the plaintiff is entitled to enter judgment in default of defence in the case of claims for liquidated demands, unliquidated damages, for detention of goods and for possession of land (other than claims which relate to a dwelling-house the rateable value of which brings it within the limits of the Rent Act 1977), or two or more such claims, his entitlement to do so is a matter of right, and not a mere matter of discretion.

---

[15] See R.S.C., Ord. 18. 18. r. 2.

[16–17] See *Practice Direction (Judgment by Default)* [1979] 1 W.L.R. 851; [1979] All E.R. 1062 which requires the plaintiff or his solicitor to certify that the time for the service of the defence by the defendant has expired and the defendant is in default in serving his defence.

[18] Thus, if the plaintiff serves an amended statement of claim *before* defence, he cannot proceed in default of defence until the expiry of 14 days after service of the amended statement of claim (R.S.C., Ord. 20, r. 3(2)), and if he serves an amended statement of claim *after* defence, the defendant is not in default by not serving an amended defence, since he is presumed to rely on his original defence (R.S.C., Ord. 20, r. 3(6)).

[19] See *Anlaby* v. *Praetorius* (1888) 20 Q.B.D. 764 at 771.

[20] *Gill* v. *Woodfin* (1884) 25 Ch.D. 707 (C.A.); *Gibbings* v. *Strong* (1884) 26 Ch.D. 66 (C.A.); and see *Graves* v. *Terry* (1882) 9 Q.B.D. 170. The defendant is in default of defence not only where he fails to serve his defence within the prescribed or duly extended period for the service of his defence, but also where his defence is struck out by order of the court for non-compliance with a previous order, *e.g.* service of further and better particulars of defence, or for discovery, inspection or production of documents (R.S.C., Ord. 24, r. 16; and see *Haigh* v. *Haigh* (1886) 31 Ch.D. 478), for interrogatories (R.S.C., Ord. 26, r. 6) or where the defence is struck out as disclosing no reasonable ground of defence (R.S.C., Ord. 18, r. 19).

(b) *Procedure*   The plaintiff must establish due default on the part of the defendant.[21] For this purpose, the plaintiff must show that the defendant is in default of the service of his defence. The plaintiff is not required to make any application to the court[22] nor is the court required to make any judicial determination as to the entitlement of the plaintiff to enter such default judgment. However, in practice, before such judgment is in fact entered, the matter may be referred to the Practice Master[23] for his direction whether the statement of claim or the relief or remedy sought is in the proper form, whether the claim is for a liquidated demand or for unliquidated damages, whether the claim is in the nature of a penalty and other such questions.

(c) *Rationale*   The entitlement of the plaintiff to enter such default judgment without any judicial determination is the sanction for failing to comply with the time provided by the rules for the service of the defence or any order extending such time. Such entitlement is also based on the ground that if the defendant makes default in the service of the defence, all the allegations in the statement of claim are deemed to be admitted.[24]

Entering judgment as of right in default of defence – analysing the categories

(a) *Liquidated demand*   If the plaintiff's claim is for a liquidated demand only[25] the plaintiff may, at any time after default of defence,

---

[21] See n. 17, above.

[22] An application to the court is necessary in the following cases in which judgment in default of defence cannot be entered without the leave of the court: (1) third party proceedings (R.S.C., Ord. 16, r. 5); (2) Crown proceedings (R.S.C., Ord. 77, r. 9); (3) actions arising out of certain consumer credit agreements (R.S.C., Ord. 83, rr. 3 and 4); and (4) actions in tort between husband and wife (R.S.C., Ord. 89, r. 2(3)). Moreover, in actions against infants and mental patients, a *guardian ad litem* must first be appointed (R.S.C., Ord. 80, r. 6). Other exceptions to entering judgment in default of defence include proceedings by originating summons (R.S.C., Ord. 28, r. 6), in admiralty actions (R.S.C., Ord. 75, r. 21), probate actions (R.S.C., Ord. 76) and mortgage actions (R.S.C., Ord. 88).

[23] See R.S.C., Ord. 63, r. 2. One of the Masters of the Queen's Bench Division is always on duty as Practice Master "for the purpose of superintending the business performed there [*i.e.* in the Central Office] and giving directions which may be required on questions of practice and procedure." In district registries, the matter is referred to the District Registrar.

[24] See R.S.C., Ord. 18, r. 13(1), and see *Cribb* v. *Freyberge* (1919) W.N. 22, C.A., though this does not apply to a person under disability, see R.S.C., Ord. 80, r. 8.

[25] A liquidated demand is a debt or other liquidated sum. It must be a specific sum of money due and payable, and its amount must be already ascertained or capable of being ascertained as a mere matter of arithmetic. Otherwise even though it be specified, or quantified, or named as a definite figure that requires investigation beyond mere calculation, it is not a "liquidated demand" but constituted "damages" (see *Knight* v. *Abbot* (1883) 10 Q.B.D. 11). A claim for a *quantum meruit* is a claim for a "liquidated demand": see *Runnacles* v. *Mesquita* (1875) 1 Q.B.D. 416) and a claim for interest under contract, express

234

enter final judgment against the defendant for a sum not exceeding that claimed in the writ and for costs.[26] A demand may be liquidated even if there is a claim for interest.[27] If there are two or more defendants, the plaintiff may enter judgment against the defendant in default of his defence and proceed with the action against the other defendant(s).[28] Where, however, two defendants are sued on a claim on which the plaintiff has a right of action alternatively, but not jointly or severally, a default judgment against one of them is equivalent to an election to sue

or implied (*Re Anglesey* [1901] 2 Ch. 548) or under statute (see Bills of Exchange Act 1882, s.57(2)(*b*)), is also a liquidated demand (R.S.C., Ord. 19, r. 2(2), and Ord. 13, r. 1(2)).

[26] R.S.C., Ord. 19, r. 2(1).

[27] See R.S.C., Ord. 13, r. 1(2). If the claim for interest indorsed on the writ, whether it is pleaded as part of the statement of claim indorsed thereon or as part of the general indorsement, is for interest on the debt or liquidated demand from the date the cause of action arose at a rate not higher than the rate payable on judgment debts at the date of the writ, and continuing at the same rate until payment or judgment, whichever is the earlier, the claim for interest will be treated for the purposes of r. 1(1) as a liquidated demand, since its amount can be duly calculated as a mere matter of arithmetic, and in such case, if the defendant fails to give notice of intention to defend within the prescribed time, the plaintiff may enter final judgment for the principal sum claimed and interest thereon as so calculated and costs under r. 1(1). The default judgment cannot include interest unless it is claimed in the writ or pleaded in the statement of claim as being due under s.35A of Supreme Court Act 1981, and the rate at which the interest is claimed is not higher than that payable on judgment debts at the date of the writ. If therefore the claim for interest is not expressed to be under s.35A, or is for a rate higher than that payable on judgment debts or is claimed "at such rate as the Court thinks fit" the default judgment will exclude any interest, but interlocutory judgment for interest to be assessed will be entered. Such interest must be assessed by the court, generally the Master or District Registrar, and the costs will be dealt with on the assessment usually consisting of the equivalent of the scale costs on the claim plus a moderate additional sum for the assessment. See *Rodway* v. *Lucas* (1855) 10 Exch. 667. If interest is in actual fact due under a contract, express or implied, the indorsement of the writ should expressly refer to the contract which contains such a term or the statement of cliam must expressly plead the contractual term, and in such case, default judgment may be entered for the agreed interest on the amount of the claim from the date of the cause of action until payment or judgment whichever is the earlier and costs. A claim for interest is often included in a claim on a promissory note payable by instalments, where it is alleged that by reason of a default the balance of principal and interest has become due. In such a case, the full amount of the claim may, and ordinarily will, contain an element of interest in respect of a period which would have fallen after the date of the judgment. The claim for such interest, *i.e.* in respect of a period after the judgment, may well be a penalty which would not be recoverable as being contrary to public policy, or it may be contrary to the proper interpretation of the promissory note itself (see *United Dominions Trust Ltd.* v. *Patterson* [1973] N.I. 142). If the plaintiff does not abandon any interest attributable to a period after judgment, he will be referred to the Practice Master who will determine whether judgment should be entered and for what sum.

[28] R.S.C., Ord. 19, r. 2(1); and see *Weall* v. *James* (1893) 68 L.T. 54 (C.A.); *Walton* v. *Topakyan & Co.* (1905) 53 W.R. 657; *Goldrei Foucard & Son* v. *Sinclair* [1918] 1 K.B. 180 (C.A.). This provision prevents the operation of the rule in *Kendall* v. *Hamilton* (1879) 4 App.Cas. 504, under which a final judgment against one joint contractor would be a bar to further proceedings against the other defendants liable under a joint contract with the defaulting defendant. See also *King* v. *Hoare* (1844) 13 M. & W. 494; *Parr* v. *Snell* [1923] 1 K.B. 1.

that one, and a bar to further proceedings against the other.[29] The plaintiff should enter judgment only for the amount actually due together with any interest claimed thereon at the date when judgment is entered, giving credit for all payments made after action brought, otherwise, the judgment will be irregular, and the defendant is entitled to have it set aside *ex debito justitiae*.[30]

(b) *Unliquidated damages* If the plaintiff's claim is for unliquidated damages only he may, at any time after default of defence, enter interlocutory judgment for damages and interest to be assessed and costs.[31] If there are two or more defendants, he may proceed with the action against the other defendants.[32]

(c) *Claim for possession of goods* If the plaintiff's claim against the defendant relates to the detention of goods only, he may, at any time after default of defence, at his option enter either, (a) interlocutory judgment against the defendant for the delivery of the goods or their value to be assessed and costs, or (b) interlocutory judgment for the value of the goods to be assessed, and if there are two or more defendants, he may proceed with the action against the other defendants.[33]

(d) *Claim for possession of land* If the plaintiff's claim is for possession of land only, he may at any time after default of defence enter judgment against the defendant for possession of the land and costs, and if there are two or more defendants he may proceed with the action against the other defendants.[34] However, the plaintiff's entitlement to enter such judgment is subject to his fulfilling two conditions, namely:

(i) producing a certificate by his solicitor, and if he sues in person an affidavit, stating that he is not claiming any relief in the action of the nature specified in R.S.C., Ord. 8. r. 1,[35]*i.e.* that the claim is not a claim arising out of a mortgage transaction; and

---

[29] *Morel Bros.* v. *Earl of Westmorland* [1903] 1 K.B. 64 (C.A.); *Moore* v. *Flanagan* [1920] 1 K.B. 919, (C.A.).

[30] *Hughes* v. *Justin* [1894] 1 Q.B. 667 (C.A.); *Muir* v. *Jenks* [1913] 2 K.B. 412 (C.A.); and see *Bolt and Nut Co. (Tipton Ltd.* v. *Nicholls (Rowland) & Co. Ltd.* [1964] 2 Q.B. 10; [1964] 2 W.L.R. 98; [1964] 1 All E.R. 137, (C.A.).

[31] For form of interlocutory judgment, see Prescribed Forms, App. A. Form No. 40. *Supreme Court Practice 1991*, Vol. 2, para. 35, and after damages assessed, Form No. 43, *ibid.*, para. 39. The term "interlocutory judgment" means that the judgment is final as to the right of the plaintiff to recover damages, but is interlocutory or provisional as to the amount of such damages.

[32] R.S.C., Ord. 19, r. 3. For the assessment of damages, see R.S.C., Ord. 37. If default judgment is entered against some but not all of the defendants, the damages should be assessed at the trial unless the court otherwise directs (R.S.C., Ord. 37, r. 3).

[33] R.S.C., Ord. 19, r. 4.

[34] R.S.C., Ord. 19, r. 5(1). If there is more than one defendant, a default judgment must not be enforced against any defendant unless and until judgment for possession of the land has been entered against all the defendants (R.S.C., Ord. 19, r. 5(5)).

[35] R.S.C., Ord. 19, r. 5(1).

(ii) producing a certificate by his solicitor, or if he sues in person an affidavit, stating either that his claim does not relate to a dwelling-house or that the claim relates to a dwelling-house of which the rateable value on every day specified by section 4(2) of the rent Act 1977 in relation to the premises exceeds the sum so specified.[36]

The object of these provisions is to prevent a default judgment for possession of land being entered in a mortgage action[37] or in an action relating to a dwelling-house where the rateable value of the premises brings it within the control of the Rent Acts, without the leave of the court.[38]

(e) *Mixed claims*   If the plaintiff makes two or more claims of the descriptions already mentioned, *i.e.* for a liquidated demand, or unliquidated damages or detention of goods or for possession of land, he may at any time after default of defence, enter judgment against the defendant in respect of any such claim as if it were the only claim made, and if there are two or more defendants, he may proceed with the action against the other defendant.[39]

(f) *Other claims*   If the plaintiff makes a claim against a defendant or defendants of a description not already mentioned,[40] *i.e.* for a claim other than for a liquidated demand or unliquidated damages or a claim for the possession of land, he may, at any time after default of defence, apply to the court for judgment, and on the hearing of the application the court may give him such judgment as he appears entitled to on his statement of claim.[41] The application may be made by summons or by motion.[42] If the defendant is in default of notice of intention to defend as well as of defence and the statement of claim was not indorsed or served with the writ, it must first be served on the defendant, even though he is

---

[36] *Ibid.* r. 5(2).

[37] R.S.C., Ord. 88, r. 1.

[38] R.S.C., Ord. 19, r. 5(3) and (4).

[39] *Ibid.* r. 6.

[40] If the plaintiff has made, in his statement of claim, a claim of a sort not already mentioned, *e.g.* for an injunction or declaration or an account, he may abandon such claim or claims and proceed to enter judgment in default. (See *Morley London Developments Ltd.* v. *Rightside Properties Ltd.* (1973) 117 S.J. 876 (C.A.)).

[41] R.S.C., Ord. 19. r. 7(1). If a claim of some other description is made against more than one defendant, the plaintiff may, if his claim against the defaulting defendant is severable from his claim against the other defendants, apply for judgment against the defaulting defendant and proceed with the action against the other defendants; otherwise he must set down the action on motion for judgment against the defaulting defendant at the time when the action is set down for trial or is set down on a motion for judgment against the other defendants (R.S.C., Ord. 19, r. 7(2)).

[42] R.S.C., Ord. 19, r. 7(3). In the Queen's Bench Division it is usual to make such application by summons to the Master, except where the claim includes an injunction which is outside a Master's jurisdiction (see R.S.C., Ord. 32, r. 11(1)(*d*)), but in the Chancery Division the ususal practice is to apply by motion for judgment.

in default of notice of intention to defend.[43] On such an application, the court will not give judgment unless and until a statement of claim has been served and neither consent of the parties nor order for directions can dispense with this necessity.[44] Moreover, on such an application, the statement of claim must show a case for the order that the applicant seeks, and the court will not generally go beyond the specific relief claimed,[45] nor will it receive any evidence, but will give judgment according to the pleadings alone.[46] The court has a discretion in the matter, *e.g.* where there are matters affecting other parties waiting to be decided, it may order the summons or motion to stand over until trial[47] or to stand over generally.[48] The entitlement of the plaintiff to apply by summons or motion for judgment in default is permissive only, and if the plaintiff cannot obtain all the relief he seeks on such summons or motion, he is entitled to proceed to trial, notwithstanding the default of the defendant in serving his defence.[49] For this purpose he may issue a summons for directions even where there is a default of defence.[50]

Default of Defence to Counterclaim

Introduction A defendant who counterclaims against the plaintiff is treated for the purposes of default of defence to counterclaim as if he were the plaintiff and the counterclaim was his statement of claim.

Practice – as in default of defence Accordingly, if the plaintiff or any other party against whom the counterclaim is made is in default in the service of defence to counterclaim, the defendant has the same rights as the plaintiff in all respects of entering or applying for judgment in default of defence. Thus default in serving a defence to counterclaim is followed by all the consequences *quoad* the counterclaim as default in service of a defence to the statement of claim.[51]

---

[43] The former practice of filing such a statement of claim has been discontinued.

[44] *Fowler* v. *White* (1961) 45 S.J. 723.

[45] *Faithful* v. *Woodley* (1890) 43 Ch.D. 287; and see *Tacon* v. *National Land Co.* (1887) 56 L.T. 165.

[46] *Smith* v. *Buchan* (1888) 58 L.T. 710; *Young* v. *Thomas* [1892] 2 Ch. 134 (C.A.); *Webster* v. *Vincent* (1898) 77 L.T. 167.

[47] *Verney* v. *Thomas* (1888) 36 W.R. 398.

[48] *Jenney* v. *Mackintosh* (1886) 61 L.T. 108.

[49] *Grant* v. *Knaresborough U.D.C.* [1928] Ch. 310.

[50] *Nagy* v. *Co-operative Press Ltd.* [1949] 2 K.B. 188; [1949] 1 All E.R. 1019; *Austin* v. *Wildig* [1969] 1 W.L.R. 67; [1969] 1 All E.R. 99.

[51] R.S.C., Ord. 19, r. 8. In respect of claims for a liquidated demand, or unliquidated damages or detention of goods or recovery of land (other than a claim relating to a dwelling-house within the rateable value limits of the Rent Act 1977) or any combination of such claims, the defendant may enter judgment in default of defence to counterclaim without the need for any application to the court, and such practice reverses the former practice as laid down in *Higgins* v. *Scott* (1888) 21 Q.B.D. 10; *Roberts* v. *Booth* [1893] 1 Ch. 52.

Setting Aside Default Judgment

Introduction   A default judgment against a defendant for default of defence is not a judgment on the merits.[52] It is entered because of his failure to comply with the requirements of the rules or orders of the court. For this reason, the defendant is given the opportunity to place the merits of his case before the court. He may do so on an application to set aside a default judgment when the court may, on such terms as it thinks fit, set aside or vary the default judgment.[53] As Lord Atkin said in *Evans* v. *Bartlam*[54]:

> "The principle obviously is that unless and until the Court has pronounced a judgment upon the merits or by consent, it is to have the power to revoke the expression of its coercive power where that has only been obtained by a failure to follow any of the rules of procedure."

However a default judgment has the same force and effect as a judgment on the merits unless and until it is set aside.[55]

Practice   The application to set aside the default judgment is made to the Master or Registrar. It is not by way of appeal, because there has been no judicial determination. The application to set aside a default judgment should of course be made promptly and within a reasonable time of the defendant knowing about it.[56] In a proper case, however, the court may disregard the lapse of time.[57] But if the delay occasions prejudice to the plaintiff or to a bona fide third party,[58] or the defendant has behaved with wilfulness in allowing the default judgment to be entered against him,[59] the court may refuse to set aside the judgment.[60] On the other hand, there is no such doctrine that the defendant, by "approbating" the judgment, *e.g.* obtaining time to pay, disables himself from

---

[52] *Openheimer & Co.* v. *Mahomed Haneef* (*decd.*) [1922] 1 A.C. 482.

[53] R.S.C., Ord. 19, r. 9. See also R.S.C., Ord. 13, r. 9 (setting aside judgment in default of notice of intention to defend). Application to set aside a default judgment may also be made where the default of defence arises by reason of its being struck out, see p. 24, *supra*, and also where the "default" consists of not appearing on the hearing of a summons for summary judgment under Ord. 14 (R.S.C., Ord. 14, r. 11) or not appearing at the trial (R.S.C., Ord. 35, r. 2).

[54] [1937] A.C. 473 at 480.

[55] For the manner and extent to which a default judgment operates as *res judicata*, see *New Brunswick Ry. Co.* v. *British and French Trust Corporation* [1939] A.C. 1; *Kok Hoong* v. *Leon Cheong Kweng Mines Ltd.* [1964] A.C. 993; [1964] 2 W.L.R. 150; [1964] 1 All E.R. 300 (P.C.).

[56] See R.S.C., Ord. 2, r. 2.

[57] *Beale* v. *Macgregor* (1886) 2 T.L.R. 311; and see *Atwood* v. *Chichester* (1878) 3 Q.B.D. 722; *Davis* v. *Ballenden* (1882) 46 L.T. 797.

[58] *Harley* v. *Samson* (1914) 30 T.L.R. 450.

[59] *Haigh* v. *Haigh* (1886) 31 Ch.D. 478.

[60] *Evans* v. *Bartlam* [1937] A.C. 437.

applying to have it set aside; and of course a default judgment e.g. obtained by fraud will be set aside, without the need for a separate action for the purpose.[61]

Irregular judgment   Where the judgment is obtained irregularly, as where it is premature or for a larger sum than is actually due[62] the defendant is entitled to have it set aside with costs *ex debito justitiae.*[63] The court should not impose any terms on the defendant (not even contingent terms, such as that costs should be costs in the cause[64]). Although not strictly necessary, the defendant should support his application by an affidavit stating the circumstances under which the default has arisen, the nature of the irregularity relied on and disclose the nature of the defence.[65] The irregularity must also be specified in the summons or notice of motion[67]

Regular judgment   If the judgment is a regular judgment, then the almost invariable practice is that the application to set aside must be supported by an affidavit of merits, *i.e.* an affidavit stating facts showing a defence on merits.[66] (If the defendant has no defence on the merits, an application to set aside the judgment would be misconceived.) The affidavit of the defendant should also state the reason or explanation why the judgment was allowed to go by default (such as mistake, accident, fraud or the like) though there is no rigid rule as to this requirement.[67]

The discretionary element   The power of the court to set aside a regular default judgment is discretionary and the court may impose terms such as ordering money to be brought into court or the payment of costs in any event or even forthwith.[68] A default judgment may be set aside as to part only and allowed to stand as to the remainder of the claim as to which there is no defence.[69]

---

[61] In the Chancery Division, such application may be by motion.

[62] R.S.C., Ord. 2, r. 2.

[63] See *Hughes* v. *Justin* [1894] 1 Q.B. 667; *Muir* v. *Jenks & Co.* [1913] 2 K.B. 412.

[64] *Anlaby* v. *Praetorius* (1888) 20 Q.B.D. 764.

[65] See *White* v. *Weston* [1968] 2 Q.B. 647; [1968] 2 W.L.R. 1459; [1968] 2 All E.R. 842, (C.A.). If the irregularity is due to an error arising from an accidental slip or omission, it may be corrected (see R.S.C., Ord. 20, r. 11 and *Armitage* v. *Parsons* [1908] 2 K.B. 410, (C.A.)).

[66] *Farden* v. *Richter* (1889) 23 Q.B.D. 124. "At any rate, when such an application is not thus supported, it ought not to be granted except for some very sufficient reason," *ibid.,* *per* Huddleston B. at 129; approving *Hopton* v. *Robertson* (1884) 23 Q.B.D. 126n; *Evans* v. *Bartlam* [1937] A.C. 473, *per* Lord Atkin at 480.

[67] *Evans* v. *Bartlam, supra, per* Lord Atkin at 480.

[68] See *Cockle* v. *Joyce* (1877) 7 Ch.D. 56; *Wright* v. *Mills* (1889) 60 L.T. 887; *Re Harley* [1891] 2 Ch. 121; *Richardson* v. *Howell* (1891) 8 T.L.R. 445.

[69] *Re Mosenthal, ex p. Marx* (1910) 54 S.J. 751 (C.A.).

CHAPTER 14

Parties and Pleadings

Necessary and Proper Parties

Introduction The system of pleadings is closely interelated with the questions concerning who are the necessary and proper parties to actions begun by writ. Since the pleadings are essentially the written statements of the parties to support their respective claims or defences, it is evident that they would not raise the real questions of controversy in the action if there is substantial defect in the manner in which the action is constituted as regards parties. Hence the law relating to parties is still[1] of great importance, for any mistake in the matter of parties will necessarily

---

[1] At common law, the law relating to parties was complex and technical and often led to difficulties and hardship. The strict rule of law was that an action should only be brought in the name of a person or persons in whom the right to sue was legally vested and only against the person or persons in whom the liability to be sued legally existed. Hence, the non-joinder or misjoinder of parties, whether as plaintiffs or defendants, and particularly in actions of contract, could be fatal, and objection could be taken either in the pleadings by a plea in abatement (see *Tidds' Practice* (9th ed., 1828), Vol. 1. pp. 634 *et seq.*) or demurrer or by motion in arrest of judgment, or if not raised on the pleadings, by objection by way of variance between evidence and verdict, leading to a non-suit or an adverse verdict (see *Chanter* v. *Leese* (1838) 4 M. & W. 295). Great improvements were introduced by the Common Law Procedure Act 1852, ss. 34–40, and the Common Law Procedure Act 1860, ss. 19–21, allowing amendments at or before the trial in the case of the non-joinder or misjoinder of plaintiffs and defendants (see *Day's Common Law Procedure Acts*, 1852–1860, pp. 70 *et seq.* and pp. 364–365, and see for an extended treatment of this subject, Dicey, *Parties to the Action* (1870)). Further reforms were made by the Supreme Court of Judicature Act 1873, s.24(3), which introduced third party procedure and counterclaims, as regulated by the rules of court which were scheduled to the Supreme Court of Judicature Act 1875 and later contained in the Rules of the Supreme Court 1883. The rule relating to the joinder of parties (Rules of the Supreme Court 1883. Ord. 16, r. 1) was restrictively construed by the House of Lords in *Smurthwaite* v. *Hannay* [1894] A.C. 494 (several holders of bills of lading refused joinder in one action against shipowners for damages for short deliveries), and see *Carter* v. *Rigby* [1896] 2 Q.B. 113), and accordingly, the rule was extended by amendment in 1899 (see *Re Beck* (1918) 87 L.J.Ch. 335, *per* Swinfen Eady L.J. at 338; and see *Thomas* v. *Moore* [1918] 1 K.B. 555, *per* Pickford L.J. at 565; *Horwood* v. *Statesman Publishing Co. Ltd.* [1929] W.N. 38. In 1962, by the Rules of the Supreme Court (Revision) 1962 (S.I. 1962 No. 2145), the rules relating to parties have been revised and re-arranged with the rules relating to causes of action and counterclaim in Ord. 15 (except for third party proceedings

involve trouble, expense and delay at some later stage of the action. The
overriding principle governing parties to an action is that all necessary
and proper parties, but no others, should be before the court. This is to
ensure that all matters in dispute in the proceedings may be effectively
and completely determined and adjudicated upon.[2] Moreover, no cause
or matter will be defeated by reason of the misjoinder or rejoinder of any
party and the court may in any cause or matter determine the issues or
questions in dispute so far as they affect the rights and interests of the
persons who are parties to the cause or matter.[2a]

Joinder by order   The court may order any person who has been
improperly or unnecessarily made a party or who has for any reason
ceased to be a proper or necessary party, to cease to be a party.[3] The
court may add a person as a party who ought to have been joined as a
party or whose presence before the court is necessary.[4]

The justification for the court's jurisdiction   The powers of the court in
respect of the parties to an action are intended to effectuate what was one
of the great objects of the Judicature Acts, namely, to bring all parties to
disputes relating to one subject-matter before the court at the same time
so that the disputes may be determined without the delay, inconvenience
and expense of separate actions and trials,[5] and to prevent justice being
defeated for want of parties.[6]

Practice   If an objection is taken that the necessary or proper parties are
not before the court, it should be taken as soon as possible by application
for the joinder of the omitted parties as co-plaintiffs or co-defendants, as
the case may be, and for a stay of proceedings unless and until they are so
joined.[7] If an objection is taken that the action is defective for want of

contained in Ord. 16 and interpleader proceedings contained in Ord. 17) and the liberty
to join parties in one action has been extended subject to the power of the court to order
separate trials (see R.S.C., Ord. 15, r. 5(1)).
[2] See R.S.C. Ord. 15, r. 6(2).
[2a] R.S.C., Ord. 15, r. 6(1).
[3] *Ibid* r. 6(2)(*a*).
[4] *Ibid*. r. 6(2)(*b*)(i).
[5] See *Byrne* v. *Brown* (1889) 22 Q.B.D. 657, *per* Lord Esher M.R. at 666–667; and again
in *Montgomery* v. *Foy* [1895] 2 Q.B. 321 at 324; and see *The W.H. Randall* [1928] P. 41
(C.A.); *McCheane* v. *Gyles* (No. 2) [1902] 1 Ch. 911; *Bentley Motors* v. *Lagonda* (1945)
114 L.J.Ch. 208; *Oesterreichische Export A.G.* v. *British Indemnity Insurance Co.*
[1914] 2 K.B. 747.
[6] *Van Gelder* v. *Sowerby Flour Society* (1890) 44 Ch.D. 374 at 394; *Moser* v. *Marsden*
[1892] 1 Ch. 487 at 490.
[7] *Sheehan* v. *Great Eastern Railway Co.* (1880) 16 Ch.D. 59; *Ruston* v. *Tobin* (1880) 49
L.J.Ch. 262; *Roberts* v. *Evans* (1877) 7 Ch.D. 830; *Wilson* v. *Balcarres Steamship Co.*
[1893] 1 Q.B. 422. After judgment, such objection is too late (see *Bullock* v. *London
General Omnibus Co.* [1907] 1 K.B. 264; *Attorney-General (and Spalding R.D.C.)* v.
Garner [1907] 2 K.B. 480).

parties, the point may be raised in the pleading, and may be ordered to be tried as a preliminary issue.[8]

Joinder of Parties

Introduction   Subject to the discretionary power to order separate trials as between parties,[9] the joinder of parties is allowed as of right in specified circumstances and in all other cases may be allowed with the leave of the court.[10]

Joinder as of right   Thus, two or more persons may be joined together in one action as plaintiffs or as defendants, without leave, where:

(a) if separate actions were brought by or against each of them, as the case may be, some common question of law or fact would arise in all the actions; and

(b) all rights to relief claimed in the action, whether they are joint, several or in the alternative, are in respect of or arise out of the same transaction or series of transactions.[11]

The whole of the transaction or series of transactions need not be the subject of the relief sought by each plaintiff.[12] Nor need every defendant be interested to the same extent in every head of relief claimed by the plaintiff. However, the "relief" in respect of which parties may be joined must be relief arising out of the same set of circumstances[13] or circumstances involving a common question of law or fact.[14]

Joinder of plaintiffs   Two or more persons may join in one action where their separate causes of action arise out of the same transaction or series of transactions *and* involve any common question of law or fact. Thus, a joinder of two or more plaintiffs will be permitted where the substantial subject-matter or grievance upon which the action is founded is common to all of them,[15] as, *e.g.*, in the case of:

---

[8] See R.S.C., Ord. 33. r. 4(2): and see *Republic of Chile* v. *Rothschild* [1891] W.N. 138; *Walters* v. *Green* [1899] 2 Ch. 696.

[9] See R.S.C., Ord. 15. r. 5(1).

[10] R.S.C., Ord. 15. r. 4(1).

[11] R.S.C., Ord. 15. r. 4(1). The rule should be construed in a liberal sense; see *Re Beck* (1918) 87 L.J.Ch. 335, *per* Swinfen Eady M.R.; *Payne* v. *British Time Recorder Co.* [1921] 2 K.B. 1.

[12] See *Markt & Co.* v. *Knight Steamship Co. Ltd.* [1910] 2 K.B. 1021, *per* Fletcher Moulton L.J.; *Stroud* v. *Lawson* [1898] 2 Q.B. 44.

[13] See *Re Beck, supra, per* Swinfen Eady M.R.

[14] *Thomas* v. *Moore* [1918] 1 K.B. 555.

[15] See *Universities of Oxford and Cambridge* v. *Gill* [1899] 1 Ch. 55.

(a) a fraudulent prospectus on the faith of which all have been induced to take shares in a company[16]; or

(b) a libel published of all the plaintiffs in relation to some conduct, business or matter common to them all[17]; or

(c) where two or more persons suffer personal injuries arising out of the same tort; or

(d) where there is some main or important question common to them all, and where some of the relief claimed by all arises:

    (i) "out of", or

    (ii) "in respect of",

some "transaction or series of transactions" in which all are involved, so that separate actions would to a substantial extent involve an unnecessary travelling over the same ground more than once.[18]

In actions for torts, where several persons are entitled to sue in respect of a wrong done to them jointly, as, for instance, in cases of injury to their joint property by trespass, conversion, or negligence they should, in general, all join as plaintiffs in the action. But it does not lie in the mouth of the wrongdoer to complain of non-joinder. It has been decided that:

(a) one of several co-owners of a patent may sue alone for an infringement of his right[19]; and

(b) so may one of several co-owners of a trade mark[20]; and

(c) in an action for conversion, one of several co-owners may sue alone, although he will be able to recover only his own share of the value of the property converted[21]; and

(d) in actions for recovery of land, all joint owners,[22] and all joint covenantees,[23] should be joined as plaintiffs.

Once two or more persons have properly been joined as plaintiffs, the question whether they can join additional causes of action with the

---

[16] *Drincqbier v. Wood* [1899] 1 Ch. 393; *Frankenburg v. Great Horseless Carriage Co.* [1900] 1 Q.B. 504.

[17] *Booth v. Briscoe* (1877) 2 Q.B.D. 496; *Horwood v. Statesman Publishing Co.* (1928) 141 L.T. 54.

[18] *Walters v. Green* [1899] 2 Ch. 696. See also *Thomas v. Moore* [1918] 1 K.B. 555 (C.A.) (eight plaintiffs suing six defendants for conspiracy and claiming also for separate slanders); *Gort v. Rowney* (1886) 17 Q.B.D. 625 (claims by owner and occupier for damages to a house). In such cases as *Smurthwaite v. Hannay* [1894] A.C. 494; *P. & O. Steam Navigation Co. v. Tsune Kijima* [1895] A.C. 661; *Carter v. Rigby* [1896] 2 Q.B. 113, and *Stroud v. Lawson* [1898] 2 Q.B. 44, the joinder there disallowed would now be permissible, and so also probably in such a case as *Sandes v. Wildsmith* [1893] 1 Q.B. 771 (slanders on mother and daughter).

[19] *Sheehan v. G.E. Ry.* (1880) 16 Ch.D. 59; *Lauri v. Renad* [1892] 3 Ch. 402.

[20] *Dent v. Turpin* (1861) 2 J. & H. 139.

[21] *Baker v. Barclays Bank* [1955] 1 W.L.R. 822.

[22] *Mitchell v. Tarbutt* (1794) 5 T.R. 649 at 651; *Lauri v. Renad* [1892] 3 Ch. 402.

[23] *Roberts v. Holland* [1893] 1 Q.B. 665.

claims in respect of which they were joined as plaintiffs depends on whether their claims come within the permissible range of the joinder of causes of action.[24]

Joinder of defendants   There is power to join several defendants in the same action for the purpose of claiming relief against them jointly or severally or in the alternative, and this power is not confined to cases in which the causes of actions alleged against the several defendants are identical. It extends to all cases in which the subject-matter of complaint against the several defendants involves the investigation of common questions, although the respective causes of action against them are different and their respective liabilities are based on different grounds.[25] Thus, a plaintiff may join in the same action as defendants any number of persons if:

(a) they are severally or jointly and severably liable to him on the same contract or tort; and

(b) he has two causes of action, one in contract and one in tort, arising out of the same subject-matter, against the same defendants.[26]

For example:

(a) where a tort has been committed by several persons jointly, *e.g.* where several persons are concerned in an assault or in the publication of a libel, their liability is several as well as joint, and the person who has suffered the wrong is entitled, at his option, to sue them all jointly, or any one or more of them separately[27];

(b) when separate and independent acts of negligence have directly contributed to cause injury, the person injured may recover damages from one or all the wrongdoers[28];

[24] See *Harris* v. *Ashworth* [1962] 1 W.L.R. 193; [1962] 1 All E.R. 438 and see p. 78, *supra.*

[25] *Bullock* v. *L.G.O. Co.* [1907] 1 K.B. 264; *Compania Sansinena de Carnes Congelades* v. *Houlder Brothers & Co. Ltd.* [1910] 2 K.B. 354; *Oesterreichische Export A.G.* v. *British Indemnity Co.* [1914] 2 K.B. 747; *Thomas* v. *Moore* [1918] 1 K.B. 555; *Re Beck, Attia* v. *Seed* (1918) 118 L.T. 629; *Payne* v. *British Time Recorder Co. Ltd.* [1921] 2 K.B. 1; *Bailey* v. *Curzon* [1932] 2 K.B. 392.

[26] *Goldrei Foucard* v. *Sinclair* [1918] 1 K.B. 180 (C.A.). In such a case, a plea by one of the defendants will enure for the benefit of the others though they do not plead it (*Pirie* v. *Richardson* [1927] 1 K.B. 448).

[27] *Sutton* v. *Clarke* (1815) 6 Taunt. 29 at 35; *The Bernina* (1888) 12 P.D. 58 at 83 and 93. It should be noted that under section 1 of the Civil Liability (Contribution) Act 1978 a plaintiff is entitled to sue two defendants as wrongdoers liable in respect of the same damage. Except where the two defendants are sued as tortfeasors liable in respect of the same damage, it is necessary for a defendant who claims against his co-defendant relief of any of the kinds mentioned in the rule to issue and serve upon him a third party notice under R.S.C., Ord. 16, r. 8 and a summons for third party directions under r. 4.

[28] The court may apportion the responsibility for the damage between the joint tortfeasors and order the proper amount of contribution be recovered one from the other: see Civil Liability (Contribution) Act 1978, s.1 and see *Croston* v. *Vaughan* [1938] 1 K.B. 540.

(c) in an action founded on tort against joint defendants one defendant must not be dismissed from the case for want of evidence against him until the whole cause is decided, as such dismissal may necessitate a new trial upon facts afterwards elicited in evidence[29];

(d) in actions for the recovery of land, strictly all persons who are actually in physical possession of the property should be made defendants. "In ejectment the tenant in possession *must* be sued."[30] But where a larger number of persons are in occupation of the premises who all claim title under the same lessor, the rule is relaxed and the plaintiff is allowed merely to make that lessor defendant.[31]

Joinder of parties in the alternative Where the plaintiff is in real doubt as to the person from whom he is entitled to redress, he may join two or more defendants in one action and make his claim against them severally or in the alternative.[32] Thus, where each of two proposed defendants blames the other, the proper course is to join both and to make the claim against them severally or in the alternative.[33] Again, where the authority of an agent is disputed or in doubt, the claim may be brought in the alternative against the principal and against the agent for breach of warranty of authority.[34] Similarly, where there is or may be a doubt as to which of two or more persons is entitled to the relief claimed, such persons may be joined as plaintiffs in one action and make their respective claims in the alternative.

Joinder of joint contractors

(a) *Joint contract—as plaintiffs* Where an action is founded on a contract made by several persons jointly, they must all, if living and entitled to sue thereon, join in the action as co-plaintiffs.[35] If any of them does

---

[29] *Hummerstone* v. *Leary* [1921] 2 K.B. 664.

[30] *Berkeley* v. *Dimery and another* (1829) 10 B. & C. 113, *per* Lord Tenterden C.J. at 113.

[31] *Minet* v. *Johnson* (1890) 63 L.T. 507; *Geen* v. *Herring* [1905] 1 K.B. 152; *Berton* v. *Alliance* Co. [1922] 1 K.B. 742.

[32] See R.S.C., Ord. 15, r. 4(1)(*b*), which effectively reproduces the express provisions of the pre-1964 R.S.C., Ord. 16, r. 7.

[33] See *The Koursk* [1924] P. 140, *per* Bankes L.J. at 153; and see *Bullock* v. *London General Omnibus Co.* [1907] 1 K.B. 264; *Compania Sansinena de Carnes Congeladas* v. *Houlder Bros. Ltd.* [1910] 2 K.B. 354; *Besterman* v. *British Motor Cab Co. Ltd.* [1914] 3 K.B. 181.

[34] See *Bennetts & Co.* v. *McIlwraith* [1896] 2 Q.B. 464; *Sanderson* v. *Blyth Theatre Co.*, [1903] 2 K.B. 533.

[35] R.S.C., Ord. 15, r. 4(2), and see *Bullen & Leake's Precedents of Pleadings* (3rd ed.), p. 471.

not consent to being joined as a plaintiff, he must, subject to any order of the court, be made a defendant.[36]

(b) *Joint contract—as defendants*   Where the liability of two or more persons is several or joint and several as well as joint, the plaintiff may choose which of them he wishes to sue and he need not join, nor can he be compelled to join, the other persons also liable to him even if their liability is under a joint contract only. If the defendant desires to obtain a contribution from the other joint contractors, he may make his claim under the Civil Liability (Contribution) Act 1978 or at common law, but this is no longer of any concern to the plaintiff. The defendant is no longer entitled to apply that all the persons jointly liable should be joined by the plaintiff as defendants in the action and that unless and until he did so, the action should be stayed.[37]

(c) *Several/joint*   If a contract made by two or more persons is several as well as joint, the plaintiff may sue all of them jointly, or any one of them separately, or may in the same action claim against all of them jointly, and also, in the alternative, against each of them separately.[38]

The construction of a contract, whether it is joint, or joint and several, or several, is often a question of difficulty. Where the contract sued upon was made by several persons jointly, and some of them have died, the action should, in general, be brought by the survivors or survivor, and if all of them have died, by the executors or administrators of the last survivor.[39]

Misjoinder and Non-joinder of Parties

The rule   The misjoinder or non-joinder of any party shall not operate to defeat any cause or matter, and the court may determine the issues or questions in dispute so far as they affect the rights and interest of the persons who are parties to the cause or matter.[40]

---

[36] *Ibid.* A tender of indemnity as to costs should first be made to a joint contractor who refuses to join as plaintiff, but such tender is not a condition precedent to his joinder as defendant where the breach alleged is due to his fraud or collusion (*Johnson* v. *Stephens & Carter Ltd. and Golding* [1923] 2 K.B. 857 (C.A.)), nor is the defendant entitled to insist on such tender first being made (*Burnside* v. *Harrison Marks Productions Ltd.* [1968] 1 W.L.R. 782). But the defendant may apply to compel the plaintiff to join his co-contractor as plaintiff if he consents or as defendant if he does not: see *Pilley* v. *Robinson* (1888) 20 Q.B.D. 155.

[37] Civil Liability (Contribution) Act 1978, s.3.

[38] See R.S.C., Ord. 15, r. 4(1); and see *Payne* v. *British Time Recorder Co.* [1921] 2 K.B. 1.

[39] See *Kendall* v. *Hamilton* (1879) 4 App. Cas. 504, *Re Hodgson* (1885) 31 Ch.D. 177.

[40] R.S.C., Ord. 15, r. 6(1). The rule was derived from the ameliorating provisions of the Common Law Procedure Act 1852.

PARTIES AND PLEADINGS

Interpretation   Misjoinder of parties is where persons who ought not to have joined as plaintiffs or defendants respectively have been so joined. Non-joinder of parties is where persons who ought to have been joined as plaintiffs or defendants respectively have not been so joined. What the rule has done is to alter the procedure by providing for an application to add the parties improperly omitted or to strike out parties improperly joined or to stay the proceedings unless and until the necessary parties are added.[41]

Rationale   The object of the rule is:

(a) to prevent justice being defeated for want of parties, by the misjoinder or non-joinder of parties, as happened under the common law[42]; and

(b) to provide for any necessary amendment in respect of the parties to an action being made at any stage of the proceedings.[43]

With the same object in view, the rule does away with the plea in abatement, by which an objection to the non-joinder of parties was raised before the Judicature Acts 1873–1875, and with demurrers for want of parties.[44]

Ambit of the court's discretion   The court, however, retains a discretionary power to refuse such an order,[45] and it may elect to deal with the matter as regards the rights and interests of the parties actually before it, especially if the action has proceeded to trial without objection as to parties.[46] If serious embarrassment would be caused to the plaintiff, the order may be refused.[47]

---

[41] See *Werderman* v. *Société Générale d'Eléctricité* (1881) 19 Ch.D. 246; *Abouloff* v. *Oppenheimer* (1882) 30 W.R. 429; *Norbury* v. *Griffiths* [1918] 2 K.B. 369 (C.A.). The object of the rule is to prevent justice being defeated for want of parties, by the misjoinder or non-joinder of parties as it appeared under the common law, and to provide for any necessary amendment in respect of the parties to an action being made at any stage of the proceedings; see *Van Gelder* v. *Sowerby Bridge Society* (1890) 44 Ch.D. 374 at 391.

[42] See *Moser* v. *Marsden* [1892] 1 Ch. 487 at 490.

[43] See *Van Gelder* v. *Sowerby Bridge Society* (1890) 44 Ch.D. 374, and *ibid.*, at 394, *per* Bowen L.J.: "it is of the essence of the procedure since the *Judicature Act* to take care that an action shall not be defeated by the non joinder of the right parties."

[44] *Wederman* v. *Société Générale d'Eléctricité* (1881) 19 Ch.D. 246 (C.A.); *Wilson* v. *Balcarres Brook S.S. Co.* [1893] 1 Q.B. 422; *Robinson* v. *Geisel* [1894] 2 Q.B. 685.

[45] *Lancaster Banking Co.* v. *Cooper* (1878) 9 Ch.D. 594; *Roberts* v. *Holland* [1893] 1 Q.B. 665.

[46] *Re Harrison* [1891] 2 Ch. 349; *Hall* v. *Heward* (1886) 32 Ch.D. 430.

[47] See *The Germanic* [1896] P. 84; *McCheane* v. *Gyles (No. 2.)* [1902] 1 Ch. 911; *Norris* v. *Beazley* (1877) 2 C.P.D. 80; *Moser* v. *Marsden* [1892] 1 Ch. 487.

Amendment as to Parties—Adding, Substituting and Striking Out

The rule At any stage of the proceedings, in any action, the court may on such terms as it thinks just and either of its own motion or on application:

(a) order any person who has been improperly or unnecessarily made a party or who has for any reason ceased to be a proper or necessary party, to cease to be a party[48]; and

(b) order any person to be added as a party who ought to have been joined as a party or whose presence before the court is necessary to ensure that all matters in dispute in the cause or matter may be effectually and completely determined and adjudicated upon.[49]

These powers are widely exercised,[50] and generally speaking the court will make all such changes in respect of parties as may be necessary to enable an effectual adjudication to be made concerning all matters in dispute.[51]

Adding/substituting plaintiffs—the court's discretion The court will ordinarily allow such an amendment:

(a) where the addition or substitution is necessary to enable the real question at issue to be determined; and

(b) where it can be done without causing the defendant to suffer injustice or prejudice which cannot be compensated for by costs.[52]

The amendment may be before or at the trial.[53]

Adding/substituting and the limitation problem Leave to add or substitute a plaintiff will not be granted where to do so would be to preclude the defendant from relying on the Limitation Acts.[54] However, leave to correct the name of a party may be given even though the effect of doing so is to substitute a new party, and even though the relevant period of

---

[48] R.S.C., Ord. 15, r. 6(2)(a).

[49] Ibid r. 6(2)(b)(i).

[50] Wilson v. Balcarres Brook S.S. Co., supra; Robinson v. Geisel [1894] 2 Q.B. 685.

[51] Van Gelder v. Sowerby Bridge Society (1890) 44 Ch.D. 374 (C.A.); Montgomery v. Foy [1895] 2 Q.B. 321; Bennetts v. McIlwraith [1896] 2 Q.B. 464; McCheane v. Gyles (No. 2) [1902] 1 Ch. 911; Ideal Films Ltd. v. Richards [1927] 1 K.B. 374; Dollfus Mieg et Compagnie S.A. v. Bank of England [1951] Ch. 33.

[52] Long v. Crossley (1879) 13 Ch.D. 388; Emden v. Carte (1881) 17 Ch.D. 169 and 768; Showell v. Winkup (1889) 60 L.T. 389; Pennington v. Cayley [1912] 2 Ch. 236; and see Ayscough v. Bullar (1889) 41 Ch.D. 341 (plaintiff's title to sue in doubt, another plaintiff added); and see Supreme Court Practice 1991, Vol. 1, para. 15/6/3.

[53] See White v. London General Omnibus Co. [1914] W.N. 78; Ives v. Brown [1919] 2 Ch. 314.

[54] Mabro v. Eagle Star and British Dominion Insurance Co. [1932] 1 K.B. 485 (C.A.).

limitation has expired, provided that the court is satisfied that the mistake[55] was genuine and was not misleading or such as to cause reasonable doubt as to the identity of the person intending to sue or be sued.[56] It follows that the correction of a mere misnomer in the name of a party will be allowed.[57]

Adding plaintiffs—the need for consent No one can be added as a plaintiff without his written consent,[58] even though he be indemnified against costs,[59] and even though the plaintiff would have been entitled, in the first instance, to have sued in his name or to have joined him on the writ as co-plaintiff in the action.[60] This difficulty may sometimes be obviated by making him a defendant to the action, for example:

(a) where a minority of shareholders have been refused the use of the name of their company as plaintiff in an action alleging misapplication of the funds of the company, the company has been made a defendant[61]; or

(b) where a co-trustee has by his personal conduct disabled himself from being a plaintiff jointly with his co-trustees.[62]

But if the court does not think fit to add as a defendant a person who refuses to be joined as a plaintiff, the proper course would appear to be for him to stay the action until the omitted person is added as plaintiff

---

[55] The word "mistake" in r. 5(3) should not be narrowly construed to mean error without fault, per Russell L.J. in *Mitchell* v. *Harris Engineering Co. Ltd.* [1967] 2 Q.B. 703 (C.A.).

[56] See R.S.C., Ord. 20, r. 5(2) and (3); and see *Rodriguez* v. *Parker* [1967] 1 Q.B. 116; [1966] 2 All E.R. 349; *Mitchell* v. *Harris Engineering Co. Ltd.* [1967] 2 Q.B. 703; [1972] 2 All E.R. 682 (C.A.); *Evans Construction Co. Ltd.* v. *Charrington & Co. Ltd.* ; *Katzenstein Adler Industries (1975) Ltd.* v. *Borchard Lines Ltd.* [1988] 2 Lloyd's Rep. 274; 138 New L.J. 94 (correcting names of plaintiffs as well as country in which they are incorporated and carry on business). See however, *Beardmore Motors Ltd.* v. *Birch Brothers (Properties) Ltd.* [1959] Ch. 298; [1958] 2 All E.R. 311; *Thistle Hotels Ltd.* v. *Sir Robert McAlpine & Son Ltd. The Times*, April 11, 1989; see also *Teltscher Brothers Ltd* v. *London and India Dock Investments Ltd.* [1989] 1 W.L.R. 770 (transposition of names of plaintiffs and defendants under genuine mistake).

[57] See *Alexander Mountain & Co.* v. *Rumere Ltd.* [1948] 2 K.B. 436; [1948] 2 All E.R. 144 (C.A.); *Belgian Economic Mission* v. *A.P. & E. Singer Ltd.* [1950] W.N. 418; *Etablissement Baudelot* v. *R.S. Graham & Co. Ltd.* [1953] 2 Q.B. 271; [1953] 1 All E.R. 149 (C.A.); and contrast *Davies* v. *Elsby Brothers* [1961] 1 W.L.R. 170, [1960] 3 All E.R. 672 (C.A.); and see also *Challinor* v. *Roder* (1885) 1 T.L.R. 527.

[58] R.S.C., Ord. 15, r. 6(2). If the consent is not in writing it may be signified "in such other manner as may be allowed," *ibid*.

[59] *Tyron* v. *National Provident Institution* (1886) 16 Q.B.D. 678; *Besley* v. *Besley* (1888) 37 Ch.D. 648.

[60] *Cullen* v. *Knowles* [1898] 2 Q.B. 380. Hence a positive order cannot be made joining him as a party in the absence of such consent. See *Wootton* v. *Joel* [1920] W.N. 28.

[61] *Silber Light Co.* v. *Silber* (1879) 12 Ch.D. 717; *Spokes* v. *Grosvenor Hotel Co.* [1897] 2 Q.B. 124 at 126, 128.

[62] *Luke* v. *South Kensington Hotel Co.*(1879) 11 Ch.D. 121; *Meldrum* v. *Scorer* (1887) 56 L.T. 471; *Cullen* v. *Knowles, supra.*

with his written consent.[63] The written consent of an agent is not sufficient.[64]

Adding defendants

(a) *On the application of the plaintiff*   The plaintiff may in general and apart from special circumstances such as unreasonable delay apply to have any persons added or substituted as defendants when he could properly have joined them as defendants in the first instance,[65] and leave may be granted to add as defendant a person against whom the plaintiff, if he fails to establish the case against the original defendant, has an alternative claim.[66]

(b) *The limitation problem*   On the other hand, leave will not be granted to add a defendant after the expiry of any relevant period of limitation affecting the proposed defendant,[67] and also of a person not already a party, and in either case against the wishes of the defendant.[68]

(c) *Third parties and counterclaims*   Third parties may be added as defendants to enable them to counterclaim,[69] and if a third party is substantially a defendant, he may be added as a defendant.[70]

Striking out parties   The court has a discretionary power to strike out a plaintiff[71] or to strike out a defendant improperly joined[72] or joined merely for discovery.[73]

Change of Parties

Introduction   Where after the commencement of an action a change takes place which affects any party to the action or the interest or liability

---

[63] *Roberts* v. *Holland* [1893] 1 Q.B. 665 at 667 and 669; *The Duke of Buccleuch* [1892] P. 201, at 211.

[64] *Fricker* v. *Van Grutten* [1896] 2 Ch. 649.

[65] See *Dollfus Mieg et Compagnie S.A.* v. *Bank of England* [1951] Ch. 33; and see *Bolingbroke* v. *Townsend* (1873) 29 L.T. 430; also see *Supreme Court Practice 1991*, Vol. 1, paras. 15/6/6 and 15/6/8.

[66] See *Oesterreichische Export A.G.* v. *British Indemnity Insurance Co.* [1914] 2 K.B. 747.

[67] *Lucy* v. *W.T. Henleys Telegraph Works Co. Ltd.* [1970] 1 Q.B. 393, [1969] 3 All E.R. 456 (C.A.); and see p. 202, *supra.*

[68] See *Dollfus Mieg et Compagnie S.A.* v. *Bank of England, supra.*

[69] *Montgomery* v. *Foy* [1895] 2 Q.B. 321.

[70] See *Edison and Swan Electric Light Co.* v. *Holland* (1886) 33 Ch.D. 497; *McCheane* v. *Gyles (No. 2)* [1902] 1 Ch. 911; *H.A. Hughes Ltd.* v. *A. Cook & Co.* [1918] W.N. 145.

[71] See *Re Matthews* [1905] 2 Ch. 460 (disagreement between plaintiffs); *Re Kent Coal Concessions* [1923] W.N. 328.

[72] *Vacher & Sons* v. *London Society of Compositors* [1913] A.C. 107; *Sadler* v. *Great Western Railway Co.* [1895] 2 Q.B. 688; *Bainbridge* v. *Postmaster-General* [1906] 1 K.B. 178 (C.A.).

[73] *Wilson* v. *Church* (1878) 9 Ch.D. 552.

of any party, the court has power to reconstitute the action on the basis of the change that has taken place.

The rule   Where at any stage of the proceedings in an action, the interest or liability of any party is assigned or transmitted to or devolves upon some other person, the court may order that other person to be made a party to the action and the proceedings to be carried on as if he had been substituted for the first mentioned party.

Object   The object of the rule is to save the pending proceedings and to avoid the multiplicity of proceedings.[74] The court will thus exercise its discretion under the rule if it thinks it necessary to do so, in order to ensure that all matters in dispute in the action may be effectually and completely determined and adjudicated upon.[75]

Examples of change in circumstances

   (a) The death or bankruptcy of a party.
   (b) The assignment, transmission or devolution of his interest or liability.

Practice/procedure   Where such changes occur:

   (a) application for an order to carry on the action is made by an *ex parte* application to the court, supported by an affidavit setting forth the relevant facts relating to the proceedings and the change that has occurred[76]; and
   (b) provision is made for the service of the order of the court on every person who is, or becomes, a party to the action, together with a copy of the original writ in the case of a person who becomes a defendant by virtue of the order.[77]

Death   On the death of a party to an action, all causes of action vested in or subsisting against him survive for the benefit of or against his estate (except in the case of a cause of action for defamation[78]). The cause of action does not abate by reason of his death.[79] Where the plaintiff dies,

---

[74] See Supreme Court Act 1981, s.49(2).
[75] R.S.C., Ord. 15, r. 7(2).
[76] *Ibid.* and *Supreme Court Practice 1991*, Vol. 1, para. 15/7/21. There is power to apply to discharge or vary an *ex parte* order so made; see R.S.C., Ord. 15, r. 7 (5).
[77] See R.S.C., Ord. 15, r. 7(4). For the consequential provisions or an order to carry on being made, see R.S.C., Ord. 15, r. 8.
[78] Law Reform (Miscellaneous Provisions) Act 1934, s. 1(1).
[79] R.S.C., Ord. 15, r. 7(1). If, of course, the death terminates the cause of action or the interest of a party, the action is at an end (see *Bowker* v. *Evans* (1885) 15 Q.B.D. 565 (C.A.); *James* v. *Morgan* [1909] 1 K.B. 564).

his executor or administrator may obtain an order to carry on the action[80] and where the defendant dies, the plaintiff may obtain an order to carry on the action against the executor or administrator of the deceased defendant or such executor or administrator may himself apply for the action to be carried on against him[81] or to carry on a counter-claim against the plaintiff.[82]

Bankruptcy   Where a party becomes bankrupt after action brought, the action does not abate by reason of the bankruptcy.[83]

(a) *Bankrupt plaintiff*   If a sole plaintiff becomes bankrupt after the action is brought and the cause of action is one which vests in his trustee,[84] the bankrupt himself cannot continue the action, only the trustee can do so, and he must obtain an order to carry it on.[85] If the trustee declines to continue the action; or does not get leave to continue it, the defendant may obtain an order to stay it or to have it dismissed.[86]

(b) *Bankrupt defendant*   If a sole defendant becomes bankrupt after an action is brought, the action cannot be continued against his trustee if it is in respect of a mere money demand in which the plaintiff can prove the bankruptcy[87] but it may be so continued where the action is wider in its scope.[88]

Assignment/transmission/devolution   Where there is an assignment, transmission or devolution of the interest or liability of a party after action brought, an order to carry on the action may be obtained by or against the person to whom such liability or interest was assigned or transmitted or upon whom it devolved.[89] Such an order to carry on,

---

[80] See *Burstall* v. *Fearon* (1883) 24 Ch.D. 126; *Long* v. *Crossley* (1879) 13 Ch.D. 388.
[81] *Duke* v. *Davis* [1893] 2 Q.B. 260.
[82] *Andrew* v. *Aitken* (1882) 21 Ch.D. 175.
[83] R.S.C., Ord. 15, r. 7(1)
[84] See *Re Berry* [1896] 1 Ch. 939 at 944, 945; *Hood's Trustee* v. *Southern Union Co.* [1928] Ch. 793. Causes of action of the bankrupt, generally speaking, vest in the trustee except causes of action in respect of injury to the person (*Stanton* v. *Collier* (1854) 23 L.J.Q.B. 116) or in respect of injury to character and having no immediate reference to the bankrupt's property (*Wilson* v. *United Counties Bank* [1920] A.C. 102).
[85] *Jackson* v. *North Eastern Railway Co.* (1877) 5 Ch.D. 844; *Emden* v. *Carte* (1881) 17 Ch.D. 768; *Farnham* v. *Milward & Co.* [1895] 2 Ch. 730; *Boaler* v. *Power* [1910] 2 K.B. 229 (C.A.).
[86] *Warder* v. *Saunders* (1882) 10 Q.B.D. 114; *Selig* v. *Lion* [1891] 1 Q.B. 513; *Reading* v. *London School Board* (1886) 16 Q.B.D. 686; *Boaler* v. *Power, supra.*
[87] *Barter & Co.* v. *Dubeux & Co.* (1881) 7 Q.B.D. 413 (C.A.).
[88] *Hale* v. *Boustead* (1881) 8 Q.B.D. 453; *Watson* v. *Holliday* (1882) 20 Ch.D. 780 (action for an account); *Borneman* v. *Wilson* (1885) 28 Ch.D. 53 (action for an injunction).
[89] See *Seear* v. *Lawson* (1880) 15 Ch.D. 426 and 16 Ch.D. 121; *Guy* v. *Churchill* (1889) 40 Ch.D. 481; *Showell* v. *Winkup* (1889) 60 L.T. 389 (assignee of plaintiff joined).

however, may only be obtained in respect of an interest or liability previously represented in the action.[90]

Order to carry on—practice and procedure

(a) Any amendments of the pleadings rendered necessary by the change affecting a party to the action must be duly made.[91]

(b) After an order has been made giving leave to carry on the action, all future proceedings should be entitled in the double form, as follows:

BETWEEN

A B .... Plaintiff

and

C D .... Defendant

(by original action)

AND BETWEEN

E F

(Executor of the Estate of the said *A B* (deceased)
(or as the case may be)).. Plaintiff

AND

G H

(Administrator of the Estate of the said *C D*, deceased) [or trustee in the bankruptcy of the said
C D, or as the case may be].................................... Defendant

(By order to carry on dated the.............day of ....19..........)

(c) The order to carry on the proceedings should contain such directions as may be requisite as to amending the pleadings, or extending the time for pleading, or any other matter necessitated by such change of parties. Where the facts relied upon as causing the transmission of interest are stated in the pleadings, they may be pleaded to, or an application may be made to discharge or vary the order.[92]

(d) In cases where an assignee is substituted for the original plaintiff, the subsequent pleadings should be headed both with the original title of the action and also with the new title, showing the name of

---

[90] *Howard* v. *Howard* (1892) 30 L.R. Ir. 430.
[91] *Seear* v. *Lawson* (1880) 16 Ch.D. 121.
[92] See R.S.C., Ord. 15, r. 7 (5).

the substituted plaintiff. There should also be shown in the body of the pleading how the plaintiff derives his title as assignee.[93]

(e) An order to carry on proceedings is not necessary where the change affecting a party after action brought arises by reason of marriage only[94] or by reason of a mere change of name,[95] nor is such an order necessary where an infant attains his majority[96] nor where a person becomes a patient after action brought.[97]

Intervention by Persons not Parties

Introduction A plaintiff who conceives that he has a cause of action against a defendant is entitled to pursue his remedy against that defendant alone and he cannot be compelled to proceed against other persons whom he has no desire to sue.[98] Nevertheless, a person who is not a party may be added as a defendant against the wishes of the plaintiff on his own intervention or on the application of the defendant or in some cases by the court of its own motion.

Ambit of court's power The court has power to add as a defendant any person not already a party between whom, and any party to the cause or matter, there may exist a question or issue arising out of or relating to or connected with any relief or remedy claimed in the cause or matter which in the opinion of the court it would be just and convenient to determine

---

[93] *Seear* v. *Lawson, supra.*

[94] The marriage of a party does not cause a transmission of interest or liability. In the case of a female party, a written notice of the change of name should be filed in the appropriate office, and a copy served on the other parties, and in all future proceedings the new surname should be substituted with the former surname mentioned in brackets, see Queen's Bench Masters' Practice Directions, No. 17 (4) (Change of name—marriage), *Supreme Court Practice 1991*, Vol. 2, para. 736.

[95] Where the name of a limited liability company is changed after an action is brought, the action is continued by or against the company under its new name (see Companies Act 1985, s.28(7)), but a written notice of the change of name must be filed at the appropriate office, and served on all other parties, and in all future proceedings, the new name of the company substituted with the former name mentioned in brackets, see Queen's Bench Masters' Practice Directions, No. 17(3) (Change of name—limited company), *Supreme Court Practice 1991*, Vol. 2, para. 736.

[96] In such case, an infant plaintiff must file at the appropriate office a notice that he is of full age and that he adopts the action, and he must serve such notice on the other parties, and the fact must be noted in the Cause Book, and should be shown in the title of all subsequent proceedings, as "*AB* (late an infant but now of full age)," see Queen's Bench Masters' Practice Directions, No. 46 (Disability), *Supreme Court Practice 1991*, Vol. 2, para. 766; and see *Carberry* v. *Davies* [1968] 1 W.L.R. 1103; [1968] 2 All E.R. 817, *per* Harman L.J.

[97] See R.S.C., Ord. 80, r. 3(5), which provides however, that where, after any proceedings have been begun, a party to the proceedings becomes a patient, an application must be made to the court for the appointment of a person to be next friend or guardian *ad litem*, as the case may be, of that party.

[98] See *Supreme Court Practice 1991*, Vol. 1, para. 15/6/6, cited in *Dollfus Mieg et Compagnie S.A.* v. *Bank of England* [1951] Ch. 33, [1950] 2 All E.R. 605.

as between him and that party as well as between the parties to the cause or matter.[99]

Rationale The main object of these powers is to prevent multiplicity of proceedings,[1] and to enable all necessary and proper parties to be brought to court who would be directly affected by the result of the proceedings.[2] A mere commercial interest, as distinct from a direct legal interest is not enough to justify a person being added as a party, however convenient this might be.[3]

When? There are broadly three classes of cases in which intervention by a person not already a party may be allowed against the wishes of the plaintiff,[4] namely:

(a) where the intervener is one of a class whom the plaintiff claims to represent in a representative action[5];

(b) where the proprietary or pecuniary rights of the intervener are directly affected by the proceedings or where the intervener may be rendered liable to satisfy any judgment either directly or indirectly[6]; and

---

[99] R.S.C., Ord. 15, r. 6(2)(b)(ii). This rule bears a close affinity to the provisions relating to third party proceedings; see R.S.C., Ord. 16, r. 1(1)(c); and may be said to have similar objects as third party procedure. To some extent, the amendment of the rule in 1971 extended its operation, and may to such extent have negatived the decision in *Vandervell's Trustees Ltd.* v. *White* [1971] A.C. 912; [1969] 3 All E.R. 16. The rule, however, does not apply to the Commissioners of Inland Revenue, unless they signify their consent in writing, or as may be authorised, to be added as parties; see R.S.C., Ord. 77, r. 8A.

[1] See *Byrne* v. *Brown* (1889) 22 Q.B.D. 657, *per* Esher M.R. at 666; *Montgomery* v. *Foy, Morgan & Co.* [1895] 2 Q.B. 321; *Bentley Motors (1931) Ltd.* v. *Lagonda Ltd.* [1945] 1 All E.R. 211 at 212.

[2] See *Amon* v. *Raphael Tuck and Sons Ltd.* [1956] 1 Q.B. 357; [1956] 2 W.L.R. 372; [1956] 1 All E.R. 273.

[3] See *Moser* v. *Marsden* [1892] 1 Ch. 487; *Hood-Barrs* v. *Frampton, Knight & Clayton* [1924] W.N. 287; *Re Farbenindustrie* [1944] Ch. 41; [1946] 4 All E.R. 486 (C.A.); *Atid Navigation Co. Ltd.* v. *Fairplay Towage and Shipping Co. Ltd.* [1955] 1 W.L.R. 336; [1955] 1 All E.R. 698.

[4] See *Supreme Court Practice 1991*, Vol. 1, paras. 15/6/9–15/6/11 inclusive.

[5] See *McCheane* v. *Gyles (No. 2)* [1902] 1 Ch. 911 at 915; *Moon* v. *Atherton* [1972] 2 Q.B. 435; [1972] 3 W.L.R. 57; [1972] 3 All E.R. 145 (C.A.); and see R.S.C., Ord. 15, r. 12.

[6] *Gurtner* v. *Circuit* [1968] 2 Q.B. 587; [1968] 2 W.L.R. 668: [1968] 1 All E.R. 328 (C.A.) (adding Motor Insurers' Bureau as parties where any judgment in the action could be legally though indirectly enforceable against him); distinguished in *White* v. *London Transport Executive* [1971] 2 Q.B. 721; [1971] 3 W.L.R. 169; [1971] 3 All E.R. 1 (C.A.); and see *Re Idenden (A Bankrupt)* [1970] 1 W.L.R. 1015; [1970] 2 All E.R. 387 (adding surety); *Vavasseur* v. *Krupp* (1878) 9 Ch.D. 351 (owner of goods infringing patent); and see *Amon* v. *Raphael Tuck & Sons Ltd.* [1956] 1 Q.B. 357; [1956] 2 W.L.R. 372; [1956] 1 All E.R. 273 (inventor of design); *Apollinaris Co.* v. *Wilson* (1886) 31 Ch.D. 632 (owner of goods infringing trade mark); *Samuel* v. *Samuel* (1879) 12 Ch.D. 152 (interest in property claimed to be forfeited); *Montgomery* v. *Foy* [1895] 2 Q.B. 321 (interest in cargo on which lien for freight is claimed).

(c) where the intervener has interest in the manner in which the contract should be performed in actions for specific performance.

Title of action   Where a person not already a party is added as a party, the proceedings and the pleadings will be required to be duly amended, so as to show the nature of the claim made by or against him or how otherwise his rights or interests are affected.

Third-Party Proceedings

Introduction   Where a defendant claims to be entitled to a relief or remedy against a person not already a party to the action, he may, in specified circumstances, make that claim (in the same action in which he is the defendant) against that other person. Such claim is made by instituting a fresh proceeding called "third party proceedings," in which he is initially the plaintiff and that other person, called "the third party" is the defendant.[7]

When?

(a) The defendant must have given notice of intention to defend.

(b) The proposed third party must not already be a party to the action,

(c) The relief sought must fall into at least one of the following categories:

   (i) claims for any contribution or indemnity. Claims for indemnity under the rule can arise only from a contract for such indemnity, express or implied, or from some equity resulting from the relation of the parties to each other.[8] Claims for contribution arise generally between co-sureties or other joint contractors or between co-trustees[9] or between co-owners,[10] or between joint tortfeasors[11];

   (ii) claims for any relief or remedy relating to or connected with the original subject-matter of the action and substantially the same as some relief or remedy claimed by the plaintiff; or

---

[7] See, however, p. 153, *supra*, "Counterclaim against plaintiff and added party," where the defendant's claim may be made by adding a person not already a party as a defendant to his counterclaim against the plaintiff.

[8] *Wynne* v. *Tempest* [1897] 1 Ch. 110 at 113; *Eastern Shipping Co.* v. *Quah Beng Kee* [1924] A.C. 177; *Bank of England* v. *Cutler* [1908] 2 K.B. 208 at 220; and see *Supreme Court Practice 1991*, Vol. 1, para. 16/1/4.

[9] *Robinson* v. *Harkin* [1896] 2 Ch. 415; *Jackson* v. *Dickinson* [1903] 1 Ch. 947.

[10] See *Von Freeden* v. *Hull* (1907) 76 L.J.K.B. 715.

[11] Civil Liability (Contribution) Act 1978, ss.1 and 3. See also the Financial Services Act 1986, s.166(1), which provides for contribution in certain cases of tort by directors; and see *Gerson* v. *Simpson* [1903] 2 K.B. 197; *Shepheard* v. *Bray* [1906] 2 Ch. 235 and [1907] 2 Ch. 571 (C.A.).

(iii) it is required that any question or issue relating to or connected with the original subject-matter of the action should be determined not only as between the plaintiff and the defendant but also as between either or both of them and such person not already a party to the action.[12]

Claims under (ii) and (iii) may well arise in a great variety of circumstances[13] as, *e.g.*, where the claim is for breach of warranty in respect of goods sold and resold under similar or substantially the same warranties, and the defendant's claim against the third party need not be co-extensive with the whole of the plaintiff's claim against the defendant.[14] Nevertheless, even though the defendant's claim against the third party may fall within the scope of the rule, the court still has a judicial discretion to disallow third party proceedings.[15]

Rationale   The objects of third party procedure are two-fold[16]:

(a) to prevent multiplicity of actions and to enable the court to settle disputes between all parties to them in one action[17]; and
(b) to prevent the same question from being tried twice with possibly different results.[18]

---

[12] R.S.C., Ord. 16, r. 1(1). The rules of Ord. 16 are founded on and intended to give effect to the provisions of section 39(1)(*b*) of the Supreme Court of Judicature (Consolidation) Act 1925 (replacing s.24(3) of the Judicature Act 1873) and now encapsulated in s.49(2)(*a*) of the Supreme Court Act 1981) which empowers the court to grant to any defendant "all such relief relating to or connected with the original subject of the cause or matter, claimed (by his pleading) against any other person, whether already a party to the cause of matter or not, who has been duly served with notice in writing of the claim pursuant to rules of court or any order of the court as might properly have been granted against that other person if he had been made a defendant to a cause duly instituted by the same defendant for the like purpose." The Rules of the Supreme Court 1875 gave effect to the provision, but the Rules of the Supreme Court 1883 materially limited that effect by confining the third party procedure to claims for "contribution or indemnity" (see *McCheane* v. *Gyles* [1902] 1 Ch. 911, per Vaughan Williams J. at 298). In 1929, new rules were introduced which considerably extended the scope of third-party procedure, though not so wide in scope as the rules of 1875. The 1929 rules were replaced by fresh rules made in 1962 by the Rules of the Supreme Court (Revision) Order 1962 (S.I. 1962 No. 2704) which simplified, but did not extend, third party procedure.

[13] See, *e.g. Standard Securities Ltd.* v. *Hubbard* [1967] Ch. 1056; [1967] 2 All E.R. 622; *Chatsworth Investments Ltd* v. *Amoco (U.K.) Ltd.* [1968] Ch. 665; [1968] 3 All E.R. 357 (C.A.); *Myers* v. *N. & J. Sherick Ltd.* [1974] 1 W.L.R. 31; [1974] 1 All E.R. 81, applying *Re Burford* [1932] Ch. 122.

[14] See *Pontifex* v. *Foord* (1884) 12 Q.B.D. 152 at 155.

[15] *Chatsworth Investments Ltd.* v. *Amoco (U.K.) Ltd.* [1968] Ch. 665; [1968] 3 All E.R. 357 (C.A.).

[16] See *Supreme Court Practice 1991*, Vol. 1, para. 16/1/1, cited by Pennycuick J. in *Standard Securities Ltd.* v. *Hubbard* [1967] Ch. 1056 at 1059; [1967] 2 All E.R. 621.

[17] See *Baxter* v. *France* [1895] 1 Q.B. 59, *per* Lord Esher M.R. at 593; and see *Barclays Bank Ltd.* v. *Tom* [1923] 1 K.B. 221 at 223 and 225; and see also s. 49(2) of the Supreme Court Act 1981.

[18] See *Benecke* v. *Frost* (1876) 1 Q.B.D. 419, *per* Blackburn J. at 422; *Ex parte Young* (1881) 17 Ch.D. 668; *Re Salmon* (1889) 42 Ch.D. 351 at 360.

The third party notice   Third party proceedings are begun by the issue by the defendant of a third party notice. It contains a statement of the nature of the claim made against the third party and the nature and grounds of the claim made by the defendant or the question or issue required to be determined.[19] In actions begun by writ, a third party notice may be issued without the leave[20]; of the court, before the defence is served. After service of the defence it may only be issued with leave[21] which may be granted on an *ex parte* application supported by the requisite affidavit.[22]

The position of the third party in the proceedings   After the service of the third party notice, the third party becomes a party to the action with the same rights in respect of his defence against any claim made against him in the notice and otherwise as if he had been duly sued in the ordinary way by the defendant by whom the notice is issued,[23] including all the liabilities of a party for costs or otherwise.[24] Thus, the third party may counterclaim against the defendant,[25] or against the plaintiff[26] or he may himself bring fourth party proceedings against a person not already a party.[27]

Acknowledging service of the third party notice   Where the third party desires to dispute the defendant's liability to the plaintiff or his own liability to the defendant, he must acknowledge service of the third party notice.[28] Such acknowledgment however, does not preclude him from raising any objections which he may have to the third party proceedings which he may raise on the hearing of the third party summons for directions.[29] The third party is allowed to defend upon any ground, other than set-off and counterclaim, which would have been available to the original

---

[19] R.S.C., Ord. 16, r. 1(1). The third party notice must be in the prescribed form; see *ibid.* and Appendix A, Prescribed Forms, Nos. 20 and 21 *Supreme Court Practice 1991*, Vol. 2, paras. 15 and 16. The third party notice must be served accompanied with a copy of the writ, and of the pleadings, if any, in the action (see R.S.C., Ord. 16, r. 3(2)).

[20] A third party notice against the Crown can only be issued with the leave of the Court; see R.S.C., Ord. 77, r. 10.

[21] R.S.C., Ord. 16, r. 1(2).

[22] *Ibid.* r. 2.

[23] *Ibid.* r. 1(3); and see *Hornby v. Cardwell* (1882) 8 Q.B.D. 329; *Greville v. Hayes* [1894] 2 Ir.R. 20; *Barclays Bank Ltd. v. Tom* [1923] 1 K.B. 221 at 223.

[24] See *Edison Light Co. v. Holland* (1889) 41 Ch.D. 28 (C.A.).

[25] *Borough v. James* [1884] W.N. 32; *Re Salmon* (1889) 42 Ch.D. 351 at 354; *Barclays Bank Ltd. v. Tom, supra.*

[26] *Eden v. Weardale Iron and Coal Co.* (1885) 28 Ch.D. 333; 35 Ch.D. 287; *Alcoy and Gandia Railway and Harbour Co. v. Greenhill* [1896] 1 Ch. 19.

[27] See R.S.C., Ord. 18, r. 9.

[28] See R.S.C., Ord. 16, r. 3.

[29] *Benecke v. Frost* (1876) 1 Q.B.D. 419 at 421; *Baxter v. France* [1895] 1 Q.B. 591.

defendant as defence to the plaintiff's claim[30]; and if he admits the defendant's claim but desires to dispute the plaintiff's claim, the third party may, if the plaintiff does not object, be substituted for the original defendant.[31]

Third party directions   After acknowledgment of service by the third party,[32] the defendant may apply for third party directions by a summons served on all the parties to the action.[33] On the hearing of such summons, and whether before or after judgment in the action has been signed by the plaintiff against the defendant:

    (a) the court may dismiss the application and terminate the third party proceedings[34]; or

    (b) if the liability of the third party to the defendant is established, the court may order such judgment as the nature of the case may require to be entered against the third party in favour of the defendant[35]; or

    (c) the court may order any claim, question or issue stated in the third party notice to be tried in such manner as the court may direct[36] and in such case, the court may give the third party leave to defend

---

[30] *Callender* v. *Wallingford* (1884) 53 L.J.Q.B. 569; *Eden* v. *Weardale Iron and Coal Co.* (1885) 28 Ch.D. 333.

[31] *Municipal Council of Sydney* v. *Bull* [1909] 1 K.B. 7; *Matthey* v. *Curling* [1922] 2 A.C. 180 at 198.

[32] For the procedure where the third party is in default of notice of intention to defend or in default in the service of a defence after having been ordered to do so, see R.S.C., Ord. 16, r. 5. The court may refuse to give directions and will dismiss the defendant's summons if the claim is outside r. 1(1): *Pontifex* v. *Ford* (1884) 12 Q.B.D. 152; *Bell* v. *Von Dadelszen* [1883] W.N. 208 (but note that these cases were decided under the former narrower rule, and that the actual decisions do not apply); or if the case is one of too great complication or difficulty to be properly tried with the original action: *Baxter* v. *France* [1895] 1 Q.B. 591; or if the plaintiff will be embarrassed or if the matters cannot be decided in one trial: *Schneider* v. *Batt* (1881) 8 Q.B.D. 701 (C.A.); if the prima facie case under r. 1(1)(a) is made out or if the case is clearly such as is contemplated by (b) or (c) it will be for the plaintiff or third party to show some special circumstances why the directions should not be given. Where a defendant fails to issue a third party summons for directions promptly but does so much later than he ought to have done, particularly where the hearing of the action between the plaintiff and the defendant is less than six months away and where the remedial works to premises which the plaintiff alleged were defective had been completed by the third party, who would thus be disabled from employing an expert to inspect the alleged defects, the court will dismiss the third party summons for directions: *Courtenay-Evans* v. *Stuart Passey & Associates* [1986] 1 All E.R. 932 *per* H.H. Judge Newey Q.C., O.R. The effect of the dismissal of the defendant's summons or refusal to give directions thereof is to put an end to the third party proceedings in *Courtenay-Evans* v. *Stuart Passey & Associates, supra.*

[33] See R.S.C., Ord. 16, r. 4(1).

[34] *Ibid.* r. 4(3)(c).

[35] *Ibid.* r. 4(3)(a).

[36] R.S.C., Ord. 16, r. 4(3) (b). For form of summons for third party directions, see Queen's Bench Masters' Practice Forms, No. PF 20, *Supreme Court Practice 1991*, Vol. 2, para. 220.

and to appear at the trial and to take such part therein as may be just.

In summary the court may make such orders and give such directions as appear proper for having the rights and liabilities of the parties most conveniently determined and enforced and as to the extent to which the third party is to be bound by any judgment or decision in the action.[37]

Usual form of directions   In practice, where the third party disputes the defendant's liability to the plaintiff or his own liability to the defendant, the court will give directions for the conduct of the third party proceedings, such as the service of pleadings and discovery and inspection of documents.[38] It is usual to order that the defendant should serve a statement of claim against the third party[39] and that the third party should serve his defence thereto within the time specified in the order.

Pleadings in third party proceedings   They may only be served pursuant to an order of the court. Where they are so ordered to be served, they will be in substantially the same form, *mutatis mutandis*, as ordinary pleadings in an action between a plaintiff and a defendant for the same cause, but the words "*EF* . . . Third Party" should be added to the title of the action and the heading of the pleadings should describe them according to the facts, as follows:

Form of Pleadings in Third Party Proceedings

IN THE HIGH COURT OF JUSTICE   19 , B. No. _____

QUEEN'S BENCH DIVISION

BETWEEN   *A B*   Plaintiff

                                and

                      C D   Defendant

                                and

                      E F   Third Party

STATEMENT OF CLAIM

Third party notice—introductory averments   It is also usual for the statement of the defendant's claim in third party notice to contain intro-

---

[37] R.S.C., Ord. 16, r. 4(4). Any such order made or direction given may be varied or rescinded by the court at any time; see R.S.C., Ord. 16, r. 4(5).

[38] For form of order for Third Party Directions, see Queen's Bench Masters' Practice Form, No. PF 21, *Supreme Court Practice 1991*, Vol. 2, para. 221.

[39] Sometimes the third party notice may be ordered to stand as the defendant's statement of claim against the third party.

ductory averments stating briefly the nature of the claim made by the plaintiff against the defendant and the nature of the claim made by the defendant against the third party or the question or issue required to be determined in the third party proceedings.

The autonomy of third party proceedings   Once third party proceedings have been duly instituted, they acquire a life of their own, quite independent of the main action. Thus if the main action is terminated by judgment[40-41] or settlement,[42] the third party proceedings can still proceed. Conversely, they may be dismissed for want of prosecution, even though the main action may still proceed.[43]

Third party procedure available to a plaintiff to a counterclaim   The third party procedure may in a proper case extend beyond the typical case of the defendant making a claim against a third party. Thus, the plaintiff against whom there is a counterclaim may, in a proper case, avail himself of the third party procedure in regard to the subject-matter of the counterclaim.[44]

As between co-defendants

(a) Third party procedure may be employed by one defendant as against a co-defendant,[45] except that in such case the defendant may issue and serve a third party notice without leave[46] and no acknowledgment of service is required by a defendant who has acknowledged·service in the action.[47]

(b) In the case of two defendants who are sued as joint tortfeasors liable in respect of the same damage, no such notice is required at all.[48] On the other hand, if it is necessary for the defendant claiming contribution to ask for discovery of documents or leave to administer interrogatories to his co-defendant, he should issue a third party notice and summons for directions under R.S.C., Ord. 16, r. 4, for until the issues are specified it will not appear whether the discovery or interrogatories relate to a matter in question.[49]

[40-41] See R.S.C., Ord. 16, r. 4(3).

[42] See *Stott* v. *West Yorkshire Road Car Co. Ltd.* [1971] 2 Q.B. 651; [1971] 3 All E.R. 534.

[43] See *Slade & Kempton (Jewellery) Ltd.* v. *Kayman Ltd.* [1969] 1 W.L.R. 1285; [1969] 3 All E.R. 786.

[44] R.S.C., Ord. 16, r. 11.

[45] *Ibid.* r. 8.

[46] *Ibid.* r. 8(1).

[47] *Ibid.* r. 8(3).

[48] s.1 of the Civil Liability (Contribution) Act 1978. In such case, however, it is convenient to write a letter warning the co-defendant of the intention to ask for the order to apportion responsibility for the damage and to award contribution.

[49] See *Clayson* v. *Rolls Royce Ltd.* [1951] 1 K.B. 746; [1950] 2 All E.R. 884.

Proceedings subsequent to third party proceedings Claims by third and subsequent parties may be made the subject of third party procedure in substantially the same way as claims by the defendant against a third party. Thus, the third party may serve a fourth party notice, and the fourth party may serve a fifth party notice and so on. Accordingly, where a defendant has served a third party notice, the third party may make such a claim or requirement as comes within the scope of third party procedure,[50] which will apply to him as if he were a defendant, and similarly the third party procedure applies to any further person as if he were a third party.[51] The fourth or subsequent party notice may be issued without leave before the expiration of 14 days after the time limited for the acknowledgment of service of the party concerned; otherwise the leave of the court would be required.[52] The pleadings in fourth or subsequent party proceedings will be in substantially the same form, *mutatis mutandis*, as ordinary pleadings in an action between a plaintiff and a defendant, but the heading of the pleadings should describe them according to the fact.[53]

Interpleader Proceedings

Introduction Interpleader proceedings are a form of relief by which a person can protect himself from legal proceedings being brought or continued against him by calling upon two claimants to the same debt or property to interplead, *i.e.* each to make his claim upon the other, in order to determine the title to the debt or property. Accordingly, where a person is under a liability in respect of a debt or in respect of any money, goods or chattels and he is, or expects to be, sued for or in respect of that debt, or money, or those goods or chattels by two or more persons making adverse claims thereto, he may apply to the court for relief by way of interpleader.[54]

Conditions precedent to interpleader relief

(a) The applicant for interpleader relief must show that he is sued or that there is a real foundation of his expectation to be sued by two

---

[50] See R.S.C., Ord. 16, rr. 1 and 8.

[51] R.S.C. Ord. 16, r. 9(1).

[52] *Ibid.* r. 9(3).

[53] See p. 262 notes 41, 42 and 43, *supra*.

[54] R.S.C., Ord. 17, r. 1(1)(*a*). As to interpleader by a sheriff who has taken or intends to take money, goods or chattels in execution under any process, see R.S.C., Ord. 17, r. 1(1)(*b*). Interpleader as between claimants was introduced by the Interpleader Act 1831, and was extended by the Common Law Procedure Act 1860, ss.12–18 (see Day's *Common Law Procedure Acts*, pp. 353 *et seq*.). These statutes were repealed by the Judicature Acts 1873–1875 and replaced by the pre-1964 R.S.C. Ord. 57, which has been replaced by R.S.C., Ord. 17.

or more persons[55] who are making adverse claims to the same debt or property.[56] Accordingly, interpleader relief will not be granted where the claims are not adverse, but may be said to be parallel, as where they arise under separate contracts[57] or where the applicant may be legally liable to both claimants.[58]

(b) Interpleader relief does not extend to unliquidated damages,[59] but it may extend to part of a debt[60] and to a debt due but not yet payable.[61]

Directions   Where an application for interpleader relief is made to the court[62] and all the persons by whom adverse claims to the subject-matter in dispute acknowledge service[63] the court may:

(a) order that any claimant be made a defendant in any pending action for or in addition to the applicant for interpleader relief;

(b) order that an issue between the claimants be stated and tried and may direct which of the claimants is to be plaintiff and which defendant[64];

(c) may, where there are issues of fact to be determined, give directions as to the conduct or further conduct of the proceedings, as by directing pleadings to be served between the claimants or between the plaintiff and the added party[65] and by directing discovery and inspection of documents between them[66] and so forth

[55] See *Watson* v. *Park Royal (Caterers)* [1961] 1 W.L.R. 727; [1961] 2 All E.R. 346; and see *Harrison* v. *Payne* (1836) 2 Hodges 107; *Diplock* v. *Hammond* (1854) 23 L.J.Ch. 550.
[56] See *Meynell* v. *Angell* (1862) 32 L.J.Q.B. 14 (claims by one person and by his undisclosed principal); and see *Tanner* v. *European Bank* (1866) L.R. 1 Ex. 261; *Attenborough* v. *London & St. Katherine's Dock Co.* (1878) 3 C.P.D. 450.
[57] *Greatorex* v. *Shackle* [1895] 2 Q.B. 249; *Sun Insurance Office* v. *Galinsky* [1914] K.B. 545.
[58] *Victor Sohne* v. *British & African Steam Navigation Co.* [1888] W.N. 84; *Sablicich* v. *Russell* (1866) L.R. 2 Eq. 441.
[59] *Walters* v. *Nicholson* (1838) 6 Dow. & L. 517; *Ingham* v. *Walker* (1887) 3 T.L.R. 448 (C.A.).
[60] *Reading* v. *London School Board* (1886) 16 Q.B.D. 686.
[61] *Ibid.*
[62] As to the mode of application, see R.S.C., Ord. 17, r. 2.
[63] For the procedure in default of notice of intention to defend by a claimant or of compliance with any order made in the proceedings, see R.S.C., Ord. 17, r. 5(3).
[64] R.S.C., Ord. 17, r.5(1). Where all the claimants consent or any of them so requests or the question at issue between them is a question of law and the facts are not in dispute, the court may summarily determine the question at issue between the claimants and make an order accordingly on such terms as may be just; see R.S.C., Ord. 17, r. 5(2), but such summary disposal is not appropriate where the goods are of considerable value and difficult questions of law arise; see *Fredericks and Pelhams Timber Buildings* v. *Wilkins, Read (Claimant)* [1971] 1 W.L.R. 1197; [1971] 3 All E.R. 545 (C.A.).
[65] In pending proceedings, the court cannot order that the defence or counterclaim of the added party be limited to such defences or counterclaims as the applicant could have pleaded (*Gerhard* v. *Montagu & Co.* (1889) 61 L.T. 564).
[66] See R.S.C., Ord. 17, r. 10.

(as in the case of a summons for directions between plaintiff and defendant).

Trial   The trial of an interpleader issue is modelled on the trial of an action,[67] and the court may give such judgment or make such order as finally to dispose of all questions arising in the interpleader proceedings.[68]

Separate Trials as Between Parties

Introduction   Where two or more plaintiffs or defendants are parties to the same action and it appears to the court that the joinder of parties may embarrass or delay the trial or is otherwise inconvenient, the court may order separate trials or make such other order as may be expedient.[69]

Making the application—when?   The application for an order for separate trials as between parties or other similar order should of course be made as soon as practicable but it may be made at the trial.[70]

Ambit of court's discretion   The power of the court under this rule is discretionary.[71] If challenged, the plaintiff must justify the joinder of parties, and the court should be satisfied that no extra burden will be imposed on the defendant through the plaintiff needlessly enlarging the area of the dispute.[72] The court will consider the convenience of all parties, and particularly whether the joinder might cause damage to one party because of evidence might be admissible in the action against a co-party which would be inadmissible in an action against him.[73]

Alternative powers of the court   The court may not only order separate trials as between the parties, it may also:

(a) confine the action to some of the parties and stay the action as to the other or others; or

(b) it may order:

  (i) the plaintiff or plaintiffs to elect which plaintiff should proceed with the action and which plaintiff should be struck out[74]; or

---

[67] See *ibid.* r. 11(1).
[68] See R.S.C., Ord. 17, r. 11(2).
[69] R.S.C., Ord. 15, r. 11(2).
[70] See *Thomas* v. *Moore* [1918] 1 K.B. 555 at 569.
[71] *Ibid., per* Pickford L.J.
[72] See *Saccharin Corporation* v. *Wild* [1903] 1 Ch. 410, *per* Collins M.R. at 422; and see *The Normar* [1968] p. 362; [1968] 1 All E.R. 753.
[73] *Sandes* v. *Wildsmith* [1893] 1 Q.B. 771 at 774.
[74] *Sandes* v. *Wildsmith, supra.*

(ii) against which of two or more defendants the plaintiff[75] or plaintiffs will proceed; or

(iii) which cause of action will be proceeded with.[76]

Pleading Where the plaintiffs are required to elect which of them should proceed with the action, the writ and the pleadings should be amended to confine the action to one plaintiff and to strike out all parts thereof referring to the claim of the other plaintiff.[77]

Particular Classes of Parties

Introduction There are a great variety of persons in relation to whom because of their special legal characteristics or other peculiar circumstances affecting them, special rules of procedure are provided which stipulate and regulate the manner in which an action by or against them can be properly constituted, *e.g.* partnership. In some instances, proceeding in one manner rather than another by or against a particular class of party may result in different legal consequences, as for example an action by or against a partnership in the name of the firm instead of by or against the individual parties in their own names.[78]

Pleading In all cases in which there are special classes of parties (whether as plaintiffs or defendants), the statement in summary form of all the material facts on which each party relies for his claim or defence[79] should remain precisely the same as in the case of pleadings between ordinary plaintiffs and defendants. However, it is almost invariably desirable to add introductory averments to explain who are the parties and what are the special circumstances affecting them.[80]

Examples of classes of persons

(a) Persons under disability (infants[81] or patients).[82]

(b) Limited companies.

(c) Partners.

(d) The Crown.

---

[75] *Vacher & Sons* v. *London Society of Compositors* [1913] A.C. 107; *Sadler* v. *Great Western Railway Co.* [1895] 2 Q.B. 688.

[76] See *Universities of Oxford & Cambridge* v. *Gill* [1899] 1 Ch. 55.

[77] See *Sandes* v. *Wildsmith, supra.*

[78] See *Ex p. Blain* (1879) 12 Ch.D. 522, *per* James L.J. at 533.

[79] See R.S.C., Ord. 18, r. 7(1).

[80] See p. 74, *supra.*

[81] See R.S.C., Ord. 80. r. 1. The terms "infant" and "minor" are interchangeable; see Family Law Reform Act 1969, but the R.S.C. still uses the term "infant." The term is a reference to one who has not attained the age of 18 years; see Family Law Reform Act 1969, s.1(1) and (2).

[82] A patient is a person who by reason of mental disorder within the meaning of the Mental Health Act 1983 is incapable of managing or administering his property and affairs.

(e) Estates.
(f) Trust property.
(g) Trades unions.
(h) Representative actions.
(i) Relator actions.

Persons under disability   The overriding rule is that such a person may not bring or make a claim in any proceedings except by his next friend and may not defend, make a counterclaim or intervene in any proceedings except by his guardian *ad litem*.[83]

So far as an infant is concerned, the name of the next friend or guardian *ad litem*, as the case may be, should appear in the body of the writ as well as in the title of the action in all the pleadings. Further, the statement of claim should aver the fact that the plaintiff or defendant is an infant suing or being sued by his next friend or guardian *ad litem* as the case may be.

So far as a patient is concerned, he must not be described in the writ as a patient but the action and the pleadings should show that he is suing or is sued by his next friend or guardian *ad litem* as the case may be.

Limited company or corporation   It sues or is sued in its corporate name which must be set out fully in the writ and in the title of each pleading.[84]

Partners and firms

(a) Partners carrying on business within the jurisdiction may sue or be sued in the name of the firm, if any, of which they were partners at the time when the cause of action accrued.[85]

(b) An individual carrying on business within the jurisdiction in a name or style other than his own name may be *sued* in that name or style as if it were the name of a firm,[86] but he must *sue* in his own name.[87]

The Crown   Civil proceedings by or against the Crown may be instituted by the appropriate government department,[88] or if none is appropriate or there is reasonable doubt, against the Attorney-General.[89]

---

[83] R.S.C., Ord. 80, r. 2(1).

[84] See p. 268, *infra*. It is essential that the name of the limited company or corporation should be fully and accurately stated in the writ.

[85] See R.S.C., Ord. 81, r. 1. A partnership firm *outside* the jurisdiction must sue or be sued in the individual names of the partners.

[86] See R.S.C., Ord. 81, r. 9.

[87] See *Mason* v. *Mogridge* (1892) 8 T.L.R. 805.

[88] Crown Proceedings Act 1947, s. 17(2). A list of authorised government departments is published by the Treasury in pursuance of s.17(1) of the Crown Proceedings Act 1947; see *Supreme Court Practice 1991*, Vol. 2, para. 6037.

[89] Crown Proceedings Act 1947, s. 17(3). The procedure relating to proceedings by and against the Crown is governed by R.S.C., Ord. 77.

Estates   In any action concerning the estate of a deceased person, all administrators or all executors who have proved the will must be joined.

Trust property   In any action concerning trust property, all the trustees within the jurisdiction must, as a rule, be joined. It is not necessary to add any of the persons beneficially interested in the trust.

Trades unions   Despite the fact that a trade union is not a special register body[90] nor a corporation, it can sue and be sued in its own name, whether in proceedings relating to property or founded on contract or tort or any other cause of action whatsoever.[91]

Representative actions   A representative action may be brought by or against one or more of numerous persons having the same interest in any proceedings as representing all or as representing all except one or more of such persons.[92] Where the plaintiff sues on behalf of a class, the formal parts of the statement of claim should be pleaded thus:

Between

A B

(suing on behalf of himself and of all the other debenture holders of the *E F* Company Limited, *or as the case may be*)   Plaintiff

and

C D(I.)

and

E F Company Limited   Defendants

STATEMENT OF CLAIM

[*The body of the Statement of Claim must show that the other persons whom the plaintiff claims to represent in the action have the same interest therein as himself, and the relief claimed should, in general, be stated to be claimed on their behalf, as well as on his own, as for instance.* The plaintiff, on behalf of himself and all the other debenture holders of the said company, claims, etc. *(stating the relief claimed).*]

---

[90] For the meaning of this term, see Trade Union and Labour Relations Act 1974, s.30(1).

[91] Trade Union and Labour Relations Act 1974, s.2(1)(c). This provision is subject to s.14 which provides for immunity from suit for certain actions in tort against trade unions and employers' associations.

[92] See R.S.C., Ord. 15, r. 12.

Relator actions   In a relator action, before the name of any person is used as a relator, he must give a written authorisation so to use his name to his solicitor and such authorisation must be filed in the Central Office or the district registry if the proceedings are issued out of the registry.[93]

---

[93] R.S.C., Ord. 15, r. 11. A relator action is one in which a person or body claiming to be entitled to restrain interference with a public right or to abate a public nuisance or to compel the performance of a public duty, is bound to bring such action in the name of the Attorney-General as the necessary party. The practice is to describe the plaintiff as "The Attorney-General at the relation of *AB* (*the relator*). Where the relator has a separate cause of action, arising out of the same facts, he may be added as a co-plaintiff. The relator is bound to bring the action in the name of the Attorney General as a necessary party for he is the only person recognised by public law as entitled to represent the public in a court of justice and he alone can maintain a suit *ex officio or ex relatione* for a declaration as to public rights: *Gouriet* v. *Union of Post Office Workers* [1978] A.C. 435; [1977] 3 All E.R. 70 (H.L.). disapproving dictum of Lord Denning M.R. in *Attorney-General ex rel. McWhirter* v. *Independent Broadcasting Authority* [1973] 1 Q.B. 626 at 649; [1973] 1 All E.R. 689. Except for the powers conferred on local authorities by s.222 of the Local Government Act 1972 only the Attorney-General can sue on behalf of the public for the purpose of preventing public wrongs and a private individual cannot do so on behalf of the public though he might be able to do so if he would sustain injury as a result of a public wrong *ibid.* The jurisdiction of the Attorney-General to decide in what cases it is proper for him to sue on behalf of relators is absolute and the court has no power to review his decision *ibid.* applying *London County Council* v. *Att.-Gen.* [1902] A.C. 165 (H.L.). When an action is commenced on behalf of the Crown, or of those who enjoy its prerogative, of for a public wrong, the action may be brought by the Attorney-General alone, or by a relator in the name of the Attorney-General on the latter's authority, or on the authority of the Solicitor-General if the Attorney-General is not available, if the conditions of s.1 of the Law Officers Act 1944 are satisfied. In order to obtain the authority of the Attorney-General to bring the action, the relator must leave at the Attorney-General's office at the Royal Courts of Justice: (a) a copy of the writ and statement of claim, with a certificate of counsel annexed thereto "that they are proper for the allowance of the Attorney-General"; (b) a second copy of the writ and statement of claim, which, if the Attorney-General sanctions the action, will be signed and returned to the relator's solicitor; and (c) a certificate of the solicitor that the relator is a proper person (or corporate body) to be relator and is competent to answer the costs of the proposed action. The writ signed by the Attorney-General must be issued as the original writ and the signed statement of claim retained and every copy of the writ, or statement of claim served must bear a copy of the Attorney-General's signature. If a statement of claim is amended the signature of the Attorney-General must be obtained in the same manner as in the case of an original statement of claim. The relator is not the plaintiff, though he may be joined as plaintiff if he has a cause of action in himself, or there are exceptional circumstances which in the opinion of the Attorney-General render it desirable that he (the relator) should be joined as plaintiff. On issuing the writ his written authority (which in the case of a corporate body must be under seal) must be filed. While the Attorney-General may have the right when suing on behalf of the Crown to select his own tribunal, that right does not extend to a case in which he sues on behalf of relators (*Attorney-General* v. *Wilson* [1900] 70 L.J.Ch. 234 (C.A.)).

269

Pleading Practice in Scotland
Alastair Mennie JH, Scots Bar

The Courts

The Scottish courts—an overview

Introduction   The principal civil courts of first instance in Scotland are the Court of Session and the sheriff courts.

The Court of Session, which sits in Edinburgh, is Scotland's superior court.

Scotland is divided into six sheriffdoms and five of the sheriffdoms are divided into six sheriffdom districts. There are approximately 50 sheriff court districts in Scotland, and in each of the sheriff court districts and in Glasgow and Strathkelvin (the sheriffdom not divided into sheriff court districts), there is one sheriff court.

Appeals and other forms of review take place in the sheriff courts, the Court of Session and the House of Lords. References for preliminary rulings can be made by certain Scottish courts in certain circumstances to the European Court of Justice.

In addition to the prinicpal courts of first instance and to which recourse may be had, there are other Scottish courts the best known of which is the Scottish Land Court.

The Court of Session—Composition   The Court of Session has at present a complement of 24 judges and is divided into an Inner House and an Outer House.

The Inner House consists of two Divisions. Four judges are members of each Division and the remaining judges sit in the outer House. The judges are styled Senators of the College of Justice. It has been said that they hold equal status and the Lord President of the Court of Session is *primus inter pares.* He presides over the First Division; the Second Division is presided over by the Lord Justice-Clerk. The other members of the divisions are the six most senior judges other than the Lord President and the Lord Justice-Clerk.

The Outer House judges are known as Lords Ordinary. The two Divisions are of equal authority: each has a quorum of three and normally three judges sit at any one time. Each Lord Ordinary sits alone.

The Senators of the College of Justice are also the judges of the High Court, the superior criminal court in Scotland. The High Court consists, strictly speaking, of the Lord Justice-General, the Lord Justice-Clerk and the Lords Commissioners of Justiciary; the Lord President of the Court of Session is Lord Justice-Clerk and the Lords Ordinary are Lords Commissioners of Justiciary. Each Senator of the College of Justice spends a significant amount of time sitting in the High Court. Certain of the Senators are also members of other courts and tribunals.

The Outer and Inner Houses: competence

Competence—general The majority of proceedings which can take place in the Court of Session begin in the Outer House. But the competence of the Inner House as a court of first instance is not insignificant.

Competence—subject matter Emslie and Welsh state that "[i]n general it may be said that all civil causes are competent in the Court of Session unless the court's power to entertain them has been excluded by statute, expressly or by plain implication." The civil causes not competent at first instance in the Court of Session can generally be divided into:

   (a) those which fall to be determined by a specialised court, such as the Scottish Land Court or Election Petition Court (if such causes can properly be considered as civil causes); and
   (b) those within.

The Court of Justice of the European Communities It is open to any Scottish court in appropriate circumstances to make a reference to the European Court in terms of article 177 of the EEC Treaty (the Treaty of Rome), article 41 of the ECSC Treaty or article 150 of the Euratom Treaty. The effect of the 1971 Protocol to the Brussels Convention is that, where a question of interpretation of the Convention is raised in an appeal before the House of Lords, it must seek a ruling from the European Court if it considers that a decision on the question is necessary before it can dispose of the case. And a sheriff principal or the Inner House may, if sitting in an appellate capacity, seek a ruling from the European Court if a decision on a question of interpretation of the Convention is necessary before the case can be disposed of. The procedure to be followed in the Scottish court in the context of any competent reference to the European Court is set out in the Rules of Court (R.C.) 296A–E for the Court of Session and R.C. 134 for the sheriff courts.

Written Pleadings in the Court of Session

Summons procedure

Proceedings begun by summons (the English equivalent being the statement of claim indorsed on the writ of summons)   R.C. 70 states:

"1. All summonses shall be on the official printed form (Form 1), which, along with the official printed backing thereon, shall be filled in and completed either in manuscript, typescript or print; provided that:

(*a*) The conclusions shall be stated in one or more of the short forms exemplified in Form 2, or in such similar short form as the circumstances may require.

(*b*) There shall be annexed to every summons a statement in the form of an articulate numbered condescendence of the averments of fact which form the grounds of the pursuer's claim, and there shall also be annexed to every summons a note of the pursuer's pleas-in-law.

(*c*) A condescendence shall include averments stating:

(i) the ground of the jurisdiction of the court, unless jurisdiction would arise only if the defender prorogated the jurisdiction of the court (without contesting jurisdiction);

(ii) where appropriate, whether there is reason to believe that there exists an agreement prorogating the jurisdiction of a court in a particular country; and

(iii) whether proceedings involving the same cause of action are in subsistence between the parties in a country to which the Convention in Schedule 1 to the Civil Jurisdiction and Judgments Act 1982 applies, unless the court has exclusive jurisdiction.

2. A summons may include:

(*a*) a warrant of inhibition which shall have the same effect as letters of inhibition;

(*b*) if the summons concludes for payment of money, a warrant to arrest the moveable property belonging to or owing to the defender."

Formal parts   Like all items of process, a summons is headed "Court of Session, Scotland." There follow "summons." "*in causa*" and the instance which contains the names and addresses of the parties, followed, as appropriate, by "Pursuer" or "Defender." This is followed by:

"ELIZABETH II, by the Grace of God, of the United Kingdom of Great Britain and Northern Ireland and of Her other Realms and Territories Queen, Head of the Commonwealth, Defender of the Faith, to the said [defender].

Whereas by this summons the pursuer crave the Lords of our Council and Session to pronounce a decree against you in terms of the conclusion appended hereto. We therefore charge you that, if you have any good reasons why such decree should not be pronounced you cause appearance to be entered on your behalf in the office of the Court, 2 Parliament Square, Edinburgh, on the calling of the Summons in Court, which calling will be not earlier than the [induciae] day from the date of service upon you of this Summons; and take warning that, if appearance is not so entered on your behalf, the pursuer may proceed to obtain decree against you in your absence."

Warrants At the foot of the first page are to be found warrants, such as warrants for arrestment and inhibition, and the embossed signet.

A warrant for arrestment is executed by a messenger-at-arms. Its purpose is to give some security to the pursuer. A debt, such as a bank account, owed to the defender will be arrested, *i.e.* frozen, so that it cannot be paid by the third party to the defender. Various rules govern arrestment, in particular the types of debts which are arrestable.

An inhibition is another form of security and significantly reduces the power of the debtor to dispose of his heritable property.

Conclusions Page two contains the conclusions. As indicated in R.C. 70, Form 2 at the end of the Rules of Court contains styles for conclusions. In the majority of actions one of these styles can be used or adapted.

Two points are worth noting. Firstly, where a sum of money by way of damages is concluded for, the sum sought should be at least the largest amount which could reasonably be expected; the court can award less, but not more, than that concluded for.

Secondly, where interdict is sought the conclusion should be as specific as possible. It is the court's practice to frame interlocutors granting interdict in terms of the conclusion in the summons and, as the court considers that it should be made quite clear to a defender what he must not do, it will not pronounce an interlocutor granting interdict if the conclusion is vague.

Strictly speaking the conclusions are the last part of the summons, but in practice the whole document, including the condescendence and pleas-in-law, is referred to as the summons.

Condescendence The condescendence begins at the top of page three. Article 1 usually briefly describes the parties and sets out the jurisdiction of the court. If jurisdiction is being based on the defender being domiciled in Scotland in terms of article 52 of the Brussels Convention and section 41 of the Civil Jurisdiction and Judgments Act 1982, then, assuming it to be the case, to comply with R.C. 70(1)(c)(i) it is sufficient to aver:

"The defender resides at [address in Scotland]. He has been resident in Scotland for more than three months immediately preceding the raising of this action. He is domiciled in [town or village]. This court accordingly has jurisdiction."

If there is no possibility of there being a prorogation agreement, and the pursuer is unaware of any proceedings elsewhere being in progress, it is not the practice for averments to this effect to be made.

The function of Scottish pleadings—the role of condescendence   The subsequent articles of the condescendence will set out the facts of the case. Macphail states that:

"it is the function of written pleadings to enable the parties and the court to ascertain with precision those matters on which the parties are at issue and those on which they are agreed, and thus to arrive at the question which the parties wish decided. Thus. . . . the conde-scendence will set out the relationship between the parties and a chronological narrative of the facts. . . . . . . Next, a link is formed between the narrative and the pleas-in-law by a separate article or articles stating the facts from which the pleas-in-law directly emerge. . . . . . . Each ground of liability, whether at common law or under statute, should be the subject of a separate article, and the relevant part of any statute or statutory instrument founded on should be quoted."

Where damages are sought, the second last article of condescendence will usually set out to explain how the figure concluded for was arrived at. The last article will state that the action is necessary as the defender has failed to make payment.

The interaction between pleadings and trial   It is very important for the pursuer's counsel to bear in mind that, at proof or jury trial, evidence can only be led on matters set out in the written pleadings. He certainly does not wish to have the defender's counsel submitting that there is no foundation in the Record for a particular line of questioning.

Pleas-in-law   Macphail describes the pleas-in-law as enunciating "[t]he legal propositions which the pursuer claims to be applicable to the facts averred in the condescendence. They are not abstract propositions of law: they must tie in with the condescendence. "When read together with the facts averred . . . the plea-in-law should substantiate the party's right to the remedy he seeks . . ." Pleas-in-law accepted by the courts are handed down from advocate to pupil, solicitor to trainee.

Signature   The summons, although drafted by counsel, is signed by the pursuer's solicitor.

Defence/procedure

Principle Rule of Court 83(b) states   Defences shall be in the form of articulate numbered answers to the condescendence annexed to the summons, and there shall be annexed to such defences a note of the defender's pleas-in-law.

Practice   A set of defences consists principally of answers to the condescendence and pleas-in -law for the defender. The answers should be in articles/paragraphs corresponding to the articles/paragraphs of the condescendence. With regard to each article of condescendence the defender should first admit what he knows to be true. He should then aver "Believed to be true that . . . " with regard to other matters which he accepts as true. If appropriate he then avers "Not known and not admitted that . . . " After that it is good practice to aver "*Quoad ultra* denied." The answer to a particular article of condescendence will often conclude with the defender's explanation of events: "Explained and averred that . . . "

Analysis of pleas-in-law   The defender's pleas-in-law can be divided into preliminary pleas and pleas on the merits.

A preliminary plea is one which, if successful, would cause the action to be dismissed without there first being a proof on the merits. Such pleas can be regarded as being principally concerned with the pursuer's written case.

Pleas on the merits, by contrast, are concerned with the pursuer's oral case and can only be disposed of after a proof or jury trial.

The first two pleas for the defender in the Open Record at the end of this Appendix are very common. The first of them is a preliminary plea and the second is a plea on the merits. It is appropriate for a defender also to insert more positive pleas bringing out the propositions which he is making. Were he believes this to be appropriate, a defender may plead "no jurisdiction," "*forum non conveniens*" and/or "*lis alibi pendens*," but many practitioners consider that such short pleas are not appropriate and that it is preferable, for example, to plead: "The defender not being subject to the jurisdiction of the court, the action should be dismissed."

Skeleton defences   Where the defender's solicitor or counsel is confronted by a lack of time and information, in order to protect his client's position he may draft simple defences denying all of the averments in each article of condescendence. Such defences are referred to as skeleton defences. The court frowns on their use and they should be expanded or withdrawn as soon as possible.

Signature   The defences are signed by counsel.

Adjustment: open and closed records

Principles   During the period that the action is on the adjustment roll, the pursuer is free to adjust his articles of condescendence and pleas-in-law and the defender may adjust his answers and pleas-in-law.

If the pursuer wishes at any stage to alter his conclusions, he can only do so by way of Minute of Amendment.

Rationale   As Macphail states, "[t]he primary object of adjustment is to make such alterations to the parties' averments and pleas-in-law as are necessary to ensure that when the record is closed the issues between the parties and the stand which each party is taking on these issues may be readily understood from a reading of the pleadings."

Pursuer practice   The pursuer usually begins the adjustment process by answering all the statements of fact made by the defender in his defences. His approach is similar to that of the defender in answering the statements in the condescendence. He may well insert at the end of more than one article of condescendence: "With reference to the defender's averments in answer, admitted that . . . . *Quoad ultra* denied except insofar as coinciding herewith." He may insert new pleas-in-law specifically concerned with the defences and he may also expand some of his initial averments.

After that the defender will adjust his pleadings and then it is the pursuer's turn again.

Logistics   So far as the logistics are concerned, a copy of the open record is treated as the adjustment copy. The adjustments prepared by counsel are added to it in the pursuer's solicitor's office. It is sent to the defender's solicitor's office. Once his adjustments have been prepared they are added to the adjustment copy record and it is sent back to the pursuer's solicitor's office. The open and closed records are printed and not signed by solicitor or counsel. It should be noted that the model open record near the end of this Appendix is one which has not had any adjustments made to it for either party.

Miscellaneous items of process in ordinary action

Introduction   In the model pleadings at page 279 there are set out various items of process which from time to time are to be found in ordinary actions. They are all signed by counsel.

Minute of amendment　If it is wished to amend the pleadings after the record has been closed, a Minute of Amendment must be prepared by the party concerned. The authority of the court must then be obtained for it to become part of the process. The other party will be given an opportunity to lodge Answers and then the Minute and Answers will be incorporated into the Record. If the amendments are lengthy, an amended closed record will be prepared.

Minute of tender, etc.　If he wishes to make an offer of settlement through the court, a Minute of Tender is prepared and lodged in process on behalf of the defender. On the other hand, he might, of course, prefer to seek an extra-judicial settlement. If a tender is acceptable, a Minute of Acceptance of Tender will be lodged on behalf of the Pursuer. If a tender is not accepted, and the pursuer eventually obtains decree for a sum less than that tendered, the non-acceptance of the tender will be taken into account by the court in awarding expenses.

Specification of documents　If it is considered appropriate to seek an order in terms of section 1 of the Administration of Justice (Scotland) Act 1972 (see Jurisdiction and related matters, above), a Specification of Documents such as that set out below will in the normal case be prepared.

Proceedings begun by petition　R.C. 191 has a function similar to that of R.C. 70. It gives directions as to the drafting of petitions and refers the reader to Form 29, a specimen petition, at the end of the Rules of Court. Several volumes of copies of petitions presented to the court, both Outer House petitions and Inner House petitions, are kept in the Advocates Library. They are used for guidance in the drafting of petitions.

　　The style and subject matter of petitions are such that in many cases no serious problems of drafting arise. Where a number of facts should be set out in the petition, the approach to drafting the averments should generally be the same as that in drafting averments for a summons. Answers are lodged on behalf of any respondent and then adjustment of the petition and answers takes place.

Model Pleadings

REVISED VERSION

ACTION FOR DAMAGES FOR BREACH OF CONTRACT

COURT OF SESSION, SCOTLAND

OPEN RECORD

I. – SUMMONS

MR. and MRS. A B C, (insert address)

PURSUERS

against

D E (Assisted Person), (insert address)

DEFENDER

ELIZABETH II [*see p. 274*]

This summons is warrant for arrestment and inhibition on the dependence of the action.

CONCLUSIONS

1. For declarator that the defender was by October 22, 1988 in material breach of his contract with the pursuers as constituted by missives between the parties' respective Agents dated June 30 and July 4 and 14, all 1988, and that the pursuers were then entitled to resile therefrom.

2. For payment by the defender to the pursuers of the sum of SEVEN THOUSAND FOUR HUNDRED AND EIGHTY-FOUR POUNDS (£7,484) Sterling with interest thereon at the rate of fifteen *per centum per annum* from the date of citation until payment.

3. For the expenses of the action.

II. – CONDESCENDENCE for PURSUERS

and

ANSWERS thereto for DEFENDER

Cond. 1.   The pursuers reside at (address). The defender resides at (address). He has been resident in Scotland for more than three months immediately preceding the raising of this action. He is domiciled in Scotland. This Court accordingly has jurisdiction.

Ans. 1.　The averments relating to the defender and to jurisdiction are admitted. *Quoad ultra* not known and not admitted.

Cond. 2.　By missives dated June 30, July 4 and 14, 1988 concluded by the parties' respective Agents, the pursuers agreed to sell to the defender the shop premises known as the Corner Shop situated at 47 Sunshine Crescent, Edinburgh for the sum of £82,000 subject to the terms and conditions contained in said missives which, or copies of which, are produced and the terms whereof are herein held incorporated *brevitatis causa*. It was agreed between the parties in terms of Condition 3 of said missive of June 30, 1988, *inter alia*, that entry and vacant possession of the subjects of sale would be given to the defender on the date of transfer to the defender of the licence relating to said shop premises. Said licence was transferred to the defender on October 5, 1988. The defender thereupon became liable to pay to the pursuers on that date the whole of the purchase price agreed upon.

Ans. 2.　Said missives are referred to for their whole terms, beyond which no admission is made. Admitted that said licence was transferred to the defender on October 5, 1988. *Quoad ultra* denied except insofar as coinciding herewith. Explained and averred that under said missives the time for payment was not of the essence of the bargain.

Cond. 3.　The defender refused or in any event failed to pay to the pursuers the purchase price on the date of entry. He failed thereafter to make any satisfactory offer to pay said sum. On October 18, 1988 the pursuers, through their Agents, Messrs. (name), gave the defender notice that, unless satisfactory proposals for the payment of said sum were made within three days, the pursuers would resile from said contract and the defender would be liable for any consequent losses resulting therefrom. No satisfactory proposals were made by the defender and accordingly the pursuers resiled from the said contract on October 22, 1988. They subsequently sold said shop to another purchaser for £75,500.

Ans. 3.　Admitted that the defender did not tender the price on October 5, 1988, under explanation that the pursuers' Agents were advised that he was finding some difficulty in raising all of the necessary finance. *Quoad ultra* denied except insofar as coinciding herewith. Explained and averred that negotiations then began between the parties' respective Agents as to how the purchase price was to be paid. By letter dated October 18, 1988 the pursuers' Agents informed the defender's Agents that the subjects were once again to be put on the market; they also informed them that no offer for the subjects would be accepted unless the defender agreed thereto. By letter dated October 22, 1988 the pursuers'

Agents intimated to the defender's Agents that a bargain had been concluded with a second purchaser and that the pursuers were resiling from the bargain with the defender. The pursuers were not entitled to do so. They did not allow a reasonable time to elapse prior to their purported resiling from the bargain. having regard to the fact that negotiations concerning the time and manner of settlement were continuing, and to the shortness of time within which the purported second bargain was concluded, the defender believes and avers that no reasonable time was permitted by the pursuers to elapse prior to their purported resiling from the bargain. Moreover at no time prior to accepting said second offer did the pursuers or their Agents call upon the defender or his Agents to implement their obligations under the missives which failing the pursuers would resile. The defender and his Agents were not informed, prior to its purported acceptance, that the second purchaser's offer had been made. At no time did the pursuers or their Agents seek to have the second purchaser increase his offer for the subjects, though the defender believes and avers that there was a substantial prospect that he would have done so. The second bargain purportedly entered into is of no effect *quoad* the bargain between the pursuers and the defender and said second bargain, and any Disposition consequent thereon, falls to be reduced.

Cond. 4.   The failure of the defender to make payment on the date specified in the Missives coupled with his failure to make any satisfactory proposals within the reasonable time limit stipulated in said letter of October 18, 1988 constituted a material breach of contract entitling the pursuers to resile. The pursuers accordingly seek declarator as first concluded for. The said breach of contract caused the pursuers loss and damage arising directly therefrom.

Ans. 4.   Denied under reference to the defender's averments in Answers 3 and 5.

Cond. 5.   The pursuers have suffered losses totalling £7,484 as a result of the defender's said breach of contract. Said losses consist of (a) £6,500, being the difference between the price agreed upon in the missives between the parties and the sum obtained as a result of the subsequent sale, (b) £350, being one month's rent of the premises which the pursuers intended opening and running as a shop, (c) £521, being additional bank interest paid and (d) £113, being loss of wages.

Ans. 5.   Denied except insofar as coinciding herewith. The pursuers are called on forthwith to vouch each and all of said purported heads of loss. At no time was the defender made aware of any circumstances such as to justify claims in respect of heads (b), (c) or (d). In any event, each of the sums respectively claimed is excessive. The pursuers continued running the subjects of sale as a business and earning profit therefrom throughout the period between October 5, 1988 and the second purchaser taking entry. They are called on to produce their accounts in relation to said period. The claim for loss of wages is not understood. The pursuers are called on to specify the nature of the claim and to vouch the amount thereof.

Cond. 6.   The defender has refused or in any event delays to make payment of the sum sued for. This action is accordingly necessary.

Ans. 6.   Denied that the action is necessary.

III.—PLEAS-IN-LAW FOR PURSUERS

1. The defender having been in material breach of contract as condescended on, the pursuers are entitled to declarator in terms of the first conclusion.

2. The pursuers having sustained loss and damage arising directly from the defender's said breach of contract are entitled to reparation therefor.

3. The sum sued for being a reasonable estimate of the pursuers' said loss and damage, decree therefor should be granted as second concluded for.

IN RESPECT WHEREOF

IV.—PLEAS-IN-LAW FOR DEFENDER

1. The pursuers' averments being irrelevant *et separatim* lacking in specification, the action should be dismissed.

2. The pursuers' averments insofar as material being unfounded in fact, the defender should be assoilzied.

3. The defender not having been in material breach of contract with the pursuers so as to entitle the pursuers to resile therefrom, decree of absolvitor should be pronounced.

4. The pursuers not having been entitled to resile from said contract in the manner in which and at the time at which they purported to do so, they are not entitled to declarator as concluded for.

5. The purported bargain between the pursuers and said second purchaser being invalid as against the defender as condescended on, the missives concerning that and any disposition following thereon should be reduced *ope exceptionis*.

6. The pursuers not being entitled to damages from the defender by reason of breach of contract, decree therefor should not be granted as concluded for.

---

7. In any event, the sum sued for not being a reasonable estimate of the loss incurred by the pursuers as a result of any breach of contract, decree therefor should not be granted as concluded for.

IN RESPECT WHEREOF

REVISED VERSION

ACTION FOR DAMAGES FOR PERSONAL INJURY RESULTING FROM FAULT ON PART OF ONE DEFENDER AND BREACH OF CONTRACT ON PART OF OTHER DEFENDER

COURT OF SESSION, SCOTLAND

I. – SUMMONS

in causa

A B, (address)

PURSUER

against

C D *plc*, (address)

FIRST DEFENDERS

AND
E F, (address)

SECOND DEFENDER

ELIZABETH II [*see p. 274*]

This summons is warrant for arrestment and inhibition on the dependence of the action.

CONCLUSIONS

1. For payment by the defenders jointly and severally or severally to the pursuer of the sum of FIFTEEN THOUSAND POUNDS STERLING (£15,000), with interest thereon at the rate of 15 *per centum per annum*

from July 13, 1987, or from such date at such rate as to the Court shall seem proper, until payment.

2. For the expenses of the action.

II.—CONDESCENDENCE

1. The pursuer lives in Glasgow. He is in his mid-fifties. The first defenders are a public limited company carrying on business as bottlers at premises at (address). for several years the second defender has been the licence holder of the International Bar, (address). He resides at (address). He has been so resident for more than three months immediately preceding the raising of this action. He is domiciled there. This Court accordingly has jurisdiction over both defenders.

2. Throughout 1987, and for some years prior thereto, the pursuer had been employed as a barman at said bar by the second defender. On about July 13, 1987 after he finished work the pursuer bought from the second defender in the course of the second defender's ordinary business in said bar a litre bottle of (proprietary brand of liquor). He took it back home with him that afternoon and then went to open it prior to drinking the contents. When he had it in his hand attempting to open it, it exploded. Pieces of broken glass from it seriously injured his left thumb.

3. The bottle was one of a crate of such bottles which had been supplied by the first defenders. They had manufactured the bottles, and thereafter bottled and capped the liquor in said bottles and delivered them to the second defender. They had no system, or at any rate no adequate system, for inspecting said bottles prior to and subsequent to their being filled to see that the bottles were sound and would not explode.

4. The accident to the pursuer was caused by fault of the first defenders. They knew or ought to have known that if a bottle which had been supplied by them exploded it would likely be that injury and damage would be sustained by persons in the vicinity. It was their duty to take reasonable care for the safety of such persons and not to expose them unnecessarily to risk of injury. It was their duty to take reasonable care to manufacture and supply bottles which could be opened in safety and which did not explode on someone attempting to open them. Bottles which are manufactured, filled and capped with reasonable care do not explode when an attempt is made to open them. Further and in any event, it was the first defenders' duty to take reasonable care to devise, institute and maintain a system for inspection of said bottles both after manufacture and after filling and capping, whereby defective bottles, in respect of which there was a risk of breakage or explosion, were spotted and removed before being delivered to a sales outlet. Such inspection was

normal and proper practice in the industry of manufacturing bottles and bottling liquids. In the fulfilment of each and all of said duties incumbent on them the first defenders failed and by their failure caused said accident. Had they fulfilled the duties incumbent on them as they ought to have done, the accident would not have occurred.

5. The accident was also caused by breach by the second defender of his duties implied in the contract of sale between him and the pursuer. It was implied in said contract that the bottle supplied would be of merchantable quality and would be fit for its purpose. It was neither. The second defender was in breach of said implied conditions and such breaches caused the accident. Had he fulfilled the duties incumbent on him as he ought to have done, the accident would not have occurred.

6. In consequence of the accident the pursuer was required to be taken in a taxi to Glasgow Royal Infirmary where 15 stitches were inserted in the cut in his left hand. He was and continues to be substantially inconvenienced. He suffers pain, discomfort and restriction of movement. He has a loss of sensation in his left thumb. His grip is diminished. While off work he lost wages. His capacity in the labour market is diminished. He received State Benefits, the amount of which will be vouched. In these circumstances the sum sued for is a reasonable estimate of his loss, injury and damage.

7. The defenders have failed to make reasonable reparation.

III.—PLEAS-IN-LAW

1. The pursuer having sustained loss, injury and damage by fault of the first defenders, *et separatim* by breach of contract by the second defender, is entitled to reparation from them or one or other of them.

2. The sum sued for being reasonable, decree therefore should be pronounced as concluded for.

IN RESPECT WHEREOF

PLEADING PRACTICE IN SCOTLAND

REVISED VERSION

ACTION FOR DAMAGES FOR RELATIVE'S DEATH RESULTING
FROM FAULT AND BREACH OF STATUTORY DUTY

COURT OF SESSION, SCOTLAND

I. – SUMMONS

in causa

(FIRST) MRS. MARY JANE SMITH or WOOD, (address) as an individ-
ual and as tutrix and administratrix-at-law of her pupil child JOHN
WOOD, who resides with her at said address, and (SECOND) PETER
WOOD, (address)

PURSUERS

against

A B CONSTRUCTION COMPANY plc, (address)

DEFENDERS

ELIZABETH II [*see p. 274*]

This summons is warrant for arrestment and inhibition on the dependence of the action and for intimation to Elaine Wood, (address) and
Agnes Wood or Elder, (address) as persons believed to have a title to sue
the defenders in an action based on the death of the late Michael Wood.

CONCLUSIONS

1. For payment by the defenders to the first pursuer (a) as an individual of
the sum of ONE HUNDRED AND FIFTY THOUSAND POUNDS
STERLING (£150,000), and (b) as tutrix and administratrix-at-law of
her pupil child JOHN WOOD of the sum of SIXTY THOUSAND
POUNDS STERLING (£60,000), with interest on each of the said sums
at the rate of 15 *per centum per annum* from December 11, 1986, or at
such rate from such date as to the Court shall seem proper, until payment.

2. For payment by the defenders to the second pursuer of the sum of
TWENTY-FIVE THOUSAND POUNDS STERLING (£25,000), with
interest thereon at the rate of 15 *per centum per annum* from December
11, 1986, or at such rate from such date as to the Court shall seem
proper, until payment.

3. For the expenses of the action.

II.—CONDESCENDENCE

1. The pursuers live in Glenrothes. The first pursuer is the widow of the late Michael Wood (hereinafter referred to as "the deceased") who died in the circumstances hereinafter mentioned on December 11, 1986 and to whom she was married on March 25, 1965. The first pursuer has two children by her said marriage, namely the second pursuer, who was born on September 6, 1968, and John Wood, who was born on September 12, 1977. The defenders are a company incorporated under the Companies Acts and having their registered office in England. The pursuers seek reparation for loss, injury and damage sustained by them as a result of fault on the part of the defenders and for which the defenders are vicariously liable. The harmful event in consequence of which the pursuers suffered said loss, injury and damage occurred in Scotland. This Court accordingly has jurisdiction. Reference is made to the Civil Jurisdiction and Judgments Act 1982, Schedule 8, Rule 2(3).

2. On about December 11, 1986 the deceased was employed by the defenders as a steel erector. On said date he was working in the course of his employment at the premises of C D Limited in Highland Road, Glenrothes. He was engaged in the erection of a large steel framed structure with two long sides and two ends. By the material time the vertical struts on which each of the four walls was to be fixed had been erected. There were horizontal steel members tied in from one vertical wall strut to the next. To the top of each of the vertical wall struts on each of the side walls, further struts were fixed to form the framework of the roof. The roof sloped upwards from each side to a central apex, forming a gable at each end. Smaller steel beams called purlins ran along the whole length of the top of the roof struts, at right angles to the roof struts and parallel to the side walls. They were fixed at intervals to the roof struts. In the middle of the gap between each roof strut, and parallel thereto, ran steel angle irons which were set at right angles through the purlins.

3. At the material time the deceased was fitting angle irons in the fifth bay from the south of the structure. He was working about 15 metres above ground level. He was working from a ladder which was laid across the roof struts, parallel to the purlins, and which served as a gangway between the roof struts. The ladder was about 300 millimetres wide. Neither end of the ladder was secured in any way. The side of the ladder nearer to the side wall of the structure was, by reason of the slope of the roof, lower than the side nearer the apex of the roof. It would not have been reasonably practicable for the deceased to carry out his job with one end of the ladder on the ground, and he was provided with no other means of access to the place at which he had to work.

287

4. As the deceased was working in said fashion, the ladder fell, and the deceased fell with it landing heavily on the ground below and sustaining injuries so severe that he died almost immediately. In consequence, the pursuers have sustained the loss, injury and damage hereinafter condescended on.

5. A few days after said accident occurred, the defenders brought a mobile scaffold to said premises. The remaining angle irons were fitted by employees working from said platform. Had such a mobile platform been provided in said premises on December 11, 1986, the deceased's accident would not have occurred. There had been no such mobile platform or any scaffold at all provided prior to the accident, nor had any instructions for the use of any such platform or scaffold been given by the defenders or anyone on their behalf. The defenders had a supervisor whose name, so far as the pursuers have been able to ascertain, was U V. He visited the site about three times each week, and the pursuers believe and aver that he was the person directly responsible to the defenders' management and employees for the way in which the job was carried out and the provision of any necessary plant and equipment. U V knew that no such mobile scaffold had been provided and that the defenders' employees, including the deceased, were required to work from ladders positioned *ad hoc*.

6. Said accident was caused by fault of the defenders. It was their duty to take reasonable care for the safety of their employees such as the deceased, and not to expose them unnecessarily to risk of injury. It was their duty to take reasonable care to provide and maintain safe plant and equipment for their employees. It was their duty to take reasonable care to ensure that their employees were provided with a safe place at which to work. It was their duty to take reasonable care to devise, institute and maintain a safe system of work. It was their duty in the exercise of such reasonable care to provide and maintain sufficient and suitable plant and equipment such that work at roof level could be carried out in safety. It was their duty to take reasonable care to instruct their supervisors, such as U V, to ensure, before instructing employees to start work, that they had sufficient and suitable equipment and plant so that they could carry out the work in safety. In particular, if work had to be carried out at heights such as 15 metres or thereby above ground level. It was their duty to take reasonable care to instruct him to ensure that there was sufficient and suitable plant and equipment to work there safely, such as a mobile platform, or scaffold and, if there was not, to see that it was obtained and that the work was not begun until it had been obtained. In the fulfilment of each and all of the said duties incumbent upon them, the defenders failed and by their failure caused said accident. Had they fulfilled the

duties incumbent upon them as they ought to have done, the accident would not have occurred.

7. The accident was caused also by fault of U V, for whose negligent acts and omissions in the course of his employment with them the defenders are responsible. It was his duty to take reasonable care for the safety of his fellow employees such as the deceased and not to expose them unnecessarily to risk of injury. It was his duty to take reasonable care to ascertain what work had to be done by the defenders' employees on said date prior to instructing them to do the job, to establish what plant and equipment were necessary in order safely to carry it out, to ensure that such plant and equipment was made available throughout the period during which it was needed, and to instruct the employees to use said plant and equipment. It was his duty to take reasonable care to see that the work was being carried out in a safe manner and, if he saw practices which were unsafe being adopted by the defenders' employees, to tell them so and to forbid the continuance of such practices. It was his duty on seeing employees working at heights from ladders positioned *ad hoc* to take reasonable care to instruct such employees to refrain from doing so, and to await scaffolding or a mobile platform being made available. In the fulfilment of each and all of said duties incumbent on him he failed and by his failure caused said accident. Had he fulfilled the duties incumbent on him as he ought to have done, the accident would not have occurred.

8. The accident was also caused by breach of statutory duty by the defenders. Said operation was one to which the provisions of the Construction (Working Places) Regulations 1966, as amended, applied, and it was the defenders' duty to comply therewith at the material time. Regulation 6(2) provides, *inter alia*, that " . . . every place at which any person at any time works shall, so far as is reasonably practicable, be made and kept safe for any person working there." Regulation 7 provides, *inter alia*, that " . . . where work cannot safely be done on or from the ground or from part of a building or other permanent structure, there shall be provided, placed and kept in position for use and properly maintained either scaffolds or where appropriate ladders or other means of support, all of which shall be sufficient and suitable for the purpose." Regulation 24(1) provides, *inter alia*, that "Every working platform, gangway and run from any part of which a person is liable to fall a distance of more than two metres shall be closely boarded, planked or plated." Regulation 27(1) provides, *inter alia*, that " . . . every gangway and run from any part of which a person is liable to fall a distance of more than two metres shall (a) . . . be at least 430 millimetres wide." Regulation 28(1) provides, *inter alia*, that "Every side of a working platform or working place, being a side thereof from which a person is liable

289

to fall a distance of more than two metres, shall . . . be provided with a suitable guard-rail or guard-rails of adequate strength to a height of between 910 millimetres and 1.15 metres above the platform or place . . . and with toe-boards or other barriers up to a sufficient height which shall in no case be less than 150 millimetres. Such guard-rails and toe-boards or other barriers shall be so placed as to prevent so far as possible the fall of persons . . . " Regulation 33 provides, in connection, *inter alia*, with any edge of any working platform, gangway or run which any person employed is liable to approach or be near, and from which any person is liable to fall more than two metres, that a guard-rail, or guard-rails, of adequate strength to a height of between 910 millimetres and 1.15 metres with toe-boards up to a sufficient height of not less than 150 millimetres shall be provided and so placed as to prevent as far as possible the fall of persons; and in addition that when work is done on or immediately above any open joisting through which a person is liable to fall a distance of more than two metres, such joisting shall be securely covered by boards or other temporary covering to the extent necessary to afford safe access to or foothold for the work, or other effective measures shall be taken to prevent persons from falling. In the fulfilment of each and all of said duties incumbent on them in terms of said statutory provisions the defenders failed and by their failure caused said accident. Had the defenders fulfilled the duties incumbent on them as they ought to have done, said accident would not have occurred.

9. As a result of the death of the deceased the pursuers and John Wood have each suffered loss, injury and damage. They suffered great grief at the sudden and tragic death of the deceased to whom they were closely attached. They have lost the society and guidance of the deceased to which they could have looked forward for many years to come. The first pursuer and John were wholly dependent on the deceased for support and the second pursuer also received support from him. At the date of his death the deceased was aged 42 and was in excellent health. He had been regularly employed as a steel erector and at the time of his death was earning about £250 net per week, of which the great majority went towards the support of the pursuers and John. Had he lived, the deceased would have received periodic wage increases throughout the remainder of his working life. In connection with the deceased's funeral the first pursuer as an individual incurred expenses totalling £487.92. In these circumstances the sums sued for are moderate estimates of the loss, injury and damage suffered by the pursuers and John respectively.

10. The defenders have been called upon to make reparation to the pursuers and John for the loss, injury and damage suffered by them but the defenders refuse or delay to do so. This action is accordingly necessary.

11. The persons named and designed in the warrant for intimation are each sisters of the deceased, and are the whole other relatives of the deceased, so far as is known to the pursuers, who have a title to sue in respect of his death in terms of the Damages (Scotland) Act 1976, as amended.

III.—PLEAS-IN-LAW

1. The pursuers and John having respectively suffered loss, injury and damage through fault for which the defenders are responsible as condescended on, are entitled to reparation from the defenders accordingly.

2. The sums respectively sued for being reasonable estimates of the said loss, injury and damage, decree therefor should be pronounced as concluded for.

IN RESPECT WHEREOF

ACTION FOR PAYMENT IN THE TERMS OF CONTRACT

COURT OF SESSION, SCOTLAND

I. – SUMMONS

in causa

OLD FASHIONED SHOES plc, 45 Leather Place, Perth,

PURSUERS

against

VENUS AND MARS LIFE ASSURANCE COMPANY plc, 32 Royal Square, Edinburgh   DEFENDERS

ELIZABETH II . . . .

This summons is warrant for arrestment and inhibition on the dependence of the action.

CONCLUSIONS

1. For payment by the defenders to the pursuers of the sum of THIRTY-FIVE THOUSAND THREE HUNDRED AND TWENTY-NINE

POUNDS STERLING (£35,329), with interest thereon at the rate of 15 *per centum per annum* from the date of citation until payment.

2. For the expenses of the action.

II.—CONDESCENDENCE

1. The pursuers are a Scottish company. The defenders are a company incorporated under the Companies Acts and having their registered office at 32 Royal Square, Edinburgh. They are domiciled in Scotland. This Court accordingly has jurisdiction.

2. The pursuers are tenants under a registered lease for a period of years expiring in 2112 of heritable subjects at 19, The Causeway, Stirling. The original lease was entered into between the pursuers as tenants and the Perth and Stirling Property Company Ltd. as landlords. By disposition in about late 1983 the said landlords disponed their interest in the subjects to the defenders, who took over their rights and obligations as landlords in the terms of the lease.

3. To the knowledge and with the approval of the landlords, the pursuers entered into sub-leases of various parts of the subjects, which constitute a building several storeys high in one of the main thoroughfares in Stirling. They sublet part of the building to Modern Sox plc and other parts to Old and New Stockings plc. The sub-leases were on terms, *mutatis mutandis*, similar to those obtaining in the principal lease.

4. On the night of August 13, 1987 there was a flood in said building. At 9.25 a.m. on August 14, Old and New Stockings notified the pursuers that their internal telephone exchange situated in the basement of the building was not functioning properly. On investigation, the lift shafts were found to be flooded and there was water throughout the basement and in part of the ground floor. The basement was under water to a depth of about one metre, and there was up to three metres of water in the lift shafts.

5. The flood was emanating from a calorifier in the boiler room in the basement of the building. There was a plug forming part of the draining system from the calorifier. The plug and sleeve of the plug had corroded. They were both made of ferrous material. The tank was of copper. It is inevitable when two different metals, such as copper and iron, are in contact, immersed in water, that galvanic corrosion will occur and that iron, which is more reactive than copper, will corrode fast. The speed of corrosion will be considerably increased when, as here, the amount of iron is very much less than the amount of copper in contact with the water. The materials of which the plug and sleeve were made were wholly unsuitable for their purpose. They should have been made from the same material, or as nearly as practicable the same material, as the tank.

6. In terms of clause Fifth (d) of the lease, it was provided, *inter alia*, as follows:

> "During the continuance of the tenancy the landlords shall replace the drains, drain pipes, water pipes, waste pipes . . . at their expense as and when required. In the event of defects in the aforementioned . . . affecting the interior of the building or the decorations the landlords shall without undue delay make good the . . . interior including the decorations at their own expense."

Clause Eighth (b) of the lease provides *inter alia* as follows:

> "The landlords shall insure and at all times during the currency of this lease keep insured all buildings, erections and fixtures of an immovable nature which are now or at any time during this lease may be erected or placed upon or affixed to the subjects let to their full replacement value . . . . . . and shall insure against loss or damage by . . . . . . bursting or overflowing of water tanks, apparatus and pipes."

7. In consequence of the flood, considerable damage was caused to the pursuers as tenants and to their sub-tenants, Modern Sox plc and Old and New Stockings plc. In terms of the sub-leases, the pursuers are under the same obligation to pay to the sub-tenants in respect of damage to the interior of the building as the defenders are to the pursuers. The damage sustained by Modern Sox was £4,297. The damage sustained by Old and New Stockings, which included the loss of part of their internal telephone exchange, was £8,191. The pursuers themselves had to pay £22,841 in respect of replacement of items damaged beyond repair in the flood. Said sums total £35,329, which is the principal sum sued for.

8. The defenders are bound, in terms of their obligations under the lease, to make payment of said sum. They have refused to do so. This action is accordingly necessary.

III.—PLEAS-IN-LAW

1. The defenders having contracted with the pursuers to be responsible for loss, injury and damage such as that condescended on, the pursuers are entitled to decree as concluded for.

2. The sum sued for being a proper assessment of the said loss, injury and damage, decree therefor should be pronounced as concluded for.

IN RESPECT WHEREOF

PLEADING PRACTICE IN SCOTLAND

REVISED VERSION

ACTION FOR DAMAGES FOR DEFAMATION

COURT OF SESSION, SCOTLAND

I. – SUMMONS

in causa

P Q, (address)

PURSUER

against

R S, (address)

DEFENDER

ELIZABETH II . . . .

This summons is warrant for arrestment and inhibition on the dependence of the action.

CONCLUSIONS

1. For payment by the defender to the pursuer of the sum of FIFTEEN THOUSAND POUNDS STERLING (£15,000), with interest thereon at the rate of fifteen *per centum per annum* from November 3, 1987, or at such rate from such date as to the Court shall seem proper, until payment.

2. For the expenses of the action.

II.—CONDESCENDENCE

1. The pursuer is an architect living and working in Aberdeen, and practising his profession principally in the Aberdeen area. The defender resides at (address). He has been resident in Scotland for more than three months immediately preceding the raising of this action. He is domiciled in Scotland. This Court accordingly has jurisdiction.

2. In about October 1987 the defender instructed Scottish Herald plc in writing to print a notice in the "Legal Notices" section of "The Scottish Herald" newspaper, being a newspaper which circulates throughout Scotland and, in particular, is widely read in the Aberdeen area. Said notice appeared in said section of all editions of said newspaper dated November 3, 1987. Said notice, the terms of which reflected accurately the defender's instructions, was in the following terms:

"P Q, ARCHITECT.—Will all creditors please submit claims immediately to Box Y 947, The Scottish Herald."

3. Some months before said date, the pursuer had carried out work and rendered professional services under contract to the defender. He had thereafter charged in accordance with the contract. The defender had not paid him. The pursuer had been required to take decree against him for the unpaid sum, with interest and expenses, which decree was pronounced at Edinburgh Sheriff Court on June 25, 1987. The defender did not pay any sum under the decree and the pursuer had to do diligence against him in August 1987. That produced nothing either, and the pursuer intimated that he was to raise an action of adjudication against the defender. It was at that stage that the defender instructed the appearance of said notice.

4. The defender's intention in so instructing was malicious, and was intended to damage the pursuer in his personal and professional reputation. It was intended to, and did, carry the imputation that the pursuer was bankrupt, or at least financially embarrassed, and that he was unable or unwilling to pay just debts. There was no substance in any such imputation. The notice was defamatory of the pursuer.

5. On account of the publication of said notice the pursuer has suffered in his personal feelings and in his personal and professional reputation. The statement contained in said notice has obtained wide currency throughout Scotland and, in particular, in the Aberdeen area. It came to the attention of a large number of the pursuer's friends, professional colleagues and clients. Said notice has caused the pursuer considerable embarrassment in his professional and social life. The pursuer's professional practice has suffered materially as a result of said notice. The sum sued for is reasonable reparation to the pursuer for the loss, injury and damage suffered by him as a result of the publication of said notice.

6. The defender has been called upon to make reparation to the pursuer for the said loss, injury and damage, but he refuses or delays to do so. This action is therefore necessary.

III.—PLEAS-IN-LAW

1. The defender having defamed the pursuer as condescended on, the pursuer is entitled to reparation from him therefor.

2. The sum sued for being reasonable reparation to the pursuer for the loss, injury and damage sustained by him in consequence of said defamation, decree should be pronounced in terms of the conclusions of the Summons.

IN RESPECT WHEREOF

PLEADING PRACTICE IN SCOTLAND

ACTION FOR DAMAGES

COURT OF SESSION, SCOTLAND

OPEN RECORD

I. – SUMMONS

T U, (insert address)	PURSUER
against	
V X, (insert address)	DEFENDER

ELIZABETH II [*see p. 274*]

This summons is warrant for arrestment and inhibition on the dependence of the action.

CONCLUSIONS

1. For payment by the defender to the pursuer of the sum of FIFTEEN THOUSAND POUNDS STERLING (£15,000), with interest thereon at the rate of fifteen *per centum per annum* from the date of citation until payment.

2. For the expenses of the action.

II.—CONDESCENDENCE FOR PURSUER
AND
ANSWERS THERETO FOR DEFENDER

Cond. 1.   The pursuer resides at——. She is in her late sixties. The defender resides at——. He has been resident in Scotland for more than three months immediately preceding the raising of this action. He is domiciled in Scotland. This Court accordingly has jurisdiction.

Ans. 1.   The averments relating to the defender are admitted. *Quoad ultra* not known and not admitted.

Cond. 2.   On or about December 18, 1987, shortly after 10 a.m., the pursuer intended to cross from the south side to the north side of the High Street in Oldburgh, at about the point where the High Street is intersected by Sea Street. She began to cross the road at a time at which it was safe to cross, the road being clear on both sides. The defender was driving at an excessive speed in an easterly direction. He accelerated away from the traffic lights at said junction and failed to notice the pursuer as she crossed. He knocked her down, causing her severe injuries.

Ans. 2. Admitted that shortly after 10 a.m. on December 18, 1987 the defender was driving in an easterly direction along the High Street in Oldburgh. Admitted that the pursuer began to cross said road, that she was knocked down by the defender's car and that she sustained certain injuries the nature and extent of which are not known and not admitted. *Quoad ultra* denied except insofar as coinciding herewith. Explained and averred that the defender drove slowly away from said traffic lights. The pursuer suddenly stepped onto said road without having any regard for traffic on the road. The defender braked instantly but was unable to avoid knocking her down.

Cond. 3. Said accident was caused by fault of the defender. It was his duty to take reasonable care for the safety of other road users, including pedestrians lawfully on the road, and not to expose them unnecessarily to risk of injury. It was his duty to take reasonable care to drive at a moderate speed, to keep a proper look out, to give warning of his approach to anyone crossing in front of him, and to keep his vehicle under proper control. It was his duty to take reasonable care to avoid colliding with pedestrians. In the fulfilment of each and all of said duties incumbent on him he failed and by his failure caused said accident. Had he fulfilled the duties incumbent on him as he ought to have done, said accident would not have occurred.

Ans. 3. Admitted that certain duties were incumbent upon the defender, under explanation that he fulfilled all of them. *Quoad ultra* denied except insofar as coinciding herewith. Explained and averred that the accident was caused or materially contributed to by fault on the part of the pursuer. It was her duty to take reasonable care for her own safety. It was her duty to keep a proper look-out and not to begin to cross the road until it was safe to cross. She saw or ought to have seen the defender's vehicle. It was her duty not to move into its path. In the fulfilment of each and all of said duties incumbent on her she failed and by her failure caused or materially contributed to said accident.

Cond. 4. The pursuer sustained severe injuries in consequence of said accident. She was rendered unconscious. She had multiple bruising and abrasions of the hands, face, legs and arms. Her left acetabulum and left interior pubic ramus were fractured. She was admitted to Oldburgh Royal Infirmary where traction was applied. She developed venous thrombosis and required anti-coagulants. She was in traction for about two months and was not released from hospital until March 1988. Since then she has been restricted in every aspect of her life. Prior to the accident she was an extremely active woman, but now she is virtually housebound. She cannot cope with her own housework. She has considerable discomfort when walking and requires the assistance of a stick. She has difficulty in bending down or remaining standing for any length of time.

At night she is kept awake by pain. Her nerves have been materially affected and she has nightmares about the accident. In these circumstances the sum sued for is a reasonable estimate of the pursuer's loss, injury and damage.

Ans. 4.   The nature, extent and consequences of any loss, injury and damage suffered by the pursuer are not known and not admitted. *Quoad ultra* denied. The sum sued for is excessive.

III.—PLEAS-IN-LAW FOR PURSUER

1. The pursuer having sustained loss, injury and damage through fault of the defender as condescended on, is entitled to reparation from him therefor.

2. The sum sued for being a reasonable estimate of the pursuer's said loss, injury and damage, decree therefor should be pronounced as concluded for.

IN RESPECT WHEREOF

IV.—PLEAS-IN-LAW FOR DEFENDER

1. The pursuer's averments being irrelevant *et separatim* lacking in specification, the action should be dismissed.

2. The pursuer's averments insofar as material being unfounded in fact, the defender should be assoilzied.

3. The pursuer not having suffered loss, injury and damage through fault of the defender, he should be assoilzied.

4. Any such accident as is averred having been caused solely by fault of the pursuer, the defender should be assoilzied.

5. *Separatim, esto* any such accident as is averred was caused to any extent by fault of the defender, it having been caused also in part by fault of the pursuer, any damages awarded should be reduced in terms of the Law Reform (Contributory Negligence) Act 1945.

6. In any event, the sum sued for being excessive, decree therefor should not be pronounced as concluded for.

IN RESPECT WHEREOF

ACTION FOR PAYMENT

COURT OF SESSION, SCOTLAND

OPEN RECORD

I. – SUMMONS

P Q, (insert address)	**PURSUER**

against

R S, (insert address)	**DEFENDER**

ELIZABETH II [*see p. 274*]

This summons is warrant for arrestment and inhibition on the dependence of the action.

CONCLUSIONS

1. For payment by the defender to the pursuer of the sum of SEVEN-TEEN THOUSAND THREE HUNDRED POUNDS STERLING (£17,300) with interest thereon at the rate of fifteen *per centum per annum* from February 17, 1988 until payment.

2. For the expenses of the action.

II.—CONDESCENDENCE FOR PURSUER

AND

ANSWERS THERETO FOR DEFENDER

Cond. 1.   The pursuer resides at——. The defender resides at——. He has been resident in Scotland for more than three months immediately preceding the raising of this action. He is domiciled in Scotland. This Court accordingly has jurisdiction.

Ans. 1.   The averments relating to the defender are admitted. The averment relating to the pursuer is not known and not admitted.

Cond. 2.   On February 17, 1988 the pursuer lent the defender the sum of seventeen thousand three hundred pounds. It was agreed by the parties that the sum would be repaid on or before February 17, 1989 and that interest at the rate of fifteen *per centum per annum* would run on the loan from February 17, 1988 until repayment.

Ans. 2.   Admitted that the pursuer lent the defender seventeen thousand three hundred pounds on February 17, 1988. *Quoad ultra* denied except

299

PLEADING PRACTICE IN SCOTLAND

insofar as coinciding herewith. Explained and averred that it was agreed by the parties that said sum would be repaid by December 31, 1990.

Cond. 3.   The pursuer has repeatedly called on the defender to make repayment in terms of said agreement, but he has failed to do so. This action is therefore necessary.

Ans. 3.   Denied that this action is necessary.

III.—PLEA-IN-LAW FOR PURSUER

The sum sued for being due and resting owing to the pursuer as condescended upon, decree therefor should be granted as concluded for.

IN RESPECT WHEREOF

IV.—PLEAS-IN-LAW FOR DEFENDER

1. The pursuer's averments being irrelevant *et separatim* lacking in specification, the action should be dismissed.

2. The pursuer's averments insofar as material being unfounded in fact, the defender should be assoilzied.

3. The sum sued for not being due and resting owing to the pursuer, decree therefor should not be granted as concluded for.

IN RESPECT WHEREOF

ACTION FOR DAMAGES

COURT OF SESSION, SCOTLAND

OPEN RECORD

I. – SUMMONS

A B, (insert address)		**PURSUER**
	against	
C D Co., (insert address)		**DEFENDER**

ELIZABETH II [*see p. 274*]

This summons is warrant for arrestment and inhibition on the dependence of the action.

CONCLUSIONS

1. For payment by the defenders to the pursuers of the sum of TWENTY-FIVE THOUSAND POUNDS STERLING (£25,000), with interest thereon at the rate of fifteen *per centum per annum* from April 3, 1988, or at such rate from such date as to the Court shall seem proper, until payment.

2. For the expenses of the action.

II.—CONDESCENDENCE FOR PURSUER

AND

ANSWERS THERETO FOR DEFENDERS

Cond. 1.   The pursuer is in his mid-twenties. He resides at——. The defenders are a company incorporated under the Companies Acts and having their registered office at——, Edinburgh. They are domiciled in Scotland.

Ans. 1.   The averments relating to the defenders are admitted. *Quoad ultra* not known and not admitted.

Cond. 2.   On about April 3, 1988 the pursuer was working in the course of his employment with the defenders as a letter press printer at their factory in——. It was his job, *inter alia*, to feed rolls of paper between two cylinders which formed part of a letter press printing machine. The loose end had to be fed between the cylinders by hand. This had to be done approximately every half hour. In the early evening of said date the paper broke in the course of its passage through the machine.

Ans. 2.   Admitted that on about April 3, 1988 the pursuer was working in the course of his employment with the defenders as a letter press printer at their factory in——. Admitted that it was his job to feed rolls of paper between two cylinders which formed part of a letter press printing machine. Admitted that approximately every half hour the loose end had to be fed between the cylinders by hand. Not known and not admitted that in the early evening of said date the paper broke in the course of its passage through said machine. *Quoad ultra* denied except insofar as coinciding herewith.

Cond. 3.   In order to feed the broken end of the paper between the cylinders, the pursuer had to get into the machine and crouch in a space about 1.5 metres high and 1 metre in width. It was dark. The only light in the space came from the small gap through which the pursuer had entered the space. There was a lamp inside the space but it had not been working for a considerable time. There was a third cylinder which blocked the pursuer's view of the gap through which he had to feed the paper. The surface of the mid-portion of each of the said two cylinders was smooth and dry. The surface of each of said two cylinders on either side of the mid-portion was sticky and tacky. There was no guard to prevent anything thicker than paper from entering the said gap. There were no metal guiding fingers to guide the paper between the appropriate parts of said two cylinders. There was a stop button inside the machine but it was gummed up and not working. It had been inoperative for a long time. The "feeding" button on the machine did not work properly. If it was pressed down for a short time, the said cylinders would turn a few degrees. If it was held down for a slightly longer time, the cylinders would turn considerably more.

Ans. 3.   Admitted that the pursuer was required to enter the machine in order to feed broken parts of the paper between the cylinders. *Quoad ultra* denied except insofar as coinciding herewith.

Cond. 4.   It was necessary for the paper to be fed through the machine between the mid-portion of each of said two cylinders. If it was fed through near the sides, it would stick and tear. To ensure that the paper would enter the gap at the appropriate point, it was necessary to hold the paper directly below the centre of the cylinders. The pursuer did so, and then shouted to a fellow employee to press a particular button to activate the machine. The fellow employee did so and the cylinders turned a large amount. They drew the fingers of the pursuer's right hand into the gap between the cylinders. Before the machine could be stopped the fingers were badly crushed.

Ans. 4.   Admitted that it was necessary for the paper to be fed between the mid-portion of each of said two cylinders. Admitted that otherwise it would stick and tear. Admitted that it was necessary to hold the paper directly below the centre of the cylinders. Not known and not admitted that the pursuer so held the paper and then shouted to a fellow employee. Not known and not admitted that the cylinders turned a large amount and that the fingers of the pursuer's right hand were drawn into the machine and badly crushed. *Quoad ultra* denied except insofar as coinciding herewith.

Cond. 5.   Said accident was caused by the fault of the defenders. It was their duty to take reasonable care for the safety of their employees, such as the pursuer, and not to expose them unnecessarily to risk of injury. It was their duty to take reasonable care to provide and maintain safe plant and equipment for their employees. It was their duty to take reasonable care to provide and maintain adequate and efficient guards against obvious dangers, such as the gap in which the pursuer's fingers were caught and crushed. It was their duty to take reasonable care to provide and maintain a lamp inside the space. It was their duty to take reasonable care to provide and maintain a stop button so as to enable employees such as the pursuer to stop the machine in any emergency. It was their duty to take reasonable care to provide and maintain metal guiding fingers so that the paper could be inserted between the appropriate parts of said cylinders without it being necessary for the hands of an employee such as the pursuer to be in close proximity to said cylinders. It was their duty to take reasonable care to ensure that the operation of the "feeding" button was consistent and that, when it was pressed, said cylinders turned a short amount which did not allow the hands of the person feeding in the paper to be caught and crushed. It was their duty to take reasonable care to devise, institute and maintain a system which prevented the risk of an operator's hands being drawn into said gap. This could have been done, for instance, by the institution of a system whereby the end of a roll of paper was reinforced by tape before being fed into the machine, or by the institution of a system whereby tape was provided to fix to broken ends. In the fulfilment of each and all of said duties incumbent on them the defenders failed and by their failure caused said accident. Had they fulfilled the duties incumbent on them as they ought to have done, the accident would not have occurred.

Ans. 5. Admitted that certain duties were incumbent upon the defenders, under explanation that they fulfilled all such duties. *Quoad ultra* denied except insofar as coinciding herewith.

Cond. 6. The accident was also caused by breach of statutory duty by the defenders. Said operation was one to which the provisions of the Factories Act 1961 applied, and it was the defenders' duty to comply therewith at the material time. Section 14(1) states that: "Every dangerous part of any machinery . . . shall be securely fenced unless it is in such a position or of such construction as to be as safe to every person employed or working on the premises as it would be if securely fenced." Section 16 thereof provides that the fencing provided in terms of section 14 must be kept in position throughout the period for which the machine is in motion or in use. In the fulfilment of each and all of the said duties incumbent upon them in terms of said statutory provisions, the defenders failed and by their failure caused said accident. The pursuer's fingers were caught in a dangerous part of the machinery which was not securely fenced. Had the defenders fulfilled the duties incumbent on them, as they ought to have done, the accident would not have occurred.

Ans. 6. Said statutory provisions are referred to for their terms under explanation that the defenders fulfilled all duties imposed on them. *Quoad ultra* denied except insofar as coinciding herewith.

Cond. 7. In consequence of the accident the pursuer has sustained severe loss, injury and damage. Immediately after the accident occurred he was taken to——Royal Infirmary and detained. He had two operations. His finger tips were cleansed and stitched. He required out-patient treatment for a considerable period thereafter. The grip in his right hand is reduced. His right hand finger tips are lacking in sensation and sensitivity. They are scarred. His whole way of life has been adversely affected by the accident. He has difficulty in picking up or handling small or thin objects. His finger tips are hypersensitive to cold. His leisure pursuits have been curtailed. He is no longer able to indulge in his former pastimes of painting, drawing and claymodelling. He was off work for nine weeks after the accident. He is unable to produce and sell works of art as he formerly did. But for the accident he would have sold a number of works. He has accordingly lost wages and other income. He has received State Benefits, which will be vouched. The sum sued for represents a moderate estimate of the pursuer's loss, injury and damage.

Ans. 7. The consequences of any accident which has occurred to the pursuer are not known and not admitted. *Quoad ultra* denied except insofar as coinciding herewith. In any event the sum sought is excessive.

Cond. 8. The defenders have been called on to make reparation to the pursuer in respect of his said loss, injury and damage, but have failed to do so, thereby rendering the present action necessary.

Ans. 8. Denied that this action is necessary.

III.—PLEAS-IN-LAW FOR PURSUER

1. The pursuer having sustained loss, injury and damage through fault of the defenders as condescended on, is entitled to reparation from them therefor.

2. The sum sued for being a reasonable estimate of the pursuer's said loss, injury and damage, decree therefor should be pronounced as concluded for.

IN RESPECT WHEREOF

IV.—PLEAS-IN-LAW FOR DEFENDERS

1. The pursuer's averments being irrelevant *et separatim* lacking in specification, the action should be dismissed.

2. The pursuer's averments insofar as material being unfounded in fact, the defenders should be assoilzied.

3. The pursuer not having sustained loss, injury and damage through the fault of the defenders, the defenders should be assoilzied.

4. Any such accident as is averred having been caused solely by the fault of the pursuer, the defenders should be assoilzied.

5. *Separatim, esto* any such accident as is averred was caused to any extent by fault of the defenders, it having been caused also in part by fault of the pursuer any damages awarded should be reduced in terms of the Law Reform (Contributory Negligence) Act 1945.

6. In any event, the sum sued for being excessive, decree therefor should not be pronounced as concluded for.

IN RESPECT WHEREOF

ACTION FOR DAMAGES

COURT OF SESSION, SCOTLAND

CLOSED RECORD

I. – SUMMONS

P Q, (insert address)   PURSUER

against

R S, (insert address)   DEFENDER

ELIZABETH II [*see p. 274*]

This summons is warrant for arrestment and inhibition on the dependence of the action.

CONCLUSIONS

1. For payment by the defender to the pursuer of the sum of THREE THOUSAND FIVE HUNDRED POUNDS STERLING (£3,500), with interest thereon at the rate of fifteen *per centum per annum* from April 4, 1988, or at such rate from such date as to the Court shall seem proper, until payment.

2. For the expenses of the action.

II.—CONDESCENDENCE FOR PURSUER
AND
ANSWERS THERETO FOR DEFENDER

Cond. 1.   The pursuer resides at——. The defender resides at——. The pursuer has been resident in Scotland for more than three months immediately preceding the raising of this action. The defender is domiciled in Scotland. This Court accordingly has jurisdiction.

Ans. 1.   The averments relating to the defender are admitted. *Quoad ultra* not known and not admitted.

Cond. 2.   The defender owns and occupies A——Farm in——. A private road crosses the land of said farm and leads to B——Farm, owned and occupied by——. The defender occupies said private road to the extent that it crosses his land. He uses it as a means of access to his own fields.

Ans. 2.   Admitted that the defender owns and occupies A——Farm and that a private road leading to B——Farm crosses his land. Admitted that the defender uses said private road as a means of access to his own fields. *Quoad ultra* denied except insofar as coinciding herewith.

Cond. 3.   On about April 4, 1988 the pursuer had cause to visit said B——Farm. He was required to use said private road in order to reach it. As he drove his motor car along said road he encountered a cattle grid. No signs indicated its presence. As the pursuer was crossing the grid in his car one of the metal bars of the grid gave way. The front of the car fell into the gap which resulted from the bar giving way. This caused the loss and damage hereinafter condescended upon. The defender's averments in answer are denied except insofar as coinciding herewith. Explained and averred that the pursuer did not use said road on a regular basis. He had used it on only two occasions between the beginning of 1983 and the date of said accident. On each of said two occasions the road was covered with snow and he was in a vehicle with greater wheel clearance.

Ans. 3.   Admitted that it was necessary to use said private road to reach B——Farm. Admitted that there was a cattle grid on said road. Not known and not admitted that the pursuer drove along said road on April 4, 1988. The nature and consequences of any accident on said date on said road involving the pursuer's car are not known and not admitted. *Quoad ultra* denied except insofar as coinciding herewith. Explained and averred that prior to April 4, 1988 the pursuer had regularly used said road. He was well aware of the existence of said cattle grid. In any event the grid was obvious to the drivers of approaching vehicles. *Esto* the pursuer's car came into contact with the grid on said date, this was the result of the pursuer failing to drive slowly and carefully across said grid.

Cond. 4.   The metal bars of the grid rested upon concrete blocks. Certain of said blocks had substantially disintegrated prior to April 4, 1988, rendering said grid unsafe.

Ans. 4.   Admitted that the metal bars of the grid rested upon concrete blocks. *Quoad ultra* denied except insofar as coinciding herewith.

Cond. 5.   Said accident was caused by the fault of the defender. As occupier of the land on which the private road and cattle grid were situated, it was his duty to take reasonable care to ensure that persons entering the land would not suffer loss and damage by reason of the state of the premises or anything done or omitted to be done on them. Reference is made to section 2(1) of the Occupier's Liability (Scotland) Act 1960. It was the defender's duty to take reasonable care to maintain the grid in a safe condition. He knew or ought to have known that if said concrete blocks were allowed to deteriorate there was a risk that vehicles crossing the grid would be damaged. It was his duty to take reasonable care to maintain said blocks and prevent them deteriorating. It was his duty to take reasonable care to erect and maintain signs warning drivers of the existence of the grid. In the fulfilment of each and all of said duties incumbent upon him the defender failed and by his failure caused said accident. Had he fulfilled the duties incumbent upon him as he ought to have done said accident would not have occurred. With reference to the defender's averments in answer, admitted that certain duties were incumbent upon the pursuer under explanation that he fulfilled all such duties. *Quoad ultra* denied except insofar as coinciding herewith. Explained and averred that the pursuer had not been aware of the existence of the grid. In any event he had been driving along said road at a reasonable speed and with due care and attention.

Ans. 5.   Admitted that certain duties were incumbent upon the defender under explanation that he fulfilled all such duties. *Quoad ultra* denied except insofar as coinciding herewith. Explained and averred that *esto* the pursuer's car came into contact with the grid on said date, this was caused or materially contributed to by fault on the part of the pursuer. It was his duty to take reasonable care for the safety of his car. It was his duty to take reasonable care not to drive at an excessive speed. It was his duty to take reasonable care to reduce the speed of his car on approaching the grid. In the fulfilment of each and all of said duties the pursuer failed and by his failure caused said accident. Had he fulfilled said duties incumbent on him as he ought to have done, the accident would not have occurred.

Cond. 6.   In consequence of the accident the pursuer suffered loss and damage. The oil sump was damaged and much oil escaped. The crank shaft was damaged beyond repair. The pursuer incurred the cost of repairing the oil sump and replacing the crank shaft. It took three months for his garage to obtain a new crank shaft and new parts for the oil sump. He bought a second-hand car to use during this period. He was put to considerable inconvenience by the accident. The sum sued for represents a reasonable estimate of his loss, injury and damage.

Ans. 6.   The nature, extent and consequences of any loss suffered by the pursuer are not known and not admitted. *Quoad ultra* denied except insofar as coinciding herewith. In any event the sum sued for is grossly excessive.

Cond. 7.   The defender has been called upon to make reparation to the pursuer in respect of his said loss, injury and damage, but has failed to do so. This action is therefore necessary.

Ans. 7.   Denied that this action is necessary.

III.—PLEAS-IN-LAW FOR PURSUER

1. The pursuer having sustained loss, injury and damage through fault of the defender as condescended on, is entitled to reparation from him therefor.

2. The sum sued for being a reasonable estimate of the pursuer's said loss, injury and damage, decree therefor should be pronounced as concluded for.

IN RESPECT WHEREOF

IV.—PLEAS-IN-LAW FOR DEFENDER

1. The pursuer's averments being irrelevant *et separatim* lacking in specification, the action should be dismissed.

2. The pursuer's averments insofar as material being unfounded in fact, the defender should be assoilzied.

3. The pursuer not having sustained loss, injury and damage through the fault of the defender, the defender should be assoilzied.

4. Any such accident as is averred having been caused solely by the fault of the pursuer, the defender should be assoilzied.

5. *Separatim, esto* any such accident as is averred was caused to any extent by fault of the defender, it having been caused also in part by fault of the pursuer, any damages awarded should be reduced in terms of the Law Reform (Contributory Negligence) Act 1945.

6. In any event, the sum sued for being excessive, decree therefor should not be pronounced as concluded for.

IN RESPECT WHEREOF

Miscellaneous Items of Process in Ordinary Action

COURT OF SESSION, SCOTLAND

MINUTE OF AMENDMENT
for the Defender

in causa

[instance]

(*name*) for the Defender craved and hereby craves leave of the Court to allow the Closed Record to be opened up and amended as follows:

1. In Answer 3, by deleting "He" and substituting: "There was a plank across it. In any event, as above set forth, he"; and

2. In Answer 5, after "excessive," by adding: "The pursuer received State Benefits in respect of said alleged accident. He is called on to specify and vouch all such payments."

IN RESPECT WHEREOF

COURT OF SESSION, SCOTLAND

SPECIFICATION OF DOCUMENTS

for the recovery of which a Commission and Dilligence is sought by the PURSUER

in causa

[instance]

1. All reports, memoranda and other written communications made to the defenders or anyone on their behalf at or about the time of the accident to the pursuer by any employee of the defenders present at the time of the accident and relative to the matters mentioned on record.

2. The wages books, cash books, wages sheets and other books, record and memoranda kept by or for the defenders for the period from January 1, 1986 to July 30, 1987, in order that excerpts may be taken therefrom

at the sight of the Commissioner of all entries therein showing or tending to show the wages earned by and the sums paid to the pursuer in consequence of his employment with them during the said period, and the extent to which basic and overtime and bonus rates of pay of H.G.V. drivers in the employment of the defenders increased during the said period, and the date or dates on which any such increases came into effect.

3. All books of the Royal Infirmary, Edinburgh, in order that excerpts may be taken therefrom at the sight of the Commissioner of all entries showing or tending to show the nature and extent of the injuries from which the pursuer was suffering when he was admitted thereto on or after June 25, 1986 and all records, notes and reports, and all X-ray and other photographs, showing or tending to how his condition and treatment whilst detained therein or attending thereat then and thereafter, and his certificate of discharge, if any.

4. Failing principals, drafts, copies or duplicates of the above or any of them.

COURT OF SESSION, SCOTLAND

MINUTE OF TENDER

in causa

[instance]

(*name*) for the defenders stated and hereby states to the Court that without admitting liability and under reservation of their whole rights and pleas the defenders tendered and hereby tender to the pursuer the sum of NINE THOUSAND SIX HUNDRED POUNDS STERLING (£9,600), together with the expenses of process to the date hereof, in full of the whole Conclusions of the Summons.

IN RESPECT WHEREOF

MISCELLANEOUS ITEMS OF PROCESS IN ORDINARY ACTION

COURT OF SESSION, SCOTLAND

MINUTE OF ACCEPTANCE OF TENDER

in causa

[instance]

(*name*) for the pursuer stated and hereby states to the Court that the pursuer accepted and hereby accepts the offer contained in the Defender's Minute of Tender (No. 15 of Process) in full of the Conclusions of the Summons.

IN RESPECT WHEREOF

COURT OF SESSION, SCOTLAND

JOINT MINUTE

in causa

[instance]

(*name*) for the pursuer and

(*name*) for the defender concurred and hereby concur in stating to the Court that parties are agreed and hereby agree that the Proof set down for May 10, 1989 and following days should be restricted to questions of liability, reserving all question of damages for subsequent determination in the event of the defender being held to be liable to make reparation to the pursuer.

IN RESPECT WHEREOF

COURT OF SESSION, SCOTLAND

JOINT MINUTE

in causa

[instance]

(*name*) for the pursuer and

(*name*) for the defender concurred and hereby concur in stating to the Court that this action has been settled extra-judicially: THEY THEREFORE craved and hereby crave the Court to find no expenses due to or by either party and *quoad ultra* to assoilzie the defender from the Conclusions of the Summons.

IN RESPECT WHEREOF

COURT OF SESSION, SCOTLAND

MINUTE OF WITHDRAWAL
OF DEFENCES

in causa

[instance]

(*name*) for the defender stated and hereby states to the Court that the defender no longer insists in her defence to this action, and hereby withdraws her defences thereto.

IN RESPECT WHEREOF

COURT OF SESSION, SCOTLAND

MINUTE OF ABANDONMENT

in causa

[instance]

(*name*) for the pursuer stated and hereby states to the Court that the pursuer no longer insists in her action and hereby abandons it at Common Law.

IN RESPECT WHEREOF

The Scottish Courts—Bibliography

On jurisdiction:

A. E. Anton, *Civil Jurisdiction in Scotland* (1984);
A. E. Anton and P. R. Beaumont, *Civil Jurisdiction in Scotland: Supplement* (1987);
R. Black, *Civil Jurisdiction: The New Rule* (1983);
G. Duncan and D. O. Dykes, *The Principles of Civil Jurisdiction* (1911).

Including sections on jurisdiction and competency:

A. E. Anton, *Private International Law* (1967), chapter 5;
E. M. Clive, *The Law of Husband and Wife in Scotland* (2nd ed., 1982) pp. 159–162, 216–222 and 640–64;
G. Maher, *A Textbook of Diligence* (1980); updating supplement (1984);
D. M. Walker, *Civil Remedies* (1974);
D. M. Walker, *The Scottish Legal System* (5th ed., 1981);
D. M. Walker, *Principles of Scottish Private Law* (4th ed., 1988) Vol. 1, chapters 1.5 and 2.2.

On the competency of, and procedure in, the Court of Session:

G. C. Emslie (Lord Emslie) and T. Walsh, *The Court of Session*, in: *The Laws of Scotland: Stair Memorial Encyclopaedia* (1988) Vol. 6;
J. A. Maclaren, *Court of Session Practice* (1916);
D. Maxwell, *The Practice of the Court of Session* (1980);
W. W. McBryde and N. J. Dowie, *Petition Procedure in the Court of Session* (2nd ed., 1988);
J. St. Clair and N. F. Davidson, *Judicial Review in Scotland* (1986);
G. R. Thomson and J. T. Middleton, *Manual of Court of Session Procedure* (1937).

On the competency of, and procedure in, the sheriff courts:

W. J. Dobie, *Law and Practice in the Sheriff Court* (1948);
I. D. MacPhail, *Sheriff Court Practice* (1988);
D. B. Smith, *The Sheriff Court*, in: *The Laws of Scotland: Stair Memorial Encyclopaedia* (1988) Vol. 6.

On written pleading:

R. Black, *An Introduction to Written Pleading* (1982);
J. M. Lees, *Handbook of Pleading* (2nd ed., 1920);
I. D. MacPhail, *supra*, chapter 9.

Style books:

S. A. Bennett, *Style Writs for the Sheriff Court Ordinary Cause* (1989);
W. J. Dobie, *Styles for Use in the Sheriff Courts in Scotland* (1951).

Pleadings in West Germany
Dr. Volker Triebel Rechtsanwalt, OLG, Barrister (Inner Temple)

Organisation of Civil Courts

Introduction   The latest census in the Federal Republic of Germany (West Germany) shows that 61.8 million people live in West Germany, among them an increasing number of foreigners. This is about the same population as in the United Kingdom. One would think that the same number of people engage in a similar volume of civil and commercial litigation and require a similar number of courts and judges to administer justice. However, statistics show that there are by far more cases, courts and judges in West Germany than in the U.K.

Some three million new actions in civil and commercial matters are filed before the lower courts (*Amtsgerichte*) each year (excluding family and non-litigious matters). All other cases are assigned to the regional high courts (*Landgerichte*), which handle more than 360,000 actions in civil and commercial matters annually spread across 1,200 civil divisions before some 1,600 judges. There are some 613 *Amtsgericthe* and 98 *Landgericthe*.

Appeals from the *Amtsgericht* in civil and commercial cases are heard by the *Landgericht*; appeals from first instance decisions of the *Landgericht* are heard by the regional courts of appeal (*Oberlandesgerichte*) before which some 94,000 appeals are filed each year (that is about 26 per cent. of the cases in the regional high courts of first instance).

Separate courts hear cases concerning labour disputes, social security, fiscal and administrative matters.

The reason for the multitude of civil and commercial cases in West Germany may be that the Germans are more litigious than their European neighbours. Certainly, the German costs system and the role of the judiciary add to the large number of cases. Most cases, however, are very

315

small and would probably not be brought in an English court of justice. If one considers the value of the claims, more than half of the cases before the *Landgerichte* concern the value of DM 25,000.00 or less. Of the 360,000 new cases in the *Landgerichte* there are only about 900 where the amount in dispute exceeds DM 1 million. Cases often are not that well prepared, and there are many actions started prematurely which would not be commenced in England, where they are conducted by the barristers and not the judges.

In West Germany there is a complete decentralisation of administration of justice. West Germany is a federation comprising 11 states (including the cities of Berlin, Bremen and Hamburg). All *Landgerichte* and *Oberlandesgerichte* are state courts. Only the Federal Supreme Court (*Bundesgerichtshof*) is a federal court. In many *Landgerichte* there is a small-town atmosphere. Judges and lawyers know each other. The presence of the judiciary varies in the different states. North Rhine Westphalia, the state with the highest population; some 17 million; and with Düsseldorf as its capital, has about a third of the courts, judges and also new cases.

Amtsgericht   The *Amtsgericht* is the lower tier of the ordinary courts. Its competence in civil matters is, in general, restricted to cases where the amount in dispute does not exceed DM 5,000. It is also competent irrespective of the value at stake for certain categories of case, such as matrimonial, maintenance and custody matters and disputes between landlord and tenant. When sitting as a civil court, the decision of the *Amtsgericht* is given by a single professional judge. The *Amtsgericht* also exercises criminal jurisdiction and in a non-contentious capacity also hears cases relating to the local commercial and land registers.

Landgericht   This is the second higher tier of ordinary civil courts and has competence over all civil cases which do not fall within the jurisdiction of the *Amtsgericht*. Many *Landgerichte* have both civil and commercial divisions. Whilst procedure in both divisions is the same, cases in the commercial division tend to be dealt with rather more expeditiously than in the civil division.

Three professional judges sit in the civil division (*Zivilkammer*) exercising jurisdiction over all matters which are not assigned to the commercial divisions. One professional judge sits in the commercial division (*Kammer für Handelssachen*) assisted by two lay judges (*Handelsrichter*) who are appointed from the business community upon the recommendation of the local chamber of commerce. Their term of office is for three years which may be extended upon reappointment.

Disputes in which both parties are merchants (*Kaufleute*) and the transaction itself can be classed as commercial, fall under commercial law. Hence, all limited companies, whether German or foreign, are deemed to be *Kaufleute*. Private individuals will only fall within this definition if they are engaged in a commercial activity and are registered accordingly in the local division if only one of the litigants is a *Kaufmann*.

Oberlandesgericht   Nineteen *Oberlandesgerichte* in West Germany exercise appellate jurisdiction over first instance decisions of the *Landgericht* and, in family law cases, of the *Amtsgericht*. It decides both on questions of law and of fact. A panel of three professional judges hears appeals on points of fact and law. Where an action results from a commercial transaction between merchants in the technical sense of the German Commercial Code, either party may refer the case to a commercial division. There are nearly 60,000 new cases filed with or referred to the Commercial Divisions each year. This large number is due to the high reputation which the Commercial Divisions enjoy amongst German businessmen.

In all three instances and particularly in the appellate courts there are a number of other very specialised divisions, *e.g.* divisions dealing solely with intellectual property, know-how, inventions and the complicated field of unfair competition. The German law of unfair competition encompasses the vast case law surrounding the Unfair Competition Act of 1909 and which goes by far beyond the English torts of passing off, libel and slander of goods. Other specialised divisions which may be found within an *Oberlandesgericht* relate to building contracts, the law surrounding brokers and estate agents, freight forwarders and carriers as well as anti-trust matters.

Bundesgerichtshof   The *Bundesgerichtshof*, which sits in Karlsruhe, is the supreme court in civil matters. It is the successor of the old *Reichsgericht* in Leipzig. Appeal against judgments of the *Oberlandesgerichte* may only be based upon error of law. Generally speaking, an appeal to the *Bundesgerichtshof* will only lie if the value at stake is more than DM 40,000, unless the *Oberlandesgericht* has given leave to appeal (where the legal issue is of fundamental importance or there is a deviation from previous judgments of the *Bundesgerichtshof*) but even then appeals on law may be rejected without any reason. Appeals against approximately one quarter of the judgments of the *Oberlandesgerichte* are made to the *Bundesgerichtshof* and are heard by a panel of five learned judges.

The Judiciary   Becoming a judge is a career and not, as in the U.K. a reward for a long and successful practice at the Bar. There are some 1,700 judges in the lower courts, some 1,600 in the *Landgerichte* and some 910 in the *Oberlandesgerichte* and some 70 judges in the *Bundesgerichtshof*.

The judges of the *Amtsgericht, Landgericht* and *Oberlandesgericht* are appointed by the respective *Land* (federal state). In the course of his professional career a judge may sit first as the junior judge of three in a *Landgericht*, and then successively as the single judge in an *Amtsgericht*, the presiding judge of a *Landgericht*, and finally as a member of an *Oberlandesgericht*. Federal judges are elected by the federal parliament and appointed to office by the government. Judges serve an initial probationary period of about three years. However, once they are permanently appointed, a judge can only be removed from office on certain statutory grounds.

Whilst other divisions of the *Oberlandesgericht* consist of one presiding and two learned judges (unless the matter is referred to a single judge alone: *Einzelrichter*), the Commercial Divisions are composed of a professional presiding judge and two lay judges. The two lay judges in a Commercial Division have the same voting power as the presiding learned judge when deliberating judgments. Their influence is highly regarded. The lay judges are appointed upon the recommendation of the local Chamber of Commerce for a tenure of three years. They must be 30 years of age and be registered as merchants in the Commercial Register or be a member of the board of directors of corporations likewise so registered (sections 105, *et seq., Gerichtsverfassungsgesetz*).

Appeals as to law and fact from judgments of Commercial Divisions will likewise be heard by specialised divisions of the *Oberlandesgerichte*, consisting of three learned judges.

What brings consistency into the decisions of first and also (though to a lesser extent) second instance is the system of promotion of judges. It is a general rule that a judge of first instance may only become a presiding judge if he has served his term as a professional judge at the *Oberlandesgericht* with distinction. Thus, a learned judge at the *Oberlandesgericht* Düsseldorf will be promoted to become a presiding judge at the Commercial Division at first instance. The presiding judge at first instance will know the views of the presiding judge at second instance and his learned two brethren in commercial transactions. The system of promotion of judges generally operates within specialised divisions of the various courts of first, second and also third instance.

The Lawyers The 52,000 German lawyers (*Rechtsanwälte*) are not divided into barristers and solicitors but form a uniform profession. Generally speaking a *Rechtsanwalt* is admitted either to one *Landgericht* and/or to one *Oberlandesgericht* or to the *Bundesgerichtshof* (to which the number of admissions is limited to 25). The *Rechtsanwalt* must have his office within the district of the court to which he is admitted. In civil and commercial matters his rights of audience are, subject to some exceptions, limited to that court of admittance, but he may appear in any *Amtsgericht*. In practice this means a that case in civil and commercial matters would require three different lawyers, one at each of the three instances. If an action has to be filed in another *Landgericht* outside the jurisdiction of the court to which the *Rechtsanwalt* handling the case is not admitted, he cannot sign the pleadings and must always be accompanied in the oral hearings by a local lawyer admitted to that *Landgericht*.

The *Rechtsanwalt* acts for his client both as a general legal adviser and as his representative in the conduct of proceedings in court. He has a monopoly in the giving of professional advice on legal matters. It is illegal for any person not so qualified to give legal advice.

The training for lawyers and judges is the same.

The training period for an intending lawyer is approximately eight years. The first five years are spent reading law at university, culminating in sitting the first *Staatsexamen*. If successful, application is then made to the Ministry of Justice of a *Land* to become a *Referendar* (trainee). For the next two and a half years the intending lawyer is classified as a civil servant working in various courts, as well as for the public prosecutor's department and in a legal practice. He will then sit the second *Staatsexamen*. After completing his studies and practical training he may choose between becoming a practising *Rechtsanwalt*, taking up a career as a judge or entering the civil service.

Partnerships are permitted and firms comprising up to 10 lawyers are to be found in all the major cities. At the same time there are very many sole practitioners, particularly in smaller towns and rural areas. Except as regards fiscal, administrative, labour or social matters, a *Rechtsanwalt* may not publicly advertise any specialisation of practice. Nevertheless, some *Anwaltsvereine* (lawyers' associations) do maintain lists of *Rechtsanwälte* who specialise in certain fields and this information will be provided upon request.

A *Rechtsanwalt* is not under a legal obligation to obtain a written power of attorney from his client. However, he will usually do so, for if there is any uncertainty as to his authority to act, proceedings may be suspended until such a power of attorney is produced.

The German Fee Ordinance for Lawyers (*Bundesrechtsanwaltsgebührenordnung* (BRAGO)) lays down the fees which a *Rechtsanwalt* may charge for services both in and out of court. Fees for work connected with litigation are discussed below (see p. 326). For advisory and other non-contentious work the *Rechtsanwalt* may agree with his client an amount calculated according to a sliding scale based on the value of the case. However, as this can lead to a disproportionately high fee, the *Rechtsanwalt* and the client will often agree upon a lump sum or hourly fee. Contingent fees are forbidden. The fees of *Rechtsanwälte* are subject to value added tax (*Mehrwertsteuer*). An exception to this rule is where a *Rechtsanwalt* acts for a client domiciled in another EEC country who itself is subject to VAT in respect of activities abroad. Hence, foreign commercial companies within the EEC do not pay VAT on legal fees, but VAT must be levied on foreign private individuals. Disputes between a *Rechtsanwalt* and client on a fee note may be referred to the local *Rechtsanwaltskammer* (law society).

Some Peculiarities of German Procedure

General   The West German Code of Civil Procedure (*Zivilprozessordnung* (ZPO)) regulates the procedure of all courts, including the *Bundesgerichtshof*.

Civil litigation, whilst adversarial in theory, is in practice dominated by the role of the judge. The judge controls the proceedings through all its stages and he has a duty to establish the truth to his own satisfaction. It is the judge who will direct whether witnesses should be called to give oral evidence if the documentary evidence is insufficient. It is he also who will decide what evidence of the parties should be given orally in support of their case. Where witnesses are called, they will be questioned, first of all by the judge, and thereafter, by the *Rechtsanwälte*. The *Rechtsanwälte* will give short argument of all the evidence that has been heard which may be followed by a short oral judgment.

The procedure for appeals before the *Oberlandesgericht*, which may involve a full re-hearing, is very similar to that of the courts of first instance.

Parties and legal representation   The main parties to an action are known respectively as the *Kläger* (plaintiff) and the *Beklagter* (defendant). All natural and legal persons as well as foreign persons and foreign corporations (irrespective of domicile) have capacity to sue and be sued. There are special rules pertaining to minors (persons under the age of 18), the mentally ill and insolvent companies. Other parties may be joined in the proceedings as either plaintiff or defendant.

A defendant may serve a third party notice on a third person against whom he has a claim, which is connected with the plaintiff's claim against him, at any time before judgment (*Streitverkündung*). The third person may then intervene in the main proceedings to protect his position. Failure on his part to do so will not result in judgment being given against him but he will be estopped in any future proceedings which the defendant may bring against him from asserting that the judgment in the main proceedings was incorrect (sections 68, 72, 73, 74 of ZPO).

A defendant may counter-claim (*Widerklage*) against the plaintiff. The counter-claim must be related in some way to the subject-matter of the claim; it may be made irrespective of whether the court has jurisdiction over the subject-matter of the counter-claim.

Hearings   A preliminary hearing or preliminary proceedings in writing will be ordered by the presiding judge of the court invoked. If a hearing is ordered, the defendant will be summoned to attend and to put forward his defence to the claim made against him immediately, or the court may set a time-limit for the filing of his defence. It is not unusual for simple cases to be dealt with at the preliminary hearing. Where this does not occur, the court will give directions on the further conduct of the proceedings.

The court will review the evidence and consider what further material it requires to reach a decision as the case proceeds. The first hearing in a case is usually a short one at which the court will announce whether the material submitted is sufficient for it to give judgment or whether oral evidence or an expert's opinion is required. Further hearings will follow should the court order the taking of oral evidence or the obtaining of an expert's report; further pleadings by the parties are then allowed.

Upon the conclusion of the hearing of evidence, the judge may give his decision or he may allow the parties to submit further pleadings commenting on the evidence and the expert's report, if any. If evidence has been taken by only one judge from a panel of three, a further formal hearing will be called before the full court. The *Rechtsanwälte* have a last opportunity to address the court at the final hearing but this is rare in practice. As there may be as many as 20 cases set down for hearing within an hour, in practice the *Rechtsanwälte* will merely refer to their pleadings and ask for judgment in favour of their client.

In most cases, the court will fix a date, normally within three weeks following the final hearing, on which it will announce its decision. On this date the court will give its decision at a hearing called for this purpose alone, the written judgment itself being issued within three weeks thereafter.

Inquisitorial versus adversarial system   Judges play a more important role in West Germany. The German judges do far more than the English ones. They also do the work done in England by the Masters, Registrars and sometimes by the Clerks. German judges prepare and set down the case and the oral hearings. They will set down time limits for filing defences and replies and censure those who do not comply. Most important, they themselves will decide whether, and if so what, evidence will be taken and in what order. They will have carefully studied the pleadings and often will have made up their mind before the oral hearings.

In many cases the judge will not hear witnesses at all, even if the lawyers insist, if he thinks their testimony irrelevant. Judges question the witnesses first and only then give the lawyers a chance to put their questions. The lawyers should easily recognise what is material in the eyes of the judge and not be tempted to ask unnecessary questions. The hearing of witnesses is thus much shorter than in England, often lasting only a couple of hours, seldom more than a day. Hence, hearings are much shorter.

The position of a German judge is best characterised by section 139 of ZPO. The section imposes a duty upon the judge to see that the parties plead all their allegations of relevant facts completely and, further, make all suitable applications in the circumstances. He is under a duty to discuss the facts and the relevant law with the parties and also to refer to legal points which the judge will consider.

Either during or after the first hearing in court the judge will often give his view on the chances of the action. Quite often the judge will initiate a settlement (*Vergleich*) between the parties and may, if requested, make a proposal as to how the settlement could be reached. He will also play an important role in the negotiations leading up to a settlement. Any settlement reached takes effect as an ordinary contract. A settlement in court has the same effect as a judgment of the court.

There is no equivalent to the English procedure of payment into court. Should the defendant acknowledge that he owes part of the claim, he must pay this sum to the plaintiff even if the plaintiff continues the action for the balance. However, such a payment on behalf of the defendant will reduce the *Streitwert* (value in dispute) on which the fees are based as from the date of payment.

Free appreciation versus strict rules of evidence There are no strict rules of evidence, such as the rule against hearsay evidence, in West German procedure. There are no instances under German law where corroboration of evidence is required. There is also no rule of evidence rendering inadmissible oral evidence to add, alter or contradict a document. On the contrary, the contract history plays an important role in construing contractual documents. Generally speaking, German judges are free under section 286 of ZPO to appraise and evaluate the evidence. When it comes to the amount of damages, there are even less constraints placed upon the judge and they may also make an estimate.

Witnesses and oral evidence Even though there are no strict rules of evidence, it is a peculiarity of West German procedure that a party to legal proceedings, generally speaking, may not be a witness. German procedure takes the viewpoint that a party cannot be an independent witness because of his interest. That rule may be circumvented. If for instance a creditor assigns his claim, then the assignee becomes the plaintiff in proceedings and the assignor may give evidence. However, the judge will attach less weight to the evidence of an assignor. Only in rare cases, where the party bearing the burden of proof has presented some evidence will the court upon its own initiative call that party to give oral evidence.

The *Rechtsanwalt* will name in his pleading any witness who can support the facts alleged. The pleadings will summarise the matters on which the witness can testify. Oral evidence will be taken only if the court so orders in a *Beweisbeschluss* interlocutory order. A witness is under a duty to appear once summoned. However, certain close relatives of the parties may refuse to give evidence.

In so-called evidential hearings, evidence is taken in private on the facts and matters stated in the *Beweisbeschluss* interlocutory order at a special hearing of the court and the witness does not hear what the other witnesses have said. The witness will first give an account in his own words of the matters in question as to facts which are within his personal knowledge. He may refuse to answer any questions which might incriminate or dishonour him or cause him financial damage or he may refuse to disclose a trade secret. He will then be questioned by the judge. Questions posed by the *Rechtsanwälte* will be designed to emphasise particular points or to clear up any ambiguities. There is no cross-examination of the kind found in common law systems. A summary of the testimony will be dictated by the judge and taken down either by a court clerk or on tape; the *Rechtsanwälte* ensuring that the resultant statement accurately summarises the evidence of the witness. The statement is then placed on the court file and copies are forwarded to the *Rechtsanwälte*. Witnesses who live a long distance from the court hearing the case may give their evidence before the judge of his local *Amtsgericht*.

The judge alone will evaluate the evidence, but there are strict rules as to the burden of proof in various factual situations. If a party carrying the burden of proof fails to prove an essential fact, the court must dismiss the case.

A party who is unable to call other evidence in support of his case may apply for the opposing party to submit to questioning. However, he runs the risk of the other party convincing the court in his favour. Alternatively, the court itself may direct one or both of the parties to make statements about the facts of the case. However, any such evidence given by the parties themselves carries less probative value than independent evidence.

Documentary evidence   Any documents which one party wishes to produce to assist his case are attached to the pleading, which are certified by the *Rechtsanwalt* as being true copies of the original. Documents in a foreign language must be submitted in certified translation. The original documents must be produced at the hearing if so requested by either the court or the other party.

PLEADINGS IN WEST GERMANY

Generally speaking there is no discovery of documents. A party may be compelled to produce documents only where the other party refers to such document or where there is a cause of action for production. Under section 810 of the German Civil Code (*Bürgerliches Gesetzbuch* (BGB)) that is the only case where the document which the person demands to examine is:

(a) made in his interest;
(b) records a legal relationship between himself and another; or
(c) contains negotiations of any legal transaction conducted between him and another person, or between one of them and a common intermediary.

The production of such documents may also be required of a third party, by a separate action. A party to proceedings (but not a third party) may also be ordered to produce specific documents of certain further limited kinds if they are known to be in his possession.

Another feature of procedure is the possibility of proceedings based upon documentary evidence (*Urkundenprozeß*) where the foreign plaintiff does not need to furnish security for the defendant's costs. Where a party is able to base and prove its claim solely by documents and by calling the other party, a summary judgment may be obtained within a very short time. These proceedings apply in particular to bills of exchange, cheques and other commercial documents. These proceedings are, to some extent, comparable to R.S.C., Ord. 14 proceedings.

Experts If a matter in issue requires to be proved by expert opinion, a party will, in his pleading, request the court to appoint an independent expert (*Sachverständiger*). If the court does not consider itself competent on the subject, it may nominate an expert from an official panel of approved experts. The expert will contact the parties to arrange for any examination of the subject-matter he considers necessary and may call the parties together to hear any representations they may wish to make to him. Upon completion of his investigations the expert will submit his report to the court with copies to the parties. Further pleadings may then be filed by either party thereon and either party may request a further hearing at which the expert may be questioned.

Foreign law: a question of law and not of fact Under section 293 of ZPO, foreign law is a question of law, and not of fact. The court is under an obligation to ascertain the foreign law and it may take into account that which the parties advance as expert evidence on foreign law. Upon its own volition it quite often appoints experts on foreign law. Contrary to the English practice, these are not practising foreign lawyers, but following the traditional high respect of German law for professors, will be

German law professors. In practice it is often a professor of the Max-Planck-Institute in Hamburg who is asked to give a detailed opinion on foreign law. An error of foreign law is no ground for appeal to the *Bundesgerichtshof*. Compared with the English practice it takes far less time and expense to ascertain the foreign law in a German court.

Judgment   Judgments of a German court are drafted impersonally in the third person contrary to the English judicial practice of pronouncing judgment in the first person.

The final judgment in an action is called an *Endurteil*. The *Rubrum* (being the first part of the judgment) identifies the court, the parties and counsel. There then follows the operative part of the decision, including any order as to costs, security and enforcement, which is called the *Tenor* or *Urteilsformel*. If the plaintiff has claimed interest it will be awarded at the rate set by law (4 per cent. per annum for civil claims; 5 per cent. per annum for commercial claims; or at a higher rate if the plaintiff has proven that he has actually paid such higher rate to a bank).

A summary of the background facts (*Tatbestand*) and a statement of the contested issues, the evidence and the court's reasons (*Entscheidungsgründe*) are contained in the next section. This will also include a statement of the basis on which the court accepted jurisdiction, if jurisdiction was disputed or doubtful. There are certain circumstances in which facts and reasoning may be omitted but these must be included if the judgment is to be enforced abroad. Dissenting opinions are not stated. The judgment will be signed by the judge or judges.

When the decision is announced it is usually only the *Tenor* which is read out in open court. The full text of the judgment is filed with the court office and copies are forwarded to the respective parties some time later.

Other types of judgment include a *Teilurteil*, by which part of a dispute is decided; a *Zwischenurteil* or interlocutory judgment by which incidental procedural matters, such as capacity to act, are decided; a *Grundurteil*, a judgment on liability only; a *Vorbehaltsurteil* a provisional judgment which is capable of being set aside on proof of further matters.

Costs   Court costs and fees and disbursements to the lawyers in a German litigation case can be summarised as follows.

Court costs   The court will recover, in advance, from the parties its own administrative costs and any allowances and expenses claimed by witnesses and experts attending a hearing where they have nominated or proposed that the court take such a step. The fee payable by the plaintiff to the court for the various stages of the action (for filing the proceedings, for the hearings and upon judgment) is determined by the amount in dispute as applied to a fixed sliding scale. If the plaintiff succeeds in full, the defendant will usually be ordered to pay all court and legal costs. Where the plaintiff recovers only a proportion of the sum claimed, the costs are apportioned between the parties accordingly. The successful party will have to meet the court costs in full if the losing party is insolvent.

Lawyers' fees These are set by the BRAGO. Fee units are calculated on a sliding scale based on the *Streitwert* (value in dispute) and charged, as court costs, for the various stages of the action: on taking initial instructions, appearances at court, when the court directs the taking of evidence and for negotiating a settlement. A sum for disbursements may also be recovered. In proceedings on appeal the fees payable to the *Rechtsanwalt* are calculated in a similar manner but are 30 per cent. higher.

Peculiarities of German Pleadings

Written pleadings versus oral advocacy There is no highly developed technique of pleading in West Germany. Due to the different role of the judge, the objective of written pleadings is not merely to define the issues, but to convince the judge.

A German lawyer drafting pleadings will throw all rules of English pleadings over board; he will set out the facts, not merely in summary form but often in great detail. He may dwell on immaterial points, as he is afraid that these may be material to the judge. A German lawyer will also plead law, and it is not unusual for the pleadings to contain elaborate theses as to a particular point of law. Further, pleadings contain not merely facts, but also the evidence by which these facts are to be proved. It is good practice to divide the facts into paragraphs and indicate after each paragraph the means of evidence. That is to say, the name and residence of witnesses, the documentary evidence (which is usually attached to the pleadings) and also whether a view of the *locus in quo* should be held or whether experts should be heard. German lawyers are thus accustomed to indicating the evidence before it is decided whether the facts are in dispute.

Such elaborate written pleadings severely reduce the need for oral argument. German judges read written pleadings. Often they are impatient and do not allow oral repetition of that which has been submitted in writing. However, by law they are required to pay lip service to oral hearings. Yet, in oral hearings there is hardly any room for oral argument. Oral hearings are quite short, often no longer than five minutes. (However, in many cases there is more than one oral hearing.) The time spent in the preparation of written pleadings therefore pays dividends.

Originating pleadings The German equivalent of originating proceedings is by filing of a *Klageschrift* (writ), which will cite the parties to the proceedings, the amount and the grounds of the claim. Any documents in support of the writ are attached to the *Klageschrift*. The amount claimed must be stated precisely except in personal injury cases where often a minimum figure only is stated. The importance of the amount claimed is apparent when one realises that this determines the *Streitwert* (value in dispute) which in turn establishes the costs of both the court and the *Rechtsanwalt*.

Three copies of the writ are forwarded by the *Rechtsanwalt* for the plaintiff to the court: one for the court file and two for service upon the defendant and his *Rechtsanwalt*. The case will be allocated to the appropriate division of the court and is entered into the court records. The presiding judge of the court invoked will then decide whether to hold a preliminary hearing or to direct preliminary proceedings in writing, the latter being the course which is usually adopted. The court will then serve a copy of the *Klageschrift* upon the defendant by post. The action becomes pending once the writ has been served upon the defendant.

Defence and further written pleadings   The court documents served on the defendant together with the *Klageschrift* lay down the action required on the part of the defendant. The defendant will either be requested to attend a preliminary hearing or to file within a period of two weeks from the date of service a notice of his intention to defend the case and to file his defence within a period of two weeks thereafter. At the same time, the judge may also fix a period within which the plaintiff is to file any reply to the defence. These periods may be extended by the court upon the application of a party.

The defendant will be deemed to have admitted all the allegations in the *Klageschrift* unless he files the intention to defend and his defence within the prescribed time period. Failure on the part of the defendant to observe the deadlines may result in a default judgment being given against him.

Where a foreign party is involved, the time periods laid down by the judge are extended. In practice the period prescribed upon service of a *Klageschrift* to a party domiciled outside West Germany between service and the hearing is one and two months.

The defendant's reply to the plaintiff's statement of claim is called a *Klageerwiderung* or a *Klagebeanwortung* which must be filed within the time period prescribed by the court. The parties may then exchange further written pleadings. All relevant documentary evidence must be attached to the pleadings at an early stage. Failure to do so may result in one party being precluded from so doing later.

Further and better particulars may be ordered by the court if it considers that a party has not pleaded his case in sufficient detail. The party must comply with this request or the court may regard the other party's allegations on the issue to have been admitted.

The defendant in his *Klageerwiderung* must either deny or admit every fact alleged in the *Klageschrift* and state every material fact upon which he intends to rely. The defendant is deemed to admit any facts alleged in the *Klageschrift*, which he does not challenge. If the defendant makes a counter-claim (*Widerklage*) this must be connected in some way with the subject-matter of the claim. If the defendant counter-claims, a plaintiff must file a defence to the counter-claim.

The pleadings are filed by the lawyer for the one party with the court, which then serves copies upon the lawyer for the other party. In practice this is done by the court clerk placing the appropriate pleadings in the pigeon-hole allocated to each lawyer admitted to the court within the court building. The lawyers may, however, send copies of their pleadings direct to each other when filing them with the court; they must indicate on the copy filed with the court that they have done so.

Specimen of Written Pleadings

Specimen of Klage The following is a translation of the text for a pleading such as would usually be adopted by a *Rechtsanwalt* for a simple claim in debt.

TR/rj/155:85–100
September 12, 1988

STATEMENT OF CLAIM

The Company ——————   ,   ,

, represented by its managing directors and ——————,
– Plaintiff –

Counsel: Attorneys: Messrs. Weil, Försterling, Petzold, Grooter-horst, Leistikow

versus

The Company ——————   ,   ,

——————, England represented by the board of directors
– Defendant –

Claim
Amount in dispute: DM 298,076.51

We bring this action in the name of and on behalf of the plaintiff. The advance on court costs in the amount of DM 2,178.00 together with service costs in the amount of DM 5.00 are paid herewith and receipted by the stamp of Court Registry. We ask that a date for oral proceedings be set down as soon as possible. At those proceedings we shall apply for

1. an order that the Defendant pay the Plaintiff DM 298,076.51 together with 5 per cent. interest from June 1, 1988;
2. in the alternative the plaintiff may provide security through one of the credit institutions associated with the security fund of the German banks and Sparkassen necessary for execution or the prevention of execution;

where preliminary written submissions are required,

3. Summary judgment in accordance with Section 331 (3) of the German Civil Code of Procedure, insofar as the Defendant does not indicate in time in accordance with Section 276 paragraph (1) sub-clause (1), sub-sub-clause (2) of the German Civil Code of Procedure that it intends to defend the claim;
4. (partial) summary judgment without oral hearing in accordance with Section 307(2) of the German Civil Code of Procedure, insofar as the Defendant admits to the claim (in Part) as provided for by Section 276(1) sub-section 1 of the German Civil Code of Procedure;

and further we seek

5. the issue of an enforceable copy of any judgment with proof of service.

PARTICULARS OF CLAIM

1. The Parties to the Action

1.1.   The Plaintiff manufactures oil and gas boilers. Since its formation in 1984 the Defendant runs a foundry and since that time has delivered to the Plaintiff end and middle sections for the manufacture of gas boilers.

1.2.   The Defendant is the successor to the Company——("old——"). The property of old—— was taken over by the defendant on——, 19——. It involved a so-called "management buy out": The management of old——, in particular——, formed the Defendant, took over the property of old——, in particular the foundry, and continued the business of old——. During a short transition period the Defendant used the name with the addition "1984," i.e. "——1984." From then the business of the Defendant was identical with that of old——.

2. Contract of October 1981

2.1.   In October 1981 the Plaintiff concluded a Contract with old——. Old—— agreed to produce the middle and end sections for the Plaintiff's gas boilers and to deliver those exclusively to the Plaintiff. After there had been two meetings in Düsseldorf to discuss the Contract the crucial discussion occurred in Autumn 1981 in Viersen at the offices of the Plaintiff. AB, the managing director of the Defendant, and CD EF and GH of the Plaintiff took part at this meeting. Verbal agreement on all points of the Contract was reached at this meeting. The conclusion of the Contract was sealed by a handshake and celebrated in Düsseldorf's Altstadt.

Proof:

1. Evidence of CD
2. Evidence of EF
3. Evidence of GH

The parties had agreed at that discussion that the Plaintiff should set out the agreement in writing and forward it in the English and German languages to the Defendant. This occurred on November 9, 1981.

Proof:

Evidence of Mrs. IJ, Export Director of the Plaintiff, c/o the Plaintiff,

correspondence from the Plaintiff dated November 9, 1981 (Annex K1).

Thereafter the Defendant did not return duly executed copies of the Contract but raised no objection with the Plaintiff that the text did not correspond with the verbally reached agreement. On the contrary as had been envisaged performance of the Contract commenced.

Proof:

Evidence of Mrs. IJ, Export Director of the Plaintiff, c/o the Plaintiff.

2.2 The Plaintiff conducted all sales and dealings pursuant to the Contract and correspondence with old——and, from 1984 onwards, with the Defendant partly in German and partly in the English language. The written Contract of October 1981 was prepared in both languages.

Proof:

Preparation of the Contract of October 1981 in German and English, Annexes K2 and K3.

2.3. The Contract of October 1981 was the basis of relations between the Plaintiff and old——and also with the Defendant—from 1984 onwards. The following provisions of the Contract are important for the dispute:

(a) This Contract set the conditions for the orders to be made by the Plaintiff (Clause 11 of the Contract). The Contract was to continue in force indefinitely. Termination was only to be available with six months prior written notice, by registered mail, terminating on either June 30 or December 31 in any particular year (Clause 11 of the Contract).

(b) In accordance with Clause 12(2) of the Contract old——(and the Defendant) could only increase its prices after six months prior notice. In the event that the parties could not reach an agreement on the new price after such notice the Contract, in accordance with Clause 11 was to be terminated after a period of six months. During this period Clause 12(2) of the Contract envisaged an obligation for the continued delivery at the old price.

(c) In Clause 13(2) of the Contract the parties agreed that German law would govern the Contract. Düsseldorf was chosen as the forum for all disputes arising out of the contract.

2.4. This Contract was not however executed. It was nevertheless clear to all parties that it was binding and set out the contractual basis for the business relationship of the parties. Since October 1981 the Contract has been adhered to and performed initially by old—and since 1984 by the Defendant.

Proof:

1. KL, Purchasing Manager of the Plaintiff, c/o the Plaintiff.
2. Mrs. IJ, Export Manager of the Plaintiff, c/o the Plaintiff.

Particulars

(a) The Plaintiff made available to old——models, designs and castings, which served as a basis for the production of the elements for the heating boilers (see Clause 1(2) and Clause 8 of the Contract). These models, drawings and castings were provided to the Defendant in 1984. In production old——and the Defendant complied with the quality and hardness prescribed in Annex 1 of the Contract (see Clause 2(1) of the Contract).

(b) Old——, *i.e.* the Defendant, carried out the certification on the construction style for the German Technical Supervisory Association (see Clause 2(2) of the Contract).

(c) Old——, *i.e.* the Defendant, gave certain warranties pursuant to Clause 3 of the Contract. The parties agreed the warranties should continue for a period of 12 months from the date of casting. The Plaintiff would keep defective boiler sections available for the examination by old——and the Defendant which would be inspected by old——, *i.e.* the Defendant, periodically. Thereafter the defective boiler sections were scraped.

(d) The Plaintiff would order February 15, May 15, August 15 and November 15 of each year its quantity for the coming quarter (see Clause 4 of the Contract).

(e) Old———, *i.e.* the Defendant, was responsible for deliveries to Vier-sen to the depot of the Plaintiff. In each case packaging, storage and ancillary costs were included in the price (see Clause 6 of the Contract).

(f) In each instance the Plaintiff would pay within 15 days and deduct 3 per cent. discount from the amount of the account.

(g) With six months notice in each instance, old———, *i.e.* the Defend-ant, announced price increases. The parties were able to come to an agreement in the past about the new prices.

Proof for the Performance of the Contract from 1981–1987:

1. Evidence of MN, Product Manager of the Plaintiff, c/o the Plain-tiff.
2. KL, Purchasing Manager of the Plaintiff, c/o the Plaintiff.

2.5.   In addition the parties have confirmed the terms of the Contract of October 1981 on many occasions. Thus, the parties extended this Con-tract to the boiler series GA 92 on January 6, 1983. This extension was confirmed by the Plaintiff to old——with a letter of January 20, 1983 (Annex K4). In this letter the Contract of October 1981 is described as the "current Contract." The exact wording is:

"6. Inclusion of GA 92 in the current Contract Insofar as there are no inconsistent provisions confirmed in this letter, the provisions of the Contract and the Annexes belonging thereto will apply so far as they are relevant to the boiler series GA 92."

2.6.   The performance of the Contract was not interrupted by the man-agement buy out in July 1984, but rather, was continued by the Defend-ant without any restrictions and in accordance with the provisions of the Contract of October 1981. In each instance in response to the written orders of the Plaintiff the Defendant delivered Contract products to the Plaintiff. The volume of orders in 1985 was DM 1,098,000.00 and in 1986 it was DM 1,232,000.00. As an example of an order, order No. 1045 of the August 12, 1987 (consisting of two sheets) is annexed hereto, Annex K5.

Proof:

1. Evidence of KL, Purchasing Manager of the Plaintiff, c/o the Plaintiff.
2. Evidence of MN, Product Manager of the Plaintiff, c/o the Plain-tiff.

2.7.   Even if the circumstances of the preparation of a contract and its forwarding to old——could be regarded as an implied agreement within the meaning of Section 154(2) of the German Civil Code, the contract has nevertheless been effectively concluded between the parties. The parties have impliedly waived any requirement of a formal agreement and abandoned a written form of contract. This can be deduced from the actual observance of the contractual agreements. None of the parties could obtain that after more than five years of continual transactions pursuant to the Contract that it had once been agreed to finalise the agreement in written form and have it executed and that this had never occurred (see in this regard BGH NJW 1983, 1727, 1728).

3. The agreement of March 12, 1987

On March 12, 1987 the parties agreed, as in the previous years, on the new prices which would be valid for one year beginning on April 1, 1987 and ending on March 31, 1988. According to this Agreement of March 12, 1988 the end sections were to cost £6.75.

Proof:

Witness KL, Purchasing Managing of the Plaintiff, c/o the Plaintiff.

By a letter of March 17, 1987 to the Defendant the Plaintiff confirmed this verbal Agreement.

Proof:

The letter of March 17, 1987, Annex K6.

As had always been the case the Defendant did not expressly confirm the newly arranged prices in a more express manner. However from April 1, 1987 onwards the Defendant invoiced in accordance with the agreed prices which had been confirmed in the letter of March 17, 1987.

Proof:

As before.

Non-performance of the Contract of October 1981 and the Agreement of March 12, 1987 by the Defendant

4.1. From March to November 1987 there were continual delays in delivery by the Defendant. The parties exchanged intensive correspondence on this point. Thus the Plaintiff complained about the delay by a telex of September 29, 1987, Annex K7.

4.2. On November 13, 1987 Mr. OP of the Defendant informed the witness Mrs. IJ of the Plaintiff on the telephone that the Defendant was intending to increase its prices. On November 16 Mr. OP informed this witness that the Defendant intended to cease production for the Plaintiff. The Plaintiff was concerned about these developments. On November 17, 1987 the witnesses Mrs. IJ and Mr. KL visited the foundry of the Defendant. On November 30, 1987 Mr. OP of the Defendant informed

Mr. HRS that the prices would double. At the same time the Plaintiff discovered that the Defendant had been taken over by the English company AB, an English public company. On December 4, 1987 Mr. AB, the managing director of the Defendant notified that acceptance of a price increase from £6.75 to "only" £12.00 had been requested. The Plaintiff rejected this price rise which was contrary to the terms of the Contract. On the afternoon of December 4, 1987, in the name of and on behalf of the Defendant Mr. OP informed the Plaintiff that the total production for the Plaintiff had finally been ceased. The Plaintiff would be able to collect its tools.

Proof:

    1. Evidence of Mrs. IJ, c/o the Plaintiff.
    2. Evidence of Mr. KL, c/o the Plaintiff.

4.3.   The Defendant is responsible to the Plaintiff for its positive failure to comply with the lawful request of the Plaintiff and also for breach of the Contract of October 1981 and the Agreement of March 12, 1987.

5. Quantum of Damages

5.1.   The Plaintiff claims damages for non-performance. The Plaintiff claims the following damages *for the time being.*

(a) *Additional Costs*   The quantities ordered by the Plaintiff from the Defendant for the 4th quarter of 1987 and for the 1st quarter of 1988 had to be obtained from another firm,———, at a higher price. The Plaintiff has made intensive enquiries for other production sources on the European and non-European markets. The firm———in———, in the——— —submitted the most favourable quote.

Proof:

    Evidence of Mr.———, c/o the Plaintiff.

The orders of August 12, 1987 (Order No. 1045, Annex K5) and of November 13, 1987 (order No. 1634, Annex K8) are for the following quantities:

Quantities not obtained from RMI for the 4th Quarter 1987

Item			Difference	Addt. Price
3,276 end sections	23.83 per item	20.25 per item	3.58	11,728.08
7,015 middle sections	14.72 per item	7.39 per item	7.34	51,490.10
	Total difference in DM			63,218.18

Quantities not delivered by for the 1st Quarter 1988

Item			Difference	Addt. Price
10.450 end sections	23.83 per item	20.25 per item	3.58	37,411.00
19.600 middle sections	14.72 per item	7.38 per item	7.34	143,864.00
	Total difference in DM			181,275.00

In total the additional costs amount to   DM 244,493.00

Proof:

     Evidence of Mr. KL, c/o the Plaintiff

(c) *Air Freight Costs*   The Plaintiff had agreed on fixed delivery dates with the client firms of ——, ——, and ——. Because the Defendant did not deliver the Plaintiff had to engage the firm of ——. Delivery delays of approximately three weeks arose. In order to keep delivery deadlines with clients the Plaintiff had to pay air freight instead of ship freight. The following costs arose therefrom:

     Invoice No. 882801 of January 28, 1988 DM 7,437.50.
     Invoice No. 882802 of February 17, 1988 DM 33,277.90.

In total the Plaintiff paid additional air freight costs of: DM 40,715.40.

Proof:

     Evidence of Mr. KL, c/o the Plaintiff.

(c) *Storage and Finance Costs of DM 12,867.93*   The Plaintiff had to store and finance over a period of five months boiler parts which could not be built into boilers (value DM 377,660.78).

     With an interest rate of 5 per cent. per annum (paragraph 353 the German Commercial Code) the finance costs are DM 7,867.93.

     The storage costs amount to a fixed amount of DM 5,000.00

Proof:

     Evidence of Mr. KL, c/o the Plaintiff.

(d) *Quantum of Damages*   The amount of damages from——, paragraph 5.1. (a)–(c) amounts to: DM 298,076.51.

     5.2.   The Plaintiff reserves its rights to amend its claim to include lost profits. The Plaintiff was unable to produce approximately 2,000 boilers.

6. Interest

The Plaintiff claims interest from June 30, 1988 and for the full legal amount by the letter of the English solicitors,——, of May 25, 1988.

PLEADINGS IN WEST GERMANY

7. *Jurisdiction of the District Court Düsseldorf*

The jurisdiction of the District Court Düsseldorf arises from Article 17 of the European Convention on Jurisdiction and Enforcement of Judgments. The Plaintiff confirmed the verbal conclusion of the Agreement by the forwarding of the Contract in October 1981.

Even if the written Contract does not confirm the verbal Agreement it has been adopted in the continuing business relations between the Plaintiff on the one hand and old——and the Defendant on the other hand. This was considered sufficient for a written confirmation by the European Court in the case of *Segoura* v. *Bonakdarian* (Judgment of December 14, 1976, printed in RIW 1977, 105 *et seq.*).

In any event the Plaintiff has again confirmed "the current Contract" together with the Agreement as to jurisdiction by the letter of January 20, 1983.

(Attorney-at-law)

APPENDIX C

The Courts and Pleadings of the United States
Michael V. Ciresi, Attorney, Minnesota

Constitutional Overview

The nature and significance of citizenship   Every American has "dual citizenship" for the purpose of judicial jurisdiction. Each American is a citizen of the United States and of the state in which he resides. Therefore, he can, in appropriate cases, sue or be sued in either the federal court system or the court system of one or more of the 50 states.

The Federal Court   The Constitution requires that there be a federal Supreme Court and such other courts as Congress creates. Within limits set by the Constitution, the United States Congress can control the jurisdiction of federal courts. The United States districts courts are the preliminary federal trial courts. There is at least one federal court present in each state, each territory and the District of Columbia. In addition, there are 12 circuit Courts of Appeal, which are intermediate appellate courts hearing appeals from district courts and federal administrative agencies. The Supreme Court is the highest court in the United States. In general, a federal court has personal jurisdiction over parties who reside in, or can be found in, the state in which the court sits, although some federal statutes may allow broader jurisdiction.

The State Court   In addition to the federal courts, each of the 50 states maintains its own court system. State courts are established by the various state governments, their jurisdiction is governed by either state constitutional or statutory authority. State courts have general jurisdiction and, with some exceptions, can hear all matters affecting citizens or residents of that state.

THE COURTS AND PLEADINGS OF THE UNITED STATES

The Supreme Court   It can review decisions of lower federal courts and also certain decisions of the highest courts of the individual states. But it can only review state decisions that affect questions of federal law or decisions of state courts that raise questions under the laws of the United States or in the United States Constitution. Most decisions affecting state law, such as tort and contract cases, products liability, estate and trusts, are governed by state law and are not subject to review by the United States Supreme Court unless initially brought in federal court under diversity jurisdiction.

The Federal/State Court distinction   While the federal courts and the court of the 50 states have many similar procedures, each are creatures of separate jurisdictions and each have their own particulars. Accordingly, each jurisdiction must be examined for its own rules.

Federal Courts

Jurisdiction   Article III of the United States Constitution governs federal judicial power. It provides that the "judicial power of the United States" shall extend to enumerated classes of "Cases" and "Controversies." The two major categories of cases and controversies that can be heard in federal courts are federal question cases (28 U.S.C. ss.1331) and diversity cases (28 U.S.C. ss.1332). Federal courts may also hear controversies between citizens of the United States and citizens and subjects of a foreign state (28 U.S.C. ss.1332(a)(2)). Other categories of significance include: "Cases of Admiralty, and Maritime Jurisdiction"; "Controversies between two or more States"; and "Controversies to which the United States shall be a Party." Federal question cases are those cases "arising under" the United States Constitution, laws of the United States (generally federal statutes and regulations), and treaties and executive agreements made by the United States. Federal question jurisdiction is based not only on the need for construing federal law but also on the necessity of enforcing federal rights.

Interaction of Federal and State jurisdiction—pendent jurisdiction
   Where federal-question jurisdiction is presented, the court may also hear related state law claims under the theory of "pendent jurisdiction." As announced by the United States Supreme Court in *United Mine Workers* v. *Gibbs* 383 U.S. 715 (1966), the doctrine of pendent jurisdiction allows federal courts to hear state-law claims whenever "the state and federal claims . . . derive from a common nucleus of operative fact," and when the considerations of judicial economy dictate having a single trial. The application of the doctrine, however, is discretionary with the trial court.

338

Diversity cases   Diversity cases are disputes between citizens of different states. Currently, federal statute provides that there is federal jurisdiction in controversies involving more than $50,000 between "citizens of different states", or between "citizens of states" and "citizens or subjects" of "foreign states". There must be "complete diversity" in order to support diversity jurisdiction: that is, every plaintiff must be "diverse" from every defendant: *Strawbridge* v. *Curtiss* 7 U.S. (3 Chranch) 267 (1806).

Removal from State Court to Federal Court   Defendants in actions originally filed in a state court, which otherwise would meet diversity criteria, may remove these actions from state court to federal court (28 U.S.C. ss.1441). A case may be removed only by defendants who are not citizens of the state in which the case is pending. All defendants must join in the petition to remove. If some defendants cannot or do not join in seeking to remove the case, the case will stay in the state court. Cases involving federal questions may also be removed from state and federal court. Removal must be sought within 30 days after service of the complaint or within 30 days after the case becomes removable, whichever is later (28 U.S.C. ss.1446).

Pleading federal jurisdiction   Defences of lack of jurisdiction over the defendant, improper venue, or failure to serve process are waived if not raised by either motion or answer. The court may on its own motion raise the question or dismiss the case if the case does not have proper federal subject matter jurisdiction (diversity or federal question). Accordingly, pleaders take great care to make certain that the basis for federal question jurisdiction are sufficiently pleaded in the complaint.

Pleading in the Federal Courts

The abolition of code pleading   In 1938 the United States Congress adopted the Federal Rules of Civil Procedure, which greatly simplified pleading. Previously pleading was governed by the complex rules of statutory codes which had their birth in the mid-nineteenth century. "Code pleading" was based upon the concept of technical "causes of action." Alternative or hypothetical pleading was prohibited, and evidence and conclusions of law could not be pleaded.

Introduction of notice pleading   The Federal Rules of Civil Procedure changed these concepts. Under these rules, a case is started by filing a complaint, which consists of "a short and plain statement of the claim showing that the pleader is entitled to relief" (Fed. R. Civ. P. 8(A)(2)). Under the rules, the complaint is required only to give notice to the opposing party of the nature and the basis or grounds of the claim and to give a general indication of the type of litigation involved. To give fair notice a complaint should provide a statement of circumstances, occurrences and events that support the claims. However, a statement of these circumstances can be quite general if the defendant is given fair notice of what is claimed. A complaint may also plead alternative and sometimes conflicting theories or claims. Lengthy recitals of "ultimate facts" are not required. Instead, the pre-trial discovery process bears the burden of filling in the details. Since the purpose of the pleading is generally to provide notice, this type of general pleading is known as "notice pleading".

Interaction of brevity and discovery   In short, the pleading must only be specific enough to allow a party to frame a response. If a pleading "so vague or ambiguous that a party cannot reasonably be required to frame a responsive pleading," the party may move for a more definite statement before imposing a responsive pleading" (Fed. R. Civ. P. 12(e)). The motion for a more definite statement will only be granted if a pleading is so vague that the defendant will not have a sufficient understanding of the claims against him and thus make it difficult or impossible to prepare an effective answer. Defendants may be able to request a specific date or event if it is necessary to form an effective response. But motions for more definite statements can usually do little more. The motion for a more definite statement is not a modern-day substitute for the bill of particulars. The motion is therefore seldom used and less often granted. The gathering of specific information for trial preparation is to be accomplished through the extensive discovery process provided for by the rules. The Federal Rules made general pleading possible, and eliminated the need for bills of particulars, by the introduction of extensive use of discovery. The discovery process fills in the specific facts generally omitted in the pleadings. Parties may obtain discovery by one or more of the following methods:

  (a) depositions upon oral examination or written questions;
  (b) written interrogatories;
  (c) production or documents or things or permission to enter upon land or other property, for inspection and other purposes;
  (d) physical and mental examinations; and
  (e) requests for admission (Fed. R. Civ. P. 26(a)).

Parties may obtain discovery regarding any matter, not privileged, which may lead to the discovery of evidence relevant to the subject matter of the action, whether relating to the claim or defence of any party. Information is discoverable even if it will not be admissible at trial so long as it appears "reasonably calculated to lead to the discovery of admissible evidence," (Fed. R. Civ. P. 26(b)(1)).

Exceptional cases requiring particularity The only areas in which the Federal Rules require particular pleading of circumstances or facts is in pleading fraud or mistake, denial of performance or occurrence, or special damages (Fed. R. Civ. P. 9(b), 9(c), 9(g)). A complaint alleging these theories must be pleaded with particularity, although all the facts need not be set forth in detail. It should also be noted that malice, intent, knowledge and other conditions of the mind may be averred generally (Fed. R. Civ. P. 9(b)).

Examples of Federal Claims

Vouchsafing the pleading by the pleader's signature Rule 11 is the major provision of the Federal Rules insuring that notice pleading does not result in instituting and conducting spurious litigation. Rule 11 requires that the pleadings, motions and other papers of a party shall be signed either by an attorney of record or, if the party is not represented by an attorney, by the party. The rule states that:

> "The signature of an attorney or party constitutes a certificate by the signer that the signer has read the pleading, motion or other paper: that to the best of the signer's knowledge, information, an belief formed after reasonable inquiry it is well-grounded in fact and is warranted by existing law or a good-faith argument for the extension, modification, or reversal of existing law, and that it is not interposed for any improper purpose, such as to harass or cause unnecessary delay or needless increase in the cost of litigation."

A violation of Rule 11 will result in sanctions which may include an order to pay the other party's reasonable attorney's fees. It has been held that the rule imposes the need for some pre-filing inquiry into both the facts and the law, and that the attorney is to be judged by a standard of reasonableness under the circumstances. In applying Rule 11, the court will avoid using the wisdom of hindsight and test the signer's conduct by inquiring into the reasonableness of the belief at the time the pleading, motion or other paper was submitted.

Personal injury Exhibit A (below) is a form of a complaint for personal injuries arising from an automobile accident, based upon the Appendix of Forms in the Federal Rules. The basis of the claim is stated in the broadest possible terms. The only specific facts pleaded are the place of the accident, the parties involved and the date. Neither the particulars of the accident, of the injuries, nor of the alleged fault or improper conduct of the defendant are alleged. In this sample pleading, the plaintiff is ignorant as to the identity of the proper defendant. The plaintiff simply alleges that one or both defendants negligently or recklessly drove over the

341

plaintiff. The specifics of the accident are not pleaded and the plaintiff's damages are recited in a general fashion so as to make the defendants aware of the general categories of damages which will be claimed.

Product liability   While Exhibit A is an example of the minimum allegations needed under the Federal Rules, in practice, complaints often contain more detail. Since the complaint is frequently the first document seen by the court, it is often a good tactic to tell the plaintiff's story in a more detailed fashion so that the court will better understand the plaintiff's position. Exhibit B (below) is a sample of a complaint prepared in a diversity action involving injuries stemming from the insertion of a contraceptive device. As can be seen in paragraphs 5 and 6, injuries are alleged in a more particular fashion than the rules require. Paragraphs 10 and 11 demonstrate a claim of fraud and misrepresentation being pleaded with particularity. Paragraphs 17 to 19 plead punitive damages. The complaint also sets forth different counts, each alleging, in general, the type of prohibited conduct engaged in by defendant.

The federal equivalent of the demurrer   When a complaint states facts which, even if true, would not entitle the plaintiff to relief under any legal theory, the defendant may move to dismiss the complaint for failure to state a claim upon which relief can be granted (Fed. R. Cov. P. 12(b)(6)). This is the Federal Rules version of the demurrer.

Other circumstances warranting dismissal   Motions to dismiss may also be made if the complaint demonstrates that there is no jurisdiction over the person of the defendant, if the federal court lacks subject matter jurisdiction (federal question or diversity jurisdiction), if the complaint was not properly served upon the defendant, or if all necessary parties to the action have not been joined in the case.

The Defendant's Answer to a Federal Claim

Timing   In most instances, defendants file answers: an answer is a response to the complaint on the merits. The answer is due 20 days after service of the complaint, unless the time is otherwise extended.

Joinder of issue   The answer must separately deny or admit each allegation of the complaint. General denials are not permitted, although answers may aver that each paragraph of the complaint which is not specifically admitted or qualified is to be considered denied. A defendant may also respond that he does not have sufficient information regarding the truth of specific allegations and, therefore, deny those allegations demanding the plaintiff prove that allegation.

Pleading an affirmative case   In addition to merely denying the complaint's allegations, an answer may also contain affirmative defences which are matters constituting a defence or set-off to the claims set forth in the complaint.[1] The complaint may also plead many of the defences which could have been raised by motion to dismiss under Rule 12, discussed above. Since motions to dismiss are so rarely granted, many defendants often prefer to answer and plead affirmative defences rather than file a motion to dismiss.

Example   Exhibit D (below) is an example of an answer to a complaint alleging personal injury and property and damage caused by the leaching of toxic chemicals into the groundwater and water supply of the plaintiff's house. In addition to answering the allegations of the complaint, this answer asserts several affirmative defences. Affirmative Defence 7 asserts contributory negligence. Affirmative Defence 4 asserts that the statute of limitation has run, and Affirmative Defence 8 asserts the doctrine of laches.

Cross-claims   An answer may also contain a cross-claim. A cross-claim is a claim made by one defendant against other defendants to the action. It may seek indemnity or contribution or set forth other matters for which the other defendants may be liable.

Counter-claims   In addition to the complaint and answer, the Federal Rules allow counter-claims (a claim by a defendant against the plaintiff) and third party complaints (a claim asserted by a defendant against a party not named in the original complaint). A plaintiff who is served with a counter-claim must also respond to that counter-claim in similar fashion. The allegations of the counter-claim need not relate to the subject-matter of the plaintiff's complaint in which it is brought. A defendant may counter-claim against a plaintiff for any claim that he may have against the plaintiff, whether it is or is not part of the same transaction. Counter-claims may plead matters in set-off of the original complaint or may seek additional recovery from the plaintiff. If a counter-claim is pleaded, the defendant may name entities that are not already parties to the suit as additional defendants to the counter-claim. No other pleading is allowed, except that the court may order a reply to an answer or a third party answer.

Third party procedure   A third party complaint can be brought against non-parties if a defendant alleges that he is entitled to indemnity or contribution from that third party for any damages that that defendant may

---

[1] Defences to be set forth affirmatively are accord and satisfaction, arbitration and award, assumption of risk, contributory negligence, discharge and bankruptcy, duress, estoppel, failure of consideration, fraud, illegality, injury by fellow servant, laches, licence, payment, release, *res judicata*, statute of frauds, statutes of limitations, waiver, and any other matter constituting an avoidance or affirmative defence (Fed. R. Civ. P. 8(c)).

ultimately owe to the plaintiff. In third party complaints, a cross-claim can be pleaded in the alternative; the defendant may deny liability to the plaintiff while claiming that the defendant is entitled to indemnity or contribution if he has to pay the plaintiff. A third party defendant who is joined by separate process in the action is required to respond to the third party complaint by either motion or answer.

Amendment

Flexibility The Federal Rules greatly simplified and liberalized the amendment of pleadings. Any pleading may be amended once as a matter of course before a responsive pleading is served. Otherwise, pleadings may be amended by written consent of the court, which is to be "freely given when justice so requires" (Fed. R. Civ. P. 15(a)). In addition, any issue not raised in the pleadings which is tried by express or implied consent shall be treated as if it had been pleaded (Fed. R. Civ. P. 15(b)).

Amendment at trial If evidence is objected to at trial because it is not within the issue raised by the pleadings, the court will generally freely allow the pleadings to be amended so long as the opposing party will not be prejudiced by the amendment. Amendment of pleadings may even be made after trial to conform the pleadings to the evidence (*ibid.*). Moreover, "every final judgment shall grant the relief to which the party in whose favour it is rendered is entitled, even if the party has not demanded such relief in the party's pleadings" (Fed. R. Civ. P. 54(c)).

Pleadings in the State Courts

Generally—notice pleading Most, but not all, states have adopted rules of civil procedure based in part or whole on the Federal Rules, including use of "notice pleading." Many state rules contain their own variations and each should be consulted for actions in those states. These variations will not be discussed here.

Exceptionally—fact pleading However, pleading in some states is still governed by code pleading statutes which require that facts be pleaded. These states require much less specificity in pleading than their nineteenth century predecessors and by and large are hybrids of notice and code pleading rules. While the varied pleading rules of states following code pleading may be confusing, national law firms have little trouble practicing in various jurisdictions with expertise.

New York State Among the states following code pleading, New York seems to have retained the greatest requirement of specificity. The New York code requires the complaint to be sufficiently particular as to "put

344

the parties and the court on notice of transactions and occurrences intended to be proven and the material elements of each cause of action or defense" (N.Y. Civ. Prac. L. and R. 3013 (McKinney 1988)). Under the New York rules, as opposed to the Federal Rules, particular facts must be pleaded which will support a specific cause of action. The New York code also contains a long list of types of actions that require extra particularity of pleading (N.Y. Civ. Prac. L. and R. 3016 (McKinney 1988)). As under the Federal Rules, the circumstances of fraud and mistake must be pleaded specifically. In addition, actions for libel or slander, separation or divorce, personal injury and negligent or intentional harm by corporate officers and trustees must also be specifically pleaded. Like all the modern code states, New York allows alternative and hypothetical pleading.

Defendant's riposte—the bill of particulars If a party to an action in New York believes that the pleading served against it lacks sufficient particularity, the party may move the court for a bill of particulars. Exhibit D is a sample New York bill of particulars for a personal injury action. In New York, personal injury actions must meet statutory guidelines for particularity. As shown in Exhibit D, defendants can often obtain details concerning the date and the approximate time and location of the occurrence, statements of the acts or omissions constituting negligence and the particular statement of the injuries. Generally, the bill of particulars must be responsive to the specific deficiencies complained of by the opposing party and recognised by the court in its order for the bill.

Examples of pleading requirements in other states In addition to New York, several other states have pleading codes that require greater particularity than do the Federal Rules. Missouri, for example, has a pleading code very similar to the Federal Rules but requiring the complaint to contain a short and plain statement of the *facts* showing that the pleader is entitled to relief (Mo. R. Civ. $ 55.05 (West 1989)). While demanding that facts be pled, Missouri does not require most causes of action to be pleaded with particularity, nor does Missouri have a provision for obtaining a bill of particulars. Illinois, on the other hand, does not require the pleading of facts, but does provide a mechanism by which a bill of particulars may be obtained "if the allegations are so wanting in details . . . " (Ill. Code Civ. Proc. $ 607(a) (Smith-Hurd 1988)). Florida has a pleading code that does not require the specificity of the New York code but nonetheless insists that the complaint contain a short and plain statement of the "ultimate facts" showing that the pleader is entitled to relief (Fla. R. Civ. P. $ 1.110(b) (West 1985)). Still other states, such as California, have retained elements of the old code and common law pleading days, such as the demurrer to the complaint, not often found in twentieth century American pleading (Cal. Civ. Proc. Code $ 472a (West 1988)).

Contrasting originating process in federal and state courts As noted above, filing of a complaint starts the action in the Federal Court. Not all states follow that practice. For example, filing of a complaint is not necessary to start a case in Minnesota; in that state simply placing the complaint with a service may suffice. In some states an action may be started by filing a summary and no complaint may be necessary in that state.

Model Pleadings

EXHIBIT A

(Case Caption)

COMPLAINT

1. (Allegation of diversity jurisdiction).
2. On June 1, 1986, on a public highway called Boylston Street in Boston, Massachusetts, defendant Sam Jones or defendant John Smith, or both defendants Sam Jones and John Smith wilfully or recklessly or negligently drove or caused to be driven a motor vehicle against plaintiff who was then crossing the highway.
3. As a result, plaintiff was thrown down and had his leg broken and was otherwise injured, was prevented from transacting his business, suffered great pain of body and mind, and incurred expenses for medical attention and hospitalization in the sum of one thousand dollars ($1,000).

Wherefore plaintiff demands judgment against Sam Jones or against John Smith or against both in the sum of————DOLLARS ($——) and costs.

_____

(Attorney)
(Attorney Number)
(Address)
(Phone)
ATTORNEY FOR PLAINTIFF

_____

EXHIBIT B

UNITED STATES DISTRICT COURT
DISTRICT OF MINNESOTA
FOURTH DIVISION

COMPLAINT
Court File No. _____

_____

_____
Plaintiff
vs.

_____
Defendant
_____

Plaintiff _____, by her counsel Robins, Kaplan, Miller & Ciresi, for her claim against defendant _____ states and alleges as follows:

INTRODUCTION

1. Plaintiff——is a citizen and resident of the State of Minnesota.

2. Defendant——is a corporation organised and existing under the laws of the State Delaware, with its post office address and principal place of business at P.O. Box 1000, 400 Main Street, New York, New York 10010. Said corporation may be served with a Summons by serving any of defendant's offices, managing agents, or agents expressly or impliedly authorised to receive service of summons.

3. This Court has jurisdiction of this action pursuant to 28 U.S.C. $ 1332 in that there is diversity of citizenship between the parties and the amount in controversy exceeds Fifty Thousand Dollars ($50,000), exclusive of interest and costs.

4. At all times material herein, defendant has been in the business of manufacturing an intra-uterine contraceptive (IUD) and promoting and selling the IUD and other pharamaceutical products in the State of Minnesota. Whenever the IUD is referred to herein, it is intended to include the IUD, its tail string, its inserter, packaging, labeling and all other materials incident to its physical make-up, distribution, sale or advertising, except where more specific reference is made to the intra-uterine contraceptive itself, or the same is apparent from the context.

5. On or about——in the State of Minnesota, (plaintiff) had inserted in her uterus, for the purpose of contraception, an IUD manufactured by defendant. On or about——in the State of Minnesota, the IUD was removed from plaintiff——. As a direct result of her use of the IUD, (plaintiff) has suffered prolonged pain and severe suffering and illnesses and injuries, including but not limited to:

  a. Chronic pelvic inflammatory disease, chronic endometritis and left tubo-ovarian abscess with adhesion formation;
  b. Primary infertility;

all resulting in hospitalization and extensive medical treatment, together with numerous incidental and consequential complications, and severe pain, suffering and mental anguish. The fore-going illnesses and injuries have continued to the present time and are likely to continue into the future, resulting in further surgery and extensive medical treatment to (plaintiff).

6. (Plaintiff) has in the past, and will in the future incur medical expense, lost income, and many other damages, all as a result of the many wrongful acts of the defendant in the design, testing, manufacturing, labeling, promotion and sale of the IUD. (Plaintiff) does not presently know the exact cost for services of physicians, surgeons and hospitals, but these services have been incurred and are reasonably likely to be required in the future, and (plaintiff) expressly reserves the right to amend this Complaint with respect to damages to conform to her exact expenses and damages. (Plaintiff) also does not presently know the full extent of past and future loss of income, and many other damages, and likewise reserves the right later to amend this Complaint to conform with those actual damages.

7. Despite the diligence of (plaintiff), she was unable to discover defendant's fraudulent and other wrongful acts until April 1988. Defendant's fraudulent acts include its efforts to conceal its wrongful acts and the true risks of the IUD from physicians and the consuming public, including (plaintiff).

COUNT ONE—NEGLIGENCE

For this Count, (plaintiff) incorporates paragraphs 1 through 7, above, and further states and alleges:

8. Defendant had a duty to use the care of an expert in all aspects of the design, testing, manufacturing, labelling, promotion, distribution and sale of the IUD to ensure the safety of the product and to ensure that the consuming public, including (plaintiff), obtained accurate information regarding both the safety and characteristics of the IUD. Special care in the exercise of these duties is especially required of the manufacturer of a

pharmaceutical product such as an IUD, designed to affect the normal functioning of the human body, and where the defects and dangers in the product cannot reasonably be discovered by persons such as (plaintiff), denied access to the specialized knowledge and expertise possessed by defendant.

9. Defendant breached all of these duties, and defendant's breach of these duties directly resulted in (plaintiff)'s damages, stated above.

COUNT TWO—FRAUD AND MISREPRESENTATION

For this Count, (plaintiff) incorporates paragraphs 1 through 7, above, and further states and alleges:

10. Defendant fraudulently, intentionally and negligently misrepresented the characteristics and safety of the IUD, and fraudulently, intentionally and negligently concealed material, adverse information regarding the characteristics and safety of the IUD. Defendant made these misrepresentations and concealed adverse information at a time when defendant knew, or should have known, that the IUD had defects, dangers and characteristics that were other than defendant had represented to physicians, the Food and Drug Administration (FDA) and the consuming public, including (plaintiff). Specifically:

a. Defendant misrepresented to plaintiff, her doctors, the FDA and the general public the IUD's efficacy, safety, and propensity to cause pelvic infection, ectopic pregnancy, infertility, and other adverse reactions.

b. Defendant misrepresented the safety and efficacy of the IUD in its labelling, advertising and promotional materials.

c. Knowing that its pre-marketing testing of the IUD was inadequate, defendant promoted and sold the IUD as if it were fully and adequately tested.

d. In its promotional brochures and journal advertising, defendant advertised the IUD as having a low incidence of side effects when in fact it knew that there was a substantial risk of serious pelvic inflammatory disease accompanying the use of the device.

e. Defendant realized and was well aware of the substantial risk of pelvic inflammatory disease associated with the use of the IUD but failed to provide adequate warnings to plaintiff, her doctors, the FDA and the general public which fairly reflected the risks known to defendant.

f. Defendant promoted the IUD as suitable for use in certain women that it knew were not appropriate candidates for the IUD, such as women who had not completed their families and still wished to have children, nulliparous women and young women.

349

g. Defendant misrepresented to plaintiff, her doctors, the FDA and to the general public that the IUD tailstring was a monofilament when it knew that the tailstring was actually a fused bundle of filaments which become frayed during the manufacturing process thereby increasing bacterial adherence to the trailstring and increasing the risk of pelvic inflammatory disease.

h. Defendant misrepresented to plaintiff, her doctors, the FDA and to the general public that the IUD was well suited for women whose uteri measured less than 7 cm when it knew that the size of the IUD was too large for these women.

i. Defendant misrepresented to plaintiff, her doctors, the FDA and to the general public that the IUD had a low incidence of pelvic inflammatory disease when it knew that the "memory" characteristic of the tailstring caused it to retract and carry bacteria from the vagina to the uterus thereby increasing the risk of pelvic inflammatory disease.

j. Defendant misrepresented to plaintiff, her doctors, the FDA and to the general public that the IUD had a low incidence of pelvic inflammatory disease when it knew that the presence of the tailstring along the outside of the inserter resulted in it becoming contaminated by bacteria in the vagina and cervix upon insertion and resulted in the IUD having a high rate of pelvic infections soon after insertion.

11. Defendant made these misrepresentations with the intention and specific desire that physicians and the consuming public would rely on them in selecting the IUD.

12. (Plaintiff) and her physician relied on and were induced by defendant's misrepresentations in selecting the IUD as a contraceptive, and (plaintiff)'s use of the IUD directly caused all her damages, stated above.

COUNT THREE—STRICT LIABILITY

For this Count, (plaintiff) incorporates paragraphs 1 through 7, above, and further states and alleges:

13. The IUDs manufactured, sold, promoted and distributed by the defendant were, at the time they left the defendant, defective products, unreasonably dangerous for use, resulting in the injuries and damages to (plaintiff) as statoducts, unreasonably dangerous for use, resulting in the injuries and damages to (plaintiff) as stated above. (Plaintiff) therefore relies upon the doctrine of strict liability in tort against defendant. (Plaintiff) used the IUD in the way defendant intended it to be used and in a manner which was reasonably foreseeable by defendant. (Plaintiff)'s injuries and reliance upon defendant's misrepresentations and expertise were reasonably foreseeable by defendant.

350

COUNT FOUR—IMPLIED WARRANTIES

For this Count, (plaintiff) incorporates paragraphs 1 through 7, above, and further states and alleges:

14. The IUD manufactured, distributed, promoted and sold by the defendant was not fit for the purpose for which it was designed and was not of merchantable quality. (Plaintiff) relied to her detriment on defendant's implied warranties, directly resulting in her injuries and damages as stated above.

COUNT FIVE—EXPRESS WARRANTIES

For this Count, (plaintiff) incorporates paragraphs 1 through 7, above, and further states and alleges:

15. Defendant, through its product literature, advertising materials, and marketing methods and tactics, expressly warranted that the IUD was safe and fit for the use for which it was intended. Defendant breached its express warranties made orally and those contained in the written or printed materials published with information coming directly and indirectly from defendant. (Plaintiff) relied to her detriment on defendant's express warranties, directly resulting in her use of the IUD and her injuries and damages, stated above.

COUNT SIX—DECEPTIVE TRADE PRACTICES

For this Count, (plaintiff) incorporates paragraphs 1 through 7, above, and further states and alleges:

16. Defendant intentionally used fraud, misrepresentation, false advertising and other deceptive practices in the promotion, distribution and sale of the IUD in violation of Minnesota Statutes, Chapters 325D and 325F, directly resulting in injury and damage to (plaintiff) as stated above.

COUNT SEVEN—PUNITIVE DAMAGES

For this Count, (plaintiff) incorporates paragraphs 1 through 7, above, and further states and alleges:

17. Defendant was grossly negligent, willful, wanton and malicious in the design, testing, manufacturing, labelling, promotion, marketing and distribution of the IUD and in the failing to warn (plaintiff), her doctors and members of the medical profession of the dangers which were well known to defendant. Defendant also intentionally used fraudulent and false statements and representations in its labelling, promotional material and marketing tactics in an effort to sell the IUD. Defendant realized the

imminence of danger to (plaintiff) and other members of the public, but continued its marketing and promotional tactics with reckless disregard and complete indifference and unconcern for the probable consequence of its acts.

18. As the direct result of the gross negligence, willful, wanton and malicious acts, misrepresentations, fraud and other wrongful acts of defendant, (plaintiff) suffered the injuries and damages stated above.

19. Defendant's acts as described herein were grossly negligent, malicious, oppressive, willful and wanton. An award of punitive and exemplary damages is therefore necessary to punish defendant and to deter any re-occurrence of this intolerable conduct. Consequently, (plaintiff) is entitled to an award of punitive and exemplary damages.

WHEREFORE, (plaintiff) demands judgment against defendant as follows:

1. Awarding plaintiff compensatory damages against defendant in an amount sufficient to compensate plaintiff fairly and completely;
2. Awarding plaintiff punitive damages against defendant in an amount sufficient to punish defendant for its wrongful conduct and deter defendant and others from similar wrongful conduct in the future;
3. Awarding plaintiff her costs and disbursements, cost of investigation, attorneys' fees and other relief as may be available under Minnesota Statutes, Chapters 325D and 325F;
4. Awarding plaintiff pre- and post- judgment interest on her award;
5. Awarding such other and further relief as the Court may deem just.

Dated this——day of——, 1989.

ROBINS, KAPLAN, MILLER & CIRESI
By: _____
(A member of the firm)

1800 International Centre
900 Second Avenue South
Minneapolis, Minnesota 55402
(612) 349–8500

PLAINTIFF HEREBY DEMANDS A TRIAL BY JURY OF ALL ISSUES.

EXHIBIT C

STATE OF WISCONSIN   CIRCUIT COURT   SAUK COUNTY

_____

_____

Plaintiffs.

v.

_____

Defendants.

*ANSWERS AND AFFIRMATIVE
DEFENSES OF
COMPANY*

_____

NOW COMES DEFENDANTS,——by their attorneys, Robins, Kaplans, Miller & Ciresi, and as their answer to the Complaint on file herein, admit, deny and show the Court the following:

1. Deny any liability to plaintiffs under the common law or the statutory provisions referred to in paragraph 1.

2. Deny having knowledge or information sufficient to form a belief as to the truth of paragraphs 2, 3 and 4.

3. Answering paragraph 5, admit that defendant——is a Wisconsin municipal corporation with its principal place of business——and deny having knowledge or information sufficient to form a belief as to the truth of the remaining allegations.

4. Deny having knowledge or information sufficient to form a belief as to the truth of paragraph 6.

5. Admit the allegations of paragraph 7.

6. Deny having knowledge or information sufficient to form a belief as to the truth of paragraphs 8, 9, 10, 11 and 12.

7. Admit the allegations of paragraph 13.

8. Answering paragraph 14, admit that defendant——owns and operates a manufacturing plant in the City of——and deny the remaining allegations set out therein.

9. Deny having knowledge or information sufficient to form a belief as to the truth of paragraphs 15 and 16.

10. Answering paragraph 17, admit that the landfill received waste from the operations of——until 1973, and deny the remaining allegations set forth therein.

11. Answering paragraphs 18, 19, 20 and 21, deny each and every allegation as it pertains to——and deny having knowledge or information sufficient to form a belief as to those allegations which pertain to the other defendants.

353

12. Deny having knowledge or information sufficient to form a belief as to the truth of paragraphs 22, 23, and 24.

13. Answering paragraphs 25, 26, 27 and 28, deny each and every allegation as it pertains to————and deny having knowledge or information sufficient to form a belief as to those allegations which pertain to the other defendants.

14. Answering paragraph 29, deny that————is liable jointly or severally to plaintiffs for their alleged damages.

FIRST CAUSE OF ACTION

15. Answering paragraph 30,————reallege and incorporate herein by reference their answers to paragraphs 1 through 29.

16. Deny the allegations of paragraph 31.

SECOND CAUSE OF ACTION

17. Answering paragraph 32,————reallege and incorporate by reference their answers to paragraphs 1 through 31.

18. Deny the allegations of paragraph 33.

THIRD CAUSE OF ACTION

19. Answering paragraph 34,————reallege and incorporate by reference their answers to paragraphs 1 through 33.

20. Deny the allegations of paragraph 35.

FOURTH CAUSE OF ACTION

21. Answering paragraph 36,————reallege and incorporate by reference their answers to paragraphs 1 through 35.

22. Deny the allegations of paragraph 37.

23. Deny having knowledge or information sufficient to form a belief as to the truth of the paragraphs 38, 39, 40, 41, 42, 44, 45, 46, 47, 48, 49, 50, 51, 52, 53, 54, 55, 56, 57, 58, 59, 60, 61, 62 and 63.

24. Admit the allegations of paragraph 43.

AFFIRMATIVE DEFENCE

As and for their affirmative defences,————alleges as follows:

1. The plaintiffs lack personal jurisdiction over————due to defective service of process.

2. The plaintiffs' Amended Complaint, authenticated on June 18, 1987, and Amended Summons, authenticated on July 31, 1987 are insufficient and defective to obtain personal jurisdiction over defendant————.

3. Plaintiffs' Amended Complaint fails to state a claim against defendant————upon which relief can be granted.

4. The plaintiffs' claims are barred in whole or in part by the applicable statutes of limitations.

5. Any injuries or damages suffered by the plaintiffs were not proximately caused by any acts or omissions of defendant————.

6. Upon information and belief, the plaintiffs' injuries and damages, if any, were and are the result of the acts or omissions of other persons, including persons and entities that have not been named as parties in this litigation, over whom these defendants exercise no control and for whom these defendants cannot be held liable.

7. Upon information and belief, the plaintiffs' injuries and damages, if any, were and are the result of their own negligence, fault or their conduct, and such contributory negligence is a complete or proportionate bar to the claims asserted.

8. Upon information and belief, the plaintiffs' claims are barred by the doctrine of laches.

9. Upon information and belief, the plaintiffs' claims have been waived.

10. Upon information and belief, the plaintiffs' have failed to mitigate, minimize or avoid part or all of their damages.

11. Upon information and belief, the plaintiffs' claims are barred by the doctrine of assumption of risk.

12. Upon information and belief, the plaintiffs have failed to join parties necessary and indispensable to a complete and just adjudication of this controversy.

13. Upon information and belief, contrary to Section 803.03 Wis. Stats., the plaintiffs have failed to join parties having an interest in the plaintiffs' claims based upon the principles of subrogation.

14. Upon information and belief, the plaintiffs have failed to exhaust their administrative remedies.

15. Upon information and belief, the plaintiffs' damages, if any, were caused by an intervening and superseding cause for which these defendants are not liable.

16. The alleged cause of the plaintiffs' damages is too remote as a matter of public policy.

17. The dump existed prior to the plaintiffs' ownership or use of the homes or wells which are the subject of this lawsuit.

WHEREFORE, the defendant————demands that this action be dismissed in its entirety on the merits and without prejudice, and that

said defendant be awarded the costs and disbursements incurred by them in defending this action.
Dated this—day of——, 1989.

> ROBINS, KAPLAN, MILLER & CIRESI
> By _____
> (A Member of the Firm)
>
> 1800 International Centre
> 900 Second Avenue South
> Minneapolis, Minnesota 55402
> (612) 349–8500
>
> ATTORNEYS FOR DEFENDANT

EXHIBIT D

BILL OF PARTICULARS

Index No.——
The following is plaintiff's bill of particulars:

1. The occurrence took place on——19—, at about——o'clock in the——noon of that day.

2. The accident occurred on the east side of——Avenue, near the intersection of——Street, southeast corner.

3. The defendants, their agents, servants and/or employees in causing, suffering and permitting and vehicle roadway located at——Avenue and Street, Borough of——, City of——, to be in a defective and dangerous condition in that they failed adequately to fill in the excavation; in permitting same to project above the level of the vehicular roadway; in failing to protect pedestrians in connection therewith; in causing and permitting same to exist so that pedestrians were liable to trip, stumble and/or fall over the aforesaid excavation; in failing to place lights, signals or other warning or protective devices at or near the said excavation or hole; in failing to place any guards, timbers or other protection around said hole or excavation, and failing to remove or remedy the said dangerous condition; in failing to have the motor bus or motor vehicle in proper condition and repair; in failing to observe the road; in failing to have

competent help; in failing to have said motor bus or vehicle under proper management and control; in failing to heed traffic conditions and/or stop; in carelessly stopping and/or parking said motor bus or vehicle to discharge passengers at a dangerous place, were negligent.

4. Upon information and belief, plaintiff sustained the following injuries:

Trimalleolar fracture of the right ankle, with dislocation of the ankle joint and displacement of fragments, necessitating operative procedures in the nature of a closed reduction, and subsequently an open reduction, with screw fixation and application of a leg cast; sprain of the left ankle, necessitating a posterior moled splint from below the knee to the toes; edema of the left ankle; swelling and deformity of the right ankle, pain, tenderness, limitation of motion and impairment of function of right and left lower extremities; injury to muscles, tendons, cartilage, ligaments, blood vessels and other soft tissue in and about fracture sites; shock; multiple bruises and contusions.

Upon information and belief, all of the fore-going injuries are of a permanent nature, except those bruises and contusions which have healed.

5. Plaintiff was confined to hospital for 13 days; to bed, house and home intermittently to date hereof, and will so continue to be confined for some time to come.

6. Plaintiff has been incapacitated from employment from date of accident to date hereof and will continue to be so incapacitated for some time to come.

7. Plaintiff's usual occupation is that of a baby-sitter and her earnings averaged about———— ($——) dollars weekly. Plaintiff had no definite employer, but was employed from time to time by various persons.

8. Plaintiff expended, or became obligated to expend, and the following sums were expended on behalf of the plaintiff: hospital expenses, approximately———— ($——) dollars. Plaintiff claims loss of earnings of approximately———— ($——) dollars to date hereof.

9. Actual and constructive notice of the condition complained of is claimed. Plaintiff claims actual notice in that the defendants caused said condition, maintained the same, permitted the same and continued same for such length of time that defendants knew or should have known said condition existed.

DATED:——, 19—.

(Attorney)
(Attorney Number)
(Address)
(Phone)
(ATTORNEY FOR PLANTIFF)

The European Courts of Justice
Philippa Watson Ph.D., Barrister, (London and Brussels)

A The Court of Justice of the European Communities

This Appendix will deal with the Court of Justice of the European Communities and the Court of First Instance of the European Communities.

Origins   The Court of Justice of the European Communities can be traced back to the Court of Justice of the European Coal and Steel Community (ECSC) set up, under the Treaty of Paris 1951 (Arts. 31–45 of the ECSC Treaty). It came into being on December 1, 1952 and delivered its first judgment on December 21, 1954.

When the European Economic Community (EEC) and the European Atomic Energy Commission (Euratom) were set up under two Treaties of Rome in 1957, a Convention on Certain Institutions common to the European Communities provided that a single court should act as the Court of Justice of those two Communities and that it should take over the function of the European Coal and Steel Community's Court of Justice.

Function   The function of the Court of the European Communities is to ensure that in the interpretation and application of the Treaties, and in the rules laid down for their implementation, the law is observed (Art. 31 of the ECSC Treaty; Art. 164 of the EEC Treaty; Art. 136 of the Euratom Treaty). In addition, jurisdiction is conferred on the court to give preliminary rulings on the interpretation of the Convention on the Jurisdiction and Enforcement of Judgments in Civil and Commercial matters (Protocol on the Interpretation by the Court of Justice of the Convention on Jurisdiction and Enforcement of Judgments in Civil and Commercial matters (Cmnd 7394. O.J. 1983 C 97/24)) and jurisdiction will be conferred on the Court to give preliminary rulings on the interpretation of the Mutual Recognition of Companies and Legal Persons (Protocol concerning the Interpretation by the Court of Justice of the Convention on the Mutual Recognition of Companies and Legal Persons) when this convention comes into force. In addition various other specific functions are conferred upon the Court.

Composition

The Judiciary The Court of Justice is composed of 13 judges. The Court sits in plenary session or in Chambers. The quorum of judges required for a plenary session is either seven, nine, 11 or 13 judges. Chambers consist of either three or six judges. At present there are four sets of Chambers of three judges and two sets of Chambers of six judges. For the rules and the principles governing the assignment of cases to the Court or Chambers see page 368.

The Court is assisted in its functions by six Advocates General. The duty of the Advocates General is to deliver, in open court, reasoned opinions on cases brought before the Court in order to assist it in the performance of its tasks (Art. 32(a)(2) of the ECSC Treaty; Protocol on the Statute of the Court of Justice, Art. II; Article 166(2) of the EEC Treaty; Article 138(2) of the Euratom Treaty).

Qualifications The judges and advocates general are selected from persons whose independence is beyond doubt and who possess qualifications required for appointment to the highest judicial office in their respective Member States or who are jurisconsults of recognised competence Art. 32(b)(1) of the ECSC Treaty; Article 167 of the EEC Treaty; Article 139(1) of the Euratom Treaty).

Appointment Judges and advocates general are appointed by the common accord of the governments of the Member States for a renewable term of six years. Every three years there is a partial replacement of the members of the Court (Art. 32(b)(1) of the ECSC Treaty; Art. 167(1) of the EEC Treaty; Art. 139(1) of the Euratom Treaty).

Disqualification A judge or an advocate general is prohibited from participating in any case in which he has previously been involved as agent or adviser, or in which he has acted for one of the parties or in which he has been called upon to pronounce as a member of a court or tribunal, of a commission of enquiry or in any other capacity (Art. 19(1) of the ECSC Treaty Protocol on the Statute of the Court of Justice; Art. 16(1) of the EEC Treaty Protocol on the Statute of the Court of Justice; Art. 16(1) of the Euratom Treaty Protocol on the Statute of the Court of Justice).

Dismissal Under the ECSC Treaty a judge may be deprived of his office only if, in the unanimous opinion of the other judges he no longer fulfils the conditions of appointment to his office. The Presidents of the EC Council and the EC Commission and the European Parliament must be notified of that decision by the Registrar Art. 7 of the ECSC Treaty Protocol on the Statute of the Court of Justice).

The EEC and Euratom Treaties provide that a judge or advocate general may be deprived of his office or his right to a pension or other benefits only if, in the unamimous opinion of the other judges and advocates general he no longer fulfils the necessary conditions of his office or meets the obligation arising from that office (Arts. 6(1) and 8 of the EEC Treaty Protocol on the Statute of the Court of Justice; Arts. 6(1) and 8 of the Euratom Treaty Protocol on the Statute of the Court of Justice).

Organisation

The President of the Court   The President is elected by the judges in a secret ballot for a term of three years. He can be re-elected (Art. 32(b) of the ECSC Treaty; Art. 167 of the EEC Treaty; Art. 135 of the Euratom Treaty Rules of Procedure of the Court of Justice, Art. 7, codified version O.J. 1982 C 39/1). The President directs the judicial business and the administration of the Court. He presides at hearings and at deliberations of the court in the Deliberation Room (Rules of Procedure of the Court of Justice, Article 8, codified version O.J. 1982 C 39/1 as amended O.J. 1987 HL165, O.J. 3 1989 2241). As soon as an application originating proceedings is lodged, the President assigns the case to one of the Chambers for any preparatory inquiries. A judge from that Chamber is designated to act as Rapporteur (Rules of Procedure, Art. 9(1)(2), codified version).

Judge-Rapporteur   The Judge-Rapporteur is primarily responsible for cases assigned to him. At the close of written proceedings, his task is to prepare a short report to be considered by his fellow judges, the advocate general and the registrar. This report identifies the main issues in the case and makes recommendations as to the way in which it should be dealt with (*e.g.* by the Court sitting in plenary session or by Chambers, the necessity for preparatory inquiries, questions to be put to the parties before the oral hearing, etc.). The Judge-Rapporteur is responsible for the preparation of the Report for the hearing, in which the main issues of the case and the pleadings of the parties are set out. Finally, after the opinion of the advocate general has been given and the court has decided the broad lines of the judgment it proposes to make, it is the Judge-Rapporteur who will draft that judgment for consideration by the members of the court in deliberation.

Presidents of Chambers   These are appointed by the President of the Court for a period of one year. Presidents of Chambers preside at hearings of the Chambers of which they are President and at deliberations in the Deliberation Room of that Chamber.

The First Advocate General   President of the Court appoints the First Advocate General for a period of one year. As soon as the Judge-Rapporteur for a particular case has been designated by the President, the First Advocate General must assign the case to an Advocate General.

The Registrar   The Registrar of the Court is appointed for a term of six years by the Court. He may be reappointed (Rules of Procedure of the Court of Justice, Art. 12, codified version). The Registrar is assisted by two *Assistant Registrars*.

Role of the Registrar   The Registrar assists the Court, The Chambers, the President and the Judges in all their official functions. He is responsible under the authority of the President for the administration of the Court, its financial management and its accounts.

Forms of action   The Court's jurisdiction is laid down in the Treaties and other instruments. These include conventions, agreements and secondary legislation, the most important of which are to be found in selected instruments published by the Court. The Court's jurisdiction may be direct, that is where a party seises the Court directly or indirect, where a case comes to the Court by way of reference for a preliminary rule from a national court or tribunal.

Direct jurisdiction: general

  (a) *Infringement Proceedings*   Infringement proceedings, that is actions against Member States for failure to fulfil their obligations under Community law, can be brought by either the Commission of the European Communities or another Member State.
  (b) *Proceedings brought by the Commission*   Art. 169 of the EEC Treaty and Art. 149 of the Euratom Treaty provide that if the Commission considers that a Member State has failed to fulfil an obligation under the Treaty, it must give a reasoned opinion on the matter, after giving the state concerned an opportunity to submit its observations. If the Member State concerned does not comply with this opinion within the period laid down by the Commission, the Commission may bring the matter before the Court.
  (c) *Proceedings brought by a Member State*   Art. 170 of the EEC Treaty and Art. 142 of the Euratom Treaty give Member States the right to bring proceedings against another Member State for failure to fulfil its obligation under the Treaty. A Member State wishing to take such proceedings must first bring the matter before the Commission. Proceedings before the Court can be com-

menced once the Commission has given a reasoned opinion on the matter. If, within a period of three months the date when the matter was brought before it, the Commission has not delivered a reasoned opinion, the Member State in question can proceed to seise the Court.

The Commission and Member States can bring proceedings directly before the Court under Art. 93(2) of the EEC Treaty and Art. 225 of the Euratom Treaty.

Under the ECSC Treaty, the Commission must establish in a reasoned decision that a Member State has failed to fulfil and obligation under the Treaty (Art. 88). The Member State has then two months to apply for a review of this decision. If a Member State fails to comply with the Commission's decision or brings an unsuccessful action against it, the Commission may then with the assent of the Council either suspend payments due under the Treaty to that Member State or authorise other Member States to take corrective measures to rectify the infringement of the Treaty (Art. 88 of the ECSC Treaty). These powers in contrast with those of the Court in infringement proceedings brought under the EEC or Euratom Treaties, where only a judgment declaring failure to fulfil obligations under Community Law can be obtained. A judgment in favour of the applicant gives rise to an obligation on the part of the defendant institution to take steps to comply with the Court's judgment (Art. 149 of the Euratom Treaty; Art. 176 of the EEC Treaty).

Failure to act

(a) Under the ECSC Treaty (Art. 35), Member States, the Council, undertakings or associations may start proceedings before the Court against the failure of the Commission to adopt a decision or recommendation in the following circumstances: (i) where the Commission is required by the Treaty on rules laid down for its implementation to adopt a decision or recommendation; or (ii) where the Commission is empowered to make such a decision or oral recommendation and where it abstains from doing so, if such a abstention constitutes a misuse of powers.

(b) The person or body wishing to bring proceedings for failure to act under the ECSC Treaty must take the matter up with the Commission in the first instance. If, after a period of two months the commission has not taken any decision or made any recommendations, proceedings may be brought against the implied decision of a refusal which is to be inferred from the silence of the commission on the matter. Such proceedings must be commenced within one month of the expiry of the two month period referred to above. Within a period of two months proceedings must be brought within one month against the implied decisions of refusal which is to be inferred from the silence (of the Commission) on the matter.

(c) By virtue of Art. 175 of the EEC Treaty and Art. 148 of the Euratom Treaty, if the Council or Commission fails to act, the Member States and other Community institutions may bring an action to have the infringement established.

An application for a declaration of failure to act is admissible only if the institution in question, that is the Council or the Commission has been called upon to act. If within two months of being called upon to act, the institution has not defined its position, the action may be brought within a further two months.

Any natural or legal person may complain to the Court that a Community institution has failed to address to that person any act other than a recommendation or opinion.

(d) A successful complaint to the Court results in a declaration of failure to act and imposes an obligation on the defendant institution to take measures to comply with the Court's judgment, and consequently to take whatever action is the subject of the complaint.

Actions for annulment of Community acts can be taken under all three Community Treaties, but the right of action is not the same under all Treaties

(a) Under the ECSC Treaty (Art. 30) an action for annulment can be brought by a Member State, the Council or an undertaking or association of undertakings against the Commission. Member States and the Council may challenge a decision or recommendation of the Commission, but undertakings and association of undertakings have more limited rights: they can only challenge decisions or recommendations concerning them which are individual in character or general decisions or recommendations which they consider to involve a misuse of powers affecting them.

(b) In general the grounds on which an act of the Commission may be declared void are:
  (i) lack of competence;
  (ii) infringement of an essential procedural requirement;
  (iii) infringement of the Treaty or any rule relating to its application; and
  (iv) misuse of powers.

However, where an action for annulment is brought by an undertaking or association of undertakings against a general decision or recommendation the only ground which may be relied upon is misuse of powers.

In considering the legality of the decision or recommendation challenged before it, the Court's powers, with respect to the evidence it may take into consideration, are somewhat limited: it cannot examine the "evolution of a situation resulting from economic facts or circumstances, in the light of which [the Commission] took its decisions or made its recommendation" (Art. 33 of the ECSC Treaty). However, where the Commission is alleged to have misused its powers or to have manifestly failed to observe the Treaty or other Community law provision, the Court is not bound by the above mentioned limitation.

Proceedings must be brought within one month of the notification or publication of the measure challenged.

(c) There are two other provisions in the ECSC Treaty which grant the right to challenge an act of a Community institution: Art. 38 provides that an action for annulment may be brought within one month of the publication of the act, where it is adopted by the Parliament or in the case of an act of the Council, one month of its notification to the Member States or the Commission. Art. 63(2) provides that a purchaser of coal and steel may institute proceedings for the annulment of an act of the Commission restricting or prohibiting temporary dealings between the purchaser and Community undertakings.

(d) Under the EEC and Euratom Treaties, an action for annulment can be brought by:
  (i) a Member State;
  (ii) the Council; or
  (iii) the Commission;
against acts of the Council or the Commission other than recommendations or opinions. In addition a natural or legal person can challenge:
  (i) a decision addressed to that person; or
  (ii) a decision which although in the form of a regulation or decision addressed to another person, is of direct and individual concern to the former.

The grounds of challenge are the same as under the ECSC Treaty as set out above (page 364).

(e) The time limit for initiation of proceedings under the Euratom and EEC Treaties is two months from the date of publication of the measure or of its notification on the plaintiff, or in the absence thereof, the day on which it came to the knowledge of the latter, as the case may be.

(f) Under all three Treaties a successful action for annulment results in a declaration by the Court that the act in question is void. Following the ECSC Treaty (Art. 34), the Court must "refer the matter" back to the Commission which must take the necessary steps to comply with the judgment. Failure to do so within a reasonable time gives rise to the right of damages before the Court.

The EEC Treaty (Art. 176) and the Euratom Treaty (Art. 149) provide that the defendant institution's obligation to take measures to comply with the judgment does not affect possible liability for non-contractual damage.

Action for damages

(a) Under the ECSC Treaty an action for damages may be brought against the Commission in respect of:
   (i) failure to comply within a reasonable time with a judgment declaring a decision or recommendation of the Commission to be void (Art. 34); and
   (ii) breach of professional secrecy (Art. 47).
      An action may be brought against the Community (Art. 40) in respect of:
   (iii) a wrongful act or omission on the part of the Community in the performance of its functions; and
   (iv) with a personal wrong committed by a servant of the Community in the performance of his duties.
(b) The EEC Treaty (Art. 215) and the Euratom Treaty (Art. 178) simply provide that in the case of non-contractual liability "the Community shall, in accordance with the general principles common to the laws of all Member States make good any damage caused by its institutions on servants in the performance of their duties."
(c) The Community's contractual liability is governed by the law applicable to the contract.
(d) In general, liability in an action for damages is established where there is proof of:
   (i) unlawful conduct on the part of the defendant;
   (ii) damage, and
   (iii) a casual connection between the damage claimed and the alleged unlawful conduct.

Staff cases The Court has jurisdiction over disputes between the Community and its officials (Art. 42 of the ECSC Treaty; Art. 152 of the Euratom Treaty; Art. 179 of the EEC Treaty).

Disputes between Member States The Court has jurisdiction over disputes between Member States which relate to the subject matter of the Treaties and which are referred to it by special agreement between the parties (Art. 89 of the ECSC Treaty; Art. 154 of the Euratom Treaty; Art. 182 of the EEC Treaty).

Disputes concerning a member of the Commission and the Court of Auditors

(a) The Commission has jurisdiction over applications made by the Council or the Commission for a ruling that a member of the Commission should be compulsorily retired or be deprived of his pension or other benefit (Article 10, Merger Treaty).

(b) The Court may compulsorily retire a member of the Commission on the application of the Council or the Commission:
   (i) if he no longer fulfils the conditions required for the performance of his duties; or
   (ii) if he has been guilty of serious misconduct (Article 13, Merger Treaty).

(c) The Court of Auditors may apply to the Court for a ruling that one of its members no longer fulfils the conditions required for office or no longer meets the obligations arising from his office (Art. 78(e)(8) of the ECSC Treaty; Art. 180 of the Euratom Treaty; Art. 206(8) of the EEC Treaty).

Arbitration   All three Treaties provide that the Court has jurisdiction to give judgment pursuant to any arbitration clause contained in a contract concluded by or on behalf of the Community, whether that contract be governed by public or private law (Art. 42 of the ECSC Treaty Art. 153 of the Euratom Treaty; Article 181 of the EEC Treaty).

Interim Relief

(a) The three Treaties provide for the possibility of an application to the court for interim relief. An application for interim measures is admissible only if it is made by a party to a case before the Court and relates to that case (Rules of Procedure Article 83). The interim measures granted must be:
   (i) restricted to what is necessary to prevent the effectiveness of the Court's final judgment from being prejudiced whoever is the successful party (Joined Cases 24, and 971/80R. *Commission* v. *France* [1980] E.C.R. 1319 at 1337 *per* Advocate-General Capotorti);
   (ii) temporary, that is they cease to have effect when final judgment is delivered (Rules of Procedure, Art. 86(3)); and
   (iii) provisional in nature in that they do not prejudice the Court's final judgment on the substance of the case (Art. 34 of the ECSC Treaty Protocol on the Statute of the Court of Justice; Art. 36 of the EEC Treaty Protocol on the Statute of the

Court of Justice; Art. 37 of the Euratom Treaty Protocol on the Statute of the Court of Justice).

(b) An application for interim relief must state:
  (i) the subject-matter of the dispute;
  (ii) the circumstances giving rise to urgency; and
  (iii) the factual and legal grounds for establishing a prima facie case for the interim measure applied for (Rules of Procedure, Art. 83(2)).

(c) It must be shown that it is necessary for the order requested to be made and to take effect before the Court's judgment on the substance of the case in order to avoid serious and irreparable damage to the party seeking relief (Case 120/83 *Raznoimport* v. *Commission* [1983] E.C.R. 2573 at 2577).

(d) A prima facie case for relief is established if the applicant shows with a sufficient degree of probability that the claims made in the main case to which the application relates are both admissible and well founded in substance (Case 118/83 *Co-operativa Muratori* v. *Commission* [1983] E.C.R. 2583 at 2595).

Proceedings in applications for interim relief are summary and usually by the president of the Court sitting alone. However, the full Court will sit in the case of an application including complex issues of Law or fact.

Assignment of cases to Chambers   The Court must sit in plenary session when it hears cases brought before it by a Member State or a Community Institution. Proceedings commenced by an official or other servant of a Community Institution with the exception of interim relief are heard by a Chamber (Rules of Procedure, Art. 95(3)). In the case of other form of actions, these may be assigned to a Chamber in so far as the difficulty or the importance of the case or particular circumstances are not such as to require the Court to decide it in plenary session (Rules of Procedure, Art. 95(1)).

Procedure

Procedural rules: source   The procedural rules of the Court of Justice are laid down in the:

(a) Protocols on the Statutes of the Court of Justice;
(b) Rules of Procedure adopted by the Court and approved by the Court and approved unanimously by the Council;
(c) Supplementary Rules adopted by the Court of Justice; and
(d) Instructions to the Registrar.

The Consolidated Rules of Procedure of the Court, the Supplementary Rules and the Instructions to the Registrar can be found in (O.J. 1982 C 39, O.J. 1987 L 165, O.J. 1989 L 24).

B Direct Jurisdiction: specific

In addition to the general heads of jurisdiction set out above, jurisdiction over specific matters is granted to the Court under a variety of Instruments.

(a) *ECSC Treaty*

    (i) Article 37 of the ECSC Treaty provides that a Member State may complain to the Commission where an act or failure to act of the latter is considered by that Member State to be "of such a nature as to provoke fundamental and persistent disturbances in the economy." Proceedings may then be brought before the Court in respect of any decision by the Commission to rectify this decision or any express or implied refusal to recognise the existence of the situation.

    (ii) Article 43 of the ECSC Treaty provides that the Court "shall have jurisdiction in any other case provided for by a provision supplementing this Treaty" and "may also rule in all cases which relate to the subject matter of this Treaty where jurisdiction is conferred on it by the law of a Member State."

    (iii) *Concentrations*

    If the Commission finds that a concentration is unlawful it has power under Article 66 (5) of the ECSC Treaty to order the separation of the undertakings involved or their assets, the cessation of joint control or any other measures it considers appropriate to return the undertakings or assets in question to independent operation and restore normal conditions of competition. Any person directly concerned may institute proceedings for the annulment of such decisions of the Commission provided he is directly concerned by the decision he challenges.

    (iv) *Opinions*

    Article 95 of the ECSC Treaty provides that the Treaty may be amended where unforeseen difficulties in its application or fundamental economic or technical charges directly affecting the common market in coal and steel make it necessary to "adapt the rules for the High Authority's exercise of its powers." Amendments are proposed jointly by the Commission and the Council and then submitted to the Court for an opinion. If the Court finds that the proposed amendments are compatible with the Treaty they are then submitted to the Parliament and come into effect if they are approved by a

369

majority of three quarters of the votes cast and two thirds of its members.

Procedure

The request for an opinion must be submitted to the Court jointly by the Commission and the Special Council of Ministers. As soon as the request has been lodged, the President assigns one of the judges to act as rapporteur. After hearing all the Advocates General, the Court delivers a reasoned opinion in the Deliberation Room. This opinion is signed by the President, the judges who participated in the Deliberation and the Registrar. It is then served on the Commission, the Special Council of Ministers and the Parliament (Rules of Procedure, Article 109).

(b) *EEC Treaty*

    (i) Disputes concerning the European Investment Bank. Article 180 of EEC Treaty gives the Court jurisdiction over certain types of dispute concerning the European Investment Bank.

   (ii) Article 228 (1) of the EEC Treaty empowers the Council, the Commission or a Member State to apply to the Court for an opinion as to whether a proposed agreement between the Community and one or more States or an international organisation is compatible with the provisions of the Treaty. Proceedings begin with the lodging of a request, by the Council, the Commission or a Member State, for an opinion. The request is served on the Council and the Member States when it is lodged by the Commission. When the request is lodged by a Member State it is served on the Council, the Commission and the other Member States. When the Council requests an opinion it is served on the Commission only (Rules of Procedure, Article 107). As soon as the request for an opinion has been lodged, the President designates a Judge to act as Rapporteur. The President prescribes a period within which the institutions and the Member States which have been served with the request may submit their observations. After hearing the Advocate General, the court, sitting in the Deliberation Room, as opposed to open Court, delivers a reasoned opinion. The Opinion is signed by the President, by the judges which took part in the deliberations and by the Registrar and served on the Council, the Commission and the Member States.

(c) *Euratom Treaty*

    (i) *Licences*

        Article 12 of the Treaty provides that Member States, persons or undertakings have the right to obtain "non-exclusive licences under patents provisionally protected patent rights, utility models or patent applications owned by the Community" and "sub-licences under patents, provisionally protected patent rights, utility models or patent. Applications where the Community holds contractual licences conferring power [to grant them]." The right to a licence or sub-licence depends on the applicant being "able to make effective use of the inventions covered thereby." The application is made to the Commission which grants the licences or sub-licences on terms agreed between it and the applicant licensee. If no such agreement is reached, the applicant licensee may apply to the Court to fix the terms of the licence or sub-licence. No special procedure for such an action is laid down.

(ii) Appeals against decisions of the Euratom Arbitration Committee.

(iii) Inspections: The Commission has power to send inspectors to the Member States for the purpose of ensuring compliance with the safeguards laid down in the Euratom Treaty (Article 77). An inspector must be granted access "to all places and data and to all persons who, by reason of their occupation, deal with materials, equipment or installations subject to the safeguards provided for." If an inspector is refused such access, the Commission may apply to the President of the Court for an order that the inspection be carried out. This order must be made within three days of the application. Alternatively, if the inspection is pressing the Commission may issue an order in writing that it proceed. This order must be submitted to the President of the Court for his approval.

Applications to the Court for compulsory inspection orders must set out the name and address of the persons or undertakings to be inspected, an indication of what is to be inspected and of the purpose of the inspection (Rules of Procedure, Article 90).

(iv) Sanctions: Article 83 (1) of the Euratom Treaty provides for sanctions to be imposed by the Commission where a person or an undertaking breaches obligations relating to the safeguards provided for in the Treaty. These decisions may be reviewed by the Court, which has unlimited jurisdiction in such cases (Euratom Treaty, Article 144 (b)). No special procedure is laid down for such cases.

(v) Articles 103–105 Euratom Treaty: These provisions lay down rules to ensure that the objectives of the Treaty are not prejudiced by agreements or contracts entered into by the

Member States, a person or an undertaking, with a third
country, an international organisation or a national of a third
country.

The Commission and the Court are entrusted with certain
powers under these provisions.

Limitation periods   The time period during which proceedings must be
commenced before the Court of Justice are, in general, defined in the provisions of the Treaties granting the Court jurisdictions (*e.g.* Art. 173 of
the EEC Treaty provides that actions for annulment must be brought
within two months of the publication or notification of the measure in
question or failing publication or notification the day on which it came to
the applicant's notice). Expiry of the time limit will not be fatal if the
plaintiff can prove unavoidable circumstances or *force majeure* (Art.
39(3) of the ECSC Treaty Protocol on the Statute of the Court of Justice;
Art. 42(2) of the EEC Treaty Protocol on the statute to the Court of Justice; Art. 43(2) of the Euratom Treaty Protocol on the Statute to the
Court of Justice).

Art. 94 of the Rules of Procedure of the Court of Justice provides that
proceedings against a measure adopted by an institution runs from the
day following receipt by the person concerned of notification of the
measure or when the measure is published, from the fifteenth day after its
publication in the Official Journal.

Procedural time limits are extended for all parties, except those habitu-
ally resident in Luxembourg, to take into account distance between the
Court of Justice and the parties' place of habitual residence by the following periods: Belgium—two days; Federal Republic of Germany, the
European territories of France and of the Netherlands—six days; Den-
mark, Greece, Ireland, Italy, Portugal, Spain and the United Kingdom—
ten days; for other European countries and territories—two weeks;
Azores and Madeira—three weeks; and for other countries, departments
and territories—one month (Rules of Procedure of the Court, Annex II).

Time begins to run on the day after the event which is the subject of
proceedings, and continues to run during the Court's vacation. If a
period ends on a Sunday or an official holiday of the Court (New Year's
Day, Easter Monday, May 1, Ascension Day, Whit Monday, June 23 (or
June 24 if June 23 falls on a Sunday), August 15, November 1, December
25, 26: Rules of Procedures of the Court, Annex I) it is extended automatically until the end of the next working day.

Language   Proceedings may be brought in any one of the official working languages of the Court which are Danish, Dutch, English, French,
German, Greek, Italian, Portuguese, Spanish and Irish.

The applicant determines the language of the case. However, where
the application is made against a Member State or a national or legal per-

son having the nationality of a Member State, the language of that State is the language of the case. Where a Member State has more than one official language, the applicant may choose between them (Rules of Procedure, Art. 29(1)).

The language of the case must be used in all written and oral addresses to the Court. Supporting documents expressed in any language other than the language of the case must be accompanied by a translation into the language of the case (Rules of Procedure, Art. 29(3)).

However, the Court may authorise the use of any one of the languages mentioned above at joint request of the parties or the request of one party (Rules of Procedure, Art. 29(2)). Applications to intervene may be made in any procedural language. Moreover a Member State is entitled to use its own official language when intervening before the Court (Rules of Procedure, Art. 29(3)). A procedural language, other than the language of the case may be used by the President of the Court, or the Presidents of Chambers when conducting oral proceedings, judges and advocates general when putting questions and advocates general in delivering opinions. Witnesses or experts may be authorised to give evidence in a language other than a procedural language of the Court, if they are unable to express themselves in the latter.

At the request of any Judge, Advocate General or party, the Registrar must arrange for anything said or written in the course of proceedings before the Court or Chambers to be translated into the languages he chooses from the Court's procedural languages. Simultaneous interpretation is provided during oral proceedings.

Proceedings   Proceedings before the Court consist of two parts: written and oral.

Proceedings before the Court begin by means of a written application addressed to the Registrar. An application need not be made on any particular form but must contain:

(a) the applicant's name and permanent address and a description of the signatory to the pleadings;
(b) the name of the party against whom the application is made;
(c) the subject matter of the dispute;
(d) the submissions of the applicant;
(e) a brief summary of the grounds on which the application is based;
(f) where the annulment of a measure is sought, a copy of that measure or where the grievance of the applicant consists of a failure to act on the part of the Commission or the Council, evidence of the date on which the institution was requested to act. (Protocol to the Statute of the Court of Justice—Art. 22(1) of the ECSC Treaty; Art. 1 of the EEC Treaty; Art. 19(1) of the Euratom Treaty). The original application must be lodged along with: five

     copies and a copy for each of the parties. Copies must be authenticated by the party lodging them; and

(g) an address for service in Luxembourg.

If an application does not comply with these requirements, the Registrar must inform the applicant and give him a reasonable period of time in which to put his application in order. If the applicant fails to do this, the Court will decide whether or not to reject the application.

Applications are lodged by means of delivery to the Registry of the Court, or outside the opening hours of the Registry with the Court's janitor who must record the date and time of such lodgment. (Instructions to the Registrar, Art. 1(1).)

Service The Application, if it complies with the requirements set out above, is served on the defendant (Rules of Procedure, Art. 29). The Registrar of the Court is responsible for service of all pleadings and other documents relating to the proceeding to all parties. Service is effected at the party's address for service either by personal delivery of a copy of the document against a receipt or by registered post with a form for acknowledgment of receipt, accompanied by a note signed by the Registrar giving the number of the case and the registration number of the document, together with a brief indication of its nature (Rules of Procedure, Art. 79(1); Instructions to the Registrar, Art. 3(2)).

If a document is very bulky and only one specimen is lodged at the Registry, the Registrar must inform the parties by registered letter that the document may be inspected by them at the Registry.

Defence With one month of service on him of the application, the defendant must lodge a defence. This time limit can be extended by the President, on a reasoned application by the defendant. The defence must state:

(a) the name and permanent residence of the defendant;
(b) the points of law and fact and the nature of any evidence relied;
(c) the form of order sought (Rules of Procedure, Art. 40);
(d) an address for service in Luxembourg.

If the defendant fails to lodge a defence with the time prescribed, the applicant may apply for a *Judgment by default* (Rules of Procedure, Art. 94(1)).

This application is served on the defendant and the President fixes a date for the opening of the oral procedure (Rules of Procedure, Art. 94(1)). The decision of the Court on the application is made after hearing the Advocate General. The Court must consider whether the procedural rules have been complied with, and whether the applicants' submissions appear to be well-founded (Rules of Procedures, Art. 94(3)).

Within one month of the date of service of a judgment by default, an application may be made to set it aside. After the application has been served, the President prescribes a period within which the other party may submit written observations. The Court will decide on the application by way of a judgment which may not be set aside (Rules of Procedure, Art. 94(5)).

Reply and rejoinder   The application originating the pleadings and the defence may be supplemented by a reply from the applicant and a rejoinder from the defendant. The President fixes the time limits within which these pleadings are to be lodged (Rules of Procedure, Art. 41). The time limit may be extended, on application.

Further evidence may be produced in the reply or rejoinder but reasons for the delay in submitting it must be given.

No fresh issue may be raised in the course of proceedings unless it is based on a matter of fact or law which comes to light in the course of the written procedure.

In such an event the President after the expiry of the normal procedural time limits, acting on a report from the Judge-Rapporteur and after hearing the Advocate General, allow the other party time to answer on that issue (Rules of Procedure, Art. 42(2)).

Admissibility

(a) No jurisdiction: Where it is clear that the Court of Justice has no jurisdiction over a particular application, it may, without serving it on the defendant, declare the application inadmissible by a reasoned order (Rules of Procedure, Art. 92).

(b) Inadmissible: Instead of lodging a defence, the defendant may apply to the Court of Justice for the action to be dismissed on the ground that it is inadmissible. The application must be made by a separate document and must state the grounds of fact and law relied upon and the form of order sought by the applicant. Supporting documents must be annexed by the application (Rules of Procedure, Art. 91(1)). After the application has been lodged, it is served on the applicant and the President prescribes a period within which observations on the application should be lodged. The application then proceeds to the oral stage unless the Court decided to treat the admissibility and substance of the action together where the admissibility issue is treated separately, the Court will decide, after hearing the parties and the opinion of the Advocate General, whether to:

(i) Uphold the application and dismiss the action;

(ii) reject the application and order proceedings on the substance of the case to continue; or

(iii) reserve its decision on admissibility until final judgment.

If the Court refuses an application or reserves its decision, the President prescribes new time limits for further steps in the proceedings.

Substance The application commencing proceedings must set out:

(a) the facts alleged and the evidence relied upon to prove them;
(b) the legal argument; and
(c) the relief sought.

The defence must contain:

(a) argument of law and fact raised in answer to the application;
(b) the relief sought.

Issues raised by the Court The Court may of its own motion raise issues not put forward by the parties.

Joinder of proceedings The Court may, at any time, after hearing the parties and the Advocate General, order a number of cases concerning the same subject-matter to be joined. The decision to join the cases may subsequently be rescinded (Rules of Procedure, Art. 43).

Joinder of parties An applicants commencing proceedings may be submitted by any number of applicants. A new defendant may not be added after the lodgment of the applicant (Case 90/77 *Helmut Stimming KG* v. *Commission* [1977] E.C.R. 2113). Third parties may not be compulsorily joined to the proceedings (Case 12/69 *Wonnerth* v. *Commission* [1969] E.C.R. 577 at 584).

Legal aid A party who is unable to meet the costs of proceedings before the Court of Justice may apply to the Court for legal aid. The application must be accompanied by evidence of the applicant's need of assistance and in particular by a document from the competent authority in his Member State certifying his lack of means. If an application is made prior to the commencement of proceedings the subject of the proceedings should be briefly set out (Rules of Procedure, Art. 76(1)).

An application made after the commencement of proceedings does not effect the running of time limits.

An application for legal aid need not be made through a lawyer. However, if before legal aid is granted the applicant lodges an application which has not been signed by a lawyer, it will be rejected as inadmissible. (Case 10/81 *Farrell* v. *Commission* [1981] E.C.R. 717). Consequently, an applicant would be advised to seek legal aid before lodging his application.

The decision to grant legal aid is made by the Chamber to which the Judge designated to act as Rapporteur belongs (Rules of Procedure, Art. 76(3)).

An order granting or refusing legal aid is unreasoned and final (Rules of Procedure, Art. 76(3)(2)).

Representation   Member States and the Community Institutions are represented before the Court by an agent appointed in each case. The agent may be assisted by an adviser or by a lawyer entitled to practice before a Court of a Member State. The agent must sign the original of every pleading (Rules of Procedure, Art. 37(1). Art. 17(1) of the ECSC Treaty Protocol on the statute of the Court of Justice; Art. 17(1) of the Euratom Treaty, Protocol on the Statute of the Court of Justice).

In proceedings brought under the ECSC Treaty, other parties must be represented by the person or persons authorised under national law, who must be assisted by a lawyer entitled to practise before a court of a Member State (Art. 20(2) of the ECSC Treaty Protocol on the Statute of the Court of Justice).

In all other proceedings parties other than the Member States and the Community Institutions must be represented by a lawyer entitled to practise before a court of a Member State. This lawyer must sign every pleading (Rules of Procedure, Art. 37(1)).

University teachers, who are nationals of a Member State and who have the right of audience in that Member State have the same rights before the Court as lawyers entitled to practice before the Court of a Member State (Art. 20(5) of the ECSC Treaty Protocol on the Statute of the Court of Justice; Art. 17 of the EEC Treaty Protocol on the Statute of the Court of Justice; Art. 17(2) of the Euratom Treaty Protocol on the Statute of the Court of Justice).

Representatives appearing before the Court enjoy the rights and immunities necessary to the independent exercise of their duties. These are:

(a) immunity in respect of words spoken or written concerning the case or the parties;
(b) exemption from search and seizure of papers and documents relating to the proceedings;
(c) entitlement to such allocation of foreign currency as may be necessary for the performance of the duties pertaining to representation; and
(d) entitlement to travel in the course of duty without hinderance (Rules of Procedure, Art. 32).

These rights, privileges and immunities may be waived by the Court (Rules of Procedure Art. 34). Qualification for rights, privileges and

377

immunity is dependent in the case of agents producing an official document issued by the state or institution which they represent. Advisers, lawyers and, where relevant, university teachers must produce a certificate signed by the Registrar of the Court (Rules of Procedure, Art. 33).

A representative may be excluded from proceedings by order of the Court or a Chamber if his conduct is incompatible with the dignity of the Court or if he abuses the rights granted to him in order to fulfil his duties. Before such an order is made, the person concerned must be given an opportunity to defend himself (Rules of Procedure, Art. 35(1)).

Preparatory inquiries   After the close of the written procedure is lodged, the Judge-Rapporteur presents his preliminary report to the Court which may recommend the holding of a preparatory inquiry or any other step before oral proceedings *e.g.* requests for further information from the parties. It The Court decides, after hearing the Advocate General what action to take on these recommendations. Any appropriate measures of inquiry are prescribed in an order served on the parties setting out the issues of fact to be determined. The essential purpose of preparatory inquiries is to resolve issues of fact raised in the course of the written procedure. It must be noted that preparatory inquiries are very rare.

The Court may, of its own motives, order measures of inquiry or it may do so following a request to that effect by a party to the proceedings. Such a request may be made in the written pleadings or raised separately and must be substantiated by facts which justify the making of such an order. (Rules of Procedure, Art. 47(1); Case 51/65 *ILFO* v. *High Authority* [1966] E.C.R. 87 at 96; Case 35/67 *Van Eick* v. *Commission* [1968] E.C.R. 329 at 342.)

In actions brought under the ECSC Treaty, the Court may:

(a) require the parties, their representatives or agents or the government of Member States to produce all documents and supply all information which the Court considers desirable; or

(b) entrust any individual body, authority, committee or other organisation it chooses with the task of holding an inquiry or granting an expert opinion (Art. 24 of the ECSC Treaty Protocol on the Statute of the Court of Justice).

In the case of actions brought under the EEC or Euratom Treaties the Court may:

(a) require the parties to produce all documents and supply all information which it considers desirable;

(b) require the Member States and the Community institutions which are *not* parties to the case to supply all information which the court considers necessary for the proceedings; or

(c) entrust any individual, body, authority, committee or other organisation it chooses with the task of giving an expert opinion (Art. 21 of the EEC Treaty Protocol or the Statute of the Court of Justice; Art. 22 of the Euratom Treaty Protocol on the Statute of the Court of Justice).

Refusal to comply with these requirements is not sanctionable.

In addition to these above mentioned powers and without prejudice to them, the Court may adopt the following measures of inquiry:

(a) the personal appearance of the parties;
(b) a request for information and production of documents;
(c) oral testimony;
(d) experts' reports; or
(e) an inspection of a place (Rules of Procedure, Art. 45).

Witnesses may be examined by the Court itself or by the judicial authorities of the place of permanent residence of the witness to be examined (Art. 28 of the ECSC Treaty Protocol on the Statute of the Court of Justice; Art. 23 of the EEC Treaty Protocol on the Statute of the Court of Justice; Art. 24 of the Euratom Treaty Protocol on the Statute of the Court of Justice).

The Court may summon a witness either of its own motion, or at the instance of the Advocate General, or on application by a party (Rules of Procedure, Art. 47). Where the Court summons a witness of its own motion, the funds necessary are advanced by the Court's cashier. It is to be noted that witnesses are in practice are very rarely summoned.

Oral procedure

Public hearing The oral procedure consists of a hearing which takes place after the close of preparatory inquiries if they have been held, otherwise after written pleadings have been closed. The oral hearing is held in public unless the Court decides otherwise (Art. 26 of the ECSC Treaty Protocol on the Statute of the Court of Justice; Art. 28 of the EEC Treaty Protocol on the Statute of the Court of Justice; Art. 29 of the Euratom Treaty, Protocol on the Statute of the Court of Justice).

The hearing begins in theory, with a reading of the Report for the Hearing, which is a summary of the written pleadings and preparatory inquiries (where they take place). This report however is, in practice, transmitted to the parties before the hearing, and is taken as read when the hearing opens. The parties may request changes in the Report.

The proceedings are opened and directed by the President of the Court who is responsible for the proper conduct of the hearing (Rules of Procedure, Art. 56(1)). Parties may address the court only through their agent, adviser or lawyers (Rules of Procedure, Art. 58(1)).

The oral submissions made before the Court are confined to the issues raised in the course of written pleadings unless the Court order states otherwise, and the parties agree (Case 730/79 *Philip Morris Holland BV v. Commission* [1980] E.C.R. 2671 at 2904). It is essential in the circumstances in which new evidence is introduced at the oral hearing by a party that the other parties have had an opportunity of considering it and are therefore in a position to plead on the points raised by it at the hearing. Consequently, a party wishing to produce new evidence at the oral hearing would be advised prior to the hearing to show it to the other parties and obtain their comment to its production.

The Advocate General's opinion   The Advocate General delivers his opinion on the case, in general four to six weeks after the hearing. The opinion consists of a reasoned assessment of the case, coupled with advice to the Court on how it should be decided.

Judgment

Delivery   The judgment of the Court is delivered in open court. The parties are given notice to attend to hear it. The original of the judgment signed by the President, the judges who participated in the deliberations and by the Registrar, is sealed and deposited in the Registry. (Rule of Procedures, Art. 64).

Unanimous   The judgment of the Court is unanimous. There are no dissenting opinions.

Form   Each judgment consists of :

    (a) a statement that it is the judgment of the court;
    (b) the date on which the judgment was delivered;
    (c) the number of the case;
    (d) the names and description of the parties and their agents, advisers and lawyers;
    (e) the cause of action, the composition of the court which dealt with the case;
    (f) a summary of the facts and arguments presented to the Court;
    (g) the grounds for the judgment; and
    (h) the operative part of the judgment including a statement as to costs.

The Report for the Hearing is attached to the judgment of the Court.

Rectification   Within two weeks of the delivery of the judgment, the Court may, either of its own motion or on the application of a party to the case, rectify clerical mistakes, errors in calculation and obvious slips (Rules of Procedure, Art. 66).

Omissions Should the Court omit to give a decision on a particular point at issue or on costs, any party may within one month of service of the judgment, apply to the court to supplement the judgment. The application is served on the other parties and the President of the Court prescribes a period within which written observations may be lodged. Following the lodging of written observations, the Council, after hearing the Advocate General, decides on the admissibility and merits of the application, Art. 67 Rules of Procedure).

Enforcement Judgments of the Court of Justice are binding from the date of their delivery (Rules of Procedure Art. 65). Judgments are enforced in accordance with the rules of civil procedure in each Member State (Art. 192 EEC Treaty). In the United Kingdom, application to append to a judgment the order for enforcement is made to the Secretary of State. The person then applies to the High Court in England and Wales, or in Northern Ireland, or the Court of Session in Scotland for the judgment to be registered, and that Court must register the judgment forthwith (European Communities (Enforcement of Community Judgments) Order 1972 (S.I. 1972 No. 1590), Art. 3(1)). Following registration a judgment of the Court of Justice has the same status as a judgment of the High Court or Court of Session.

Discontinuance If before the Court has given its judgment the parties reach a settlement of their dispute and inform the Court of the abandonment of their claims, the Court orders the case to be removed from the Register (Rules of Procedure, Art. 77).

Proceedings cannot be discontinued in the case of an application for the annulment of acts of the Commission or the Council, or request for a declaration of failure to act on the part of a Community Institution.

The Court may, of its own motion, declare at the end of proceedings that there is no necessity for it to proceed to judgment.

Revision Judgments of the Court are not subject to appeal or review on points of law. However, within 10 years of the date of a judgment, an application may be made to the court for a revision of it, if a new fact, unknown to the Court and to the party applying for the revision at the time of the judgment, which is of "such a nature as to be a decisive factor" is discovered (Art. 38(1) of the ECSC Treaty Protocol on the Statute to the Court of Justice; Art. 41(1) of the EEC Treaty Protocol to the statute of the Court of Justice; Art. 42(1) of the Euratom Treaty Protocol on the Statute of the Court of Justice).

An application for revision of a judgment must be made within three months of the date on which the applicant receives the knowledge of the facts on which he bases his application (Rules of Procedure, Art. 98).

The application must comply with the general rules governing written pleadings and must:

(a) specify the judgment contested;
(b) indicate the points on which the judgment is contested;
(c) set out the facts on which the application is based; and
(d) indicate the nature of the evidence to show that there are facts justifying the revision of the judgment, and that the application was lodged within three months of the discovery of the facts (Rules or Procedure, Art. 99).

All the parties to the case are entitled to submit written observations on the application (Rules of Procedure, Art. 100(1)). The Court decides on the admissibility of the application after considering the parties written pleadings and hearing the Advocate General (Rules of Procedure, Art. 100(1)). If the Court admits the application, it will then proceed to decide on its merits (Rules of Procedure, Art. 100(2)). The original of the revising judgment is annexed to the original of the judgment revised. A note of the revising judgment is made in the margin of the original of the judgment revised (Rules of Procedure, Art. 100(3)).

Costs

Court costs   The final judgment or order of the Court makes an award of courts (Rules of Procedure, Art. 69(1)). Proceedings before the Court are free of charge. However, the Court may recover:

(a) avoidable costs which a party has caused the Court to incur;
(b) copying or translation work carried out at the request of a party to the extent to which the Registrar considers the work excessive;
(c) sums advanced to witnesses and experts by the cashier of the Court; and
(d) the expense of letters rogatory (Rules of Procedure, Arts. 71 and 72; Art. 26 of the EEC Treaty Protocol on the Statute of the Court of Justice; Art. 27 of the Euratom Treaty Protocol on the Statute of the Court of Justice).

Other recoverable costs   Costs recoverable by the parties include:

(a) sums payable to witnesses and experts;
(b) expenses incurred by the parties for the purpose of the proceedings, in particular, the travel and subsistence expenses and the remuneration of agents, advisers and lawyers;

(c) fees incurred in providing an address for service in Luxembourg; (Joined Cases 20, 21/63 *Maudet* v. *Commission* [1964] E.C.R. 621 at 622);
(d) postal telecommunications and photocopying charges (Case 238/78 *Ireks—Arcady GmbH.* v. *EEC* [1981] E.C.R. 1723 at 1726); and
(e) taxes due on recoverable costs (Case 75/69 *Hake & Co* v. *Commission* [1970] E.C.R. 901 at 9036) (Rules of Procedure, Art. 73).

Costs which may not be recoverable The travel expenses of the party himself are recoverable only if his presence at the hearing was necessary (Case 24/79 *Oberthur* v. *Commission* [1981] E.C.R. 2229 at 2230). The remuneration of an agent or adviser who is an official or servant of the party (*e.g.* a Commission official) is not recoverable.

Award of costs The unsuccessful party will be ordered to pay the costs if they have been asked for by the successful party in its pleadings. Where there are several unsuccessful parties the Court will decide how the costs are to be shared. (Rules of Procedure, Art. 69(2)). The unsuccessful party usually bears all the costs of interveners who support the successful party. An intervener who supported the unsuccessful party will bear his own costs and that part of the costs of the successful party attributable to his intervention (Case 133/77 *NTW Toyo Bearing Co Ltd* v. *Council* [1979] E.C.R. 1185).

A successful party may be ordered to pay costs where these have been unreasonable or vexatious (Rules of Procedure, Art. 69(3)). It is considered to be vexatious to bring or continue proceedings where there is manifestly no interest or useful purpose in doing so. (Joined Cases 6, 97/79 *Granni* v. *Council* [1980] E.C.R. 2142; Joined Cases 122, 123/79 *Schiavo* v. *Council* [1981] E.C.R. 473.)

A party who discontinues or withdraws from proceedings will be ordered to pay the costs unless the discontinuance or withdrawal is justified by the conduct of the opposing party. (Rules of Procedure, Art. 69.) If the opposing party has not asked for costs the parties will bear their own costs.

Discontinuance or withdrawal is justified by the conduct of the opposing party if, for example, it occurs because the defendant satisfies the applicant's claims after the commencement of proceedings (Cases 123/81 and 123/81 R *Krupp Stahl AG* v. *Commission* [1981] E.C.R. 2391).

Where for reasons other than withdrawal or discontinuance a case does not proceed to judgment, the costs are at the discretion of the Court (Rules of Procedure, Art. 69(5)).

In proceedings brought by an official or other servant of an institution against that institution, the institution bears its own costs. However, the applicant may be ordered to pay costs which he has unreasonably or vexatiously caused the defendant institutions to incur (Rules of Procedure, Art. 70).

Taxation of costs   The party awarded costs by the Court of Justice should submit to the other party an account of costs claimed within a reasonable time after the making of the Court order. Unreasonable delay may be construed as a waiver of the right to costs (Case 126/79 *Dretz* v. *Commission* [1979] E.C.R. 2131).

Where there is a dispute between the parties as to the costs the Chamber to which the case has been assigned will, on application by the party concerned, and after hearing the opposite party and the Advocate General, make an order. There is no appeal from this order.

Intervention: who may intervene?   The rules vary under the different Treaties. Natural or legal persons, including the Member States and the Community Institutions may intervene in actions in the Court brought under the ECSC Treaty if they can establish an interest in the outcome of the case (Art. 34(1) of the ECSC Treaty Protocol on the Statute of the Court of Justice).

Member States and Community Institutions may intervene in actions brought under the EEC or Euratom Treaties by establishing an interest in the result of the case (Art. 37(1) of the EEC Treaty Protocol on the Statute of the Court of Justice; Art. 38(1) of the Euratom Treaty Protocol on the Statute of the Court of Justice).

Any person other than a Member State or a Community institution may intervene in actions under the EEC or Euratom Treaty except in:

(a) actions between Member States;
(b) actions between the Community Institutions; or
(c) actions between the Member States and the Community Institutions;

provided an interest in the outcome of the case can be proved. Intervention is confined to supporting the submission of one of the parties (Art. 37(2)(3) of the EEC Treaty Protocol on the Statute of the Court; Art. 38(2)(3) of the Euratom Treaty Protocol on the Statute of the Court).

An application to intervene in a case must be made within three months of the publication of the notice of the case in the Official Journal.

The application must comply with the general rules governing pleadings and representations and the rules governing originating actions (Rules of Procedure, Art. 93(2)(3)). It must set out, in addition:

(a) the description of the case;
(b) the description of the parties;
(c) the name and permanent residence of the intervener;

(d) the reasons for the intervener's interest in the result of the case, where this is required;

(e) submission supporting or opposing the submission of the one of parties to the original case;

(f) an indication of evidence relied upon, in the annex, supporting documents; and

(g) the intervener's address for service in Luxembourg.

The application to intervene is served on the parties to the original case, who can submit observations either orally or in writing (Rules of Procedure, Art. 95(3)).

The Court decides on the application after hearing the Advocate General (Rules of Procedure, Art. 93(3)). If the application is allowed the intervener receives a copy of all the documents served on the parties. On the application of one of the parties the Court may withhold secret or confidential documents.

The intervener must take the case as it stands at the time of his intervention: no earlier stages in the proceedings can be re-opened.

C Indirect Jurisdiction

One of the main roles of the Court of Justice is to interpret Community law when requested to do so by national courts. Such interpretations are given in the form of preliminary rulings, that is rulings on questions of Community law which arise in the course of national proceedings and which are referred to the Court for guidance as to their meaning.

Nature of the Proceedings   The proceedings are essentially in the nature of a co-operation between the European Court of Justice and national courts, the primary objective of which is to ensure the uniform interpretation and application of Community law in all the Member States. In addition, given the limited means of redress open to individuals against Community acts, the preliminary ruling procedure is an important means of legal redress for natural and legal persons wishing to challenge the validity of Community acts or the compatibility of national rules and practices with Community law.

Jurisdiction of the Courts of Justice

Article 177 of the EEC Treaty   Requests for preliminary rulings are made to the Court most frequently under Article 177 of the EEC Treaty which gives the Court Jurisdiction to give rulings concerning:

(a) the interpretation of the Treaty;

    (b) the validity and interpretation of acts of the institutions of the Community;

    (c) the interpretation of statutes of bodies established by an act of the Council where those statutes so provide.

Although references for interpretation are commonly made under Article 177 of the EEC Treaty, preliminary rulings may be referred under Article 41 of the ESCS Treaty which gives the Court of Justice jurisdiction to give preliminary rulings on acts of the Commission and the Council when these are in issue in proceedings before a national court or tribunal.

Article 150 of the Euratom Treaty empowers the Court of Justice to give preliminary rulings on the interpretation of the Euratom Treaty and the validity and interpretation of the acts of the institutions of the Community.

The Protocol on the Interpretation by the Court of Justice of the Convention on Jurisdiction and the Enforcement of Judgments in Civil and Commercial Matters empowers the Court to give preliminary rulings on the interpretation of the Convention, the Conventions of Accession and the Protocols. However the power to refer question is limited to specified courts (O.J. 1983 C97/24).

Similarly the Protocol concerning the Interpretation by the Court of Justice of the Convention on the Mutual Recognition of Companies and Legal Persons gives the Court power to interpret the provisions. (EC Bull Supp 7/71). This Convention has not yet come into force.

Referral at Discretion of the National Court   It is for the national court to decide whether there is a point of Community law in issue in the proceedings before it which requires interpretation and if so, whether it will ask the Court of Justice for a ruling on the matter. The parties to the national proceedings cannot make a reference nor can they prevent the Court from making a reference if it wishes to do so. (Joined Cases 31 and 33/62 *Milchwerke Heinz Wohrmann & Sohn KG* v. *EEC Commission* [1962] E.C.R. 501 at 507. Case 93/78 *Mattheus* v. *Doego Fruchtimport und Tiefkühl Kost* [1978] E.C.R. 2203 at 2220.) The Court of Justice cannot compel a national court to make a reference to it: it must respect the national court's discretion in the matter.

Similarly it is for the national court to decide whether to withdraw a reference for a preliminary ruling. Neither the parties to the main proceedings nor the Court of Justice itself can compel the withdrawal of a reference for a preliminary ruling.

Which courts can refer and when   The provisions in the Euratom and EEC Treaties governing preliminary rulings provide:

"1. Where a question on any of these matters (interpretation of the Treaty, validity and interpretation of arts of Community institutions, statutes of bodies established by the Council) arises before any court or tribunal of a Member State that court or tribunal may, if it considers that a decision on the question is necessary to enable it to give judgment request the Court of Justice to give a ruling therein.

2. Where any such question is raised in a case pending before a court or tribunal of a Member State, against whose decisions there is no judicial remedy under national law, that court or tribunal must bring the matter before the Court of Justice. The ECSC Treaty simply refers to 'A national court or tribunal.' "

Any court or tribunal of a Member State   A body set up by a Member State with jurisdiction to decide questions of law or fact will, in general, constitute a court or tribunal within the meaning of the Treaties. Thus in the United Kingdom courts of criminal or civil jurisdiction including specialist tribunals may refer questions of Community law to the Court of Justice.

It is a question of fact in each case whether a body is a court or tribunal competent to refer questions to the Court of Justice. The Court itself has given some indications, in its case-law of what entities have the right to refer questions to it:

(a) bodies which give opinions as opposed to decisions are not competent to refer questions to the Court (Case 138/80 *Borker* [1980] E.C.R. 1975);

(b) an appeal committee which operated with the consent of the public authorities and with their co-operation, which handed down final decisions after an adversarial procedure, was to be considered a court or tribunal within the meaning of Article 177 (case 246/80 *Broekmeulen* v. *Huisarts Registratie Commissie* [1981] E.C.R. 2311).

Three essential criteria appear from the Court's judgments:

(a) the court or tribunal in question must be linked to the state;
(b) its proceedings must be adversarial;
(c) its decisions must be binding.

Thus the Court has held that private arbitrators cannot refer questions under Article 177. (Case 102/81 *Nordsee* [1982] E.C.R. 1095) Courts against whose decisions there is no judicial remedy "shall refer questions of Community Law to the Court of Justice" (Article 177 EEC Treaty and Article 150 Euratom Treaty).

This simply means that such a court, in cases in which a question of Community law arises can refer the question to the Court of Justice if it is in doubt as to its meaning or application (case 34/79 *R. v. Henn and Darby* [1979] E.C.R. 3795). The Court, adopting the French doctrine of "acte claire" has held that a court of final appeal is not obliged to make a referral to the Court of Justice where the " . . . the Community provision in question has already been interpreted by the Court of Justice or that the correct application of Community law is so obvious as to leave no scope for any reasonable doubt (Case 283/81 *CILFIT* [1982] E.C.R. 3415).

Other Courts   Courts against whose decisions, an appeal will lie, are not under an obligation to refer questions of Community law but may do so. The reference can be made at any stage in the proceedings; it is not necessary that there should be a finding of fact before a reference is made (Case 72/83 *Campus Oil Ltd.* v. *Minister for Industry and Energy* [1984] E.C.R. 2727).

Interlocutory proceedings   Whether there is an obligation on a national court to refer questions to the Court of Justice in interlocutory proceedings depends on whether the interlocutory order is one in respect of which there is no further remedy under national law. If there is no further remedy, and the matter does require some interpretation of Community law then the question ought to be referred at the interlocutory stage, otherwise it can be referred at a later stage in the proceedings (Cases 35 and 36/82 *Morson and Jhanjan* v. *Netherlands* [1982] E.C.R. 3723).

Procedure   A national court which is obliged or willing to refer a question for a preliminary ruling to the Court of Justice, must suspend proceedings before it and notify its question to the Court (EEC Treaty, Protocol on the Statute of the Court of Justice Article 20(1), Euratom Treaty Protocol on the Statute of the Court of Justice Article 21(1)) in the United Kingdom.

Order 114 rule 5 of the Rules of Procedure of the Supreme Court lay down that when an order referring a question to the European Court for a preliminary ruling has been made, the Senior Master must send a copy to the Registrar of the Court of Justice. However, in the case of an order made by the High Court, he must not do so, unless the Court otherwise orders, until the time for appealing against the order expired or, if an appeal is entered into within that time, until the appeal has been determined or otherwise disposed of.

An order made by the High Court is deemed to be a final decision and accordingly an appeal against it shall lie to the Court of Appeal without leave; but the period within which a notice of appeal must be served under Order 59 rule 4(1) is 14 days. It seems that a refusal to make an order of reference remains interlocutory in character and therefore leave to appeal against such a refusal will be required.

When the notification is received by the Court of Justice the Registrar must notify the parties to the case before the national court, all the Member States and the EC Commission. The EC Council must also be informed if the validity of an act originating from the Council is in issue.

The parties, the Member States, the Commission and the Council (where the question is notified to it) may then submit written observations to the Court within two months of the notification (EEC Treaty, Protocol on the Statute of the Court of Justice Article 20(2), Euratom Treaty, Protocol on the Statute of the Court of Justice Article 21(2)).

Language The order of the court or tribunal making the reference must be communicated to the Member States in the original language version of the reference and in the official language of the Member State to which they are addressed (Rules of Procedure of the Court, Article 104(1)).

The language of the case is the language of the national court or tribunal making the reference (Rules of Procedure Article 29(2)).

Member States are entitled to use their own official language in making written submissions to the Court and at the oral hearing.

No form is prescribed under Community law for making a reference to the Court. However the question put to the Court has to fall within the terms of Article 177 of the Treaty. But the Court will not in general reject a request for preliminary ruling, on a point of Community law, on the ground that it is not correctly formulated, rather it will re-word the request to fit in with the terms of that provision.

Although there is no form laid down by Community law for the making of references for preliminary rulings, national rules may prescribe the form in which such references are to be made. References from Superior Courts in the United Kingdom are made on Form App. A. 109. The order will set out the request for a preliminary ruling in a schedule which will be prepared and directed by the Court. In practice, in the United Kingdom it is frequently the parties' counsel and solicitors who draft the references but obviously the final decision as to the content and wording is that of the referring court.

Written submissions on the reference must be made to the Court of Justice within two months of the notification of the decision making the reference to the parties. Only one written pleading is permitted. The parties may make oral submissions to the Court at a hearing fixed by the Court at the end of the written procedure.

The oral hearing When the written procedure has finished the Judge-Rapporteur in the case will, as in the case of direct actions, make a preliminary report on the case which will be considered by the Court in an administrative meeting. The Court will then decide on what further information it needs to have before the oral hearing and whether the case should be heard by plenary session or in Chambers.

After the oral hearing, the Advocate General delivers his opinion and the Court proceeds to judgment. The answers to the national court's questions are then sent to the referring court or tribunal.

Representation As regards representation and attendance of the parties to the main proceedings, in the preliminary ruling procedure, the Court must take account of the rules of procedure of the national court or tribunal which made the reference (Rules of Procedure Art. 104 (2)). A person entitled to be heard by the referring court or tribunal with respect to the proceedings to which the preliminary ruling relates is entitled to appear in those proceedings before the Court of Justice.

Costs The costs of references are decided upon by the national court or tribunal (Rules of Procedure Article 104(3)). In special circumstances the Court may grant legal aid to facilitate the representation or attendance of a party.

Effect of a Reference for a Preliminary Ruling When a reference for a preliminary ruling to the Court is made proceedings before the national court are suspended (EEC Treaty Protocol on the Statute to the Court of Justice Article 20(1) RSC Order 114). An order referring a question to the Court of Justice can be appealed if national law permits an appeal from a decision of the referring court or tribunal (Case 146/83 *Rhein-muhlen-Dusseldorf* v. *Einfuhr-und Vorratsstelle für Getreide und Futtermittel* [1974] E.C.R. 139).

Refusal to accept a Reference The Court of Justice has the right to refuse to deal with a request for a preliminary ruling on the ground that it has no jurisdiction to do so, for example because the question referred concerns a matter of national law only or that the referring court is not a body competent to refer a question to the Court. The Court may also refuse to consider a question which is not genuinely put in the interest of solving a real dispute between the parties in national proceedings but rather as a means of inducing the Court to give its views on a hypothetical problem *e.g.* the compatibility of the law of a Member State other than that of the court or tribunal referring the case, with Community law (Case 104/79 *Foglio* v. *Novello* [1980] E.C.R. 745 Case 244/80 *Foglio* v. *Novello* [1981] E.C.R. 3045).

D The Court of First Instance of the European Communities

Introduction The Treaties, as amended by the Single European Act provide for the creation of a Court attached to the Court of Justice.

"1. At request of the Court of Justice and after consulting the Commission and the European Parliament, the Council may, acting unanimously, attach to the Court of Justice a court with jurisdiction to hear and determine at first instance, subject to a right of appeal to the Court of Justice on points of law only and in accordance with the conditions laid down by the Statute, certain classes of action or proceeding brought by natural or legal persons. That court shall not be competent to hear and determine actions brought by Member States or by Community institutions or questions referred for a preliminary ruling under Article 177.

2. The Council, following the procedure laid down in paragraph 1, shall determine the composition of that court and adopt the necessary adjustments and additional provisions to the Statute of the Court of Justice. Unless the Council decides otherwise, the provisions of this Treaty relating to the Court of Justice, in particular the provisions of the Protocol on the Statute of the Court of Justice, in particular the provisions of the Protocol on the Statute of the Court of Justice, shall apply to that court.

3. The members of that court shall be chosen from persons whose independence is beyond doubt and who possess the ability required for appointment to judicial office; they shall be appointed by common accord of the Governments of the Member States for a term of six years. The membership shall be partially renewed every three years. Retiring members shall be eligible for reappointment.

4. That court shall establish its rules of procedure in agreement with the Court of Justice. Those rules shall require the unanimous approval of the Council."

(Article 32 (d), ECSC Treaty, Article 168 (b) EEC Treaty, Article 140 (a) Euratom Treaty)

Council Decision   Council Decision 88/591 of October 24, 1988 established a Court of First Instance of the European Communities (OJ 1988 L 319, OJ 1989 L241/4). The Decision laid down the seat of the Court, its composition, its jurisdiction, the relationship between the Court of First Instance and the Court of Justice, the right of appeal from decisions of the Court of First Instance to the Court of Justice and the effect of such an appeal.

The Court of First Instance started functioning on September 1, 1989. It will adopt its own Rules of Procedure (Decision 88/591, Article 1). Until these rules have been adopted, the Rules of Procedure of the Court of Justice will apply.

Composition   The Court has twelve members. The Court sits in chambers of either five or three judges. However, in certain cases, the

Court may sit in plenary session. The first President which Court was appointed in the same way as the members of the court, that is by the Member States.

Advocates General No advocates general are appointed to the Court of First Instance. However the Rules of Procedure of the Court of First Instance will lay down cases in which an advocate general is to be appointed. The advocate general will be chosen from among the members of the Court of First Instance. He may not take part in the judgment of the cases (Decision 88/591, Article 2 (3)).

Registrar The Court of First Instance will appoint its registrar and lay down the rules governing his service (Protocols on the statutes of the Court of Justice as amended on Article 5, Decision 88/591).

Jurisdiction The Court of First Instance had jurisdiction over:

(a) Staff cases, that is disputes between the personnel of the institutions of the European Communities and associated institutions, and their employers;
(b) competition decisions adopted by the European Commission;
(c) actions brought to establish failure to act in competition matters by a Community institution;
(d) actions for damages caused by a Community institution through an act or failure to act over which the Court of First Instance has jurisdiction.
(Decision 88/591, Article 3, Decision of 31 October 1989 of the President of the Court, OJ 1989 L 317/48). The Council, will examine the jurisdiction of the Court of First Instance after two years of its operation until a view to broadening it. (Decision 88/591, Article 3 (3)).

Relationship between the Court of Justice and the Court of First Instance

1. Where an application or other procedural document addressed to the Court of First Instance is lodged, in error, with the Registrar of the Court of Justice, it must be transmitted at once to the Registrar of the Court of First Instance; likewise where an application or any procedural document addressed to the Court of Justice is lodged by mistake with the Registrar of the Court of First Instance, it must be transmitted immediately by that Registrar to the Registrar of the Court of Justice (Decision 88/591, Article 9).
2. Where the Court of First Instance finds that it does not have jurisdiction to hear a case in which the Court of Justice had jurisdiction it must refer the case to the Court of Justice. Similarly, when the Court of Justice finds that an action falls within the jurisdic-

tion of the Court of First Instance, it shall refer the action to the Court of First Instance. That Court may not decline jurisdiction.

3. Where the Court of Justice and the Court of First Instance are seised of cases in which the same issues or remedies are sought, the Court of First Instance may, after hearing the parties, stay the proceedings before it, unitl the Court of Justice has delivered judgment (Decision 88/591, Article 5).

4. *Right of Appeal: Point of law only*

(i) The amended provision of the Treaties state that decisions of the Court of First Instance shall be "subject to a right of appeal to the Court of Justice on points of law only and in accordance with the conditions laid down by the statute (ECSC Treaty, Article 32 (d), EEC Treaty Article 168 (a) Euratom Treaty, Article 104 (a)). The amended provision of the Protocol on the Statute of the Court of Justice amplify this statement further. Appeals to the Court of Justice are to be limited to points of law and will lie on the following grounds:

(a) lack of competence of the Court of First Instance;
(b) a breach of precedure before it which adversely affects the interests of the appellant;
(c) infringement of Community law by the Court of First Instance.
(Decision 88/591, Article 5, 7, 9).

(ii) No appeal lies to the Court of Justice with respect to the question of costs only.

(iii) An appeal from a final decision of the Court of First Instance must be brought within two months of the notification of the decision appealed against.

(iv) An appeal may be brought by any party which has been unsuccessful. Interveners, other than the Member States and the Community institutions may bring an appeal only against a decision which directly affects them.

(v) With the exception of staff cases, an appeal may also be brought by Member States and Community institutions when did not intervene in the proceedings before the Court of First Instance.

(vi) A person whose application to intervene has been dismissed by the Court of First Instance may appeal to the Court of Justice within two weeks of the notification of the decision dismissing the application.

(vii) An appeal does not have suspensory effect. Decisions of the Court of First Instance declaring a regulation null and void will take effect only after the period allowed for lodging the appeal has expired or where an appeal has been lodged within that period, from the date of dismissal of the appeal without prejudice, to the right of a party to apply to the Court of Justice for the suspension of the effects of the annulled regulation or any other interim measure.

8. If an appeal is well founded, the Court of Justice may quash the decision of the Court of First Instance. It may give final judgment in the matter or refer the case back to the Court of First Instance for final judgment. Where a case is referred back to the Court of First Instance that court is bound by the decision of the Court of Justice on points of law.

Appeals Procedure Rules of Procedure (Article 110–129 OJ 1989 L 241) An appeal against a decision of the Court of First Instance is brought in the language of that decision, by lodging an appreciation of the Registry of the Court of Justice or the Court of First Instance.

The Court of First Instance must transmit immediately to the Regulation of the Court of Justice, the papers in the case of First Instance and the appeal has been lodged with it, there papers
an appeal must contain:

(a) the name and permanent address of the appellant
(b) the names of the other parties to the proceedings before the Court of First Instance;
(c) the grounds on which the appeal is based and the arguments relied on.
(d) the form of order sought by the appellant;
(e) the decision which is being appealed must be annexed to the appeal.

An appeal must seek

(a) to quash in whole or in part the decision of the Court of First Instance,
(b) the same form of order, either in whole or in part as that sought at first instance. A different form of order may not be sought.

There must be no charge in the subject matter of the proceedings before the Court of First Instance.

Response Any party to the proceedings before the Court of First Instance may lodge a response within two months after the notice of appeal is served on him. There can be no extension in the time limit for lodging a response. The response must contain:

(a) the name and permanent address of the party lodging it;
(b) the date on which notice of the appeal was served on him;
(c) the grounds relied on and arguments of law raised;

(d) the form of order sought.

A response must seek the dismissal of the appeal in whole or in part or to quash in whole or in part the decision of the Court of First Instance. The subject matter of the proceedings before the Court of First Instance may not be changed in the response.

The appeal and response may be supplemented by a reply and rejoinder or any other pleading where the President allows such further pleadings.

After the submission of the written pleadings the Court, may acting upon the report of the Judge Rapporteur and after hearing the opinion of the Advocate-General decide to dispense with the oral procedure unless are of the parties objects or the ground that the written procedure alone did not enable him to express his point of view fully.

The Court will give final judgment in the case, after hearing the opinion of the Advocate General and will make an order as to costs.

Index

INDEX

INDEX

INDEX

INDEX